THE AUTHENTIC LITERATURE
OF ISRAEL

THE MACMILLAN COMPANY
NEW YORK · BOSTON · CHICAGO · DALLAS
ATLANTA · SAN FRANCISCO

MACMILLAN & CO., Limited
LONDON · BOMBAY · CALCUTTA
MELBOURNE

THE MACMILLAN CO. OF CANADA, Ltd.
TORONTO

THE
AUTHENTIC LITERATURE
OF ISRAEL

*FREED FROM THE DISARRANGEMENTS, EXPANSIONS AND
COMMENTS OF EARLY NATIVE EDITORS*

EDITED WITH AN INTRODUCTION

BY

ELIZABETH CZARNOMSKA, A.M.

PROFESSOR OF BIBLICAL AND COMPARATIVE LITERATURE
IN SWEET BRIAR COLLEGE, VIRGINIA

FORMERLY PROFESSOR OF ENGLISH LITERATURE IN SMITH COLLEGE, MASS.
LATER, OF HEBREW LANGUAGE AND LITERATURE IN THE UNIVERSITY OF CINCINNATI, OHIO;
HONORARY SECRETARY OF THE EGYPT EXPLORATION SOCIETY

PART ONE

FROM THE EXODUS TO THE EXILE

New York
THE MACMILLAN COMPANY
1924

TO THE MEMORY
OF THE GUIDES OF MY YOUTH
AND MY LIFE-LONG INSPIRATION

GEORGE WASHINGTON COAKLEY, LL.D.
MATHEMATICIAN, PHYSICIST AND ASTRONOMER

AND

ELIZA JULIANA COAKLEY
(SISTER ELIZA)

PIONEER IN MANY GOOD WORKS
IN THE
DIOCESE OF LONG ISLAND

ERRATA

Page xv, Booklet VI. line 2 : for Jeremiahan, read Jeremianic

Page xv, Poem of Nahum, title : for or, read on

Page xxxv, Introd. line 36 to the right : for prophets, read prophecies

Page 25, Proverbs, Ref. to A. V. : for xxi, 17–xxiii ; read xxii, 17–xxiii

Page 86, line 38 should be a blank space ; verse intruded from 1. 54, below

Page 119, line 14 : for eahweh, read Yahweh

Page 164, last line of note ; for xvii, read xviii

Page 270, X. strophe 3, line 4 : for give up, read, give thee up

Page 279, III. 4 : for eaves, read leaves

Page 288, I. strophe 4, line 4 : for plate, read gate

Page 312, Ref. to A. V. for Exordium : for iii, 1 ; iv, 28 read, iii, 1–iv, 28

Page 419, Append. A, II, b : for Aqila, read Aquila

PREFACE

The rapid advance of Science in the last century and the discovery of the high civilization of the Ancient Empires of the Near East, before only known through the Hebrew Scriptures and the discredited accounts of Herodotus, occasioned revision of these works. That of the Greek historian was thorough and largely restored faith in his accuracy; but the eminent theologians selected to put forth the "Revised Editions" concerned themselves only with the amending of the text and the substitution of modern terms for the obsolete words and phrasing of the Authorized Version. Reverence for the traditional view of the Inspiration of the Hebrew writings must have prevented the majority of the revisers from accepting the views of those collaborators who are now recognised as authorities in the study of the Bible. Hence all sorts of blemishes arising from the uncritical editing of the earliest native revisers still cling to the current editions like barnacles to a ship, of no worth in themselves and impeding its usefulness.

This is by no means the first attempt to acquaint the public with the results of applying scientific methods to the study of the Sacred Scriptures. Thirty-two years ago the late Dr. Samuel R. Driver, Canon of Christ Church, Oxford, England, gave the English-speaking world a masterly "Introduction to the Literature of the Old Testament"; wherein, by means of schematic analyses of the Hexateuch and copious lists of words and phrases peculiar to each author, editor or group of collaborators in the whole Canon, accompanying them by his own felicitous criticisms, he supplied everyone interested, and who had time to use it, with a sufficient apparatus for estimating not only the work so far accomplished, but its incomparable value. American scholars were not slow to perceive the advantages of Dr. Driver's method and to make it more practical. Dr. Benjamin W. Bacon, now of Yale University, published in 1894 "The Triple Tradition of the Exodus", in which he distinguished typographically from each other and from the interpolations of post-exilic editors the two accounts of the Flight from Egypt contained in the books of Exodus and Numbers. Dr. Paul Haupt, of the Johns Hopkins University, had already planned a remarkable edition in which the books of the Old Testament were to be "newly translated and annotated by eminent scholars of Europe and America, *and printed in colors exhibiting the composite structure of each book*", thereby enabling the reader to grasp in their integrity the argument and style of the original author. The first volumes of this "Polychrome edition" appeared in 1898, and took the literary world by storm. No such royal road to learning had enticed the young student or delighted the Bible-teacher before. Unfortunately, the enterprise was soon abandoned, owing, it was said, to the heavy cost of production; and this unique aid to the study of the Sacred Scriptures as literature remains incomplete. However, in 1904 appeared the first volume of the "Student's Bible" by Dr. Charles F. Kent, Professor of Biblical Literature in Yale

University, which sets side by side, in proper sequence and with their approximate dates, the several contributions to the text of each book in the Old Testament. Dr. Kent has also assembled the opinions of the highest authorities on still disputed points; and, with his able introductions to the several volumes, together with excellent charts and maps, he has almost obviated the necessity for any other book of reference for the lay student.

But these volumes and others of their sort are at once too cumbrous and too costly for the ordinary reader,—for the busy man of affairs who consecrates some of his precious leisure to a Sunday Bible-class, for the mother who asks how she shall answer her children's questions, or for the instructor who would have his pupils gain their impression of these great writers from their own words and not from hearsay. The "Revised Editions" do indeed distinguish between poetry and prose by inset lines and capitals in the Historical Books, but not in the books of the Prophets, whose teachings are mostly embodied in noble poems. The "Temple Edition" (Oxford, 1902) of the Authorized Version, and the "Modern Reader's Bible" (Moulton, R. G. 1904), have remedied this oversight, but present little more of the now established results of critical analysis than did the "Paragraph Bible" (Nourse, James, 1834), published before such analysis was begun. Perhaps the time was not then ripe for a bolder advance. New discoveries in Bible-lands, new results from younger scholars might any day upset seemingly well-grounded conclusions. But for twenty years past, every product of continuous research has only confirmed these conclusions. The preacher, the lecturer, even the daily press frequently refer to and build upon them as received truths. Moreover, the political problems in the Near East and new inquiries into the basis and development of our religion demand that the original documents of the Hebrew writers, of the keen-sighted politicians and inspired leaders of thought known to us as the Hebrew Prophets, should be in the hands of every thoughtful student of affairs.

For these reasons the present simple edition, unencumbered with notes, is offered. The references at the head of each separate division are always to the Authorized Version (A.V.). A short list of works of reference easily obtainable at most public libraries, and some points in the development of criticism which the editor has found useful in class-work are put at the end of the volume. The few words necessary to supply connecting links between passages ruthlessly separated by the native compilers are put in brackets. Otherwise, no foreign matter has been introduced into the text, and that omitted in Part I. will be found in its proper chronological order in Part II., which will present the Exilic and Post-exilic writings.

I find no words to express adequately my gratitude to my inspiring teachers, Dr. Irving F. Wood, of Smith College; Dr. Richard Gottheil, of Columbia University, and Dr. Charles P. Fagnani, of the Union Theological Seminary, New York, for their kind encouragement and valuable criticism; also, without their casual agreement or suggestion in and out of class, the work would never have been attempted. They can never know how often memory has recalled their very voices as I have come across a passage on which they gave the final word which I have thankfully adopted; but whatever mistakes I have made cannot be laid at their door; they are all my own.

To other friends most dear, among them many of my former pupils, I am indebted for their enthusiastic encouragement and their insistence upon the immediate completion of the work, for which they themselves have felt the need. To each and all of these I tender my heartfelt thanks. I will not chronicle their names; each will know his or her own share. But to Mr. Elmer Hunter Scott, of Omaha, Neb. and Washington, D. C., and to Prof. C. Alphonso Smith, of the Naval Academy, Annapolis, Md., I owe special thanks for their examination of my plan and introduction and their favorable verdict upon them.

ELIZABETH CZARNOMSKA.

Sweet Briar College, 1924.

CONTENTS

THE LITERATURE OF ISRAEL

THE HISTORY OF THE CHILDREN OF ISRAEL

SUPPLEMENT TO THE HISTORY OF THE
CHILDREN OF ISRAEL

I.   The death of Jeroboam II, King of Israel, and the
accession of Azariah (Uzziah) in Judah. The
fall of the Northern Kingdom, conquered by
Assyria, (722 B.C.)

II.   The reign of Hezekiah in Judah. Isaiah the
Prophet his counsellor. Death of Hezekiah,
(694 B.C.)

SUPPLEMENT II. THE LAST KINGS OF JUDAH

The abominable reigns of Manasseh and his son
Amon. The righteous reign of JOSIAH; the
Finding of the Book of the LAW, and the Conse-
quent Religious Reform. The reigns of his
Apostate Sons and details of the Final Catas-
trophe. (584 B.C.)

MAPS

INTRODUCTION

The Need for a Thorough Rearrangement of the Text of the Old Testament, and How the Necessary Apparatus for So-doing was Obtained.

THE LITERATURE OF A NATION can be fully estimated only in the light of its history. Conversely, it is only from the literature of any given period that the historian learns the social and political conditions, the conflicting aims and opinions of the people, which vivify and explain the movements stated baldly in their annals, for every author is the product of his age, and consciously or unconsciously reflects it. Now, if these annals are lost, and the literature has been tampered with by editors, however well-meaning, to accord with their personal convictions; if poetry has been mistaken for prose, and much of it presented in fragments assigned to a period or author regardless of evident date or inherent probability; if overzealous copyists have worked into the text explanatory marginal notes or have otherwise marred the integrity of the original manuscripts, only a miracle could bring order out of the resultant confusion, restore the true sequence of events, and show convincingly the germs and growth of whatever noble ideals or invaluable truths the nation had evolved. Such was the condition of classic Hebrew Literature at the opening of the nineteenth century. Then, wonderfully, miracles came to pass.

Two powerful organizations were then aiming to exploit the East for their own aggrandizement, the English East India Company, and the armies of France under Napoleon in Egypt. But the most astonishing and permanent gain of each resulted from the interest of an obscure employé in a casual find.

The first came from India. A clerk in the offices of the East India Company found in its lumber-rooms, among its unconsidered spoils of war, a mass of well-ordered manuscript written in an unknown tongue. He brought it to the attention of Sir William Jones, recently appointed Head of the Supreme Court of Caicutta, and already famed for his linguistic attainments, especially for his profound knowledge of Persian. Sir William announced in 1785 that these MSS. were part of the Sacred Books of the ancient Hindus written in Sanskrit, hitherto unknown to Europeans, and evidently the mother-tongue from which the principal modern languages of Hindustan were derived; moreover, that its grammar and vocabulary were closely akin, not only to those of Old Persian, but also to those of Greek, Latin and the Teutonic languages; and he inferred that all the peoples who spoke those languages were originally of the same stock. Sir William died in 1794, but not before he had shown that Arabic and its congeners, though also highly inflected languages, differed radically from the above-mentioned Indo-European tongues. Following these suggestions and tracing modern languages to their several sources, Jakob Grimm, of the University of Göttingen, published in 1820 his famous "Law of Phonetic Change in Languages", a change inevitable in time.   The first great triumph of the application of this law was the recovery of the Avestan language, older than any Old Persian before known, in which *Zoroaster* and his disciples had written the principles of their noble religion.   Upon the basis of these discoveries, Franz Boppe, of Mainz, published, between 1829 and 1833, the four volumes of his "Analytical and Comparative Study of the Grammars of Sanskrit, Greek, Latin and the Teutonic Languages", following it up in 1837 with "A Comparison of Slavic, Gothic and German."   Meanwhile, H. F. W. Gesenius, Professor of Theology in the University of Halle, had published his exhaustive "Dictionary of Hebrew and Chaldaic" and a "History of the Hebrew Tongue".   Thus was built up a splendid apparatus for the thorough analysis and emendation of all the then known texts in ancient languages.

Napoleon opened the way for the second astonishing discovery.   All literatures show at various periods the influence of their contemporaries. English literature affords a striking example.   Leaving out of account its general tendency, due to the blending of many races in the forming of the nation and to the centuries of Christian teaching by the Monastic Orders, the impulse for every new departure since Chaucer's time has come from Italy, France, Spain, France again, Germany and Norway; yet in every case the persistence of English characteristics and the philosophical trend of English thought have moulded the new influence into conformity with English ideals.   So was it with Hebrew literature. As we now know, it successively absorbed elements from the literatures of Egypt, Assyria and Persia; but the sources of these elements were unsuspected by either Jews or Christians.   Native and assimilated ideas were alike attributed to direct divine inspiration of the Children of Israel alone.   Nor until late in the nineteenth century was any literature older than the Hebrew known.   Greek legends, indeed, traced the Pythagorean philosophy to Egypt, and the earliest laws of the Greeks and their knowledge of music to Crete; but even Herodotus (450 B.C.), who closely observed the physical characteristics and present conditions of the eastern lands he visited, and gave detailed accounts of the laws, customs and religions of their peoples, said nothing of their literatures. Now Napolean was a man of insatiable curiosity, intent always upon fathoming a subject to its depths.   He landed in Egypt in 1798, Bible and Herodotus in hand, and accompanied by a body of *savants* whose business it should be to reveal the truth about Egypt to the world.   They did indeed tear away the veil which had so long enshrouded her and reveal her manifold superficial charms, even the daily life and occupations of her working-classes and the sports of her Pharaohs in past millenniums, pictured for any one to see upon her temple-walls.   But they found no means of either verifying or disproving the legends concerning her rulers.   There were no writings or even numbers that the *savants* could understand; and Napoleon left Egypt in 1802, disappointed in his archæological investigations as well as in his martial aims.

But in 1799, a young lieutenant of engineers named Broussard, who knew something of Greek, had found on the Rosetta branch of the Nile a block of basalt on which were inscribed many lines of Greek in an almost perfect condition, many other lines, slightly defaced, in an unknown cursive writing, and fourteen regularly arranged lines of those birds and serpents and lions and arms and legs, &c., so liberally distributed about the figures of men and gods upon the temple-walls.   He suspected that the unknown characters might be a transcription of the Greek, and made known his find to the French authorities in Alexandria;

but little did he dream that here was the key to a buried treasure of
Egyptian history and literature. The way to it was long and difficult.
Not until five years after Napoleon's death did *Champollion* publish the
Egyptian alphabet, determinatives and ideograms obtained from the
"Rosetta Stone" and nearly contemporary inscriptions. Fortunately, all
were of the Ptolemaic period, *i.e.*, after the Macedonian Conquest; for
at no other period would Greek and Egyptian inscriptions have been
engraved together. But it was quite another thing to read the papyri
and inscriptions found in the tombs of kings and nobles buried one to
three thousand years before. Still, the clue was now in the hands of
a little army of workers; and, after fifty years of individual study,
comparison of results, disputes and final agreement, scholars were ready
to give accurate translations of accumulated documents, and of new
ones from Tell el Amarna and elsewhere towards the end of the century.

Meanwhile, *Henry Rawlinson*, an English scholar as well as soldier,
had found on the "Rock of Behistun", far to the east of the Tigris,
another tri-lingual inscription in Old Persian, Susian, and the wedge-
shaped characters that had long intrigued travelers in Mesopotamia, and
which we now call *Cuneiform*. Well-versed in Old Persian, he succeeded
in deciphering the Cuneiform inscription, and published a translation
of it in 1846-7. At the same time, Henry Austen Layard, inspired by the
notable finds in Egypt, had obtained a firman from the Turkish government to open a remarkable mound near Mosul on the Tigris. (It had
been opened before by a Frenchman named Botta, but without great
results.) Mounds do not belong to the geological formation of the Meso-
potamian plateau; and those which have since been excavated have
revealed long-buried villages and cities of an early date. This one proved
to contain the palace of Sargon II., king of Assyria in the eighth
century B.C. The numerous inscriptions in Cuneiform characters on
the walls proved that this was the Assyrian form of writing. Later it
was learned that the Assyrians had adopted it from Babylonia; and that
thus the laws, literature and science and even the mercantile transac-
tions of private citizens from 3800 B.C. to the fall of Assyria in 606 B.C.
could be read. Also, from the glossaries used by the Babylonians in
their temple-schools, as schoolboys to-day use those in their Latin
textbooks, we can learn something of the language of the Sumerians,
the predecessors of the Semitic Babylonians, and, so far as we yet
know, the Founders of Civilization.

The value of the discovery of these languages is incalculable. Thereby, ancient history has been overturned and reset upon a sure foundation, and each nation fitted into its proper place; science recognizes her
debt to these first inventors; and the development of the literature and
religion of all Christendom is now traceable to their origins. For the
CHILDREN OF ISRAEL built up their kingdoms upon the ruins of
those of their kinsmen, the Canaanites, in the very centre of civilization,
assimilated it, and passed it on through the medium of Christianity to
the western world. North, east, south and west of them lay the great
empires that had created it,—the Hittite, the Babylonia-Assyrian, Egypt,
and the Naval Hegemony of the Ægæan (immortalized by Homer), whose
leader was Crete. The first and the last were on the verge of extinc-
tion when the Israelites appeared. The Hittites had fought their last
great battle at Kadesh-on-the-Orontes between the Lebanons; and a
remnant of the Cretans, fleeing before the barbarian hordes who were
to create Greece, had sought the eastern coast of the Mediterranean,
and were now settled in its southeastern corner, where they remained

a constant thorn in the flesh for Israel, and, as Philistines, became the type of everything opposed to idealism and spiritual growth. There remained Egypt and Assyria; the latter now in the ascendant in the dual Semitic empire between the Euphrates and the Persian Gulf; the former, under Rameses II., of the Nineteenth Dynasty, had just harrowed her rebellious Syrian provinces into subjection, and almost depopulated Canaan, already reduced by inroads of Hittites and Philistines. It may be that the great leader of the Israelites saw herein a heavensent opportunity to establish his brethren in the home of their forefathers, amidst the ancient culture of their race.

The mutilation and disarrangement of the Hebrew writings could not greatly obscure the superb genius of their authors, their keen observation of the life and character of their contemporaries, their clear foresight of the results of unbridled self-indulgence, wanton disregard of the sufferings of the poor and disobedience to the primary laws of God. So also stand forth boldly the beautiful expansions of the Ten Words attributed to Moses, and the insistence upon the only social and economic relations between man and man upon which the world's progress to stable government can be based. Here are masterpieces of prose and poetry whose manifold perfections of style have been the standard for all the literatures of Christendom; here, too, that recognition of one Creator and Ruler of the universe, just, unchangeable and true, the Father of all mankind without distinction of race or degree, which was proclaimed by the prophets of the eighth century B.C., when all other peoples, civilized or barbarous, were steeped in superstition, and worshiping gods who were at best but supermen. Portions of these writings, selected to be read or commented upon in temple or synagogue or as "lessons" in Christian churches, are incomparable for instruction, warning or consolation, or for inspiration to high endeavor. But read or studied consecutively as the writing of the single author to whom they are attributed,—as Moses, Joshua, Samuel or the prophets— they are full of defects. The "Historical Books" (Genesis to 2 Kings) give variant versions of the same incidents which involve strange discrepancies, sometimes flat contradictions; and in the "Books of the Prophets" (Isaiah to Malachi) occur abrupt changes of style and subject, interpolations of foreign matter and sometimes passages of utter bathos, impossible to ascribe to such masters of form and treatment of subject-matter as the bulk of the work reveals.

Devoted and clear-thinking students, both Jew and Christian, strove to reconcile these anomalies by various theories of interpretation which only served to "darken counsel by words without knowledge". They could only propound theories, for they had no facts to go upon. The Jews fell back upon the dictum of Josephus, that the writers "spake some things wisely but enigmatically and others by decent allegory". In the Christian Church it became the custom to ascribe all difficulties to the loss of parts of the original documents during the terrible vicissitudes which the nation had undergone. Yet it was fully demonstrable that no change had been made in the "Canon of the Law" (the first five books of the Old Testament, closed c. B.C. 400) nor in the "Canon of the Prophets" (closed much later), without the consent of the *Sanhedrim,* the governing body in Judæa after the Persian Conquest. The whole collection of Hebrew writings was early translated into Aramaic (the *Targums*) for the use of the laity in Palestine and Syria, since that was the language of Damascus, the centre of trade between the East and the West; for, long before the present era, Hebrew had become a dead language, used only in the temple-service and by the priests. In Egypt, the first Ptolemies (B.C. 323-171), lovers and patrons of learning, caused it to be translated into Greek (the *Septuagint*) for the use of their Jewish subjects, who then formed one-third of the population of Alex-.andria, had a flourishing colony and a temple in Upper Egypt and another twenty miles north of the present city of Cairo,—a little replica of Jerusalem and her Temple. Later, when Christianity had come into favor with the Roman Emperors and was soon to be the State religion, Saint Jerome (*Hieronymus*) went to Jerusalem and, with the aid of learned rabbis, made a translation of the Hebrew Canon into Latin which became the authorized version of the Roman Church. Small wonder that these translations, as well as the original, soon became sacrosanct; and any one who charged them with defect ran the risk of excommunication in both the Jewish Church and the Christian. Such was the fate of Pelagius, Abelard, Spinoza and others; while Maimonides, Galileo and, in the nineteenth century, St. George Mivart escaped it only by recantation or specious argument. In view of the number of exceptions to the text taken by the greatest scholars of the Middle Ages, the Christian Church withdrew the Scriptures from common use, and the majority of the priests studied and taught only Peter Lombard's "Sentences" (*Sententiarum Libri Quattuor*), books of "Opinions" drawn from the writings of the early "Fathers of the Church".

Analysis of the So-Called "Historical Books"

HISTORY is not usually classified as Literature. Their domains are too far asunder. The one recounts facts, the other gives expression to thoughts and emotions. History searches out and tells the course of past events; Literature interweaves the ideals of the past with those of the present, and gives inspiration for the future. The tone of History is unimpassioned, judicial; Literature, even when most tranquil and tranquilizing, is penetrated with feeling. The Hebrew Historical Books are all highly emotional. It is as literature, therefore, that we are compelled to regard them and apply to them the same method of analysis and criticism as to other literature.

The Historical Books, taken as a whole, are the work of four major writers, all anonymous, but distinguished by scholars as J, E, D, and P. The bulk of it up to 850 B.C. comes from J; to P (priestly writer or band of writers) is due the annalistic framework in which are set the writings of the other three, each of which had been edited and re-edited before P combined them and interpolated statistics and geographical and genealogical details. None of the editing was like that of the present day, which aims to discover and hold intact the original text of the author; rather it resembles that of the Elizabethan and Restoration playwrights, who cut out or added scenes to meet the needs of some special representation, or to cater to the tastes of another age. As P's combination was made after both kingdoms had fallen, and the Exile was a thing of the past, the consideration of his share in the completed Canon will be given in Part II. of this edition.

A prime requisite of history is continuity. In the Historical Books it is conspicuously lacking. Instead, we have a series of dramatic scenes, vigorously drawn. The actors in them live. We hear their word-combats, we can weigh their arguments. Comments are dispensed with. Pathetic situations and stirring deeds are left to make their own impression. But many decades, even centuries, during which the conditions and animus of the next scene were preparing, are passed over in silence, or with the brief formula, "and the land had rest forty years" (or forty-five or thirty-one or four-score as the case might be), or with some slight mention of the reigns of intervening rulers.   The life of the nation, from the Exodus to the conquest of all southwestern Asia by Alexander of Macedon, covered some nine hundred years.   As given in this panorama, begun by J and carried on by P and the Chronicler, it divides into seven periods of each of which the beginning is pictured with profuse detail and the end strongly condensed.   These periods are:

1. The Exodus from Egypt and the Settlement in Canaan (c. 1220-1160 B.C.);
2. The Rise of Monarchy under Saul, its expansion under David and consolidation under Solomon (c. 1050-960 B.C.);
3. The Division of the kingdom after the death of Solomon into the twin kingdoms of Israel (N.) and Judah (S.) (937-850 B.C.);
4. The Predominance of Israel until conquered by Assyria in 722 B.C.;
5. The Brilliant Literary Period in Judah until its conquest by Nebuchadrezzar the Chaldean, and the Deportation of its higher classes into Babylonia (765-586 B.C.);
6. The Conquest of Babylonia and its dependencies by Cyrus the Persian (538 B.C.);
7. The Second great Literary Period in Judæa under Persian rule, and the re-establishment of Theocracy (535-332 B.C.).

There is a supplementary period which begins with the rule of the Greeks, includes the Revolt of the Maccabees (167 B.C.) and ends with the death of Herod the Great (4 B.C.); but its history is consigned to the Apocrypha, because it adds nothing to the development of the Religion of Israel.   It enters into Biblical Literature, however, as part of the Apocalyptic Vision in "Daniel", and because it furnishes the background of much of the late "Wisdom Literature" of the Jews.

IT WAS IN the ninth century B.C., when Ahab was king in Israel and Jehoshaphat in Judah, that a literary genius and philosopher of the first order originated the above arrangement of the material at his command for the solution of a problem of absorbing interest.   His name is unknown, but scholars call him J because he was evidently of the southern kingdom (Judah), and because he invariably calls the national God *Yahweh* or *Yah* (Heb. Jahweh or Yah).   J was not primarily interested in historical research.   The Israelites knew already all the facts he could give them.   In the long peaceful years of their tribal life, broken only by the few forays that furnished the subjects for their folk-songs and tales, they had reveled in stories of the prowess of their tribal heroes, and sung the victories of Yahweh: How Joshua and Caleb, the tribe of Judah, and Deborah "the prophetess, wife of Lapidoth, who judged Israel" had successively brought the Canaanites into subjection; How Jephthah had defended their northeastern frontier, and Gideon had driven from the heart of the land the marauding Bedouin; How Samson paid for his youthful exploits against the hated Philistines, but later took an awful reprisal for the same.   All these were done in the name of their militant God, Yahweh.   From the Canaanites in their midst— ("For, when Israel became strong, they subjected the Canaanites to forced labor but did not dispossess them, . . . the Canaanites lived in the midst of them"), they learned the old Babylonian legends of the early world, which were probably current in writing before they entered the land.   Those of their own heroes had been collected, probably in Solomon's time, in two anthologies, "The Wars of Yahweh" and "The Book of the Upright" (Heb. *Jashar.*)   In creating his Cabinet, David had appointed a Recorder, and Solomon, after building his temple, had appointed scribes among its officials; so that State and Temple Records were available for Israelite writers as for those of other nations. Chronicles of these two kings and Commentaries upon the *Acts* of the non-literary prophets (or teachers) had also been written. All of these works, now lost, were at the disposal of J when he set himself to answer the question: Why have not the promises of Moses been fulfilled? For now, in this ninth century B.C. and the third since their complete possession of Canaan, Assyria, the great empire in the east, was again upon the war-path and had already overthrown Babylonia. But the Israelites were not alarmed. If Assyria should come west of the Euphrates, Damascus would turn her northward as she had done before. If necessary, however, the Twin Kingdoms would bring to her aid their unconquerable God, Yahweh, who, according to His promises, would always lead the Children of Israel to victory when they called upon Him.

It was an unwarranted assumption. No such unconditioned promise had Moses brought them. Well he knew that his brethren were enfeebled in body and dulled in soul by the long oppression they had undergone. All that he could build on to raise their morale was the tenacity with which they clung to traditions of their forefathers and of the promises their God had given them—traditions of Abraham, their progenitor, noble in character, strong in self-control, obedient to the promptings of his conscience; of Jacob (Israel), to whom God had promised the land of Canaan for his descendants; of Joseph, whom his brethren had sold into Egypt, and whom his native sagacity and diligence had raised to the highest office in the land, whereby he saved its people and his own family from starvation, and fixed the royal revenue on a firm basis. Relying on these examples to inspire his brethren with faith and courage, Moses brought them a *Covenant* with Yahweh, who had revealed Himself to him on Sinai as the God of the Patriarchs, the Creator of heaven and earth, by whatever name He might be called. Yahweh would deliver the Children of Israel from their task-masters, guide them to the Promised Land and protect them therein, provided that they would obey His laws. These laws were simple. They ordained little outward observance. Their substance could be summed in one command; *Obey and be loyal to Yahweh, your benefactor, and do to others as you would have them do to you.* They were not prescribed for emergencies, but for daily living. As interpreted by Moses, they demanded the exercise of reason and aroused the conscience. Doubtless, few of the Israelites understood at first to what they bound themselves; probably only those "elders" to whom Moses first submitted the Covenant, and who later ratified it in the presence of Jethro, priest of Midian; for, almost on the morrow of their escape, many of the fugitives were complaining of the hardships of the journey and stirring up sedition, and few months passed without a mutiny. With inexhaustible patience Moses endured their insubordination and open insolence, put them under strict discipline, and appointed judges to settle their disputes. Then, after two years of training, he brought them to the southern border of the Promised Land.

Did Moses believe that the sight of it would make the tribes pluck up spirit to fight for it? Not they. Not only did they refuse to make the attempt, but they proposed *to elect another leader to guide them back to Egypt.* Like many a later philanthropist, Moses was at last compelled to recognize that gratitude, which prompts the noble soul to ready obedience, is practically dead in those who have only obeyed the lash. Perforce he gave up the adults, and turned them all back to the

simple life and invigorating climate of the steppes, there to bring up
the children to a sense of the high mission he dreamed for them,—to
uphold the liberty and equal rights of all men under the rule of their
powerful though invisible God and King.   More than a generation later,
Joshua and Caleb, who alone had sympathized with and staunchly sup-
ported him during the whole migration, carried out the first condition
of his plan and brought into Canaan a stalwart and eager band of
warriors prepared to keep and spread the knowledge of their Covenant
with Yahweh.   Alas, in a few decades, the beauty of the land with its
rich gifts of corn and wine and ease of living had allured their descendants to a laxity of morals and distinction of classes utterly opposed to
His laws.

Looking back from his standpoint of the ninth century through many
such lapses, consequent humiliations and new beginnings, J found the
answer to his question in the blind indifference of his brethren to the
teachings of experience (teachings embodied in the very tales they so
delighted in), and hence the constant repetition of the old self-indulgence, old disobedience to the laws of right living, old ingratitude to
God and injustice to their fellows.   He set himself, therefore, not only
to assemble these scattered lessons and show their meaning, but to
trace Man's growth in intelligence, dignity and worth to the world
through obedience to the inner promptings of right reason; and the
inevitable disaster to himself and the world through a weak yielding
to every selfish impulse.

The thesis of J begins with the condition of primitive man, newly
conscious of free agency and the power of invention, not yet competent
to see cause for gratitude, and therefore for obedience, in the gift of
reason.   Next he shows the *innate sense of justice* displayed by Abel
in his grateful offering to the Giver of all good things, and the dire
destruction of all social life which Cain's breach of the *innate bond of
kinship* would entail.   How small a percentage of men make a right
use of privilege he shows in the story of the preservation of righteous
Noah and his family; and how futile the presumptuous dependence
upon the righteousness of ancestors as a shield against just punishment,
in that of the Tower of Babel.   He portrays the Patriarchs, none of
them perfect, but always growing towards perfection by living in close
communion with God; and he shows how far below them the immi-
grants from Egypt had fallen, in spite of the inspired teaching of
Moses, their advance in material prosperity and culture, and the constant efforts of many teachers, such as Samuel and Nathan, to keep
them to their covenant.   He brings in examples of the evil bred of evil
from recent events in the sister kingdom of Israel, contrasting them
with the wisdom of their own king Asa and the consequent peace in
Judah; but he feels sure that neither of the Twin Kingdoms can hope
for help from Yahweh against onslaughts of "heathen peoples", unless
they both reform.

The place of J is not among historians, though necessarily he has
given us many historical incidents, and the ancestors of his nation live
in his pages; but he must be classed with the great philosophers and
religious reformers of all ages.   Twenty-five hundred years before Vico
published his *Scienza Nuova,* and initiated the modern method of writing
history, J brilliantly illustrated its highest uses.   And, for command
of dramatic situation, powerful delineation of character and subtle distinction of motive, he is still unsurpassed.

The next great writer came from the Northern Kingdom.   Like J
he is anonymous, and is called E because he uses the word Elohim

(Strong ones) as the name of Deity. Hence the two are also distinguished as the "Yahwist" and the "Elohist". The latter wrote in the eighth century, about a hundred years after J. He too found his material in current traditions; but either those of the north differed greatly from those of the south, or the two authors differed widely in their preferences. So far as we can judge, E had no thesis to sustain, but gathered various interesting stories of the heroes of the northern tribes, and was careful to determine the scenes of their activity. E leans to narrative as J to the dramatic. Unlike J, he gives little foundation for psychological study in his accounts of the Exodus. J is careful to give natural causes for the wonders wrought in Egypt; E delights in the miraculous. For E, Moses is a mere mouthpiece for the Divine message; a messenger who reports *verbatim;* but he is a great enchanter, who governs the winds and waves, and brings disasters to pass by the waving of a wand. He even converts the wand into a serpent, as Pharaoh's magicians can also do; but Moses is greater than they. Evidently E was well acquainted with Egyptian folk-lore, which abounds in miracles; he also uses Egyptian titles and gives several of his characters Egyptian names. He draws few philosophical conclusions from his facts.

As J was contemporary with Elijah and possibly one of his disciples, yet left it to another hand to give the striking account of his career, so E, who was contemporary with at least three of the four literary prophets of his century who carried on and accentuated J's exhortations to religious reform, makes no mention of them. Apparently his interest was in the past, or he was too timid to chronicle actions and words so unpopular at court as those of Amos and Hosea; but we are greatly indebted to him for many an intimate detail in the lives of Israel's heroes, and for his masterly presentment of both humor and pathos. While by no means the equal of J for profound insight and clear reasoning, he is a most graphic narrator, and his style is both graceful and pungent.

Less than twenty years after E had finished his work, Tiglath Pileser III., king of Assyria, appeared on the northern frontier of Israel, captured a few towns and deported their inhabitants, replacing them with his own people, and thus securing the head waters of the Jordan. Then he retired for a time. But, finding that Hoshea, king of Israel, was negotiating with Egypt to withstand him, he reappeared and laid siege to Samaria, the great fortress-capital of Israel and the rival of Jerusalem. The siege lasted three years; and when the city was finally taken, the Kingdom of Israel, which for over two hundred years had been the barrier between Egypt and Assyria, came to an end; the leading men of the tribes, the "Ten Lost Tribes", were deported, and no trace of them has ever been found. Yet, only forty years before, Jeroboam II., their greatest warrior-king, had regained all the neighboring territory conquered by David and left to Solomon; and he was contemplating the conquest of Judah and the reunion of the two kingdoms when he died. Had his plan been carried out, all the tribes of Israel might have perished together, the great uplifting power of Hebrew literature might have been strangled in its birth, the very name of its instigator forgotten, and we might still be openly worshiping Melech and Astarte, or such gods as Tiberius, Nero and Caligula. But Judah in her mountain fastnesses was spared; for "God meant it for good, to bring to pass the saving of many people alive."

The immediate result for Hebrew literature of the devastation of the Northern Kingdom, the destruction of its records and the deportation of all who might have recalled its cherished traditions and replaced its writings, was a unique production which it is safe to say has caused more misunderstanding and discussion than any other work in literature. The Kingdom of Israel fell in 722 B.C. Before the end of the century, a patriotic but undiscriminating writer, striving to preserve at least its most sacred traditions, had grafted upon J's noble thesis the narratives of E in such fashion as to produce those strange discrepancies and contradictions already spoken of, the explanation of which has necessitated nearly a century of close study. The well-intentioned author of this confusion is appropriately called JE. How much of J's impressive argument and graphic illustration he sacrificed to his admiration of E, it is impossible to tell; but we are indebted to him not only for all we know of the latter, but also for the preservation of the two very ancient law-codes, the "Book of the Covenant" and the "Law of Holiness", both attributed with great probability to Moses, but later distributed by P among the laws that the tribes found in Canaan.

The awful object-lesson in the fate of the Ten Tribes, "which kept not the commandments of Yahweh their God, but walked in the statutes of the heathen and of the kings of Israel", had not been without effect upon Judah. The Assyrian army was nearing Jerusalem, and its heralds were stirring up the populace to revolt against their king and put themselves under the protection of Assyria. Therefore, acting upon the counsels of Isaiah, the cousin and couniellor of the king, Hezekiah and his Court rushed to the Temple, and with solemn prayer and sacrifice besought Yahweh for the honor of His name to save His Chosen People, And, marvelous to relate, Sennacherib raised the siege (whether because of a plague in the camp, as one writer gives it, or, according to another, because of tidings of a revolt at home), and Judah was saved. The deliverance was followed by a reform which lasted till Hezekiah's death; but his son and successor, Manasseh, did his utmost to root out the pure worship of Yahweh, substituting for it the licentious and cruel rites of the "gods of the nations". The rich resumed their old habits of luxurious living with its attendant evils; the poor were hideously oppressed; and the king "filled Jerusalem with innocent blood". Tradition ascribes to him the martyrdom of the venerable Isaiah. The fifty-seven years of the reigns of Manasseh and his son Amon were an orgy of all that is most vile in irresponsible tyranny, the worst blot on the history of David's line. Nevertheless, from it was born, through revulsion of popular feeling, and the immediate instrumentality of D, the great reformation of Josiah's reign which established the Law on which was to be founded that "New Covenant" (Jer. xxxi, 31-34) which is the basis of all spiritual religion, and which Christ came "not to destroy, but to fulfil".

The graphic account of the occasion and completion of this reform is given in 2 Ki. xxi, 23—xxiii, 25. It begins: "The servants of Amon conspired against him and slew him in his own house; and the people of the land slew all that had conspired against King Amon, and made Josiah his son king in his stead". Thus the people cleared the way for the return of the priests of the ancient faith, under whose training and advice the boy-king grew up. Evidently he came to an impoverished kingdom; but in his twenty-sixth year he commanded that the people's voluntary offerings to the Temple should be used to remove every vestige of the altars to all sorts of foreign gods with which Manasseh had defiled it, to repair the breaches in its walls, and thoroughly to restore its dignity and beauty. At some time during this restoration, the High Priest announced: "I have found the Book of the Law in the House of Yahweh"; and Josiah accepted it and acted upon it.

What is this epoch-making "Book of the Law"? It purports to give *verbatim* Moses' farewell words of counsel, warning and encouragement to the sons of the bondmen whom he had brought out of Egypt, and whom he had trained from childhood to establish a unique nation of freemen, self-governed under the promptings of gratitude to their beneficent God and King. But it is a late work, and no hint of any such address is given by any previous writer. Its language, free from archaisms, its form and its easy, flowing rhythm bear the stamp of high literary culture, the outcome of a long period of previous use. Jeremiah and later writers show its influence, notably in their adoption of its marked phraseology, of which there is no trace in the previous century; while its author is as evidently imbued with the lofty idealism first voiced by the poet-prophets of that century. It also presupposes forms of idolatry unmentioned by the same prophets, and presumably unknown in Judah before the apostasy of Manasseh. From this and other evidence we conclude that it could not have been written before the reign of Manasseh, nor, in all likelihood, long before it was found. It is free from those "redactions" from which it would surely have suffered had it not come fresh from the author's hand to the eye and heart of the king. A very few foreign lines, mostly repetitions, have crept into the text, and a later hand inserted the superb "Song of Moses" and "Blessing of Moses"; part of chapter xxvii, also, is either an interpolation or has lost a connecting link; but the main body of the work is a unit, apparently written *currente calamo* under the urgency of a special need. It falls easily into the divisions of a great oration, of which, indeed, it is the earliest known.

A noble EXORDIUM briefly reviews the Exodus, and brings the hearer to the time and place of delivery,—the ford of the Jordan, and the eve of the Crossing into Canaan. The force of the aged leader is spent; he must not set foot in the Promised Land; Joshua must complete his work. But how will it be when his voice is hushed and no one else may have the same sense of intimate communion with God? when no one can say: Yahweh bade me speak this and this? He himself, therefore, must once more impress upon his beloved children the laws of right reason and right living, adjuring them by all they hold most dear to love their God "with all their heart and with all their soul and with all their strength", and gratefully to obey Him for love's sake. Next comes the STATEMENT of the original laws, the Decalogue, and of the People's choice of him, Moses, to be their intermediary between them and Yahweh and the expositor of His will. Then come the EXPOSITIONS; first, of the inner meaning of the laws of the First Table,—*their Duty towards God;* secondly, the detailed application of the other six laws,—*their Duty towards their Fellow-men.* Then comes the DEDUCTION or COROLLARY,—the blessings that shall reward their obedience, and the evils that will be their curse if they disobey. Finally, with a magnificent PERORATION (ch. xxix, 2-9 and xxx, 11-20), the oration ends, and with it the work of D.

A superb piece of oratory! but far more—a dramatic creation of the imagination in a supreme effort to deliver the once "holy nation" from a slavery as much worse than that of Egypt as sin eats deeper than hard labor into the forces of life. With the audacity of genius, D brings before them in their degradation the figure of their great leader at the most heart-moving crisis of his career. Not for a moment does he let them forget Moses' advanced age and failing powers as he repeats again and again his anxious forebodings and pathetic entreaties. (It was another hand that wrote "his eye was not dimmed nor his natural force abated".) By impassioned sympathy D has entered into the mind of the great law-giver, has comprehended the wisdom and ideals implicit in his laws, and emphasized them by appeals not to the reason but to the heart. At the fitting moment, for which doubtless he had watched as Moses had watched for the moment to advance upon Canaan, D prudently placed the document where it would certainly be found; but not too easily, since it must be believed to come out of the sacred past, and its author must remain forever unknown or his purpose could not be achieved. How far otherwise it might have been received we may learn from the treatment of Amos by the High Priest of Bethel (Am. vii, 10-13), or of Jeremiah's scroll by Jehoiakim, son of Josiah (Jer. xxxvi, 21-25). The form of the work has been a model for orators. As a Dramatic Monologuist, D was the forerunner of such literary artists as Walter Mapes, Marlowe and Pope, Tennyson and Browning; but he remains for all time as far greater than they as his aim was higher; and when Theocracy was revived after the Exile, it was built up upon this Book of Deuteronomy, thought to be Moses' *Second Giving* of the Law.

King Josiah carried out a drastic reform not only in Judah but in the cities of Samaria, and among the rural population of Israel whom Shalmaneser IV. had left when he deported the prominent families of the Ten Tribes. But Josiah could not renew the dread of Yahweh's mysterious power which had aforetime held "the heathen peoples" in awe. That had disappeared forever when Ahaz, father of Hezekiah, scorning the counsels of Isaiah, then a young man, had turned to the "arm of flesh" for protection, and offered tribute to Assyria, paying it by despoiling the Temple of Solomon of its treasures. Later in his career, Isaiah saw considerable merit in Ahaz's policy in view of the changed conditions of the age, and used it as the basis of his doctrine of pacifism. Judah had neither army nor abundant food-supplies to compete with either of the great empires. Her eminence henceforth would lie in the superior nobility of her religion. Yahweh would determine when the "yoke of her burden" should be broken. Meanwhile, her "strength was to sit still". In the eyes of his contemporaries, it had been happy for Judah if Josiah and his sons had obeyed this warning. Josiah died all too young in a futile attempt to turn back the invading army of the Egyptians. On the other hand, his son and grandson, siding with Egypt, brought upon themselves the wrath of Nebuchadrezzar, the destruction of Jerusalem and her temple, and the same fate that had befallen Israel in the deportation of her people. But God sees not as man sees. Josiah's reform, like Hezekiah's, had affected only the outward aspect of her national life; it had neither touched the heart nor inspired sound morality in the majority of the people. Such reform cannot be brought about by mandate. But, from the bitter sorrows of exile; from the compulsory abolition of caste; from intimate acquaintance with despotic military government and a fatalistic religion, the Children of Israel were to return in the third generation to the land of their fathers with a strong conviction of the wisdom of their prophets and of the high value of their own laws and religion for ensuring happiness and the highest development of mankind.

When the populace slew the murderers of King Amon, brought back the priesthood of their ancient faith to the Temple and set a promising young prince upon the throne, they prepared the way for a brilliant literary period analogous to that of the Stuarts in England. The land was at peace. The language was at its best, purified from archaisms and as yet free from Aramaisms. The poets of the eighth century, Amos, Hosea, Isaiah and Micah, had set a high standard which those of the seventh must needs emulate. Literature of all kinds, therefore, flourished. Of it have been preserved poems by several authors interested in the fate of their neighboring enemies, though remaining blind to any danger for themselves; the noble "Praise of Wisdom" (Prov. i-ix), the forerunner of the "Wisdom-literature" of the Persian period; also after Nebuchadrezzar had made his first attack upon Jerusalem and carried away the king, the queen-mother and all the Court-officials, Habakkuk's striking impeachment of the justice of Yahweh, which started the question worked out later in the Book of Job. But of far greater interest than any of these, not excepting the Book of Deuteronomy on which they all turned, is the "Book of Jeremiah", which covers the period of Josiah's maturity and the troublous reigns of his successors, and throws a searching light upon the proud self-sufficiency of the Court and Temple officials and the degeneracy of the people, which brought the kingdom of Judah to an end. The prose portions of it, however, are from a Biography of the Prophet, written some while after the catastrophe of the Exile, and after all trace of him had probably been lost, for there is no mention of his death. It comes properly, therefore, under consideration with the other pre-exilic Prophetical Books.

Revision of the Books of the Prophets

A SPECIAL DIFFICULTY met the critics in the analysis of the prophetical books. When Jerusalem was besieged by the Romans (67-70 B.C.) the Sanhedrim fled to *Jamnia* near the sea coast (as the French Government fled during the late war from Paris to Bordeaux) taking with them three copies of their Sacred Scriptures rescued from the Temple. These furnished the material for a careful emendation of the text early in the next century by the Rabbi Aqiba; which excellent version was authorized for use in the synagogues of the *Diaspora* (the Dispersed). Now classic Hebrew, like all the other languages of the Western Semites, was written without vowels. Vowels are not necessary to any living language; they merely facilitate rapid reading at sight. The meaning of any combination of letters is determined by the context (*e.g.*, álly, n., and allý, v.; cóntract, n., and contráct, v.); if this were not so, understanding of the spoken word would be impossible. But when a language is no longer in daily use, and when these differences of meaning have not been familiar from childhood, there is large room for mistake. Also, the sound of the letters changes in time; rough breathings become smooth, vowels are flattened, strong dentals become sibilants and gutturals vanish. There are even two modern nations that have the same grammar and vocabulary and noble literatures equally intelligible to the eye for both, who yet can not converse with each other without considerable practice. The Norwegian says: We speak the language as it is written, the Danes slur it over. To obviate such mutilation of their scriptures in reading or cantilation, a band of Jewish scholars of the fifth century A.D. who called themselves *Masoretes* (followers of tradition), devised a system of vowel-points and accent-signs which should fix for all time the sonorous beauty of the language as it had been used in the Temple. It may be doubted if they even nearly succeeded; but at least it fixed for modern ears the pronunciation of their own day. But these tiny points and accents introduced a new possibility of error when applied by even the most painstaking copyists, and modern scholars are still at work correcting misplaced points that have converted nouns into verbs or participles and *vice versa*, to the obvious distortion of the meaning.

But the Masoretes made a grave error of their own. Not satisfied with one system of accents for prose, they made, as was well, another for poetry; but they limited its use to the so-called "Poetical Books" (Psalms, Proverbs and Job) and to certain passages in the Historical Books distinctly called "Songs". It was not until 1753 that an Enlgishman, Robert Lowth, then Professor of Poetry in Oxford, electrified both England and the Continent by publishing lectures upon Hebrew Poetry which pointed out its laws, and later illustrated their use in a thorough analysis of the Book of Isaiah. In consequence, there soon appeared a "Paragraph Bible" in which the poetry (by far the larger part) of the Prophetical Books was distinguished by insetting the lines and beginning each with a capital. This method was first followed in the "Revised Version" and more fully developed in Prof. Moulton's "Modern Reader's Bible" and in the Temple edition of the Authorized Version; but it remained for Wellhausen and the later critics to discover, while emending the text and excising the foreign matter now rejected, the great aid afforded by their knowledge of these laws. They are as follows:

a. Each line has two distinct parts, which together have from five to seven accented syllables, or stresses, separated by one, two or more unaccented syllables, and not by a fixed number as in our modern poetry. The lines are also grouped in couplets with an occasional triplet.

b. Between the two parts of a line, or between the two lines of a couplet, is a marked *Parallelism* in thought or structure. This parallelism is of three kinds: *Synonymous, Anthithetic,* and *Synthetic.* Later critics have added a fourth, *Climactic.*

c. The Parallelism is *Synonymous* if the second half-line, or second line, enforces the thought by repeating it in almost the same words as in the first, but with an added detail which enhances the meaning. If the second line, or second half-line enforces the original statement by a contrasting one given in similar form, the parallelism is Antithetic. In *Synthetic* parallelism, there is necessary only a parallel order of grammatical forms; *i.e.,* noun answering to noun, verb to verb, phrase to phrase, while the thought is expanded or confirmed. Climactic parallelism may be carried through a triplet or group of couplets, longer or shorter as the emotion to be expressed requires. This form corresponds in great measure with the Greek *strophe.*

d. A refrain of one or more lines may be used either at the beginning or the end of a strophe or of a succession of strophes.

The growth and perfecting of these varieties of parallelism, grouping and stress of lines is well illustrated in "Proverbs", the only one of the Poetical Books of which any part was written before the Exile. It is made up of collections of ethical teachings coming from widely separated periods. The oldest consists of chapters x to xv, and is a series of aphorisms connected only by their general purpose and stereotyped verse-form. The latter has all the rigidity of a first conscious attempt at literary style. Each aphorism is expressed in a single line (in the Hebrew), of which each half-line is three-stressed and in perfect *antithetic parallelism* with the other half. The collection is a treasury of shrewd common-sense and worldly wisdom directed towards the attainment of health, wealth, comfort and length of days; but of poetry there is not a whit. It bears the simple heading, "The Proverbs of Solomon".

Evidently of a later period are chapters xvi—xxii, 16. The language is more flexible, the parallelism is *synonymous*, tending to expand the thought, which is no longer confined to a single line, but is carried through a couplet. Metaphors appear and one or two similes. There is warmth of feeling and a higher moral tone than before. Stress is laid upon righteousness. The presence of Yahweh to shield, to guide, to justify the righteous man is constantly assumed, and the king is His mouthpiece. But between this collection and the next two chapters (seemingly a father's counsels to his son, chapter xxii, 17—xxiv), are striking differences which indicate a further advance in literary art. The tone is gracious, even intimate. Figures abound. The monotonous succession of *three-three stressed* lines is broken by *three-two* or *four-four* stressed lines. The subject is now confined to a couplet, now over-flows into a longer or shorter strophe. Sometimes a half-line is left without its parallel, thus marking the conclusion all the more strongly. One is reminded of Shakespeare's or Dryden's powerful uncompleted lines. Many critics hold that this "appendix", which amplifies the subjects of the second collection, is from the hand or at least by a contemporary of the editor who, just before the Exile, gathered together all the current maxims of the "Wise Men" (including those "copied out by the men of Hezekiah"), and prefaced them with the superb "Praise of Wisdom" (ch. i-ix) which exhibits the mastery of subject and graceful presentment of the best writings of the Golden Age. The rest of the book is made up of short collections from a very late period.

No loss of any early literature is more to be regretted than that of the two Hebrew anthologies, "The Wars of Yahweh" and "The Book of the Upright", frequently referred to and sometimes quoted in the Historical Books. Compiled towards the end of David's reign or the beginning of Solomon's, they must have contained much of the popular poetry which furnished material for J and E. (An interesting glimpse of their use of it is given in the Book of Judges (ch. iv-v), where the ancient martial ode of Deborah is set side by side with the prose account of the same facts drawn from it some four hundred years later.) One beautiful dirge and fragments of others are from the hand of "the sweet singer of Israel" himself. But the priests who made the final collection of the national literature were only solicitous to preserve what concerned their religion or the lives of the heroes who advanced it. Fortunately, certain snatches of song escaped their notice or were read as history. Some of these are now known to be fragments of Babylonian myths current in Canaan. Their originals are now in our hands. Notable features of all this folk-lore are the excellent handling of rhythms and the frequent use of *Apostrophe*. From our present knowledge of Assyrian poetry, we are compelled to infer that to its influence is due the early perfection of these poetical forms in Hebrew.

The discovery that several collections compiled by different editors were assembled in the canonical Book of Proverbs, was interesting and easy to verify; but it was of slight importance compared with that of the composite nature of the Books of the Prophets. As we can now read them in their true succession and (except for occasional *lacunae*) in their original integrity, they abundantly answer the questions, (1): How and when was the highly spiritual religion on which Christianity is founded evolved from the gross materialism of the eighth century B.C., when the supreme end in life for the rich seemed to be pleasure and luxurious ease, and the means for enjoying it were wrung from the misery of the poor? And (2): By what magic could so sophisticated and degenerate a people have been restored to the personal purity and unselfish fraternity inculcated by Moses?   This was to be the self-appointed though none-the-less-inspired work of the Prophets of the Golden Age.

THE GOLDEN AGE opened with the irruption of Poetry into the alien fields of economics and social ethics.   A hundred years had elapsed since J and Elijah the Tishbite[1] had shown the necessity for reform and the essence of true religion.   Not by magnificent ritual and impressive holocausts copied from the forms of pagan worship, but by spiritual communion with God, and obedience to the "still, small voice" of conscience was Israel to regain her great heritage,—a heritage not to be measured in territory, but by the spread of her early moral and religious standards.   It does not appear that J's teachings had been heeded by his contemporaries; the proverbs of the Wise Men seemed more serviceable in the daily struggle to get on in the world.   They were destined, however, to inspire and direct the efforts of the great reformers known as the "Literary Prophets of Israel".   These were all *admirable poets* though of different degrees of merit.   Each approached the common problem from a different point of view according to the conditions of his day; but the pioneers whom after ages have set highest on the roll, —Amos, a landed proprietor of Tekoa; Isaiah of Jerusalem, companion and counsellor of kings; Micah the Morasthite, spokesman for the peasantry of the Judæan lowlands,—had the least immediate influence. Possessed of every poetic gift, all three mistook the office of poetry and alienated those whose selfish and short-sighted policies and habits they hoped to reform.   Poetry has always swayed the multitude, but only when it delights the senses or inspires the down-trodden and despondent with hopes of better conditions.   These poets employed all the devices of rhetoric, every variety of rhythm, and a wealth of imagery drawn from the beauties and forces of nature to intensify the withering irony with which they laid bare existing evils, and to picture the terrible vengeance of their offended God.   For Amos unflinchingly proclaims the inflexible justice of Yahweh; Micah foretells the speedy fall of the aristocrats to the level of those they now oppress; and though Isaiah shows a touch of tenderness in one early poem and, in almost his last utterance, a gleam of hope for his own little band of disciples, these stand alone against the torrent of denunciation he pours upon the capitalists who "despoil the wretched . . . and lay field to field till there is no more room"; upon the thoughtless and frivolous women who flaunt their jewels, "leering as they go"; upon the dissolute *gilded youth*, only "valiant in drinking wine".   But the condemnation was too wholesale to be accepted, the picture too lifelike to be recognized.   "For what" (we can fancy them saying) "have we done?   We go to the temple-services, we pay our tithes, we give alms to beggars, we obey the laws, we reverence the priests".   Nay, but the priests are like the people; they are faithless to their duty, lax in morals; they "reel with wine".   The judges despoil the widow and the orphan; they "stagger while giving false judgment".   Therefore Isaiah exclaims, "Thus saith Yahweh: Because this people draw near and honor me with their lips, but their heart is far from me,—who say to the prophets: 'Speak to us smooth things, . . . trouble us no more with Israel's Holy One!' therefore I will turn my hand against them and will smelt out in the furnace their dross.   Verily, never can this your iniquity be canceled till ye die".

Yet Isaiah is still as world-famed for tenderness and hopefulness as

[1] See Story of Elijah in the "Notable Deeds of Israel's Heroes" by E.

for stern invective, for prophecies of future glory for the nation as for those of its immediate and permanent dissolution. Exact criticism has removed these discrepancies; first, by showing the wide differences in style and historical background between chapters i—xxxvi and xl—lxvi, which verdict has long been accepted and the two parts ascribed respectively to Isaiah I. and Isaiah II.,—authors separated in date by over two hundred years. But secondly, while the stern grandeur of Isaiah I. never appears in the later division, the gracious charm and glowing pictures of peace and prosperity for a redeemed people, characteristic of Isaiah II., stand in all versions side by side with the fierce denunciations of Isaiah I. Clearer knowledge of contemporary history through the discovery of Assyrian records, and of linguistics through the advance of philology, now prove that both parts are composite; and that fragments of poems by anonymous authors belonging to the joyous, optimistic Persian period have been fathered upon Isaiah to relieve his otherwise unbroken pessimism. For the same incontrovertible reasons, the "Book of Amos" loses its editorial introduction (ch. i, 1-2), its conclusion (ch. ix, 5-6, 8b-15) and a few other lines; while at least half of the "Book of Micah" must be ascribed to an author of the Persian period now called Micah II., and even the three noble poems of Micah I., the youthful contemporary of Isaiah I., are shown to have been meddled with. Such meddling not only blemished the style and falsified the opinions of all the major poets of the Golden Age, but introduced obstacles to our comprehension of their respective contributions to the slow development of spiritual religion. These obstacles have now for the most part been removed.

Stripped of all incongruities, the writings of the Judæan poets of the eighth century B.C. reveal their authors' uncompromising creed and its limitations. They laid stress upon the righeousness of Yahweh, which demanded fair-dealing of man with man and obedience to the primal laws of well-ordered social living; they also proclaimed Yahweh as the Holy One who required personal purity of His people; but they made no further attempt to comprehend the nature and purposes of their God. They had advanced so far as to believe Him *supreme* over all other gods whatever, while yet recognizing the gods of other nations as legitimate but inferior rulers; but they drew the deduction that if the Chosen People should cling to inferior gods tolerant of every soul-destroying vice, Yahweh would wipe them off the face of the earth and raise up others to reveal His will; for He was a Jealous God and a God of Vengeance; the instruments of His vengeance, the armies of Assyria, were even now at the doors. In their passionate haste to reinstate their brethren in His favor, these prophets forgot the teachings of their own philosopher of the preceding century, the stress he had laid upon Yahweh's mercy, His long-suffering and faithfulness to His pledged word. They strove to drive men into just-dealing and high morality through the agency of fear. Therefore the reform that Isaiah accomplished was neither lasting nor fundamental. The people multiplied their sacrifices and petitions, but their hearts remained unchanged.

But in the Northern Kingdom, in the mountain-land of Ephraim, had appeared a poet of far different temperament to that of the Judæans, —Hosea, the son of Beeri. His career had begun a few years before Isaiah's, and it lasted till the time of Micah. Ignorant of the ways of courts and the methods of the schools, he had learned from personal experience the compelling power of a great love to forgive, seek out and cherish one who had grievously sinned against him. Possibly it was the daring venture of Amos into the stronghold of idolatry to inveigh against the vices of Israel (Am. vii, 10) that turned his attention to the degeneracy of his nation. Therein he saw a striking likeness to his own experience; and, looking into his own heart and reasoning from "Man's nothing-perfect to God's all-complete" he pronounced authoritatively in the name of Yahweh: My people are destroyed for lack of *knowledge; . . .* they have not *known* Yahweh". Yet how should they know without a teacher? Priests and prophets were alike recreant to their duty, and barefacedly committing deliberate crimes. Therefore Hosea revives J's teaching. With even fuller detail than Amos, but without his bitterness, he recounts the sins of Israel for which Yahweh must needs punish them; nay, the punishment is the fruit of their own misdoings; "they have sown the wind, they shall reap the whirlwind". But, with outbursts of passionate pleading, he reviews the benefits they have received from Yahweh, His loving care of them in danger, the preventives and defenses He gave them against their personal weaknesses in His laws. These laws Israel has rejected. "My people are *bent* upon backsliding; they call to the Most High for help, yet none at all will *lift himself* up". But as the prophet had pardoned and brought home his erring wife, though shorn of all dignity and honor in the eyes of her neighbors, so he foresees salvation in the end for Israel, and a possibility of her regaining her spiritual heritage. "I will not return to destroy Ephraim, saith Yahweh, for I am God and not man, the Holy One in the midst of thee. I will *not* come in wrath".

No Hebrew poet, even among the post-exilic writers, has written with greater pathos and with more exquisitely appropriate and delicate figures than Hosea. But it remained for the great prose-writer of the next century, the author of Deuteronomy, to build upon that *Knowledge* of Yahweh's love and fidelity inculcated by Hosea, and to devise the effectual means of reaching the hearts of the people. There was no time for Hosea's teaching to produce results for Ephraim. As he laid down his pen, Tiglath Pileser was entering the Northern Kingdom, and her punishment had begun.

The accession of Manasseh in the Southern Kingdom in 698 B.C., his disgraceful reign and his relentless persecution of the followers of Yahweh put an end to all attempts at reform. His excesses, however, roused his subjects to the reasonableness of their prophets' strictures; and no sooner was his grandson Josiah established upon the throne than poets and prophets sprang up, even before the finding of the "Book of the Law", who proclaimed Hosea's gospel of the mercy and lovingkindness as well as the justice of Yahweh. First among them was Zephaniah, who extended the threats of Amos and Isaiah to all workers of wickedness in high places, but encouraged the righteous and the meek to expect salvation. The one fine poem of Zephaniah's that has been preserved shows perfect unity of plan and handling, save for two or three interpolated couplets and the final strophe, which were evidently added after the Captivity.

Far different is the case of the "Book of Jeremiah" in which prose and poetry, genuine utterances of the prophet and late additions are closely interwoven. Tradition asserts that it was written down at Jeremiah's dictation by his secretary, Baruch; but there is no evidence to confirm the assertion. Baruch was not Jeremiah's secretary, but his confidential friend and co-worker; and though from stress of circumstances he once acted as his amanuensis, no part of the famous *scroll* he then wrote has been identified in the extant book. The latest verdict of scholars is that, like Socrates and Epictetus, and like the Greatest of All Teachers, Jeremiah never wrote at all. His words bear the stamp of immediate, spontaneous utterance. Probably they were taken down, more or less *verbatim*, at different times and places by enthusiastic disciples, who passed their several booklets from hand to hand during his lifetime; but they were not brought together until the middle of the Persian period. These booklets are distinguishable by their headings; in spite of which clear indications of their proper order they were jumbled together without regard to date, and are also marred by the introduction into their text of marginal glosses and additions by various readers. Interspersed among the booklets are detailed accounts of Jeremiah's personal experiences which seem to have been derived from a Biography.

The greatest aid in revising and rearranging this important book is its translation into Greek as found in the Alexandrian Codex of the Septuagint. Thence we learn that the Hebrew text of "Jeremiah" was shorter in the third and second centuries B.C. than our present text by 2,700 words, or one-eighth of its whole contents. We are thus enabled to state definitely not only how many lines have been added, but just where they were inserted, and to deduce from contemporary history the feelings that prompted their insertion. Their phraseology also shows their authors' full acquaintance with Persian and Greek words and idioms that only crept into Hebrew long after Jeremiah's day.

THE BABYLONIAN CAPTIVITY (586-538 B.C.) was an unexampled humiliation. The nation founded on the principles of Truth, Justice and Fraternity between man and man, and sworn allegiance to a Supreme Ruler of all the world, of whom there could be no similitude among created things, has betrayed its trust and is uprooted. On the acropolis of Jerusalem, Solomon's Temple, which has symbolized for centuries to all the surrounding kingdoms the majesty, power and steadfastness of Yahweh, now lies in ruins. The King, Court, Priests and Notables of Judah are captives far in the East in the midst of the sordid and depraving conditions from which Abraham had turned away; the rest of the turbulent and rebellious leaders of the population have fled to Egypt, almost to the very spot from which Moses had delivered their fathers. Never again shall they be an independent nation. So their prophets have foretold, all of whose other prophets have been fulfilled. This too they must perforce believe. But their religion, the noblest yet seen in the world, remains; they are still the *chosen people* of a Holy God who will cleanse and heal every faithful heart, and bring back to Zion a chastened and grateful "remnant" to do Him loyal service, whatever that service may be. This is the hope inspiring the noblest minds among the Exiles, and this the Mission whose scope they will strive to foresee. And this it was that carried the Golden Age of their literature through and over the catastrophic downfall of the nation without lapse and to ever higher mountains of vision, as the subjected Israelites passed successively from the depressing but not unkindly rule of the Chaldæans to the sympathetic protection of the Persians and the colder fellowship in philosophic inquiry of the Greeks, until it reached the very threshold of the Christian Era. The first stage, characterized by much beauty, tenderness and pathos, attained force and grandeur. In the second, Hebrew Lyrism will voice every emotion of the heart,—towards men, towards God, and towards His handiwork; and Hebrew Philosophy, analyzing the bases of morality, the office of suffering, the possibility of personal communion with God, and the mission of Israel to the world at large, will rise to the Sublime.

EXTANT WORKS IN HEBREW LITERATURE

TO THE

OPENING OF THE GOLDEN AGE, 850 B.C.

THE DECALOGUE

A FIRST COLLECTION OF PROVERBS

A SECOND COLLECTION OF PROVERBS

THE HISTORY OF THE CHILDREN OF ISRAEL, BY J.

THE DECALOGUE

THE TEN WORDS BROUGHT BY MOSES
TO THE CHILDREN OF ISRAEL

I. I AM YAHWEH, THY GOD; thou shalt have no other gods before Me.

II. Thou shalt not make unto thee any graven image, or any likeness of any thing that is in heaven above, or in the earth beneath, or in the water under the earth.

III. Thou shalt not take the name of Yahweh, thy God, in vain.

IV. Remember the Sabbath-day to keep it holy.

V. Honor thy father and thy mother.

VI. Thou shalt not kill.

VII. Thou shalt not commit adultery.

VIII. Thou shalt not steal.

IX. Thou shalt not bear false witness.

X. Thou shalt not covet thy neighbor's house, nor any thing that is his.

[Expositions of these laws, as applied to every circumstance in the life of a simple agricultural people, are to be found in Exodus, xx, 19—xxiii, 33, and in Leviticus, xvii-xxvi. The former group is known as the Book of the Covenant, and the latter as the Law of Holiness. The Law of Holiness is held to be the more ancient; but whether it came from the Mosaic age or not cannot be proved. The Book of the Covenant closes with the exhortation coupled with a promise, which forms the basis of the Book of Deuteronomy:

"Behold, I send a messenger before thee to keep by the way, and to bring thee into the place which I have prepared. Take ye heed of him, and hearken unto his voice; provoke him not, for I will not pardon thy transgression, for My name is in him. But, if thou wilt indeed obey his voice and do all that I speak, then will I be an enemy to thy enemies, and an adversary to thy adversaries. And ye shall serve Yahweh our God; and I will bless thy bread and thy water, and I will take sickness away from the midst of thee. None shall cast their young nor be barren in thy land; the number of thy days I will fulfil. And I will send a hornet before thee which shall drive out the Hivite and the Canaanite and the Hittite from before thee. By little and little I will drive them out before thee, until thou be increased and possess the land. And I will set thy bounds from the Red Sea even unto the sea of the Philistine, and from the wilderness unto the River (the Euphrates)".—ED.]

THE FIRST COLLECTION OF PROVERBS

(Proverbs, x, 1-xv, c. 950 B.C.)

THE PROVERBS OF SOLOMON

i

A wise son maketh a glad father, but a foolish son is the grief of his mother.

ii

Treasures of wickedness profit nothing, but righteousness delivereth from death.

iii

Yahweh will not suffer the righteous to famish, but He thrusteth away the desire of the wicked.

iv

He becometh poor that dealeth with a slack hand, but the hand of the diligent maketh rich.

v

A wise son gathereth in summer, but he that sleepeth in harvest causeth shame.

vi

Blessings are upon the head of the righteous, but the mouth of the wicked concealeth violence.

vii

The memory of the just is blessed, but the name of the wicked shall rot.

viii

The wise in heart will receive commands, but a prating fool shall fall.

ix

He that walketh uprightly walketh surely, but he that perverteth his ways shall be known.

x

He that winketh with the eye causeth sorrow, but a prating fool shall fall.

xi

The mouth of the righteous is a well of life, but the mouth of the wicked covereth violence.

xii

Hatred covereth up strife, but love covereth all transgression.

xiii

In the lips of him that hath discernment, wisdom is found;
But a rod for the back of him that hath no understanding.

xiv

Wise men lay up knowledge, but the mouth of the foolish is an imminent ruin.

xv

The rich man's wealth is his strong city; the ruin of the poor is their poverty.

xvi

The labor of the righteous tendeth to life; the increase of the wicked, to sin.

xvii

He is in the way of life that heedeth instruction, but he that forsaketh reproof, erreth.

xviii

He that hideth hatred is of lying lips, and he that uttereth a slander is a fool.

xix

In the multitude of words there lacketh not transgression,
But he that restraineth his lips is wise.

xx

The tongue of the righteous is as choice silver; the heart of the wicked is worth little.

xxi

The lips of the righteous feed many, but the foolish die for want of understanding.

xxii

The blessing of Yahweh, it maketh rich, and toil addeth nothing thereto.

xxiii

It is as sport to a fool to do wickedness; so is wisdom to a man of discernment.

xxiv

The heart of the wicked, it shall come upon him; the desire of the righteous shall be granted.

xxv

When the whirlwind passeth, the wicked is no more, but the righteous is a lasting foundation.

xxvi

As vinegar to the teeth and as smoke to the eyes, so is the sluggard to them that send him.

xxvii

The fear of Yahweh prolongeth days, but the years of the wicked shall be shortened.

xxviii

The hope of the righteous shall be gladness, but the expectation of the wicked shall perish.

xxix

The way of Yahweh is a stronghold to the upright, but ruin to the workers of iniquity.

xxx

The righteous shall never be removed, but the wicked shall not dwell in the land.

xxxi

The mouth of the righteous uttereth wisdom, but the froward tongue shall be cut off.

xxxii

The lips of the righteous uttereth wisdom, but those of the wicked speak frowardness.

xxxiii

A false balance is abomination to Yahweh, but a just weight is His delight.

xxxiv

When pride cometh, then cometh shame; but with the lowly is wisdom.

xxxv

The integrity of the upright shall guide them;
But the perverseness of the faithless shall destroy them.

xxxvi

Riches profit not in the day of wrath, but righteousness delivereth from death.

xxxvii

The righteousness of the sincere shall direct his way,
But the wicked shall fall by his own wickedness.

xxxviii

The righteousness of the upright shall deliver them; but they that deal treacherously shall be taken in their own mischief.

xxxix

When the wicked man dieth, his expectation shall perish, and the hope of iniquity perisheth.

xl

The righteous is delivered out of trouble, and the wicked cometh in his stead.

xli

With his mouth the impious man destroyeth his neighbor, but through knowledge shall the righteous be delivered.

xlii

When it goeth well with the righteous, the city rejoiceth, and when the wicked perish, there is joy.

xliii

By the blessing of the upright the city is exalted, but it is overthrown by the mouth of the wicked.

xliv

He that despiseth his neighbor is void of wisdom, but a man of discernment holdeth his peace.

xlv

He that goeth about as a talebearer revealeth secrets;
But he that is of a faithful spirit concealeth a matter.

xlvi

Where no wise guidance is, a people falleth, but in the multitude of counsellors there is safety.

xlvii

He that is surety for a stranger shall smart for it, but he that hateth suretiship is sure.

xlviii

A gracious woman obtaineth honor, and strong men obtain riches.

xlix

The merciful man doeth good to his own soul, but he that is cruel troubleth his own flesh.

l

The wicked earneth deceitful wages, but he that soweth righteousness hath a sure reward.

li

Steadfast righteousness tendeth to life, but he that pursueth evil doth it to his own death.

lii

They that are perverse in heart are an abomination to Yahweh;
But such as are upright in their way are His delight.

liii

Though hand join in hand, the evil man shall not be unpunished;
But the seed of the righteous shall escape.

liv

As a jewel of gold in a swine's snout, so is a fair woman without discretion.

lv

The desire of the righteous is only good, but the expectation of the wicked is wrath.

lvi

There is that scattereth, and increaseth yet more;
And there is that withholdeth more than is meet, but it tendeth only to want.

lvii

The liberal soul shall be made fat, and he that satisfieth abundantly shall be satisfied himself.

lviii

He that withholdeth corn, the people shall curse him;
But blessing shall be upon the hand of him that selleth it.

lix

He that diligently seeketh good, seeketh favor; but he that searcheth after mischief, it shall come upon him.

lx

He that trusteth in his riches shall fall; but the righteous shall flourish like the green leaf.

lxi

He that troubleth his own house shall inherit the wind; and the foolish shall be servant to the wise of heart.

lxii

The fruit of the righteous is a tree of life; and he that is wise winneth souls.

lxiii

Behold, the righteous shall be requited in the earth; how much more the wicked and the sinner!

lxiv

Whoso loveth knowledge loveth correction, but he that is brutish hateth reproof.

lxv

A good man shall obtain favor from Yahweh, but a man of wicked devices will He condemn.

lxvi

A man shall not be established by wickedness, but the root of the righteous shall never be moved.

lxvii

A virtuous woman is a crown to her husband; but she that doth shamefully is as rottenness in his bones.

lxviii

The thoughts of the righteous are just; but the counsels of the wicked are deceit.

lxix

The words of the wicked are to lie in wait for blood, but the mouth of the righteous shall deliver them.

lxx

Overthrow the wicked and they are not; but the house of the righteous shall stand.

lxxi

A man shall be commended according to his wisdom, but he that is of a perverse mind shall be despised.

lxxii

Better is he that is lightly esteemed and hath a servant,
Than he that honoreth himself and lacketh bread.

lxxiii

A righteous man regardeth the life of his beast; but the tender mercies of the wicked are cruel.

lxxiv

He that tilleth his land shall have plenty of bread,
But he that followeth after vain things is void of understanding.

lxxv

The wicked desireth the prey of evil men, but the root of the righteous yieldeth fruit.

lxxvi

The transgression of the lips is a snare to the evil man;
But the righteous shall come out of trouble.

lxxvii

A man shall be satisfied with good by the fruit of his mouth,
And the doings of a man's hands shall be rendered unto him.

lxxviii

The way of a fool is right in his own eyes, but he that is wise hearkeneth unto counsel.

lxxix

A fool's vexation is presently known, but a prudent man concealeth shame.

lxxx

He that uttereth truth uttereth righteousness; but a false witness, deceit.

lxxxi

There is that speaketh like the piercings of a sword, but the tongue of the wise is health.

lxxxii

The lip of truth shall be established for ever; but a lying tongue is but for a moment.

lxxxiii

Deceit is in the mind of them that devise evil; but to the counsellors of peace belongeth joy.

lxxxiv

No mischief shall befall the righteous; but the wicked shall be filled with evil.

lxxxv

Lying lips are an abomination to Yahweh; but they that deal truly are His delight.

lxxxvi

A prudent man concealeth knowledge; but the heart of fools proclaimeth foolishness.

lxxxvii

The hand of the diligent shall bear rule; but the slothful shall be under tribute.

lxxxviii

Care in the heart of a man boweth it down, but a good word maketh it glad.

lxxxix

The righteous is a guide to his neighbor; but the way of the wicked leadeth them astray.

xc

The slothful man shall not hunt the prey; but the precious substance of men cometh to the diligent.

xci

In the way of righteousness is life; and in the pathway thereof there is no death.

xcii

A wise son hearkeneth to his father's instruction, but a scorner heareth not rebuke.

xciii

A man shall eat good from the fruit of his mouth, but the desire of the faithless is violence.

xciv

He that guardeth his mouth keepeth his life, but he that openeth wide his lips shall be ruined.

xcv

The soul of the sluggard desireth and hath nothing, but the desire of the diligent shall be abundantly gratified.

xcvi

A righteous man hateth lying; but a wicked man behaveth vilely and shamefully.

xcvii

Righteousness guardeth him that is upright, but wickedness overthroweth the sinner.

xcviii

There is that pretendeth himself rich and hath nothing; there is that voucheth himself poor, yet hath great wealth.

xcix

The ransom of a man's life are his riches; but the poor heareth no threatening.

c

The light of the righteous rejoiceth; but the lamp of the wicked shall be put out.

ci

By pride cometh only contention; but with the well-advised is wisdom.

cii

Wealth gotten by vanity shall be diminished, but he that gathereth by toil shall have increase.

ciii

Hope deferred maketh the heart sick; but desire fulfilled is a tree of life.

civ

Whoso despiseth the word shall suffer thereby; but he that feareth the law shall be rewarded.

cv

The law of the wise is a fountain of life, to depart from the snares of death.

cvi

Good understanding giveth favor; but the way of the treacherous is rugged.

cvii

Every prudent man worketh with forethought, but a fool unfoldeth folly.

cviii

A wicked messenger falleth into evil; but a faithful ambassador is health.

cix

Poverty and shame shall be to him that refuseth instruction;
But he that regardeth reproof shall be honored.

cx

The desire accomplished is sweet to the soul; but it is an abomination to fools to depart from evil.

cxi

Walk with wise men, and thou shalt be wise; but the companion of fools shall smart for it.

cxii

Evil pursueth sinners; but the righteous shall be repaid with good.

cxiii

A good man leaveth an inheritance to his children's children;
But the wealth of the sinner is laid up for the righteous.

cxiv

Much food is in the tillage of the poor; but there is that is destroyed by reason of injustice.

cxv

He that spareth his rod hateth his son; but he that loveth him chasteneth him betimes.

cxvi

The righteous eateth to the satisfying of his desire; but the belly of the wicked shall want.

cxvii

Every wise woman buildeth her house; but the foolish plucketh it down with her own hands.

cxviii

He that walketh in his uprightness feareth Yahweh; but he that is perverse in his ways despiseth Him.

cxix

In the mouth of the foolish is a rod of pride; but the lips of the wise shall preserve them.

cxx

Where no oxen are, the crib is clean; but much increase is by the strength of an ox.

cxxi

A faithful witness will not lie, but a false witness uttereth lies.

cxxii

A scorner seeketh wisdom and findeth it not; but knowledge is easy unto him of discernment.

cxxiii

Go into the presence of a foolish man, and thou shalt not perceive the lips of knowledge.

cxxiv

The wisdom of the prudent is to understand his way; and the folly of fools is deceit.

cxxv

The foolish make a mock at guilt, but among the upright there is good will.

cxxvi

The heart knoweth its own bitterness, and with its joy no stranger can intermeddle.

cxxvii

The house of the wicked shall be overthrown, but the tent of the upright shall flourish.

cxxviii

There is a way which seemeth right unto a man, but the end thereof are the ways of death.

cxxix

Even in laughter the heart is sorrowful, and the end of mirth is heaviness.

cxxx

The dissembler in heart shall have his fill from his own ways, and a good man shall be satisfied from himself.

cxxxi

The thoughtless believeth every word; but the prudent man looketh well to his going.

cxxxii

A wise man feareth, and departeth from evil; but the fool beareth himself insolently and is confident.

cxxxiii

He that is soon angry will act foolishly; and a man of wicked devices is hated.

cxxxiv

The simple inherit folly; but the prudent are crowned with knowledge.

cxxxv

The evil bow before the good, and the wicked at the gates of the righteous.

cxxxvi

The poor is hated even of his own neighbor, but the rich hath many friends.

cxxxvii

He that despiseth his neighbor sinneth; but he that hath pity upon the poor, happy is he.

cxxxviii

Shall they not go astray that devise evil? but mercy and truth shall be for them that devise good.

cxxxix

In all labor there is profit; but the talk of the lips tendeth only to penury.

cxl

The crown of the wise is their riches; but the folly of fools is only folly.

cxli

A true witness delivereth souls; but he that uttereth lies is full of deceit.

cxlii

In the fear of Yahweh is strong confidence; and His children shall have a place of refuge.

cxliii

The fear of Yahweh is a fountain of life, to depart from the snares of death.

cxliv

In the multitude of people is the king's glory; but in the want of people is the ruin of the prince.

cxlv

He that is slow to anger is of great understanding; but he that is hasty of spirit exalteth folly.

cxlvi

A tranquil heart is the life of the flesh; but envy is the rottenness of the bones.

cxlvii

He that oppresseth the poor reproacheth his Maker; but he that hath mercy on the needy honoreth Him.

cxlviii

The wicked is thrust down in his calamity; but the righteous hath a refuge in his death.

cxlix

Wisdom resteth in the mind of him that hath discernment; but whatever is in the heart of fools is made known.

cl

Righteousness exalteth a nation; but sin is a reproach to any people.

cli

The king's favor is toward a servant that dealeth wisely; but his wrath shall strike him that dealeth shamefully.

clii

A soft answer turneth away wrath; but a grievous word stirreth up anger.

cliii

The tongue of the wise uttereth knowledge aright; but the mouth of fools poureth out folly.

cliv

The eyes of Yahweh are in every place, keeping watch upon the evil and the good.

clv

A wholesome tongue is a tree of life, but perverseness therein is a wound to the spirit.

clvi

A fool despiseth his father's correction; but he that regardeth reproof gaineth prudence.

clvii

In the house of the righteous is much treasure; but in the revenues of the wicked is trouble.

clviii

The lips of the wise dispense knowledge; but the mind of the foolish doth not so.

clix

The sacrifice of the wicked is an abomination to Yahweh; but the prayer of the upright is His delight.

clx

The way of the wicked is an abomination to Yahweh; but He loveth him that followeth after righteousness.

clxi

There is grievous correction for him that forsaketh the way; and he that hateth reproof shall die.

clxii

Sheol and destruction are before Yahweh; how much more then the hearts of the children of men!

clxiii

A scorner loveth not to be reproved; he will not go unto the wise.

clxiv

A merry heart maketh a cheerful countenance, but by sorrow of heart the spirit is broken.

clxv

The heart of him that hath discernment seeketh knowledge; but the mouth of fools feedeth on folly.

clxvi

All the days of the afflicted are evil; but he that is of a cheerful heart hath a continual feast.

clxvii

Better is little with the fear of Yahweh, than great treasure and trouble therewith.

clxviii

Better is a dinner of herbs where love is, than a stalled ox and hatred therewith.

clxix

A wrathful man stirreth up contention; but he that is slow to anger appeaseth strife.

clxx

The way of the sluggard is as a hedge of thorns; but the path of the upright is as a highway.

clxxi

A wise son maketh a glad father; but a foolish man despiseth his mother.

clxxii

Folly is joy to him that is void of wisdom; but a man of discernment walketh in a straight path.

clxxiii

For want of counsel purposes are frustrated; but in the multitude of counsellors they are established.

clxxiv

A man hath joy in the answer of his mouth; and a word in season, how good it is!

clxxv

The path of life goeth upward for the wise, that he may depart from Sheol beneath.

clxxvi
Yahweh will root up the house of the proud, but He will establish the border of the widow.

clxxvii
Evil devices are an abomination to Yahweh, but pleasant words are pure.

clxxviii
He that is greedy of gain troubleth his own house; but he that hateth gifts shall live.

clxxix
The mind of the righteous studieth to answer; but the mouth of the wicked poureth out evil.

clxxx
Yahweh is far from the wicked, but He heareth the prayer of the righteous.

clxxxi
The light of the eyes rejoiceth the heart, and good tidings make the bones fat.

clxxxii
The ear that hearkeneth to the reproof of life shall abide among the wise.

clxxxiii
He that refuseth correction despiseth his own soul; but he that hearkeneth to reproof getteth understanding.

clxxxiv
The FEAR of YAHWEH is the Teaching of WISDOM,
And before HONOR goeth HUMILITY.

THE SECOND COLLECTION OF PROVERBS

(Proverbs, xvi, 1—xxii, 16)

i
The preparations of the heart belong to man, but the answer of the tongue is from Yahweh.

ii
All the ways of a man are clean in his own eyes, but Yahweh weigheth the spirit.

iii
Commit thy works unto Yahweh, and thy thoughts shall be established.

iv
Yahweh hath made everything for its own end; yea, even the wicked for the day of evil.

v
Every one that is proud in heart is an abomination to Yahweh.
My hand upon it! he shall not go unpunished.

vi
By mercy and truth iniquity is purged, and by the fear of Yahweh men turn from evil.

vii
When a man's ways please Yahweh, He maketh even his enemies to be at peace with him.

viii

Better is a little with righteousness than great revenues with injustice.

ix

A man's heart deviseth his way, but Yahweh directeth his steps.

x

A divine sentence is in the lips of the king; his mouth shall not transgress in judgment.

xi

A just balance and scales are Yahweh's; all the weights of the bag are His work.

xii

To do wickedness is an abomination in kings, for the throne is established by righteousness.

xiii

Righteous lips are the delight of kings, and they love him that speaketh right.

xiv

The wrath of a king is as messengers of death, but a wise man will pacify it.

xv

In the light of the king's countenance is life, and his favor is as a cloud of the latter rain.

xvi

How much better it is to get wisdom than gold! yea, to get understanding is rather to be chosen than silver.

xvii

The highway of the upright is to depart from evil; he that keepeth his way preserveth his soul.

xviii

Pride goeth before destruction, and a haughty spirit before a fall.

xix

Better it is to be of a lowly spirit with the poor, than to divide the spoil with the proud.

xx

He that giveth heed unto the word shall find good; and whoso trusteth in Yahweh, happy is he.

xxi

The wise in heart shall be called discerning, and the sweetness of the lips increaseth learning.

xxii

Understanding is a wellspring of life to him that hath it; but the chastisement of fools is their folly.

xxiii

The heart of the wise teacheth his mouth, and addeth learning to his lips.

xxiv

Pleasant words are as a honeycomb, sweet to the soul and health to the bones.

xxv

There is a way which seemeth right to a man, but the end thereof are the ways of death.

xxvi

The hunger of the laboring man laboreth for him, for his mouth craveth it of him.

xxvii

A worthless man deviseth mischief, and in his lips there is a burning fire.

xxviii

A froward man soweth strife, and a whisperer separateth close friends.

xxix

A man of violence enticeth his neighbor, and leadeth him in a way that is not good.

xxx

He that shutteth his eyes, it is to devise froward things;
He that compresseth his lips bringeth evil to pass.

xxxi

The hoary head is a crown of glory if it be found in the way of righteousness.

xxxii

He that is slow to anger is better than the mighty;
And he that ruleth his spirit than he that taketh a city.

xxxiii

The lot is cast into the lap; but the whole disposing thereof is of Yahweh.

xxxiv

Better is a dry morsel and quietness therewith than a house full of feasting with strife.

xxxv

A servant that dealeth wisely shall have rule over a son that causeth shame,
And shall have part in the inheritance among the brethren.

xxxvi

The refining-pot is for silver and the furnace for gold; but Yahweh trieth the hearts.

xxxvii

An evil-doer giveth heed to wicked lips, and a liar giveth ear to a mischievous tongue.

xxxviii

Whoso mocketh the poor reproacheth his Maker and he that is glad at calamity shall not be unpunished.

xxxix

Children's children are the crown of old men, and the glory of children are their fathers.

xl

Overbearing speech becometh not a churl, much less do lying lips a prince.

xli

A gift is as a precious stone in the eyes of him that hath it; withersoever he turneth, he prospereth.

xlii

He that covereth a transgression seeketh love; but he that harpeth on a matter estrangeth a close friend.

xliii

A rebuke sinketh deeper into an understanding mind, than a hundred stripes into a fool.

xliv

A rebellious man seeketh only evil; therefore a cruel messenger shall be sent against him.

xlv

Let a man meet a bear robbed of her whelps, rather than a fool in his folly.

xlvi

Whoso rewardeth evil for good, evil shall not depart from his house.

xlvii

The beginning of strife is as when one letteth out water; therefore leave off contention before quarreling break out.

xlviii

He that justifieth the wicked and he that condemneth the righteous, both alike are an abomination to Yahweh.

xlix

Wherefore is there a price in the hand of a fool to buy wisdom, seeing he hath no understanding?

l

A friend loveth at all times, and a brother is born for adversity.

li

A man void of understanding is he that striketh hands, and becometh surety in the presence of his neighbor.

lii

He loveth transgression that loveth strife; he that raiseth high his gate seeketh destruction.

liii

He that hath a froward heart findeth nothing good; and he that hath a perverse tongue falleth into mischief.

liv

He that begetteth a fool doth it to his sorrow; the father of a fool hath no joy.

lv

A merry heart is a good medicine, but a broken spirit drieth up the bones.

lvi

A wicked man taketh a gift out of the bosom to pervert the ways of judgment.

lvii

Wisdom is present with him that hath understanding, but the eyes of a fool are in the ends of the earth.

lviii

A foolish son is a grief to his father, and a bitterness to her that bare him.

lix

To punish the righteous is not good, nor to strike the noble for their uprightness.

lx

He that spareth his words hath knowledge, and he that hath a cool spirit is a man of discretion.

lxi

Even a fool when he holdeth his peace is accounted wise; he that shutteth his lips is held to be prudent.

lxii
He that separateth himself seeketh his own desire; and rageth against all sound wisdom.

lxiii
A fool hath no delight in understanding, but only that his heart may lay itself bare.

lxiv
When the wicked cometh, there cometh also contempt, and with ignominy cometh reproach.

lxv
The words of a man's mouth are as deep waters; the wellspring of wisdom is as a flowing brook.

lxvi
To respect the person of the wicked is not good, nor to turn aside the righteous in judgment.

lxvii
A fool's lips enter into contention, and his mouth calleth for stripes.

lxviii
A fool's mouth is his destruction, and his lips are the snare of his soul.

lxix
The words of a whisperer are as dainty morsels, and they go down into the innermost parts of the belly.

lxx
He also that is slack in his work is brother to him that is a destroyer.

lxxi
The name of Yahweh is a strong tower; the righteous runneth into it, and is safe.

lxxii
The rich man's wealth is his strong city, and as a high wall in his own imagination.

lxxiii
Before destruction, the heart of a man is haughty, and before honor goeth humility.

lxxiv
He that giveth answer before he heareth, it is folly and confusion unto him.

lxxv
The spirit of a man will sustain his infirmity; but a broken spirit who can bear?

lxxvi
The mind of the prudent getteth knowledge; and the ear of the wise seeketh knowledge.

lxxvii
A man's gift maketh room for him, and bringeth him before great men.

lxxviii
He that first pleadeth his cause seemeth just; but his neighbor cometh and searcheth him out.

lxxix
The lot causeth strife to cease, and parteth asunder the contentious.

lxxx
A brother offended is harder to be won than a strong city;
And such contentions are like the bars of a castle.

lxxxi

A man's belly shall be filled with the fruit of his mouth; with the increase of his lips shall he be satisfied.

lxxxii

Death and life are in the power of the tongue; and they that love it shall eat the fruit thereof.

lxxxiii

Whoso findeth a wife findeth a great good, and obtaineth favor of Yahweh.

lxxxiv

The poor useth entreaties. but the rich answereth roughly.

lxxxv

There are friends that one hath to his own hurt; but there is a friend that sticketh closer than a brother.

lxxxvi

Better is the poor that walketh in integrity than he that is perverse in his lips and is a fool.

lxxxvii

Also, that the soul be without knowledge is not good, and he that hasteth with his feet sinneth.

lxxxviii

The foolishness of man perverteth his way, and his heart fretteth against Yahweh.

lxxxix

Wealth addeth many friends; but as for the poor, his friend separateth himself from him.

xc

A false witness shall not go unpunished, and he that uttereth lies shall not escape.

xci

Many will entreat the favor of the liberal man, and every man is a friend to him that giveth gifts.

xcii

All the brethren of the poor do hate him; how much more do his friends go far from him! He pursueth them with words, but they are gone.

xciii

He that getteth wisdom loveth his own soul; he that keepeth understanding shall find good.

xciv

A false witness shall not go unpunished; and he that breatheth forth lies shall perish.

xcv

Luxury is not seemly for a fool; much less, for a servant to have rule over princes.

xcvi

It is discretion in a man to be slow to anger, and it is his glory to pass over a transgression.

xcvii

The king's wrath is as the roaring of a lion; but his favor is as dew upon the grass.

xcviii

A foolish son is the calamity of his father; and the contentions of a wife are a continual dropping.

xcix

House and riches are an inheritance from fathers; but a prudent wife is from Yahweh.

c

Slothfulness casteth into a deep sleep; and the idle soul shall suffer hunger.

ci

He that keepth the commandment keepeth his soul; but he that is careless of his ways shall die.

cii

He that hath pity upon the poor lendeth to Yahweh, and his good deed will He repay him.

ciii

Chasten thy son, seeing there is hope, and set not thine heart upon his destruction.

civ

A man of great wrath shall bear the penalty; for if thou interpose, thou wilt add thereto.

cv

Hear counsel, and receive instruction, that thou mayest be wise at the end of thy days.

cvi

There are many devices in a man's heart; but the counsel of Yahweh, that shall stand.

cvii

The lust of a man is his shame; and a poor man is better than a liar.

cviii

The fear of Yahweh tendeth to life, and he that hath it shall abide satisfied; He shall not be visited with evil.

cix

The sluggard burieth his hand in the dish, and will not so much as bring it back to his mouth.

cx

Smite a scorner, and the ignorant will become prudent;
Reprove one that hath discernment, and he will understand knowledge.

cxi

He that despoileth his father and chaseth away his mother, is a son that causeth shame and bringeth reproach.

cxii

Cease, my son, to hear the instruction that causeth to err from the words of knowledge.

cxiii

An ungodly witness mocketh at judgment; and the mouth of the wicked devoureth iniquity.

cxiv

Judgments are prepared for scorners, and stripes for the back of fools.

cxv

Wine is a mocker, strong drink a brawler; and whoso erreth thereby is not wise.

cxvi

The terror of a king is as the roaring of a lion; he that provoketh him to anger forfeiteth his own life.

cxvii

It is an honor for a man to keep aloof from strife; but every fool will be quarreling.

cxviii

The slothful will not plough when winter setteth in; therefore he shall beg in harvest, and have nothing.

cxix

Counsel in the heart of man is like deep water; but a man of understanding will draw it out.

cxx

Most men will proclaim every one his own goodness; but a faithful man who can find?

cxxi

A just man that walketh in his integrity, blessed are his children after him.

cxxii

A king that sitteth on the throne of judgment winnoweth away all evil with his eyes.

cxxiii

Who can say: I have made my heart clean, I am pure from sin?

cxxiv

Diverse weights and diverse measures, both alike are an abomination to Yahweh.

cxxv

Even a child can be known by his doings, whether his work be pure and whether it be right.

cxxvi

The hearing ear and the seeing eye, Yahweh hath made even both of them.

cxxvii

Love not sleep, lest thou come to poverty; open thine eyes, and thou shalt have bread in plenty.

cxxviii

It is naught, it is naught, saith the buyer; but when he is gone his way, then he boasteth.

cxxix

There is gold and abundance of rubies; but the lips of knowledge are a precious jewel.

cxxx

Take his garment that is surety for a stranger; and hold him in pledge that is surety for an alien woman.

cxxxi

Bread of falsehood is sweet to a man; but afterwards his mouth shall be filled with gravel.

cxxxii

Every purpose is established by counsel; and by good advice carry thou on war.

cxxxiii

He that goeth about as a tale-bearer revealeth secrets;
Therefore meddle not with him that openeth wide his lips.

cxxxiv

Whoso curseth his father or his mother, his lamp shall be put out in the blackest darkness.

cxxxv

An estate may be gotten hastily at the beginning, but the end thereof shall not be blessed.

cxxxvi

Say not thou: I will recompense evil; wait for Yahweh, and He will save thee.

cxxxvii

Diverse weights are an abomination to Yahweh, and a false balance is not good.

cxxxviii

A man's goings are of Yahweh; how then can man understand his way?

cxxxix

It is a snare to a man rashly to say: It is holy! and after vows to make inquiry.

cxl

A wise king winnoweth the wicked, and bringeth the threshing-wheel over them.

cxli

The spirit of man is the lamp of Yahweh, searching all the innermost parts of him.

cxlii

Mercy and truth preserve the king, and his throne is upholden by mercy.

cxliii

The glory of young men is their strength, and the beauty of old men is the hoary head.

cxliv

Sharp wounds cleanse away evil; so do stripes that reach the inward parts.

cxlv

The king's heart is in the hand of Yahweh like the watercourses; He turneth it whither He will.

cxlvi

Every way of a man is right in his own eyes; but Yahweh weigheth the hearts.

cxlvii

To do judgment and justice is more acceptable to Yahweh than sacrifice.

cxlviii

A haughty look and a proud heart—even the tillage of the wicked is sin.

cxlix

The thoughts of the diligent tend only to plenteousness; but he that is hasty hasteth only to want.

cl

The getting of treasures by a lying tongue is a vapor driven to and fro; they that seek them seek death.

cli

The violence of the wicked shall sweep them away, because they refuse to do justly.

clii

The way of the guilty is exceeding crooked; but as for the pure, his work is right.

cliii

It is better to dwell in a corner of the housetop than in a large house with a contentious woman.

cliv

The soul of the wicked desireth evil; his neighbor findeth no favor in his eyes.

clv

When the scorner is punished, the thoughtless is made wise;
And when the wise is instructed, he receiveth knowledge.

clvi

The righteous one considereth the house of tthe wicked, how the wicked are overthrown to their ruin.

clvii

Whoso stoppeth his ears at the cry of the poor, he also shall cry but shall not be heard.

clviii

A gift in secret pacifieth anger, and a present in the bosom strong wrath.

clix

It is joy to the righteous to do justly; but it is ruin to the workers of iniquity.

clx

The man that strayeth out of the way of discretion shall rest in the congregation of the dead.

clxi

He that loveth pleasure shall be a poor man; he that loveth wine and oil shall not be rich.

clxii

The wicked is a ransom for the righteous, and the treacherous cometh in the stead of the upright.

clxlii

It is better to dwell in a desert land than with a contentious and fretful woman.

clxiv

There is precious treasure and oil in the dwelling of the wise; but a foolish man swalloweth it up.

clxv

He that followeth after righteousness and mercy findeth life, prosperity and honor.

clxvi

A wise man scaleth the city of the mighty, and bringeth down the stronghold wherein it trusteth.

clxvii

Whoso keepeth his mouth and his tongue keepeth his soul from troubles.

clxviii

The proud and haughty man, scorner is his name; he dealeth in the arrogance of pride.

clxix

The desire of the slothful killeth him, for his hands refuse to labor.

clxx

There is that coveteth greedily all the day long; but the righteous giveth and spareth not.

clxxi

The sacrifice of the wicked is an abomination. How much more, when he bringeth it to atone for wickedness!

clxxii
A false witness shall perish; but the man that obeyeth shall speak unchallenged.

clxxiii
A wicked man hardenth his face; but as for the upright, he looketh well to his way.

clxxiv
There is no wisdom nor understanding nor counsel against Yahweh.

clxxv
The horse is prepared against the day of battle; but victory is of Yahweh!

clxxvi
A good name is rather to be chosen than great riches, and loving favor rather than silver and gold.

clxxvii
The rich and the poor meet together; Yahweh is the maker of them all.

clxxviii
A prudent man seeth the evil and hideth himself; but the thoughtless pass on, and suffer.

clxxix
The reward of humility and the fear of Yahweh is riches and honor and life.

clxxx
Thorns and snares are in the way of the froward; he that guardeth his soul shall be far from them.

clxxxi
Train up a child in the way he should go, and, even when he is old, he will not depart from it.

clxxxii
The rich ruleth over the poor, and the borrower is servant to the lender.

clxxxiii
He that soweth iniquity shall reap calamity; and the rod of his wrath shall fail.

clxxxiv
He that hath a bountiful eye shall be blessed, for he giveth of his bread to the poor.

clxxxv
Cast out the scorner, and contention will go out; yea, strife and ignominy will cease.

clxxxvi
He that loveth pureness of heart, for the grace of his lips the king shall be his friend.

clxxxvii
The eyes of Yahweh preserve him that hath knowledge, but He overthroweth the words of the treacherous man.

clxxxiii
The sluggard saith: There is a lion without; I shall be slain in the streets.

clxxxix
The mouth of strange women is a deep pit; he that is abhorred of Yahweh shall fall therein.

cxc

Foolishness is bound up in the heart of a child, but the rod of correction shall drive it far from him.

cxci

He that oppresseth the poor to increase his gain, and he that giveth to the rich, come only to want.

A FATHER'S ADVICE TO HIS SON [1]

Proverbs, xxi, 17-xxiii; xxiv, 1-22, 23-34.

Incline thine ear and hear the words of the wise
    And apply thy heart unto my knowledge;
For it is a pleasant thing if thou keep them within thee.
Let them be established altogether on thy lips.
    That thy trust may be in Yahweh
I make them known unto thee this day, even to thee.
Have not I written unto thee excellent things
    of counsel and knowledge,
That I might make thee know the certainty
    of the words of truth,
That thou mightest bring back words of truth
    to them that send thee?

Rob not the weak because he is weak, neither crush the poor in the gate,
    For Yahweh will plead their cause,
    And despoil of life them that despoil them.

Make no friendship with one given to anger, nor go with a wrathful man;
    Lest thou learn his ways,   and get a snare to thy soul.

Be not thou of them that strike hands, or of them that go surety for debts;
If thou hast not wherewith to pay,
    Why should thy bed be taken from under thee?

Remove not the ancient landmark   which thy fathers have set.

Seest thou a man diligent in his business? He shall stand before kings.
    He shall not stand before mean men.

When thou sittest to eat with a ruler,
    Consider well him that is before thee,
And put a knife to thy throat,   if thou be a man given to appetite.
Be not desirous of his dainties,   seeing they are deceitful meat.

Weary not thyself to be rich; cease from thine own wisdom.
Wilt thou set thine eyes upon it? It is gone.
For riches surely make themselves wings,
    Like an eagle that flieth toward heaven.

Eat thou not his bread that hath an evil eye
    Neither desire thou his dainties;
For as one that reckoneth within himself, so is he.
Eat and drink, saith he to thee; but his heart is not with thee.
The morsel thou hast eaten shalt thou cast up, and lose thy sweet words.

Speak not in the ears of a fool, for he will despise
    The wisdom of thy words.

[1] Written late in the seventh century B.C. and added by the editors of the Canon in the fifth or fourth century to the "Proverbs of Solomon."

Remove not the ancient landmark; enter not the fields of the fatherless,
For their Redeemer is strong; He shall plead their cause with thee.

Apply thy heart to wisdom, and thine ears to the words of knowledge.

Withhold not correction from the child;
    For if thou beat him with a rod, he will not die;
Thou shalt beat him with the rod, and wilt deliver his soul from Sheol.

My son, if thy heart be wise, my heart will be glad,—even mine:
Yea, my reins will rejoice when thy lips speak right things.

Let not thy heart envy sinners, but be in fear of Yahweh alway:
For surely there is a reward, and thy hope shall not be cut off.

Hear thou, my son, and be wise, and guide thy heart in the way.
Be not among wine-bibbers, among gluttonous eaters of flesh.
For the drunken and the glutton shall come to poverty,
    And drowsiness shall clothe a man in rags.

Hearken unto thy father that begat thee,
And despise not thy mother when she is old.

Buy truth and sell it not; yea, wisdom and instruction and discretion.

The father of the righteous will greatly rejoice,
And he that begetteth a wise child shall have joy of him.
Let thy father and thy mother be glad; let her that bare thee rejoice.

My son, give me thine heart,   and let thine eyes observe my ways.
For a harlot is a deep ditch,   and an alien woman is a narrow pit.
Yea, she lieth in wait as a robber,
    And increaseth the faithless among men.

Who crieth: Woe! Woe! Alas! Who hath contentions? Who is raving?
Who hath wounds without cause? Who hath redness of eyes?
They that tarry long at the wine, that go to seek mixed wine.
Look not on the wine when it is red, when it giveth its color to the cup,
    When it glideth down smoothly.

At last it biteth like a serpent, and stingeth like an adder.
    Thine eyes shall behold strange things
    And thy heart shall utter froward things;
Yea, thou shalt be as he that lieth down in the midst of the sea.
    Or as he that lieth on the top of a mast.

    They have struck me,   and I felt it not,
    They have beaten me,   and I knew it not,
    When shall I awake?   I will seek it yet again.

Be not thou envious of evil men, neither desire to be with them;
For their heart studieth destruction, and their lips talk of mischief.

Through wisdom is a house builded,
And by understanding it is established.
By knowledge are its halls filled with precious and pleasant riches.

A wise man is strong; yea, a man of knowledge increaseth strength;
For by wise advice thou shalt make thy war,
And in the multitude of counsellors is victory.

Wisdom is unattainable for a fool; he openeth not his mouth in the gate.

He that deviseth to do evil, men shall call a mischievous person.

The thought of the foolish is sin;
And the scorner is an abomination to men.

If thou faint in the day of adversity, thy strength is small indeed.

Deliver them that are being drawn to death;
And those about to be slain, wilt thou not rescue?

If thou sayest: Behold, we know not this,
Doth not He that weigheth hearts consider it?
And He that knoweth thy soul, doth not He know it?
And shall not He render to every man according to his works?

My son, eat thou honey, for it is good,
    And the honeycomb, which is sweet to the taste.
So know thou wisdom to be unto thy soul;
    If thou hast found it, then there shall be a reward,
        And thy hope shall not be cut off.

Lie not in wait, O wicked man, against the home of the just;
    Spoil not his resting-place.
For a righteous man falleth seven times and riseth up again;
    But the wicked are overthrown by calamity.

Rejoice not when thine enemy falleth,
    Let not thine heart be glad when he stumbleth;
Lest Yahweh see it, and it displease Him,
    And He turneth away His wrath from him.

Fret not thyself because of evil-doers,
    Neither be thou envious of the wicked;
For their calamity shall rise suddenly,
    The lamp of the wicked shall be put out.

My son, fear thou Yahweh and the king,
    And meddle not with them that are given to change;
For their calamity shall rise suddenly;
    And who knoweth the destruction of their years?

These also are Sayings of the Wise.[1]

To have respect of persons in judgment is not good;
He that saith unto the wicked: Thou art righteous,
Peoples shall curse him, nations shall execrate him.
But to them that justly decide shall be delight,
And a good blessing shall come upon them.

He kisseth the lips that give a right answer.

Prepare thy work without, and make it ready for the field,
    And afterwards build thy house.

Be not a witness against thy neighbor without cause,
    And deceive not with thy lips;
Say not I will do so to him as he hath done unto me;
    I will render to the man according to his work.

[1] An appendix to an appendix, possibly edited by the same writer.

THE FATE OF THE SLOTHFUL

An Apologue.

I went by the field of the slothful
And by the vineyard of the man void of understanding;
And lo, it was all grown over with thistles;
The face thereof was covered with nettles,
And the stone wall thereof was broken down.

Then I beheld and considered well;
I saw and received instruction.
Yet a little sleep and a little slumber,
A little folding of the hands to sleep!
So shall thy poverty come as a robber, and thy want
As an armed man.

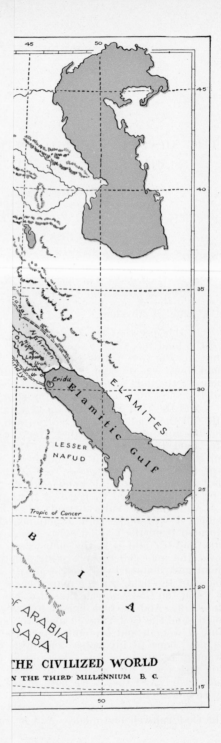

THE CIVILIZED WORLD
IN THE THIRD MILLENNIUM B. C.

THE HISTORY OF THE PEOPLE OF ISRAEL TO THE MIDDLE OF THE NINTH CENTURY, B. C.

By the Judaic Author, J.

CHAPTER I

TO THE DEATH OF JACOB (ISRAEL)

Section I.—From the Creation of Man to the Confounding of Language and the Consequent Separation of Nations. (Genesis ii, 4b-iv; vi, 1-9; vii, 1-5, 10, 12, 15b, 20-23; ix, 18-28; xi, 1-9.)

Materials used by J. Myths preserved in early Semitic Epics in Babylonia, and probably current among the Canaanites before the time of Abraham.

In the day that the God Yahweh made heaven and earth, no plant of the field was yet in the earth, and no herb of the field had yet sprung up; for the God Yahweh had not yet caused it to rain upon the earth, and there was no man to till the ground. And the God Yahweh formed man of the dust of the ground, and breathed into his nostrils the breath of life; and man became a living soul.

And the God Yahweh planted a garden eastward in Eden, and there He put the man whom He had formed. And the God Yahweh caused to spring up out of the ground every tree pleasant to the sight and good for food, the tree of life also in the midst of the garden, and the tree of the knowledge of good and evil. And the God Yahweh commanded the man, saying: Of every tree of the garden thou mayest freely eat; but of the tree of the knowledge of good and evil thou shalt not eat, for in the day that thou eatest thereof thou shalt surely die.

And the God Yahweh said: It is not good that the man should be alone; I will make him a helpmeet for him. And the God Yahweh formed from the ground every beast of the field and every fowl of the air, and brought it to the man to see what he would call it; and whatever the man called each living creature, that was its name. And the man gave names to all cattle and to the fowl of the air and to every beast of the field, but for man there was not found a helpmeet for him.

And the God Yahweh caused a deep sleep to fall upon the man, and he slept. And He took one of his ribs and closed up the flesh in place of it; and the God Yahweh made the rib which He had taken from man into a woman and brought her to the man. And the man said: This is now bone of my bones and flesh of my flesh; she shall be called woman, because she was taken out of man; therefore shall a man leave his father and his mother and cleave unto his wife, and they shall be one flesh. And they were both naked, the man and his wife, and they were not ashamed.

Now the serpent was more subtle than any beast of the field that the God Yahweh had made. And he said unto the woman: Truly hath

29

God said, ye shall not eat of any tree of the garden? And the woman said unto the serpent: Of the fruit of the trees of the garden we may eat; but of the fruit of the tree which is in the midst of the garden God hath said: Eat ye not of it nor touch it, lest ye die. And the serpent said unto the woman: Surely ye will not die; but God knoweth that in the day ye eat thereof your eyes shall be opened, and ye shall be as gods, knowing good and evil. When the woman saw that the tree was good for food, and that it was pleasing to the eyes and desirable to make one wise, she took of its fruit and ate, and she gave also unto her husband with her and he ate. And the eyes of them both were opened, and they knew that they were naked; and they sewed together fig leaves and made themselves girdles.

And they heard the voice of the God Yahweh, walking in the garden in the cool of the day; and the man and his wife hid themselves from the presence of the God Yahweh amongst the trees of the garden. And the God Yahweh called unto the man and said unto him: Where art thou? And he said: I heard thy voice in the garden, and I was afraid because I was naked, and I hid myself. And He said: Who told thee thou wast naked? Hast thou eaten of the tree whereof I commanded thee that thou shouldest not eat? And the man said: The woman whom thou gavest to be with me, she gave me of the tree, and I did eat. And the God Yahweh said unto the woman: What is this that thou hast done? And the woman said: The serpent beguiled me, and I did eat. And the God Yahweh said unto the serpent: Because thou hast done this,

Cursed be thou above all beasts   and above all creatures of the field;
   Upon thy belly shalt thou go,   and dust shalt thou eat
       All thy life long.
  Enmity I put between thee and the woman,
    Between thy seed and seed of her.
He shall bruise thee on the head,   and thou shalt bite him in the heel.
  Unto the woman He said:

  Very sore will I make thy travail-pains; in sorrow shalt thou bring
    forth sons;
Yet toward thy husband shall be thy desire, and over thee shall he rule.

  And to Adam He said: Because thou hast hearkened to the voice of thy wife and hast eaten of the tree concerning which I commanded thee, saying: Eat not of it,

  Cursed is the ground because of thee; by toil shalt thou eat from it
    all the days of thy life.
  Thorns and thistles shall it bear, and thou shalt eat of the herb
    of the field.
  In the sweat of thy face shalt thou eat bread, until thou return
    unto the ground,
      For from it wert thou taken; for dust thou art,
      And unto dust shalt thou return.

And for Adam and his wife the God Yahweh made tunics of skins and clothed them. And the God Yahweh said: Behold, the man is become like one of us, to know good and evil. Therefore, that he should not put forth his hand and take also of the tree of life and eat and live for ever, the God Yahweh sent him forth from the garden of Eden to till the ground from which he was taken. So He drove out the man; and He placed at the east of the garden of Eden Cherubim, and the flame of a sword which turned every way to guard the way of the tree of life.

And Adam knew his wife, and she conceived and bare Cain, and said: I have gotten a man-child from Yahweh. And again she bare his brother Abel. And Adam called his wife's name Eve,[1] because she was the mother of all living.

And Abel became a keeper of sheep, but Cain was a tiller of the ground. And in process of time it came to pass that Cain brought of the fruit of the ground an offering to Yahweh; and Abel, he also brought of the firstlings of his flock and the fat thereof. And Yahweh had respect unto Abel and his offering, but unto Cain and his offering He had no respect. And Cain was very wroth, and his countenance fell. And Yahweh said unto Cain:

Why art thou wroth, and why is thy face fallen?
If thou doest well, shall it not be lifted up?
And if thou doest not well, lurketh not sin at the door?
Unto thee is its desire, but thou shouldest rule over it.

Then said Cain to Abel his brother: Let us go into the field. And when they were in the field, Cain rose up against Abel his brother and slew him. Then said Yahweh unto Cain: Where is Abel, thy brother? And he said: I know not; am I my brother's keeper? And He said: What hast thou done? The voice of thy brother's blood crieth unto me from the ground. And now:

Cursed art thou from the ground which hath opened wide her mouth
To receive thy brother's blood from thy hand.
When thou shalt till the ground no more shall it
Yield thee its strength.
A wanderer and a fugitive shalt thou be in the earth.

And Cain said unto Yahweh: My punishment is greater than I can bear. Behold Thou hast driven me out this day from the face of the ground, and from Thy face shall I be hid. A wanderer and a fugitive shall I be in the earth; and it shall come to pass, whosoever findeth me shall slay me. And Yahweh said unto him:

Therefore, if anyone slayeth Cain, sevenfold shall he be avenged.

And Yahweh appointed a sign for Cain, lest anyone finding him should kill him. And Cain went forth from the presence of Yahweh and dwelt in the land of Nod, on the east of Eden.

(Then Cain knew his wife; and she conceived and bare Enoch; and he builded a city and he called the city after the name of his son, Enoch. And unto Enoch was born Irad and Irad begat Mehujael; and Mehujael begat Methusael; and Methusael begat Lamech. And Lamech begat a son; and he called his name Noah, saying: This one shall comfort us for our work, and for the labor of our hands because of the ground which Yahweh hath cursed.

And Lamech took unto him two wives; the name of the one, Adah; and the name of the other, Zillah. And Adah bare Jabal; he was the father of such as dwell in tents and have cattle. And his brother's name was Jubal; he was the father of all such as handle the harp and pipe. And Zillah, she also bare Tubal-cain, the father of all those who forge copper and iron; and the sister of Tubal-cain was Naamah. And Lamech said unto his wives:

---

[1] Eve, (Heb. *Havvah*, life). The verse is brought forward from Ch. iii, 20, where it is clearly misplaced, having no proper antecedent.

Adah and Zillah, hear my voice!
>   Ye wives of Lamech, hearken to my speech!
For I have slain a man for wounding me,
>   And a young man for injuring me.
If Cain shall be avenged sevenfold,
>   Then Lamech seventy-and-sevenfold.)

And Adam knew his wife again; and she bare a son and called his name Seth, for she said: God hath appointed me yet another child. And to Seth, to him also there was born a son; and he called his name Enosh. . . .

And Lamech[1] lived a hundred and eighty and two years, and begat a son. And he called his name Noah, saying: This same shall comfort us in our work, and in the toil of our hands, which cometh from the ground which Yahweh hath cursed. . . . And Noah was five hundred years old; and Noah had sons, Shem, Ham and Japheth.

And it came to pass, when men began to multiply on the face of the earth and daughters were born unto them, that the sons of God saw the daughters of men that they were fair, and they took them wives of all whom they chose. Then said Yahweh: "My spirit shall not remain in man forever, seeing that he is only flesh; yet his days shall be an hundred and twenty years. The Nephilim were upon the earth in those days and also afterwards, when the sons of God came in unto the daughters of men, and they bare children unto them; these were the mighty men who of old were men of renown. And Yahweh saw that the wickedness of man was great in the earth, and that every plan devised in his heart was only evil continually; and Yahweh repented that he had made man on the earth, and it grieved him to his heart. And Yahweh said: I will destroy man whom I have created from the face of the ground, both man and beast and creeping thing, and the fowls of the air; for it repenteth Me that I have made them.

But Noah found favor in the eyes of Yahweh. . . .

And Yahweh said unto Noah: Come thou and all thy house into the ark, for thee have I seen righteous before Me in this generation. Of every clean beast thou shalt take unto thee by sevens, the male and his female; and of beasts that are not clean by twos, the male and his mate. Of fowls also of the air by seven and seven, male and female, to keep seed alive upon the face of all the earth. For yet seven days and I will cause it to rain upon the earth forty days and forty nights; and every living thing that I have made will I destroy from off the face of the earth.

And Noah did according to all that Yahweh commanded him. And it came to pass, after the seven days, that the waters of the flood were upon the earth. And Noah went in, and his sons and his wife, and his son's wives with him, into the ark because of the waters of the flood. Of clean beasts and of beasts that were not clean, and of fowls, and of every thing that creepeth on the earth, there went in by pairs, male and female, unto Noah into the ark; and Yahweh shut him in.

And the rain was upon the earth forty days and forty nights. And the waters increased and bare up the ark, and it was lift up above the

---

[1] Ch. v, 1-27 gives a list of the sons of Adam in the line of Seth, parallel to the briefer one of the line of Cain in ch. iv, 17-22. It is unmistakably in the style of P, but must also be based on a very old tradition, as it brings in Methusaleh and Enoch, both of whom are mentioned by earlier authors than P. Each list makes special mention of a Lamech, the one as father of the inventors of arts and industries, and the other as the father of Noah: both are inserted here, the first in parenthesis.

earth. All in whose nostrils was the breath of life, of all that was on the dry land, died; and every living thing was destroyed which was on the face of the ground, both men and cattle and creeping thing and fowl of the air. And they were destroyed from the earth and only Noah remained, and they that were with him in the ark.

And God made a wind to pass over the earth, and the waters assuaged; the fountains also of the deep and the windows of heaven were stopped. And it came to pass at the end of forty days, that Noah opened the window of the ark which he had made, and he sent forth a raven which went to and fro until the waters were dried up from off the earth. Also he sent forth from him a dove, to see if the waters were abated from off the face of the ground, but the dove found no rest for the sole of her foot, and she returned unto him into the ark, for the waters were on the face of the whole earth. Then he put forth his hand and took her, and pulled her in unto him into the ark. And he stayed yet other seven days, and again he sent forth the dove out of the ark, and the dove came in to him in the evening, and lo, in her mouth was an olive leaf plucked off. So Noah knew that the waters were abated from off the earth. And he waited yet other seven days and sent forth the dove; and she returned not unto him any more.

Then Noah removed the covering of the ark, and looked; and behold, the face of the ground was dry. And Noah builded an altar unto Yahweh, and took of every clean beast and of every clean fowl, and he offered burnt offerings on the altar. And Yahweh smelled a sweet savor; and Yahweh said in His heart: I will never apain curse the ground for man's sake, for the imagination of man's heart is evil from his youth. Neither will I ever again smite every living thing as I have done. While the earth remaineth, seedtime and harvest, and cold and heat, and summer and winter, and day and night shall not cease.

Now the sons of Noah that went forth out of the ark were Shem and Ham and Japheth; (and Ham was the father of Canaan). These are the three sons of Noah, and unto them were sons born after the flood, and of them was the whole earth overspread. And Noah began to be an husbandman, and he planted a vineyard. And he drank of the wine and was drunken; and he was uncovered in his tent. And Ham, the father of Canaan, saw the nakedness of his father and told his brethren without. Then Shem and Japheth took a garment and laid it upon both their shoulders, and went backward and covered the nakedness of their father; and their faces were backward, and they saw not their father's nakedness. And Noah awoke from his wine, and knew what his younger son had done unto him; and he said:

Cursed be Canaan! Servant of servants   let him be to his brethren.
Blessed of Yahweh be the tents of Shem, and Canaan shall be subject unto him.
Japheth! God shall enlarge him; he shall dwell in the tents of Shem;
And it shall be that Canaan   shall be servant also to him.

Now the whole earth was of one language and of one speech. And it came to pass as they journeyed from the east, that they found a plain in the land of Shinar, and they dwelt there. And they said one to another: Come, let us make brick and burn them thoroughly. And they had brick for stone and bitumen had they for mortar. And they said: Come, let us build us a city, and a tower with its summit in the heavens; and let us make us a name, lest we be scattered abroad over the face of the whole earth. And Yahweh came down to see the city and the tower which the children of men had built. And Yahweh said: Behold, the people is one, and they have all one language, and this they begin to do; and now nothing will be impossible for them which they may plan to do. Come, let us go down and there confound their language, that they may not understand one another's speech. So Yahweh scattered them abroad from thence over the face of the whole earth; and they ceased to build the city. Therefore is the name of it called *Babel* (Gate of God); because Yahweh did there confound the language of all the earth, and thence did Yahweh scatter them abroad upon the face of all the earth.

SECTION II.—The Origin of the *B'ne Israel*, and their progenitor, Abram.

> *Materials:* The Cherished Traditions of his Descendants. (Gen. xi, 27-xii, 18; xvi, 1b-14; xviii-xix; xxiv-xxv, 6.)

Now these are the generations of Terah.[1] Terah begat Abram, Nahor and Haran; and Haran begat Lot. And Haran died in the presence of his father Terah in the land of his nativity, in Ur of the Chaldees. And Abram and Nahor took them wives; the name of Abram's wife was Sarai, and the name of Nahor's wife, Milcah, the daughter of Haran the father of Milcah and of Iscah. And Sarai was barren; she had no child.

Now Yahweh had said unto Abram: Get thee out of thy country and from thy kindred and from thy father's house unto a land that I will show thee; and I will make of thee a great nation; and I will bless thee and make thy name great, and thou shalt be a blessing. And I will bless them that bless thee, and curse him that curseth thee; and in thee shall all the families of the earth be blessed. So Abram went, as Yahweh had said unto him, and Lot went with him. And Abram passed through the land unto the place of Shechem, unto the terebinth of Moreh. And the Canaanite was then in the land. And Yahweh appeared unto Abram, and said: Unto thy seed will I give this land. And he builded there an altar unto Yahweh who had appeared unto him. And he removed from thence unto the mountain on the east of Bethel, and pitched his tent, having Bethel on the west and Ai on the east; and he builded there an altar unto Yahweh, and called on the name of Yahweh. And Abram journeyed, going on still toward the south.

Now there was a famine in the land; and Abram went down into Egypt to sojourn there, for the famine was sore in the land. And it came to pass, when Abram was about to enter Egypt, that he said unto Sarai, his wife: Behold, now, I know that thou art a woman fair to look upon; and it will come to pass that when the Egyptians shall see thee, that they shall say: This is his wife; and they will kill me, but thee they will keep alive. Say, I pray thee, that thou art my sister; that it may be well with me for thy sake, and my life shall be spared because of thee.

And it came to pass when Abram was come into Egypt, that the Egyptians beheld the woman, that she was very fair. And Pharaoh's

---

[1] According to P, who here inserts a genealogical table (ch. xi, 10-26) Terah was in the ninth generation from Shem in the line of Arphaxad. What is more important, Haran, his youngest son, is said to have died in Ur before the family removed to Haran in Aram. It corroborates another tradition of Abraham's birth and upbringing in the great metropolis and trading mart of Babylonia.

princes saw her and praised her to Pharaoh, and the woman was taken into Pharaoh's house. And he treated Abram well for her sake; and he had sheep and oxen and he-asses, and man-servants and maid-servants and she-asses and camels.

And Yahweh plagued Pharaoh and all his house with great plagues because of Sarai, Abram's wife. And Pharaoh called Abram, and said: What is this that thou hast done unto me? Why didst thou not tell me that she was thy wife? Why saidst thou: She is my sister, so that I took her to be my wife? Now, therefore, behold thy wife. Take her and go. And Pharaoh gave men charge concerning him, and they sent him away and his wife, and all that he had.

And Abram went up out of Egypt, he and his wife and all that he had, and Lot with him, into the south. And Abram was very rich in cattle, in silver and in gold. And he went on his journeys from the south even to Bethel, unto the place where his tent had been at the beginning, between Bethel and Ai; unto the place of the altar which he had made there at first; and there Abram called on the name of Yahweh. And Lot also, who went with Abram, had flocks and herds and tents. And there was a strife between the herdmen of Abram's cattle and the herdmen of Lot's cattle. (And the Canaanite and the Perizzite dwelled then in the land.) And Abram said unto Lot: Let there be no strife, I pray thee, between me and thee, and between my herdmen and thy herdmen, for we are brethren. Is not the whole land before thee? If thou wilt take the left hand, then I will go to the right; or if thou take the right hand then I will go to the left. And Lot lifted up his eyes and beheld all the plain of Jordan, that it was well watered everywhere (before Yahweh destroyed Sodom and Gomorrah) like the garden of Yahweh, like the land of Egypt, as thou goest unto Zoar. Then Lot chose him all the plain of Jordan; and Lot journeyed east, and pitched his tent toward Sodom. Now the men of Sodom were wicked, and sinners against Yahweh exceedingly.

And Yahweh said unto Abram, after that Lot was separated from him: Lift up now thine eyes, and look from the place where thou art northward and southward and eastward and westward; for all the land which thou seest, to thee will I give it and to thy seed forever. And I will make thy seed as the dust of the earth; so that, if a man can number the dust of the earth, thy seed also shall be numbered. Arise, walk through the land in the length of it and in the breadth of it, for I will give it thee. Then Abram moved his tent and came and dwelt by the oaks of Mamre, which are in Hebron, and built there an altar to Yahweh.

Now Sarai, Abram's wife, had a handmaid, an Egyptian, whose name was Hagar. And Sarai said unto Abram: Behold, now, Yahweh hath restrained me from bearing; I pray thee, go in unto my maid; it may be that I may obtain children by her. And Abram hearkened to the voice of Sarai. And he went in unto Hagar, and she conceived. And when she saw that she had conceived, her mistress was despised in her eyes. And Sarai said unto Abram: My wrong be upon thee. I have given my maid into thy bosom; and when she saw that she had conceived, I was despised in her eyes. Yahweh judge between me and thee. But Abram said unto Sarai: Behold, thy maid is in thy hand; do to her as it pleaseth thee. And when Sarai dealt hardly with her, she fled from her face.

And the messenger of Yahweh found her by a spring of water in the wilderness, by the spring on the way to Shur. And he said: Hagar,

Sarai's handmaid, whence comest thou? And she said: I flee from
the face of my mistress, Sarai. And the messenger of Yahweh said
unto her: Return to thy mistress, and submit thyself under her hands.
And the messenger of Yahweh said unto her: I will greatly multiply
thy seed, that it shall not be numbered for multitude. And the messenger of Yahweh said unto her: Behold, thou art with child and shalt
bear a son. And thou shalt call his name *Ishmael* (God heareth), for
Yahweh hath heard of thy affliction. And he shall be an untamed man,
his hand against every man and every man's hand against him; and
he shall dwell in the presence of all his brethren. And she called the
name of Yahweh who spake unto her: Thou art a God that seest; for
she said: Even here have I looked upon Him who seeth me? Wherefore the well was called *Beer-la-hai-roi* (Well of the Living One Who
seeth me); behold, it is between Kadesh and Bered. And Hagar bare
Abram a son, and he called his name, Ishmael. And Yahweh appeared
unto him [Abraham] by the oaks of Mamre; and he sat in the tent
door in the heat of the day. And he lifted up his eyes and looked,
and lo, three men standing by him; and when he saw them, he ran
to meet them from the tent door, and bowed himself to the earth, and
said: My lord, if now I have found favor in thy sight, pass not away,
I pray thee, from thy servant. Let a little water be fetched, I pray,
and wash your feet, and rest yourselves under the tree; and I will fetch
you a morsel of bread that ye may refresh yourselves; afterwards ye
shall pass on, as ye have visited your servant. And they said: So do
as thou hast said.

[1] Then Abraham hastened into the tent unto Sarah and said: Make
ready quickly three measures of fine meal; knead it and make cakes.
And Abraham ran unto the herd and fetched a calf, tender and good,
and gave it unto the servant; and he hasted to dress it. And he took
butter and milk and the calf which he had dressed and set it before
them; and he stood by them under the tree, and they did eat. And
they said unto him: Where is Sarah, thy wife? And he said: Behold,
in the tent. And he said: I will certainly return to thee when the
season cometh round, and lo, Sarah shall have a son. And Sarah heard
in the tent door which was behind him. Now Abraham and Sarah
were old, well-stricken in age; it had ceased to be with Sarah after
the manner of women. And Sarah laughed within herself, saying:
After I am waxed old shall I have pleasure, my lord being old also?
And Yahweh said unto Abraham: Wherefore did Sarah laugh, saying,
Shall I of a surety bear a child, which am old? Is anything too hard
for Yahweh? At the set time will I return unto thee when the season
cometh round, and Sarah shall have a son. Then Sarah denied, saying:
I laughed not; for she was afraid. And he said: Nay, but thou didst
laugh.

And the men rose up from there and looked towards Sodom; and
Abraham went with them to bring them on their way. And Yahweh
said: Shall I hide from Abraham that which I do, seeing that Abraham
shall surely become a great and mighty nation, and all the nations of the
earth shall be blessed in him? For I know him, that he will command
his children and his household after him, that they may keep the
way of Yahweh to do righteousness and justice, that Yahweh may
bring upon Abraham that which He hath spoken of him. And Yahweh
said: Verily, the cry of Sodom and Gomorrah is great; their sin is

[1] From this point the names of the Patriarch and his wife are changed to Abraham
and Sarah. The occasion for the change is given in ch. xvii, A. V. inserted by P.

very grievous; I will go down now, and see whether they have done altogether according to the cry of it which is come to Me, if not, I will know. And the men turned thence and went toward Sodom; but Abraham stood yet before Yahweh.

And Abraham drew near, and said: Wilt Thou consume the right-eous with the wicked? Peradventure there be fifty righteous within the city, wilt Thou consume and not spare the place for the fifty righteous that are therein? That be far from Thee to do after this manner, to slay the righteous with the wicked, that so the righteous should be as the wicked; that be far from Thee. Shall not the Judge of all the earth do right?

And Yahweh said: If I find in Sodom fifty righteous within the city, then I will spare all the place for their sake.

And Abraham answered and said: Behold now, I have taken upon me to speak unto Yahweh, which am but dust and ashes; peradventure there shall lack five of the fifty righteous; wilt Thou destroy all the city for lack of five? And He said: I will not destroy it, if I find there forty and five. And he spake unto Him yet again, and said: Peradven-ture there shall be forty found there; and He said: I will not do it for the forty's sake. And he said: O, let not Yahweh be angry, and I will speak; peradventure there shall thirty be found there? And He said: I will not do it if I find thirty there. And he said: Behold, I have taken upon me to speak unto Yahweh; peradventure there shall twenty be found there? And He said: I will not destroy it for the twenty's sake. And he said: O, let not Yahweh be angry, and I will speak yet but this once; peradventure ten shall be found there. And He said: I will not destroy it for the ten's sake. And Yahweh went his way, as soon as he had left communing with Abraham; and Abraham returned to his own place.

And there came two messengers to Sodom at even, and Lot sat in the gate of Sodom. And Lot saw them and rose up to meet them; and he bowed himself with his face to the earth, and he said: Behold now, my lords, turn aside, I pray you, into your servant's house and tarry all night and wash your feet; and ye shall rise up early and go on your way. And they said: Nay, but we will abide in the street all night. And he urged them greatly, and they turned in unto him and entered his house. And he made them a feast, and did bake unleavened bread, and they did eat. But, before they lay down, the men of the city, even the men of Sodom, compassed the house around, both young and old, all the people from every quarter; and they called unto Lot, and said unto him: Where are the men which came in to thee this night? Bring them out unto us that we may know them. And Lot went out unto them to the door, and shut the door after him. And he said: I pray you, brethren, do not so wickedly. Behold now, I have two daughters which have not known man; let me, I pray you, bring them out unto you, and do ye to them as is good in your eyes; only unto these men do nothing, forasmuch as they are come under the shadow of my roof. And they said: Stand back. And they said: This one came in to sojourn, and he will need be a judge; now will we deal worse with thee than with them. And they pressed sore upon the man Lot, and drew near to break the door. But the men put forth their hand and brought Lot into the house to them, and shut to the door. And they smote the men that were at the door with blindness, both small and great, so that they wearied themselves to find the door. And the men said unto Lot: Hast thou any here besides? son-in-law, and thy sons and thy daughters, and whomsoever thou hast in the city, bring out of this place; for we will destroy this place, for the cry of them is great before Yahweh, and Yahweh hath sent us to destroy it.

And Lot went out and spake unto his sons-in-law which married his daughters, and said: Up, get you out of this place, for Yahweh will destroy this city. But he seemed as one that mocked unto his sons-in-law. And when the morning dawned, the messengers hastened Lot, saying: Rise, take thy wife and thy two daughters which are here, lest thou perish in the punishment of the city. But he lingered; and the men laid hold upon his hand and upon the hand of his wife and upon the hand of his two daughters, Yahweh being merciful to him, and they brought him forth and set him without the city. And it came to pass, when they had brought them forth outside, that He said: Escape for thy life; look not behind thee, and stay not in all the plain. Escape to the mountain, lest thou be consumed. And Lot said unto him: Oh, not so, my Lord. Behold now, thy servant hath found grace in thy sight, and thou hast magnified thy mercy which thou hast showed unto me in saving my life. And I cannot escape to the mountain, lest evil overtake me and I die. Behold now, this city is near to flee unto, and it is a little one. Oh, let me escape thither (is it not a little one?) and my soul shall live. And he said unto him: See, I have accepted thee concerning this thing also, that I will not overthrow the city of which thou hast spoken. Haste thee, escape thither; for I cannot do any thing till thou be come thither. Therefore the name of the city was called *Zoar* (little).

The sun was risen upon the earth when Lot came unto Zoar. Then Yahweh rained upon Sodom and upon Gomorrah brimstone and fire from Yahweh out of Heaven, and He overthrew those cities and all the plain and all the inhabitants of the cities, and that which grew upon the ground. But his wife looked back from behind him, and she became a pillar of salt. And Abraham gat up early in the morning to the place where he had stood before Yahweh; and he looked toward Sodom and Gomorrah, and toward all the land of the plain, and beheld; and lo! the smoke of the land went up as the smoke of a furnace.

And Lot went up out of Zoar and dwelt in the mountain, and his two daughters with him, for he feared to dwell in Zoar; and he dwelt in a cave, he and his two daughters. And the firstborn said under the younger: Our father is old, and there is not a man in the earth to come in unto us after the manner of all the earth. Come, let us make our father drink wine, and we will lie with him, that we may preserve seed of our father. And they made their father drink wine that night, and the firstborn went in and lay with her father; and he knew not when she lay down nor when she arose. And it came to pass on the morrow, that the firstborn said unto the younger: Behold, I lay yesternight with my father; let us make him drink wine this night also, and go thou in and lie with him, that we may preserve seed of our father. And they made their father drink wine that night also; and the younger arose and lay with him; and he knew not when she lay down nor when she arose. Thus were both the daughters of Lot with child by their father. And the firstborn bare a son and called his name Moab; the same is the father of the Moabites unto this day. And the younger, she also bare a son and called his name Ben-ammi; the same is the father of the children of Ammon unto this day.

And Yahweh visited Sarah as he had said; for Sarah conceived and bare Abraham a son in his old age. And he called the name of his son that Sarah bare to him, Isaac. And he planted a tamarisk tree in

Beersheba, and called there on the name of Yahweh, the Everlasting God.[1]

2 *   *   *   *   *   *   *

And Abraham was old, and well stricken in age; and Yahweh had blessed Abraham in all things. And Abraham said unto his servant, the elder of his house, who ruled over all that he had: Put, I pray thee, thy hand under my thigh; for I will make thee swear by Yahweh, the God of heaven and the God of the earth, that thou wilt not take a wife for my son of the daughters of the Canaanites among whom I dwell. But thou shalt go unto my country and to my kindred, and take a wife for my son Isaac. And the servant said unto him: Peradventure the woman will not be willing to follow me unto this land. Must I needs bring thy son again unto the land which thou camest from? And Abraham said unto him: Beware that thou bring not my son thither again. Yahweh, the God of heaven, that took me from my father's house and from the land of my nativity, and that spake unto me, saying: Unto thy seed will I give this land; He shall send His messenger before thee, and thou shalt take a wife for my son from thence. And if the woman be not willing to follow thee, then thou shalt be clear from this my oath, but thou shalt not bring my son thither again. And the servant put his hand under the thigh of Abraham, his master, and sware unto him upon this matter.

And the servant took ten camels of the camels of his master, and departed, for all his master's goods were in his hand. And he arose and went into Aram Naharaim, unto the city of Nahor. And he made the camels to kneel down without the city by the well of water at the time of evening, the time that women go out to draw water. And he said: O Yahweh, God of my master Abraham, I pray Thee, order Thou what shall befall me this day, and show kindness unto my master Abraham. Behold, I stand by the fountain of water, and the daughters of the men of the city are coming out to draw water. Now, let it come to pass that the damsel to whom I shall say: Let down thy pitcher, I pray thee, that I may drink; and she shall say: Drink, and I will give thy camels drink also; let her be whom Thou appointest for thy servant Isaac and thereby shall I know Thou hast showed kindness to my master.

And it came to pass that he had not done speaking, when behold, Rebekah came out (who was born to Bethuel the son of Milcah, the wife of Nahor, Abraham's brother), with her pitcher upon her shoulder. And the damsel was very fair to look upon, a virgin, neither had any man known her. And she went down to the fountain and filled her pitcher, and came up. And the servant ran to meet her, and said: Give me to drink, I pray thee, a little water of thy pitcher. And she said: Drink, my lord; and she hasted and let down her pitcher upon her hand, and gave him drink. And when she had done giving him drink, she said: I will draw for thy camels also until they have done drinking. And she hasted and emptied her pitcher into the trough, and ran again unto the well to draw, and drew for all his camels, while the man looked steadfastly on her, pondering, seeking to know whether Yahweh had made his journey prosperous or not. And it

---

[1] The "Expulsion of Hagar", the doublet of the "Sojourn in Egypt" (set this time in Gerar of the Philistines), and the "Sacrifice of Isaac", are all apparently told only by E; but that other versions may also have been in J's history and excised by JE in favor of E's, is suggested by a passage in ch. xxii (vv. 14-18), evidently by J, which presupposes his own version of the tradition.

[2] Chapter xxiii, containing the account of the death and burial of Sarah, is a late addition.

came to pass, as the camels finished drinking, that the man took a ring of gold of half a shekel weight, and two bracelets for her hands of the weight of ten shekels of gold, and said: Whose daughter art thou? tell me, I pray thee. Is there room in thy father's house for us to lodge in? And she said unto him: I am the daughter of Bethuel, son of Milcah, whom she bare unto Nahor. She said moreover unto him: We have both straw and provender enough, and room to lodge in. And the man bowed his head and worshipped Yahweh. And he said: Blessed be Yahweh, the God of my master Abraham, who hath not relaxed his mercy and his truth toward my master. As for me, Yahweh hath led me in the way to the house of my master's brethren.

And the damsel ran and told her mother's house of these words. And Rebekah had a brother, and his name was Laban; and Laban ran to the man to the fountain outside. And seeing the ring and the bracelets upon his sister's hands and hearing the words of Rebekah his sister, saying: Thus spake the man unto me, he came unto the man; and behold, he stood by the camels at the fountain. And he said: Come in, thou blessed of Yahweh, why standest thou without? for I have prepared the house, and room for the camels. And the man came into the house, and he ungirded the camels and gave straw and provender for the camels, and water to wash his feet and the feet of the men who were with him. And there was set meat before him to eat; but he said: I will not eat until I have told mine errand. And he said: Speak on. And he said: I am Abraham's servant. And Yahweh hath blessed my master greatly, and he is become great; and He hath given him flocks and herds and silver and gold, and men-servants and maid-servants and camels and asses. And Sarah, my master's wife, bare a son to my master when she was old, and unto him hath he given all that he hath. And my master made me swear, saying: Thou shalt not take a wife for my son of the daughters of the Canaanites in whose land I dwell, but thou shalt go to my father's house and to my kindred and take a wife for my son. And I said unto my master: Peradventure the woman will not follow me. And he said unto me: Yahweh, before whom I walk, will send his messenger with thee and prosper thy way. And thou shalt take a wife for my son of my kindred, and of my father's house; then shalt thou be clear from my oath when thou comest to my kindred; and if they give her not to thee, then thou shalt be clear from my oath. And I came this day unto the fountain, and said: Yahweh, God of my master Abraham, if now it please Thee to prosper the way which I am taking in this matter; behold, I take my stand by the fountain of water. Now, may it be that the maiden who cometh forth to draw to whom I shall say: Give me, I pray thee, a little water from thy pitcher to drink; and she shall say: both drink thou, and also will I draw for thy camels; she shall be the woman whom Yahweh hath appointed for my master's son. Scarcely had I finished speaking in my heart, when lo, Rebekah came forth with her pitcher on her shoulder, and she went down to the fountain and drew. And I said unto her: Let me drink, I pray thee. And she made haste and let down her pitcher from her shoulder, and said: Drink, and I will give thy camels drink also. So I drank, and she made the camels drink also. And I asked her, and said: Whose daughter art thou? And she said: The daughter of Bethuel, Nahor's son, whom Milcah bare unto him. And I put the ring upon her nose, and the bracelets upon her hands. And I bowed my head and worshipped Yahweh, and blessed Yahweh, the God of my master Abraham, which had led me in the right way to take my master's brother's daughter for his son. And now, if so be that ye will deal kindly and truly with my master, tell me; and if not, tell me: that I may turn to the right hand or to the left.

Then Laban and Bethuel answered and said: From Yahweh the thing has come, we cannot speak to thee bad or good. Behold, Rebekah is before thee; take her and go, and let her be the wife of thy master's son, as Yahweh hath spoken. And it came to pass, that when Abraham's servant heard their words, he bowed himself down to the earth unto Yahweh. And the servant brought forth jewels of silver and jewels of gold and raiment and gave them to Rebekah; he gave also to her brother and to her mother precious things. And they did eat and drink, he and the men that were with him, and tarried all night. And they rose up in the morning, and he said: Send me away to my master. And her brother and her mother said: Let the damsel abide with us a few days, at the least ten; after that she shall go. And he said unto them: Detain me not, since Yahweh hath prospered my way; send me away that I may go to my master. And they said: We will call the damsel and inquire at her mouth. And they called Rebekah and said unto her: Wilt thou go with this man? and she said: I will go. And they sent away Rebekah, their sister, and her nurse and Abraham's servant and his men. And they blessed Rebekah, and said unto her: Be thou, our sister, the mother of myriads of thousands, and may thy seed possess the gates of those that hate them. And Rebekah arose and her damsels, and they rode upon the camels and followed the man. So the servant took Rebekah and went his way.

And Isaac came from the way of Beer-lahai-roi, for he dwelt in the south country. And Isaac went out to meditate in the field at eventide. And he lifted up his eyes and saw, and behold, there were camels coming. And Rebekah lifted up her eyes, and when she saw Isaac, she lighted from the camel; and she said unto the servant: What man is this that walketh in the field to meet us? And the servant said: It is my master; and she took her veil and covered herself. And the servant made known to Isaac all the things that he had done. And Isaac brought her into the tent of Sarah his mother, and took Rebekah, and she became his wife, and he loved her. And Isaac was comforted after his mother's death.

Then Abraham took another wife, and her name was Keturah. And she bare him Zimran and Jokshan and Medan and Midian and Ishbak and Shuah. All these were the children of Keturah. And Abraham gave all that he had unto Isaac. But unto the sons of the concubines that Abraham had, Abraham gave gifts, and sent them away from Isaac his son, while he yet lived, eastward into the east country.

SECTION III.—From the Birth of Esau and Jacob to the Death of Their Father Isaac. (Genesis xxv, 11b, 21-34; xxvi; 1-14, 16-17, 19-25; xxvii, 1-45; xxviii, 10, 15-16, 19; xxix, 1a, 2-14, 31-35; xxx, 4, 5, 7, 9-16, 25-45; xxxi, 1, 3, 17-18a, 21a, c, 25b, 27, 30, 32-40, 45a-44, 46-49; xxxii, 4-23, 25-32; xxxiii, 1-17; xxxiv, 1-5, 7, 11-12, 25b-26, 30-31.)

Materials: Traditions and folksongs of the Israelites.

And Isaac dwelt by the well La-hai-roi. And Isaac entreated Yahweh for his wife, because she was barren; and Yahweh hearkened unto him, and Rebekah conceived. And the children struggled together within her, and she said: If it be so, why do I live? And she went to inquire of Yahweh; and Yahweh said unto her:

> Two nations are in thy womb,
>   And two peoples shall be separated from thy bowels;
> And one people shall be stronger than the other,
>   And the Elder shall serve the Younger.

And when her days to be delivered were fulfilled, behold there were twins in her womb. And the first came forth red all over like a hairy garment. And they called him Esau. And after that came forth his brother, and his hand had hold on Esau's heel. And the boys grew; and Esau was a cunning hunter, a man of the fields; but Jacob was a quiet man, dwelling in tents. Now Isaac loved Esau, because he did eat of his venison; and Rebekah loved Jacob.

Now Jacob sod pottage; and Esau came in from the field, and he was faint; and Esau said to Jacob: Feed me, I pray thee, with that very red stuff, for I am faint (therefore was his name called *Edom*). And Jacob said: Sell me this day thy birthright. And Esau said: Behold, I am at the point of death, and what profit shall the birthright be to me? And Jacob said: Swear to me this day; and he sware unto him; and he sold his birthright to Jacob. Then Jacob gave Esau bread and pottage of lentils; and he did eat and drink, and rose up and went his way. Thus did Esau despise his birthright.

And there was a famine in the land besides the first famine that was in the days of Abraham. And Isaac went unto Abimelech, king of the Philistines, unto Gerar. And Yahweh appeared unto him, and said: Go not down into Egypt. Dwell in the land which I shall tell thee of; sojourn in this land, and I will be with thee, and will bless thee. For unto thee and unto thy seed I will give all these lands, and I will establish the oath which I sware unto Abraham thy father; and I will multiply thy seed as the stars of heaven and will give unto thy seed all these lands. And in thy seed shall all the nations of the earth be blessed, because that Abraham obeyed my voice, and kept my charge, my commandments, my statutes and my laws.

(And Isaac dwelt in Gerar; and the men of the place asked him of his wife. And he said: She is my sister; for he feared to say, My wife, lest the men of the place should kill him for Rebekah, because she was fair to look upon. And it came to pass when he had been there a long time, that Abimelech, king of the Philistines, looked out at a window and saw, and behold, Isaac was sporting with Rebekah, his wife. And Abimelech called Isaac, and said: Behold, of a surety she is thy wife; and how saidst thou, She is my sister? And Isaac said unto him: Because I said, Lest I die for her. And Abimelech said: What is this thou hast done unto us? one of the people might lightly have lain with thy wife, and thou shouldst have brought guiltiness upon us. And Abimelech charged all the people, saying: He that toucheth this man or his wife shall surely be put to death.)

And Isaac sowed in that land and reaped in the same year a hundredfold; and Yahweh blessed him. And the man waxed great and grew more and more, until he became very great; and he had possessions of flocks and possessions of herds and a great household. And the Philistines envied him. And Abimelech said unto Isaac: Go from us, for thou art much mightier than we. And Isaac departed thence, and encamped in the valley of Gerar, and dwelt there. And Isaac's servants digged in the valley, and found there a well of springing water. And the herdmen of Gerar strove with Isaac's herdmen, saying: The water is ours. And he called the name of the well Esek (*contention*), because they contended with him. And they digged another well, and they strove for that also and he called the name of it Sitnah (*hatred*). And he removed from there and digged another well; and for that they strove not. And he called the name of it Rehoboth (*room*), and he said: For now Yahweh hath made room for us, and we shall be fruitful in the land. And he went up thence to Beersheba.

Now it came to pass, that when Isaac was old and his eyes were dim so that he could not see, he called Esau, his eldest son, and said unto him: My son! and he said unto him: Behold, here am I. And he said: Behold now, I am old, and I know not the day of my death. Now therefore take, I pray thee, thy weapons, thy quiver and thy bow, and go out to the field and get me venison and make me savory meat, such as I love, and bring it to me that I may eat so that my soul may bless thee before I die. And Rebekah heard when Isaac spake to Esau his son. And Esau went to the field to hunt for venison and to bring it. And Rebekah spake unto Jacob her son, saying: Behold, I heard thy father speak unto Esau thy brother, saying: Bring me venison and make me savory meat, that I may eat and bless thee before Yahweh before my death. Now therefore, my son, obey my voice according to that which I command thee. Go now to the flock and fetch me from it two good kids of the goats, and I will make them savory meat for thy father, such as he loveth; and thou shalt bring it to thy father, that he may eat, and that he may bless thee before his death. And Jacob said to Rebekah his mother: Behold, Esau my brother is a hairy man, and I am a smooth man. My father peradventure will feel me, and I shall be in his eyes a deceiver; and I shall bring a curse upon me, and not a blessing. And his mother said unto him: Upon me be the curse, my son; only obey my voice, and go fetch me them. And he went and took and brought them to his mother; and his mother made savory meat, such as his father loved. And Rebekah took the goodly raiment of her eldest son Esau, which was with her in the house, and put it upon Jacob her younger son; and she put the skins of the kids of the goats upon his hands and upon the smooth of his neck, and she gave the savory meat and the bread, which she had prepared, into the hand of her son Jacob.

And he came unto his father, and said: My father! and he said: Here am I; who art thou, my son? And Jacob said unto his father: I am Esau, thy firstborn. I have done according as thou badest me. Arise, I pray thee, sit and eat of my venison that thy soul may bless me. And Isaac said unto his son: How is it that thou hast found it so quickly, my son? And he said: Because Yahweh, thy God, brought it to me. And Isaac said unto Jacob: Come near, I pray thee, that I may feel thee, my son, whether thou be my very son Esau or not. And Jacob went near unto Isaac his father, and he felt him, and said: The voice is Jacob's voice, but the hands are the hands of Esau. And he discerned him not, because his hands were hairy, as his brother Esau's hands; so he blessed him. And he said: Art thou my very son Esau? And he said: I am. And he said: Bring it near to me, and I will eat of my son's venison, that my soul may bless thee. And he brought it near to him, and he did eat; and he brought him wine, and he drank. And his father Isaac said unto him: Come near now, and kiss me, my son. And he came near and kissed him. And he smelled the smell of his raiment, and blessed him, and said:

> See, the smell of my son is as the smell of a field that Yahweh
>   hath blessed.
> Let the peoples serve thee! let nations bow down before thee.
> Let him that curseth thee be cursed, and him that blesseth
>   thee be blessed.

And it came to pass, as Isaac had made an end of blessing Jacob, that Esau, his brother, came in from his hunting and said unto his father: Let my father arise and eat of his son's venison, that thy soul may bless me. And Isaac his father said unto him: Who are thou? And he said: I am thy son, thy firstborn Esau. And Isaac trembled violently and said: Who, then, is he that hunted game and brought it me before thou camest, and I ate of it all and blessed him? Verily, he shall be blessed.

When Esau heard the words of his father, he cried out with a very great and exceeding bitter cry and said unto his father: Bless me, even me also, my father! and said unto his father: Bless me too, even me, my father! And he said: Thy brother came with guile and hath taken away my blessing. And he said: Is he not rightly named Jacob (*Supplanter*)? for he hath supplanted me these two times. He took away my birthright, and behold, now he hath taken away my blessing. And he said: Hast not thou reserved a blessing for me? And Isaac answered and said unto Esau: Behold, I have made him thy lord, and all thy brethren have I given unto him for servants, and with corn and wine have I sustained him; and what shall I do for thee, my son? And Esau said unto his father: Hast thou but one blessing, my father? Bless me also, even me, O my father! And Esau lifted up his voice and wept. And Isaac his father answered and said unto him:

> Behold, of the fat places of the earth shall be thy dwelling;
>   And of the dew of heaven above.
> And by thy sword thou shalt live, and shalt serve thy brother.
>   But it shall be, when thou shalt break loose,
> Thou shalt shake off his yoke from thy neck.

And Esau hated Jacob, because of the blessing wherewith his father had blessed him. And Esau said in his heart: Let the days of mourning for my father be at hand, then will I slay my brother Jacob. And the words of Esau, her elder son, were told unto Rebekah; and she sent and called Jacob, her younger son, and said unto him: Behold, thy brother Esau is comforting himself, purposing to kill thee. Now therefore, my son, heaken to my words. Arise, flee thou unto Laban, my brother, and tarry with him a while, until thy brother's fury turn away from thee, and he forget what thou hast done unto him; then will I send, and fetch thee from thence. Why should I be bereaved of you both in one day?

And Jacob went out from Beersheba, and went toward Haran. . . . And behold, Yahweh stood near him and said: I am Yahweh, the God of Abraham thy father and the God of Isaac. The land whereon thou liest, to thee will I give it and to thy seed. And thy seed shall be as the dust of the earth; and thou shalt spread abroad to the west and to the east, to the north and to the south; and in thee and in thy seed shall all the families of the earth be blessed. And behold, I am with thee and will keep thee withersoever thou goest; and I will bring thee back to this land, for I will not leave thee until I have done what I have promised thee.

And Jacob awoke from his sleep, and said: Surely, Yahweh is in

this place, and I knew it not.   And he called the name of that place
Beth-El (*House of God*) ; but the name of that city was Luz at the first.
   Then Jacob went on his way

*   *   *   *   *   *   *

and he looked, and behold, a well in the field, and lo, three flocks of
sheep lying by it, for out of that well they watered the flocks; and a
great stone was upon the mouth of the well.   And thither were all the
flocks gathered.   And they rolled the stone from the well's mouth and
watered the sheep, and put the stone again upon the well's mouth in
its place.   And Jacob said unto them: My brethren, whence be ye?
And they said: Of Haran are we.   And he said unto them: Know ye
Laban, the son of Nahor?   And they said, We know him.   And he said
unto them: Is he well?   And they said: He is well, and behold, Rachel
his daughter cometh with the sheep.   And he said: Lo, it is yet high
day, neither is it time that the cattle should be gathered together;
water ye the sheep and go and feed them.   And they said: We may not,
until all the flocks be gathered together, and they roll the stone from
the well's mouth; then we water the sheep.   And while he yet spake
with them, Rachel came with her father's sheep, for she kept them.
And it came to pass, when Jacob saw Rachel, the daughter of Laban his
mother's brother, and the sheep of Laban his mother's brother, that
Jacob went near and rolled the stone from the well's mouth and watered
the flock of Laban his mother's brother.   And Jacob kissed Rachel, and
lifted up his voice and wept.   And Jacob told Rachel that he was her
father's brother, and that he was Rebekah's son; and she ran and told
her father.   And it came to pass, when Laban heard the tidings of
Jacob, his sister's son, that he ran to meet him and embraced him and
kissed him, and brought him to his house.   And he told Laban all these
things.   And Laban said unto him: Surely thou art my bone and my
flesh.   And he abode with him the space of a month.[1]   .   .   .

*   *   *   *   *   *   *

   And when Yahweh saw that Leah was hated, he opened her womb;
but Rachel was barren.   And Leah conceived and bare a son, and she
called his name Reuben (*See, a son!*), for she said: Surely, Yahweh
hath looked upon my affliction; now, therefore, my husband will love
me.   And she conceived again and bare a son, and said: Because Yahweh
hath heard that I was hated, he hath given me this son also.   And she
called his name, Simeon (*Hearing*).   And she conceived again and bare
a son, and said: Now this time will my husband be joined unto me,
because I have born him three sons.   Therefore was his name called
Levi (*Joined*).   And she conceived again and bare a son, and she said:
Now will I praise Yahweh.   Therefore she called his name Judah
(*Praising*), and ceased bearing.   And Rachel gave Bilhah, her maid,
to Jacob, and she said: That I also may have children by her.   And
she gave him Bilhah, her handmaid, to wife; and Jacob went in unto
her, and Bilhah conceived and bare Jacob a son.   And Bilhah, Rachel's
maid, conceived again, and bare Jacob a second son.
   When Leah saw that she had ceased bearing, she took Zilpah, her
maid, and gave her to Jacob to wife.   And Zilpah, Leah's maid, bare Jacob
a son.   And Leah said: By good fortune! and she called his name Gad

---

   [1] Jacob's various contracts with Laban, first for his wives and then for his flocks, and
the details of the jealousies of his wives are given by E.   Except for a few phrases, all
the omissions in this section will be found in E's Collection.

(*Fortune*). And Zilpah, Leah's maid, bare Jacob a second son. And Leah said: Happy am I, for women will call me happy. And she called his name Asher (*Happy*).

And Reuben went in the days of wheat-harvest and found love-apples in the field, and he brought them to his mother Leah. Then Rachel said unto Leah: Give me, I pray thee, of thy son's love-apples. But she said unto her: Is it a small matter that thou hast taken away my husband, and wouldest thou take away my son's love-apples also? And Rachel said: Therefore shall he lie with thee tonight for thy son's love-apples. And Jacob came out of the field in the evening, and Leah went out to meet him, and said: Thou must come in unto me, for surely I have hired thee with my son's love-apples. And he lay with her that night. And Leah said: Now will my husband dwell with me, because I have borne him six sons.

And Rachel conceived and bore a son, and she called his name Joseph (*Adding*), and said: Yahweh will add to me another son.

And it came to pass, when Rachel had borne Joseph, that Jacob said unto Laban: Send me away, that I may go unto mine own place and to my country. Give me my wives and my children for whom I have served thee, and let me go; for thou knowest my service which I have done thee. And Laban said unto him: If now I have found favor in thine eyes, stay; I have divined that Yahweh hath blessed me because of thee. And he said: Appoint thine own wage, and I will give it. And he answered him: Thou knowest how I have served thee, and how thy cattle have prospered with me; for little belonged to thee before I came, and now it is increased to a multitude; and Yahweh hath blessed thee since my coming. And now, when shall I provide for my own house also?

Then said he: What shall I give thee? And Jacob said: Thou shalt not give me anything; if thou wilt do for me this thing, I will again keep thy flock. I will pass through all thy flock to-day, removing thence every speckled and spotted one, and every black one among the lambs and the speckled and spotted among the goats, and this shall be my hire. So shall my uprightness answer for me in future, when thou comest to consider my wages; every one that is not speckled and spotted among the goats and black among the sheep, will have been stolen by me.

And Laban said: behold, let it be according to thy word. And he removed that day the he-goats that were striped and spotted, and all the she-goats that were speckled and spotted, every one that had white on it, and all the black among the sheep, and gave them into the hands of his sons. And he put three days' journeys between himself and Jacob; and Jacob fed the rest of Laban's flock.

Then Jacob took him rods of fresh poplar and of the almond and the plane-tree, and peeled white streaks in them and made the white on the rods appear; and he set the rods which he had peeled before the flocks in the gutters [watering-troughs] where the flocks came to drink, that they should conceive when they came to drink. And the flocks conceived before the rods, and the flocks brought forth striped, speckled and spotted. And Jacob separated the lambs . . . and put all the black in Laban's flock; and he set his own flock apart, and did not put them near Laban's cattle. And when the stronger conceived, Jacob laid the rods before the eyes of the cattle in the gutters, that they might conceive among the rods; but when the cattle were feeble, he put them not in. So the feebler were Laban's and the stronger,

Jacob's. And the man increased exceedingly in wealth and had much cattle, and maid-servants and men-servants, and camels and asses.

Then he heard the words of Laban's sons, saying: Jacob hath taken away all that was our father's, and from that which was our father's hath he gotten all this wealth. And Yahweh said unto Jacob: Return unto the land of thy fathers and to thy kindred, and I will be with thee. Then Jacob rose up, and set his sons and his wives upon camels; and he drove away all his cattle. Now Laban had gone to shear his sheep. And Rachel stole the teraphim (*household gods*) which were her father's So he fled with all that he had; and set his face toward the mount of Gilead. Then Laban took his kinsmen with him and pursued after him seven days' journey, and overtook him in the mountain. Now Jacob had pitched his tent in the mount; and Laban with his kinsmen also pitched in Mount Gilead. And Laban said unto Jacob: Why didst thou flee secretly and steal away from me; and didst not tell me, that I might have sent thee away with mirth and with songs, with tabret and with harp? And now, if thou wouldst needs be gone, because thou didst long sorely for thy father's house, why hast thou stolen my gods? And Jacob said to him: With whomsoever thou findest thy gods, let him not live; seek out for thyself whatever of thine is with me, and take it (for Jacob did not know that Rachel had stolen them). So Laban went into Jacob's tent and into Leah's tent and into the tents of the two maid-servants; but he found them not. Then went he out of Leah's tents, and entered into Rachel's. Now Rachel had taken the teraphim and put them in the camel's saddle, and was sitting upon them. And Laban searched all the tent but found them not. And she said to her father: Let not my lord be angry that I cannot rise in thy presence, for the custom of women is upon me. And he searched, but found not the teraphim.

Then Jacob was wroth and chode with Laban; and Jacob answered and said to Laban: What is my trespass, what my sin, that thou hast so hotly pursued after me? Now thou hast explored through all my household goods, what hast thou found of all the furnishings of thy house? Set it here before my kinsmen and yours, that they judge betwixt us two. These twenty years have I been with thee; thy ewes and thy she-goats have not cast their young, and the rams of thy flock have I not eaten. That which was torn of wild beasts I brought not to thee; I myself bare the loss of it; of my hand didst thou require it, whether stolen by day or by night. Thus I was; by day the drought consumed me and the frost by night; and my sleep fled from mine eyes.

Then answered Laban and said: Come, let us make a covenant between us, I and thou, and let it be a witness between me and thee. Then Jacob said unto his people: Gather stones. And they took stones and made a heap; and they did eat there upon the heap. And Laban said: This heap is a witness between me and thee this day. And Laban called it Jegar-sahadutha (*Heap of Witness*, Aram.) but Jacob called it Galeed (*Heap of Witness*, Heb.) and Mispah (*Watchtower*); for he said: May Yahweh watch between me and thee, when we are absent one from another. And Laban said to Jacob: Behold this heap (and behold this pillar), which I have set up between me and thee. This heap be witness that I will not pass over this heap to thee, and that thou shalt not pass over this heap unto me for harm. The God of Abraham and the God of Nahor, the God of our fathers judge between us.

Then Jacob sent messengers before him to Esau his brother unto the land of Seir, the country of Edom. And he commanded them, saying:

Thus shall ye speak unto my lord Esau. Thy servant Jacob saith thus: I have sojourned with Laban, and stayed there until now. And I have oxen and asses and men-servants and women-servants; and I have sent to tell my lord, that I may find grace in his sight. And the messengers returned to Jacob, saying: We came to thy brother Esau, and he also is coming to meet thee, and four hundred men with him. Then Jacob was greatly afraid and distressed; and he divided the people that were with him, and the flocks and the herds and the camels into two bands, and said: If Esau come to the one company and smite it, then the other company which is left shall escape. And Jacob said: O God of my father Abraham and God of my father Isaac, Yahweh! which didst say unto me, Return unto thy country and to thy kindred, and I will do thee good; I am not worthy of the least of all Thy mercies and of all the truth which Thou hast showed unto Thy servant; for with my staff passed I over this Jordan, and now I am become two bands. Deliver me, I pray Thee, from the hand of my brother Esau; for I fear him, lest he come to smite me and the mother with the children. And Thou didst say, Surely I will do thee good, and make thy seed as the sand of the sea, which cannot be numbered for multitude. And he rose up that night and took his two wives and his two women-servants and his eleven sons, and passed over the ford Jabbok.

And Jacob was left alone. And there wrestled a man with him until the breaking of the day. And when he saw that he prevailed not against him, he touched the hollow of his thigh; and the hollow of Jacob's thigh was strained as he wrestled with him. And he said: Let me go, for the day breaketh. And he said: I will not let thee go unless thou bless me. And he said unto him: What is thy name? And he said: Jacob. And he said: Thy name shall no more be called Jacob, but Israel; for thou hast striven with God and with man and hast prevailed. And Jacob asked him, and said: Tell me, I pray, thy name. And he said: Wherefore is it that thou dost ask after my name? And he blessed him there. And Jacob called the name of the place, Peniel (*The face of God*); for he said: I have seen God face to face, and my life is preserved. And the sun rose upon him as he passed over Peniel, and he limped upon his thigh.

And Jacob lifted up his eyes and looked, and behold, Esau came and with him four hundred men. And he divided the children unto Leah and unto Rachel, and unto the two handmaids. And he put the handmaids and their children foremost, and Leah and her children after, and Rachel and Joseph hindermost. And he himself passed over before them, and bowed himself to the ground seven times until he came near to his brother. And Esau ran to meet him and embraced him, and fell on his neck and kissed him; and they wept. And he lifted up his eyes, and saw the women and the children, and said: Who are these with thee? And he said: The children which God hath graciously given to thy servant. Then the handmaidens came near, they and their children, and they bowed themselves. And Leah also with her children came near and bowed themselves; and after came Joseph near and Rachel, and they also bowed themselves. And Esau said: What is all this band of thine that I met? And he said: To find grace in the sight of my lord. And he said: I have enough, my brother; Let that thou hast be thine. And Jacob said: Nay, I pray thee, if now I have found grace in thy sight, then take thou my present at my hand; forasmuch as I have seen thy face, as one seeth the face of God, and thou wast pleased with me. Take, I pray thee, my gift that is brought to thee; because God hath dealt graciously with me, and because I have enough. And he urged him, and he took it. And he said: Let us take our journey and let us go, and I will go before thee. And he said unto him: My lord knoweth that the children are tender, and I have flocks and herds with their young, and if they overdrive them one day all the flock will die. Let my lord, I pray thee, pass over before his servant; and I will lead on softly, according to the pace of the cattle that are before me, and according to the pace of the children, until I come unto my lord unto Seir. And Esau said: Let me now leave with thee some of the folk that are with me. And he said: Why so? let me find grace in the sight of my lord. So Esau turned back that day on his way unto Seir. But Jacob journeyed to Succoth and built him booths for his cattle; therefore the name of the place is called Succoth (*booths*). And Jacob came in peace to the city of Shechem.

Now Dinah the daughter of Leah, which she bare unto Jacob, went out to see the daughters of the land. And when Shechem, the son of Hamor the Hivite, prince of the land, saw her, he took her and lay with her and humbled her. And his soul clave unto Dinah, the daughter of Jacob, and he loved the damsel and spake kindly to her. And Jacob heard that he had defiled Dinah his daughter. Now his sons were with his cattle in the field; and Jacob held his peace until they were come. And the sons of Jacob came in from the field and when the men heard it they were very grieved, and their anger burned exceedingly because he had wrought folly in Israel in lying with Jacob's daughter, which thing ought not to be done. But Shechem said unto her father and unto her brethren: Let me find grace in your eyes, and what ye shall say unto me, that will I give. Ask me never so much dowry and gift, and I will give according as ye shall say unto me; but give me the damsel to wife. And they said unto him: We can not do this thing, to give our sister to one that is uncircumcised; for this were a reproach unto us. Only under this [condition] will we consent; if ye will be like us and circumcise every male among you. And the young man delayed not to do so, because he had delight in Jacob's daughter. And he was honored above all the house of his father.

Then two of the sons of Jacob, Simeon and Levi, Dinah's brethren, took each man his sword and came upon the city unawares, and slew all the males. And they slew Hamor and Shechem, his son, with the edge of the sword, and took Dinah out of Shechem's house, and went out. Then said Jacob unto Simeon and Levi: Ye have troubled me in making me loathsome among the inhabitants of the land, among the Canaanites and the Perizzites; and I being few in number, they will gather themselves together against me, and slay me, I and my house. And they answered: Should he deal with our sister as with a harlot?

Then Jacob came to Luz, which is in the land of Canaan, that is, Beth-el, he and all the people with him. And he built there an altar, and called the place El-Beth-el (*the God of Bethel*); because there God had appeared unto him when he fled from the face of his brother. And Jacob set up a pillar in the place where He had talked with him, even a pillar of stone; and he poured a drink-offering thereon, and he poured oil thereon. And Israel journeyed, and spread his tent beyond Migdol-Eder (*the Tower of the flock*). And it came to pass, while Israel dwelt in that land, that Reuben went and lay with Bilhah, his father's concubine, and Israel heard of it.

And Jacob came to Mamre, unto Isaac his father. And Isaac died; and his sons Esau and Jacob buried him.

SECTION IV.—The Sale of Joseph to the Ishmaelites and his Career in
Egypt. (Genesis, xxxvii, 3a, 4, 13-18, 25-27, 28c, 31-35; xxxix-xli,
41-44, 46b-48, 54-56; xliii-xliv; xlv, 1a, 4, 5a, 7a, 9b, 10-12, 14, 19,
21b, 27a, 28; xlvi, 1a, 28ff; xlvii, 1-4, 5d-6, 27a, 13-26, 29-31; xlviii,
1-2, 8-11; l, 1-11, 14.

Materials. The same as before.

Now Israel loved Joseph more than all his children, because he was
the son of his old age. And when his brethren saw that their father
loved him more than all his brethren, they hated him and could not
speak to him peaceably.

And Israel said unto Joseph: Are not thy brethren shepherding the
flock in Shechem? Come, and I will send thee unto them. And he said:
Here am I. And he said to him: Go, I pray thee, and see if it be well
with thy brethren and well with the flocks, and bring me word again.
So he sent him out of the vale of Hebron and he came to Shechem. And
a certain man found him and behold, he was wandering in the fields.
And the man asked him, saying: What seekest thou? And he said: I
seek my brethren; tell me, I pray thee, where they are shepherding.
And the man said: They are departed hence; for I heard them say, Let
us go to Dothan. And Joseph went after his brethren, and found them
in Dothan.

Now when they saw him afar off, even before he came near unto
them, they conspired against him to slay him. And they sat down to
eat bread. And they lifted up their eyes and looked; and behold, a
company of Ishmaelites coming from Gilead with their camels bearing
spicery and balm and myrrh, going to carry it down to Egypt. And
Judah said unto his brethren: What profit is it if we slay our brother
and conceal his blood? Come, let us sell him to the Ishmaelites; and
let not our hand be upon him, for he is our brother and our flesh. And
his brethren were content, and sold Joseph to the Ishmaelites for twenty
pieces of silver. And they took Joseph's tunic, and killed a buck of the
goats, and dipped the tunic in his blood, and brought it to their father,
and said: This have we found. Know now whether it be thy son's
tunic or not. And he knew it, and said: It is my son's tunic; an evil
beast hath devoured him. Joseph is without doubt torn in pieces.

And Jacob rent his clothes and put sackcloth upon his loins and
mourned for his son many days. And all his sons and all his daughters
rose up to comfort him; but he refused to be comforted, and he said:
I will go down into the grave to my son, mourning. And his father
wept for him.

But Joseph was brought down to Egypt; and Potiphar, an officer of
Pharaoh, captain of the guard, an Egyptian, bought him out of the
hands of the Ishmaelites which had brought him down thither. And
Yahweh was with Joseph, and he was a prosperous man; and he was
in the house of his master the Egyptian. And his master saw that Yahweh was with him, and that Yahweh made all that he did to prosper in
his hand. And Joseph found grace in his sight, and he served him; and
he made him overseer over his house, and all that he had he put into
his hand. And from the time that he made him overseer in his house
and over all that he had, Yahweh blessed the Egyptian's house for
Joseph's sake; and the blessing of Yahweh was upon all that he had in
the house and in the field. And he left all that he had in Joseph's hand;
and he knew not what he possessed, save the bread that he did eat. And
Joseph was of a fine figure, and goodly to look upon.

Now it came to pass after these things, that his master's wife cast her eyes[1] upon Joseph, and said: Lie with me. But he refused, and said unto his master's wife: Behold, my master knoweth not what is with me in the house, and he hath committed all that he hath to my hand. There is none greater in this house than I, neither hath he kept back anything from me but thee, because thou art his wife. How, then, can I do this great wickedness and sin against God? And it came to pass, as she spake to Joseph day by day, that he hearkened not unto her to lie by her or to be with her. And it came to pass about this time, as he went into the house to do his work and none of the men of the house were within, that she caught him by his garment saying, Lie with me; and he left his garment in her hand and fled, and got out of the house. And it came to pass, when she saw that he had left his garment in her hand and had escaped, that she called unto the men of her house and spake unto them, saying: See, he hath brought in a Hebrew unto us to mock us. He came in to lie with me, and I cried with a loud voice. And it came to pass, when he heard that I lifted up my voice and cried, that he left his garment with me and fled and got away. And she laid up his garment near her until his master should come home. Then she spake to him according to these words, saying: The Hebrew servant which thou hast brought unto us came in unto me to mock us; and it came to pass, when I lifted up my voice and cried aloud, that he left his garment with me and fled. And it came to pass, when his master heard the words of his wife, saying: After this manner did thy servant to me, his wrath was kindled. And Joseph's master took him and put him into the prison, a place where the king's prisoners were bound; and he was there in the prison.

But Yahweh was with Joseph and showed him mercy and gave him favor in the sight of the keeper of the prison. And the keeper of the prison committed to Joseph's hand all the prisoners that were in the prison; and whatsoever was done there, he was the doer. The keeper of the prison saw to nothing whatever that was under his hand; and whatever he did, Yahweh made it prosper.[2] . . .

* * * * * * *

Then Pharaoh said unto Joseph: See, I have set thee over all the land of Egypt. And Pharaoh took off his ring from his hand and put it on Joseph's hand, and clothed him in vesture of fine linen and put a chain of gold about his neck, and made him ride in the second chariot which he had. And they cried before him: Bow the knee! Thus he set him over all the land of Egypt. And Pharaoh said unto Joseph: I am Pharaoh; but without thee shall no man lift up his hand or foot in all the land of Egypt.

And Joseph went out from the presence of Pharaoh and went throughout all the land of Egypt; and he gathered up all the food of the seven years (of plenty) which were in the land of Egypt, and laid up the food in the cities; the food of the fields round about every city laid he up in the same. And the seven years of dearth began to come, according as Joseph had said. And when all the land of Egypt was famished, the people cried unto Pharaoh for bread; and Pharaoh said unto all the

[1] A strikingly similar tale is found in Egyptian folk-lore. See "Egyptian Tales", translated by Wm. T. Flinders-Petrie.

[2] The two stories of Joseph's experiences in Egypt were so dovetailed together by JE and afterwards revised by P, that it is scarcely possible to separate them. The account of his rise to power is given only from E; but the references to it and to the earlier visit of his brethren in J establish the existence of J's earlier though perhaps not so detailed version. In J's account, Judah is the chief spokesman for the brethren; in E's, it is Reuben. J's account of Joseph's introduction to Pharaoh is missing.

Egyptians: Go unto Joseph; what he saith unto you, do. And the famine was over all the face of the earth. Then Joseph opened all the storehouses and sold to the Egyptians. And the famine waxed sore in the land of Egypt.

＊　　＊　　＊　　＊　　＊　　＊　　＊

Now the famine was sore in the land [of Canaan]. And it came to pass, when they had eaten up the corn which they had brought out of Egypt, their father said: Go again, buy us a little food. And Judah spake unto him, saying: The man did solemnly charge us, saying, Ye shall not see my face except your brother be with you. If thou wilt send our brother with us, we will go down and buy thee food. But if thou wilt not send him, we will not go down; for the man said unto us, Ye shall not see my face except your brother be with you. And Israel said: Wherefore dealt ye so ill with me as to tell the man whether ye had yet a brother? And they said: The man asked us straitly of our state and of our kindred, saying: Is your father yet alive? Have ye another brother? and we told him according to the words of his mouth. Could we certainly know that he would say, Bring down your brother? And Judah said unto Israel his father: Send the lad with me, and we will arise and go; that we may live and not die, both we and thou and also our little ones. I will be surety for him. Of my hand shalt thou require him. If I bring him not to thee and set him before thee, then let me bear the blame forever. And except we had lingered, surely now we had returned the second time. And their father Israel said unto them: If it must be so now, do this. Take of the best fruits in the land in your vessels and carry down a present to the man, a little balm and a little honey; spicery and myrrh, nuts and almonds, and take double money in your hand; and the money that was returned in the mouth of your sacks carry again in your hand; peradventure it was an oversight. Take also your brother and arise, go again to the man. And the men took that present, and they took double money in their hand, and Benjamin, and rose up and went down to Egypt and stood before Joseph. And when Joseph saw Benjamin with them, he said to the steward of his house: Bring these men into the house, and slay and make ready; for these men shall dine with me at noon. And the man did as Joseph bade; and the man brought the men into Joseph's house. And the men were afraid because they were brought into Joseph's house; and they said: Because of the money that was returned in our sacks at the first time are we brought in; that he may seek occasion against us, and fall upon us, and take us for bondmen, and our asses. And they came near to the steward of Joseph's house, and they communed with him at the door of the house, and said: Oh, my lord, verily we came down at the first to buy food; and it came to pass when we came to the lodging-place, that we opened our sacks, and behold, every man's money was in the mouth of his sack, our money in full weight. Now we have brought it again in our hand. And other money have we brought down in our hands to buy food. We cannot tell who put our money in our sacks. And he said: Be at peace. Fear not; your God, and the God of your father hath given you treasure in your sacks. Your money came to me. And the man brought the men into Joseph's house and gave them water, and they washed their feet; and he gave their asses provender. And they made ready the present against Joseph came at noon, for they heard that they should eat bread there.

Now when Joseph came home, they brought him the present which was in their hand into the house, and bowed themselves to the earth. And he asked them of their welfare, and said: Is your father well, the old man of whom ye spake? Is he yet alive? And they answered: Thy servant our father is in good health, he is yet alive. And they bowed down their heads and made obeisance. And he lifted up his eyes and saw his brother Benjamin, his mother's son, and said: Is this your younger brother, of whom ye spake unto me? And he said: God be gracious unto thee, my son. And Joseph made haste, for his bowels did yearn upon his brother. And he sought where to weep; and he entered his chamber, and wept there. And he washed his face and went out, and refrained himself, and said: Set on bread. And they set on for him by himself and for them by themselves, and for the Egyptians which did eat with him by themselves; because the Egyptians might not eat bread with the Hebrews, for that is an abomination unto the Egyptians. And they sat before him, the firstborn according to his birthright and the youngest according to his youth; and the men marvelled one with another. And portions were taken from him for them, but Benjamin's portion was five times as much as any of theirs. And they drank and were merry with him.

And he commanded the steward of his house, saying: Fill the men's sacks with food, as much as they can carry, and put every man's money in his sack's mouth. And put my cup, the silver cup, in the sack's mouth of the youngest, and his corn-money. And he did according to the word that Joseph had spoken.

As soon as the morning was light, the men were sent away, they and their asses. And when they were gone out of the city, not far, Joseph said unto his steward: Up, follow after the men; and when thou dost overtake them, say unto them, Wherefore have ye rewarded evil for good? Is not this it in which my lord drinketh and whereby indeed he divineth? Ye have done evil in so doing. And he overtook them, and he spake unto them these same words. And they said unto him: Wherefore said my lord these words? God forbid that thy servants should do such a thing. Behold, the money which we found in our sacks' mouths we brought again to thee out of the land of Canaan; how then should we steal out of thy lord's house silver or gold? With whomsoever of thy servants it be found, both let him die, and we also will be my lord's bondmen. And he said: Now let it be according unto your words; he with whom it is found shall be my servant, and ye shall be blameless. Then they hasted and took down every man his sack to the ground, and every man opened his sack. And he searched, and began at the oldest and ended with the youngest; and the cup was found in Benjamin's sack. Then they rent their clothes and laded every man his ass and returned to the city.

And Judah and his brethren came to Joseph's house, for he was yet there; and they fell before him on the ground. And Joseph said unto them: What deed is this that ye have done? wot ye not that such a man as I can certainly divine? And Judah said: What shall we say unto my lord? What shall we speak, or how shall we clear ourselves? God hath found out the iniquity of thy servants. Behold, we are my lord's servants, both we and he also with whom this cup is found. And he said: God forbid that I should do so; the man in whose hand the cup is found, he shall be my servant. And as for you, get you in peace unto your father.

Then Judah came near unto him, and said: Oh, my lord, let thy servant, I pray thee, speak a word in my lord's ears, and let not thine anger burn against thy servant; for thou art even as Pharaoh.   My lord asked his servants, saying, Have ye a father, or a brother?   And we said unto my lord, We have a father, an old man, and a child of his old age, a little one; and his brother is dead, and he alone is left of his mother, and his father loveth him.   And thou saidst unto thy servants: Bring him down unto me, that I may set mine eyes upon him.   And we said unto my lord: The lad cannot leave his father; for, if he should leave his father, his father would die.   And thou saidst unto thy servants: Except your youngest brother come down with you, ye shall see my face no more.   And it came to pass, when we came up unto thy servant our father, we told him the words of my lord.   And our father said: Go again, and buy us a little food.   And we said: We cannot again go down.   If our youngest brother be with us, then will we go down; but we may not see the man's face except our youngest brother be with us.   And thy servant, our father, said unto us: Ye know that my wife bare me two sons.   And the one went out from me, and I said: Surely he is torn in pieces.   And I have not seen him since; and if ye take this one also from me, and mischief befall him, ye shall bring down my gray hairs with sorrow to the grave.   Now therefore, when I come to thy servant, my father, and the lad is not with us, seeing that his life is bound up in the lad's life, it shall come to pass, when he seeth that the lad is not with us, that he will die; and thy servants shall bring down the gray hairs of thy servant, our father, with sorrow to the grave.   For thy servant became surety for the lad unto my father, saying: If I bring him not unto thee, then I shall bear the blame to my father forever.   Now therefore, I pray thee, let thy servant abide instead of the lad a bondman to my lord; and let the lad go up with his brethren. For how shall I go up to my father, and the lad not with me, and see the sorrow that shall come upon my father?

Then Joseph could not refrain himself before all them that stood by him; and he cried: Cause every man to go out from me.   And Joseph said unto his brethren: Come near to me, I pray you.   And they came near.   And he said: I am Joseph your brother, whom ye sold into Egypt.   Now therefore, be not troubled that ye sold me hither; for God sent me before you to preserve you a remnant in the earth.   Go up to my father and say unto him: Come down unto me, and tarry not; and thou shalt dwell in the land of Goshen, thou and thy children and thy children's children, and thy flocks and thy herds and all that thou hast. And there will I provide for thee, for still there are five years of famine; lest thou and thy household and all that thou hast come to poverty.   And behold, your eyes see, and the eyes of my brother Benjamin, that it is my mouth that speaketh unto you.   (And he fell upon his brother Benjamin's neck, and wept; and Benjamin wept upon his neck.)   Now I command you, this do; take you wagons out of the land of Egypt for your little ones and for your wives, and bring your father and come.   And the sons of Israel did so.   And they told their father all the words of Joseph which he had said unto them.   And Israel said: It is enough; Joseph, my son, is yet alive; I will go and see him before I die.

And Israel took his journey with all that he had.   And he sent Judah before him unto Joseph, to direct his face unto Goshen, and they came into the land of Goshen.   And Joseph made ready his chariot, and went up to Goshen to meet his father, and presented himself unto him; and he fell on his neck, and wept on his neck a good while.   And Israel said unto Joseph: Now let me die since I have seen thy face, that thou art yet alive. And Joseph said unto his brethren and unto his father's house: I will go up and show Pharaoh, and say unto him, My brethren and my father's house, which were in the land of Canaan, are come unto me. And the men are shepherds, for their trade hath been to feed cattle; and they have brought their flocks and their herds, and all that they have. And it shall come to pass, when Pharaoh shall call you and say: What is your occupation? that ye shall say, Thy servants have been keepers of cattle from our youth up until now, both we and also our fathers; that ye may dwell in the land of Goshen, for every shepherd is an abomination unto the Egyptians.

Then Joseph came and told Pharaoh and said: My father and my brethren, and their flocks and their herds and all that they have, are come out of the land of Canaan, and behold, they are in the land of Goshen. And he took some of his brethren, five men, and presented them unto Pharaoh. And Pharaoh said unto his brethren: What is your occupation? And they said unto Pharaoh: Thy servants are shepherds, both we and also our fathers. They said moreover unto Pharaoh: For to sojourn in the land are we come, for thy servants have no pasture for their flocks; for the famine is sore in the land of Canaan. Now therefore, we pray thee, let thy servants dwell in the land of Goshen. And Pharaoh spake unto Joseph, saying: In the land of Goshen let them dwell; and, if thou knowest any capable men among them, then make them rulers over my cattle. And Joseph provided his father and his brethren and all his father's household with food according to the number of children. And Israel dwelt in the land of Egypt, in the province of Goshen.

And there was no bread in all the land, for the famine was very sore; so that the land of Egypt and the land of Canaan fainted by reason of the famine. And Joseph gathered up all the money to be found in the land of Egypt and in the land of Canaan by reason of the corn which they bought; and Joseph brought the money into Pharaoh's house. And when money failed in the land of Egypt and in the land of Canaan, all the Egyptians came unto Joseph, and said: Give us bread; for why should we die in thy presence? for the money faileth. And Joseph said: Give your cattle, and I will give you grain for your cattle, if money fail. And they brought their cattle unto Joseph. And Joseph gave them in exchange for horses and for the flocks, and for the herds of cattle and the asses. And he fed them with bread for that year in exchange for their cattle. When that year was ended, they came unto him the second year, and said unto him: We will not hide it from my lord, that our money is spent; my lord also hath our cattle. There is nought left in the sight of my lord but our bodies and our lands. Wherefore shall we die before thine eyes, both we and our land? Buy us and our land for bread, and we and our land will be servants unto Pharaoh. And give us seed, that we may live and not die, that the land be not desolate.

And Joseph bought all the land of Egypt for Pharaoh; for the Egyptians sold every man his field, because the famine prevailed over them. So the land became Pharaoh's. And as to the people, he removed them to cities from one end of Egypt even to the other end thereof. Only the land of the priests bought he not; for the priests had a portion from Pharaoh, and did eat their portion which Pharaoh gave them; hence they did not sell their lands. Then Joseph said unto the people: Behold, I have bought you and your land this day for Pharaoh; lo, here is seed for you, and ye shall sow the land. And it shall come to pass at the ingatherings, that ye shall give a fifth part unto Pharaoh, and four parts shall be your own, for seed of the field, and for your food and for them of your households, and for food for your little ones. And they said: Thou hast saved our lives; let us find grace in the sight of my lord, and we will be the servants of Pharaoh. And Joseph made it a law for the land of Egypt unto this day, that Pharaoh should have the fifth part; only the land of the priests became not Pharaoh's.

Now the time drew nigh that Israel must die. And he called his son Joseph, and said unto him: If now I have found grace in thy sight, Put, I pray thee, thy hand under my thigh, and deal kindly and truly with me. Bury me not, I pray thee, in Egypt; but I would lie with my fathers; and thou shalt carry me up from Egypt and bury me in their burying place. And he said: I will do as thou hast said. And he said: Swear unto me. And he sware unto him. And Israel bowed down upon the head of the bed.

And Joseph fell upon his father's face, and wept upon him, and kissed him. Then Joseph commanded his servants the physicians to embalm his father, and forty days were fulfilled for him, for so are fulfilled the days for those which are embalmed, and the Egyptians mourned for him three-score and ten days. And when the days of his mourning were past, Joseph spake unto the house of Pharaoh, saying: If now I have found favor in your eyes, speak, I pray you, in the ears of Pharaoh, saying: My father made me swear, saying: Lo, I die; in the grave which I have digged for me in the land of Canaan, there shalt thou bury me. Now, therefore, let me go up, I pray thee, and bury my father, and I will come again. And Pharaoh said: Go up and bury thy father, according as he made thee swear.

And Joseph went up to bury his father; and with him went up all the servants of Pharaoh, the elders of his house, and all the elders of the land of Egypt, and all the house of Joseph, and his brethren, and his father's house. Only their little ones, and their flocks and their herds they left in the land of Goshen. And there went up with him both chariots and horsemen, and it was a very great company.

And they came to the threshing-floor of Atad, which is beyond Jordan; and there they mourned with a very great and sore lamentation, and he made a mourning for his father for seven days. And when the inhabitants of the land, the Canaanites, saw the mourning in the Floor of Atad, they said: This is a grievous mourning for the Egyptians. Wherefore the name of it was called Abel-Misraim (*the Mourning of the Egyptians*), which is beyond Jordan.

And Joseph returned into Egypt, he and his brethren, and all that went up with him to bury his father, after that he had buried his father.

CHAPTER II

THE EXODUS FROM EGYPT

Section I.—From the Flight of Moses to Midian, to his last Interview with the Pharaoh, and the Institution of the Feast of the Passover. (Exodus i, 6-14; ii, 15-22, 25a; iii, 2-4a, 5, 7-8, 16-18; iv, 1-16, 19-20, 22-26, 29-31; v, 1-3, 5-23; vii, 14, 16, 17b-18, 26, 24-28; viii, 4-6, 8-11, 16-20, 21-28; ix, 1-7, 13-21, 23c, 24b-34; x, 1-11, 13b, 14b-15a, 16-19, 24-26; xi, 4-8; xii, 24-27, 37a; xii, 20-24, 3-16.)
Materials: Still largely traditions transmitted orally.

And Joseph died, and all his brethren and all that generation. Now there rose up a new king over Egypt which knew not Joseph. And he said to his people: Behold, the people of the Children of Israel are more and mightier than we. Come, let us deal wisely with them lest they multiply, and it come to pass that, when there falleth out any war, they join also with our enemies and fight against us, and so get them out of the land.

Therefore they did set over them taskmasters to afflict them with their burdens. And they built for Pharaoh treasure-cities, Pithom and Ramses. But the more they oppressed them, the more they multiplied and spread. And they feared the Children of Israel.[1]

* * * * * * *

Now when Pharaoh heard this thing, he sought to slay Moses; but Moses fled from the face of Pharaoh and dwelt in the land of Midian; and he sat down by a well. Now the priest of Midian had seven daughters, and they came and drew water and filled the troughs to water their father's flock. And the shepherds came and drove them away; but Moses rose up and helped them and watered their flock. And when they came to Reuel, their father, he said: How is it that ye are come so soon to-day? And they said: An Egyptian delivered us out of the hand of the shepherds, and also drew enough for us and watered the flock. And he said to his daughters: And where is he? Why is it ye have left the man? Call him, that he may eat bread. And Moses was content to dwell with the man; and he gave Zipporah, his daughter, to Moses. And she bare him a son, and he called his name Gershom; for he said: A stranger have I been in a foreign land.

And it came to pass in process of time, that the king of Egypt died. Then the Messenger of Yahweh appeared to him [Moses] in a flame of fire out of the midst of a bush; and he looked, and behold, the bush burned with fire, and the bush was not consumed. And Moses said: I will now turn aside and see this great sight, why the bush is not

[1] The Birth of Moses and the occasion of the Pharaoh's anger were taken by JE from E's work (pp. 196-7). The older pharaoh has been identified as Rameses II. of the XIXth dynasty. The one with whom Moses pleaded was Mer-en-Ptah (B.C. 1225-1215), his son, and possibly a school-mate of the great Leader.

consumed. And Yahweh saw that he turned aside to see, and He said: Put off thy shoes from off thy feet, for the place whereon thou standest is holy ground.

And Yahweh said: I have surely seen the affliction of My people which are in Egypt, and have heard their cry for help because of their task-masters, for I know their suffering. And I am come down to deliver them out of the hand of the Egyptians and to bring them up out of that land unto a good land and a large, a land flowing with milk and honey; unto the place of the Canaanite and the Hittite and the Amorite and the Perizzite and Hivite and the Jebusite. Go and gather together the elders of Israel, and say unto them: Yahweh the God of your fathers, the God of Abraham, of Isaac and of Jacob appeared unto me, saying: I have surely visited you and seen that which is done unto you in Egypt. And I have said, I will bring you up out of the affliction of Egypt unto the land of the Canaanites and Hittites and the Amorites and Perizzites and the Hivites and Jebusites, unto a land flowing with milk and honey. And they shall hearken to thy voice. And thou shalt come, thou and the elders of Israel, unto the King of Egypt; and ye shall say unto him: Yahweh, the God of the Hebrews, hath met with us; and now let us go, we beseech thee, three days' journey into the wilderness, that we may sacrifice unto Yahweh our God.

And Moses answered and said: But, behold, they will not believe me nor hearken unto my voice, for they will say: Yahweh hath not appeared unto thee. And Yahweh said unto him: What is that in thine hand? And he said: A rod. And He said: Cast it upon the ground. And he cast it on the ground, and it became a serpent, and Moses fled before it. And Yahweh said unto Moses: Put forth thine hand and take it by the tail (and he put forth his hand and caught it, and it became a rod in his hand), that they may believe that Yahweh, the God of their fathers, the God of Abraham, the God of Isaac and the God of Jacob hath appeared unto thee. And Yahweh said furthermore unto him: Put now thine hand into thy bosom; and when he took it out, behold, his hand was leprous, as white as snow. And He said: Put thine hand into thy bosom again; and he put his hand into his bosom again, and plucked it out of his bosom; and behold, it was restored as his flesh; and it shall come to pass, if they will not believe thee, neither hearken to the voice of the first sign, that they will believe the voice of the latter sign. And it shall be, if they will not believe even these two signs neither hearken to thy voice, that thou shalt take of the waters of the river and pour it upon the dry land; and the water which thou takest out of the river shall become blood upon the dry land.

And Moses said unto Yahweh: O, my Lord, I am not eloquent, neither heretofore nor since thou hast spoken unto Thy servant, for unready of speech and slow of tongue am I. And Yahweh said unto him: Who hath given man speech, or who maketh the dumb or the deaf or the open-eyed or the blind? Is it not I, Yahweh? And now, go, and I will be with thy speech, and will teach thee what thou shalt say. And he said: O, Yahweh, send, I pray thee, by the hand Thou wilt send! And the anger of Yahweh was kindled against Moses, and He said: Is not Aaron the Levite thy brother? I know that he can speak well; and, also, behold, he cometh forth to meet thee; and when he seeth thee, he will be glad in his heart. And thou shalt speak unto him and put words in his mouth; and I will be with thy mouth and with his mouth, and will teach you what ye shall do. And he shall be thy spokesman unto the people, and verily he shall be as a mouth for thee, and thou shalt be for him as God. And Yahweh said unto Moses in Midian: Go, return into Egypt, for all the men are dead which sought thy life. (And Moses took his wife and his sons and set them upon an ass, and he returned to the land of Egypt.) And thou shalt say unto Pharaoh: Thus saith Yahweh, Israel is My son, even My firstborn. And I say unto thee, Let My son go, that he may serve Me; and, if you wilt not let him go, behold, I will slay thy son, even thy firstborn.

And it came to pass by the way in the inn, that Yahweh met him and sought to kill him. Then Zipporah took a sharp stone and cut off the foreskin of her son and cast it at his feet, and said: Surely, a bloody husband art thou to me. So He let him go. Then she said: A bloody husband art thou! (because of the circumcision).

And Moses and Aaron went and gathered together all the elders of the Children of Israel, and Aaron spake all the words which Yahweh had spoken unto Moses, and did the signs in the sight of the people. And the people believed. And when they heard that Yahweh had visited the Children of Israel and had seen their affliction, they bowed their heads and worshiped. And afterward, Moses and Aaron went in and told Pharaoh: Thus saith Yahweh, the God of Israel, Let my people go, that they may hold a feast to me in the wilderness. And Pharaoh said: Who is Yahweh that I should obey his voice to let Israel go? I know not Yahweh, neither will I let Israel go. And they said: The God of the Hebrews hath met with us. Let us go, we pray thee, three days' journey into the wilderness and sacrifice unto Yahweh, our God, lest He fall upon us with pestilence or with the sword. And the king of Egypt said unto them: Why do ye, Moses and Aaron, hinder the people from their work? get ye to your tasks. And Pharaoh said: Behold, the people of the land now are many, and ye make them cease from their tasks. And the same day, Pharaoh commanded the taskmasters of the people and their officers, saying: Ye shall not continue to give the people straw for moulding the bricks as heretofore. Let them go and gather straw for themselves. And the tale of the bricks which they did make heretofore, ye shall lay upon them. Ye shall not diminish aught thereof, for they be idle. Therefore they cry, saying: Let us go and sacrifice to our God. Let more work be laid upon the men that they may toil over it, and let them not regard vain words.

Then the taskmasters of the people went out and their officers, and they spake to the people, saying: Thus saith Pharaoh, I will not give you straw. Go ye, get you straw where ye can find it, but naught shall be deducted from your service therefor. So the people were scattered abroad throughout all the land of Egypt to gather chaff instead of straw. And the taskmasters were urgent, saying: Fulfil your tasks, the tale of each day, as when there was straw. And the officers of the Children of Israel, whom Pharaoh's taskmasters had set over them, were beaten and were asked: Wherefore have ye not finished as heretofore your tale of bricks either yesterday or to-day? And the officers of the Children of Israel came to Pharaoh and cried for help, saying: Why dost thou act thus toward thy servants? no straw is given us, yet they say: Make brick. And behold, thy servants are beaten when it is the fault of thine own people. But he said: Ye are idle, ye are idle; therefore do ye say, Let us go and sacrifice to Yahweh. Go now, and work; for no straw shall be given you, yet ye shall deliver the full tale of brick.

And the officers of the Children of Israel saw that they were in evil case when they were told: Ye shall not lessen the daily tale of your bricks. And they came to Moses and Aaron who had stationed themselves to meet them as they should come out from Pharaoh, and they said unto them: May Yahweh look upon you and judge you, for ye have made our savor odious in the eyes of Pharaoh and in the eyes of his servants to put a sword in their hands to slay us. And Moses turned to Yahweh, and said: Lord, why hast Thou done evil to this people, and why is it that Thou hast sent me? for, since I came to Pharaoh to speak in Thy name, he hath done evil to this people, and Thou hast done nothing to deliver Thy people.

Then said Yahweh to Moses: Pharaoh's heart is hardened; he refuseth to let the people go. Now, thou shalt say unto him: Yahweh, God of the Hebrews, sent me unto thee, saying, Let My people go that they may serve Me in the wilderness; and behold, hitherto thou wouldst not hear. Thus saith Yahweh: Behold I will smite the river; and the fish that is in the river shall die, and the river shall stink, and the Egyptians shall loathe to drink of the river. And the fish that was in the river died, and the river stank, and the Egyptians could not drink the water from the river (and all the Egyptians digged round about the river for water to drink, for they could not drink of the water of the river). And seven days were fulfilled after that Yahweh had smitten the river.

And Yahweh said unto Moses: Go unto Pharaoh, and say unto him, Thus saith Yahweh: Let My people go that they may serve Me; and if thou refuse to let them go, behold, I will smite all thy borders with frogs; and the river shall swarm with frogs, and they shall come into thy house and into thy bedchamber and upon thy bed, and into the house of thy servants, and upon thy people, and into thine ovens and into thy kneading troughs; and the frogs shall come up both upon thee and upon thy people and upon all thy servants.

Then Pharaoh called for Moses and Aaron, and said: Entreat Yahweh that he take away the frogs from me and from my people, and I will let the people go, that they may sacrifice unto Yahweh. And Moses said unto Pharaoh: Tell me plainly, when shall I entreat for thee, for thy servants and for thy people, that the frogs shall be withdrawn from thee and thy house, and shall remain only in the river? And he said: To-morrow. And he said: According to thy word shall it be, that thou mayest know that there is none like unto Yahweh, our God. And the frogs shall depart from thee and from the houses and from the servants and from the people; they shall remain in the river only. And Moses and Aaron went out from Pharaoh, and Moses cried unto Yahweh because of the frogs which he had brought upon Pharaoh. And Yahweh did according to the word of Moses; and the frogs died out of the houses, out of the villages and out of the fields. And they gathered them in heaps together, and the land stank. But, when Pharaoh saw that there was respite, he hardened his heart.

Then said Yahweh unto Moses: Rise up early in the morning and stand before Pharaoh, (lo, he cometh forth to the water), and say unto him: Thus saith Yahweh: Let My people go that they may serve me. Else, if thou wilt not let My people go, behold, I will send the gadfly upon thee and upon thy servants and upon thy people and into thy houses; and the gadflies shall fill the houses of the Egyptians and even the ground upon which they rest. And I will sever in that day the land of Goshen where My people dwell, that there shall not be a gadfly there; that thou mayest know that I, Yahweh, am in the midst of the earth. And I will put a division between My people and thy people. To-morrow shall this sign be.

And Yahweh did so. And the gadfly came in swarms into the house of Pharaoh and into his servants' houses, and in all the land of Egypt the land was corrupted by reason of the gadflies. And Pharaoh called for Moses and for Aaron, and said: Go, sacrifice to your God in the land. And Moses said: It is not fitting so to do, for we shall sacrifice the abomination of the Egyptians to Yahweh our God; lo, shall we sacrifice the abomination of the Egyptians before their eyes, and shall they not stone us? We will go three days' journey into the wilderness and sacrifice to Yahweh our God, as He shall command us. And Pharaoh said: I will let you go, that ye may sacrifice to Yahweh your God in the wilderness; only ye shall not go very far away. Entreat for me. And Moses said: Behold, I go out from thee, and I will entreat Yahweh that the gadfly may depart from Pharaoh and from his servants and from his people to-morrow; only, let not Pharaoh continue to deceive by not letting the people go to sacrifice to Yahweh. And Moses went out from Pharaoh and entreated Yahweh. And Yahweh did according to the word of Moses, and he removed the gadflies from Pharaoh, from his servants and from his people. There remained not one. But Pharaoh hardened his heart this time also, and he did not let the people go.

Then Yahweh said unto Moses: Go in unto Pharaoh and tell him, Thus saith Yahweh, the God of the Hebrews: Let My people go that they may serve Me. For, if thou refuse to let them go and still wilt hold them fast, behold, the hand of Yahweh is upon thy cattle which are in the field, upon the horses, upon the asses, upon the oxen and upon the sheep, a very grievous plague. And Yahweh will distinguish between Israel's cattle and the cattle of Egypt, and nothing shall die of all that belongeth to the Children of Israel. And Yahweh appointed a set time, saying: To-morrow Yahweh shall do this thing in the land. And Yahweh did that thing on the morrow, and all the cattle of Egypt died; but of the cattle of the Children of Israel died not one. And Pharaoh sent, and behold, of Israel's cattle not one was dead. And the heart of Pharaoh was hardened, and he did not let the people go.

And Yahweh said unto Moses: Rise up early in the morning and stand before Pharaoh and say unto him, Thus saith Yahweh, God of the Hebrews: Let My people go that they may serve Me; for this time I will send all my plagues upon thy heart and upon thy servants and upon thy people, that thou mayest know there is none like me in all the earth. For now I have stretched out My hand and, verily, thou and thy people in a pestilence shall disappear from the earth. And in very deed, for this cause have I raised thee up to show thee My power, and to make known My name through all the earth. Still art thou exalting thyself against My people, that thou wilt not let them go? Behold, at this time to-morrow will I pour down a very grievous hail, the like of which hath not been in Egypt from the day of its foundation until now. Send therefore now, hasten to gather all thy cattle and all that thou hast in the field; every man and beast which shall be found in the field and shall not be brought home, upon them the hail shall come down and they shall die. He that feared the word of Yahweh among the servants of Pharaoh made his servants and his cattle flee into the houses, and he who regarded not the word of Yahweh left his servants and cattle in the field.

And Yahweh rained down hail upon the land of Egypt such as there was none like it in all the land of Egypt since it became a nation; and the hail smote every herb of the field and brake every tree of the field.

Only in the land of Goshen, where the Children of Israel were, was there no hail.

And Pharaoh sent and called for Moses and Aaron, and said unto them: I have sinned this time; Yahweh is righteous, and I and my people are transgressors. Make supplication to Yahweh, for there has been enough of mighty thunderings and hail; and I will let you go, and ye shall no longer delay. And Moses said unto him: As soon as I am gone out of the city, I will spread abroad my hands to Yahweh, the thunderings shall cease and there shall be no more hail; that thou mayest know that the earth belongs to Yahweh. But as for thee and thy servants, I know that not yet will ye fear the God Yahweh. Now the flax and the barley were smitten, for the barley was in the ear and the flax was bolled; but the wheat and the spelt were not smitten, for they ripen late. And Moses went out of the city from Pharaoh and spread forth his hands to Yahweh, and the thunders and hail ceased, and the rain was not poured upon the earth. But when Pharaoh saw that the rain and the hail and the thunder had ceased, he sinned yet more and hardened his heart, he and his servants.

And Yahweh said unto Moses: Go in unto Pharaoh, for I have hardened his heart and the heart of his servants that I might show these My signs before him, and that thou may tell in the ears of thy son and of thy son's son what things I have wrought in Egypt and the signs which I have done among them, that ye may know that I am Yahweh. And Moses and Aaron went in unto Pharaoh and said unto him: Thus saith Yahweh, the God of the Hebrews, How long wilt thou refuse to be humbled before Me? Let My people go that they may serve Me. For, if thou refuse to let My people go, behold, to-morrow I will bring the locusts into thy border, and they shall cover the face of the earth, so that one will not be able to see the earth; and they shall eat the residue of that which escaped, which remaineth unto you from the hail; and they shall eat every tree that groweth up in your fields. And they shall fill thy houses and the houses of all thy servants and the house of all the Egyptians, as neither thy fathers nor thy fathers' fathers have seen, from the day they came upon the earth to this day. And he turned and went out from Pharaoh.

And the servants of Pharaoh said unto him: How long shall this man be a snare unto us? Let the men go that they may serve Yahweh their God. Knowest thou not yet that Egypt is ruined? And Moses and Aaron were brought back unto Pharaoh, and he said unto them: Go, serve Yahweh your God; but who and what shall go? And Moses said: With our young and with our old will we go, with our sons and our daughters, with our flocks and with our herds will we go; for us it is a feast unto Yahweh. And he said unto them: So may Yahweh be with you, as I shall let you and your little ones go. Look out, for evil is before you. Not so! Go now, ye that be men, and serve Yahweh, for that is what ye asked. And they drove them from Pharaoh's presence. And Yahweh brought an east wind over the land all that day and all the night; when it was morning, the east wind brought locusts; very grievous were they; before them were no such locusts as they, neither after them shall be such; for they covered the face of the whole earth so that the land was darkened; and there remained no green thing in the trees or in the herbs of the field through all the land of Egypt.

Then Pharaoh called for Moses and Aaron in haste, and he said: I have sinned against your God and against you. Now, therefore, forgive, I pray thee, my sin but this once and entreat Yahweh your God, that he will turn away from me just this death. And he went out from Pharaoh and entreated Yahweh; and Yahweh turned a mighty strong west wind which bore away the locusts and cast them into the Red Sea. There remained not one locust within all the borders of Egypt. And Pharaoh called Moses and said: Go, serve Yahweh; only your flocks and your herds shall be left behind; your little ones may also go with you. And Moses said: Thou must also give into our hands sacrifices and burnt offerings, that we may sacrifice to Yahweh, our God. Our cattle also shall go with us; not a hoof shall be left behind, for thereof must we take to serve Yahweh, our God; and we know not with what we must serve Yahweh until we come thither. And Pharaoh said unto him: Get thee from me; take heed unto thyself; see my face no more, for in that day thou seest my face thou shalt die.

Then Moses said: Rightly hast thou spoken; I will see thy face no more. Thus saith Yahweh: About midnight I will go forth into the midst of Egypt, and all the firstborn of Egypt shall die, from the firstborn of Pharaoh that sitteth upon his throne unto the firstborn of the maidservant that is behind the mill, and all the firstborn of beasts. And there shall be a great cry throughout all the land of Egypt, such as there hath been none like it, nor shall be like it any more. But against any of the Children of Israel shall not a dog move his tongue, against man or beast; that ye may know that Yahweh doth put a difference between the Egyptians and Israel. And all these thy servants shall come down unto me, saying, Get thee out, and all the people that follow thee. And after that, I WILL GO OUT. And he went out from Pharaoh in a great anger.

Then Moses called for all the elders of Israel, and said unto them: Draw out and take ye lambs according to your families and kill the Passover. And ye shall take a bunch of hyssop and dip it in the blood which is in the basin, and strike the lintel and the two side-posts with the blood that is in the basin; and none of you shall go out of the door of his house until the morning. For Yahweh will pass over to smite the Egyptians; and when he seeth the blood upon the lintel and on the two side-posts, Yahweh will pass over the door, and will not suffer the destroyer to come in unto your houses to smite you. And ye shall observe this thing for an ordinance to thee and to thy sons for ever. And it shall be, when ye have come into the land which Yahweh will give you, according as he hath promised, that ye shall keep this service. And it shall be, when your children shall say unto you: What mean ye by this service? that ye shall say: This is the sacrifice of Yahweh's Passover, who passed over the houses of the Children of Israel in Egypt when he smote the Egyptians and delivered our houses. And the people bowed the head and worshiped; as Yahweh had commanded Moses and Aaron, so did they.

And it came to pass, at midnight, that Yahweh smote all the firstborn in the land of Egypt, from the firstborn of Pharaoh that sat on the throne unto the firstborn of the captive that was in the dungeon, and all the firstborn of cattle. And Pharaoh rose up in the night, he and all his servants, and all the Egyptians; and there was a great cry in Egypt, for there was not a house where there was not one dead. And he summoned Moses and Aaron by night, and said: Rise up, get you forth from among my people, both ye and the Children of Israel; and go, serve Yahweh as ye have said. Take both your flocks and your herds, as ye have said, and begone!

And the Children of Israel took their journey from Ramses to Succoth, and from Succoth they took their journey and encamped in Etham, in the edge of the wilderness. And Yahweh went before them by day in a pillar of cloud, to lead the way for them; and by night in a pillar of fire, to give them light. The pillar of cloud by day and the pillar of fire by night departed not from before the people. Then Moses said unto the people: Remember this day in which ye came out from Egypt, out of the house of bondage; for by strength of hand Yahweh brought you out from this place. This day are ye going out, in the month Abib. And it shall be when Yahweh shall bring you into the land of the Canaanites and the Hittites and the Amorites and the Jebusites which he sware unto thy fathers to give thee, a land flowing with milk and honey, that thou shalt keep this service in this month. Seven days shalt thou eat unleavened bread, and in the seventh day shall be a feast to Yahweh. Unleavened bread shall be eaten seven days; and there shall be no leavened bread seen with thee, neither shall there be leaven seen with thee in all thy quarters. And thou shalt explain to thy son in that day, saying: This is because of what Yahweh did for me in bringing me out of Egypt. And it shall be a sign for thee upon thy hand and for a memorial between thine eyes, that the law of Yahweh may be in thy mouth; for with a strong hand hath Yahweh brought thee out of Egypt. Therefore shalt thou keep this ordinance in its season from year to year.

And it shall be when Yahweh shall bring thee into the land of the Canaanites, as He sware unto thee and to thy fathers, and shall give it thee, that thou shalt set apart all that openeth the womb, every firstling that cometh of a beast that belongeth to thee; the males shall belong to Yahweh. And every firstling of an ass thou shalt redeem with a lamb; and if thou wilt not redeem it, thou shalt break his neck. And all the firstborn of man among thy children thou shalt redeem. And it shall be when thy son asketh thee in time to come, saying: What is this? that thou shalt say unto him, By strength of hand Yahweh brought us out of Egypt, from the house of bondage. And it came to pass when Pharaoh would hardly let us go, that Yahweh slew all the firstborn in the land of Egypt, both of man and beast. Therefore I sacrifice to Yahweh all that openeth the matrix, being males: but all the firstborn of my children I redeem. And it shall be for a sign upon thine hand, and for frontlets between thine eyes; for by strength of hand, Yahweh brought us out of Egypt.

Section II.—The Egyptians pursue the Israelites. The Crossing of the Red Sea, and the Destruction of the Pursuers. The Journey along the Seacoast to Sinai. (Ex. xiv, 5-7, 10a, 11-14, 19b-20, 21b, 24-25, 27b, 30-31; xv, 22-27; xvi, 4-5, 25-30; xvii, 1b-2, 7; xix, 20-25.)

Materials: Still only oral traditions, with some possible records by Moses and Aaron. The only Egyptian record found so far mentions Israel as already in Syria in the reign of Mer en Ptah; this may or may not be taken for their stay in Kadesh, before they turned back to the Syrian Desert.

And it was told the king of Egypt that the people fled. And the heart of Pharaoh and of his servants was turned against the people, and they said: Why have we done this, that we have let Israel go from serving us? And he made ready his chariot and took his people with him; and he took six hundred chosen chariots, all the chariots of Egypt, and captains over every one of them. And when Pharaoh drew nigh, the Children of Israel lifted up their eyes and, behold, the Egyptians marched after them, and they were sore afraid. And they said unto Moses: Were there no graves in Egypt that thou hast brought us out to die in the wilderness? What is this thou hast done unto us in bringing us out of Egypt? Is not this the word that we spake unto thee in Egypt, saying: Let us alone that we may serve the Egyptians, for it is better for us to serve the Egyptians than that we should die in the wilderness? And Moses said unto the people: Fear not; stand still and see the salvation of Yahweh which He will work for you to-day; for the Egyptians whom ye have seen to-day, ye shall see them again no more for ever. Yahweh shall fight for you, and ye shall hold your peace. And the pillar of cloud removed from before them and stood behind them. And it came between the camp of the Egyptians and the camp of Israel; and it was cloud and darkness to them, but it gave light by night to these, so that the one came not nigh the other all the night.

And Yahweh caused the sea to go back by a strong east wind all that night and made the sea dry land. And it came to pass in the morning watch that Yahweh looked through the pillar of fire and cloud upon the host of the Egyptians and discomfited the Egyptians, and took off their chariot wheels and made them go heavily, so that the Egyptians said: Let us flee from the face of Israel, for Yahweh is fighting for them against the Egyptians. And the sea returned to its strength when morning dawned, and the Egyptians, fleeing, encountered it, and Yahweh overthrew the Egyptians in the midst of the sea.

Thus Yahweh saved Israel that day out of the hand of the Egyptians, and Israel saw the Egyptians dead upon the seashore. And Israel saw the great work which Yahweh did upon the Egyptians; and the people feared Yahweh, and believed in Yahweh, and in Moses his servant.

So Moses brought Israel from the Red Sea, and they went into the wilderness of Shur; and they went three days in the wilderness and found no water. And when they came to Marah they could not drink of the waters of Marah, for they were bitter; (therefore the name of it was Marah). And the people murmured against Moses, saying: What shall we drink? And he cried unto Yahweh, and Yahweh showed him a tree which he caused to be thrown into the waters, and the waters became sweet. There he laid down a statute for them and an ordinance, and there he tested them, and said: If thou wilt diligently hearken to the voice of Yahweh, thy God, and wilt do that which is right in His sight, and wilt give ear to His commandments and keep all His statutes, I will put none of those diseases upon thee which I have brought upon the Egyptians; for I, Yahweh, am He who healeth thee.

And they came to Elim, where were twelve wells of water and threescore and ten palmtrees; and they encamped there by the waters.

Then said Yahweh unto Moses: Behold, I will rain bread[1] from heaven for you, and the people shall go out and gather a certain rate each day, that I may prove them whether they will walk in My law or not. And it shall be that on the sixth day, they shall prepare what

[1] E gives full details of the murmurings of the people barely mentioned by J. Chapters xvii and xix are largely the work of P, the priestly group of editors in the Persian period.

they shall bring in, and it shall be twice as much as they gather daily. And Moses said: Eat that to-day, for to-day is the sabbath unto Yahweh; to-day ye shall not find it in the field. Six days shall ye gather it; but on the seventh day, the sabbath, in it there shall be none. (And it came to pass that some of the people went out on the seventh day in order to gather, and they found none.) And Yahweh said unto Moses: How long will ye refuse to keep my commandments and my laws? See, because Yahweh hath given you the sabbath, therefore he giveth you on the sixth day bread for two days. Let every man remain at home; let no man go out of his place on the seventh day. So the people rested on the seventh day.

And there was no water for the people to drink. Wherefore the people did chide with Moses and said: Give us water that we may drink. And Moses said unto them: Why chide ye with me? Why tempt ye Yahweh? And he called the name of the place Massah and Meribah, because of the chiding of the Children of Israel, and because they tempted Yahweh, saying: Is Yahweh among us or not?

And Yahweh came down upon Mount Sinai, to the top of the mount. And Yahweh called Moses to the top of the mount; and Moses went up. And Yahweh said unto Moses: Go down, charge the people, lest they break through unto Yahweh to gaze, and many of them perish. And let the priests also that come near unto Yahweh sanctify themselves, lest Yahweh break through upon them. And Moses said unto Yahweh: The people cannot come up to Mount Sinai; for Thou didst charge us, saying: Set bounds about the mount and sanctify it. And Yahweh said unto him: Go, get thee down; and thou shalt come up, thou and Aaron with thee; but let not the priests and the people break through to come up unto Yahweh, lest He break forth upon them. So Moses went down unto the people and told them.

SECTION III.—The Feast of the Covenant on Sinai. Yahweh's anger against the swift Apostasy of the People appeased by Moses. The Second Tables of the Law. The Departure from Sinai. Renewed murmurings against Moses. The consequent Plague. The journey to Kadesh. Spies sent to Survey the Hill country as far as Hebron; their report. The people refuse to enter Canaan, and are turned back to the Desert (Steppes). (Exod. xxiv, 1-2; xxxii, 9-44; xxxiii, 12-23; xxxiv, 1-26. Numb. x, 28b-32; xi, 4-16a, 18-23, 31-35; xiii, 1, 3a, 17b-20, 22-23, 26-31; xiv, 1b, 3-4, 8-9, 11-24, 31-33, 25, 39-42, 44-45.)

Materials: The written Laws. Possible records. Folk-songs and traditions.

[1] Then Yahweh said unto Moses: Come up unto Yahweh, thou and Aaron, Nadab and Abihu and seventy of the elders of Israel, and let these worship afar off; Moses alone shall come near unto Yahweh; they shall not come near, neither shall the people go up with him. Then went up Moses and Aaron, Nadab and Abihu, and seventy of the elders of Israel. And they saw the God of Israel; and there was under his feet the likeness of a paved work of sapphire stone, and the like of the very heaven for clearness. And upon the chiefs of the Children

---

[1] Ch. xx, 1-21, which gives the Decalogue and the accompanying scene, will be found in E's "Deeds of Moses". Ch. xxi-xxiii give the "Book of the Covenant".

of Israel He laid not His hand; but they beheld God, and did eat and drink.[1]

* * * * * * *

Yahweh spake unto Moses, saying: I have seen this people, and behold, it is a stiff-necked people. Now therefore, let Me alone, that My wrath may wax hot against them and that I may consume them; and I will make a great nation of thee.

And Moses besought his God, and said: O Yahweh, why doth Thy wrath wax hot against Thy people whom Thou hast brought forth out of the land of Egypt with great power and with a mighty hand? Wherefore should the Egyptians speak, saying: For evil did He bring them forth to slay them in the mountains, and to consume them from the face of the earth? Turn from Thy fierce wrath, and repent of this evil against Thy people. Remember Abraham, Isaac and Israel, Thy servants, to whom Thou didst swear by Thine own self, and saidst unto them: I will multiply your seed as the stars of heaven, and all this land that I have spoken of will I give unto your seed; and they shall inherit it forever.

And Yahweh repented of the evil which He had said He would do unto His people.

And Moses said unto Yahweh: See, Thou sayest unto me, Bring up this people, and Thou hast not let me know whom Thou wilt send with me. Yet Thou hast said: I know thee by name, and thou hast also found favor in My sight. Now, therefore, if I have found grace in Thy sight, show me now Thy way, that I may know Thee; to the end that I may find grace in Thy sight. And consider that this nation is Thy people. And he said: I beseech Thee, show me Thy Glory![2]

And He said: I will make all My goodness pass before thee; and I will proclaim the name of Yahweh before thee; and I will be gracious to whom I will be gracious, and will show mercy on whom I will show mercy. And He said: Thou canst not see My face, for man shall not see Me and live. And Yahweh said: Behold, there is a place by Me, and thou shalt stand upon the rock; and it shall come to pass while My glory passeth by, that I will put thee in a cleft of the rock, and will cover thee with My hand while I pass by; and I will take away My hand, and thou shalt see My back; but My face shall not be seen.

And Yahweh said unto Moses: Hew thee two tables of stone like unto the first, and I will write upon these tables the words that were upon the first tables which thou brakest. And be ready in the morning, and come up in the morning unto mount Sinai, and present thyself there to Me in the top of the mount. And no man shall come up with thee, neither let any man be seen throughout all the mount. And Moses hewed two tables of stone like unto the first, and rose up early in the morning and went up unto mount Sinai, as Yahweh had commanded him, and took in his hand the two tables of stone. And Yahweh descended in the cloud and stood with him there and proclaimed the name of Yahweh.

And Yahweh passed before him and proclaimed: Yahweh! Yahweh the merciful and gracious God, long-suffering and plenteous in goodness and truth; keeping mercy for thousands, forgiving iniquity and sin,

[1] The rest of ch. xxiv is by E save for three verses at the end, added by P. Also E alone gives the story of the Golden Calf, and the breaking of the first Tables of the Law.
[2] Chapters xxxii-xxxiv, 28 were so amalgamated by JE that the usual criteria for separating the work of J and of E avail little; one can but recognize the evident repetitions, but their rearrangement is a matter of individual opinion.

and that will by no means clear the guilty; visiting the iniquity of the fathers upon the children and upon the children's children unto the third and unto the fourth generation.

And Moses made haste and bowed his head toward the earth and worshiped; and he said: If now I have found grace in Thy sight, O Yahweh, let my Lord, I pray thee, go among us, for it is a stiff-necked people; and pardon our iniquity and our sin, and take us for thine inheritance. And He said: My presence shall go with thee, and I will give thee rest. And He said unto Him: If Thy presence go not with us, carry us not up hence. For wherein shall it be known that I and Thy people have found grace in Thy sight? Is it not that Thou goest with us so that we shall be separated, I and Thy people, from all the people that are on the face of the earth? And Yahweh said unto Moses: I will do this thing also that thou hast spoken, for thou hast found favor in My sight, and I know thee by name.

And He said: Behold, I make a covenant. Before all thy people, I will do marvels such as have not been done in all the earth nor in any nation; and all the people among whom thou art shall see the work of Yahweh, for it is a wonderful thing that I am about to do with thee. Observe thou that which I command thee this day. Behold, I drive out before thee the Amorite and the Hittite and the Perizzite and the Hivite and the Jebusite. Take heed to thyself lest thou make a covenant with the inhabitants of the land whither thou goest, lest it be for a snare in the midst of thee. But ye shall destroy their altars, break their images and cut down their groves. For thou shalt worship no other god. For Yahweh, whose name is Jealous, is a jealous God; lest thou make a covenant with the inhabitants of the land, and they go astray after their gods and do sacrifice unto their gods; and they shall call thee and thou eat of their sacrifice, and thou take of their daughters unto thy sons, and their daughters go astray after their gods and make thy sons go astray after their gods.

Thou shalt have no molten gods.

The feast of unleavened bread shalt thou keep. Seven days thou shalt eat unleavened bread, as I commanded thee, in the time of the month Abib; for in the month Abib thou camest out from Egypt.

All that openeth the womb is Mine; and of all thy cattle thou shalt sanctify the males, the firstlings of ox and sheep. And the firstling of an ass thou shalt redeem with a lamb; and if thou wilt not redeem it thou shalt break its neck. All the firstborn of thy sons thou shalt redeem. And none shall appear before Me empty. Six days thou shalt work, but on the seventh day thou shalt rest; in ploughing-time and in harvest thou shalt rest.

And thou shalt observe the feast of weeks, even of the firstfruits of wheat harvest, and the feast of ingathering at the turn of the year. Three times in the year shall all thy males appear before the God Yahweh, the God of Israel. For I will cast out nations before thee and enlarge thy borders; neither shall any man covet thy land, when thou goest up to appear before Yahweh thy God three times in the year.

Thou shalt not offer the blood of My sacrifice with leavened bread; neither shall the sacrifice of the feast of the passover be left until the morning.

The choicest firstfruits of thy land thou shalt bring unto the house of Yahweh thy God.

Thou shalt not seethe a kid in its mother's milk.

And Yahweh said unto Moses: Write thou these words; for after the tenor of these words have I made a covenant with thee and with Israel. And he was there with Yahweh forty days and forty nights; he did neither eat bread nor drink water. And he wrote upon the tables the words of the covenant—THE TEN WORDS.

And the Children of Israel set forward. And Moses said unto Hobab, the son of Reuel the Midianite, Moses' father-in-law: We are journeying unto the place of which Yahweh hath said: I will give it you. Come thou with us, and we will do thee good; for Yahweh hath spoken good concerning Israel. And he answered: I will not go, but I will depart to mine own land and to my kindred. And he said: Leave us not, I pray thee, forasmuch as thou knowest how we are to encamp in the wilderness, and thou mayest be to us instead of eyes. And it shall be, if thou go with us—yea, it shall be that what goodness Yahweh shall do unto us, the same will we do to thee.

Now the mixed multitude that was among them fell a lusting; and the children of Israel also repented and wept, and said: Who shall give us flesh to eat? We remember the fish which we did eat freely in Egypt, the cucumbers and the melons, and the leeks and the onions and the garlic. But now, our soul is dried away; there is nothing at all besides this manna before our eyes. Then Moses heard the people weeping throughout their families, every man in the door of his tent. And the anger of Yahweh was kindled greatly. Moses also was displeased; and Moses said unto Yahweh: Why hast thou afflicted Thy servant, and why have I not found favor in Thy sight, that Thou layest the burden of all this people upon me? Have I conceived all this people? Have I begotten them, that thou shouldest say unto me: Carry them in thy bosom, as a nursing father carries the sucking child, unto the land which Thou swarest unto their fathers? Whence should I have flesh to give unto all this people? for they weep unto me, saying, Give us flesh that we may eat. Now, if Thou deal thus with me, kill me, I pray thee, out of hand, if I have found favor in Thy sight; and let me not see my wretchedness.

Then Yahweh said unto Moses: Say unto the people, Sanctify yourselves against to-morrow, and ye shall eat flesh; for ye have wept in the ears of Yahweh, saying, Who shall give us flesh to eat? for it was well with us in Egypt. Therefore Yahweh will give you flesh, and ye shall eat. Ye shall not eat one day nor two days nor five days, neither ten days nor twenty days; but even a whole month, until it come out at your nostrils and it be loathsome unto you; because that ye have despised Yahweh who is among you, and have wept before Him, saying: Why came we forth out of Egypt? And Moses said: The people among whom I am are six hundred thousand footmen;[1] and Thou hast said: I will give them flesh, that they may eat a whole month. Shall the flocks and the herds be slain for them, to suffice them? or shall all the fish of the sea be gathered together for them, to suffice them? And Yahweh said unto Moses, Is the hand of Yahweh weakened? Thou shalt see now whether My word shall come to pass or not. And there went forth a wind from Yahweh, and it brought quails from the sea and scattered them upon the camp, as it were a day's journey on this side and as it were a day's journey on that side round about the camp, two cubits deep on the face of the earth. And the people stood

[1] This enormous number would have almost depopulated the Delta. Bishop Colenso was the first to question it. Dr. Flinders-Petrie has shown that it came from the misreading of the Hebrew word *Aleph* which means both *one thousand* and *family*. In accordance with his clear exposition, we now read, five thousand five hundred men on foot, (*i.e.*, soldiers).

up all that day and all that night and all the next night, and they gathered the quails; he that gathered least gathered ten homers; and they spread them out thickly for themselves about the camp.

The flesh was still between their teeth, not yet swallowed, when the wrath of Yahweh flamed against the people, and Yahweh smote the people with a very great plague. And the name of that place was called Kibroth-hattaavah (*Graves of Lust*), because there they buried the people that lusted.

From Kibroth-hattaavah the people journeyed to Hazeroth, and rested at Hazeroth; afterward the people journeyed from Hazeroth and encamped in the wilderness of Paran.

And Yahweh spake unto Moses, saying: Send thou men that they may spy out the land of Canaan, which I give unto the Children of Israel. And Moses sent them from the wilderness of Paran, and said unto them: Get you into the South country (*Negeb*) and see the people that dwell therein, whether they be strong or weak, few or many, and what the land is that they dwell in, whether it be good or bad; and what cities they are dwelling in, in camps or in strongholds, and what the land is—whether it is fat or lean, whether there is wood therein or not. And be of good courage, and bring of the fruit of the land. Now the time was the time of the first-ripe grapes.

So they went up into the Negeb and came to Hebron; and Ahiman and Sheshai and Talmai, children of Anak, were there. (Now Hebron was built ten years before Zoan in Egypt.) And they came into the valley of Eshcol, and cut down from thence a branch with one cluster of grapes, and they bore it on a pole between two; they took also of the pomegranates and of the figs.

And they returned to the congregation of the Children of Israel to Kadesh, and brought back word unto all the congregation, and showed them the fruit of the land. And they said: We came unto the land whither thou didst send us, and truly it floweth with milk and honey, and this is the fruit of it. Howbeit, the people that dwell in the land are fierce and the cities are fortified and very great, and moreover we saw the children of Anak there. Amalek dwelleth in the Negeb; and the Hittite and the Jebusite and the Amorite dwell in the mountains; and the Canaanite dwelleth by the sea and alongside of the Jordan.

Then Caleb quieted the people before Moses, and said: Let us go up quickly and take possession of it, for we are well able to do it. But the men who had gone up with him said: We are not able to go up against this people, for they are stronger than we. And the people wept that night, and said: Wherefore hath Yahweh brought us unto this land to fall by the sword? Our wives and our little ones will be for a prey. Were it not better for us to return to Egypt? And they said one to another: Let us make a captain, and let us return into Egypt. But Caleb the son of Jephunneh said: If Yahweh delights in us, then He will bring us into this land and give it to us, a land that floweth with milk and honey. Only rebel not against Yahweh, neither fear ye the people of the land; for they are bread for us; their defense is departed from them, and Yahweh is with us. Fear them not.

And Yahweh said unto Moses: How long will this people provoke Me? And how long will they not trust Me after all the signs which I have given them? I will smite them with the pestilence and disinherit them, and I will make of thee a greater and a mightier nation than they.

And Moses said unto Yahweh: Then the Egyptians will hear it—

for Thou broughtest up this people in Thy might from among them—
and they will tell it to the inhabitants of this land. They have heard
that Thou, O Yahweh, art in the midst of this people, for Thou, O
Yahweh, art seen face to face; and Thy cloud standeth over them and
in a pillar of cloud Thou goest before them by day, and in a pillar of
fire by night. Now if Thou kill this people as one man, then the
nations which have heard the fame of Yahweh will say: Because He
was wholly unable to bring this people into the land which He sware
unto them, therefore hath He slain them in the wilderness. And now,
I pray Thee, let the power of my Lord be great, as Thou hast spoken,
saying: Yahweh is slow to wrath and of great mercy, forgiving iniquity
and transgression, but never leaving it unpunished; visiting the iniquity
of the fathers upon the children unto the third and fourth generation.
Forgive, I pray Thee, the iniquity of this people, according to the
greatness of Thy mercy, and as Thou hast done unto this people
until now.

And Yahweh said: I have forgiven, according to thy word. Nevertheless, as I live—and all the earth shall be filled with the glory of
Yahweh—verily, all those men who have seen My glory and My signs
which I did in Egypt and in the wilderness, yet have tempted Me these
ten times, and have not hearkened to My voice; verily, they shall not
see the land which I sware unto their fathers, neither shall any of
those who despised Me see it. But My servant Caleb, because he had
another spirit in him and he hath followed Me fully, him will I bring
into the land whither he went, and his seed shall possess it. But your
little ones, which ye said should be for a prey, them will I bring in,
and they shall know the land which ye have despised. But as for
you, your carcasses shall fall in this wilderness, and your children
shall be wanderers in the wilderness forty years, and shall bear your
apostasies until your dead bodies shall be utterly consumed in the
wilderness. Now, the Amalekite and the Canaanite dwell in the vale.
To-morrow, turn ye, and get you into the wilderness by the way of the
Red Sea.

And Moses told all these words unto all the Children of Israel, and
the people mourned greatly. And they rose up early in the morning,
and got them up to the top of the mountain, saying: Lo, we are here,
and will go up unto the place Yahweh hath promised, for we have
sinned. And Moses said: Wherefore do ye now transgress the commandment of Yahweh, seeing it shall not prosper? Go not up, for
Yahweh is not among you; that ye may not be smitten down before
your enemies.

But they presumed to go up. Then the Amalekites and the Canaanites who dwelt in that hill-country came down and smote them, and
beat them even to Hormah.

SECTION IV.—The Rebellion of Dathan and Abiram.[1] The Journey Northward of the Second Generation, the original fugitives having proved their unfitness for self-government, and died in the Syrian steppes. Edom refuses the young host passage; they make a difficult detour, and reach Mount Hor. They conquer Arad and destroy the Canaanites in the South Country (*the Negeb*); also Sihon and Og, and dwell in their cities. Moab fears them and sends to Aram for a Seer to curse them. Judaic account of Balaam's prophecy. The Israelites reach the foot of Mount Pisgah. (Numb. xvi, 1a, 2a, 25-26, 27b-34; xx, 19-20, 21b-22; xxi, 1-4, 16-20, 25b-35; xxii, 3-4, 5b, 5a, c, 6a, b, 11, 17-18, 21b-36b, 39; xxiii, 28-36; xxiv, 1-19, 25; xxv, 1-4.)

Materials: Traditions and Folksongs as before. Possible records of incidents of their journeys. Quotations from "The Book of *Jashar* (the Upright)", a collection of lyrics made either in the time of David or of Solomon.

Then Dathan and Abiram, the sons of Eliab the son of Pallu the son of Reuben,[1] took men and rose up against Moses. And Moses sent to summon Dathan and Abiram, the sons of Eliab; and they said: We will not come up. Is it a small thing that thou hast brought us up out of a land flowing with milk and honey to kill us in the wilderness, but thou wilt make thyself altogether a prince over us? Also thou hast not brought us into a land flowing with milk and honey, nor given us possession of fields and vineyards. Wilt thou put out the eyes of these men? We will not come up. Then Moses was very wroth, and said to Yahweh: Respect not Thou their offering. Not one ass have I taken from them, neither have I hurt one of them. And Moses rose up and went unto Dathan and Abiram, and the elders of Israel followed him. And he spake unto the congregation, saying: Turn aside, I pray you, from the tents of these wicked men, and touch nothing that is theirs, lest ye be carried away in all their sins. And Dathan and Abiram came out and stood in the door of their tents, and their wives and their sons, and their little ones.

And Moses said: Hereby shall ye know that Yahweh hath sent me to do all these things, and that they are not of my devising. If these men die the common death of all men, or if the visitation of all men come upon them, then Yahweh hath not sent me. But if Yahweh make a new thing, and the ground opens its mouth and swallows them up and all that belongs to them, and they go down alive into Sheol, then ye shall know that these men have rejected Yahweh.

And it came to pass as he finished speaking, that the ground under them was riven; and the earth opened its mouth and swallowed up them and their houses; they and all that belonged to them went down alive into Sheol, and the earth closed upon them. And they perished out of the midst of the congregation. And all Israel that were round about them fled at the cry of them, for they said: Lest the earth swallow us up alive also.

Now the Children of Israel said unto the king of Edom: Let us pass, I pray thee, through thy country. We will go by the highway; and if I and my cattle drink of thy water, then I will pay for it; I ask nothing else than to pass through on foot. And he said: Thou shalt not pass through. And Edom came out against him with much people

---

[1] The rebellion of Korah and his 250 men, here omitted, is dextrously blended with that of the sons of Reuben in the received texts, but is a late interpolation of P. The one is based on the assumption by the Levites of superior authority; the other is directly opposed to the authority of Moses. It will be remembered that Reuben was the oldest son of Jacob (Israel), and Levi, only the third.

and with a strong hand; wherefore Israel turned away from him. And the Children journeyed from Kadesh and came unto mount Hor.

Now when the Canaanite king of Arad who dwelt in the Negeb heard that Israel was coming by way of Atharim, he fought against Israel, and took some of them captive. And Israel vowed a vow unto Yahweh, and said: If Thou wilt surely give this people into my hands, then will I utterly destroy their cities. And Yahweh hearkened to the voice of Israel and delivered up the Canaanites; and they utterly destroyed them and their cities. And the name of the place was called Hormah (*utter destruction*).

And they journeyed from mount Hor, by the way to the Red Sea, and they compassed the land of Edom. And from thence the Israelites journeyed to Beer (that is the well whereof Yahweh said unto Moses: Gather the people together, and I will give them water). Then sang Israel this song:

> Spring up, O well! Sing ye unto it!
> The well the princes sought out,
> And the nobles of the people did dig
> With a sceptre and with their staves.

And thence they journeyed to Mattanah, and from Mattanah to Nahaliel and from Nahaliel to Bamoth, and from Bamoth to the valley that is in the field of Moab near the peak of Pisgah, which looketh down upon the desert.

And Israel dwelt in all the cities of the Amorites, in Heshbon and in all the environs thereof. For Heshbon was the capital city of Sihon, the king of the Amorites, who had fought against the former king of Moab, and taken all his land out of his hand even to Arnon. Therefore do the poets say:

> Come to Heshbon!
> Rebuilt let it be.   re-established be the city of Sihon.
> For fire went forth from Heshbon,   flame from Sihon's town.
>   It consumed Ar of Moab,   the chiefs of the high places of Arnon.
>   Woe to thee, Moab!   Lost art thou, people of Chemosh!
> His sons hath he made outcasts,   his daughters,
>   Captives to the Amorite king.
> Their rich fields are destroyed   from Heshbon to Dibon;
> We have laid them waste even to Nophah, which is even to Medeba.

Then Moses sent to spy out Jazer, and they took the towns thereof, and drave out the Amorites that were there. And they turned and went up by the way of Bashan; and Og the king of Bashan went out against them, he and all his people, to battle at Edrei. And Yahweh said unto Moses: Fear him not, for I have delivered him into thy hand, him and all his people and all his land; and thou shalt do unto him as thou didst unto Sihon,[1] the king of the Amorites who dwelt at Heshbon. So they smote him and his sons and all his people, until there were none remaining to him; and they possessed his land.

Now Moab was filled with fear because of the Children of Israel. And Moab said unto the elders of Midian: Now will this multitude lick up all that is round about us, as the ox licketh up the grass of the field. And Balak the son of Zippor was king of Moab at that time. He sent therefore to the land of the children of his people to summon Balaam the son of Beor, saying: Behold, a people has come out from Egypt;

---

[1] The full account of the conflict with Sihon is given by E. It was sung with rapture by the populace, as is seen above, and D uses it as the starting-point for his great exposition of the Law.

lo, they cover the face of the earth, and they are abiding over against me. Come now, I pray thee, curse me this people, for they are too mighty for me; peradventure I shall prevail, and we may smite them and drive them out of the land.

So the elders of Moab and the elders of Midian departed with the rewards of divination in their hands; and they came to Balaam, and spake unto him the words of Balak: Behold, a people has come out of Egypt which covereth the face of the earth; come now, curse me them; peradventure I shall be able to overcome them and drive them out. For I will promote thee to very great honor, and whatsoever thou sayest unto me I will do. Come therefore, I pray thee, curse me this people.

And Balaam answered the servants of Balak: If Balak would give me his house full of silver and gold, I can not go beyond the word of Yahweh, my God, to do less or more. And Balaam saddled his ass, and went.

And God's anger was kindled because he went. And the messenger of Yahweh took his stand in the way, as an adversary against him. Now he was riding upon his ass, and his two servants were with him. And the ass saw the messenger of Yahweh standing in the way, with his sword drawn in his hand; and the ass turned aside out of the way and went into the field. And Balaam smote the ass to turn her into the way. But the messenger of Yahweh stood in a path between the vineyards, a wall being on this side, and a wall on that side. And when the ass saw the messenger of Yahweh, she thrust herself against the wall and crushed Balaam's foot against the wall; and he smote her again. And the messenger of Yahweh went farther and stood in a narrow place where there was no way to turn to the right hand or to the left. And when the ass saw the messenger of Yahweh, she lay down under Balaam; and Balaam's anger was kindled, and he smote the ass with his staff. And Yahweh opened the mouth of the ass, and she said unto Balaam: What have I done unto thee that thou hast smitten me these three times? And Balaam said unto the ass: Because thou hast mocked me; I would there were a sword in my hand, for now I would kill thee. And the ass said unto Balaam: Am not I thine ass, upon which thou hast ridden all thy life unto this day? was I ever wont to do thus unto thee? And he said: Nay.

Then Yahweh opened Balaam's eyes, and he saw the messenger of Yahweh standing in the way, and his sword drawn in his hand. And he bowed down and prostrated himself on his face. And the messenger of Yahweh said unto him: Wherefore hast thou smitten thine ass these three times? Behold, I have come out to be thine adversary, because thy way is perverse before me. And the ass saw me and turned away from me these three times. Unless she had turned from me, surely now I would even have slain thee, and saved her alive. And Balaam said unto the messenger of Yahweh: I have sinned, for I knew not that thou wert standiing against me in the way. But now, if it displeases thee, I will get me back again. But the messenger of Yahweh said: Go! but only the word that I shall speak unto thee, that shalt thou speak.

Now when Balak heard that Balaam was coming, he went out to meet him unto a city of Moab which is in the border of Arnon, which is in the utmost coast. And Balaam went with Balak, and they came to Kirjath-huzzoth. And Balak brought Balaam unto the top of Peor, which looketh out towards the desert. And Balaam said unto Balak: Build me here seven altars, and prepare me here seven bullocks and seven rams. And Balak did as Balaam said, and offered a bullock and a ram on every altar. And Balaam saw that it pleased Yahweh to bless Israel; and he went not as at other times to seek omens, but he turned his face towards the wilderness. And Balaam lifted up his eyes and saw Israel encamped according to their tribes; and the spirit of God came upon him; and he took up his parable and said:

Balaam the son of Beor saith, and the man whose eyes are open saith;
  He saith who heareth the word of God,
  Who seeth the vision of the Almighty,
  Prostrate, but his eyes are open;
How goodly are thy tents, O Jacob! thy dwelling-places, O Israel!
Like valleys are they extended wide, like gardens along a river;
Like fragrant aloes by Yahweh planted, like cedars beside the waters.
Water shall he pour from his buckets, and his seed into many waters.
  And his king shall be higher than Agag,
  And his kingdom shall be exalted.
God, who bringeth him forth from Egypt is for him
  As the strength of the wild ox.
He shall eat up nations, his oppressors, their bones shall he crush,
  His arrows shall pierce them.
He couched, he lay down as a lion, and like a lioness,
  Who shall arouse him?
Blessed be he that blesseth thee, and cursed be he that curseth thee.

Then was Balak's anger kindled against Balaam, and he smote his hands together, and Balak said unto Balaam: I summoned thee to curse mine enemies, and behold, thou hast altogether blessed them. Therefore now, flee thee to thy place. I thought to promote thee to great honor; but lo, Yahweh hath kept thee back from honor. And Balaam said unto Balak: Spake I not unto thy messengers whom thou didst send unto me, saying: If Balak should give me his house full of silver and gold, I cannot go beyond the word of Yahweh to do either bad or good of mine own will? What Yahweh speaketh, that will I speak. And now, behold, I go to mine own people; come, I will advertise thee what this people shall do unto thy people in days to come.

And he took up his parable, and said:

Balaam the son of Beor saith, and the man whose eyes are open saith;
  He saith who heareth the word of God,
  And knoweth the knowledge of the Most High.
  Who seeth the vision of the Almighty,
  Prostrate, but having his eyes open.
I shall see him, but not now; I behold him, but not nigh!
  A star shall come forth out of Jacob,
  And a sceptre shall arise out of Israel,
  And shall smite the borders of Moab
  And destroy all the sons of tumult.
And Edom shall be a possession, and Seir,
  His enemies shall be a possession.
Israel shall do deeds of valor; from Jacob one shall rule.
  And destroy the remnant from the city.

And Balaam rose up and returned to his place; and Balak also went his way.

Now Israel abode in Shittim, and began to commit whoredom with the daughters of Moab. For these called the people to the sacrifices of their gods; and the people did eat, and bowed down to their gods. Thus did Israel join himself unto the Baal of Peor, and the anger of Yahweh was kindled against Israel. And Yahweh said unto Moses: Take all the leaders of the people, and execute them unto Yahweh in the face of the sun, that the fierce anger of Yahweh may turn away from Israel.

CHAPTER III.

THE ADVANCE INTO CANAAN AND THE SETTLEMENTS OF THE TRIBES

SECTION I.—Joshua becomes the leader. Sends out spies to study the situation of Jericho and its defenses. They lodge with Rahab and bring back a favorable report. The solemn Crossing of the Jordan. Circumcision of the male children born since the departure from Egypt. The encampment at Gilgal. The advance upon Jericho. The fall of Jericho. The taking of Ai. The treaty with the Gibeonites. (Joshua, i, 1-2a; ii, 1, 4a, 6b, 2, 3b, 4b-5, 8-9, 12, 14, 18, 19, 21, 25b, 24; iii, 7a, 8-10a, 13-17; iv, 1-3, 8, 20; v, 2-3, 8-9, 13-19; vi, 2-3, 5c, 7, 10-12, 14-16a, 16c-17, 20a, 21, 25-27; vii, 2-26; viii, 1a, 3-10, 14, 15, 16b, 17b, 19a, c, 21b-22, 23, 29; ix, 3-6b, 12-13a, 16, 22-23a.)

Materials: Oral traditions. Possible records of the priests. The "Book of Jashar".

Now it came to pass after the death of Moses, the servant of Yahweh, that Yahweh spake unto Joshua the son of Nun, Moses's minister, saying: Moses, My servant is dead; now, therefore, arise, go over this Jordan, thou and all thy people. Then Joshua the son of Nun sent out of Shittim two spies secretly, saying: Go, view the land and Jericho. And they went and came to the house of a harlot whose name was Rahab, and lay there. And the woman took the two men and hid them among the stalks of flax which she had spread out upon the roof.

Now it was told the king of Jericho: Behold, there came men in hither to-night of the Children of Israel to search out the land. And the king of Jericho sent unto Rahab, saying: Bring forth the men that are come to thee. And she said: Yea, the men came to me; but it came to pass when it was dark the men went out; whither the men went I know not. Pursue them quickly, and ye will overtake them. And the men pursued them by the way to the Jordan. And before they were laid down, she came up to the men on the roof, and said: I know that Yahweh hath given you the land, and fear of you hath fallen upon us, for all the inhabitants of the land melt away before you. Now, therefore, I pray you, swear unto me by Yahweh, since I have dealt kindly with you, that ye also will deal kindly with my father's house, and give me a true token. And the men said unto her: Our life for yours; if ye tell not this our business, it shall be, that when Yahweh giveth us this land, we will deal kindly and truly with thee. Behold, when we come into the land, thou shalt bind this line of scarlet thread in the window; and thou shalt gather unto thee into the house thy father and thy mother and thy brethren, and all thy father's household. And it shall be that whosoever shall go out of the doors of thy house into the street, his blood shall be upon his head, and we will be guiltless; and whosoever shall be with thee in the house, his blood shall be on our

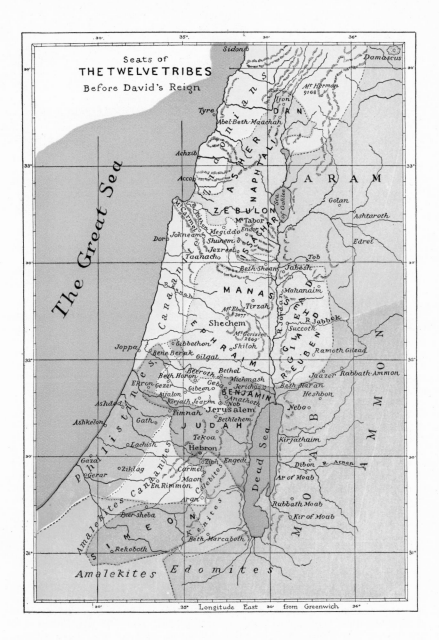

Seats of
THE TWELVE TRIBES
Before David's Reign

The Great Sea

Sidon
Damascus
Tyre
Ijon
DAN
Mt Hermon
9166
Abel-Beth-Maachah
Achzib
ASHER
NAPHTALI
Accho
ARAM
Golan
Sea of Galilee
ZEBULON
Ashtaroth
Mt Carmel
Mt Tabor
ISSACHAR
Edrei
Jokneam
Megiddo
Ender
Dor
Shunem
Jezreel
Taanach
Tob
Beth-Shean
Jabesh
MANASSEH
Mahanaim
Kanah
GILEAD
Mt Ebal
Tirzah
3077
Shechem
R. Jabbok
Succoth
Mt Gerizim
2869
Shiloh
Ramoth Gilead
Joppa
Gibbethon
EPHRAIM
Bene Berak
Gilgal
Beeroth
Bethel
Jaazer
Rabbath-Ammon
Beth Haron
Michmash
Ekron
Gezer
Geba
Jericho
Beth-Haran
AMMON
Gibeon
REUBEN
Heshbon
Aijalon
BENJAMIN
Ashdod
Kirjath Jearim
Anathoth
Nob
Nebo
Timnah
Jerusalem
Ashkelon
Gath
Bethlehem
JUDAH
Kirjathaim
Lachish
Tekoa
Hebron
Gaza
Ziph
Engedi
Dibon
R. Arnon
Gerar
Ziklag
Carmel
Ar of Moab
MOAB
Maon
En Rimmon
Beer-sheba
Rabbath Moab
SIMEON
Kir of Moab
Beth Marcaboth
Rehoboth
Amalekites
Edomites

Longitude East from Greenwich

head if any hand be on him. And she said: according unto your words, so be it. And she sent them away; and they departed, and she bound the scarlet line in the window. Then the men returned and said to Joshua: Truly Yahweh hath delivered into our hands all the land; and, moreover, all the inhabitants of the land do melt away before us.

Then Joshua rose up early in the morning, and he and all the people of Israel removed from Shittim and came to the Jordan, and lodged there before they passed over. And Joshua spake unto the priests, saying: Take up the ark of the covenant and pass on before the people. And they took up the ark of the covenant and went before the people. And Yahweh said unto Joshua: Thou shalt command the priests that bear the ark of the covenant, saying: When ye come to the brink of the waters of the Jordan, ye shall stand still in the Jordan. And Joshua said unto the Children of Israel: Come hither and hear the words of Yahweh your God. And Joshua said: Hereby ye shall know that the living God is among you. Behold, the ark of the covenant of Yahweh passeth on before you, over the Jordan. And it shall come to pass, when the soles of the feet of the priests that bear the ark of Yahweh shall rest in the waters of the Jordan, that the waters of the Jordan shall be cut off, even the waters that come down from above, and they shall stand in one heap. And it came to pass, when the people removed from their tents to pass over the Jordan, the priests that bore the ark of the covenant being before the people, and when they that bore the ark were come unto the Jordan, and the feet of the priests that bore the ark were dipped in the brink of the water,—for the Jordan overfloweth all its banks all the time of harvest—that the waters which came down from above stood, and rose up in one heap, a great way off from Adam, the city that is beside Zarethan; and those that went down toward the sea of the Arabah, even the Salt Sea, were wholly cut off; and the people passed over right opposite Jericho. And the priests that bore the ark of the covenant of Yahweh stood firm on dry ground in the midst of the Jordan, while all Israel passed over, until all the nation had passed clean over the Jordan.

And it came to pass, when all the people were passed over Jordan, that Yahweh spake unto Joshua, saying: Take you twelve men out of the people, out of every tribe a man, and command them, saying: Take you hence out of the midst of the Jordan, out of the place where the priests' feet stood, twelve stones made ready, and carry them over with you and lay them down in the lodging-place where ye shall lodge this night.

And the Children of Israel did as Joshua commanded, and took up twelve stones out of the midst of the Jordan, as Yahweh spake unto Joshua, according unto the number of the tribes of the Children of Israel; and they carried them over with them unto the place where they lodged, and they laid them down there. And those twelve stones which they took out of the Jordan did Joshua set up in Gilgal.

At that time, Yahweh said unto Joshua: Make thee knives of flint, and circumcise the Children of Israel. And Joshua made him knives of flint, and circumcised the Children of Israel at Gibeah-ha-Araloth (*the Hill of the Foreskins*). And it came to pass, when all the nation was circumcised, every one of them, that they abode in their places in the camp until they were whole. And Yahweh said unto Joshua: This day have I rolled away the reproach of Egypt from off you. Wherefore the name of that place was called *Gilgal* (rolling), to this day.

And it came to pass, when Joshua was by Jericho, that he lifted up his eyes and looked, and behold, there stood a man over against him with his sword drawn in his hand; and Joshua went unto him and said unto him: Art thou for us, or for our adversaries? And he said: Nay, but as leader of the host of Yahweh am I now come. And Joshua fell on his face to the earth, and bowed down, and said unto him: What saith my lord unto his servant? And the leader of Yahweh's host said unto Joshua: Put off thy shoes from off thy feet, for the place whereon thou standest is holy. And Joshua did so. And Yahweh said unto Joshua: See, I have given into thy hand Jericho and the king thereof, even the mighty men of valor. And ye shall compass the city, all the men of war, going around the city once. This shalt thou do six days. And the seventh day the people shall go up, every man straight before him. And he said unto the people: Pass on and compass the city, and let the armed men pass on before the ark of Yahweh. And Joshua commanded the people, saying: Ye shall not shout, nor let your voice be heard, neither shall any word proceed out of your mouth, until the day I bid you shout; then shall ye shout. So he caused the ark of Yahweh to compass the city going about it once; and they came into the camp, and lodged in the camp. And Joshua rose up early in the morning, and the priests took up the ark of Yahweh. And the second day they compassed the city once, and returned into the camp. Thus they did six days.

And it came to pass on the seventh day, that they rose early at the dawning of the day and compassed the city after the same manner seven times. Only on that day did they compass the city seven times. And it came to pass at the seventh time that Joshua said unto the people: Shout! for Yahweh hath given you the city! And the city shall be devoted, even it and all that is therein, to Yahweh; only Rahab the harlot shall live, she and all that are with her in the house, because she hid the messengers that we sent. So the people shouted with a great shout and went up into the city, every man straight before him, and they took the city. And they utterly destroyed all that was in the city, both men and women, both young and old, and ox and sheep and ass, with the edge of the sword. But Rahab the harlot, and her father's household, and all that she had, did Joshua save alive; and she dwelt in the midst of Israel unto this day, because she hid the messengers whom Joshua sent to spy out Jericho.

And Joshua charged the people with an oath at that time, saying:

Cursed before Yahweh be the man   that riseth to build up this city.
With the loss of his first-born son   shall he lay foundation thereof;
And with the loss of his youngest son   shall he set up its gates.

So Yahweh was with Joshua, and his fame was in all the land.

And Joshua sent men from Jericho to Ai, which is beside Beth-Aven on the east of Bethel, and spake unto them, saying: Go up and spy out the land. And the men went up and spied out Ai. And they returned to Joshua, and said unto him: Let not all the people go up; but let two or three thousand men go up and smite Ai; make not all the people go up, for they are but few. So there went up thither of the people about three thousand men; and they fled before the men of Ai. And the men of Ai smote of them about thirty-six men; and they chased them from before the gate even unto Shebarim, and smote them at the descent. And Joshua rent his clothes and fell to the earth upon his face before the ark of Yahweh until the evening, he and the elders of Israel; and they put dust upon their heads. And Joshua said: Alas,

O God Yahweh! wherefore hast Thou brought this people at all over
the Jordan? Would that we had been content, and dwelled beyond the
Jordan! O Yahweh! what shall I say, after that Israel hath turned
their backs before their enemies? For when the Canaanites hear of it,
they will compass us round and cut off our name from the earth; and
what wilt Thou do for Thy great name?[1]

But Yahweh said unto Joshua: Get thee up! wherefore now art
thou fallen upon thy face? Israel hath sinned; yea, they have even taken
of the devoted thing, and have stolen and dissembled also, and they
have even put it among their own stuff. Therefore the Children of
Israel cannot stand before their enemies; they turn their backs upon
their enemies because they are accursed. I will not be with you any
more, except ye destroy the accursed from among you. Up! Sanctify
the people, and say: Sanctify yourselves against to-morrow; for thus
saith Yahweh, the God of Israel: There is a curse in the midst of you,
O Israel; thou canst not stand before thine enemies, until ye take away
the accursed thing from among you. In the morning, therefore, ye
shall draw near by your tribes; and the tribe which Yahweh taketh
shall come near by families; and the family which Yahweh shall take
shall come near by households; and the household which Yahweh shall
take shall come near man by man. And it shall be, that he that is taken
with the devoted thing shall be burnt with fire, he and all that he hath.

So Joshua rose up early in the morning, and brought Israel near
by their tribes, and the tribe of Judah was taken. And he brought near
the families of Judah, and He took the family of the Zerahites; and he
brought near the family of the Zerahites, man by man, and Zabdi was
taken; and he brought near his household, man by man, and Achan
was taken. And Joshua said unto Achan: My son, give, I pray thee,
glory to Yahweh, the God of Israel, and make confession unto Him; and
tell me now what thou hast done; hide nothing from me. And Achan
answered Joshua and said: Of a truth, I have sinned against Yahweh,
the God of Israel; thus and thus have I done. When I saw among the
spoil a goodly Shinar mantle, and two hundred shekels of silver, and
a wedge of gold of fifty shekels weight, then I coveted them and took
them; and behold they are hid in the earth in the midst of my tent,
and the silver under it. So Joshua sent messengers, and they ran into
the tent; and behold, it was hid in the tent, and the silver under it.
And they took them forth from the midst of the tent and brought them
to Joshua, and unto all the Children of Israel; and they laid them
down before Yahweh. And Joshua took Achan the son of Zerah and all
that he had, and they brought them up unto the valley of Achor. And
Joshua said: Why hast thou troubled us? Yahweh shall trouble thee
this day; and they burned them with fire. And they raised over him
a great heap of stones; and Yahweh turned away from the fierceness of
His anger. Wherefore the name of that place was called The Valley
of Achor (*troubling*) unto this day.

And Yahweh said unto Joshua: Fear not, neither be thou dismayed;
take all the men of war with thee, and arise, go up to Ai. So Joshua
arose and all the men of war, to go up to Ai; and Joshua chose out thirty
thousand men, the mighty men of valor, and sent them forth by night;
and he commanded them, saying: Behold, ye shall lie in ambush against
the city, behind the city; be ye not very far from the city, but be ye
all ready. And I, and all the people that are with me, will approach

[1] With the exception of a repetition or two and some slight additions by a late writer,
the account of the first assault upon Ai seems to be wholly from the Judaic author.

unto the city; and it shall come to pass, when they come out against us, we will flee before them as at the first. And they will come out after us until we have drawn them away from the city; for they will say: They flee before us as at the first. So we will flee before them. And ye shall rise up from the ambush, and take possession of the city; for Yahweh, your God will deliver it into your hand. And it shall be, when ye have seized upon the city, that ye shall set the city on fire; see, I have commanded you. And Joshua sent them forth, and they went to the place of ambush, between Bethel and Ai, on the west side of Ai; but Joshua lodged that night among the people.

And Joshua rose up early in the morning, and numbered the people, and went up, he and the elders of Israel, before the people to Ai. And it came to pass, when the king of Ai saw it, that the men of the city hastened and went out against Israel to battle, he and all his people to a certain place fronting the Arabah; but he knew not that there was an ambush against him behind the city. And Joshua and his people fled by the way of the wilderness; and they pursued after Joshua, and were drawn away from the city. And they left the city open and pursued after Israel.

Then the men in ambush rose quickly out of their place, and they hastened and set the city on fire. And when the men of Ai looked behind them, behold, the smoke of the city ascended up to heaven; and they had no power to flee this way or that way, for the people that were fleeing to the wilderness turned back upon the pursuers, and they slew the men of Ai. And the others came forth out of the city against them; so they were in the midst of Israel, some on this side, some on that side; and they smote them, so that they let none of them remain or escape. And the king of Ai they took alive, and brought him to Joshua. And Joshua hanged the king of Ai on a tree until eventide; and at the going down of the sun, Joshua commanded, and they took his body down from the tree and cast it at the entrance of the gate of the city, and raised thereon a great heap of stones [which is] there to this day.

Now when the inhabitants of Gibeon heard what Joshua had done unto Jericho and Ai, they did work wilily, and went and took old sacks upon their asses and wineskins worn and rent and patched, and worn shoes and clouted upon their feet and worn garments upon their backs; and all the bread of their provisions was dry and become crumbs. And they went to the men of Israel and said: We are come from a far country; now therefore, make ye a covenant with us. And the men of Israel said: Peradventure ye dwell among us; and how shall we make a covenant with you? And they said: This our bread we took hot for our provision out of our houses on the day we came forth to go unto you; behold it is dry and is become crumbs; and these wineskins, which we filled, were new; and behold, they are rent. And these our garments and our shoes are worn by reason of the very long journey. Then the men took of their provision and asked not counsel at the mouth of Yahweh, but made a covenant with them, to let them live.

And it came to pass at the end of three days, after they had made a covenant with them, that they heard they were their neighbors, and that they dwelt among them. And Joshua called for them and he spake unto them, saying: Wherefore have ye beguiled us, saying, We are very far from you, when ye dwell among us? Now, therefore, ye are cursed; and there shall never fail to be of you bondmen.

SECTION II.—Joshua's Conquests in the North. He assigns the lots of Judah and of the children of Joseph. Urges the other tribes to explore and divide the rest of the land among themselves, and bring them to him at Shiloh for confirmation. Receives for himself the city of Timnath-Serah, and dwells there. (Joshua, x, 1a, c, 2-7, 9-10, 12a, c-13a, 16-24, 26-27; xi, 1, 2a, 3-7, 8a, c, 9; xiii, 1, 7; xiv, 3-13; xv, 1-2, 5, 12a; xvi, 1-3, 9-10; xvii, 1b-2a, 5, 9-10; xviii, 1, 2-6, 8-10; xix, 9, 47, 49-50.)

Materials: No more certain than before; but it is evident that the body of traditions was large from which later writers culled important items. The "Book of Jashar" is again quoted from.

Now it came to pass when Adoni-Zedek, king of Jersualem, heard how Joshua had taken Ai and utterly destroyed it, and how the inhabitants of Gibeon had made peace with Israel and were among them, that he feared greatly; because Gibeon was a great city, as one of the royal cities, and because it was greater than Ai, and all the men thereof were mighty. Wherefore Adoni-Zedek, king of Jerusalem, sent unto Hoham, king of Hebron, and unto Piram, king of Jarmuth, and unto Japhia, king of Lachish, and unto Debir, king of Eglon, saying: Come up unto me and help me, and let us smite Gibeon, for it hath made peace with Joshua and with the Children of Israel. Therefore these five kings gathered themselves together and went up, they and all their hosts, and encamped against Gibeon and made war against it. And the men of Gibeon sent unto Joshua to the camp at Gilgal, saying: Slack not thy hands from thy servants; come up to us quickly and help us and save us; for all the kings of the Amorites that dwell in the hill-country are gathered together against us. So Joshua went up from Gilgal, he and all the people of war with him, all the mighty men of valor. And Joshua came upon them suddenly, for he went up from Gilgal by night. And Yahweh discomfited them before Israel, and slew them with a great slaughter at Gibeon; and they chased them by the way of the ascent of Beth-horon, and smote them to Azekah and unto Makkedah.

Then spake Joshua to Yahweh; and he said in the presence of Israel:

> Sun, stand thou still upon Gibeon,
> And thou, Moon, in the valley of Aijalon!
> Then the sun stood still,   and the moon stayed
> Until the nation had taken vengeance upon its foes.

(Is not this written in the Book of Jashar?) So the sun stayed in the midst of heaven, and hasted not to go down for a whole day. And there was no day like that before it or after it, that Yahweh hearkened to the voice of a man; for Yahweh fought for Israel.

Now it was told Joshua: The five kings are found hidden in the cave at Makkedah. And Joshua said: Roll great stones to the mouth of the cave, and set men by it to keep them; but stay not ye; pursue after your enemies, and smite the hindmost of them. Suffer them not to enter into their cities, for Yahweh hath delivered them into your hand. And it came to pass, when Joshua and the Children of Israel had made an end of slaying them with a very great slaughter till they were consumed, and the remnant which remained of them had entered the fortified cities, that all the people returned to the camp to Joshua at Makkedah in peace,—none whetted his tongue against any of the Children of Israel. Then said Joshua: Open the mouth of the cave, and bring forth those five kings unto me out of the cave, the king of Jerusalem, the king of Hebron, the king of Jarmuth, the king of Lachish, the king of Eglon. And it came to pass, when they brought forth these kings unto Joshua, that Joshua called for all the men of Israel, and said unto the chiefs of the men of war that went with him: Come near, put your feet upon the necks of these kings. And they came near and put their feet upon the necks of them. And afterward, Joshua smote them and put them to death, and hanged them on five trees; and they were hanging upon the trees until the evening. And it came to pass, at the time of the going down of the sun, that Joshua commanded, and they took them down off the trees, and cast them into the cave wherein they had hidden themselves, and laid great stones on the mouth of the cave. And they are there to this day.

And it came to pass when Jabin, king of Hazor heard thereof, that he sent to Jobab king of Madon, and to the king of Shimron, and to the king of Achashaph, and to the kings that were in the north in the hill-country, to the Canaanite on the east and on the west and the Hivite under Hermon; and they went out, they and all their hosts with them, much people, even as the sands upon the seashore in multitude, with horses and chariots very many. And all these kings met together; and they came and pitched together at the waters of Merom to fight with Israel. And Yahweh said unto Joshua: Be not afraid of them; tomorrow thou shalt hough their horses, and burn their chariots with fire. So Joshua came and all the people of war with him, and fell upon them suddenly by the waters of Merom; and they smote them until they left them none remaining. And Joshua did unto them as Yahweh bade him; he houghed their horses and burned their chariots with fire.

Now Joshua was old, well-stricken in years; and Yahweh said unto him: Thou art old and well-stricken in years, and there remaineth very much land to be possessed. Now therefore, divide this land for an inheritance unto the nine tribes and the half-tribe of Manasseh.[1]

[For Moses had given the inheritance of the two tribes Reuben and Gad and the half-tribe of Manasseh beyond the Jordan; but unto the Levites he gave no inheritance. For the children of Joseph were two tribes, Manasseh and Eprhaim. And they gave no portion unto the Levites in the land, save cities to dwell in, with the open land about them for their cattle and their sustenance.[2]]

Then the children of Judah drew nigh unto Joshua in Gilgal; and Caleb the Kenite said unto him: Thou knowest the thing that Yahweh spake unto Moses, the Man of God, concerning thee and concerning me in Kadesh-Barnea. Forty years old was I when Moses the servant of Yahweh sent me up from Kadesh-Barnea to spy out the land; and I brought him back word as it was in my heart. Nevertheless, my brethren that went up with me made the heart of the people melt; but I wholly followed Yahweh my God. And Moses sware on that day, saying: Surely the land whereon thy foot hath trodden shall be an inheritance to thee and to thy children forever, because thou hast wholly followed Yahweh thy God. And now, behold, Yahweh hath kept me alive these forty and five years while Israel walked in the wilderness; and now, lo, I am this day fourscore and five years old. And yet I am as strong this day as I was in the day that Moses sent me. As my strength was then, even so is my strength now for war, and to go out and to come in. Now therefore, give me this mountain whereof Yahweh spake in that day; for thou didst hear in that day how the Anakim were there, and cities

---

[1] Chapters xiii-xxiii are mainly from D2 and P. In the few passages from JE, but a small portion can be distinguished as from E, and this so insignificant that it is not worth while to separate them.

[2] Ch. xiv, 3-5, are by P, but are retained here for the sake of clearness concerning the allotments for all the tribes. Compare also Numb. xxxiv, 13-15, and xxxv, 2, 6-7.

great and fortified; it may be that Yahweh will be with me, and I shall
drive them out, as Yahweh spake.

And Joshua blessed him; and he gave Hebron unto Caleb, the son of
Jephunneh the Kenite, for an inheritance, for a portion among the
children of Judah.

Now the lot for the tribe of Judah according to its families was
unto the borders of Edom, even to the wilderness of Zin southward, at
the uttermost part of the south. And their southern border was from
the uttermost part of the Salt Sea, and it went out at the Brook of Egypt,
and its goings out were at the sea. And the east border was the Salt
Sea even unto the end of the Jordan. And the border of the north
side was from the bay of the sea at the end of the Jordan; and as for
the west border, the Great Sea was the border thereof.

And the lot for the children of Joseph went out from the Jordan
at Jericho, at the waters of Jericho on the east going up through the
hill-country to the wilderness even to Bethel. And it went out from
Bethel-Luz, and passed unto the border of the Archites to Ataroth. And
it went down westward to the border of the Japhletites unto the border
of Beth-horon the nether, even unto Gezer; and the goings out thereof
were at the Great Sea. This is the inheritance of the tribe of the
children of Ephraim according to their families; together with the cities
separated for the children of Ephraim in the midst of the inheritance
of the children of Manasseh, all the cities with their villages. And they
drove not out the Canaanites that dwelt in Gezer; but the Canaanites
dwell in the midst of Ephraim unto this day, and became servants to
do task-work.

As for Machir the firstborn of Manasseh, the father of Gilead, because
he was a man of war therefore he had Gilead and Bashan. And the lot
was for the rest of the children of Manasseh according to their families.
And there fell ten parts to Manasseh, besides the land of Gilead and
Bashan which are beyond the Jordan. But Tappuah, on the border of
Manasseh, belonged to the children of Ephraim. And the border went
down unto the brook of Kanah; but the border of Manasseh was on the
north side of the brook; southward it was Ephraim's, and northward
it was Manasseh's; and the sea was his border; and they reached to
Asher on the north, and to Issachar on the east.

And there remained among the children of Israel seven tribes which
had not yet received their inheritance. And Joshua said unto the Children of Israel: How long are ye slack to go in and possess the land
which Yahweh, the God of your fathers, hath given you? Appoint for
you three men for each tribe, and I will send them; and they shall arise
and walk through the land and describe (write) it according to their
inheritance; and they shall come unto me. And they shall divide it
into seven portions; Judah shall abide within his border on the south,
and the house of Joseph shall abide in their border on the north. And
ye shall write of the land in seven portions, and bring the writing
hither to me; and I will cast lots for you here before Yahweh. And
the men arose and went; and Joshua charged them that went to write
of the land: Go and walk through the land and describe it, and come
back to me and I will cast lots for you here before Yahweh in Shiloh.[1]
And the men went and passed through the land and described it in
seven divisions in a book; and they came to Joshua unto the camp at
Shiloh. And Joshua cast lots for them in Shiloh before Yahweh; and

---

[1] Verse 1, as prefixed by P, indicates that the ark had been removed to Shiloh, its
first permanent resting-place, where it remained till the death of Eli. Samuel the Seer
spent his childhood and youth there.

there Joshua divided the land unto the Children of Israel according to their divisions. Out of the allotment of the children of Judah was the inheritance of Simeon; for the portion of the children of Judah was too much for them, therefore the children of Simeon had inheritance in the midst of their inheritance. And the territory of the children of Dan was too strait for them; so the children of Dan went up and fought against Leshem and took it; and they smote it with the edge of the sword and possessed it and dwelt therein; and they called Leshem, Dan, after the name of Dan their father.

When they had made an end of distributing the land for inheritance by the borders thereof, the Children of Israel gave an Inheritance to Joshua the son of Nun in the midst of them; according to the commandment of Yahweh, they gave him the city which he asked, even Timnath-serah in the hill-country of Ephraim; and he built the city and dwelt therein.

Section III.—Judah and Simeon win their allotments. Othniel, son-in-law of Caleb, governs the southeast. Repels the Aramæans. The other tribes make terms with the earlier inhabitants of Canaan. Having disobeyed the laws of Yahweh, they are subjugated by their neighbors. Ehud delivers them from the Moabites. Deborah and Barak overthrow the Canaanites. These force the Danites out of their western allotment, and they move to the far north. Gideon frees Central Canaan from the annual raids of the Midianites (Bedouin). (Judges, i, 1-3, 5-7, 11a, 12-17, 19-36; ii, 1a, 5b, 25a; iii, 5-11, 16-27a, 28-30; iv, 1a, 2a, 3b, 4, 6a, 7b, 23; v, 1-31; xvii, 1, 5-13; xviii, 1-30a; vi, 1, 6b, 11-19, 21a, 22-24, 34; vii, 1, 9-17a, 20-21; viii, 4-9, 10a, 11-21, 24-28.)

Materials: Current songs and stories; the "Book of Jashar"; probably, some tribal records, for a writer of the seventh century (D_2) adds many undisputed details. His additions, when necessary to the sequence of events, are here put in parentheses.

Now it came to pass (after the death of Joshua) that the children of Judah asked of Yahweh: Who shall go up first against the Canaanites to fight against them? And Yahweh answered them: Judah shall go up; I will give the land into his hand. And the tribe of Judah said to their brethren the Simeonites: Come up with us into our lot that we may fight against the Canaanites; then we will go up with you into your lot. So the Simeonites went with them. And they came upon Adoni-bezek in Bezek and they fought against him, and they defeated the Canaanites and the Perizzites. But Adoni-Bezek fled, and they pursued after him and took him and cut off his thumbs and great toes. And Adoni-Bezek said: Threescore and ten kings, having their thumbs and great toes cut off, used to pick up food under my table. As I have done, so God hath requited me. Then they went up against the inhabitants of Debir. (Now the older name of Debir was Kirjah-sepher.) And Caleb said: He that attacketh Debir and taketh it, to him will I give Achsah my daughter to wife. And Othniel, the son of Kenaz the younger brother of Caleb, took it; and he gave him Achsah his daughter to wife. And it came to pass when she came to him, that she moved him to ask her father for a piece of land. So she alighted from her ass; and Caleb said unto her: What wouldest thou? and she said: Give me a blessing; thou hast put me off in the Negeb, therefore give me also springs of water. And Caleb gave her the Upper Springs and the Lower Springs.

Now the children of the Kenite, Moses's father-in-law, went up with the children of Judah out of the City of Palm-trees to the wilderness which is in the south of Arad, and dwelt with the Amalekites. Then the tribe of Judah went with their brethren the Simeonites, and they smote the Canaanites which dwelt in Zephath and utterly destroyed it. Hence the city was called Hormah. And Yahweh was with Judah; and they conquered the hill-country, but could not drive out the inhabitants of the plain because they had chariots of iron. And they gave Hebron unto Caleb, as Moses had bidden, and Caleb drove therefrom the three giants, Sheshai, Ahiman and Talmai. But the Judahites did not dispossess the Jebusites which inhabited Jerusalem; for the Jebusites dwelt with the Judahites in Jerusalem unto this day.

And the tribes of Joseph, they also went up against Bethel; and Yahweh was with them. And the house of Joseph sent to spy out Bethel; and the scouts saw a man coming out of the city, and they said to him: show us, we pray thee, how to enter the city, and we will deal kindly with thee. And he showed them the entrance to the city, and they smote the city with the edge of the sword; but they let the man go and all his family; and they went into the land of the Hittites and built a city and called its name Luz, which is the name thereof unto this day.

Manasseh did not cónquer Beth-shean with the villages belonging thereto, nor Taanach with its villages, nor the inhabitants of Dor nor of Ibleam with their villages, nor of Megiddo with its villages; for the Canaanites maintained themselves resolutely in that region. But it came to pass that when Israel became strong, they put the Canaanites to taskwork, but did by no means cast them out. Nor did Ephraim dispossess the Canaanites that dwelt in Gezer, but the Canaanites remained in Gezer in the midst of them.

Zebulon drove not out the inhabitants of Kitron nor of Nahaloi; but the Canaanites dwelt in the midst of them and became tributary. Asher did not dispossess the inhabitants of Accho nor of Zidon, nor of Helbah nor of Aphik nor of Rehob; but the Asherites settled among the Canaanites, for they did not dispossess them. Naphtali drove not out the inhabitants of Beth-shemesh nor of Beth-anath; he dwelt among the Canaanite inhabitants of the land; nevertheless they became tributary to him. The Amorites forced the Danites into the hill-country; they would not suffer them to come down to the valley, but maintained themselves resolutely in Har-heres, in Aijalon and in Shaalbim; yet the hand of the house of Joseph prevailed, so that they became tributary. And the border of the Amorites was the pass of Akrabbim, from Sela and upward. And the Messenger of Yahweh came up from Gilgal to Bethel, and they offered sacrifice there to Yahweh.

So Yahweh left these peoples, not dispossessing them at once. And the Israelites dwelt among the Canaanites, the Hittites, the Amorites, the Perizzites, the Hivites and the Jebusites; and they took their daughters to be their wives and gave their own daughters to their sons; and they served their gods.

(And the Children of Israel did that which was evil in the sight of Yahweh, and forgat Yahweh their God, and worshipped the Baalim and the Asheroth. Therefore the anger of Yahweh was kindled against Israel, and He gave them over into the hand of Cushan-Rishathaim, king of Aram-Naharaim; and the Israelites served him eight years. Then the Israelites cried to Yahweh for help, and Yahweh raised up a saviour for Israel, even Othniel son of Kenaz, Caleb's younger brother. And his hand prevailed over Cushan-Rishathaim; and the land had rest forty years. And after Othniel died, the Israelites again did evil in the sight of Yahweh; and Eglon, king of Moab, gathered unto him the children of Ammon and of Amalek, and he went and smote Israel, and took possession of the City of Palm-trees. And the Israelites served Eglon eighteen years. Then the Israelites cried unto Yahweh for help; and He raised up for them another saviour, Ehud, the son of Gera, a Benjamite, a man left-handed, by whom the Israelites sent their tribute to the king of Moab.)

And Ehud made him a two-edged dagger, the length of a cubit; and he girded it under his raiment on his right thigh. And he offered the tribute unto Eglon, king of Moab. Now Eglon was a very fat man. And when Ehud had made an end of offering the tribute, he sent away the people that had borne it. But he himself turned back at the quarries that were at Gilgal, and said: I have a secret errand unto thee, O King. Then the king said: Silence! And all that stood by him went forth from him. And Ehud came up to him, and he was sitting by himself in his cool upper chamber. And Ehud said unto him: I have a divine message unto thee. And he arose from his seat. And Ehud put forth his left hand, and took the dagger from his right thigh and thrust it into his belly. And the haft also went in after the blade, and the fat closed upon the blade, for he drew not the sword out of his belly, and it came out behind. Then Ehud went forth into the porch and closed the doors of the upper chamber upon him, and locked them. Now when he was gone out the servants came; and they saw that the doors of the upper chamber were locked, and they said: Surely he is covering his feet in the cabinet of the cool chamber. And they tarried until they were ashamed, for, behold, he opened not the doors of the upper chamber; therefore they took the key and opened them; and behold, their lord was fallen down dead on the ground. But Ehud made his escape while they were waiting, and having passed the quarries escaped unto Seirah. And it came to pass when he was come, that he blew a horn in the hill-country of Ephraim, and said: Follow me, for Yahweh hath delivered your enemies, the Moabites, into your hand. And they went down after him and took the fords of the Jordan against the Moabites, and suffered not a man to pass over. (Thus Moab was subdued that day and brought under the hand of Israel. And the land had rest fourscore years.)

The mountains quaked at the presence of Yahweh,

(And the Israelites again did evil in the sight of Yahweh, and He sold them into the hand of Jabin king of Canaan, who mightily oppressed the Children of Israel twenty years. Now a prophetess, Deborah the wife of Lapidoth, was judging Israel at that time; and she summoned Barak and the Israelites to battle against Jabin; and Yahweh enabled the Israelites to subdue Jabin, king of Canaan.)

Then sang Deborah with Barak the son of Abinoam on that day:

For the taking of the lead by the chieftains of Israel;
For the volunteering of the people, bless ye Yahweh!

Hear, O ye kings! Give ear, O ye princes!
I to Yahweh will address my song;
I will sing praise to Yahweh, the God of Israel.

Yahweh, when Thou didst go forth out of Seir,
When Thou didst march out of the fields of Edom,
The earth trembled, the heavens dropped, yea the clouds dropped water.
The mountains quaked at the presence of Yahweh,
Even yon Sinai at the presence of Yahweh, the God of Israel.

In the days of Shamgar ben-Anath, in the days of Jael, highways ceased,
    And solitary travelers took roundabout ways.
    Rulers ceased in Israel, yea they ceased
Till thou didst arise, O Deborah, till thou didst arise, a mother in Israel.

    They chose them new gods; then was war in the gates.
    Was any spear seen, or even a shield
        Among forty thousand in Israel?
    My heart is with the rulers of Israel!
Ye volnnteers among the people, bless ye Yahweh!
Ye that ride on white asses, ye that sit on rich cloths,
And ye that walk by the way, tell of it!
Louder than the voice of them that divide booty beside the watering-
        troughs,
There shall they rehearse the righteous acts of Yahweh,
        Even the righteous acts of His rulers in Israel
    When the people of Yahweh marched down to the gates.

        Awake, awake, Deborah!
    Awake, awake, utter a song!
    Arise, Barak, and lead thy captives captive,
        Thou son of Abinoam!
Then made He a remnant to have dominion over a people.
Yahweh made me have dominion over the mighty.

    Out of Ephraim came those whose root is in Amalek;
        After thee, Benjamin, among thy peoples;
Out of Machir came down governors, out of Zebulon, those who wield
    the marshal's staff.
        And the chiefs of Issachar were with Deborah;
        As was Issachar, so was Barak.
Into the valley they rushed down on foot.

    Great were the dissensions in the divisions of Reuben.
Why sattest thou among the sheepfolds listening to the pipings of flocks?
    At the divisions of Reuben were great searchings of heart!
    Gilead abode beyond the Jordan;
    And Dan, why did he sojourn by the ships?
    Asher tarrieth on the shore of the Sea,
    Sitting still by his places of landing.
But Zebulon and Naphtali were tribes that jeoparded their lives to the
    death,
    Upon the heights of the battlefield.

    The kings came, they fought;
    Then fought the kings of Canaan,
    In Taanach by the waters of Megiddo;
    They took no gain of money!
        Heaven itself fought,
    The stars of heaven fought against Sisera.
    The brook Kishon swept them away,
    That ancient stream, the stream of Kishon.
O my soul! Tread them down with strength!
    Then stamped the hoofs of his horses
    In the furious galloping of his warriors.

    Curse ye Meroz, said the messenger of Yahweh,
    Curse ye bitterly the inhabitants thereof,
    Because they came not to the help of Yahweh
    To the help of Yahweh against the mighty.

Blessed above women shall Jael be
The wife of Heber the Kenite!
Above all women in tents shall she be blessed.
Water he asked, she gave him milk;
In a noble bowl she brought him curds.
Her hand she put to the tent-pin, her right hand to the workman's mallet.
She smiteth Sisera, she crusheth his head; yea, she shatters, pierces his temples.
At her feet he sank, he fell, he lay;
Where he sank, where he fell, there he lay down, dead.

Through the window peered and called aloud
The mother of Sisera, through the lattice:
Why is his chariot so long in coming? Why tarry the wheels of his chariot?
The wisest of her princesses reply,
Yea, she returneth answer to herself:
They must be finding, dividing the spoil, a damsel or two to every man;
To Sisera a spoil of dyed garments, a spoil of embroidered garments,
A piece or two of embroidery for the neck of every spoiler!

So perish all thine enemies, O Yahweh!
But be Thy friends as the sun, when he goeth forth in his might.

Now there was a man of the hill-country of Ephraim, whose name was Micah; and the man Micah had a little temple; and he made an ephod and teraphim and consecrated one of his sons who became his priest. And there was a young man of Bethlehem in Judah who was a Levite, and sojourned there. And this man departed out of the city of Bethlehem to sojourn wherever he might find a place; and he came to the hill-country of Ephraim, and as he journeyed he came to the house of Micah. And Micah said unto him: Dwell with me, and be unto me a father and a priest, and I will give thee ten pieces of silver by the year and a suit of apparel and thy victuals. So the Levite went in. And the Levite was content to dwell with the man; and the young man was unto him as one of his sons. And Micah consecrated the Levite; and the young man became his priest, and was in the house of Micah. Then said Micah: Now know I that Yahweh will do me good, seeing I have a Levite as my priest.

Now in those days, the Danites were seeking a possession to dwell in; for unto that day there had nothing been allotted unto them among the tribes of Israel for their dwelling; and the children of Dan sent five men from the whole number of their families, men of valor from Zorah and from Eshtaol, to explore the land and to examine it; and they said unto them: Go, search the land. And they came to the hill-country of Ephraim, unto the house of Micah, and lodged there. And they said to the Levite: What art thou here for? And he answered: The man hired me, and I have become his priest. And they said unto him: Ask counsel of God, we pray thee, that we may know whether our way on which we are going shall be prosperous. And the priest said unto them: Go in peace; your way wherein ye go is before Yahweh. Then the five men departed and came to Laish, and found the people dwelling in the city quiet and secure; for there was none in the land possessing authority that could put them to shame in any thing, and they were far from the Zidonians, and had no dealings with any others. Then they returned to Zorah and Eshtaol, and said: Arise, let us march against [Laish]; when ye go, ye shall find a people secure; and the land is large, a place wherein there is nothing lacking; it hath everything that is in the earth. Then there set forth from thence, from Zorah and from Eshtaol, six hundred men girt with weapons of war. And they went up and encamped in Kirjath-jearim in Judah; wherefore it is called Mahaneh-Dan to this day. And they passed thence to the hill-country of Ephraim, and came to the house of Micah. And the five men that had explored the land said unto their brethren: Do ye know that in these houses is an ephod and Teraphim? Now consider what ye will do. And the six hundred armed men came to Micah's house and took the ephod and the Teraphim; and when the priest said unto them: What do ye? they said unto him: Hold thy peace; lay thy hand upon thy mouth and go with us, and be to us a father and a priest. Is it better for thee to be a priest unto the household of one man, or to be priest unto a tribe and a family in Israel? And the priest's heart was glad; and he took the ephod and the Teraphim, and went in the midst of the people. So they turned and departed and put the little ones and the cattle and the goods before them.

When they were a good way from Micah's house, the men that were in the houses near Micah's house gathered together and overtook the children of Dan. And they shouted to the Danites; and they turned their faces, and said unto Micah: What aileth thee, that thou comest with such a company? And he said: Ye have taken the gods that I made and the priest and have gone away; and what have I more? How then say ye unto me: What aileth thee? And the Danites said unto him: Let not thy voice be heard among us, lest angry fellows fall upon you and thou lose thy life and the lives of thy household. And the Danites went their way; and Micah, seeing that they were too strong for him, turned and went back to his house. But they took that which Micah had made and the priest whom he had, and came to Laish, upon a people quiet and secure, and smote them with the edge of the sword, and they burnt the city with fire. And there was no one to save it, for it was far from Zidon and they had no dealings with any other.

And they rebuilt the city and dwelt therein. And they called it Dan; and the Danites set up for themselves the idol, and Jonathan, the son of Gershom, the son of Moses, and his sons, were priests to the tribe of Dan.

(And the Children of Israel again did that which was evil in the sight of Yahweh, and Yahweh delivered them into the hand of the Midianites seven years, until the Israelites cried for help unto Yahweh.) And the Messenger of Yahweh came and sat under the terebinth which was in Ophrah, which belonged to Joash the Abi-ezrite; and his son Gideon was beating out wheat in the wine-press to hide it from the Midianites. And the Messenger of Yahweh appeared unto him and said unto him: Yahweh is with thee, thou mighty man of valor! And Gideon answered him: O, my lord, if Yahweh be with us, why then is all this befalling us, and where are all His wondrous works of which our fathers told us, saying: Did not Yahweh bring us up from Egypt? But now, Yahweh hath cast us off and given us into the hands of Midian. Then Yahweh turned towards him, and said: Go in this thy might, and save Israel from the hand of Midian. But he answered: O, my lord, wherewith shall I save Israel? Behold, my family is the poorest in Manasseh, and I am the least in my father's house. And He answered: Surely, I will be with thee, and thou shalt smite the Midianites as one man. And he said unto Him: If now I have found favor in Thy sight, depart not hence, I pray Thee, until I come again and bring forth my offering and lay it before Thee. And He said: I will tarry until thou come back. And Gideon went in and made ready a kid, and unleavened cakes of an ephah of meal; the flesh he put in a basket, and he put the broth in a pot, and brought it to the man under the terebinth. And the Messenger of Yahweh reached out the staff that was in his hand, and touched the flesh and the unleavened cakes; and there went up fire out of the rock and consumed the flesh and the unleavened cakes. When Gideon perceived that it was the Messenger of Yahweh, he said: Alas, O God Yahweh! I have seen the Messenger of Yahweh, face to face. And Yahweh said unto him: Peace be unto thee; fear not! thou shalt not die. Then Gideon built an altar there to Yahweh, and called it Yahweh-shalom (*Yahweh is peace*); it is yet in Ophrah of the Abi-ezrites.

And the spirit of Yahweh possessed Gideon; and he sounded the alarm and the men of Abiezer were gathered together to follow him. And Jerubbael (that is, Gideon) and all the people that were with him rose up early and encamped beside En-harod; and the camp of Midian was north of Gibeath-moreh. And it came to pass the same night, that Yahweh said unto him: Arise, get thee down upon the camp, for I have delivered it into thy hand. But if thou fear to go down, go thou with Purah thy servant into the camp and hear what they shall say; afterwards shall thy hand be strengthened to descend upon the camp. Then went he down with Purah his servant to the outermost part of the armed men that were in the camp. Now the Midianites were lying in the plain like the sand upon the seashore for multitude. And as Gideon came near, a man was telling a dream unto his fellow, and saying: Behold, I dreamed a dream, and lo, a great cake of barley-bread tumbled into the camp of Midian; and it came to the tent and struck it that it fell, and turned it upside down so that the tent lay flat. And his companion said: this is nothing else than the men of Israel; into their hand hath Yahweh delivered all the host. And it was so, when Gideon heard the telling of the dream, and the interpretation thereof, that he worshiped; and he returned into the camp of Israel and said: Arise, for Yahweh hath delivered into your hand the host of Midian. And Gideon had three hundred men, and he divided them into three companies, and put into the hand of all of them empty pitchers and lamps in their pitchers. And he said: Look at me, and when I blow the horn do as I do. And he blew his horn and the three companies shattered their pitchers, grasping the torches, and shouted: For Yahweh and Gideon! And they stood where they were about the camp; and all the camp awoke and sent up a wild cry and fled to Zeredah, to the border of Abel-Meholah near Tabbath.

And Gideon came to the Jordan, he and the three hundred men with him, faint yet pursuing. And he said to the inhabitants of Succoth: Give loaves of bread, I pray you, unto the people that follow me; for they are faint. I am pursuing Zebah and Zalmunna, the kings of Midian. But the rulers of Succoth said: Are the hands of Zebah and Zalmunna now in thy power, that we should give thy soldiers bread? And Gideon said: When Yahweh hath delivered Zebah and Zalmunna into my power, then will I tear your flesh with the thorns of the wilderness and with briers. And he went up thence to Penuel, and spake in like manner; and the men of Penuel answered him as the men of Succoth had done. And he spake also unto the men of Penuel: When I come back in peace, I will break down this tower.

Now Zebah and Zalmunna were at Karkor, and their hosts with them, about fifteen thousand men; and Gideon went up by the way east of Nobah and Jogbehah, and attacked the host, for the host felt secure; and Zebah and Zalmunna fled. And he pursued after them; and he took the two kings of Midian, Zebah and Zalmunna, and discomfited all the host. And Gideon the son of Joash returned from the battle, from the ascent of Heres. And he caught a young man of the men of Succoth, and inquired of him; and he wrote down for him the princes of Succoth and the elders thereof, seventy and seven men. And he came unto the men of Succoth, and said: Behold, Zebah and Zalmunna, concerning whom ye did taunt me, saying: Are the hands of Zebah and Zalmunna now in thy power, that we should give bread unto thy men that are weary? And he took the elders of the city, and thorns of the wilderness and briers, and with them he taught the men of Succoth. And he brake down the tower of Penuel, and slew the men of the city. Then said he unto Zebah and Zalmunna: Who, then, were the men whom ye slew at Tabor? And they answered: As thou art, so were they; in stature like king's sons, every one. And he said: They were my brethren, the sons of my mother. As Yahweh liveth, if ye had saved them alive, I would not kill you. And he said unto Jether, his first-born: Up, and slay them. But the youth drew not his sword; for he feared, for he was yet a youth. Then said Zebah and Zalmunna: Rise thou, and fall upon us; for as the man is, so is his strength. And Gideon arose and slew Zebah and Zalmunna, and took the crescents that were on the necks of their camels. And Gideon said to his men: I will make a request of you, that ye would give me every man the earrings of his spoils. (For they had golden earrings, because they were Ishmaelites.) And they answered: We will give them willingly. And they spread a garment, and did cast therein every man the earrings of his spoil. And the weight of the golden rings was a thousand and seven hundred shekels of gold. And Gideon made thereof an ephod, and put it in his city, even in Ophrah. And all Israel went astray after it there; and it became a snare unto Gideon and to his family. Thus the Midianites were subdued by the Israelites, and litfed not their heads again. And the land had rest forty years in the days of Gideon.

Section IV.—The Last of the Warrior-Judges. The story of Samson: his birth; his provocation of the Philistines; his death. The outrage at Gibeah, and the punishment and reduction in power of Benjamin. The First Recorded Aggressions of the Phillistines; their capture of the Ark of the Covenant; their punishment by Yahweh; the Return of the Ark. (Judges, xiii-xviii; xix, 1-6a, 8b-10a, 11, 12, 14, 15b-16a, 17-23, 25-30; xx, 1a, c, 3-8, 14, 19, 29, 36b-37a, 38-41, 44a, 47; xxi, 1, 15, 16-19a, 21-25. 1 Samuel, iv, 2a, c, 3a, 4a, 5a, c, 6b, 7b, 9a, c, 10b; v, 1-11a; vi, 2-4, 6-14, 16, 19-21; vii, 1.)

Materials: As before, traditions and folk-songs; probably, also, priestly records from the temple at Shiloh.

Now there was a certain man of Zorah of the tribe of the Danites whose name was Manoah; and his wife was barren, and bare no child. And the messenger of Yahweh appeared unto the woman and said unto her: Behold now, thou art barren and hast borne no child; but thou shalt conceive and bear a son. Now, therefore, I pray thee, drink no wine nor strong drink, and eat not any unclean thing. For lo, thou shalt conceive and bear a son; and no razor must come upon his head; for the child shall be a Nazarite from his mother's womb, and he shall begin to save Israel out of the hands of the Philistines.

Then the woman came to her husband and told him, saying: A

man of God came to me, and his countenance was like the countenance of a messenger of God, very terrible; and I asked him not whence he came, neither told he me his name. But he said: Behold, thou shalt conceive and bear a son; and now, drink no wine nor strong drink, nor eat any unclean thing; for the child shall be a Nazarite from the womb to the day of his death.

Then Manoah entreated Yahweh, and said: O Yahweh, I pray Thee, let the man of God whom Thou didst send come again unto me and teach us what we shall do unto the child that shall be born. And God hearkened to the voice of Manoah; and the messenger of God came again to the woman as she sat in the field; but Manoah her husband was not with her. And the woman made haste, and ran and told her husband, and said unto him: Behold, the man hath appeared unto me that came unto me that day. And Manoah rose and went after his wife, and came upon the man and said: Art thou the man that spake unto the woman? And he said: I am. And Manoah said: Now, when thy word cometh to pass, what shall be the rules for the child, and what shall be done with him? And the messenger of Yahweh said unto Manoah: Of all that I said unto the woman let her be mindful. She may not eat of any product of the vine, nor let her drink any strong drink nor eat any unclean thing; all that I commanded her let her observe. And Manoah said unto the messenger of Yahweh: I pray thee, let us detain thee, that we may make ready a kid for thee. And the messenger of Yahweh said unto Manoah: Though thou detain me, I will not eat of thy bread; and if thou wilt make a burnt-offering, thou must offer it to Yahweh. For Manoah knew not that he was the messenger of Yahweh. And Manoah said unto him: What is thy name, that when thy words come to pass we may do thee honor? And the messenger of Yahweh said unto him: Wherefore askest thou after my name, seeing it is hidden? So Manoah took the kid and offered it upon the rock unto Yahweh. And the man did wondrously; for it came to pass when the flame went up toward heaven from off the altar, that the messenger of Yahweh ascended in the flame of the altar; and Manoah and his wife looked on; and they fell on their faces to the ground. Then Manoah knew that he was the messenger of Yahweh; but the messenger of Yahweh did no more appear to Manoah or to his wife. And Manoah said unto his wife: We shall certainly die, because we have seen God. But his wife said unto him: If Yahweh were pleased to kill us, He would not have received the burnt-offering at our hand, neither would He have shown us all these things, nor would at this time have announced to us such a thing.

And the woman bare a son and called his name Samson; and the boy grew up, and Yahweh blessed him. And the spirit of Yahweh began to move him.

And Samson went down to Timrath and saw a woman of the daughters of the Philistines there. And he came back and told his father and his mother: I have seen at Timnath a daughter of the Philistines; now therefore get her for me to wife. Then his father said unto him: Is there never a woman of the daughters of thy brethren, or among all my people, that thou goest to take a wife of the uncircumcised Philistines? And Samson said unto his father: Get her for me, for she pleaseth me well. But his father and his mother knew not that it was of Yahweh, that He sought an occasion against the Philistines. So Samson went down to Timnath and came to the vineyards of Timnath; and behold, a young lion roared against him. And the spirit of Yahweh came mightily upon him, and he rent him as one would rend a kid; he had nothing in his hand. Then he went down and talked with the woman; and she pleased Samson well. And after a while, he returned to take her, and he turned aside to see the carcass of the lion; and behold, there was a swarm of bees in the body of the lion and honey. And he scraped out the honey into his hands, and went on eating as he went; and he came to his father and mother and gave unto them, and they did eat; but he told them not he had scraped the honey out of the body of the lion. And Samson went down to the woman, and he made there a feast; for so used the bridegrooms to do. And it came to pass that thirty companions were with him. And Samson said unto them: Let me now put forth a riddle to you; if ye can declare it me within the seven days of the feast, I will give you thirty linen garments and thirty changes of raiment; but if ye cannot declare it unto me, then shall ye give me thirty linen garments and thirty changes of raiment. And they said: Put forth thy riddle, that we may hear it. And he said:

> Out of the eater came forth food,
> And out of the strong came forth sweetness.

And they could not solve the riddle. And it came to pass on the seventh day that they said unto Samson's wife: Entice thy husband, that he may declare unto us the riddle, lest we burn thee and thy father's house with fire; have ye called us hither to impoverish us? And Samson's wife wept before him, and said: Thou dost but hate me, and lovest me not; thou hast put forth a riddle to my people, and wilt thou not tell it me? And he said unto her: I have not told even my father and mother, and shall I tell it thee? But she wept before him the seven days that they held the feast; and it came to pass on the seventh day that he told her, because she pressed him sore; and she told the riddle to the children of her people. And the men of the city said unto him on the seventh day, before the sun went down:

> What is sweeter than honey?
> And what is stronger than a lion?

And he said unto them:

> If with my heifer ye had not ploughed,
> Ye had not found out my riddle.

And the spirit of Yahweh came mightily upon him; and he went down to Ashkelon and smote thirty men of them and took their spoil, and gave the changes of raiment unto them that declared the riddle. And his anger was kindled, and he went up to his father's house. But Samson's bride was given to his companion whom he had had for his groomsman.

But it came to pass after a while, in the time of wheat-harvest, that Samson went to visit his wife with a kid; and he said: I will go in to my wife in her chamber. But her father said: I verily thought that thou didst hate her utterly, therefore I gave her to thy friend. Is not her younger sister fairer than she? take her, I pray thee, instead. And Samson said: This time shall I be quits with the Philistines when I do them a mischief. And Samson went and caught three hundred foxes, and took torches, and turned the foxes tail to tail and put a torch between every two tails. And when he had set the torches a-fire, he let them go into the standing grain of the Philistines, and burnt up both the shocks and the standing grain. Then the Philistines said: Who hath done this? and they said: Samson, the son-in-law of the Timnathite; because he hath taken Samson's wife and given her to his friend. And the Philistines came up and burned her and her father with fire. And Samson said: If ye do after this manner, surely I will be avenged of you; and after that I will cease. And he smote them hip and thigh with a great slaughter. Then he went down and dwelt in the cleft of the rock of Etam.

Then the Philistines went up and pitched in Judah, and spread themselves against Lehi. And the men of Judah said: Why are ye come up against us? And they said: To bind Samson are we come up, to do to him as he hath done to us. Then three thousand men of Judah went down to the cleft of the rock Etam, and said to Samson: Knowest thou not that the Philistines are rulers over us? what then is this that thou hast done unto them? And he said: As they did to me, so have I done unto them. And they said unto him: We are come down to bind thee, that we may deliver thee into the hands of the Philistines. And Samson said: Swear unto me that ye will not fall upon me yourselves. And they spake unto him, saying: No; but we will bind thee fast and deliver thee into their hand; but surely we will not kill thee. And they bound him with two new ropes, and brought him up from the rock. When he came unto Lehi, the Philistines shouted as they met him; and the spirit of Yahweh came mightily upon him, and the ropes upon his arms became as flax that was burnt with fire, and his bonds dropped from off his hands. And he found a new jaw-bone of an ass, and put forth his hand and took it, and smote a thousand therewith. And Samson said:

With the jawbone of an ass, heaps upon heaps,
With the jawbone of an ass have I slain a thousand men.

And it came to pass, when he had finished speaking, that he cast away the jawbone out of his hand; therefore that place was called Ramath-lehi. And he was sore athirst, and called Yahweh, and said: Thou hast given this great deliverance by the hand of Thy servant; and now shall I die for thirst, and fall into the hands of the uncircumcised? But God clave the hollow place that is in Lehi, and there came out water; and when he had drunk, his spirit revived; wherefore the name of that place is called En-hakkore which is in Lehi to this day.[1]

Samson went to Gaza, and he saw there a harlot and went in unto her. [And it was told] the Gazites: Samson is come hither. And they were quiet all the night, saying: Let be till the morning light; then we will kill him. But Samson lay till midnight; and at midnight he rose and laid hold of the doors of the city-gate and the two posts, and plucked them up, bar and all, and put them on his shoulders and carried them to the top of the mountain that is before Hebron.

Afterward it came to pass, that Samson loved a woman in the valley of Sorek, whose name was Delilah. And the lords of the Philistines came up unto her and said: Entice him, and find wherein his great strength lieth, and by what means we may prevail against him and bind him that we may afflict him, and each of us will give thee eleven hundred pieces of silver. And Delilah said to Samson: Tell me, I pray thee, wherein thy great strength lieth, and wherewith thou mightest be bound to overpower thee. And Samson said unto her: If they bind me with seven fresh bowstrings that have never been dried, then shall I become weak like any other man. Then the lords of the Philistines brought her seven fresh bow-strings which had not been

---

[1] The redactor adds: "And he (Samson) judged Israel in the days of the Philistines twenty years."

dried, and she bound him with them. And she said: The Philistines
are upon thee, Samson! And he broke the bowstrings as a string of
tow is broken when it toucheth the fire. So the secret of his strength
was not known. And Delilah said unto Samson: Behold, thou hast
mocked me, and told me lies; now tell me wherewith thou canst be bound.
And he said: If they only bind me with new ropes wherewith no work
hath been done, then shall I become weak, and be as other men. So
Delilah took new ropes and bound him therewith, and said to him: The
Philistines are upon thee, Samson. And the men were lying in wait in
the inner chamber. And he snapped the ropes from his arms like thread.
And Delilah said to Samson: Hitherto thou hast mocked me and told
me lies; tell me wherewith thou mightest be bound. And he said: If
thou weavest the seven locks of my head with the web and fastenest it
with a pin, I shall become weak and like any other man. So, while he
was asleep, she took the seven locks of his hair and wove them with
the web, and fastened it with the pin, and said to him: The Philistines
are upon thee, Samson. And he awoke out of his sleep, and plucked
away the pin from the beam and the web.

Then she said unto him: How canst thou say, I love thee, when thy
heart is not with me? Thou hast mocked me these three times, and hast
not told me wherein thy great strength lieth. And it came to pass, when
she pressed him daily with her words and urged him, that his soul was
vexed unto death; and he told her all his heart and said unto her:
There hath not come a razor upon my head, for I have been a Nazarite
unto God from my mother's womb. If I be shaven, then my strength
will go from me, and I shall become weak and be like any other man.

Now when Delilah saw that he had told her all his heart, she sent
and called for the lords of the Philistines, saying: Come up this once,
for he hath told me all his heart. And the lords of the Philistines came
up to her, and brought the money in their hands. And she put him
to sleep upon her knees. And she called for a man, and had the seven
locks of his hair shaven off; and she began to torment him, and his
strength went from him. And she said: The Philistines are upon thee,
Samson. And he awoke out of his sleep and said: I will go out as at other
times and shake myself. But he knew not that Yahweh had departed
from him. And the Philistines laid hold on him, and put out his eyes;
and they brought him down to Gaza and bound him with fetters of
brass; and he did grind in the prison-house. Howbeit, the hair of his
head began to grow again after he was shaven.

And the lords of the Philistines assembled to offer a great sacrifice
unto Dagon their god and to rejoice; for they said: Our god hath delivered Samson, our enemy, into our hands. And when the people saw
him, they praised their god, for they said: Our god hath given into our
hand our enemy, the destroyer of our country who hath killed many
of us. And it came to pass when their hearts were merry, that they
said: Call for Samson, that he may make us sport. And they called
for Samson out of the prison-house, and he made sport before them;
and they set him between the pillars.

Then Samson said to the lad that held him by the hand: Suffer me
to feel the pillars whereupon the house resteth, that I may lean upon
them. Now the house was full of men and women, and all the lords
of the Philistines were there,[1] who were looking on while Samson made
sport. Then Samson prayed unto Yahweh, and said: O God Yahweh,

---

[1] P adds, to make the disaster greater "and there were upon the roof three thousand
men and women".

remember me, I pray thee, and strengthen me, I pray thee, only this once, O God, that I may be avenged of the Philistines for one of my two eyes! Then Samson grasped firmly the two middle pillars upon which the house rested, and leaned upon them, the one with his right hand, the other with his left. And he said: Let me die with the Philistines. And he bowed himself with all his might, and the house fell upon the lords and upon all the people who were therein. So those that he killed at his death were more than those whom he slew in his life.

Then his brethren and all the house of his father came down and took him and brought him up and buried him between Zorah and Eshtaol, in the burial-place of Manoah, his father.

Now it came to pass in those days, that there was a certain Levite sojourning in a remote part of the hill-country of Ephraim, who took him a concubine from Bethlehem in Judah. And his concubine became angry with him and left him, and went to her father's house in Bethlehem in Judah, and was there the space of four months. Then her husband followed her to speak kindly to her and to bring her back, having with him his servant and a couple of asses; and he came to her father's house, and she brought him in. And when the father of the damsel saw him, he came to meet him rejoicing. And his father-in-law, the girl's father, detained him, and he abode with him three days. So they did eat and drink and lodged there. On the fourth day when he arose in the morning, he was about to set out; but the damsel's father said unto his son-in-law: Stay thy heart with a morsel of bread, and then ye shall go your way. So they sat down and did eat and drink, both of them together; and so they tarried till the close of day. And when the man rose to go, he and his concubine and his servant, his father-in-law, the damsel's father, said: Behold now, the day draweth toward the evening; tarry, I pray you, to-night; behold, the day is declining; lodge here and be merry, and to-morrow get you early on your way, that thou mayest go home. But the man would not tarry that night, but rose up and set out. When they were near Jebus, and the day was far spent, the servant said unto his master: Come, let us turn aside to this town of the Jebusites, and pass the night in it. But his master said: We will not turn aside into the city of a stranger that belongeth not to the Children of Israel. So they went on their way; and the sun went down as they were near Gibeah, which belongeth to Benjamin. And they entered it, and sat down in the market-place of the town; for no one took them to lodge in his house.

And behold, an old man was coming home at evening from his work in the fields. And he lifted up his eyes and saw the traveler in the market-place of the city, and the old man said: Whither goest thou, and whence comest thou? And he said unto him: We are passing from Bethlehem-Judah to the farther side of the hill-country of Ephraim. From thence am I, and I went to Bethlehem in Judah, and I am now going to my house, and no man taketh me into his house. Yet we have here both chopped straw and provender for our asses, and there is also bread and wine for us and for thy handmaid, and for the young man that is with thy servant; there is no lack of anything. Then said the old man: Peace be to thee; however, let all that thou needest be at my charge, only lodge not in the market-place. So he brought them to his house, and gave the asses fodder; and they washed their feet and did eat and drink.

As they were making their hearts merry, behold certain base fellows of the city beset the house round about, beating on the door and commanding the master of the house, saying: Bring forth the man that came into thy house. And the master of the house went out to them, and said to them: Nay, my brethren, be not so wicked, seeing that this man is come into my house; do not this wanton deed. But the men would not listen to him. Then the man laid hold on his concubine and thrust her out to them in the street; and they laid hold on her and abused her all night until the morning; and when the day began to dawn, they let her go. Then came the woman at the dawning of the day, and fell down at the door of the man's house where her lord was till it was light. And when her lord rose in the morning, and opened the door of the house to go his way, behold, the woman his concubine was fallen down at the door of the house, and her hands were on the sill. And he said unto her: Up, and let us be going. But none answered. Then the man put her upon an ass, and rose up and gat him unto his place.

And when he came to his house, he took a knife and laid hold of his concubine and divided her joint by joint into twelve pieces, and sent them throughout all the borders of Israel. And he commanded the men whom he sent out, saying: Thus shall ye say to all the men of Israel: Did ever a thing like this happen from the time that the Children of Israel came up from the land of Egypt until this day? Consider it, take counsel, and speak.

Then all the Israelites went out for war to the sanctuary of Yahweh at Mizpah. And the Benjamites heard that all the Children of Israel were gone up to Mizpah. And the Children of Israel said: Tell us, how did this wickedness come about? And the Levite, the husband of the woman who was murdered said: I came with my concubine to Gibeah, which belongeth to Benjamin, to lodge for the night. And the men of Gibeah rose against me, and beset the house round about by night, and thought to have slain me; and they ravished my concubine so that she died. Then I took my concubine and cut her in pieces, and sent them throughout all the country of Israel, because they have committed lewdness and wantonness in Israel. Behold, ye are all here, ye Children of Israel; give your word and counsel here. Then all the people stood up, saying: We will none of us go to his tent, nor any of us to his home. So all the men of Israel were gathered against the city, knit together as one man.

Now the children of Benjamin gathered from their cities to Gibeah to make war against the Israelites. So the Israelites set out in the morning, and encamped against Gibeah; and Israel put men in ambush against Gibeah on all sides. And the men of Israel gave ground to Benjamin, relying upon the ambush which they had set for Gibeah. Then the ambush made haste and rushed upon Gibeah. Now it had been agreed between the men of Israel and the ambush that, when they should make a great flame with smoke rise out of the city, then the men of Israel should turn about to the battle. And Benjamin had begun to make slaughter among the men of Israel, and killed about thirty persons; and they said: We have surely beaten them. But when the flame began to rise out of the city with a pillar of smoke, the Benjamites looked back and behold, the flame of the whole city ascended up to heaven. Then the men of Israel turned again, and the men of Benjamin were dismayed, for they saw that evil was come upon them, and there fell of Benjamin eighteen thousand men. But six hundred men turned and fled to the rock of Rimmon, and abode on the rock of Rimmon four months.

Now the men of Israel had sworn in Mizpah, saying: No one of us shall give his daughter to Benjamin to wife. But the people were sorry for Benjamin, because Yahweh had made a breach in the tribes of Israel; for women had been utterly destroyed out of Benjamin; and they said: Those that are escaped must be inheritors for Benjamin, that a tribe be not wholly blotted out from Irsael. Howbeit, we may not give them wives of our daughters. For the Children of Israel had sworn: Cursed be he that giveth a wife to Benjamin.

Then they said (to the Benjamites): Behold, there is a feast of Yahweh from year to year at Shiloh; go, lie in wait in the vineyards; and lo, if the daughters of Shiloh come out to dance in the dances, then come ye out of the vineyards and catch you every man his wife of the daughters of Shiloh, and go to the land of Benjamin. And it shall be, if their fathers or their brethren come to us to complain, then we will say to them: Grant them graciously unto them; for had ye given them to them, ye would now be guilty.

And the Benjamites did so; and they took them wives of them that danced, whom they carried off. And they went back again to their possession, and rebuilt their cities, and dwelt in them.

Now it came to pass in those days, that the Philistines gathered together to make war upon Israel; and they slew of the army in the field about four thousand men. So when the Israelites had come back into the camp, they sent to Shiloh and brought thence the ark of the covenant of Yahweh Sabaoth. And when the ark came into the camp, the earth rang; and the Philistines knew that the ark of Yahweh was come into the camp, and they cried: Woe unto us! for there hath not been such a thing before. But be ye valiant; quit yourselves like men, and fight. And the Philistines fought, and there was a very great slaughter.

Now the Philistines had taken the ark of God; and they brought it from Ebenezer to Ashdod. And they took the ark of God, and brought it into the House of Dagon and set it by Dagon. And when they of Ashdod arose early on the morrow, behold, Dagon was fallen on his face to the ground before the ark of Yahweh. And they took Dagon and set him in his place again. And when they arose early on the morrow morning, behold, Dagon was fallen upon his face to the ground before the ark of Yahweh; and the head of Dagon and both the palms of his hands lay cut off upon the threshold; only the trunk of Dagon was left to him. Therefore, neither the priests of Dagon, nor any that come into Dagon's house, tread on the threshold of Dagon in Ashdod to this day.

But the hand of Yahweh was heavy upon them of Ashdod, and He destroyed them and smote them with emerods, even Ashdod and all the borders thereof. And when the men of Ashdod saw that it was so, they said: The ark of the god of Israel shall not abide with us, for his hand is sore upon us and upon Dagon our god. They sent therefore and gathered all the lords of the Philistines unto them, and said: What shall we do with the ark of the god of Israel? And they answered: Let the ark of the god of Israel be carried about unto Gath. And they carried the ark of the God of Israel thither. And it was so that, after they had carried it thither, the hand of Yahweh was against the city with a very great destruction; and He smote the men of the city, both small and great, and they had emerods in their secret parts. Therefore they sent the ark of God to Ekron.

And it came to pass, as the ark of God came to Ekron, that the Ekronites cried out, saying: They have brought the ark of the God of Israel to us, to slay us and our people. So they sent and gathered together all the lords of the Philistines and said: Send away the ark of the God of Israel, and let it go again to its own place that it slay not us and our people; for there was a deadly pestilence throughout all the city; the hand of God was very heavy there. And the men that died not were smitten with the emerods; and the cry of the city went up to heaven.

Then the Philistines called for the priests and the diviners, saying: What shall we do with the ark of Yahweh? tell us wherewith we shall send it to its place. And they said: If ye send away the ark of the God of Israel, send it not empty, but in any wise return Him a trespass-offering; then ye shall be healed, and it shall be known to you why His hand is not removed from you. Then said they: What shall be the trespass-offering which we must return to Him? They answered: Five golden emerods and five golden mice, according to the number of the lords of the Philistines; for one plague was on you all and on your lords. Wherefore do ye harden your hearts, as the Egyptians and Pharaoh hardened their hearts? When He had wrought wonderfully among them, did they not let the people go, and they departed?

Now, therefore, take a new cart, and take two milch kine on which there hath come no yoke, and tie the kine to the cart and bring their calves home from them; and take the ark of Yahweh and lay it upon the cart; and put the jewels of gold, the trespass-offering which ye return Him, in a coffer by the side thereof, and send it away that it may go. And see if it goeth up by the way of His own border to Beth-shemesh; then He hath done us this great evil; but if not, then we shall know that it is not His hand that hath smitten us; it was a chance that happened to us.

And the men did so. They took two milch kine and tied them to the cart, and shut up their calves at home; and they laid the ark of Yahweh upon the cart, and the coffer with the mice of gold and with the images of the emerods. And the kine took the straight way by the road to Beth-shemesh, and they went along the highway, lowing as they went. They turned not away to the right hand or to the left; and the lords of the Philistines went after them unto the border of Beth-shemesh. And they of Beth-shemesh were reaping their wheat-harvest in the valley: and thy lifted up their eyes and saw the ark, and rejoiced to see it. And the cart came to the field of Joshua, a Beth-shemite, where was a great stone; and it stood there; and they cleaved the wood of the cart, and offered the kine a burnt-offering unto Yahweh. And when the five lords of the Philistines had seen it, they returned to Ekron the same day.

And Yahweh smote of the men of Beth-shemesh three score and ten men, because they looked into the ark of Yahweh; and the people mourned because He had smitten so many of the people. And the men of Beth-shemesh said: Who is able to stand before this holy God, Yahweh? And to whom shall He go up from us? And they sent messengers to the inhabitants of Kiriath-jearim, saying: The Philistines have brought back the ark of Yahweh; come ye down and fetch it up to you. And the men of Kiriath-jearim came and fetched up the ark of Yahweh, and brought it into the house of Abinadab in the hill, and sanctified Eleazer his son to keep the ark of Yahweh.

CHAPTER IV

THE KINGSHIP OF SAUL, THE BENJAMITE

SECTION I.—The Israelites demand a king. Saul, seeking his father's asses, appears before Samuel the Seer. Samuel anoints him king. Saul saves Jabesh-Gilead from the Ammonites. The people hail him as king in Gilgal. He orders his forces for an attack upon the Philistines. His son Jonathan makes the first foray upon their garrison. The great exploit of Jonathan, followed by an earthquake and the rout of the Philistines. Saul builds his first altar to Yahweh. (1 Samuel, ix-x, 7, 9-16; xi, 1-7, 9-11, 15; xiii, 1-5a, 7a, 16-18, 25; xiv, 1-4.)

Materials: Oral traditions, the "Book of Jashar", the "Wars of Yahweh", Priestly Records, "Acts of Samuel the Seer".

Now there was a man of Benjamin whose name was Kish the son of Abiel, the son of Zerar, the son of Bechereth, the son of Aphiah; a Benjamite, a mighty man of valor. And he had a son whose name was Saul, a choice young man and a goodly; and there was not among the Children of Israel a goodlier person than he; for from his shoulders upward he was taller than any of the people.

And the asses of Saul's father, Kish, were lost. And Kish said to Saul his son: Take now one of the servants with thee, and arise, go seek the asses. And he passed through mount Ephraim, and passed through the land of Shalim, and passed through the land of the Benjamites, and found them not. And when they were come to the land of Zuph, Saul said to his servant that was with him: Come, let us return, lest my father leave caring for the asses, and take thought for us. And he answered him: Behold now, there is in this city a man of God, an honorable man; all that he saith cometh to pass. Now let us go thither; peradventure he can show us the way that we should go.

Then said Saul to his servant: But behold, if we go, what shall we bring to the man? for the bread is spent in our vessels, and we have no present to bring to the man of God. What have we? And the servant answered Saul again, and said: Behold, I have here at hand the fourth part of a shekel of silver; that will I give to the man of God to tell us our way. (Aforetime in Israel, when a man went to inquire of God, he said: Come let us go to the Seer; for he that is now called a prophet was aforetime called a Seer.) Then said Saul to his servant: Well said, let us go. So they went into the city where the man of God was.

And as they went up to the city, they found young maidens going out to draw water, and said unto them: Is the Seer here? And they answered them and said: He is; behold, he is ahead of you; make haste now, for he came to-day to the city; for there is a sacrifice of the people to-day in the high place; as soon as ye be come into the city ye shall straightway find him, before he go up to the high place to eat;

for the people will not eat until he come, because he doth bless the sacrifice; afterwards they eat that are bidden.

And they went up into the city; and when they were come into the city, behold, Samuel came out against them to go up unto the high place.[1]

Now Yahweh had told Samuel in his ear a day before Saul came, saying: To-morrow about this time I will send thee a man out of the land of Benjamin, and thou shalt anoint him captain over My people Israel, that he may save My people out of the hand of the Philistines; for I have looked upon My people, because their cry hath come unto Me. And when Samuel saw Saul, Yahweh said unto him: Behold the man of whom I spake unto thee; this same shall reign over My people.

Then Saul drew near unto Samuel in the gate, and said: Tell me, I pray thee, where the seer's house is. And Samuel answered Saul, and said: I am the seer; go up before me unto the high place, for ye shall eat with me to-day, and to-morrow I will let thee go, and will tell thee all that is in thy heart. As for thine asses that were lost three days ago, set not thy mind on them, for they are found. And on whom is all the desire of Israel? Is it not on thee, and on all thy father's house?

And Saul answered and said: Am not I a Benjamite, of the smallest of the tribes of Israel? and my family least of all the families of the tribe of Benjamin? Wherefore then speakest thou so to me?

And Samuel took Saul and his servant and brought them into the chamber, and made them sit in the chiefest place among them that were bidden, which were about thirty persons. And Samuel said unto the cook: Bring the portion that I gave thee, of which I said: Set it by thee. And the cook took up the shoulder and that which was upon it, and set it before Saul. And Samuel said: Behold that which was left; set it before thee and eat; for unto this time hath it been kept for thee since I said: I have invited the people. So Saul did eat with Samuel that day.

And when they were come down from the high place into the city, Samuel communed with Saul on the top of the house. And they arose early. And it came to pass about the spring of the day, that Samuel called to Saul on the top of the house, saying: Up, that I may send thee away. And Saul arose; and they went out both of them, he and Samuel, abroad. And as they were going down to the end of the city, Samuel said to Saul: Bid the servant pass on (and he passed on), but stand thou still awhile, that I may show thee the word of God.

Then Samuel took a vial of oil and poured it upon his head, and kissed him, and said: Is it not because Yahweh hath anointed thee to be prince over His inheritance? When thou art departed from me to-day, thou shalt find two men by Rachel's tomb in the border of Benjamin at Zelzah; and they will say unto thee: The asses which thou wentest to seek are found; and lo, thy father hath left off caring for the asses, and is sorrowing for you, saying: What shall I do for my son? Then thou shalt go forward from thence, and thou shalt come to the plain of Tabor, and there shall meet thee three men going up to God to Bethel, one carrying three kids, and another carrying three loaves

---

[1] In this version, the introduction of Samuel is as abrupt as that of Melchizedek; but it is improbable that J had given no account of his origin and early history. We may rather infer that JE preferred the fuller and more romantic account of E; and, as has happened before, no later editor seems to have thought a connecting link necessary. E left Samuel a judge in a small circuit of four cities only, but of considerable importance. He appears here as a revered Seer, exercising priestly functions, whose verdict is accepted in the highest civic affairs.

of bread, and another carrying a bottle of wine; and they will salute thee, and give thee two loaves of bread, which thou shalt receive at their hands. After that, thou shalt come to the hill of God where is the garrison of the Philistines. And it shall come to pass when thou art come thither to the city, that thou shalt meet a company of prophets coming down from the high place with a psaltery and a tabret and a pipe and a harp before them; and they shall prophesy. And the Spirit of Yahweh shall come upon thee, and thou shalt prophesy with them, and shalt be turned into another man. And let it be, when these signs are come unto thee, that thou do as occasion serve thee; for God is with thee.

And it was so, that, when he had turned his back to go from Samuel, God gave him another heart; and all those signs came to pass that day. And when they came to the hill, behold, a company of prophets met him; and the Spirit of God came upon him, and he prophesied with them. And it came to pass, when all that knew him aforetime saw that he prophesied among the prophets, then the people said one to another: What is this that hath come unto the son of Kish? Is Saul also among the prophets? And one of the same place answered and said: But who is their father? Therefore it became a proverb, Is Saul also among the prophets? And when he had made an end of prophesying, he came to the high place.

And Saul's uncle said unto him and to his servant: Whither went ye? And he said: To seek the asses; and when we saw them nowhere, we went to Samuel. And Saul's uncle said: Tell me, I pray thee, what Samuel said unto thee? And Saul said unto his uncle: He told us plainly that the asses were found. But of the matter of the kingdom whereof Samuel spake, he told him not.

Then Nahash the Ammonite came up and encamped against Jabesh-Gilead; and all the men of Jabesh said unto Nahash: Make a covenant with us, and we will serve thee. And Nahash the Ammonite answered them: On this will I make it with you, that I may thrust out all your right eyes, and lay it for a reproach to all Israel. And the elders of Jabesh said unto him: Give us seven days 'respite, that we may send messengers unto all the coasts of Israel; and then, if there be none to save us, we will come out to thee. Then came the messengers to Gibeah of Saul, and told the tidings in the ears of the people; and all the pople lifted up their voices and wept.

And behold, Saul came after the herd out of the field; and Saul said: What aileth the people that they weep? And they told him the tidings of the men of Jabesh. And the Spirit of God came upon Saul when he heard those tidings, and his anger was kindled greatly. And he took a yoke of oxen, and hewed them in pieces, and sent them throughout all the coasts of Israel by the hands of messengers, saying. Whosoever cometh not forth after Saul and after Samuel, so shall it be done unto his oxen. And the fear of Yahweh fell upon the people, and they came out with one consent.

And they said unto the messengers that came: Thus shall ye say unto the men of Jabesh-Gilead: To-morrow, by that time the sun be hot, ye shall have help. And the messengers came and showed it to the men of Jabesh; and they were glad. Therefore the men of Jabesh said: To-morrow we will come out to you, and ye shall do with us all that seemeth good unto you.

And it was so, that on the morrow Saul put the people into three companies, and they came into the midst of the host in the morning watch, and slew the Ammonites until the heat of the day; and it came to pass that they which remained were scattered so that two of them were not left together. And all the people went to Gilgal; and there they made Saul king before Yahweh in Gilgal; and there they offered sacrifices of peace-offerings before Yahweh; and there Saul and all the men of Israel rejoiced greatly.

[1] Now when Saul had reigned two years over Israel, he chose him three thousand men of Israel, whereof two thousand were with Saul in Michmash and in mount Bethel, and a thousand with Jonathan in Gibeah of Benjamin; and the rest of the people he sent every man to his tent. Now some of the Hebrews had gone over the Jordan to the land of Gad and Gilead; but Saul and Jonathan his son, and the people who were with them, abode in Gibeah of Benjamin. And the Philistines encamped in Michmash. And the spoilers came out of the camp of the Philistines in three companies: one company turned unto the way that leadeth to Ophrah, unto the land of Shual; another company turned the way of Beth-horon; and another turned the way of the border that looketh down upon the valley of Zeboim toward the wilderness. And the garrison of the Philistines went out unto the pass of Michmash.

Now it came to pass upon a day, that Jonathan the son of Saul said to the young man who bare his armor: Come, let us go over to the Philistine garrison that is on the other side. But he told not his father. And Saul was tarrying in the uttermost part of Gibeah under a pomegranate-tree which is in Migron; and the people that were with him were about six hundred men, and Ahiah the son of Ahitub (Ichabod's brother, the son of Phinehas, the son of Eli who had been the priest of Yahweh in Shiloh), wearing an ephod. And the people knew not that Jonathan had gone.

Now between the passages by which Jonathan sought to go over to the Philistines' garrison was a sharp rock on the one side, and a sharp rock on the other side; and the name of the one was Bozez, and the name of the other Seneh. The fore-front of the one was situate northward over against Michmash, and the other eastward over against Gibeah. And Jonathan said to the young man that bare his armor: Come and let us go over unto the garrison of these uncircumcised; it may be that Yahweh will work for us, for to Yahweh there is no restraint to save by many or by few. And his armor-bearer said unto him: Do all that is in thine heart; turn thee; behold, I am with thee, according to thy heart. Then said Jonathan: Behold, we will pass over unto these men, and we will discover ourselves to them. If they say thus unto us: Tarry until we come to you; then we will stand still in our place and will not go up unto them. But if they say thus: Come up unto us,— then we will go up; for Yahweh hath delivered them unto us; and this shall be the sign unto us.

And both of them discovered themselves unto the garrison of the Philistines; and the Philistines said: Behold, the Hebrews come forth out of the holes where they had hid themselves. And the men of the garrison answered Jonathan and his armor-bearer, and said: Come up, and we will show you a thing.

And Jonathan said unto his armor-bearer: Come up after me; for Yahweh hath delivered them into the hand of Israel. And Jonathan climbed up upon his hands and upon his feet, and his armor-bearer

[1] Chapter xii is interpolated by a Deuteronomist. The style and manner of Samuel's address are out of harmony with the simple account of the selection and grateful acceptance of the first king, given by J. It is therefore omitted.

after him; and they fell before Jonathan, and his armor-bearer slew after him. And the first slaughter which Jonathan and his armor-bearer made was about twenty men, within as it were half an acre of land. And there was trembling in the host, in the field, and among all the people; the garrison and the spoilers, they also trembled, and the earth quaked; so it was a very great trembling. And the watchmen of Saul in Gibeah of Benjamin looked; and behold, the multitude melted away, and they went on beating one another down.

Then said Saul unto the people who were with him: Number now, and see who is gone from us. And when they had numbered, behold, Jonathan and his armor-bearer were not there. And Saul said unto Ahiah: Bring hither the ark of God (for the ark of God was there with them at that time); and it came to pass, while Saul was talking unto the priest, that the noise in the host of the Philistines went on and increased; and Saul said unto the priest: Withdraw thy hand. And Saul and all the people that were with him assembled themselves, and came to the battle; and behold, every man's sword was against his fellow, and there was a very great discomfiture. Moreover the Israelites that were with the Philistines before that time, which went up with them into the camp from round about, even they also turned to be with the Israelites that were with Saul and Jonathan. Likewise, all the men of Israel who had hid themselves in mount Ephraim, when they heard that the Philistines fled, even they also followed hard after them in battle.

So Yahweh saved Israel that day; and the battle passed over unto Bethaven.

And the men of Israel were distressed that day; for Saul had adjured the people, saying: Cursed be the man that taketh any food until the evening, that I may be avenged on mine enemies. So none of the people tasted any food. And all they of the land came to a wood; and there was honey on the ground. And when the people were come into the wood, behold, the honey was dropping; but no man put his hand to his mouth; for the people feared the oath. But Jonathan heard not when his father straitly charged the people with the oath; wherefore he put forth the end of the rod that was in his hand and dipped it in the honeycomb, and put his hand to his mouth; and his eyes were enlightened.

Then said one of the people: Thy father straitly charged the people with an oath, saying: Cursed be the man that eateth any food this day. Now the people were faint. Then said Jonathan: My father hath troubled the land; see, I pray you, how mine eyes have been enlightened, because I tasted a little of this honey. How much more, if haply the people had eaten more freely to-day of the spoil of their enemies which they found; for had there not been a much greater slaughter among the Philistines?

And they smote the Philistines that day from Michmash to Aijalon, and the people were very faint. And the people flew upon the spoil, and took sheep and oxen and calves, and slew them on the ground; and the people did eat them with the blood.

Then they told Saul, saying: Behold, the people sin against Yahweh, in that they eat with the blood. And he said: Ye have transgressed; roll a great stone unto me this day. And Saul said: Disperse yourselves among the people, and say unto them: Let every man bring me hither his ox, and every man his sheep, and slay them here and eat; and sin not against Yahweh, by eating with the blood. And all the people brought, every man with him that night, his ox, and they slew them there.

And Saul built an altar unto Yahweh; the same was the first altar that he built unto Yahweh.

And Saul said: Let us go down after the Philistines by night, and spoil them until the morning light, and let us not leave a man of them. And they said: Do whatsoever seemeth good to thee. Then said the priest: Let us draw near unto God. And Saul asked counsel of God: Shall I go down after the Philistines? wilt Thou deliver them into the hand of Israel? But He answered him not that day. And Saul said: Draw ye near hither, all the chief of the people; and know and see wherein this sin hath been this day; for, as Yahweh liveth, which saveth Israel, though it be in Jonathan my son, he shall surely die. But there was not a man among all the people that answered him. Then said he unto all Israel: Be ye on one side, and I and Jonathan my son will be on the other side. And the people said unto Saul: Do what seemeth good unto thee. Therefore Saul said unto Yahweh: God of Israel, give a perfect lot! And Saul and Jonathan were taken, but the people escaped. And Saul said: Cast lots between me and Jonathan my son. And Jonathan was taken.

Then Saul said to Jonathan: Tell me what thou hast done. And Jonathan told him, saying: I did but take a little honey with the end of the rod that was in my hand; lo, I must die. And Saul answered: God do so unto me, and more also; for thou shalt surely die, Jonathan.

And the people said unto Saul: Shall Jonathan die, who hath wrought this great salvation in Israel? God forbid; as Yahweh liveth, there shall not one hair of his head fall to the ground; for he hath wrought with God this day. So the people rescued Jonathan, that he died not.

Then Saul went up from following the Philistines; and the Philistines went to their own land.

SECTION II.—Samuel brings Saul a command to annihilate the Amalekites. Saul spares the king, and gives the best of the spoil to his men. Thereby, he loses the kingdom of Israel. He becomes a victim of melancholia. His men advise music as a remedy, and introduce David, a skilled musician and an able warrior. Saul welcomes him; but becomes jealous of his prowess, and tries to kill him. David escapes to Nob, "the city of the priests". Is seen there by the spy, Doeg the Edomite, who later, at Saul's command, slaughters all the priests of Nob, and destroys the city. David saved from Saul's enmity by his wife Michal, Saul's daughter. A band of outlaws gathers about him in the cave of Adullam. He provides for the safety of his father and mother in Moab; then becomes the head of the outlaws. Saul pursues him relentlessly, but is at last overcome by David's generosity. (1 Sam'l, xv, 1-25, 32-35; xvi, 14-23; xviii, 19-29; xix, 11-17; xxi, 2-16; xxii, 1-23; xxiii, 1-14a; xxvi, 1-25.)

Materials: Abundant folk-songs. A collection called "Wars of Yahweh". A "Chronicle of King David". The "Acts of Samuel the Seer"; possibly, also, the "Acts of Gad", and the "Chronicles of the Kings of Judah" often referred to by the late writer called the Chronicler.

Then Samuel said unto Saul: Yahweh sent me to anoint thee to be king over his people, over Israel. Now, therefore, hearken thou unto the voice of Yahweh. Thus saith Yahweh Sabaoth: I remember what Amalek did to Israel; how he set himself against him in the way when he came up out of Egypt. Now go and smite Amalek, and utterly destroy all that they have, and spare them not; but slay both men and women, infant and suckling, ox and sheep, camel and ass.

And Saul summoned the people and numbered them in Telaim, two hundred thousand footmen, and ten thousand men of Judah. And Saul came to the city of Amalek, and lay in wait in the valley. And Saul said unto the Kenites: Go, depart, get you down from among the Amalekites, lest I destroy you with them; for ye showed kindness to all the Children of Israel, when they came up out of Egypt. So the Kenites departed from among the Amalekites. And Saul smote the Amalekites, from Havilah as thou goest to Shur, that is in front of Egypt. And he took Agag, the king of the Amalekites, alive; and utterly destroyed all the people with the edge of the sword. But Saul and the people spared Agag, and the best of the sheep, and of the oxen, even the youngest of the second birth, and the lambs, and all that was good; but everything that was of no account and feeble, that they destroyed utterly.

Then came the word of Yahweh to Samuel, saying: It repenteth Me that I have set up Saul to be king; for he is turned back from following Me, and hath not performed My commandments. And it grieved Samuel; and he cried unto Yahweh all night. And when Samuel rose early to meet Saul in the morning, it was told Samuel, saying: Saul came to Carmel; and behold, he is setting him up a monument, and is gone about and passed on, and gone down to Gilgal.

And Samuel came to Saul; and Saul said unto him: Blessed be thou of Yahweh; I have performed the commandment of Yahweh. And Samuel said: What meaneth then this bleating of the sheep in mine ears, and the lowing of the oxen that I hear? And Saul said: They have brought them from the Amalekites; for the people spared the best of the sheep and of the oxen to sacrifice unto Yahweh thy God; and the rest we have utterly destroyed. Then Samuel said unto Saul: Stay, and I will tell thee what Yahweh hath said unto me this night. And he said unto him: Say on.

And Samuel said: Though thou be little in thine own sight, art thou not head of the tribes of Israel? And Yahweh anointed thee king over Israel. And Yahweh sent thee on a journey, and said: Go and utterly destroy the sinners the Amalekites, and fight against them until they be consumed. Wherefore then didst thou not hearken to the voice of Yahweh? but thou didst fly upon the spoil, and didst that which was evil in the sight of Yahweh.

And Saul answered Samuel: Yea, I have hearkened to the voice of Yahweh, and have gone the way Yahweh sent me, and have brought Agag, the king of Amalek, and have utterly destroyed the Amalekites. But the people took the spoil, sheep and oxen, the chief of the devoted things, to sacrifice unto Yahweh thy God in Gilgal. And Samuel said:

Hath Yahweh as great delight in burnt-offerings and sacrifices,
    As in hearkening to the voice of Yahweh?
Behold, to obey is better than sacrifice,
    And to hearken than the fat of rams.
    For rebellion is as the sin of Witchcraft,
    And Stubbornness is as idolatry and teraphim.

Because thou hast rejected the word of Yahweh, He hath also rejected thee from being king.

Then said Samuel: Bring ye hither to me Agag the king of the Amalekites. And Agag said: Surely the bitterness of death is at hand. And Samuel said:

As thy sword hath made women childless,
So shall thy mother be childless among women.

And Samuel hewed Agag in pieces before Yahweh in Gilgal.

Now the Spirit of Yahweh had departed from Saul, and an evil spirit from Yahweh terrified him. And Saul's servants, said unto him: Behold now, an evil spirit from God troubleth thee. Let our lord now command his servants that are before him to seek out a man who is a skilful player on the harp; and it shall be when the evil spirit from God cometh upon thee, that he shall play with his hand, and thou shalt be well. And Saul said unto his servants: Provide me now a man that can play well, and bring him to me. Then aswered one of the young men, and said: Behold, I have seen a son of Jesse the Bethlehemite, that is skilful in playing, and a mighty man of valor, and a man of war, and prudent in affairs, and a comely person, and Yahweh is with him. Wherefore Saul sent messengers unto Jesse, and said: Send me David thy son. And Jesse took an ass laden with bread, and a bottle of wine and a kid, and sent them by David his son unto Saul. And David came to Saul and stood before him; and he loved him greatly; and he became his armor-bearer. And Saul sent to Jesse, saying: Let David, I pray thee, stand before me; for he hath found favor in my sight. And it came to pass, that when the evil spirit from God was upon Saul, that David took the harp and played with his hand; so Saul found relief and was well and the evil spirit departed from him.

Now it came to pass on a day, that an evil spirit from God came mightily upon Saul, and he raved in the midst of the house, and David played with his hand, as at other times; and Saul had his spear in his hand. And Saul cast the spear, for he said: I will smite David even to the wall. And David stepped aside out of his presence twice. And Saul was afraid of David, because Yahweh was with him, and was departed from Saul. Therefore Saul removed him from him, and made him his captain over a thousand; and he went out and came in before the people. And David had great success in all his doings; and Yahweh was with him. Wherefore, when Saul saw that he acted very wisely, he was afraid of him. But all Israel and Judah loved David, because he went out and came in before them. And David went out whithersoever Saul sent him, and behaved himself wisely; and Saul set him over the men of war, and he was accepted in the sight of all the people, and also in the sight of Saul's servants.

And Saul said unto David: Behold my elder daughter Merab, her will I give thee to wife; only be thou valiant for me and fight Yahweh's battles. For Saul said: Let not mine hand be upon him, but let the hand of the Philistines be upon him. And David said unto Saul: Who am I, and what is my life, or my father's family in Israel, that I should be son-in-law to the king? But it came to pass at the time when Merab, Saul's daughter, should have been given to David, that she was given to Adriel the Meholathite to wife.

Now Michal, Saul's daughter, loved David; and they told Saul, and the thing pleased him. And he said: I will give her to him, that she may be a snare unto him, and that the hand of the Philistine may be against him. Wherefore Saul said unto David: Thou shalt this day be my son-in-law through one of the twain. And Saul commanded his servants: Speak with David secretly, and say: Behold, the king hath delight in thee, and all his servants love thee; now therefore, be the king's son-in-law. And Saul's servants spake these words in the ears of

David. And David said: Seemeth it to you a light thing to be the king's
son-in-law, seeing that I am a poor man, and lightly esteemed? And the
servants of Saul told him, saying: In this manner spake David. And
Saul said: Thus shall ye say to David. The King desireth not any
dowry, but an hundred foreskins of the Philistines, to be avenged of
the king's enemies. For Saul thought to make David fall by the hand
of the Philistines. And when his servants told David these words, it
pleased David well to be the king's son-in-law. And the days were not
expired; and David arose and went, he and his men, and slew of the
Philistines two hundred men; and David brought their foreskins, and
they gave them in full number to the king, that he might be the king's
son-in-law. And Saul gave Michal his daughter to him to wife. And
Saul saw and knew that Yahweh was with David. And Michal, Saul's
daughter, loved him. And Saul was yet the more afraid of David; and
Saul remained David's enemy continually.

Then the princes of the Philistines came forth; and as often as they
came forth David prospered more than all the servants of Saul, so that
his name was much set by.

And Saul sent messengers to David's house to watch him, and to slay
him in the morning. And Michal, David's wife, told him, saying: If
thou save not thy life this night, to-morrow thou shalt be slain. So
Michal let David down through the window; and he went and fled and
escaped. And Michal took the teraphim, and laid it in the bed and put
a pillow of goats' hair at the head thereof and covered it with a cloth.
And when Saul sent messengers to take David, she said: He is sick.
Then Saul sent messengers to see David, saying: Bring him up to me
in the bed, that I may slay him. And when the messengers came in,
behold, the teraphim was in the bed with the pillow of goats' hair at
the head thereof. And Saul said unto Michal: Why hast thou deceived me, and sent mine enemy away so that he has escaped? And
Michal answered Saul: He said unto me: Let me go. Why should I
kill thee?

(Now David fled and escaped and came to Samuel to Ramah and
told him all that Saul had done to him. And he and Samuel went and
dwelt in Naioth. And it was told Saul: Behold, David is at Naioth in
Ramah. And Saul sent messengers to take David; and when they saw
the company of the prophets prophesying, and Samuel standing as chief
of them, the spirit of God came upon the messengers of Saul, and they
also prophesied. And when this was told Saul, he sent other messengers,
and they also prophesied. And Saul sent messangers again the third
time, and they also prophesied. Then went he also to Ramah, and came
to the great cistern that is in Secu; and he asked and said: Where are
Samuel and David? And one said: Behold, they are at Naioth in
Ramah. And he went thither to Naioth in Ramah; and the spirit of
God came upon him also, and he went on and prophesied, until he came
to Naioth in Ramah. And he stripped off his clothes, and he also
prophesied before Samuel, and lay down naked all that night. Where-
for they say: Is Saul also among the prophets?)[1]

Then came David to Nob to Ahimelech the priest; and Ahimelech
came to meet David trembling, and said unto him: Why art thou alone
and no man with thee? And David said unto the priest Ahimelech:

---

[1] A Deuteronomist has interpolated here (vv, 18-24) a variant of the legend given
by J as a result of the anointing of Saul (ch. x, 9-13). The repetition of this and other
events in the lives of their heroes in different settings, speaks strongly for their popularity.
Each version shows an attempt to find a new reason for the widely quoted saying. Sometimes it has even reached the ears of aliens who understand the allusion at a word.

The king hath commanded me a business, and hath said unto me: Let no man know anything of the business whereabout I send thee, and what I have commanded thee; and the young men have I appointed to such and such a place. Now therefore, what is under thy hand? five loaves of bread? give them into my hand, or what there is at hand. And the priest answered David, and said: There is no common bread here under my hand, but there is hallowed bread,—if the young men have kept themselves from women. And David answered the priest, and said unto him: Of a truth, women have been kept from us about these three days, since I came out; and the vessels of the young men are holy, and it [the bread] is in a manner common, yea, though it were this day sanctified in the vessel. So the priest gave him hallowed bread; for there was no bread there but the showbread, that was taken from before Yahweh, to put in hot bread the day when it was taken away.

Now a certain man of the servants of Saul was there that day, detained before Yahweh; and his name was Doeg the Edomite, the chief of the herdsmen that belonged to Saul. And David said unto Ahimelech: And is there here peradventure under thy hand spear or sword? for I have neither brought my sword nor my weapons with me, because the king's business required haste. And the priest said: The sword of Goliath the Philistine, whom thou slewest in the vale of Elah, behold it is here wrapped in a cloth behind the ephod; if thou wilt take that, take it; for there is no other save that here. And David said: There is none like that; give it me.

And David arose and fled that day for fear of Saul, and went to Achish, king of Gath. And the servants of Achish said unto him: Is not this David, the king of the land? Did not they sing of him one to another in the dances, saying:

Saul hath slain his thousands, and David his ten thousands!

And David laid up these words in his heart, and was sore afraid of Achish, king of Gath. And he changed his demeanor before them, and feigned himself mad in their hands, and scrabbled on the doors of the gate, and let his spittle fall down upon his beard. Then said Achish to his servants: Lo, when ye see a man is mad, wherefore do ye bring him unto me? Do I lack madmen, that ye have brought this fellow to play the madman in my presence? Shall this fellow come into my house?

David therefore departed thence, and escaped to the cave of Adullam; and when his brethren and all his father's house heard it, they went down thither unto him. And every one that was in distress, and every one that was in debt, and every one that was discontented, gathered themselves unto him; and he became captain over them; and there were with him about four hundred men.

And David went thence to Mizpeh of Moab; and he said unto the king of Moab: Let my father and my mother, I pray thee, come forth and be with you, till I know what God will do for me. And he brought them before the king of Moab; and they dwelt with him all the while that David was in the stronghold. And the prophet Gad said unto David: Abide not in the stronghold; depart, and get thee into the land of Judah. Then David departed, and came into the forest of Hereth. And Saul heard that David was discovered and the men that were with him. Now Saul was sitting under the holy tree in Ramah with his spear in his hand, and all his servants were standing about him. And Saul said unto his servants that stood about him: Hear now, ye Benjamites: will the son of Jesse give every one of you fields and vineyards? will he make you all captains of thousands and captains of hundreds, that all of you have conspired against me, and there was none that disclosed it to me, when my son made a league with the son of Jesse? and there is none that is sorry for me, or discloseth unto me that my son hath stirred up my servant against me, to lie in wait as at this day? Then answered Doeg the Edomite who was set over the servants of Saul; and he said: I saw the son of Jesse coming to Nob, to Ahimelech the son of Ahitub. And he inquired of Yahweh for him, and gave him victuals, and gave him the sword of Goliath the Philistine.

Then the king sent to call Ahimelech the priest, the son of Ahitub, and all his father's house, the priests that were in Nob [1]; and they came all of them to the king. And Saul said: Hear now, thou son of Ahitub. And he answered: Here I am, my lord. And Saul said unto him: Why have ye conspired against me, thou and the son of Jesse, in that thou hast given him bread and a sword, and hast inquired of God for him, that he should rise against me to lie in wait as at this day? Then Ahimelech answered the king, and said: And who among all thy servants is so trusted as David, who is the king's son-in-law, and giveth heed unto thy bidding and is honorable in thy house? Have I begun to-day to inquire for him? Be it far from me; let not the king impute anything unto his servant, nor to all the house of my father; for thy servant knoweth nothing of all this, less or more. And the king said: Thou shalt surely die, Ahimelech, thou and all thy father's house.

Then the king said unto the guard that stood about him: Turn and slay the priests of Yahweh; because their hand is also with David, and because they knew that he fled and did not disclose it unto me. But the servants of the king would not put forth their hand to fall upon the priests of Yahweh. And the king said unto Doeg: Turn thou, and fall upon the priests. And Doeg the Edomite turned, and he fell upon the priests, and he slew on that day fourscore and five persons that did wear a linen ephod. And Nob [Gibeon], the city of the priests, smote he with the edge of the sword, both men and women, children and sucklings, and oxen and asses and sheep, with the edge of the sword. And one of the sons of Ahimelech, the son of Ahitub, named Abiathar, escaped and fled after David. And Abiathar told David that Saul had slain Yahweh's priests. And David said: I knew on that day when Doeg the Edomite was there, that he would surely tell Saul; I have brought about the death of all the persons of thy father's house. Abide thou with me; fear not; for he that seeketh my life seeketh thy life; so with me thou shalt be in safeguard.

And they told David, saying: Behold, the Philistines are fighting against Keilah, and they rob the threshing-floors. Therefore David inquired of Yahweh, saying: Shall I go up and smite these Philistines? And Yahweh said unto David: Go and smite the Philistines, and save Keilah. And David's men said unto him: Behold we are afraid here in Judah; how much more then if we go to Keilah against the armies of the Philistines. Then David inquired of Yahweh once again. And Yahweh answered him and said: Arise, go down to Keilah, for I will deliver the Philistines into thy hand. And David and his men went to Keilah, and fought with the Philistines and brought away their cattle and slew them with a great slaughter. So David saved the inhabitants of Keilah.

----

[1] The word translated *Nob* is a corrupt form of *Gibeon*, a city already well known from the covenant made with Joshua by fraud by its inhabitants, who thus escaped the fate of Jericho and Ai. It was the seat of an ancient Canaanitish sanctuary, whose priests had accepted the worship of Yahweh. That they were Canaanites, may have been the plea by which Saul justified himself for the wholesale massacre he commanded.

And it came to pass, when Abiathar the son of Ahimelech fled to David to Keilah that he brought an ephod in his hand. And it was told Saul that David was come to Keilah. And Saul said: God hath delivered him into my hand; for he is shut in, by entering into a town that hath gates and bars. And Saul summoned all the people to war, to go down to Keilah and besiege David and his men. And David knew that Saul was devising evil against him; and he said to Abiathar the priest: Bring hither thine ephod. Then said David: O Yahweh, God of Israel, Thy servant hath surely heard that Saul seeketh to come to Keilah, to destroy the city on my account. Will the men of Keilah deliver me up into his hand? Will Saul come down as Thy servant hath heard? O Yahweh, the God of Israel, I beseech thee, tell thy servant. And Yahweh said: They will come down. Then said David: Will the men of Keilah deiver me up? And Yahweh said: They will deliver thee up. Then David and his men, who were about six hundred, arose and departed, and went whithersoever they could go. And it was told Saul that David was escaped from Keilah, and he forbare to go forth.

Then the Ziphites came unto Saul at Gibeah, saying: Doth not David hide himself in the hill of Hachilah, which is before Jeshimon? Then Saul arose and went down to the wilderness of Ziph, having three thousand chosen men of Israel with him, to seek David in the wilderness of Ziph. And Saul pitched in the hill of Hachilah, which is before Jeshimon, by the roadside. But David abode in the wilderness; and he saw that Saul had come after him into the wilderness. David therefore sent out spies, and understood that Saul was certainly come. And David arose and came to the place where Saul had pitched; and David beheld the place where Saul lay, and Abner, the son of Ner, the captain of the host, and Saul lay within the barricade, and the people pitched round about him.

Then said David to Ahimelech the Hittite, and to Abishai the son of Zeruiah, brother to Joab, saying: Who will go down with me to Saul in the camp? And Abishai said: I will go down with thee. So David and Abishai came to the people by night; and behold, Saul lay sleeping within the barricade, with his spear stuck in the ground at his head; and Abner and the people lay round about him. Then said Abishai to David: God hath delivered up thine enemy into thy hand this day; now therefore, let me smite him, I pray thee, with the spear to the earth at one stroke, and I will not smite him the second time. And David said to Abishai: Destroy him not; for who can put forth his hand against Yahweh's anointed, and be guiltless? And David said: As Yahweh liveth, nay; but Yahweh shall smite him, or his day shall come to die; or he shall go down into battle, and be swept away. Yahweh forbid it me, that I should put forth my hand against Yahweh's anointed. But now, take, I pray thee, the spear that is at his head, and the cruse of water, and let us go. So David took the spear and the cruse of water from Saul's head; and they gat them away and no man saw it or knew it, neither did any awake, for they were all asleep; because a deep sleep from Yahweh was fallen upon them.

Then David went over to the other side of the mountain, and stood on the top afar off; a great space being between them. And David cried to the people and to Abner the son of Ner, saying: Answerest thou not, Abner? Then Abner answered and said: Who art thou that criest to the king? And David said unto Abner: Art not thou a valiant man? and who is like unto thee in Israel? Wherefore then, hast thou not kept watch over thy lord the king? for there came one of the people in to destroy the king, thy lord. This thing is not good that thou hast done. As Yahweh liveth, ye deserve to die, because ye have not kept watch over your lord, Yahweh's anointed. And now, see where the king's spear is, and the cruse of water that was at the king's head.

And Saul knew David's voice, and said: Is this thy voice, my son David? And David said: It is my voice, O my lord the king. And he said, Wherefore doth my lord pursue his servant? for what have I done? or what evil is in my hand? Now therefore, I pray thee, let my lord the king listen to the words of his servant. If it be Yahweh that hath stirred thee up against me, let him accept an offering; but if the children of men, cursed be they before Yahweh; for they have driven me out this day from abiding in the inheritance of Yahweh, saying: Go, serve other gods. Now, therefore, let not my blood fall to the earth before the face of Yahweh; for the king of Israel is come out to seek a flea, or as when one doth hunt a partridge in the mountains.

Then said Saul: I have sinned; return, my son David, for I will no more do thee harm, because my life was precious in thine eyes this day. Behold, I have played the fool, and have erred exceedingly.

And David answered and said: Behold, the king's spear, and let one of the young men come over and fetch it. May Yahweh render to every man according to his righteousness and fidelity; for Yahweh delivered thee into my hand this day, but I would not stretch forth my hand against Yahweh's anointed. And behold, as thy life was much set by this day in mine eyes, so let my life be much set by in the eyes of Yahweh, and may He deliver me out of all tribulation.

Then said Saul unto David: Blessed be thou, my son David; thou shalt both do great things, and shalt also surely prevail.

So David went his way, and Saul returned to his place.

SECTION III.—The Philistines advance in great force to Shunem. Saul is terrified. Yahweh does not answer his appeals, and Samuel is dead. Saul seeks a prophecy of good fortune from the sorceress of Endor. The battle is joined on mount Gilboa. Three of Saul's sons are killed; and, having lost the battle, Saul falls upon his sword. David receives these tidings at Ziklag. He goes to Hebron, where he is anointed King of Judah. Abner, Saul's captain, raises the standard of Ishbosheth, Saul's remaining son, as King of Ephraim and Benjamin. Joab is made captain of David's forces. Abner, alienated by Ishbosheth, comes to the support of David. Is killed by Joab. Ishbosheth is slain by two of his own captains. The northern tribes seek alliance with Judah. David is anointed king of the twelve tribes. With their aid, David takes the stronghold of the Jebusites, and rules thenceforth from Jerusalem. (1 Sam'l., xxvii, 4-16, 19b-25; 2 Sam'l., i, 1-16, 17-27; iii, 1-29, 30-39; iv, 1-2a, 3-12; v, 1-3, 6-12.)

Materials: Popular traditions; "Chronicles of King David"; "Acts of Gad"; "Wars of Yahweh"; Priestly Records; State Records.

The Philistines gathered themselves together and came and pitched in Shunem; and Saul gathered all Israel[1] together, and they pitched in Gilboa. And when Saul saw the host of the Philistines, he was afraid,

---

[1] "All Israel" must here be interpreted, *all of the southern tribes,* who had fought with Saul against the Philistines before.

and his heart trembled greatly. Now Saul had put away those that divined by a ghost or by a familiar spirit out of the land. But, when Saul inquired of Yahweh, Yahweh answered him not, neither by dreams, nor by Urim nor by prophets. Then Saul said unto his servants: Seek me a woman that divineth by a ghost, that I may go and inquire of her. And his servants said: Behold, there is a woman that divineth by a ghost at Endor. And Saul disguised himself, and put on other raiment, and went, he and two men with him, and they came to the woman by night; and he said: Divine unto me, I pray, thee, by a ghost, and bring me up whomsoever I shall name unto thee. And the woman said unto him: Behold, thou knowest what Saul hath done; how he hath cut off those that divine by a ghost or by a familiar spirit out of the land; wherefore then layest thou a snare for my life, to cause me to die? And Saul sware to her by Yahweh, saying: As Yahweh liveth, there shall no punishment happen to thee for this thing. Then said the woman: Whom shall I bring up unto thee? And he said: Bring me up Samuel. And when the woman saw Samuel, she cried with a loud voice; and the woman spake to Saul, saying: Why hast thou deceived me? for thou art Saul. And the king said unto her: Be not afraid; what seest thou? And the woman said unto Saul: I see a godlike being coming up out of the earth. And he said unto her: What form is he of? And she said: An old man cometh up; and he is covered with a robe. And Saul perceived that it was Samuel; and he bowed with his face to the ground, and prostrated himself.

And Samuel said to Saul: Why hast thou disquieted me, to bring me up? And Saul answered: I am sore distressed; for the Philistines make war against me, and God is departed from me and answereth me no more, neither by prophets, nor by dreams; therefore have I called thee, that thou mayest make known unto me what I shall do.

Then said Samuel: Wherefore then dost thou ask of me, seeing Yahweh is departed from thee, and is become thine adversary? To-morrow shalt thou and thy sons be with me; Yahweh will deliver the host of Israel, also, into the hand of the Philistines.

Then Saul fell straightway his full length upon the earth, and was sore afraid, because of the words of Samuel; and there was no strength in him, for he had eaten no bread all the day nor all the night. And the woman came unto Saul and saw that he was sore affrighted, and said to him: Behold, thy handmaid hath hearkened unto thy voice, and I have put my life in thy hand, and have hearkened unto thy words which thou spakest unto me. Now therefore, hearken thou also, I pray thee, unto the voice of thy handmaid, and let me set a morsel of bread before thee; and eat, that thou mayest have strength when thou goest on thy way. But he refused, and said: I will not eat. But his servants together with the woman urged him, and he hearkened unto their voice. So he rose from the earth, and sat upon the bed. And the woman had a fatted calf in the house; and she made haste and killed it; and she took flour and kneaded it, and did make unleavened bread thereof; and she brought it before Saul and before his servants; and they did eat. Then they rose up, and went away that night.

Then the Philistines fought against Israel, and the men of Israel fled from before the Philistines, and fell down slain in Mount Gilboa. And the Philistines followed hard upon Saul and upon his sons; and the Philistines slew Jonathan and Abinadab and Malchishua, the sons of Saul. And the battle went sore against Saul, and the archers over-took him; and he was in great anguish by reason of the archers. Then said Saul to his armor-bearer: Draw thy sword, and thrust me through therewith, lest these uncircumcised ones come and thrust me through and make a mock of me. But his armor-bearer would not, for he was sore afraid. Therefore Saul took his sword and fell upon it. And when his armor-bearer saw that Saul was dead, he likewise fell upon his sword, and died with him. So Saul died, and his three sons, and his armor-bearer and all his men that day together. And when the men of Israel that were on the other side of the valley, and they that were beyond the Jordan, saw that the men of Israel fled, and that Saul and his sons were dead, they forsook the cities and fled; and the Philistines came and dwelt in them.

And it came to pass on the morrow, when the Philistines came to strip the slain, they found Saul and his three sons fallen in Mount Gilboa. And they cut off his head and stripped off his armor, and sent into the land of the Philistines round about to carry the tidings unto the house of their idols and to the people. And they put his armor in the house of the Ashtaroth, and they fastened his body to the wall of Beth-shean.

Now when the inhabitants of Jabesh-Gilead heard concerning him that which the Philistines had done to Saul, all the valiant men arose and went all night, and took the body of Saul and the bodies of his sons from the wall of Beth-shean; and they took their bones and buried them under the holy tree in Jabesh; and they fasted seven days.

After the death of Saul, when David had returned from the slaughter of the Amalekites and had abode two days in Ziklag, it came to pass that behold, a man came out of the camp of Saul with his clothes rent and earth upon his head; and so it was, when he came to David, that he fell to the earth and prostrated himself. And David said unto him: Whence comest thou? And he said unto him: Out of the camp of Israel am I escaped. And David said unto him: How went the matter? I pray thee, tell me. And he answered: The people are fled from the battle, and also many of the people are fallen and dead; and Saul and Jonathan his son are dead also. And David said unto the young man that was telling him: How knowest thou that Saul and Jonathan his son are dead? And the young man that told him said: As I happened by chance upon Mount Gilboa, behold, Saul leaned upon his spear; and lo, the chariots and the horsemen pressed hard upon him. And when he looked behind him, he saw me, and called unto me. And I answered: Here am I. And he said unto me: Who art thou? And I answered him: I am an Amalekite. And he said unto me: Stand, I pray thee, beside me and slay me, for the agony hath taken hold of me, because my life is yet whole in me. So I stood beside him and slew him, because I was sure that he could not live after he was fallen. And I took the crown that was upon his head and the bracelet that was on his arm, and I have brought them hither unto my lord.

Then David took hold on his clothes and rent them; and likewise did all the men who were with him, and they mourned and wept, and fasted until even for Saul and for Jonathan his son, and for the people of Yahweh and for the house of Israel, because they were fallen by the sword.

And David said unto the young man who told him: Whence art

thou? And he answered: I am the son of a stranger, an Amalekite. And David said unto him: How wast thou not afraid to put forth thy hand to destroy Yahweh's anointed? And David called one of the young men, and said: Go near, and fall upon him. And he smote him that he died. And David said unto him: Thy blood be upon thy head; for thy mouth hath testified against thee, saying: I have slain Yahweh's anointed.

And David lamented with this lamentation over Saul and over Jonathan his son. (Also, he bade them teach the children of Judah "The Bow"; behold, it is written in the "Book of Jashar"):[1]

Tell it not in Gath, Publish it not in the streets of Ashkelon,
    Lest the daughters of the Philistines rejoice,
    Lest the daughters of the uncircumcised triumph.

Ye mountains of Gilboa, let there be no dew nor rain upon you,
    Neither fields of choice fruits;
For there the shield of the mighty was vilely cast away,
The shield of Saul, as though he had not been anointed with oil!

From the blood of the slain, from the fat of the mighty,
    The bow of Jonathan turned not back,
    And the sword of Saul returned not empty,—
Saul and Jonathan, the lovely and pleasant in their lives,
    And in their death they were not divided.
They were swifter than eagles, they were stronger than lions.

Ye daughters of Israel, weep over Saul, who clothed you in scarlet,
Who put ornaments of gold upon your apparel, with other delights.
    How are the mighty fallen in the midst of the battle?
    Jonathan is slain upon the high places!

I am distressed for thee, my brother Jonathan.
    Very pleasant hast thou been to me!
    Thy love to me was wonderful,
    Passing the love of women.
    How are the mighty fallen
    And the weapons of war perished!

And it came to pass after this, that David inquired of Yahweh, saying: Shall I go up into any of the cities of Judah? And Yahweh said unto him: Go up. And David said: Whither shall I go? And He said: Unto Hebron. So David went up thither and his two wives also, Ahinoam the Jezreelitess, and Abigail, the wife of Nabal the Carmelite; and his men that were with him did David bring up, every man with his household; and they dwelt in the cities of Hebron. And the men of Judah came, and they there anointed David king over the house of Judah.

And they told David, saying: The men of Jabesh-Gilead were they that buried Saul. And David sent messengers unto the men of Jabesh-Gilead, and said unto them. Blessed be ye of Yahweh, that ye have shown this kindness unto your lord, even unto Saul, and have buried him. And now, may Yahweh show kindness and truth unto you; and I also will requite you this kindness, because ye have done this thing. Now, therefore, let your hands be strong, and be ye valiant; for Saul your lord is dead, and also, the house of Judah have anointed me king over them.

    [1] Although it is now held that this beautiful elegy is one of the latest insertions in 2 Sam'l, it is preserved here, because it is so apposite to the preceding account, and could not be severed from it without loss. It was of course known to J, but all the poems in this book were inserted late.

Now Abner the son of Ner, captain of Saul's host, had taken Ish-bosheth the son of Saul, and brought him over to Mahanaim; and he made him king over Gilead and over the Ashurites, and over Jezreel, and over Benjamin, and over all Israel. And Ishbosheth reigned two years. But the house of Judah followed David.

And Abner the son of Ner, and the servants of Ishbosheth the son of Saul, went out from Mahanaim to Gibeon. And Joab the son of Zeruiah and the servants of David went out, and they met together by the pool of Gibeon, and sat down, the one on the one side of the pool, and the other on the other side of the pool. And Abner said to Joab: Let the young men, I pray thee, arise and play before us. And Joab said: Let them arise. Then there arose and went over by number twelve of Benjamin and for Ishbosheth, the son of Saul, and twelve of the servants of David. And they caught each one his fellow by the head, and thrust his sword in his fellow's side; so they fell down together; wherefore that place was called Helkath-hazzurim (*the field of the sharp knives*) which is in Gibeon. And the battle was very sore that day, and Abner was beaten and the men of Israel before the servants of David.

Now the three sons of Zeruiah were there: Joab and Abishai and Asahel; and Asahel was as light of foot as one of the roes that are in the wilds. And Asahel pursued Abner; and in going he turned not to the right hand nor to the left in following Abner. Then Abner looked behind him, and said: Is it thou, Asahel? And he answered: It is I. And Abner said unto him: Turn thee aside to the right hand or to the left and lay hold on one of the young men, and take his armor. But Asahel would not turn aside from following him. And Abner said to Asahel: Turn thee aside from following me; wherefore should I smite thee to the ground? How then could I hold up my face to Joab, thy brother? Howbeit he refused to turn aside; wherefore Abner with the hinder end of his spear smote him in the groin, that the spear came out behind him; and he fell down there and died in that same place; and it came to pass, that as many as came to the place where Asahel fell down and died stood still.

But Joab and Abishai pursued after Abner; and the sun went down when they were come to the hill of Ammah, that lieth before Giah by the way of the wilderness of Gibeon. And the children of Benjamin gathered themselves together after Abner and became one band, and stood on the top of a hill. Then Abner called to Joab and said: Shall the sword devour for ever? Knowest thou not that it will be bitter-ness in the end? how long shall it be then, ere thou bid the people return from following their brethren? And Joab said: As God liveth, if thou hadst not spoken, surely then only after the morning had the people gone up from following every one his brother. And Joab blew the horn, and all the people stood still and pursued after Israel no more. And Abner and his men went all that night through the Arabah; and they passed over the Jordan, and went through all Bithron, and came to Mahanaim.

And Joab returned from following after Abner, and when he had gathered all the people together, there lacked of David's servants nine-teen men and Asahel. But the servants of David had smitten of Ben-jamin, even of Abner's men, three hundred and threescore men. And they took up Asahel, and buried him in the sepulchre of his father, which was in Beth-lehem. And Joab and his men went all night, and the day broke upon them in Hebron.

Now there was long war between the house of Saul and the house of David; and David waxed stronger and stronger, but the house of Saul, weaker and weaker. And unto David were sons born in Hebron; and his firstborn was Ammon, of Ahinoam the Jezreelitess; and his second, Chileab, of Abigail the wife of Nabal the Carmelite; and the third, Absalom the son of Maachah the daughter of Talmai, king of Geshur; and the fourth, Adonijah the son of Haggith; and the fifth, Shephatiah, the son of Abitai; and the sixth, Ithream, of Eglah David's wife.

And it came to pass, while there was war between the house of Saul and the house of David, that Abner showed himself strong in the house of Saul. Now Saul had a concubine whose name was Rizpah, the daughter of Aiah; and Ishbosheth said to Abner: Wherefore hast thou gone in unto my Father's concubine? Then was Abner very wroth for the words of Ishbosheth, and said: Am I a dog's head that belongeth to Judah? this day do I show kindness unto the house of Saul thy father, to his brethren, to his friends, and have not delivered thee into the hand of David, and yet thou chargest me this day with a fault concerning this woman. God do so to Abner, and more also, if, as Yahweh hath sworn unto David, I do not even so to him; to transfer the kingdom from the house of Saul, and to set up the throne of David over Israel and over Judah, from Dan even to Beersheba. And he could answer Abner not another word, because he feared him.

And Abner sent messengers to David straightway, saying: Whose is the land? saying also: Make thy league with me, and behold, my hand shall be with thee, to bring over all Israel unto thee. And he said: Well, I will make a league with thee; but one thing I require of thee, that is, thou shalt not see my face, except thou first bring Michal, Saul's daughter when thou comest to see my face. And David sent messengers to Ishbosheth, Saul's son, saying: Deliver me my wife Michal, whom I betrothed unto me for a hundred foreskins of the Philistines. And Ishbosheth sent and took her from her husband, Paltiel the son of Laish. And her husband went with her, weeping as he went, and followed her to Bahurim. Then said Abner to him: Go, return; and he returned.

And Abner had communication with the elders of Israel, saying: In times past ye sought for David to be king over you; now then do it; for Yahweh hath spoken of David, saying: By the hand of my servant David will I save My people Israel out of the hand of the Philistines, and out of the hand of all their enemies. And Abner spake also in the ears of Benjamin; and Abner went also to speak in the ears of David in Hebron all that seemed good to Israel, and to the whole house of Benjamin. So Abner came to David to Hebron, and twenty men with him. And David made Abner and the men who were with him a feast. And Abner said unto David: I will arise and go, and will gather all Israel unto my lord the king, that they may make a covenant with thee, and that thou mayest reign over all that thy soul desireth. And David sent Abner away; and he went in peace.

Now behold, the servants of David and Joab came from a foray, and brought in a great spoil with them; but Abner was not with David in Hebron, for he had sent him away, and he was gone in peace. When Joab and all the host that was with him were come, they told Joab, saying: Abner the son of Ner came to the king, and he hath sent him away; and he hath gone in peace. Then Joab came to the king and said: What hast thou done? Behold, Abner came unto thee;

why is it that thou hast sent him away, and he is quite gone? Thou knowest Abner the son of Ner, that he came to deceive thee, and to know thy going out and thy coming in, and all that thou doest. And when Joab was come out from David, he sent messengers after Abner, and they brought him back from Bor-sirah; but David knew it not.

And when Abner was returned to Hebron, Joab took him aside into the midst of the gate to speak with him quietly; and he smote him there in the groin so that he died, for the blood of Asahel his brother. And afterward, when David heard it, he said: I and my kingdom are guiltless before Yahweh for ever from the blood of Abner son of Ner. Let it fall upon the head of Joab and of all his father's house; and let there not fail from the house of Joab one that hath an issue, or that is a leper, or that leaneth on a staff, or that falleth by the sword, or that lacketh bread. And David said to Joab and to all the people that were with him: Rend your clothes, and gird you with sackcloth, and wail before Abner. And King David followed the bier. And they buried Abner in Hebron; and the king lifted up his voice and wept at the grave of Abner; and all the people wept. And the king lamented for Abner, and said: Should Abner die as a churl dieth? And all the people wept again over him. And all the people came to cause David to eat bread while it was yet day; but David sware, saying: God do so to me and more also, if I taste bread or aught else till the sun be down. And all the people took notice of it, and it pleased them. Whatsoever the king did pleased all the people. So all the people and all Israel understood that day, that it was not of the king to slay Abner the son of Ner. And the king said unto his servants: Know ye not that there is a prince and a great man fallen in Israel to-day? And I am this day weak, and just anointed king; and these men, the sons of Zeruiah, are too hard for me. May Yahweh reward the evil-doer according to his wickedness.

Now when Saul's son heard that Abner was dead in Hebron, his hands became feeble, and all the Israelites were affrighted. And Saul's son had two men who were captains of bands; the name of the one was Baanah, and the name of the other, Rechab, sons of Rimmon the Beerothite.

Now Jonathan, Saul's son, had a son that was lame on his feet. He was five years old when the tidings came of Saul and Jonathan out of Jezreel; and his nurse took him up and fled. And it came to pass, as she made haste to flee, that he fell and became lame. And his name was Mephibosheth.

And the sons of Rimmon the Beerothite, Rechab and Baanah, went, and came about the heat of the day to the house of Ishbosheth, as he took his rest at noon. And they came into the midst of the house, as though they would have fetched wheat; and they smote him in the groin; and Rechab and Baanah his brother escaped. Now when they came into his house, as he lay on his bed in the bedchamber, they smote him and slew him and beheaded him, and took his head and went by the way of the Arabah all night. And they brought his head unto David to Hebron, and said unto the king. Behold the head of Ishbosheth, the son of Saul thine enemy who sought thy life; and Yahweh hath avenged my lord the king this day of Saul and of his seed.

And David answered Rechab and Baanah his brother, the sons of Rimmon the Beerothite, and said unto them: As Yahweh liveth, who hath redeemed my soul out of all adversity, when one told me, saying: Behold, Saul is dead, and he was in his own eyes as one who brought good tidings, I took hold of him and slew him in Ziklag, instead of giving him a reward for his tidings. How much more, when wicked men have slain a righteous person in his own house upon his bed. Shall I not now require his blood of your hand, and take you away from the earth? And David commanded his young men, and they slew them and cut off their hands and their feet, and hanged them up over the pool in Hebron. But they took the head of Ishbosheth and buried it in the grave of Abner in Hebron.

Then came all the tribes of Israel to David in Hebron, and spake, saying: Behold, we are thy bone and thy flesh. In times past, when Saul was king over us, it was thou that didst lead out and bring in Israel; and Yahweh said unto thee: Thou shalt feed My people Israel, and thou shalt be prince over Israel. So all the elders of Israel came to the king in Hebron before cahweh, and they anointed David King over Israel.

And the king and his men went to Jerusalem against the Jebusites, the inhabitants of the land, who spake unto David, saying: Except thou take away the blind and the lame, thou shalt not come in hither. Thinking: David cannot come in hither. Nevertheless, David took the stronghold of Zion—the same is the city of David. And David said on that day: Whosoever smiteth the Jebusites, and getteth up to the gutter, and . . . the blind and the lame, hated of David's soul, . . . Wherefore they say: There are the blind and the lame; he cannot come into the house.[1] And David dwelt in the stronghold, and called it, The City of David. And David built round about from Millo and inward. And David waxed greater and greater; for Yahweh, the God of Hosts, was with him.

And Hiram, king of Tyre, sent messengers to David, and cedar-trees, and carpenters and masons; and they built David a house. And David perceived that Yahweh had established him KING OVER ISRAEL; and that He had exalted his kingdom for His people Israel's sake.

[1] The text is here defective, and there are no means of knowing how David took a city that has resisted so many assaults. There is a hint only of his having escaladed the walls, and opened the gates from within. The LXX uses the defective passage only as the occasion of a by-word.

CHAPTER V

THE REIGN OF DAVID
WARRIOR-KING AND ORGANIZER OF THE UNITED KINGDOM

SECTION. I.—David establishes himself in Jerusalem. Surprises the Philistines in two attempts against him and defeats them. Brings up the Ark of God to Jerusalem, and dances before it. Subdues the Philistines in a third battle, subjects Moab and the king of Zobah, puts garrisons in Damascus and Aram and Edom. Regulates the internal affairs of the kingdom and forms a Cabinet. Fulfils his promise to Jonathan to care for his children. His nephew, Joab, achieves great distinction as general of David's forces. David's intrigue with Uriah's wife. Nathan's rebuke, and David's repentance. The birth of Solomon. (2 Samuel, iv, 4a, 5; v, 13, 17-35; vi, 1-23; viii-xi, 20, 21b-27; xii, 1-7a, b, 9b-25.)

Materials: Folk-tales; "Chronicles of King David"; "Chronicles of the Kings of Judah"; "Acts of Nathan"; "Acts of Gad"; State Records.

(David was thirty years old when he began to reign. In Hebron he reigned over Judah seven years and six months; and in Jerusalem he reigned thirty and three years over all Israel and Judah.[1]) And David took him more concubines and wives out of Jerusalem, when he was come from Hebron; and there were yet more sons and daughters born to David.

Now when the Philistines heard that David was anointed king over Israel, all the Philistines went up to seek David; and David heard of it and went down to the hold. And the Philistines had come and spread themselves in the valley of Rephaim. And David inquired of Yahweh: Shall I go up against the Philistines? Wilt Thou deliver them into my hand? And Yahweh said unto David: Go up; for I will certainly deliver the Philistines into thy hand. And David came to Baal-perazim, and smote them there; and he said: Yahweh hath broken mine enemies before me, like the breach of waters. Therefore the name of that place was called Baal-perazim (*Master of breaches*). And they left their images there, and David and his men burned them.

And the Philistines came up yet again, and spread themselves in the valley of Rephaim. And when David inquired of Yahweh, He said: Thou shalt not go up; make a circuit behind them, and come upon them over against the mulberry trees. And it shall be when thou hearest the sound of rustling in the tops of the mulberry trees, that thou shalt bestir thyself; for then is Yahweh gone out before thee to smite the host of the Philistines. And David did so, as Yahweh commanded him, and he smote the Philistines from Geba until thou comest to Gerar.

And David again gathered together all the chosen men of Israel,

[1] These statistics bear the mark of late editing; but they are a needed link between the old and the new conditions of David's kingship.

thirty thousand. And David arose and went with all the men who were with him from Baale-judah to bring up from thence the ark of God, whose name is called by the name of Yahweh Sabaoth (that dwelleth between the cherubim). And they set the ark of God upon a new cart, and brought it out of the house of Abinadab that was in Gibeah; and Uzzah and Ahio, the sons of Abinadab drove the new cart. And they brought it out of the house of Abinadab, which was in Gibeah, with the ark of God; and Ahio went before the ark. And David and all the house of Israel played before Yahweh with all manner of instruments made of cyprus-wood, and with harps and with psalteries, and with timbrels and with sistra and with cymbals.

And when they came to the threshing floor of Nacon, Uzzah put forth his hand to the ark of God, and took hold of it; for the oxen stumbled. And the anger of Yahweh was kindled against Uzzah; and God smote him there for his error; and there he died by the ark of God. And David was displeased, because Yahweh had broken forth upon Uzzah; and that place was called Perez-uzzah to this day. And David was afraid of Yahweh that day; and he said: How shall the ark of God come unto me? So David would not remove the ark of Yahweh unto him into the city of David; but David carried it aside into the house of Obed-edom the Gittite. And the ark of Yahweh remained in the house of Obed-edom the Gittite three months; and Yahweh blessed Obed-edom, and all his house.

And it was told David: Yahweh hath blessed the house of Obed-edom, and all that pertaineth unto him, because of the ark of God. And David went and brought up the ark of God from the house of Obed-edom into the city of David with gladness. And it was so, that when they that bore the ark of Yahweh had gone six paces, he sacrificed an ox and a fatling. And David danced before Yahweh with all his might, and David was girded with a linen ephod. So David and all the house of Israel brought up the ark of Yahweh with shouting and with the sound of the horn.

And it was so, as the ark of Yahweh came into the city of David, that Michal the daughter of Saul looked out of the window, and saw king David leaping and dancing before Yahweh; and she despised him in her heart. And they brought in the ark of Yahweh and set it in its place, in the midst of the tent that David had pitched for it; and David offered burnt-offerings and peace-offerings before Yahweh. And when David had made an end of offering the burnt-offerings and the peace-offerings, he blessed the people in the name of Yahweh Sabaoth. And he dealt among all the people, even among the whole multitude of Israel, both to men and women, to every one a cake of bread and a good piece from the pan and a flagon of wine. So all the people departed every one to his own house.

Then David returned to bless his household. And Michal, Saul's daughter, came out to meet David, and said: How glorious was the king of Israel to-day, who uncovered himself in the eyes of the handmaids of his servants, as one of the base fellows shamelessly uncovers himself! And David said unto Michal: Before Yahweh, who chose me above thy father and above all his house, to appoint me prince over the people of Yahweh, over Israel—before Yahweh will I make merry. And I will be yet more vile than this, and will be base in mine own sight; and with the handmaids thou hast spoken of, with them will I get me honor. And Michal the daughter of Saul had no child to the day of her death.

[1]After this it came to pass that David smote the Philistines and subdued them; and David took Metheg-ammah out of the hand of the Philistines.

And he smote Moab, and measured them out with a line, making them to lie down on the ground; and he measured two lines to be put to death, and one full line to keep alive. And the Moabites became David's servants, and brought gifts. David smote also Hadadezer the son of Rehob, king of Zobah, as he went to establish his dominion at the river Euphrates. And David took from him a thousand and seven hundred horsemen, and twenty thousand footmen; and David houghed all the chariot-horses, but reserved of them for a hundred chariots. And when the Aramæans of Damascus came to succor Hadadezer king of Zobah, David smote of the Aramæans two and twenty thousand men. Then David put garrisons in Aram of Damascus, and the Aramæans became servants to David and brought gifts. And Yahweh gave victory to David whithersoever he went. And David took the shields of gold that were on the servants of Hadadezer, and brought them to Jerusalem. And from Betah and from Berothai, cities of Hadadezer, David took exceeding much brass.[2]

And when Toi, king of Hamath heard that David had smitten all the host of Hadadezer, then Toi sent Joram his son unto king David to salute him and to bless him (because he had fought against Hadadezer and smitten him; for Hadadezer had wars with Toi); and he brought with him vessels of silver and vessels of brass. These also did David dedicate unto Yahweh, with all the silver and gold that he dedicated of all the nations which he subdued; of Aram and of Moab and of the children of Ammon, and of the Philistines, and of Amalek, and of the spoil of Hadadezer, son of Rehob, king of Zobah. And David got him a name when he returned from smiting the Aramæans in the valley of Salt, even eighteen thousand men. And he put garrisons in Edom; throughout all Edom he put garrisons, and all the Edomites became servants [i.e., tributaries] to David. And Yahweh gave victory to David, whithersoever he went.

And David reigned over all Israel, and David executed justice and righteousness unto all his people. And Joab the son of Zeruiah was over the army; and Jehoshaphat the son of Ahilud was Recorder; and Zadok the son of Ahitub, and Ahimelech, the son of Abiathar, were priests; and Seraiah was Scribe; and Benaiah the son of Jehoiada was over the Cherethites and the Pelethites; and David's sons were chief ministers.

And David said: Is there yet any that is left of the house of Saul, that I may show him kindness for Jonathan's sake? Now there was of the house of Saul a servant whose name was Ziba, and they summoned him to David; and the king said unto him: Art thou Ziba? And he said: Thy servant is he. And the king said: Is there not any of the house of Saul, that I may show the kindness of God unto him? And Ziba said unto the king: Jonathan hath yet a son, who is lame on his feet. And the king said: Where is he? And Ziba said unto the king: Behold, he is in the house of Machir the son of Ammiel, in Lodebar.

[1] Ch. vii not only breaks the very homogeneous narrative of the older writer, but has distinctive marks of the hand of a Deuteronomist. Also, it neither accords with the trend of David's mind, as it has been shown, nor has it a fit setting. David is in the very midst of his struggles.

[2] This account of the conflict with the king of Zobah sounds apocryphal, especially as to the numbers killed or taken captive, and the amount of the spoil. The source in this case seems to have been a folk-tale, and not an official record. It will be remembered that David's army is stated to have been thirty thousand men.

Then King David sent and fetched him out of the house of Machir the son of Ammiel, from Lodebar. And Mephibosheth, the son of Jonathan the son of Saul, came unto David, and fell on his face and prostrated himself. And David said: Mephibosheth! And he answered: Behold, thy servant. And David said unto him: Fear not; for I will surely show thee kindness for Jonathan's, thy father's sake, and will restore thee all the land of Saul thy father; and thou shalt eat bread continually at my table. And he bowed down, and said: What is thy servant, that thou shouldst look upon such a dead dog as I am?

Then the king called to Ziba, Saul's servant, and said unto him: Thou shalt till the land for thy master's son, thou and thy sons and thy servants: and thou shalt bring in the fruits, that thy master's son may have bread to eat; but Mephibosheth, thy master's son shall eat bread continually at my table. Now Ziba had fifteen sons and twenty servants. Then said Ziba unto the king: According to all that my lord the king commandeth his servant, so shall thy servant do; but Mephibosheth eateth at my table as one of the king's sons. Now Mephibosheth had a young son, whose name was Mica. And all that dwelt in the house of Ziba were servants unto Mephibosheth. But Mephibosheth dwelt in Jerusalem; for he did eat continually at the king's table; and he was lame on both his feet.

And it came to pass after this that the king of the Ammonites died, and Hanun his son reigned in his stead. And David said: I shall show kindness unto Hanun the son of Nahash, as his father showed unto me. So David sent by the hand of his servants to comfort him concerning his father. And David's servants came into the land of the children of Ammon. But the princes of the children of Ammon said unto Hanun, their lord: Thinkest thou that David doth honor thy father, that he hath sent comforters unto thee? hath not David sent his servants unto thee to search the city, and to spy it out and to overthrow it? So Hanun took David's servants and shaved off the one-half of their beards, and cut off their garments in the middle, even to their buttocks, and sent them away. When it was told unto David, he sent to meet them for the men were greatly ashamed. And the king said: Tarry at Jericho until your beards be grown, and then return.

Now, when the children of Ammon saw that they were become odious to David, they sent and hired the Aramæans of Beth-rehob and the Aramæans of Zobah, twenty thousand footmen, and the king of Maacah with a thousand men, and the men of Tob, twelve thousand men. And when David heard of it, he sent Joab and all the host of his warriors. And the children of Ammon came out and put the battle in array at the entrance of the gate, and the Aramæans of Zobah and of Rehob, and the men of Tob and of Maacah were by themselves in the field. Now when Joab saw that the battle was set against him before and behind, he chose of all the choice men of Israel and put them in array against the Aramæans, and the rest of the people he committed into the hand of Abishai his brother, and he put them in array against the Ammonites. And he said: If the Aramæans be too strong for me, then thou shalt help me; but if the Ammonites be too strong for thee, then I will come and help thee. Be of good courage, and let us prove strong for our people, and for the cities of our God; and Yahweh shall do what seemeth to Him good.

So Joab and the people that were with him drew nigh unto the battle against the Aramæans, and they fled before him. And when the children of Ammon saw that the Aramæans had fled, they likewise fled before Abishai, and entered into the city. Then Joab returned from the children of Ammon, and came to Jerusalem.

Now, when the Aramæans saw that they were put to the worse before Israel, they gathered themselves together. And Hadadezer sent and brought out the Aramæans that were beyond the River, and they came to Helam with Shobach, the captain of the host of Hadadezer at their head. And it was told David, and he gathered all Israel together and passed over the Jordan, and came to Helam. And the Aramæans set themselves in array against David, and fought with him. And the Aramæans fled before Israel; and David slew of the Aramæans seven hundred drivers of chariots, and forty thousand horsemen, and smote Shobach the captain of their host, so that he died there. And when all the kings that were servants to Hadadezer saw that they were put to the worse before Israel, they made peace with Israel and served them. So the Aramæans feared to help the children of Ammon any more.

And it came to pass at the return of the time of the year when kings go out to battle, that David sent Joab and his servants with him and all Israel, and they destroyed the children of Ammon, and besieged Rabbah. But David tarried at Jerusalem. And it came to pass at eventide, that David arose from his bed and walked upon the roof of the king's house; and from the roof he saw a woman bathing; and the woman was very beautiful to look upon. And David went and inquired after the woman. And one said: Is not this Bath-sheba the daughter of Eliam, the wife of Uriah the Hittite? And David sent messengers, and took her; and she came in unto him, and he lay with her, for she was purified from her uncleanness; and she returned unto her house. And the woman conceived; and she sent and told David, and said: I am with child.

Then David sent to Joab, saying: Send me Uriah the Hittite. And Joab sent Uriah to David. And when Uriah was come unto him, David asked of him how Joab did and how the people fared, and how the war prospered. And David said unto Uriah: Go down to thy house, and wash thy feet. And Uriah departed out of the king's house, and there followed him a mess of food from the king. But Uriah slept at the door of the king's house with all the servants of his lord, and went not down to his house. And when they had told David, saying: Uriah went not down to his house, David said unto Uriah: Art thou not come from a journey? Wherefore didst thou not go down unto thy house? And Uriah said unto David: The ark and Israel and Judah abide in booths; and my lord Joab and the servants of my lord are encamped in the open field; shall I then go into my house to eat and to drink and to lie with my wife? As thou livest, and as thy soul draweth breath, I will not do this thing. And David said to Uriah: Tarry here to-day also, and to-morrow I will let thee depart. So Uriah abode in Jerusalem that day and the morrow. And when David had called him, he did eat and drink before him, and he made him drunk; and at even he went out to lie on his bed with the servants of his lord, but went not down to his house.

And it came to pass in the morning, that David wrote a letter to Joab, and sent it by the hand of Uriah. And he wrote in the letter, saying: Set ye Uriah in the forefront of the hottest battle, and retire ye from him, that he may be smitten and die. And it came to pass, when Joab kept watch upon the city, that he assigned Uriah unto the place where he knew that valiant men were. And the men of the city came out and fought with Joab; and there fell some of the people, even of the servants of David; and Uriah the Hittite died also. Then Joab sent and told David all the things concerning the war; and he charged the messenger, saying: When thou hast made an end of telling all the things concerning the war unto the king, it shall be, that if the king's wrath arise, and he say unto thee: Wherefore went ye so nigh unto the city to fight? knew ye not that they would shoot from the wall? why went ye so nigh the wall? then thou shalt say: Thy servant Uriah the Hittite is dead also.

So the messenger went, and came and told David all that Joab had sent him for. And the messenger said unto David: Surely the men prevailed against us and came out to us in the field, but we were upon them even unto the entering of the gate. And the shooters shot from off the wall upon thy servants; and some of the king's servants are dead, and thy servant Uriah the Hittite is dead also. Then said David unto the messenger: Thus shalt thou say unto Joab, Let not this thing displease thee, for the sword devoureth one as well as another; make thy battle more strong against the city, and overthrow it. Thus encourage thou him.

And when the wife of Uriah heard that Uriah her husband was dead, she made lamentation for her husband. But when the mourning was past, David sent and took her home to his house; and she became his wife, and she bare him a son.

But the thing that David had done displeased Yahweh.

And Yahweh sent Nathan unto David. And he came unto him, and said unto him: There were two men in one city; the one rich, and the other poor. The rich man had exceeding many flocks and herds; but the poor man had nothing save one little ewe lamb which he had bought and nourished up; and it grew up together with him and with his children; it did eat of his own meat, and drank of his own cup, and lay in his bosom, and was to him as a daughter. And there came a traveller unto the rich man, and he spared to take of his own flock and of his own herd, to dress for the wayfaring man that was come unto him, but took the poor man's lamb and dressed it for the man that was come to him.

And David's anger was greatly kindled against the man; and he said to Nathan: As Yahweh liveth, the man that hath done this shall surely die; and he shall restore the lamb fourfold, because he did this thing, and because he had no pity.

And Nathan said unto David: Thou art the man. Thus saith Yahweh the God of Israel: [1] Thou hast smitten Uriah the Hittite with the sword, and hast taken his wife to be thy wife, and hast slain him with the sword of the children of Ammon. And David said unto Nathan: I have sinned against Yahweh. And Nathan said unto David: Yahweh also hath put away thy sin; thou shalt not die. Howbeit, because by this deed thou hast given occasion to the enemies of Yahweh to blaspheme, the child that is born unto thee shall surely die. And Nathan returned to his own house.

And Yahweh struck the child that Uriah's wife bare unto David, and it was very sick. David therefore besought God for the child; and David fasted, and went in, and lay all night upon the earth. And the elders of his house arose and stood beside him to raise him up from the earth; but he would not, neither did he eat bread with them. And it

[1] The Deuteronomist has greatly added to Nathan's arraignment of David and to the judgment pronounced against him, to the weakening of the simple and most impressive account of the incident.

came to pass on the seventh day, that the child died. And the servants of David feared to tell him that the child was dead; for they said: Behold, while the child was yet alive, we spake unto him, and he would not hearken unto our voice; how then will he vex himself, if we tell him that the child is dead? But when David saw that his servants whispered, David perceived that the child was dead; therefore David said unto his servants: Is the child dead? And they said: He is dead. Then David arose from the earth and washed and anointed himself, and changed his apparel, and came into the house of Yahweh and worshiped. Then he came to his own house; and when he required, they set bread before him, and he did eat. Then said his servants unto him: What is this that thou hast done? Thou didst fast and weep for the child while it was alive; but when it was dead, thou didst rise and eat bread.

And he said: While the child was yet alive, I fasted and wept; for I said: Who knoweth whether Yahweh will be gracious to me, that the child may live? But now he is dead, wherefore should I fast? Can I bring him back again? I shall go to him, but he will not return to me.

And David comforted Bathsheba his wife, and went in unto her and lay with her; and she bare him a son, and called his name Solomon. And Yahweh loved him; and He sent by the hand of Nathan the prophet, and he called his name Jedidiah (*Beloved of Yahweh*), because of Yahweh.

SECTION II.—David continues to expand Israel's possessions, but he has begun to pay the penalty for breaking the laws of the Covenant meant to preserve the purity of family life. His eldest son, Amnon, dishonors his half-sister, Tamar. Absalom bides his time, but finally avenges her by killing her betrayer. All the king's sons flee from Jerusalem; the others return, but Absalom remains away three years. Joab causes Absalom to be recalled. Absalom wins over the people to his side and revolts against David. David flees before him with a great part of his people. Old adherents of Saul join Absalom. Shimei curses David, as he passes on his way. But Hushai, David's friend, joins Absalom in order to befriend David. By which means David safely crosses the Jordan to Mahanaim, where he prepares his forces to meet Absalom's. Absalom's forces are routed, and Joab kills him. The tidings are brought to David, and he mourns for his best loved son. (Ch. xii, 26ff; xiii-xiv, 24; xiv, 28-xix, 9a.)

Materials: The same as for the preceding section.

Now Joab fought against Rabbah of the Ammonites, and took the royal city. And Joab sent messengers to David, and said: I have fought against Rabbah, yea, I have taken the city of waters. Now therefore, gather the rest of the people together, and encamp against the city, and take it; lest I take the city, and it be called by my name. And David gathered all the people together and went to Rabbah, and fought against it and took it. And he took the crown of Malcam from off his head; and the weight thereof was a talent of gold, and in it were precious stones; and it was set on David's head. And he brought forth the spoil of the city, exceeding much. And he brought forth the people that were therein, and put them under saws, and under harrows of iron, and under axes of iron, and made them pass through the brick-kiln; and thus did he unto all the Ammonites. And David and all the people returned unto Jerusalem.

Now Absalom the son of David had a fair sister whose name was Tamar; and Amnon the son of David loved her. And Amnon was so distressed that he fell sick because of his sister Tamar; for she was a virgin, and it seemed hard to Amnon to do anything unto her. But Amnon had a friend whose name was Jonadab, the son of Shimeah, David's brother; and Jonadab was a very subtle man. And he said unto him: Why, O son of the king, art thou thus becoming leaner from day to day? Wilt thou not tell me? And Amnon said unto him: I love Tamar, Absalom's sister. And Jonadab said unto him: Lay thee down on thy bed and feign thyself sick; and when thy father cometh to see thee, say unto him: Let my sister Tamar come, I pray thee, and give me bread to eat, and dress the food in my sight, that I may see it and eat it at her hand. So Amnon lay down and feigned himself sick; and when the king was come to see him, Amnon said unto the king: Let my sister Tamar come, I pray thee, and make a couple of cakes in my sight, that I might eat at her hand.

Then David sent home to Tamar, saying: Go now to thy brother Amnon's house, and dress him food. So Tamar went to her brother Amnon's house; and he was lying down. And she took dough and kneaded it, and make cakes in his sight, and did bake the cakes. And she took the pan and poured them out before him; but he refused to eat. And Amnon said unto Tamar: Have all men out from me. And they went out every man from him. And Amnon said unto Tamar: Bring the food into the chamber, that I may eat of thy hand. And Tamar took the cakes which she had made, and brought them into the chamber of Amnon her brother. And when she had brought them near unto him to eat, he took hold of her, and said unto her: Come, lie with me, my sister. And she answered him: Nay, my brother, do not force me; for no such thing ought to be done in Israel. Do not this wanton deed. And I, whither shall I carry my shame? And as for thee, thou wilt be as one of the base men in Israel. Now, therefore, speak unto the king; for he will not withhold me from thee. Howbeit, he would not hearken to her voice; but being stronger than she, he forced her and lay with her.

Then Amnon hated her with exceeding great hatred; for the hatred with which he hated her was greater than the love wherewith he had loved her. And Amnon said unto her: Arise, begone. And she said unto him: Not so, because this great wrong in putting me forth is worse than the other that thou didst unto me. But he would not hearken unto her. Then he called his servant that ministered unto him, and said: Put this woman out from me now, and bolt the door after her. And his servant brought her out, and bolted the door after her. And Tamar put ashes on her head, and went her way crying aloud as she went. And Absalom her brother said unto her: Hath Amnon thy brother been with thee? but now hold thy peace, my sister; take not this thing to heart. So Tamar remained desolate in her brother's house.

But when king David heard these things, he was very wroth. And Absalom spake unto Amnon neither good nor bad; for Absalom hated Amnon, because he had forced his sister Tamar. And it came to pass after two full years, that Absalom had sheep-shearers in Baal-hazor which is beside Ephraim; and Absalom invited all the king's sons. And Absalom came to the king and said: Behold now, thy servant hath sheep-shearers; let the king, I pray thee, and his servants go with thy servant. And the king said: Nay, my son, let us not all go, lest we be burdensome to thee. And he pressed him; however he would not go, but blessed him. Then said Absalom: If not, I pray thee, let my brother Amnon go with us. And the king said unto him: Why should he go with thee? And Absalom pressed him, and he let Amnon, and all the king's sons go with him. And Absalom commanded his servants, saying: Mark ye now, when Amnon's heart is merry with wine; and when I say unto you, Smite Amnon! then kill him, fear not; have I not commanded you? be courageous, yea, be valiant. And the servants of Absalom did unto Amnon as Absalom had commanded. Then all the king's sons arose, and every man gat him upon his mule, and fled.

And it came to pass, while they were in the way, that the tidings came to David, saying: Absalom hath slain all the king's sons, and there is not one of them left. Then the king arose and rent his garments, and lay on the earth; and all his servants stood by with their clothes rent. And Jonadab, the son of Shimeah David's brother, answered and said: Let not my lord suppose that they have killed all the young men the king's sons; for Amnon only is dead; for by the appointment of Absalom this hath been determined from the day that he forced his sister Tamar. Now therefore, let not my lord the king take the thing to heart, to think that all the king's sons are dead; for Amnon only is dead.

But Absalom fled. And the young man that kept the watch lifted up his eyes and looked; and behold, there came much people running in a roundabout way by the hillside. And Jonadab said unto the king: Behold, the king's sons are come; as thy servant said, so it is. And it came to pass, as soon as he had made an end of speaking, that behold, the king's sons came, and lifted up their voice and wept; and the king also, and all his servants wept very sore.

Then Absalom fled, and went to Talmai, the son of Ammihud, king of Geshur. And David mourned for his son every day.

So Absalom fled, and went to Geshur, and was there three years. And the soul of David failed with longing for Absalom; for he was comforted for Amnon, seeing he was dead.

Now Joab the son of Zeruiah perceived that the king's heart was toward Absalom. And Joab sent to Tekoa and fetched thence a wise woman, and said unto her: I pray thee, feign thyself to be a mourner, and put on mourning apparel, I pray thee, and anoint not thyself with oil, but be as a woman that had a long time mourned for the dead; and go in unto the king, and speak on this manner to him. So Joab put the words in her mouth.

And when the woman of Tekoa spake to the king, she fell on her face to the ground, and prostrated herself, and said: Help, O King! And the king said unto her: What aileth thee? And she answered: Of a truth I am a widow, my husband being dead. And thy handmaid had two sons, and they two strove together in the field, and there was none to part them, but the one smote the other and killed him. And behold, the whole family is risen against thy handmaid and have said: Deliver him that smote his brother, that we may kill him for the life of his brother whom he slew, and so destroy the heir also. Thus will they quench my coal which is left, and will leave to my husband neither name nor remainder upon the earth.

And the king said unto the woman: Go to thy house, and I will give charge concerning thee. And the woman of Tekoa said unto the king: My lord, O king, the iniquity be on me and on my father's house;·and the king and his throne be guiltless. And the king said: Whosoever saith aught unto thee, bring him unto me, and he shall not touch thee any more. Then said she: I pray thee, let the king remember Yahweh thy God, that the avenger of blood destroy not any more, lest they destroy my son. And he said: As Yahweh liveth, there shall not a hair of thy son fall to the ground.

Then the woman said: Let thy handmaid, I pray thee, speak a word more to the king. And he said: Say on. And the woman said: Wherefore then hast thou devised such a thing against the people of God? for in speaking this word the king is as one who is guilty; in that the king doth not fetch home again his banished son. For we must needs die, and are as water spilt on the ground which cannot be gathered up again; neither doth God respect any person; but let him devise means, that he that is banished be not an outcast from him. Now then, seeing that I am come to speak this word unto my lord the king, it is because the people have made me afraid; and thy handmaid said: I will now speak unto the king; it may be that the king will perform the request of his servant. For the king will hear, to deliver his handmaid from the hand of the man who would destroy me and my son together out of the inheritance of God. Then thine handmaid said: The word of my lord the king shall now be comfortable; for as a messenger of God, so is the king to discern good and bad; therefore Yahweh thy God will be with thee.

Then the king answered and said unto the woman: Hide not, I pray, from me the thing that I shall ask thee. And the woman said: Let my lord the king now speak. And the king said: Is not the hand of Joab with thee in all this? And the woman answered and said: As thy soul liveth, my lord the king, none can turn to the right hand or to the left from aught that my lord the king hath spoken; for thy servant Joab, he bade me and he put all these words in the mouth of thy handmaid; to change the face of the matter hath thy servant Joab done this thing; and my lord is wise, according to the wisdom of a messenger of God, to know all things that are in the earth.

Then the king said unto Joab: Behold now, I have granted this request; go, therefore, bring the young man Absalom back. And Joab fell to the ground on his face, and prostrated himself, and blessed the king; and Joab said: To-day thy servant knoweth that I have found grace in thy sight, my lord, O king, in that the king hath performed the request of thy servant. So Joab arose and went to Geshur, and brought Absalom to Jerusalem. And the king said: Let him turn to his own house but let him not see my face. So Absalom turned to his own house, and saw not the face of the king.

So Absalom dwelt two full years in Jerusalem, and he saw not the king's face. Then Absalom sent for Joab to send him to the king, but he would not come to him; and he sent a second time, but he would not come. Therefore he said unto his servants: See, Joab's field is near mine, and he hath barley there; go and set it on fire. And Absalom's servants set the field on fire. Then Joab arose and came to Absalom unto his house, and said unto him: Wherefore have thy servants set my field on fire? And Absalom answered Joab: Behold, I sent unto thee, saying: Come hither that I may send thee unto the king, to say: Wherefore am I come from Geshur? It were better for me to be there still. Now therefore, let me see the king's face; and if there be iniquity in me, let him kill me. So Joab came to the king and told him; and when he had called for Absalom, he came to the king, and bowed himself on his face to the ground before the king; and the king kissed Absalom.

Now it came to pass after this, that Absalom prepared him a chariot and horses and fifty men to run before him. And Absalom used to rise up early and stand beside the way of the gate; and it was so, that when any man came to the king for judgment, that Absalom called unto him and said: Of what city art thou? And if he said: Thy servant is of such a one of the tribes of Israel, Absalom would say unto him: See, thy matters are good and right; but there is no man deputed of the king to hear thee. He said moreover: O that I were made judge in the land, that every man who hath any suit or cause might come unto me, and I would do him justice! And it was so, that when any man came nigh to prostrate himself before him, he put forth his hand, and took hold of him and kissed him. And on this manner did Absalom to all Israel that came to the king for judgment. Thus Absalom stole the hearts of the men of Israel.

And it came to pass, at the end of his fortieth year, that Absalom said unto the king: I pray thee, let me go and pay the vow which I have vowed unto Yahweh, in Hebron. For thy servant did vow a vow while I abode at Geshur in Aram, saying: If Yahweh will indeed bring me back to Jerusalem, then I will serve Yahweh. And the king said: Go in peace. So he arose and went to Hebron. But Absalom sent spies throughout all the tribes of Israel, saying: As soon as ye hear the sound of the horn, then ye shall say: Absalom is king in Hebron. And with Absalom went two hundred men out of Jerusalem, that were invited, and went in their simplicity; and they knew not anything. And Absalom sent for Ahithophel, the Gileadite, David's counselor, from his city, even from Giloh, while he offered sacrifices. And the conspiracy was strong; for the people increased continually with Absalom.

And there came a messenger to David, saying: The hearts of the men of Israel are gone after Absalom. And David said unto all the servants that were with him in Jerusalem: Arise and let us flee, for else none of us shall escape from Absalom; make speed to depart, lest he overtake us quickly and bring down evil upon us, and smite the city with the edge of the sword. And the king's servants said unto the king: Behold, thy servants are ready to do whatsoever the king my lord shall choose. And the king went forth, and all his household with him. And the king left ten women that were concubines to keep the house. And the king went forth, and all the people after him; and they tarried in Beth-merhak. And all his servants passed on beside him; and all the Cherethites and all the Pelethites, and all the Gittites, six hundred men that came after him from Gath, passed on before the king.

Then said the king to Ittai, the Gittite: Wherefore goest thou also with us? return and abide with the king; for thou art a foreigner, and also an exile from thine own place. Whereas thou camest but yesterday, should I this day make thee go up and down with us, seeing I go whither I may? Return thou and take back thy brethren with thee in kindness and truth. And Ittai answered the king, and said: As Yahweh liveth, and as my lord the king liveth, surely in what place my lord the king shall be, whether for death or for life, even there also will thy servant be. And David said to Ittai: Go and pass over. And Ittai the Gittite passed over, and all his men, and all the little ones that were with him. And all the country wept with a loud voice as all the people passed over; and as the king passed over the brook Kidron, all the people passed over toward the way of the wilderness.

And lo, Zadok also came, bearing the ark of the covenant of God; and they set down the ark of God until all the people had done passing out of the city. And the king said unto Zadok: Carry back the ark of God into the city; if I shall find favor in the eyes of Yahweh, He will bring me back, and show me both it and His habitation; but if He say thus: I have no delight in thee, behold, here am I; let Him do as seemeth good unto Him. The king also said unto Zadok the priest: Seest thou? return into the city in peace and your two sons with you, Ahimaaz, thy son, and Jonathan, the son of Abiathar. See, I will tarry in the plains of the wilderness until there cometh word from you to announce to me. Zadok therefore, and Abiathar, carried the ark back to Jerusalem, and they abode there.

And David went up by the ascent of Olivet and wept as he went up; and he had his head covered, and went barefoot; and all the people that were with him covered every man his head, and they went up, weeping as they went up. And one told David, saying: Ahithophel is among the conspirators with Absalom. And David said: O Yahweh, turn the counsel of Ahithophel into foolishness. And it came to pass, that when David was come to the top of the ascent, where he was wont to worship God, behold, Hushai the Archite came to meet him with his coat rent and earth upon his head. And David said unto him: If thou passest on with me, then thou wilt be a burden unto me; but if thou will return to the city, and say unto Absalom: I will be thy servant, O king; then thou wilt defeat for me the counsel of Ahithophel. And hast thou not there with thee Zadok and Abiathar, the priests? there-fore it shall be, that what thing soever thou shalt hear out of the king's house, thou shalt tell it to Zadok and Abiathar the priests. Behold, they have there with them their two sons, Ahimaaz, Zadok's son, and Jona-than, Abiathar's son; and by them ye shall send unto me everything that ye shall hear. So Hushai, David's friend, came into the city; and Absalom was at the point of entering Jerusalem.

And when David was a little past the top, behold, Ziba, the servant of Mephibosheth, met him with a couple of asses saddled, and upon them two hundred loaves of bread, and a hundred clusters of raisins, and a hundred of summer fruits, and a bottle of wine. And the king said unto Ziba: What meanest thou by these? And Ziba said: The asses are for the king's household to ride on, and the bread and summer fruit for the young men to eat, and the wine that such as are faint in the wilder-ness may drink. And the king said: And where is thy master's son? And Ziba said unto the king: Behold, he abideth in Jerusalem; for he said, To-day will the house of Israel restore me the kingdom of my father. Then said the king to Ziba: Behold, thine is all that pertaineth to Mephibosheth. And Ziba said: I prostrate myself; let me find favor in thy sight, my lord O king.

And when king David came to Bahurim, behold, there came out thence a man of the family of Saul, whose name was Shimei, the son of Gera; he came out and kept on cursing as he came. And he cast stones at David, and at all the servants of king David; and all the people and all the mighty men were on his right hand and on his left. And thus said Shimei when he cursed: Begone, begone, thou bloody man and base fellow! Yahweh hath returned upon thee all the blood of the house of Saul, in whose stead thou hast reigned; and Yahweh hath delivered the kingdom into the hand of Absalom thy son; and behold, thou art taken in thine own mischief, because thou art a man of blood.

Then said Abishai the son of Zeruiah to the king: Why should this dead dog curse my lord the king? Let me go over, I pray you, and take off his head. And the king said: What have I to do with you, ye sons of Zeruiah? So let him curse because Yahweh hath said unto him: Curse David; who then shall say: Wherefore hast thou done so? And David said to Abishai, and to all his servants: Behold! my son, who came forth of my body, seeketh my life; how much more this Benjamite now? Let him alone, and let him curse, for Yahweh hath bidden him. It may be that Yahweh will look into my eye, and that Yahweh will requite me with good for his cursing this day. So David and his men went by the road, and Shimei went along on the hillside over against him, and cursed as he went, and threw stones at him and cast dust. And the king and all the people that were with him became weary, and refreshed themselves there.

Now Absalom and all the people, the men of Israel, came to Jerusalem, and Ahithophel with him. And it came to pass, when Hushai the Archite, David's friend, was come unto Absalom, that Hushai said unto Absalom: Long live the king, Long live the king! And Absalom said unto Hushai: Is this thy kindness to thy friend? why wentest thou not with thy friend? And Hushai said unto Absalom: Nay, but whom Yahweh and this people and all the men of Israel have chosen, his will I be, and with him will I abide. And again, whom should I serve? should I not serve in the presence of his son? As I have served in thy father's presence, so will I be in thy presence.

Then said Absalom to Ahithophel: Give your counsel what we shall do. And Ahithophel said unto Absalom: Go in unto thy father's concubines, that he hath left to keep the house; and all Israel will hear that thou art abhorred of thy father; then will the hands of all that are with thee be strong. So they spread Absalom a tent upon the top of the house; and Absalom went in unto his father's concubines in the sight of all Israel. Now the counsel of Ahithophel which he counselled in those days was as if a man inquired of the word of God; so was the counsel of Ahithophel both with David and with Absalom.

Moreover Ahithophel said unto Absalom: Let me now choose out twelve thousand men, and I will arise and course after David this night; and I will come upon him while he is weary and weak-handed, and will make him afraid; and all the people that are with him shall flee, and I will smite the king only; and I will bring back all the people unto thee; when all the people shall have returned save the man whom thou seekest, all the people will be at peace. And the saying pleased Absalom well and all the elders of Israel.

Then said Absalom: Call now Hushai the Archite also, and let us hear likewise what he says. And when Hushai was come to Absalom, Absalom spake unto him, saying: Ahithophel hath spoken after this fashion; shall we do after his saying? if not, speak thou. And Hushai said unto Absalom: The counsel that Ahithophel hath given is not good. Hushai said moreover: Thou knowest thy father and his men that they are mighty men, and they are embittered in their minds, as a bear robbed of her whelps in the field. And thy father is a man of war, and will not lodge with his people. Behold, he is hid now in some pit, or in some other place; and it will come to pass, when they fall upon them at the first, whosoever heareth it shall say: There is a slaughter among the people that follow Absalom. Then even he that is valiant, whose heart is as the heart of a lion, will utterly melt; for all Israel knoweth that thy father is a mighty man, and mighty men are with him. But I counsel that all Israel be gathered together unto thee, from Dan even to Beersheba, as the sand that is by the sea for multitude; and that thou go to battle in thine own person. So shall we come upon him in some place where he shall be found; and we will light upon him as the dew falleth on the ground; and of him and of all the men that are with him we will not leave so much as one. Moreover, if he withdraw himself into a city, then shall all Israel bring ropes to that city, and we will draw it into the valley until there be not one small stone found there. And Absalom and all the men of Israel said: The counsel of Hushai the Archite is better than the counsel of Ahithophel. For Yahweh had ordained to defeat the good counsel of Ahithophel, to the intent that Yahweh might bring evil upon Absalom.

Then said Hushai to Zadok and to Abiathar, the priests: Thus and thus did Ahithophel counsel Absalom and the elders of Israel, and thus and thus have I counselled. Now, therefore, send quickly and tell David, saying: Lodge not this night in the plains of the wilderness, but in any wise pass over; lest the king be swallowed up, and all the people that are with him. Now Jonathan and Ahimaaz were staying by Enrogel, that they might not be seen coming into the city; and a maid went out and told them; and they went and told king David. Nevertheless, a lad saw them and told Absalom; but they went away both of them quickly, and came to a man's house in Bahurim which had a well in its court, into which they went down. And the woman took and spread a covering over the well's mouth, and spread ground corn thereon; and the thing was not known. And when Absalom's servants came to the woman to the house they said: Where are Ahimaaz and Jonathan? And the woman said unto them: they are gone over the brook of water. And when they had sought and could not find them, they returned to Jerusalem.

And it came to pass after they were departed, that they came up out of the well and went and told David, and they said unto him: Arise, and pass quickly over the water, for thus hath Ahithophel counselled against you. Then David arose, and all the people which were with him, and they passed over the Jordan; by the morning light there lacked not one of them that was not gone over the Jordan.

Now when Ahithophel saw that his counsel was not followed, he saddled his ass, and arose and gat him home to his city, and set his house in order and strangled himself; and he died, and was buried in the sepulchre of his father.

When David was come to Mahanaim, Absalom passed over the Jordan, he and all the men of Israel with him. And Absalom had set Amasa over the host instead of Joab. (Now Amasa was the son of a man whose name was Ithra the Jezreelite, who married Abigail, the daughter of Nahash, sister to Zeruiah, Joab's mother.) And Israel and Absalom pitched in the land of Gilead.

And it came to pass that when David was come to Mahanaim, Shob, the son of Nahash of Rabbah, of the Ammonites, and Machir the son of Ammiel of Lo-debar, and Barzillai the Gileadite of Rogelim, brought beds and basins and earthen vessels, and wheat and barley and meal, and parched corn and beans and parched pulse, and honey and curd and cheese of kine and sheep for David, and for the people that were with him to eat; for they said: The people is hungry and faint and thirsty in the wilderness.

And David numbered the people that were with him, and set captains of thousands and captains of hundreds over them. And David sent forth the people, a third part under the hand of Joab, and a third part under the hand of Abishai the son of Zeruiah, Joab's brother, and a third part under the hand of Ittai the Gittite. And the king said unto the people: I will surely go forth with you myself also. But the people said: Thou shalt not go forth; for if we flee away, they will not care for us; neither if half of us die will they care for us; but thou art worth ten thousand of us; therefore it is better that thou be ready to succor us out of the city. And the king said unto them: What seemeth you best, I will do. And the king stood by the gate-side, and all the people came out by hundreds and by thousands. And the king commanded Joab and Abishai and Ittai, saying: Deal gently for my sake with the young man, even with Absalom. And all the people heard when the king gave all the captains charge concerning Absalom.

So the people went out into the field against Israel; and the battle was in the wood of Ephraim; and the people of Israel were smitten there before the servants of David, and there was a great slaughter there that day of twenty thousand men. For the battle there was spread over the face of all the country; and the forest devoured more people that day than the sword devoured.

And Absalom chanced to meet the servants of David. And Absalom was riding upon his mule, and the mule went under the thick boughs of a great terebinth, and he was taken up between the heaven and the earth; and the mule that was under him went on. And a certain man saw it and told Joab, and said: Behold, I saw Absalom hanging in a terebinth. And Joab answered the man that told him: And behold, thou sawest it; and why didst thou not smite him there to the ground? I would have given thee ten pieces of silver, and a girdle. And the man said to Joab: Though I should receive a thousand pieces of silver in my hand, yet would not I put forth my hand against the king's son; for in our hearing the king charged thee and Abishai and Ittai, saying: Beware that none touch the young man Absalom. Otherwise I should have wrought falsehood against mine own life; for there is no matter hid from the king; then thou thyself wouldst have stood aloof. Then said Joab: I may not tarry with thee. And he took three darts in his hand, and thrust them through the heart of Absalom, while he was yet alive in the midst of the terebinth. And ten young men that bare Joab's armor compassed about and smote Absalom, and slew him.

And Joab blew the trumpet, and the people returned from pursuing after Israel; for Joab held back the people. And they took Absalom, and cast him into the great pit in the forest, and raised over him a very great heap of stones; and all Israel fled, every one to his tent. Now Absalom in his lifetime had taken and raised up for himself the pillar which is in the king's dale; for he said: I have no son to keep my name in remembrance; and he called the pillar after his own name, and it is called Absalom's place unto this day.

Then said Ahimaaz the son of Zadok: Let me now run and bear the king tidings, how that Yahweh hath avenged him of his enemies. And Joab said unto him: Thou shalt not be the bearer of tidings this day, but thou shalt bear tidings another day; but this day thou shalt bear no tidings, forasmuch as the king's son is dead. Then said Joab to the Cushite: Go, tell the king what thou hast seen. And the Cushite bowed down to Joab, and ran. Then said Ahimaaz the son of Zadok yet again to Joab: But, come what may, let me, I pray, also run after the Cushite. And Joab said: Wherefore wilt thou run, my son, seeing that thou wilt have no reward for the tidings? But, howsoever (he said), let me run. And he said unto him: Run. Then Ahimaaz ran by the way of the plain, and overran the Cushite.

Now David sat between the two gates; and the watchman went up to the roof of the gate unto the wall, and lifted up his eyes and looked, and behold, a man running alone. And the watchman cried, and told the king. And the king said: If he be alone, there is tidings in his mouth. And he came apace, and drew near. And the watchman saw another man running; and the watchman called unto the porter, and said: Behold, another man runneth alone. And the king said: He also bringeth tidings. And the watchman said: Methinks, the running of the foremost is like the running of Ahimaaz, the son of Zadok. And the king said: He is a good man, and he bringeth good tidings.

And Ahimaaz called and said to the king: All is well. And he bowed down before the king with his face to the earth, and said: Blessed be Yahweh thy God, who hath delivered up the men that lifted up their hand against my lord the king. And the king said: Is it well with the young man Absalom? And Ahimaaz answered: When Joab sent the king's servant and me thy servant, I saw a great tumult, but I knew not what it was. And the king said: Turn aside, and stand here. And he turned aside, and stood still.

And behold, the Cushite came; and the Cushite said: Tidings for my lord the king; for Yahweh hath avenged thee this day of all them that rose up against thee. And the king said unto the Cushite: Is it well with the young man Absalom? And the Cushite answered: The enemies of my lord the king, and all that rise up against thee to do thee hurt, be as that young man is.

And the king was much moved, and went up to the chamber above the gate, and wept; and as he wept, thus he said: O my son Absalom, my son, my son Absalom! Would God I had died for thee, O Absalom, my son, my son!

And it was told Joab: Behold, the king weepeth and mourneth for Absalom. And the victory that day was turned into mourning unto all the people; for the people heard say that day: The king grieveth for his son. And the people gat them by stealth that day into the city, as people that are ashamed steal away when they flee in battle. But the king covered his face, and the king cried with a loud voice: O my son, Absalom, O my son, my son! And Joab came into the house to the king, and said: Thou hast shamed this day the faces of all thy servants, who this day have saved thy life, and the lives of thy sons and of thy daughters, and the lives of thy wives, and the lives of thy concubines; in that thou lovest them that hate thee, and hatest them that love thee. For thou hast declared this day, that princes and servants are naught unto thee; for this day I perceive that, if Absalom had lived and all we had died this day, then it had pleased thee well. Now, therefore, arise, go forth, and speak to the heart of thy servants; for I swear by Yahweh if thou go not forth, there will not tarry a man with thee this night; and that will be worse unto thee than all the evil that hath happened unto thee from thy youth until now.

Then the king arose and sat in the gate. And they told unto all the people, saying: Behold, the king sitteth in the gate; and all the people came before the king.

SECTION III.—All Israel plans to bring David back to Jerusalem. The tribe of Judah forestalls the rest, and with them come Shimei and Ziba, the Benjamites, and their following. But Sheba, the Benjamite, incites the northern tribes through their jealousy of Judah to abandon David. David sends Joab with the men of Judah to put down the revolt. He conciliates the disaffected tribes, and causes the death of Sheba. David reconstructs his Cabinet. How David pays the blood-penalty demanded by the Gibeonites, the first Canaanite allies of Joshua, for Saul's breach of their covenant. The story of Rizpah. The last attack of the Philistines; David resigns his leadership of the army. He takes a census of all Israel, in spite of Joab's protest. Having made it, he repents of this trespass upon tribal liberty. Is rebuked by the prophet Gad. In sign of repentance, he builds an altar for all Israel on the site, later occupied by the Temple of Solomon. The last days of David. Adonijah, his oldest living son, assumes the state of heir-apparent. Nathan stirs Bath-sheba to obtain the succession for Solomon. David calls for Zadok the priest to anoint Solomon king. Adonijah seeks sanctuary at the new altar, from which Solomon summons him, and sends him home in peace. David gives Solomon his last admonitions, and dies. He is buried in Jerusalem. (2 Sam'l, xix, 9b-44; xx-xxi, 15; xxiv, 1-4, 8-25; 1 Ki., i-ii, 10.)

Materials: A wealth of oral tradition concerning the Hero-king; a "Chron. of King David"; the "Acts of Nathan" and "Acts of Gad"; Poems on the "Wars of Yahweh"; and the State Records. Possibly also the "Book of Jashar".

Now Israel had fled, every man to his tent. And all the people were at strife among all the tribes of Israel, saying: The king delivered us out of the hands of our enemies, and he saved us out of the hands of the Philistines; and now he is fled out of the land from Absalom; and Absalom whom we anointed over us is dead in battle. Now, therefore, why speak ye not a word of bringing back the king? And king David sent to Zadok and to Abiathar the priests, saying: Speak to the elders of Judah, and say: Why are ye the last to bring the king back to his house? Ye are my brethren, ye are my bone and my flesh; wherefore then should ye be the last to bring back the king? And say ye to Amasa: Art thou not my bone and my flesh? God do so to me and more also, if thou be not captain of the host before me continually in the place of Joab. And he bowed the heart of all the men of Judah, even as the heart of one man; so that they sent unto the king, saying: Return thou, and all they servants.

So the king returned and came to the Jordan. And Judah came to Gilgal to go to meet the king, to bring the king over the Jordan. And Shimei the son of Gera, the Benjamite, who was of Bahurim, made haste and came down with the men of Benjamin to meet king David. And there were a thousand men of Benjamin with him; and Ziba, the servant of the house of Saul and his fifteen sons and his twenty servants with him. And they rushed into the Jordan before the king. And the ferry-boat passed to and fro to carry over the king's household, and to do what he thought good. And Shimei the son of Gera fell down before the king, as he was come over Jordan; and he said unto the king: Let not the king impute iniquity unto me; neither do thou remember that which thy servant did iniquitously the day that my lord the king went out of Jerusalem, that the king should take it to heart. For thy servant doth know that I have sinned; therefore have I come, indeed, this day, the first of all the house of Joseph to go down to meet my lord the king.

But Abishai, the son of Zeruiah, answered and said: Shall not Shimei be put to death for this, because he cursed Yahweh's anointed? And David said: What have I to do with you, ye sons of Zeruiah, that ye should this day be adversaries unto me? shall there any man be put to death this day in Israel? for do not I know that I am this day king over Israel? And the king said to Shimei: Thou shalt not die. And the king sware unto him.

And Mephibosheth the son of Saul came down to meet the king; and he had neither dressed his feet nor trimmed his beard nor washed his clothes, from the day the king departed until the day he came home in peace. And it came to pass, when he was come to Jerusalem to meet the king, that the king said unto him: Wherefore wentest thou not with me, Mephibosheth? And he answered: My lord, O king! my servant deceived me; for thy servant said: I will saddle me an ass, that I may ride thereon, and go with the king, because thy servant is lame. And he hath slandered thy servant unto my lord, the king. But my lord the king is as a messenger of God; do therefore what is good in thine eyes. For all my father's house were deserving of death at the hand of my lord the king; yet didst thou set thy servant among them that did eat at thine own table. What right have I yet, therefore; or why should I cry any more unto the king? And the king said unto him: Why speakest thou any more of thy matters? I have said: Thou and Ziba divide the land. And Mephibosheth said unto the king: Yea, let him take all, forasmuch as my lord the king is come in peace unto his own house.

And Barzillai the Gileadite came down from Rogelim; and he passed on to the Jordan with the king, to bring him on the way over the Jordan. Now Barzillai was a very aged man, even four-score years old; and he had provided the king with sustenance while he lay at Mahanaim; for he was a very great man. And the king said to Barzillai: Come over with me, and I will sustain thee with me in Jerusalem. And Barzillai said unto the king: How many are the days of the years of my life, that I should go up with the king unto Jerusalem? I am this day four-score years old; can I discern between good and evil? can thy servant taste what I eat, or what I drink? can I hear any more the voice of singing men and women? wherefore then should I be a burden unto my lord the king? Thy servant would but just go over the Jordan with the king; and why should the king recompense it to me with such a reward? Let thy servant go back, I pray thee, that I may die in mine own city, by the grave of my father and my mother. But behold thy servant Chimham, let him go over with my lord the king; and do to him that which shall seem good unto thee; and whatsoever thou shalt require of me, that will I do for thee. And the king said: Chimham shall go with me, and I will do to him that which shall seem good unto thee; and whatsoever thou shalt require of me, that will I do for thee.

And all the people went over Jordan, and the king went over; and the king kissed Barzillai and blessed him; and he returned to his own place.

So the king went over to Gilgal, and Chimham went over with him; and all the people of Judah brought the king over, and also half of the people of Israel. And behold, all the people of Israel came to the king, and said unto the king: Why have our brethren the men of Judah stolen thee away, and brought the king and his household over the Jordan, and all David's men with him? And all the men of Judah answered the men of Israel: Because the king is near of kin to us;

wherefore then are ye angry for this matter? have we eaten at all of the king's cost, or hath any gift been given us? And the men of Israel answered the men of Judah, and said: We have ten parts in the king, and we have also more right in David than ye; why then did ye despise us, that our advice should not be first had in bringing back our king? And the words of the men of Judah were fiercer than the words of the men of Israel.

Now there happened to be there a man of Belial whose name was Sheba the son of Bichri, a Benjamite; and he blew the horn and said: We have no portion in David, neither have we inheritance in the son of Jesse; every man to his tents, O Israel. So all the men of Israel went up from following David and followed Sheba, the son of Bichri; but the men of Judah did cleave unto their king, from the Jordan even to Jerusalem.

And David came to his house at Jerusalem; and the king took the ten women his concubines, whom he had left to keep the house, and put them in ward and provided them with sustenance, but went not in unto them. So they were shut up unto the day of their death in widowhood.

Then said the king to Amasa: Call me the men of Judah together within three days, and be thou here present. So Amasa went to call the men of Judah together; but he tarried longer than the set time which he had appointed him. And David said to Abishai: Now will Sheba the son of Bichri do us more harm than did Absalom; take thou thy lord's servants and pursue after him; lest he get him fortified cities and escape out of our sight. And there went out after him Joab's men, and the Cherethites, and the Pelethites, and all the mighty men; and they went out of Jerusalem to pursue after Sheba the son of Bichri. When they were at the great stone which is in Gibeon, Amasa came to meet them. And Joab was girded with his apparel of war that he had put on, and thereon was a girdle with a sword fastened upon his loins in the sheath thereof; and as he went forth it fell out. And Joab said to Amasa: Is it well with thee, my brother? And Joab took Amasa by the beard with his right hand to kiss him. But Amasa took no heed to the sword that was in Joab's hand; so he smote him therewith in the groin, and shed out his bowels on the ground, and struck him not again; and he died.

And Joab and Abishai his brother pursued after Sheba the son of Bichri. And there stood by him [Amasa] one of Joab's young men, and said: He that favoreth Joab and he that is for David, follow Joab. And Amasa lay wallowing in his blood in the midst of the highway. And when the man saw that all the people stood still, he carried Amasa out of the highway into the field, and cast a garment over him. When he was removed out of the highway, all the people went on after Joab, to pursue after Sheba the son of Bichri. And he went through all the tribes of Israel unto Abel, and to Beth-Maacah, and they cast up a mound against the city, and it stood in the moat; and all the people that were with Joab battered the wall to throw it down.

Then cried a wise woman out of the city: Hear, Hear! say, I pray you, unto Joab: Come near hither, that I may speak with thee. And he came near unto her; and the woman said: Art thou Joab? And he answered: I am. Then she said: Hear the words of thy handmaid. And he answered: I hear. Then she spake, saying: They were wont to say of old time, saying: They shall surely ask counsel at Abel; and so they ended the matter. We are peaceable and loyal in Israel; seekest thou to destroy a city and a mother in Israel? Why wilt thou swallow up the inheritance of Yahweh? And Joab answered and said: Far be it from me that I should swallow up or destroy. The matter is not so. But a man of the hill-country of Ephraim, Sheba the son of Bichri by name, hath lifted up his hand against the king, even against David. Deliver him only, and I will depart from the city. And the woman said unto Joab: Behold, his head shall be thrown to thee over the wall. Then the woman went unto all the people in her wisdom. And they cut off the head of Sheba the son of Bichri and threw it down to Joab. And he blew the horn, and they were dispersed from the city, every man to his tent. And Joab returned to Jerusalem unto the king.

Now Joab was over all the host of Israel; and Benaiah the son of Jehoiada was over the Cherethites and the Pelethites; and Adoram was over the levy; and Jehoshaphat the son of Ahilud was the recorder; and Sheva was scribe; and Zadok and Abiathar were priests; and Ira also the Jairite was chief minister unto David.

Now there was a famine in the days of David three years, year after year; and David sought the face of Yahweh. And Yahweh said: It is for Saul, and for his bloody house, because he put to death the Gibeonites. And the king called the Gibeonites, and said unto them (now the Gibeonites were not of the children of Israel but of the remnant of the Ammonites; and the Children of Israel had sworn unto them; and Saul had sought to slay them in his zeal for the Children of Israel and of Judah). Wherefore David said unto the Gibeonites: What shall I do for you? and wherewith shall I make atonement, that ye may bless the inheritance of Yahweh? And the Gibeonites said unto him: We will have no silver nor gold of Saul, nor of his house, neither for us shalt thou slay any man in Israel. And he said: What ye shall say, that will I do for you. And they answered the king: The man that consumed us, and that devised against us that we should be destroyed from remaining in any of the coasts of Israel,—let seven men of his sons be delivered unto us, and we will hang them up unto Yahweh in Gibeah of Saul, the chosen of Yahweh. And the king said: I will give them.

But the king spared Mephimosheth the son of Jonathan the son of Saul, because of Yahweh's oath that was between them, between David and Jonathan the son of Saul. But David took the two sons of Rizpah, whom she bare unto Saul, Armoni and Mephibosheth, and the five sons of Michal whom she bare unto Adriel the son of Barzillai the Meholathite; and he delivered them into the hands of the Gibeonites, and they hanged them in the mountain before Yahweh; and they fell all seven together; and they were put to death in the days of harvest,—in the first days, at the beginning of barley-harvest.

And Rizpah the daughter of Aiah took sackcloth, and spread it for her on the rock from the beginning of harvest until water was poured upon them from heaven, and she suffered neither the birds of the air to rest on them by day, nor the beasts of the fields by night. And it was told David what Rizpah the daughter of Aiah, the concubine of Saul, had done. And David went and took the bones of Saul and the bones of Jonathan his son from the men of Jabesh-gilead, who had stolen them from the open square of Beth-shan, where the Philistines had hanged them, in the day that the Philistines slew Saul in Gilboa; and he brought up from thence the bones of Saul and the bones of Jonathan his son; and they gathered the bones of them who were hanged. And they buried the bones of Saul and of Jonathan his son in the country of

Benjamin in Zela, in the sepulchre of Kish, his father; and they performed all that the king commanded. And after that, God was entreated for the land.

And the Philistines had war again with Israel; and David went down and his servants with him, and fought against the Philistines; and David waxed faint. And Ishi-benob, who was of the sons of the giant, the weight of whose spear was three hundred shekels of brass in weight, he, being girded with new armor, thought to have slain David. But Abishai, the son of Zeruiah, succored him, and smote the Philistine and killed him. Then the men of David sware unto him, saying: Thou shalt go no more out with us to battle, that thou quench not the lamp of Israel.

And again the anger of Yahweh was kindled against Israel; and He moved David against them, saying: Go, number Israel and Judah. And the king said to Joab, the captain of the host, who was with him: Go, now, to and fro through all the tribes of Israel, from Dan even to Beer-sheba, and number ye the people, that I may know the sum of the people. And Joab said unto the king: Now Yahweh thy God add unto the people, how many soever they may be, a hundredfold; and may the eyes of my lord the king see it: but why doth my lord the king delight in this thing? Notwithstanding, the king's word prevailed against Joab, and against the captains of the host. And Joab and the captains of the host went out from the presence of the king to number the people of Israel. And they passed over the Jordan, and pitched in Aroer, on the right side of the city that is in the middle of the valley of Gad, and unto Jazer; then they came to Gilead, and to the land of Tahtim-hodshi; and they came to Dan-jaan, and round about to Zidon and to all the cities of the Hivites and of the Canaanites; and they went out to the south of Judah at Beer-sheba.

So when they had gone to and fro through all the land, they came to Jerusalem at the end of nine months and twenty days. And Joab gave up the sum of the numbering of the people unto the king. And there were in Israel eight hundred thousand valiant men that drew the sword; and the men of Judah were five hundred thousand men.

And David's heart smote him after that he had numbered the people. And David said unto Yahweh: I have sinned greatly in what I have done; but now, O Yahweh, put away, I beseech Thee, the iniquity of thy servant; for I have done very foolishly. And when David rose up in the morning, the word of Yahweh came unto the prophet Gad, David's seer, saying: Go and speak unto David: Thus saith Yahweh: I lay upon thee three things; choose thee one of them, that I may do it unto thee. So Gad came to David, and told him, and said unto him: Shall seven years of famine come unto thee in thy land? or wilt thou flee for three months before thine enemies while they pursue thee? or that there be three days' pestilence in thy land? Now advise thee and consider what answer I shall return to Him that sent me. And David said unto Gad: I am in a great strait; let us fall now into the hand of Yahweh, for His mercies are great; and let me not fall into the hand of man.

So Yahweh sent a pestilence upon Israel from the morning even to the time appointed and there died of the people from Dan even to Beersheba seventy thousand men. And when the messenger of death stretched out his hand toward Jerusalem to destroy it, Yahweh repented Him of the evil, and said to the messenger that destroyed the people: It is enough; now stay thy hand. And the messenger of Yahweh was by the threshing-floor of Araunah, the Jebusite. And David spake unto Yahweh when he saw the messenger that smote the people, and said: Lo, I have sinned, and I have done iniquitously; but these sheep, what have they done? Let Thy hand, I pray Thee, be against me, and against my father's house.

And Gad came that day to David, and said unto him: Go up, rear an altar unto Yahweh in the threshing-floor of Araunah the Jebusite. And David went up according to the saying of Gad, as Yahweh commanded. And Araunah looked forth, and saw the king and his servants coming on toward him; and Araunah went out, and bowed down before the king, with his face to the ground. And Araunah said: Wherefore is my lord the king come to his servant? And David said: To buy the threshing-floor of thee, to build an altar unto Yahweh, that the plague may be stayed from the people. And Araunah said unto David: Let my lord the king take and offer up what seemeth good unto him; behold the oxen for the burnt-offering, and the threshing instruments and the gear of the oxen for the wood. All this doth Araunah give unto the king. And Araunah said unto the king: Yahweh, thy God, accept thee. And the king said unto Araunah: Nay, but I will verily buy it of thee at a price; neither will I offer burnt-offerings unto Yahweh my God which cost me nothing.

So David bought the threshing-floor and the oxen for fifty shekels of silver. And David built there an altar unto Yahweh, and offered burnt-offerings and peace-offerings. So Yahweh was entreated for the land, and the plague was stayed from Israel.

Now king David was old and stricken in years; and they covered him with clothes but he could get no heat. Wherefore his servants said unto him: Let there be sought a young virgin, and let her stand before the king and cherish him, and let her lie in thy bosom, that my lord the king may get heat. So they sought throughout all the borders of Israel and found Abishag, a Shunammite, and brought her to the king. And the damsel was very fair, and she cherished the king and ministered unto him; but the king knew her not.

Now, Adonijah, the son of Haggith, exalted himself, saying: I will be king; and he prepared him chariots and horsemen, and fifty men to run before him. And his father had not grieved him in all his life by saying: Why hast thou done so? and he was also a very goodly man; and he was born after Absalom. And he conferred with Joab the son of Zeruiah, and with Abiathar the priest; and they that followed Adonijah helped. But Zadok the priest and Benaiah the son of Jehoiada, and Nathan the prophet, and Shimei and Rei, and the mighty men that belonged to David, were not with Adonijah. And Adonijah slew sheep and oxen and fatlings by the stone of Zoheleth, which is by En-rogel; and he called all his brethren the king's sons, and all the men of Judah the king's servants; but Nathan the prophet and Benaiah and the mighty men, and Solomon his brother, he called not.

Then Nathan spake unto Bath-sheba the mother of Solomon, saying: Hast thou not heard that Adonijah the son of Haggith doth reign, and David our lord knoweth it not? Now therefore, come, let me, I pray thee, give thee counsel, that thou may save thine own life and the life of thy son Solomon. Go and get thee in unto king David, and say unto him: Didst thou not, my lord, O king, swear unto thy handmaid, saying: Assuredly Solomon thy son shall reign after me, and he shall sit upon my throne? Then why doth Adonijah reign? Behold, while thou yet talkest there with the king, I also will come in after thee, and confirm thy words.

And Bath-sheba went in unto the king into the chamber. (Now the king was very old, and Abishag the Shunammite ministered unto the king.) And Bath-sheba bowed, and prostrated herself before the king. And the king said: What wouldst thou? And she said unto him: My lord, thou didst swear by Yahweh thy God unto thine hand-maid: Assuredly Solomon thy son shall reign after me, and he shall sit upon my throne. And now, behold, Adonijah reigneth; and thou, my lord the king, knowest it not. And he hath slain oxen and fatlings and sheep in abundance, and hath called all the sons of the king, and Abia-thar the priest, and Joab the captain of the host; but Solomon thy servant hath he not called. And thou, my lord the king, the eyes of all Israel are upon thee, that thou shouldest tell them who shall sit on the throne of my lord the king after him. Otherwise it will come to pass, when my lord shall sleep with his fathers, that I and my son shall be counted offenders.

And lo, while she was yet talking with the king, Nathan the prophet came in. And they told the king, saying: Behold, Nathan the prophet. And when he was come in before the king, he bowed down before the king with his face to the ground. And Nathan said: My lord, O king, hast thou said: Adonijah, my son, shall reign after me, and he shall sit upon my throne? For he is gone down this day, and hath slain oxen and sheep and fatlings in abundance, and hath called all the king's sons and the captains of the host, and Abiathar the priest; and behold, they eat and drink before him, and say: God save king Adonijah. But me, even me thy servant, and Zadok the priest, and Benaiah the son of Jehoiada, and thy servant Solomon, hath he not called. Is this thing done by my lord the king, and thou hast not declared unto thy servant who should sit on the throne of my lord the king after him?

Then king David answered and said: Call me Bath-sheba. And she came into the king's presence, and stood before the king. And the king sware and said: As Yahweh liveth who hath redeemed my soul out of all adversity, verily, as I sware unto thee by Yahweh, the God of Israel, saying: Assuredly, Solomon thy son shall reign after me, and he shall sit on my throne in my stead; verily, so will I do this day. Then Bath-sheba bowed with her face to the earth, and prostrated herself before the king, and said: Let my lord king David live forever.

And king David said: Call me Zadok the priest, and Nathan the prophet, and Benaiah the son of Jehoiada. And they came before the king. And the king said unto them: Take with you the servants of your lord, and cause Solomon my son to ride upon mine own mule, and bring him down to Gihon. And let Zadok the priest and Nathan the prophet anoint him there king over Israel; and blow ye with the horn, and say: Long live King Solomon. Then ye shall come up after him, and he shall come and sit upon my throne; for he shall be king in my stead, and I have appointed him to be ruler over Israel and over Judah. And Benaiah the son of Jehoiada answered the king, and said: Amen; may Yahweh, the God of my lord the king, say so also. As Yahweh hath been with my lord the king, even so may He be with Solomon and make his throne greater than the throne of my lord, King David.

So Zadok the priest and Nathan the prophet and Benaiah the son of Jehoiada, and the Cherethites and the Pelethites, went down and caused Solomon to ride on King David's mule, and brought him to Gihon. And Zadok the priest took the horn of oil out of the Tabernacle, and anointed Solomon. And they blew the ram's horn; and all the people said: Long live King Solomon. And all the people came up after him, and the people piped with pipes, and rejoiced with great joy, so that the earth rent with the sound of them.

And Adonijah and all the guests that were with him heard it as they made an end of eating. And when Joab heard the sound of the horn, he said: Wherefore is this noise of the city in an uproar? While he yet spake, behold, Jonathan the son of Abiathar the priest came; and Adonijah said: Come in, for thou art a worthy man and bringest good tidings. And Jonathan answered and said to Adonijah: Verily, our lord King David hath made Solomon king. And the king hath sent with him Zadok the priest, and Nathan the prophet, and Benaiah the son of Jehoiada, and the Cherethites and the Pelethites, and they have caused him to ride on the king's mule. And Zadok the priest and Nathan the prophet have anointed him king in Gihon; and they are come up from thence rejoicing, so that the city is in an uproar. This is the noise that ye have heard. And also Solomon sitteth on the throne of the kingdom. And moreover, the king's servants came to bless our lord king David, saying: God make the name of Solomon better than thy name, and make his throne greater than thy throne; and the king bowed down upon his bed. And also thus said the king: Blessed be Yahweh, the God of Israel, who hath given one to sit on my throne this day, mine eyes even seeing it.

And all the guests of Adonijah were afraid, and rose up and went, every man his way. And Adonijah feared because of Solomon; and he arose and went and caught hold on the horns of the altar. And it was told Solomon, saying: Behold, Adonijah hath laid hold on the horns of the altar, saying: Let King Solomon swear unto me first of all that he will not slay his servant with the sword. And Solomon said: If he shall show himself a worthy man, there shall not a hair of him fall to the earth; but if wickedness be found in him, he shall die. So king Solomon went, and they brought him down from the altar. And he came and prostrated himself before king Solomon; and Solomon said unto him: Go to thy house.

Now the days of David drew nigh that he should die; and he charged Solomon his son, saying: I go the way of all the earth; be thou strong therefore, and show thyself a man; and keep the charge of Yahweh thy God, to walk in His ways, to keep His statutes and His commandments and His ordinances and His testimonies, according to that which is written in the book of Moses; that thou mayest prosper in all that thou doest, and whithersoever thou turnest thyself; that Yahweh may establish His word which He spake concerning me, saying: If Thy children take heed to their way, to walk before Me in truth with all their heart and with all their soul, there shall not fail thee, said He, a man on the throne of Israel. Moreover thou knowest also what Joab the son of Zeruiah did unto me, even what he did to the two captains of the hosts of Israel, unto Abner the son of Ner and unto Amasa the son of Jether, whom he slew, and shed the blood of war in peace, and put the blood of war upon his girdle that was about his loins, and in his shoes that were on his feet. Do therefore according to thy wisdom, and let not his hoar head go down to the grave in peace. But show kindness unto the sons of Barzillai the Gileadite, and let them be of those who eat at thy table; for so they drew nigh unto me when I fled from Absalom thy brother. And behold, there is with thee Shimei the son of Gera, the Benjamite, of Bahurim, who cursed me with a grievous curse in the day when I went to Mahanaim; but he came down to meet me at the Jordan, and I sware unto him by Yahweh, saying: I will not put thee to death with the sword. Now therefore, hold him not guilt-less, for thou art a wise man; and thou wilt know what thou oughtest to do unto him, and thou shalt bring his hoar head down to the grave with blood.

And David slept with his fathers, and was buried in the city of David. And the days that David reigned were forty years. Seven years he reigned in Hebron, and thirty and three years reigned he in Jeru-salem.

CHAPTER VI

THE REIGN OF SOLOMON
THE ACCESSION OF REHOBOAM AND THE DIVISION
OF THE KINGDOM

SECTION I.—Solomon establishes his rule by putting to death Adonijah
and Joab. Makes alliance with Egypt, and marries Pharaoh's
daughter. Dreams that Yahweh endows him with great wisdom.
Judges justly between two women. Appoints his Cabinet and household officials. Contracts with Hiram, king of Tyre, for materials
and workmen for building the Temple of Yahweh. Description of
the Temple and its furnishings. Builds his own palace and that
of the Egyptian princess. The installing of the ark in the Temple;
the dedication of the Temple, and Solomon's address to the people.
(1 Kings, ii, 12-iv, 7; v, 7, 8, 15, 19a, 20, 22-25, 26b, 32; vi, 1b-10,
15-20, 22, 29, 31-38; vii, 13, 15-18, 20b-45, 47, 57; viii, 1, 3b, 4, 7-9a,
10, 55-66.)

Materials: Besides popular traditions, much written matter; "Acts
of Solomon", "Sayings of the Seers", and other works now lost; also,
undoubtedly, State and Temple Records.

And Solomon sat upon the throne of David his father. Then Adonijah
the son of Haggith came to Bathsheba, the mother of Solomon. And she
said: Comest thou peaceably? and he said: Peaceably. He said, moreover: I have somewhat to say unto thee. And she said: Say on. And
he said: Thou knowest that the kingdom was mine, and that all Israel
set their faces on me that I should reign; howbeit, the kingdom is turned
about, and is become my brother's, for it was his from Yahweh. And
now, I ask one petition of thee; deny me not. And she said unto him:
Say on. And he said: Speak, I pray thee, unto Solomon the king,—for
he will not say thee nay,—that he give me Abishag the Shunammite to
wife. And Bathsheba said: Well, I will speak for thee unto the king.

Bathsheba, therefore, went unto King Solomon, to speak unto him
for Adonijah. And the king rose up to meet her, and bowed down before
her, and sat down on his throne, and caused a throne to be set for the
king's mother; and she sat on his right hand. Then she said: I ask
one small petition of thee; deny me not. And the king said unto her:
Ask on, my mother; for I will not deny thee. And she said: Let
Abishag the Shunammite be given to Adonijah thy brother to wife. And
king Solomon answered and said unto his mother: And why dost thou
ask Abishag the Shunammite for Adonijah? Ask for him the kingdom
also, for he is my elder brother; even for him and for Abiathar the
priest, and for Joab the son of Zeruiah. Then king Solomon sware by
Yahweh, saying: God do so unto me, and more also, if Adonijah hath
not spoken this against his own life. Now therefore, as Yahweh liveth,
who hath established me and set me on the throne of David my father,

and who hath made me a house as He promised, surely Adonijah shall be put to death this day. And King Solomon sent by the hand of Benaiah the son of Jehoiada; and he fell upon him so that he died.

And unto Abiathar the priest said the king: Get thee to Anathoth unto thine own fields, for thou art deserving of death; but I will not at this time put thee to death, because thou didst bear the ark of Yahweh before David my father, and because thou wast afflicted in all wherein my father was afflicted. So Solomon thrust out Abiathar from being priest unto Yahweh; that the word of Yahweh might be fulfilled which He spake concerning the house of Eli, at Shiloh.

And the tidings came to Joab, for Joab had turned after Adonijah, though he turned not after Absalom. And Joab fled unto the Tabernacle of Yahweh, and laid hold on the horns of the altar. And it was told king Solomon: Joab is fled unto the tabernacle of Yahweh, and behold, he is by the altar. Then Solomon sent Benaiah the son of Jehoiada, saying: Go, fall upon him. And Benaiah came to the tabernacle of Yahweh, and said unto him: Thus saith the king: Come forth. And he said: Nay, but I will die here. And Benaiah brought back word unto the king, saying: Thus said Joab, and thus he answered me. And the king said unto him: Do as he hath said, and fall upon him and bury him; that thou mayest take away the blood, which Joab shed without cause, from me and from my father's house. And Yahweh will return his blood upon his own head, because he fell upon two men more righteous and better than he, and slew them with the sword, and my father David knew it not, Abner the son of Ner, captain of the host of Israel, and Amasa the son of Jether, captain of the host of Judah. So shall their blood return upon the head of Joab, and upon the head of his seed for ever; but unto David and unto his seed and unto his house, and unto his throne, shall there be peace for ever from Yahweh. Then Benaiah the son of Jehoiada went up and fell upon him, and slew him; and he was buried in his own house in the wilderness. And the king put Benaiah the son of Jehoiada in his room over the host; and Zadok the priest did the king put in the room of Abiathar.

And the king sent and called for Shimei, and said unto him: Build thee a house in Jerusalem, and dwell there; and go not thence any whither. For on the day thou goest out, and dost pass over the brook Kidron, know thou for certain that thou shalt surely die; thy blood shall be upon thine own head. And Shimei said unto the king: The saying is good; as the king my lord hath said, so will thy servant do, and Shimei dwelt in Jerusalem many days.

And it came to pass, at the end of three years, that two of the servants of Shimei ran away unto Achish, son of Maachah, king of Gath. And Shimei arose and saddled his ass and went to Achish to seek his servants; and Shimei went and brought his servants from Gath. And it was told Solomon that Shimei had gone from Jerusalem to Gath, and was come back. And the king sent and called for Shimei, and said unto him: Did I not make thee to swear by Yahweh, and forewarn thee, saying: Know for certain, that on the day thou goest out and walkest abroad any whither, thou shalt surely die? and thou saidst unto me: The saying is good; I have heard it. Why then hast thou not kept the oath of Yahweh, and the commandment that I charged thee with? The king said moreover to Shimei: Thou knowest all the wickedness which thou didst to David my father; therefore Yahweh shall return thy wickedness upon thine own head. But king Solomon shall be blessed, and the throne of David shall be established before Yahweh for ever. So the king commanded Benaiah the son of Jehoiada; and he went out and fell upon him, so that he died.

So the kingdom was established in the hand of Solomon. And Solomon became allied to the Pharaoh of Egypt by marriage, and took Pharaoh's daughter, and brought her into the city of David, until he had made an end of building his own house, and the House of Yahweh, and the wall of Jerusalem round about. Only the people sacrificed in the high places, because there was no house built for the name of Yahweh until those days. And Solomon loved Yahweh, walking in the statutes of David his father; only he sacrificed and burnt incense in high places.

And the king went to Gibeon to sacrifice there; for that was the great high place; a thousand burnt-offerings did Solomon offer upon that altar. In Gibeon Yahweh appeared to Solomon in a dream by night; and God said: Ask what I shall give thee. And Solomon said: Thou hast shown unto Thy servant David my father great kindness. And now, O my God, Yahweh, Thou hast made Thy servant king instead of David my father; and I am but a child; I know not how to go out or to come in. Give Thy servant, therefore, an understanding heart to judge Thy people, that I may choose aright between good and evil; for who is able to judge this Thy great people? And the speech pleased Yahweh, that Solomon had asked this thing. And God said unto him: Because thou hast asked this thing, and hast not asked for thyself long life, neither hast asked riches for thyself nor hast asked the life of thine enemies, but hast asked for thyself understanding to discern justice; behold, I have done according to thy word. Lo, I have given thee a wise and understanding heart. And I have also given thee that which thou hast not asked, both riches and honor.

And Solomon awoke, and behold, it was a dream. And he returned to Jerusalem.

Then came there unto the king two women that were harlots, and stood before him. And the one woman said: O my lord, I and this woman dwell in one house; and I was delivered of a child with her in the house. And it came to pass the third day after I was delivered, that this woman was delivered also; and we were together; there was no stranger with us in the house save we two in the house. And this woman's child died in the night, because she overlay it. And she arose at midnight and took my son from beside me while thy handmaid slept, and laid it in her bosom, and laid her dead child in my bosom. And when I rose in the morning to give my child suck, behold, it was dead; but when I had looked well at it in the morning, behold, it was not my son whom I did bear. And the other woman said: Nay, but the living is my son, and the dead is thy son. Thus they spake before the king.

Then said the king: The one saith, This is my son that liveth, and thy son is the dead; and the other saith: Nay, but thy son is the dead, and my son is the living. And the king said: Fetch me a sword. And they brought a sword before the king. And the king said: Divide the living child in two, and give half to the one, and half to the other. Then spake the woman whose the living child was unto the king, for her heart yearned upon her son, and she said: O my lord, give her the living child, and in no wise slay it: But the other said: It shall be neither thine nor mine; divide it. Then the king answered and said: Give her the living child and in no wise slay it; she is the mother thereof. And all Israel heard of the judgment which the king had judged; and they feared the king, for they saw that the wisdom of God was in him to do justice.

So king Solomon was king over all Israel. And these were the princes that he had. Azariah the son of Zadok, the priest; Elihoreph and Ahijah, the sons of Shisha, scribes; Jehoshaphat the son of Ahilud, the recorder; and Benaiah the son of Jehoiada was over the army; and Zadok and Abiathar were priests; and Azariah the son of Nathan was over the officers; and Zabud the son of Nathan was chief minister and the king's friend; and Ahishar was over the household; and Adoniram the son of Abda, was over the levy.

And Solomon had twelve officers over all Israel, who provided victuals for the king and his household; each man had to make provision for a month in the year, and one officer was over all the officers in the land. And these officers provided victual for king Solomon, and for all that came unto king Solomon's table, each man in his month; they let nothing be lacking. Barley also and straw for the horses and swift steeds brought they into the place where it should be, every man according to his charge.

Hiram, king of Tyre, sent his servants unto Solomon; for he had heard that they had anointed him king in the room of his father; for Hiram was ever a lover of David. And Solomon sent to Hiram, saying: I purpose to build a house to the name of Yahweh my God. Now therefore, command thou that they hew me cedar-trees out of Lebanon; and my servants shall be with thy servants; and I will give thee hire for thy servants according to all that thou shalt say; for thou knowest that there are not among us any that hath skill to hew timber like unto the Zidonians. And Hiram sent unto Solomon, saying: I have heard that which thou hast sent unto me; I will do all thy desire concerning timber of cedar, and concerning timber of cypress. My servants shall bring them down from Lebanon to the sea, and I will make them into rafts to go by sea unto the place that thou shalt appoint me, and will cause them to be broken up there, and thou shalt receive them. And thou shalt accomplish my desire in giving food for my household. So Hiram gave Solomon timber of cedar and timber of cypress according to all his desire; and Solomon gave Hiram twenty thousand measures of wheat for food to his household, and twenty measures of beaten oil; thus gave Solomon to Hiram, year by year. And there was peace between Hiram and Solomon; and they two made a league together.

And king Solomon raised a levy out of all Israel; and the levy was thirty thousand men. And he sent them to Lebanon, ten thousand a month by course; a month they were in Lebanon, and two months at home; and Adoniram was over the levy. And Solomon had threescore and ten thousand that bare burdens, and fourscore thousand that were hewers in the mountains; besides Solomon's chief officers that were over the work,—three thousand and three hundred who bare rule over the people that wrought in the work. And the king commanded, and they quarried great stones to lay the foundations of the house with cut stone. And Solomon's builders and Hiram's builders and the Gebalites did fashion them, and prepared the timber and the stones to build the house.

Now it came to pass in the fourth year of Solomon's reign over Israel, he began to build the house of Yahweh; and the length thereof was threescore cubits, and the breadth thereof twenty cubits, and the height thereof thirty cubits. And the porch before the temple of the house, twenty cubits was the length thereof, according to the breadth of the house; and ten cubits was the breadth thereof before the house.

And for the house he made windows broad within, and narrow without. And against the wall of the house, he built a side-structure round about, against the walls both of the house and of the Sanctuary; and he made side-chambers round about. The nethermost story of the side-structure was five cubits broad, and the middle was six cubits broad, and the third was seven cubits broad; for on the outside he made abutments round about, that the beams should not be fastened in the walls of the house. The door for the lowest row of chambers was in the right side of the house; and one went up by winding stairs into the middle row, and out of the middle into the third. So he built the house and finished it; and he covered in the house with planks of cedar over beams. And he built the stories of chambers, each five cubits high, against the walls of the house, and they rested on the house with timber of cedar.

And Solomon built the walls of the house within with boards of cedar; from the floor of the house to the joists of the ceiling, he covered them on the inside with wood; and he covered the floor of the house with boards of cypress. And he built twenty cubits on the hinder part of the house with boards of cedar from the floor to the joists; he built them within for a Sanctuary; and the temple before it was forty cubits long. And the cedar on the house within was carved with knops and open flowers; all was cedar; there was no stone seen. And he prepared the Sanctuary in the midst of the house within, to set there the ark of Yahweh, twenty cubits in length and twenty cubits in breadth, and twenty cubits in the height thereof. And before it he set an altar which he covered with cedar; and the whole altar which belonged to the Sanctuary he overlaid with gold.

And for the Sanctuary he made two cherubim of olive-wood, each ten cubits high. And five cubits was the one wing of the cherub, and five cubits the other wing of the cherub; from the uttermost part of the one wing to the uttermost part of the other were ten cubits. And the other cherub was ten cubits; both the cherubim were of one measure and one form. And he set the cherubim within the Sanctuary; and the wings of the cherubim were stretched forth, so that the wing of the one touched one wall and the wing of the other touched the other wall; and their [other] wings touched in the midst of the house. And he overlaid the cherubim with gold.

And he carved all the walls of the house round about with figures of cherubim and palm-trees and open flowers, both in the inner and outer rooms. And for the entrance of the Sanctuary he made doors of olive-wood, the door-posts within the frame having five hinges. And on the two doors of olive-wood he carved carvings of cherubim and palm-trees and open flowers, and overlaid them with gold. So also he made for the entrance of the temple door-posts of olive-wood within a frame four-square, and two doors of cypress-wood; the two leaves of the one door were folding, and the two leaves of the other door were folding. And he carved thereon cherubim and palm-trees and open flowers; and he overlaid them with gold fitted upon the graven work.

In the fourth year was the foundation of the house of Yahweh laid, in the month Ziv; and in the eleventh year in the month Bul was the house finished throughout all the parts thereof, and according to all the plan of it. So was he seven years in finishing it.

Then Solomon sent and fetched Hiram of Tyre, a worker in brass; and he was filled with wisdom and understanding and skill to work all sorts of work in brass. And he came to King Solomon, and wrought all his works. Thus he fashioned the two pillars of brass, each eighteen cubits high; and a line of twelve cubits did compass one about, and so the other pillar. And he made two capitals of molten brass to set upon the tops of the pillars; the height of the one capital was five cubits, and the height of the other capital was five cubits. He also made nets of checker-work and wreaths of chain-work for the capitals which were upon the top of the pillars, seven for the one capital and seven for the other. And he made the pomegranates; and there were two rows round about upon the one network to cover the capital that was above the pomegranates. And the pomegranates were two hundred in rows round about under the capital, close above the swelling of the pillar. And so he did also for the other pillar. And he set up the pillars at the porch of the temple; and he set up the right pillar, and called the name thereof *Jakin;* and he set up the left pillar, and called the name thereof, *Boaz.* And upon the top of the pillars was lily-work. So was the work of the pillars finished.

And he made the molten sea of ten cubits from brim to brim, round in compass, and the height thereof was five cubits; and a line of thirty cubits did compass it round about. And under the brim of it round about there were knops which did encompass it for ten cubits, compassing the sea round about; the knops were in two rows, cast when it was cast. It stood upon twelve oxen, three looking toward the north, and three looking toward the west, and three looking toward the south, and three looking toward the east; and the sea was set upon them above, and all their hinder parts were turned inward. And it was a handbreadth thick; and the brim thereof was wrought like the brim of a cup, like the flower of a lily; it held two thousand baths.

And he made the ten bases of brass; four cubits was the length of one base, and four cubits the breadth thereof, and three cubits the height of it. And the work of the bases was on this manner; they had borders, and the borders were between the stays; and on the borders that were between the stays were lions, oxen and cherubim; and upon the stays it was in like manner above; and beneath the lions and oxen were wreaths of hanging work. And every base had four brazen wheels, and axles of brass; and the four feet thereof had undersetters; beneath the laver were the undersetters molten, with wreaths at the side of each. And the mouth of it within the crown and above, was a cubit high; and the mouth thereof was round like the work of a pedestal, a cubit and a half; and also upon the mouth of it were gravings; and their borders were foursquare, not round. And the four wheels were underneath the borders, and the axle-trees of the wheels were in the base; and the height of a wheel was a cubit and half a cubit. And the work of the wheel was like the work of a chariot-wheel; their axle-trees, and their felloes, and their spokes, and their hubs were all molten. And there were four undersetters at the four corners of each base; the undersetters thereof were of one piece with the base itself. And in the top of the base was a round compass of half a cubit high; and on the top of the base, the stays thereof and the borders thereof were of one piece therewith. And on the plates of the stays thereof and on the borders thereof, he graved cherubim and palm-trees, and lions according to the space of each, with wreaths round about. After this manner he made the ten bases; all of them had one casting, one measure, and one form. And he made ten lavers of brass; one laver contained forty baths; and every laver was four cubits, and upon every one of the ten bases, one laver. And he set the bases, five on the right side of the house, and five on the left side of the house; and he set the sea on the right side of the house, eastward towards the south. And Hiram made the pots and the shovels and the basins.

So Hiram made an end of doing all the work that he wrought for king Solomon in the house of Yahweh; the two pillars and the two bowls of the capitals that were on the top of the pillars; and the two networks to cover the two bowls of the capitals that were on the top of the pillars; and the four hundred pomegranates for the two networks, two rows of pomegranates for each network to cover the two bowls of the capitals that were upon the top of the pillars; and the ten bases, and the ten lavers on the bases; and the one sea, and the twelve oxen under the sea; and the pots, and the shovels, and the basins; even all these vessels which Hiram made for king Solomon were of burnished brass. In the plain of the Jordan did the king cast them, in the clay ground between Succoth and Zarethan. And Solomon left all the vessels unweighed, because they were exceeding many; the weight of the brass could not be found out.

But Solomon made all the vessels in the House of Yahweh of gold: the golden altar, and the table where the show-bread was; and the candlesticks, five on the right side and five on the left before the Sanctuary; the flowers and the lamps and the tongs; and the cups and the snuffers and the basins and the pans and the fire-pans, of pure gold; and the hinges, both for the doors of the inner house, the most holy place, and for the doors of the House, that is, of the Temple.

Thus all the work that king Solomon wrought for the House of Yahweh was finished. And Solomon brought in the things which David his father had dedicated, the silver and the gold, and the vessels, and put them in the treasuries of the House of Yahweh.

Then Solomon assembled the elders of Israel, and all the heads of the tribes, the princes of the father's houses of the Children of Israel, unto king Solomon in Jerusalem to bring the ark of Yahweh out of the City of David at the feast in the month Ethanim. And the priests took up the ark of Yahweh, and brought in the ark of Yahweh unto its place, into the Sanctuary of the house, even under the wings of the cherubim. For the cherubim spread forth their wings over the place of the ark, and the cherubim covered the ark and the staves thereof above. And the staves were so long, that the ends of the staves were seen from the holy place, even in front of the Sanctuary; but they could not be seen without, and there they are unto this day. There was nothing in the ark save the two tables of stone which Moses put there at Horeb. And it came to pass, when the priests were come out of the holy place, that the cloud filled the House of Yahweh, so that the priests could not stand to minister by reason of the cloud; for the glory of Yahweh filled the House of Yahweh. Then spake Solomon:

Yahweh hath said that He would dwell in the thick darkness.
I have surely built Thee   a house of habitation,
      A place for Thee to dwell in for ever.

Then the king turned about and blessed all the congregation of Israel; and all the congregation of Israel stood. And he said: Blessed be Yahweh, the God of Israel, who spake with His mouth unto David my father, and hath with His hand fulfilled it, saying: Since the day that I brought forth My people Israel out of Egypt, I chose no city out of all the tribes of Israel to build a house that My name might be there; but I chose David to be over My people Israel. And Yahweh said unto David my father: Thy son that shall come forth out of thy loins, he shall build the house for My name. And Yahweh hath established His word that He spake; for I am risen up in the room of David my father and sit on the throne of Israel, as Yahweh promised, and have built the House for the name of Yahweh, the God of Israel. And there I have set a place for the ark, wherein is the covenant of the Lord, which He made with our fathers, when He brought them out of the land of Egypt.

And Solomon stood before the altar of Yahweh, and blessed all the congregation of Israel with a loud voice, saying: Blessed be Yahweh that hath given rest unto His people Israel, according to all that He promised; there hath not failed one word of all His good promise, which He promised by the hand of His servant Moses. May Yahweh, our God be with us, as He was with our fathers; let Him not leave us nor forsake us. Let your heart, therefore, be whole with Yahweh your God, to walk in His statutes and to keep His commandments, as at this day.

And the king and all Israel with him offered sacrifice before Yahweh. And Solomon offered for the sacrifice of peace-offerings which he offered unto Yahweh, two and twenty thousand oxen, and a hundred and twenty thousand sheep. Thus did the king and all the Children of Israel dedicate the House of Yahweh. The same day did the king hallow the middle of the court that was before the House of Yahweh; for there he offered the burnt-offering and the meal-offering, and the fat of the peace-offerings; because the brazen altar that was before Yahweh was too little to receive the burnt-offering and the meal-offering and the fat of the peace-offerings.

So Solomon held the feast at that time, and all Israel with him—a great congregation from the entrance of Hamath unto the brook of Egypt,—before Yahweh, our God, seven whole days; and on the eighth day he sent the people away. And they blessed the king, and went unto their tents joyful and glad of heart, for all the goodness that Yahweh had shown unto David His servant and to Israel His people.

Section II.—Solomon builds his own palace, the House of the Forest of Lebanon, and that of his Egyptian queen. Settles his accounts with Hiram, king of Tyre. Rebuilds Gezer and other cities. Establishes a fleet of trading-vessels. Trades on the Red Sea, with Egypt, and even Tarshish (Spain). The visit of the queen of Sheba. His luxurious living, and breach of the laws of the Covenant. Enemies arise in Edom and Damascus. Jeroboam, son of Nebat, whom Solomon had made head of the levy from the northern tribes for his building operations, arouses the king's jealousy and flees into Egypt. Rehoboam succeeds his father Solomon, and the northern tribes appeal for relief from their heavy taxes. Jeroboam, recalled from Egypt, heads their embassy. Rehoboam scornfully refuses, and the tribes revolt, making Jeroboam their king. Rehoboam summons his army, but Yahweh forbids a war. (1 Ki. vii, 1-12; ix, 11b-19, 23, 26-29; x, 11, 12, 14-21, 1-10, 13; xi, 1-9, 14-25, 16-34, 40-43; xii, 1-19, 21-24.)

Materials: As for Section I.

Now Solomon was building his own house thirteen years before he had finished all his house, for he built the House of the Forest of

Lebanon. The length thereof was a hundred cubits, and the breadth thereof fifty cubits, and the height thereof thirty cubits upon four rows of cedar pillars with cedar beams upon the pillars. And it was covered with cedar above upon the side-chambers, that lay on forty and five pillars, fifteen in a row. And there were beams in three rows, and light was over against light in three ranks. And he made the Hall of Pillars; the length thereof was fifty cubits, and the breadth thereof thirty cubits; and before it a porch with pillars, and a threshold before them. Then he made a porch for the throne where he should judge, even the Porch of Judgment; and it was covered with cedar from one side of the floor to the other. His house where he dwelt, in another court, was of like work. Solomon made also for Pharaoh's daughter, whom he had taken to wife, a house like unto this. And Pharaoh's daughter came up out of the City of David unto her house which Solomon had built for her. Then he built Millo.

All these were of costly stones, according to the measure of hewn stones, sawed with saws, within and without, even from the foundation unto the coping, and so on the outside to the great court. And the foundation was of costly stones, even of great stones; stones of ten cubits and stones of eight cubits. And above were costly stones, after the measure of hewn stones, and cedar-wood. And the great court round about had three rows of hewn stone and a row of cedar beams, like as the inner court of the House of Yahweh, and the court of the porch of the House.

Then Solomon gave Hiram [king of Tyre] twenty cities in the land of Galilee. And Hiram came from Tyre to see the cities which Solomon had given him, and they pleased him not. And he said: What cities are these which thou hast given me, my brother? And they are called the land of Cabul unto this day. And Hiram gave unto the king six-score talents of gold.

Now this is the account of the levy which king Solomon raised to build the House of Yahweh, and his own house, and Millo, and the wall of Jerusalem, and Hazor and Megiddo, and Gezer. (Now Pharaoh king of Egypt had gone up and taken Gezer and burnt it with fire, and slain the Canaanites that dwelt in the city, and given it as a portion unto his daughter, Solomon's wife.) And Solomon rebuilt Gezer and Bethhoron the nether, and Baalath, and Tadmor in the wilderness, in the land; and all the store-cities that Solomon had, and cities for his chariots and for his horsemen, and what Solomon desired to build in Jerusalem and in Lebanon, and in all' his dominion. And the chief officers that were over Solomon's work were five hundred and fifty, who bare rule over the people that wrought in the work.

And King Solomon made a fleet of trading vessels in Ezion-geber, which is beside Eloth on the shore of the Red Sea, in the land of Edom. And Hiram sent in them of his servants, shipmen that had knowledge of the sea, with the servants of Solomon. And they came to Ophir, and fetched from thence gold, four hundred and twenty talents, and brought it to King Solomon. And Hiram's navy that brought in gold from Ophir, brought in from Ophir great plenty of sandal-wood and precious stones. And the king made of the sandalwood pillars for the king's house, harps also and psalteries; there came no such sandal-wood, nor was seen, unto this day.

Now the weight of gold that came to Solomon in one year was six hundred threescore and six talents of gold, besides that which came of the merchants and of the traffic of the traders, and of all the kings of the mingled people and of the governors of the country. And King Solomon made two hundred targets of beaten gold; six hundred shekels of gold went to one target. And he made three hundred shields of beaten gold; three pounds of gold went to one shield; and the king put them in the House of the Forest of Lebanon.

Moreover the king made a great throne of ivory, and overlaid it with the finest gold. There were six steps to the throne, and the top of the throne was round behind; and there were arms on either side on the place of the seat, and two lions standing beside the arms. And twelve lions stood there on the one side and on the other on the six steps; there was not the like made in any kingdom. And all King Solomon's drinking-cups were made of gold, and all the vessels of the House of the Forest of Lebanon were of pure gold; none were of silver; it was nothing accounted of in the days of Solomon. For the king had at sea a navy of Tarshish with the navy of Hirom; once every three years came the navy of Tarshish, bringing gold and silver, ivory and apes and peacocks. And they brought every man his present, vessels of silver and vessels of gold, and raiment and armor and spices, horses and mules,—a rate year by year. And Solomon gathered together chariots and horsemen; and he had a thousand and four hundred chariots, and twelve thousand horsemen that he bestowed in the chariot cities, and with the king in Jerusalem. Now the horses which Solomon had were brought out of Egypt; also out of Keveh, the king's merchants buying them of the men of Keveh at a price. And a chariot came up and went out of Egypt for six hundred shekels of silver, and a horse for a hundred and fifty; and so for all the kings of the Hittites, and for the kings of Aram did they bring them out by their means.

Now when the queen of Sheba [1] heard of the fame of Solomon, because of the name of Yahweh, she came to prove him with hard questions. And she came to Jerusalem with a very great train, with camels that bare spices and very much gold, and precious stones; and when she was come to Solomon, she spake to him of all that was in her heart. And Solomon answered all her questions; there was not anything hid from the king, which he told her not. And when the queen of Sheba had seen the wisdom of Solomon, and the house that he had built, and the food of his table, and the seating of his servants; and the attendance of his ministers, and their apparel; and his cup-bearers, and his burnt-offerings which he offered in the house of Yahweh; there was no more spirit in her. And she said to the king: It was a true report that I heard in mine own land of thine acts and of thy wisdom. Howbeit, I believed not the words until I came, and mine eyes had seen it; and behold, the half was not told me; thou hast wisdom and prosperity exceeding the fame that I heard. Happy are thy men, happy are these thy servants that stand continually before thee, and that hear thy wisdom. Blessed be thy God Yahweh, who delighted in thee to set thee on the throne of Israel. Because Yahweh loved Israel for ever, therefore made he thee king, to do justice and righteousness.

And she gave the king a hundred and twenty talents of gold, and of spices very great store, and precious stones. There came no more such abundance of spices as those which the queen of Sheba brought to King Solomon. And King Solomon gave to the queen of Sheba all her desire; whatsoever she asked, besides that which Solomon gave

[1] The story of the Queen of Sheba, though added late, seems to have come from the same source as the rest of J's account; it is only another detail, however, of the dizzy height of fame and glory attributed to Solomon, which brought about the fall of his kingdom. It is a tradition greatly cherished by the Arabs.

her of his royal bounty. So she turned, and went to her own land, she and her servants.

Now King Solomon loved many foreign women besides the daughter of Pharaoh, Moabites, Ammonites, Edomites, Zidonians, and Hittites; of the nations concerning which Yahweh said unto the Children of Israel: Ye shall not go among them, neither shall they come among you; for surely they will turn away your heart after their gods. Solomon did cleave unto these in love. And he had seven hundred wives, princesses, and three hundred concubines. For it came to pass, when Solomon was old, that his heart was not perfect with Yahweh his God, as was the heart of David his father. For Solomon did build a high place for Chemosh, the abomination of the Moabites, in the mount that is before Jerusalem, and for Melech, the abomination of the children of Ammon. And so did he for all his foreign wives, who offered and sacrificed unto their gods.

And Yahweh was angry with Solomon because his heart was turned away from Yahweh the God of Israel. And Yahweh raised up an adversary unto Solomon, Hadad the Edomite; he was of the king's seed in Edom. For it came to pass, when David was in Edom, and Joab, the captain of the host, had gone up to bury the slain, and had smitten every male in Edom (for Joab and all Israel remained there six months until he had cut off every male in Edom), that Hadad fled, he and certain Edomites of his father's servants with him, to go into Egypt, Hadad being yet but a little child. And they arose out of Midian and came to Paran; and they took men with them out of Paran and came to Egypt, unto Pharaoh, king of Egypt, who gave him a house and appointed him victuals, and gave him land. And Hadad found great favor in the sight of Pharaoh, so that he gave him to wife the sister of his own wife, the sister of Tahpahnes, the queen. And the sister of Tahpahnes bare him Genubath, his son, whom Tahpahnes weaned in Pharaoh's house; and Genubath was in Pharaoh's house among the sons of Pharaoh. But when Hadad heard in Egypt that David slept with his fathers and that Joab, the captain of the host, was dead, Hadad said unto Pharaoh: Let me depart that I may go into mine own country. Then Pharaoh said unto him: But what hast thou lacked with me that thou makest to go to thine own country? And he answered: Nothing; howbeit, let me depart in any wise.[1]

And God raised up another adversary unto him, Rezon, the son of Eliada, who had fled from his lord, Hadadezer, King of Zobah. And he gathered men unto him, and became captain over a troop, when David slew them [of Zobah]; and they went to Damascus, and dwelt therein; and he reigned in Damascus. And he was an adversary to Israel all the days of Solomon, *besides the mischief that Hadad did;* and he abhorred Israel, and reigned over Aram.

And Jeroboam, the son of Nebat, an Ephrathite of Zeredah, whose mother's name was Zeruiah, a widow, he also lifted up his hand against the king. And this was the cause that he lifted up his hand against the king. Solomon built Millo and repaired the breach in the wall of the city of David, his father. And the man Jeroboam was a man of great vigor; and Solomon saw that the young man was industrious, and he gave him charge over all the levy of the house of Joseph. And it came to pass at that time, when Jeroboam went out of Jerusalem, that the prophet Ahijah of Shiloh found him in the way. Now Ahijah had clad himself in a new garment; and they two were alone in the field. And

---

[1] The sequel is hinted at in the next paragraph, and therefore put in Italics there.

Ahijah laid hold of the new garment that was on him, and rent it into twelve pieces. And he said to Jeroboam: Take thee ten pieces; for thus saith Yahweh, the God of Israel. Behold, I will rend the kingdom out of the hand of Solomon, and will give ten tribes to thee. But he shall have one tribe, for My servant David's sake, and for the sake of Jerusalem, the city which I have chosen out of all the tribes of Israel.

Solomon sought therefore to kill Jeroboam. Then Jeroboam arose and fled to Egypt, unto Shishak, King of Egypt, and was in Egypt until the death of Solomon. And Solomon slept with his fathers, and was buried in the city of David his father; and Rehoboam, his son, reigned in his stead.

Now Rehoboam went to Shechem; for all Israel were come to Shechem to make him king. And it came to pass, when Jeroboam the son of Nebat heard it, that Jeroboam and all the congregation of Israel came and spake unto Rehoboam, saying: Thy father made our yoke grievous; now, therefore, make thou the grievous service of thy father and the heavy yoke which he put upon us lighter, and we will serve thee. And he said unto them: Depart for yet three days, then come again unto me. And the people departed. And King Rehoboam took counsel with the old men that had stood before his father Solomon while he yet lived, saying: What counsel give ye me to return answer to this people? And they spake unto him and said: If thou answer them and speak good words unto them, then will they be thy servants for ever. But he forsook the counsel of the old men, which they had given him, and took counsel with the young men that had grown up with him that stood before him. And he said unto them: What counsel give ye, that we may return answer to this people who have spoken to us, saying: Make the yoke that thy father did put upon us lighter. And the young men that were grown up with him spake unto him, saying: Thus shalt thou say unto this people that spake unto thee, saying: Thy father made our yoke heavy, but do thou make it lighter unto us; thus shalt thou say unto them: My little finger is thicker than my father's loins. And now, whereas my father did burden you with a heavy yoke, I will add to your yoke; my father chastised you with whips, but I will chastise you with scorpions.

So Jeroboam and all the people came to Rehoboam on the third day, as the king had bidden, saying: Come to me again the third day. And the king answered the people roughly, and forsook the counsel of the old men which they had given him; and spake to them after the counsel of the young men, saying: My father made your yoke heavy, but I will add to your yoke; my father chastised you with whips, but I will chastise you with scorpions. So the king hearkened not unto the people; for the cause was from Yahweh, that He might establish His word which Yahweh had spoken through Ahijah the Shilonite to Jeroboam the son of Nebat.

And when all Israel saw that the king hearkened not unto them, the people answered the king, saying:

> What share have we in David?
> Or rights in the son of Jesse?
> To your tents, O Israel!
> Now look to thy own house, David!

So Israel departed to their tents.

Then king Rohoboam sent Adoram, who was over the levy; and all Israel stoned him with stones that he died. And king Rehoboam made speed to get him up to his chariot, to flee to Jerusalem. So Israel rebelled against the house of David unto this day; there was none that followed the house of David but the tribe of Judah only.

And when Rehoboam was come to Jerusalem, he assembled all the house of Judah and the tribe of Benjamin, a hundred and fourscore thousand chosen warriors, to fight against the house of Israel to bring the kingdom back to Rehoboam, the son of Solomon. But the word of God came unto Shemaiah the man of God, saying: Speak unto Rehoboam the son of Solomon, king of Judah, and unto all the house of Judah and of Benjamin, and to the rest of the people, saying: Thus saith Yahweh: Ye shall not fight against your brethren the children of Israel; return every man to his house, for this thing is of Me. So they hearkened unto the word of Yahweh, and returned and went their way, according to the word of Yahweh.

CHAPTER VII

THE APOSTASY OF REHOBOAM AND HIS SON ABIJAH AND THE REIGNS OF ASA AND JEHOSHAPHAT, KINGS OF JUDAH

SECTION I.—The evil-doings of Rehoboam and his people. The invasion of the Pharaoh Shishak. Accession of Abijah. His character. The long and righteous rule of Asa. His war with Baasha, king of Israel. His alliance with Ben-Hadad, king of Aram. The successful conclusion of the war. Rebuilds the cities of Geba and Mizpah. The struggle for the throne in apostate Israel; the establishing of the House of Omri. Omri builds the fortress-city, Samaria. Ahab succeeds him as king of Israel. Jehoshaphat succeeds his father Asa in Judah. (1 Ki. xiv, 21b-28, 30-31; xv, 2-5, 7b, 8, 10-15, 33, 18-22; xvi, 15-19, 21-26, 28-34; xv, 24; xxii, 41-45.)

Materials: Chiefly, State and Temple Records immediately preceding the author's day, and tidings of contemporary events both in Judah and Israel.

Rehoboam was forty and one years old when he began to reign; and he reigned seventeen years in Jerusalem; and his mother's name was Naamah, the Ammonitess. And Judah did that which was evil in the sight of Yahweh; and they provoked him to jealousy with their sins that they committed above all that their fathers had done. For they also built high places and pillars, and Asherim on every high hill, and under every leafy tree. And there were also sodomites in the land; and they did according to all the abominations of the nations which Yahweh drove out from before the Children of Israel.

And it came to pass in the fifth year of king Rehoboam, that Shishak king of Egypt came up against Jerusalem. And he took away the treasures of the house of Yahweh, and the treasures of the king's house; he even took away all the shields of gold which Solomon had made. And king Rehoboam made in their stead shields of brass and committed them to the hands of the captains of the guard who kept the door of the king's house. And it was so that, as oft as the king went into the house of Yahweh, the guard bare them, and brought them back into the guard-chamber. Now there was war between Rehoboam and Jeroboam continually.

And Rehoboam slept with his fathers and was buried with his fathers in the city of David; and Abijah his son reigned in his stead. Three years he reigned in Jerusalem; and his mother's name was Maacah, the daughter of Abishalom. And he walked in all the sins of his father, which he had done before him; and his heart was not perfect with Yahweh, his God, like the heart of David his father. Nevertheless for David's sake did Yahweh, his God, give him a lamp in Jerusalem, to set up his son after him and to establish Jerusalem, because David had done what was right in the eyes of Yahweh, and turned not aside from anything that He commanded him all the days of his life, save only in the matter of Uriah the Hittite. And there was war also between Abijah and Jeroboam, all the days of his life.

And Abijah slept with his fathers, and they buried him in the city of David; and Asa his son reigned in his stead. Forty and one years reigned he in Jerusalem; and his mother's name was Maacah. And Asa did that which was right in the eyes of Yahweh, as did David his father. And he put away the sodomites out of the land, and removed all the idols that his father had made. And also Maacah, his mother, he removed from being queen, because she had made an abominable symbol for an Asherah. And Asa cut down her image, and burnt it at the brook Kidron. But the high places were not taken away. Nevertheless the heart of Asa was perfect before Yahweh all his days. And he brought into the house of Yahweh the things that his father had hallowed, and the things that himself had hallowed, silver and gold and vessels.

In the third year of Asa, king of Judah, began Baasha the son of Ahijah to reign over all Israel in Tirzah, and he reigned twenty and four years. And there was war between Asa and Baasha, king of Israel, all their days. And Baasha, king of Israel, went up against Judah and built Ramah, that he might not suffer any one to go out or come in to Asa, king of Judah. Then Asa took all the treasures that were left in the house of Yahweh, and the treasures of the king's house, and delivered them into the hands of his servants; and king Asa sent them to Ben-Hadad, the son of Tabrimmon, the son of Hezion, king of Aram, that dwelt at Damascus, saying: There is a league between thee and me, between thy father and my father; behold, I have sent thee a present of silver and gold; go, break thy league with Baasha, king of Israel, that he may depart from me. And Ben-Hadad hearkened unto king Asa, and sent the captains of his armies against the cities of Israel, and smote Ijon and Dan and Abel-ben-maacah, and all Chinneroth and all the land of Naphtali. And it came to pass, when Baasha heard thereof, that he left off building Ramah, and dwelt in Tirzah. Then king Asa made a proclamation unto all Judah; none was exempted; and they carried away the stones of Ramah and the timber thereof wherewith Baasha had builded; and king Asa rebuilt therewith Geba of Benjamin and Mizpah.

In the twenty and seventh year of Asa, king of Judah, did Zimri reign seven days in Tirzah. Now the people were encamped against Gibbethon, which belonged to the Philistines. And the people that were encamped heard say: Zimri hath conspired and hath smitten the king; wherefore all Israel made Omri, the captain of the host, king over Israel that day in the camp. And Omri went up from Gibbethon, and all Israel with him, and they besieged Tirzah. And it came to pass, when Zimri saw that the city was taken, that he went into the castle of the king's house, and burnt the king's house over him with fire, and died.

Then were the people of Israel divided into two parts: half of the people followed Tibni the son of Ginath, to make him a king; and half followed Omri. But the people that followed Omri prevailed against the people that followed Tibni the son of Ginath; so Tibni died, and Omri reigned.

In the thirty and first year of Asa, king of Judah, began Omri to reign over Israel, and reigned twelve years; six years he reigned in Tirzah. And he bought the hill Samaria of Shemer for two talents of silver; and he built on the hill, and he called the name of the city which he built Samariah after the name of Shemer, the owner of the hill. And Omri did that which was evil in the sight of Yahweh, and dealt wickedly above all that were before him. For he walked in all the way of Jeroboam the son of Nebat, and in his sins wherewith he made Israel to sin, to provoke Yahweh, the God of Israel, with their vanities.

And in the thirty and eighth year of Asa, king of Judah, began Ahab the son of Omri to reign over Israel; and Ahab the son of Omri reigned over Israel in Samaria twenty and two years. And Ahab the son of Omri did that which was evil in the sight of Yahweh above all that were before him. And it came to pass, as if it had been a light thing for him to walk in the sins of Jeroboam the son of Nebat, that he took to wife Jezebel the daughter of Ethbaal, king of the Zidonians, and went and served Baal, and worshipped him. And he reared up an altar for Baal in the house of Baal which he had built in Samaria. And Ahab made the Asherah; and Ahab did yet more to provoke Yahweh, the God of Israel, than all the kings of Israel that were before him.

In his days did Hiel the Bethelite build Jericho. With Abiram his first-born he laid the foundations thereof, and with his youngest son Segub he set up the gates thereof; according to the word of Yahweh, which He spake by the hand of Joshua the son of Nun (Josh. vi, 26).

And Asa slept with his fathers, and was buried with his fathers in the city of David his father; and Jehoshaphat his son reigned in his stead.

And Jehoshaphat the son of Asa began to reign over Judah in the fourth year of Ahab, king of Israel. Jehoshaphat was thirty and five years old when he began to reign; and his mother's name was Azubah, the daughter of Shilhi. And he walked in all the way of Asa his father; he turned not aside from it, doing always that which was right in the sight of Yahweh. Howbeit the high places were not taken away; the people sacrificed and offered in the high places. And Jehoshaphat made peace with the king of Israel.

Section II.—Ben-Hadad of Aram continues the war against Israel. Through the advice of a prophet of Yahweh, Ahab defeats him twice. For his league with the king of Aram, Ahab is warned of his death. The king of Judah, Jehoshaphat, joins Ahab in an attack upon Ramoth-Gilead. Ahab is killed. His son Ahaziah succeeds him. Tries to join Jehoshaphat in trading with Ophir. Jehoshaphat refuses. (1 Ki. xx, 1-43; xxii, 1-38, 40.)
Materials: As for preceding section.

Ben-Hadad, the king of Aram, gathered all his host together; and there were thirty and two kings with him, and horses and chariots; and he went up and besieged Samaria, and fought against it. And he sent messengers to Ahab, king of Israel, into the city, and said unto them: Thus saith Ben-Hadad: Thy silver and thy gold are mine; thy wives also and thy children, even the goodliest are mine. And the king of Israel answered and said: It is according to thy saying, my lord O king; I am thine and all that I have. And the messengers came again, and said: Thus speaketh Ben-Hadad, saying: I sent unto thee, indeed, saying: Thou shalt deliver me thy silver and thy gold, thy wives and thy children; but I will send my servants unto thee to-morrow about this time, and they shall search thy house and the houses of thy servants; and it shall be, that whatever is pleasant in thine eyes, they shall put it in their hand, and take it away.

Then the king of Israel called all the elders of the land, and said: Mark, I pray you, and see how this man seeketh mischief; for he sent unto me for my wives and for my children, and for my silver and my gold; and I denied him not. And all the elders and all the people said unto him: Hearken not thou, neither consent. Wherefore he said unto the messengers of Ben-Hadad: Tell thy master the king: All that thou didst send for to thy servant at the first I will do; but this thing I may not do. And Ben-Hadad sent unto him, and said: The gods do so to me, and more also, if the dust of Samaria shall suffice for handfuls for all the people that follow me. And the king of Israel answered and said: Tell him: Let not him that girdeth on his armor boast himself as he that putteth it off. And it came to pass, when he heard this message as he was drinking, he and the kings, in the booths, that he said unto his servants: Set yourselves in array. And they set themselves in array against the city.

And behold, a prophet came near unto the king of Israel, and said: Thus saith Yahweh: Hast thou seen this great multitude? Behold, I will deliver it into thy hand this day; and thou shalt know that I am Yahweh. And Ahab said: By whom? And he said: Thus saith Yahweh: By the young men of the princes of the provinces. Then he said: Who shall begin the battle? And he answered: Thou. Then he numbered the young men of the princes of the provinces, and they were two hundred and thirty-two; and after them he numbered all the people, even all the children of Israel, being seven thousand.

And they went out at noon. But Ben-Hadad was drinking himself drunk in the booths, he and the kings, the thirty and two kings that helped him. And the young men of the provinces went out first; and Ben-Hadad sent out, and they told him, saying: There are men come from Samaria. And he said: Whether they are come out for peace, take them alive; or whether they are come out for war, take them alive. And they slew every one his man; and the Aramæans fled, and Israel pursued them; and Ben-Hadad the king of Aram escaped on a horse with horsemen. And the king of Israel went out and smote the horses and chariots, and slew the Aramæans with a great slaughter. And the prophet came near to the king of Israel, and said unto him: Go, strengthen thyself, and see and mark what thou doest; for at the return of the season the king of Aram will come up against thee.

And the servants of the king of Aram said unto him: Their God is a God of the hills; therefore they were stronger than we; but let us fight against them in the plain, and surely we shall be stronger than they. And do this thing: take the kings away, every man out of his place, and put captains in their room; and number thee an army, like the army thou hast lost, horse for horse, and chariot for chariot; and we will fight them in the plain, and surely we shall be stronger than they. And he hearkened unto their voice, and did so.

And it came to pass at the return of the season, that Ben-Hadad mustered the Aramæans, and went up to Aphek to fight against Israel. And the children of Israel were mustered and victualled, and went against them; and the children of Israel encamped before them like two little flocks of kids; but the Aramæans filled the country. And a man of God came near and spake unto the king of Israel, and said: Thus saith Yahweh: Because the Aramæans have said: Yahweh is a God of the hills, but he is not a God of the valleys; therefore will I deliver all this great multitude into thy hand; and ye shall know that I am Yahweh. And they encamped one over against the other seven days. And so it was, that in the seventh day the battle was joined; and the children of Israel slew of the Aramæans a hundred thousand footmen in one day. But the rest fled to Aphek into the city; and the wall fell upon twenty and seven thousand men that were left. And Ben-Hadad fled, and came into the city, into an inner chamber.

And his servants said unto him: Behold now, we have heard that the kings of the house of Israel are merciful kings; let us, we pray thee, put sackcloth on our loins, and ropes upon our heads, and go out to the king of Israel; peradventure he will save thy life. So they girded sackcloth on their loins, and put ropes on their heads, and came to the king of Israel, and said: Thy servant Ben-Hadad saith: I pray thee, let me live. And he said: Is he yet alive? he is my brother. Now the men took it for a sign, and hastened to catch it; and they said: Thy brother Ben-Hadad. Then he said: Go, bring him. Then Ben-Hadad came forth to him; and he caused him to come up into his chariot. And Ben-Hadad said unto him: The cities which my father took from thy father, I will restore; and thou shalt make streets for thee in Damascus, as my father made in Samaria. Then said Ahab: I will send thee away with this covenant. So he made a covenant with him and let him go.

And a certain man of the sons of the prophets said unto his neighbor by the command of Yahweh: Smite me, I pray thee. And the man refused to smite him. Then said he unto him: Because thou hast not hearkened to the voice of Yahweh, behold, as soon as thou art departed from me, a lion shall slay thee. (And, as soon as he was departed from him, a lion found him and slew him.) Then he found another man, and said: Smite me, I pray thee. And the man smote him, smiting and wounding him. So the prophet departed, and waited for the king by the way, and disguised himself with his headband over his eyes. And as the king passed by, he cried unto the king, and said: Thy servant went out into the midst of the battle; and behold, a man turned aside and brought a man unto me, and said: Keep this man; if by any means he be missing, then shall thy life be for his life, or else thou shalt pay a talent of silver. And as thy servant was busy here and there, he was gone. And the king of Israel said unto him: So shall thy judgment be; thyself hast decided it. And he hastened and took the headband away from his eyes; and the king of Israel discerned that he was one of the prophets. And he said unto him: Thus saith Yahweh: Because thou hast let go out of thine hand the man whom I had devoted to destruction, therefore thy life shall go for his life, and thy people for his people. And the king of Israel went to his house sullen and displeased, and came to Samaria.

And three years passed without war between Aram and Israel. And it came to pass in the third year, that Jehoshaphat, the king of Judah, came down to the king of Israel. And the king of Israel said unto his servants: Know ye that Ramoth-Gilead is ours? and we are still, and take it not out of the hand of the king of Aram. And he said unto Jehoshaphat: Wilt thou go with me to battle to Ramoth-Gilead? And Jehoshaphat said to the king of Israel: I am as thou art, my people as thy people, my horses as thy horses.

And Jehoshaphat said unto the king of Israel: Inquire, I pray thee, at the word of Yahweh to-day. Then the king of Israel gathered the prophets together, about four hundred men, and said unto them:

Shall I go against Ramoth-Gilead to battle, or shall I forbear? And they said: Go up, for Yahweh will deliver it into the hand of the king. But Jehoshaphat said: Is there not here besides a prophet of Yahweh, that we might inquire of him? And the king of Israel said unto Jehoshaphat: There is yet one man by whom we may inquire of Yahweh, Micaiah the son of Imlah; but I hate him, for he doth not prophesy good concerning me but evil. And Jehoshaphat said: Let not the king say so. Then the king of Israel called an officer, and said: Fetch quickly Micaiah the son of Imlah. Now the king of Israel and Jehoshaphat, the king of Judah, were sitting each on his throne, arrayed in their robes, in the open place before the entrance of the gate of Samaria; and all the prophets prophesying before them. And Zedekiah the son of Chenaanah made him horns of iron, and said: Thus saith Yahweh: With these shalt thou gore the Aramæans until they be consumed. And all the prophets prophesied thus, saying: Go up to Ramoth-Gilead and prosper; for Yahweh will deliver it into the hand of the king.

Now the messenger that went to call Micaiah spake to him, saying: Behold now, the words of the prophets declare with one mouth good unto the king; let thy word, I pray thee, be like the word of one of them, and do thou speak good. And Micaiah said: As Yahweh liveth, what Yahweh saith unto me, that will I speak. And when he was come unto the king, the king said unto him: Micaiah, shall we go to Ramoth-Gilead to battle, or shall we forbear? And he answered him: Go up, and prosper; and Yahweh will deliver it into the hand of the king. And the king said unto him: How oft shall I adjure thee that thou speak unto me nothing but the truth in the name of Yahweh? And he said: I saw all Israel scattered upon the mountain as sheep that have no shepherd; and Yahweh said: These have no master; let them return every man to his home in peace. (And the king of Israel said unto Jehoshaphat: Did I not tell thee that he would not prophesy good concerning me, but evil?) And he continued: Therefore, hear thou the word of Yahweh. I saw Yahweh sitting on a throne, and all the host of heaven standing by Him on His right hand and on His left. And Yahweh said: Who shall entice Ahab, that he may go up and fall at Ramoth-Gilead? And one said on this manner, and another on that manner. And there came forth a spirit and stood before Yahweh, and said: I will entice him. And Yahweh said unto him: Wherewith? And he said: I will go forth, and will be a lying spirit in the mouth of all his prophets. And He said: Thou shalt entice him, and shalt prevail also. Go forth and do so. Now, therefore, behold, Yahweh hath put a lying spirit in the mouth of all these thy prophets; and Yahweh hath spoken evil concerning thee.

Then Zedekiah the son of Chenaanah came near, and smote Micaiah on the cheek, and said: Which way went the spirit of Yahweh from me to speak unto thee? And Micaiah said: Behold, thou shalt see on that day, when thou goest into an inner chamber to hide thyself. And the king of Israel said: Take Micaiah, and carry him back to Amon the governor of the city, and to Joash the king's son, and say: Thus saith the king: Put this fellow in the prison, and feed him on the bread of affliction and the water of affliction until I come in peace. And Micaiah said: If thou return at all in peace, Yahweh hath not spoken by me.

So the king of Israel and Jehoshaphat, the king of Judah, went up to Ramoth-Gilead. And the king of Israel said to Jehoshaphat: I will disguise myself and go into the battle; but put thou on thy robes. And the king of Israel disguised himself.

Now the king of Aram had commanded the thirty and two captains of his chariots, saying: Fight neither with small nor great, save only with the king of Israel. And it came to pass, when the captains of the chariots saw Jehoshaphat, that they said: Surely it is the king of Israel; and they turned aside to fight against him; but Jehoshaphat cried out. And it came to pass, when the captains of the chariots saw that it was not the king of Israel, that they turned back from pursuing him. And a certain man drew a bow at a venture, and smote the king of Israel between the joints of his armor; wherefore he said unto the driver of his chariot: Turn thy hand and bear me out of the host; for I am sore wounded. And the battle increased that day; and the king was stayed up in his chariot against the Aramæans, and died at even; and the blood ran out of the wound into the bottom of the chariot. And there went up a cry throughout the host, about the going down of the sun: Every man to his city, and every man to his country.

So the king died and was brought to Samaria; and they buried the king in Samaria. And they washed the chariot by the pool of Samaria; and the dogs licked up his blood; the harlots also washed themselves there; according to the word that Yahweh had spoken. So Ahab slept with his fathers, and Ahaziah his son reigned in his stead.

[But in Judah] Jehosophat put away out of the land the remnant of the sodomites that remained in the days of his father Asa. Now there was no king in Edom; a deputy was ruler. Jehoshaphat made ships of Tarshish to go to Ophir for gold; but they went not, for the ships were broken in Ezion-geber. Then said Ahaziah the son of Ahab unto Jehoshaphat: Let my servants go with thy servants in the ships; but he would not[1] . . .

[1] Here ends the great work of J,—abruptly, as if the pen had just fallen from his hand. The Ephraimite author E, having covered the same ground from Abraham to Ahab and given most vital traditions of the national heroes, rounds out the history of the usurpers in Israel during Asa's reign in Judah from the Ephraimitic point of view; and, in his accounts of Elisha's activities and the reign of Joash in Judah (Stories xvii and xvii), brings history to the reign of Jeroboam II in the middle of the eighth century B.C.

THE
GOLDEN AGE OF HEBREW LITERATURE

FIRST PERIOD

PROSE AND POETRY OF THE EIGHTH CENTURY, B.C.

NOTABLE DEEDS OF ISRAEL'S HEROES

POEMS OF AMOS OF TEKOA IN JUDAH

POEMS OF HOSEA, THE EPHRAIMITE

POEMS OF ISAIAH, THE COUNSELLOR OF HEZEKIAH

POEMS OF MICAH, THE MORASTHITE

SUPPLEMENT OF J'S HISTORY OF ISRAEL, BY JE

WITH A LATE ADDITION BY P.

NOTABLE DEEDS OF THE PATRIARCHS AND HEROES OF ISRAEL

BY THE EPHRAIMITE AUTHOR E

I

OF ABRAHAM, THE PROGENITOR OF THE ISRAELITES

The birth of Isaac. The abolition for his descendants of human sacrifice. (Genesis, xv, 1-18; xvi, 1a, 3, 15; xx, 1-17; xxi, 1b, 2b, 6-21; xxii, 1-13.)

The word of Yahweh came to Abram in a vision, saying: Fear not, Abram; I am thy shield. Thy reward shall be exceeding great. And Abram said: O God Yahweh, what wilt Thou give me, seeing I go childless, and he that shall be the possessor of my goods is this Eliezer of Damascus? Behold, to me Thou hast given no seed, and one born in my house is mine heir. Then behold, the word of Yahweh came to him saying: This shall not be thine heir, but he that shall come forth of thine own bowels shall be thine heir. And He brought him forth abroad, and said: Look now toward heaven and count the stars, if thou be able to count them. And He said unto him: So shall thy seed be. And he believed in Yahweh, and it was counted to him for righteousness.

And He said unto him: I am Yahweh, that brought thee out of Ur of the Chaldees to give thee this land for an inheritance. And he said: O God Yahweh, whereby shall I know that I shall inherit it? And He answered him: Take Me a heifer of three years old, and a turtle-dove and a young pigeon. And he took unto him all these and divided them in the midst, and laid each piece, one against the other; but the birds he divided not. And when the fowls came down upon the carcasses, Abram drove them away.

Now, when the sun was going down, a deep sleep fell upon Abram, and lo, a horror of great darkness fell upon him. And He said unto Abram: Know of a surety that thy seed shall be a stranger in a land that is not theirs, and shall serve them; and they shall afflict them four hundred years. And that nation also whom they shall serve will I judge; and afterward shall they come out with great substance. But thou shalt go to thy fathers in peace; thou shalt be buried in a good old age. But in the fourth generation shall they come hither again; for the iniquity of the Amorites is not yet full.

And it came to pass that when the sun went down and it was dark, behold! a smoking furnace and a burning torch that passed between the pieces.

In the same day, Yahweh made a covenant with Abram, saying: Unto thy seed will I give this land from the river of Egypt to the great river, the river Euphrates.

167

Now Sarai, Abram's wife, bare him no children. And Sarai, Abram's wife, took Hagar the Egyptian, her maid, after Abram had dwelt twelve years in the land of Canaan, and gave her to her husband to be his wife. And Hagar bare Abram a son. And Abram called the name of his son whom Hagar bare, Ishmael. And Abraham[1] journeyed from thence and dwelled between Kadesh and Shur, and sojourned in Gerar. And Abraham said of Sarah his wife: She is my sister. And Abimelech, king of Gerar, sent and took Sarah. But God came to Abimelech in a dream by night, and said unto him: Behold, thou art a dead man on account of the woman thou hast taken, for she is a man's wife. And Abimelech had not come near her; and he said: Lord, wilt thou slay even a righteous person? Said he not unto me, She is my sister? and she, even she herself said: He is my brother. In the integrity of my heart and innocency of my hands have I done this. And God said unto him in a dream: Yea, I know that thou didst this in the integrity of thy heart, for I also withheld thee from sinning against me; therefore suffered I thee not to touch her. Now therefore, restore to the man his wife, for he is a prophet; and he shall pray for thee, and thou shalt live. But, if thou restore her not, thou shalt surely die, thou and all that is thine.

Then Abimelech rose early in the morning and called his servants, and told all these things in their ears. And the men were sore afraid. And Abimelech called Abraham, and said unto him: What hast thou done unto us? and how have I offended thee, that thou hast brought upon me and on my kingdom a great sin? Thou hast done deeds unto me that ought not to be done. And Abimelech said unto Abraham: What sawest thou, that thou hast done this thing? And Abraham said: Because I thought, Surely the fear of God is not in this place, and they will slay me for my wife's sake. And yet she is indeed my sister; she is the daughter of my father, but not the daughter of my mother; and she became my wife. And it came to pass when God caused me to wander from my father's house, that I said unto her: This is the kindness which thou shalt show me; at whatever place whither we come, say of me: He is my brother.

And Abimelech took sheep and oxen and man-servants and maid-servants, and gave them unto Abraham, and restored him Sarah his wife. And Abimelech said: Behold, my land is before thee; dwell where it pleaseth thee. And unto Sarah he said: Behold, I have given thy brother a thousand pieces of silver. Behold, he is to thee a covering of the eyes, unto all that are with thee and to all other, and before all men thou art righted. And Abraham prayed unto God; and God healed Abimelech and his wife and his maid-servants, and they bare children.

And God did to Sarah as he had spoken, at the set time of which He had spoken. And Sarah said: God hath made me to laugh; every one that heareth will laugh with me. And she said: Who would have said unto Abraham that Sarah should give children suck? for I have borne him a son in his old age. And the child grew and was weaned. And Abraham made a great feast the day Isaac was weaned. And Sarah saw the son of Hagar the Egyptian, which she had borne to Abraham, mocking. Wherefore she said unto Abraham: Cast out the bondwoman and her son; for the son of this bondwoman shall not be heir with my son, with Isaac. And the thing was very grievous in

[1] The circumstances of the change of the names of Abram and Sarai are told by P, in ch. xvii, A. V.

Abraham's sight, because of his son. And God said unto Abraham: Let it not be grievous in thy sight because of the lad and because of the bondwoman; in all that Sarah hath said unto thee, hearken unto her voice; for in Isaac shall thy seed be called. And also of the son of the bondwoman will I make a nation, because he is thy seed.

And Abraham rose up early in the morning and took bread and a bottle of water, and gave them unto Hagar, putting them on her shoulder and the child, and sent her away. And she departed, and wandered in the wilderness of Beersheba. When the water was spent in the bottle, she cast the child under one of the shrubs. And she went and sat her down over against him a good way off, as it were a bow-shot; for she said: Let me not see the death of the child. And she sat over against him, and lifted up her voice and wept. And God heard the voice of the lad; and the angel of God called unto Hagar out of heaven and said unto her: What aileth thee, Hagar? fear not, for God hath heard the voice of the lad where he is. Arise, lift up the lad, and hold him in thine hand; for I will make him a great nation. And God opened her eyes, and she saw a well of water; and she went and filled the bottle with water, and gave the lad drink. And God was with the lad; and he grew and dwelt in the wilderness, and he became an archer. And he dwelt in the wilderness of Paran; and his mother took him a wife out of the land of Egypt.

And it came to pass at that time, that Abimelech and Phicol the chief captain of his host spake unto Abraham, saying: God is with thee in all that thou doest. Now therefore swear unto me by God that thou wilt not deal falsely with me, nor with my son, nor with my son's son. According to the kindness that I have done to thee, thou shalt do unto me and to the land wherein thou hast sojourned. And Abraham said, I will swear. And Abraham reproved Abimelech because of a well of water which Abimelech's servants had violently taken away. And Abimelech said: I wot not who hath done this thing; neither didst thou tell me, neither yet heard I of it but to-day. And Abraham took sheep and oxen and gave them to Abimelech, and they two made a covenant. And Abraham set seven ewe-lambs of the flock by themselves. And Abimelech said unto Abraham: What mean these seven ewe-lambs which thou hast set by themselves? And he said: These seven ewe-lambs shalt thou take of my hand, that it may be a witness unto me, that I have digged this well. Wherefore he called that place Beersheba (Well of an oath); because there they sware, both of them. So they made a covenant at Beersheba.

And it came to pass after these things, that God did tempt Abraham, and said unto him: Abraham! And he said: Behold, here I am. And he said: Take now thy son, thine only son Isaac whom thou lovest, and get thee into the land of Moriah, and offer him there for a burnt-offering upon one of the mountains which I shall tell thee of. And Abraham rose up early in the morning and saddled his ass, and took two of his young men with him, and Isaac his son, and clave the wood for the burnt-offering, and rose up and went unto the place of which God had told him. Then, on the third day Abraham lifted up his eyes and saw the place afar off. And Abraham said unto his young men: Abide ye here with the ass, and I and the lad will go yonder and worship, and come again to you. And Abraham took the wood of the burnt offering and laid it upon Isaac, his son; and he took the fire in his hand, and a knife; and they went both of them together. And Isaac spake unto Abraham, his father, and said: My father! And he said: Here am I, my son. And he said: Behold the fire and the wood, but where is the lamb for a burnt-offering? And Abraham said: My son, God will provide himself a lamb for a burnt-offering. So they went both of them together. And they came to the place which God had told him of; and Abraham built an altar there and laid the wood in order, and bound Isaac his son and laid him on the altar upon the wood. And Abraham stretched forth his hand and took the knife to slay his son. And the messenger of Yahweh called unto him out of heaven, and said: Abraham, Abraham! And he said: Here am I. And he said: Lay not thine hand upon the lad, neither do thou anything unto him; for now I know that thou fearest God, seeing thou hast not withheld thy son, thine only son from me. And Abraham lifted up his eyes and looked, and behold, behind him a ram caught in a thicket by his horns. And Abraham went and took the ram, and offered him up for a burnt-offering instead of his son.[1] Then Abraham returned unto his young men, and they rose up and went together to Beersheba. And Abraham dwelt at Beersheba.

II

OF ESAU AND JACOB, TWIN SONS OF ISAAC

(Genesis, xxvii, 41a, 43, 44b-45; xxviii, 10-12, 17-18, 20-22; xxix, 15-23, 25-31; xxx, 1-5, 17-24; xxxi, 2, 4-16, 20-22, 24-25a, 26-29, 31, 41-43, 45-50, 53b-54; xxxii, 2-5, 14b-22, 24-33; xxxiii, 18-20; xxxv, 1-20.)

Now Esau hated Jacob, because of the blessing wherewith his father had blessed him; and Rebekah told Jacob and said: Now therefore, my son, hear my voice; flee thou to Laban until thy brother's anger turn away from thee, and he forget what thou hast done to him. Then I will send and fetch thee thence. Why should I be bereaved of you both in one day? And Jacob went out from Beersheba, and went toward Haran. And he lighted upon a certain place and tarried there all that night, because the sun was set. And he took one of the stones of the place, and put it under his head and lay down to sleep. And he dreamed; and behold, a ladder set up on the earth, and the top of it reached to heaven; and behold, the messengers of God ascending and descending upon it. And he was afraid, and said: How dreadful is this place! This is none other than the house of God, and this is the gate of heaven. And Jacob rose up early in the morning, and took the stone that he had put under his head and set it up for a pillar, and poured oil on the top of it. And Jacob vowed a vow, saying: If God will be with me, and will keep me in this way that I go, and will give me bread to eat and raiment to put on, so that I come to my father's house in peace; then shall Yahweh be my God, and this stone, which I have set up for a pillar, shall be the house of God. And of all that Thou shalt give me I will surely give the tenth unto thee.[2]

*   *   *   *   *   *

Then Laban said unto Jacob: Because thou art my kinsman, shouldest thou therefore serve me for naught? tell me, what shall thy wages

---

[1] "And the messenger of Yahweh called unto Abraham a second time out of heaven, and said: By myself have I sworn, saith Yahweh, because thou hast done this thing, and hast not withheld thy son, thine only son; that in blessing I will bless thee, and in multiplying I will multiply thy seed as the stars of heaven and as the sand upon the seashore; and thy seed shall possess the gates of his enemies. And in thy seed shall all the nations of the earth be blessed; because thou hast obeyed my voice." (xxii, 15-18.) (Fragment from a Judaic form of the same narrative.)

[2] The meeting of Jacob and Rachel and his introduction to Laban are given by J.

be? Now Laban had two daughters; the name of the elder was Leah, and the name of the younger was Rachel. Leah's eyes were weak; but Rachel was beautiful in form and fair to look upon. And Jacob loved Rachel, and said: I will serve thee seven years for Rachel, thy younger daughter. And Laban said: It is better that I give her to thee than to another man; abide with me. And Jacob served seven years for Rachel; and they seemed to him but a few days, for the love he had to her.

And Jacob said unto Laban: Give me my wife, for my days are fulfilled, that I may go in unto her. And Laban gathered together all the men of the place and made a feast. And it came to pass in the evening, that he took Leah his daughter, and brought her to him; and he went in unto her. And it came to pass that in the morning, behold, it was Leah. And he said to Laban: What is this thou hast done unto me? Did I not serve with thee for Rachel? Wherefore hast thou deceived me? And Laban said: It must not be so done in our country, to give the younger before the firstborn. Fulfil her week and I will give thee Rachel also for the service which thou shalt do for me for seven more years. And Jacob did so, and fulfilled the week for the one and he gave him Rachel his daughter to wife also. And he went in also unto Rachel, but he loved Rachel more than Leah; and he served him yet another seven years.

And when Rachel saw that she bare Jacob no children, Rachel envied her sister; and she said unto Jacob: Give me children, or else I die. And Jacob's anger was kindled against Rachel, and he said: Am I in God's stead, who hath withheld from thee the fruit of the womb? And she said: Behold my maid Bilhah, go in unto her, and she shall bear upon my knees. And Bilhah conceived and bare Jacob a son; and Rachel said: God hath judged me, but hath also heard my voice, and given me a son. Therefore called she his name Dan (*He judged*). And Bilhah, Rachel's maid, conceived again, and bare Jacob a second son. And Rachel said: With mighty wrestlings have I wrestled with my sister, and I have prevailed. And she called his name Naphthali (*My wrestling*). And God hearkened unto Leah; and she conceived and bare Jacob a fifth son. And Leah said: God hath given me my hire, because I have given my handmaid to my husband. And she called his name Issachar (*Bought*). And Leah conceived again and bare Jacob a sixth son. And Leah said: God hath endowed me with a good dowry; now will my husband dwell with me. And she called his name Zebulun (*Dwelling*). And afterwards she bare a daughter and called her name Dinah.

And God remembered Rachel, and God hearkened unto her and opened her womb. And she conceived and bare a son, and said: God hath taken away my reproach. And she called his name Joseph, (*He will add*), and said: Yahweh shall add to me another son:

And Jacob beheld the countenance of Laban, and behold, it was not toward him as before. And Jacob sent and called Rachel and Leah to the field unto his flock, and said unto them: I see your father's countenance, that it is not toward me as before; but the God of my father hath been with me; and ye know, that with all my power I have served your father. And your father hath deceived me and changed my wages ten times; but God suffered him not to hurt me. If he said: The speckled shall be your wages; then all the flock bare speckled; and if he said thus: The striped shall be thy hire; then all the flock bare striped. Thus hath God taken away the flocks of your father, and given them to me. And it came to pass at the time that the flocks conceived, that I lifted up mine eyes and saw in a dream, and behold, the he-goats which leaped upon the flock were striped, speckled and spotted. And the angel of God said unto me in a dream: Jacob! And I said: Here am I. And he said: Lift up thine eyes now and see, all the he-goats which leap upon the flock are striped, speckled and spotted; for I have seen all that Laban doeth unto thee. I am the God of Bethel, where thou didst anoint the pillar, and where thou didst vow a vow unto me. Now arise, get thee out from this land and return to the land of thy kindred. And Rachel and Leah answered and said unto him: Is there yet any portion or inheritance for us in our father's house? Are we not counted of him strangers? for he hath sold us and hath quite devoured our money. But all the riches which God hath taken from our father belongs to us and to our children. Now, then, whatsoever God hath said unto thee, do. Then Jacob deceived Laban the Aramæan, in that he did not tell him that he was about to flee away. And he rose up and passed over the River. And it was told Laban on the third day that Jacob had fled. But God came to Laban the Aramæan in a dream by night, and said unto him: Take heed that thou speak not to Jacob, good or bad. Then Laban overtook Jacob and said unto Jacob: What hast thou done, that thou hast stolen away unawares, and carried away my daughters as captives by the sword? Thou hast not suffered me to kiss my sons and my daughters. Now hast thou acted foolishly. It is in the power of my hand to do thee harm; but the God of your father spake unto me yesternight, saying: Take thou heed that thou speak not to Jacob either good or bad. And Jacob answered Laban saying: I was afraid lest thou shouldst tear thy daughters from me. These twenty years have I been in thy house. I served thee fourteen years for thy two daughters and six years for the flock, and thou hast changed my wages ten times. Except the God of my father, the God of Abraham and the Fear of Isaac had been with us, surely thou hadst sent me away empty. God hath seen my affliction and the labor of my hands and rebuked thee yesternight. And Laban answered and said unto Jacob: The daughters are my daughters and the children are my children, and the flock is my flock, and all thou seest is mine; and what can I do unto these my daughters and unto their children which they have borne?

Then Jacob took a stone and set it up for a pillar. Then Laban said: If thou shalt afflict my daughters, or if thou shalt take wives besides my daughters, no man is with us; understand, God is witness between me and thee. And Jacob sware by the Fear of his father Isaac. Then Jacob offered a sacrifice upon the mount, and called his kinsmen to eat bread. And they did eat bread and tarried all night in the mount. And early in the morning Laban rose up and kissed his sons and his daughters and blessed them. And Laban departed and returned to his place.

And Jacob went on his way, and the messengers of God met him. And when Jacob saw them, he said: This is God's host. And he called the name of that place Mahanaim, (*Encampments*).

*   *   *   *   *   *   *

And Jacob took of that which came to his hand a present for Esau his brother; two hundred she-goats and twenty he-goats, two hundred ewes and twenty rams, thirty milch camels with their colts, forty kine and ten bulls, twenty she-asses and ten foals; and he delivered them into the hands of his servants, drove by drove, and said unto his servants: Pass over before me, and put a space between drove and drove. And he commanded the foremost, saying: When Esau my brother meeteth thee and asketh thee, saying: Whose man art thou? and whither art thou going? and whose are these droves before thee? then thou shalt say: Thy servant Jacob's. It is a present sent unto my lord Esau; and behold, he himself is behind us. And so commanded he the second and the third and all that followed the droves, saying: In this manner shall ye speak unto Esau, when ye find him. And say ye moreover, Behold, thy servant Jacob is behind us. (For he said to himself: I will appease him with the present that goeth before me, and afterward I will see his face; peradventure he will look favorably upon me.) So the present passed over before him, but he remained that night in the camp. And he took them [his family] and sent them over the brook and all his possessions; and Jacob was left alone. And there wrestled a man with him until the break of day. And when he saw that he prevailed not over him, he touched the hollow of his thigh; and the hollow of Jacob's thigh was out of joint as he wrestled with him. And he said: Let me go! for the day breaketh. And he said: I will not let thee go unless thou bless me. And he said unto him: What is thy name? And he said: Jacob. And he said: Thy name shall be called no more Jacob (*Supplanter*), but Israel (*Prince of God*); for as a prince hast thou striven with God and with men, and hast prevailed. And Jacob asked him and said: Tell me, I pray thee, thy name. And he said: Why dost thou ask my name? and he blessed him there. And Jacob called the name of the place, Peniel (*Face of God*); for I have seen God face to face, and my life is spared. And as he passed over Peniel, the sun rose over him, and he halted upon his thigh. Therefore the Children of Israel eat not of the sinew that shrank, which is upon the hollow of the thigh, unto this day, because he touched the hollow of Jacob's thigh in the sinew that shrank. And Jacob came in peace to the city of Shechem, which is in the land of Canaan, when he came from Padan Aram, and pitched his tent before the city. And he bought the piece of land where he had spread his tent at the hand of the children of Hamor, Shechem's father, for a hundred pieces of money. And he erected there an altar, and called it El-Elohe-Israel (*El, God of Israel*).

And God said unto Jacob: Arise, go up to Bethel and dwell there; and make there an altar unto God who appeared unto thee when thou didst flee from the face of Esau, thy brother. Then Jacob said unto his household, and to all that were with him: Put away the strange gods that are among you, and be clean and change your garments; and let us arise and go up to Bethel. And I will make there an altar unto God who answered me in the day of my distress, and was with me in the way which I went. And they gave unto Jacob all the strange gods which were in their hand, and the earrings which were in their ears, and Jacob hid them under the oak which was by Shechem. And they journeyed; and a great terror was upon the cities that were around about them, and they did not pursue after the sons of Jacob. So Jacob came to Luz, which is in the land of Canaan, (that is, Bethel), he and all the people with him. And he built there an altar and called the place El-Bethel (*God of Bethel*), because there God appeared unto him when he fled from the face of his brother. But Deborah,

Rebekah's nurse, died, and she was buried below Bethel under the oak. And its name was called Allon-Bacuth (*Oak of weeping*).

And they journeyed from Bethel, and there was still some little distance to come to Ephrath when Rachel travailed, and she had hard labor. And it came to pass when she was in hard labor, that the midwife said unto her: Fear not: thou shalt have this son also. And it came to pass, as her soul was departing (for she was dying), that she called his name Benoni (*The son of my sorrow*); but his father called him Benjamin. And Rachel died and was buried in the way to Ephrath, which is Bethlehem. And Jacob set a pillar upon her grave: that is the pillar of Rachel's grave to this day.

III

OF JOSEPH, VIZIR OF EGYPT

A.—The older sons of Jacob give Joseph to the Midianites, who sell him in Egypt. He has a gift for interpreting dreams. After some years, he interprets the dreams of the Pharaoh and is made Vizir. (Gen. xxxvii, 2b, 6-12, 19-20, 22-24, 28a, c, 29, 30, 36; xl, 1-23; xli, 1-40.)

Joseph, who was about seventeen years of age, was feeding the flock with his brethren. And the lad was with the sons of Bilhah and with the sons of Zilpah, his father's wives; and Joseph brought an evil report of them to his father. And Joseph dreamed a dream, and he told it to his brethren; and they hated him. And he said unto them: Hear, I pray you, this dream that I have dreamed. For we were binding sheaves in the field; and lo, my sheaf arose and stood upright, and lo, your sheaves stood round about and made obeisance to my sheaf. And his brethren said to him: Shalt thou indeed reign over us? or shalt thou indeed have dominion over us? And they hated him yet the more for his dreams and for his words. And he dreamed yet another dream and told it to his brethren, and said: Behold, I have dreamed another dream; and behold, the sun and the moon and eleven stars made obeisance unto me. And he told it to his father and to his brethren; and his father rebuked him and said unto him: What is this dream that thou hast dreamed? Shall I and thy mother and thy brethren indeed come to bow down ourselves to the earth to thee? And his brethren envied him, but his father kept the saying in mind.

And his brethren went to feed their father's flock in Shechem; and they said one to another: Behold, this dreamer cometh. Come now, and let us slay him and cast him into some pit; and we will say: Some beast hath devoured him. Then we shall see what will become of his dreams. But Reuben said unto them: Shed no blood; cast him into this pit that is in the wilderness, and lay no hand upon him. This he said that he might deliver him out of their hands, and restore him to his father. And it came to pass, when Joseph was come unto his brethren, that they stripped Joseph of his coat, the striped coat that was on him, and they took him and cast him into the pit; and the pit was empty, there was no water in it. Then there passed by Midianites, merchantmen; and they drew up Joseph and lifted him out of the pit; and they [the Midianites] brought him into Egypt.

And Reuben returned unto the pit; and behold, Joseph was not in the pit; and he rent his clothes. And he returned unto his brethren and said: The child is not; and I, whither shall I go? But the Midianites sold him in Egypt to Potiphar, an officer of Pharaoh's, a captain of the guard.

Now it came to pass after these things, that the butler of the king of Egypt and his baker had offended their lord, the king of Egypt. And Pharaoh was wroth against his two officers; and he put them in a ward in the house of the chief executioner. And the chief executioner entrusted them to Joseph, and he waited on them; and they continued some time in ward.

And they dreamed a dream, both of them, each man his dream in one night, each man according to the interpretation of his dream, the chief butler and the chief baker of the king of Egypt who were bound in the prison. And Joseph came in unto them in the morning, and saw them; and behold, they were sad. And he asked Pharaoh's officers that were in ward in his master's house, saying: Why look ye so sad to-day? And they said unto him: We have dreamed a dream, and there is no interpreter of it. And Joseph said unto them: Do not interpretations come from God? Tell me them, I pray you.

Then the chief butler told his dream to Joseph, and said to him: In my dream, behold, a vine was before me, and in the vine three shoots; and, as if it were blooming, its blossoms burst forth, its clusters brought forth ripe grapes. And Pharaoh's cup was in my hand. And I took the grapes and pressed them into Pharaoh's cup, and I gave the cup into Pharaoh's hand. And Joseph said unto him: This is the interpretation of it. The three shoots are three days; within three more days, Pharaoh shall lift up thy head and restore thee to thine office, and thou shalt give Pharaoh's cup into his hand after the former manner when thou wast his cupbearer. But O, remember me when it shall be well with thee, and do me a kindness, I pray thee, and mention me to Pharaoh, and bring me out of this house. For indeed, I was stolen from the land of the Hebrews, and here, too, I have done nothing that they should put me into a dungeon.

When the chief baker saw that the interpretation was good, he said unto Joseph: I also was dreaming, and behold, three baskets of white bread were upon my head, and in the uppermost basket all kinds of food for Pharaoh that a baker prepares; and birds were eating them from the baskets over my head. And Joseph answered and said: This is the interpretation thereof. The three baskets are three days; within the next three days shall Pharaoh lift up thy head from off thee, and shall hang thee on a tree; and the birds shall eat thy flesh from off thee.

And it came to pass on the third day, which was Pharaoh's birthday, that he made a feast unto all his servants. And he lifted up the head of the chief butler and of the chief baker among his servants. And he restored the chief butler unto his office so that he gave the cup into Pharaoh's hand; but he hanged the chief baker, as Joseph had interpreted to them. And the chief butler did not remember Joseph, but forgot him.

Now it came to pass, at the end of two years, that Pharaoh dreamed; and behold, he was standing by the river, and, behold, coming up from the river were seven heifers good to look upon and fat of flesh; and they had been feeding in the Nile-grass. And behold, coming up after them from the river, seven other heifers, ill-favored and lean of flesh;

and they stood near the other heifers on the brink of the river. And the ill-favored and lean-fleshed heifers did eat up the seven well-favored and fat heifers. And Pharaoh awoke. And he slept and dreamed again. And behold, seven ears of grain growing on one stalk, full and good; and behold, seven ears, thin and blasted by the east wind, sprouting forth after them. And the seven thin ears swallowed up the seven thick and full ears. And Pharaoh awoke and behold, it was a dream. And it came to pass in the morning, that his spirit was troubled; and he sent and called for all the magicians of Egypt and all the wise men thereof; and Pharaoh told them his dreams, but there was no one who could interpret them to Pharaoh. Then spake the chief butler to Pharaoh, saying: This day do I remember my sin. Pharaoh was wroth with his servants and put me in ward in the house of the chief executioner, me and the chief baker. And we dreamed a dream the same night, I and he; each according to the interpretation of his dream that he dreamed. And there was with us a Hebrew youth, a servant of the chief executioner; and we told him, and he interpreted to us our dreams; to each according to his dream did he interpret. And it came to pass, as he interpreted to us, so it was; me he restored to mine office, and him he hanged.

Then Pharaoh sent and called Joseph (and they brought him hastily out of the dungeon); and he shaved himself and changed his raiment and came in unto Pharaoh. And Pharaoh said unto Joseph: I have dreamed a dream, and there is no one who can interpret it. Now I have heard it said of thee that when thou hearest a dream, thou canst interpret it. And Joseph answered Pharaoh, saying: Not I; God will answer Pharaoh in full. And Pharaoh said unto Joseph: In my dream, behold, I was standing on the brink of the river. And behold, coming up from the river were seven heifers, fat of flesh and well formed; and they had been feeding in the river-grass. And lo, coming up after them, seven other heifers exceeding poor and lank and lean, worse than I have ever seen in all the land of Egypt. And the lean and ill-favored heifers did eat up the first seven fat heifers; and when they had eaten them up, it could not be known that they had eaten them, for they were as ill-favored as in the beginning. So I awoke. And I saw in my dream, and behold, seven ears growing on one stalk, full and good; and behold, seven ears, withered, thin and blasted by the east wind sprouted forth after them, and the thin ears swallowed up the seven good ears. And I have told it to the magicians, and there is no one who can expound it to me.

Then Joseph said unto Pharaoh: The dream of Pharaoh is one; what God is about to do he hath declared unto Pharaoh. The seven good heifers are seven years, and the seven good ears are seven years; the dream is one. And the seven lean and ill-favored heifers that came up after them are seven years, and also the seven empty ears blasted with the east wind; they shall be seven years of famine. That is the thing which I spake unto Pharaoh; what God is about to do, he hath showed unto Pharaoh. Behold, there are coming seven years of great plenty throughout all the land of Egypt. And there shall arise after them seven years of famine; and all the plenty shall be forgotten in the land of Egypt; and the famine shall consume the land; (and the plenty shall not be known in the land by reason of the famine which followeth, for the famine shall be very severe). And that the dream was repeated unto Pharaoh, it is because the thing is established by God, and God will shortly bring it to pass. Now therefore let Pharaoh look out a man discreet and wise, and set him over the land of Egypt. And let them gather all the food of these good years that come, and let them keep it. And that food shall be a store for the land against the seven years of famine which shall be in the land of Egypt; that the land perish not because of the famine. And the thing was good in the eyes of Pharaoh and in the eyes of all his servants. And Pharaoh said unto his servants: Can we find a man like this, in whom is the spirit of God?

And Pharaoh said unto Joseph: Forasmuch as God hath showed thee all this, there is none so discreet and wise as thou. Thou shalt be over my house, and according to thy word shall all my people be ruled. Only in the throne will I be greater than thou.

B.—Joseph's political career. His provision for his family. The coming of Jacob and his sons to Egypt. Their settlement in Goshen. (Gen. xli, 45b, 47, 49, 50-53, 54b, 57; xlii, 1-38; xliii, 14; xlv, 1b, 2-3, 5b, 6, 7b-9a, 9c, 10b, 13, 15-18, 21b-26, 27b; xlvi, 1b, 2-5; xlvii, 5-6a; xlviii, 1-2, 8-22; l, 15-20.)

Then Joseph went out over all the land of Egypt. And in the seven plenteous years the earth brought forth abundantly. And Joseph gathered grain as the sand of the sea in great quantities, until he ceased to keep account, for there was no counting it. And to Joseph were born two sons before the years of famine came, whom Asenath, the daughter of Potiphera, priest of On, bare unto him. And Joseph called the name of the firstborn Manasseh (*Forgetting*), for God, said he, hath caused me to forget all my suffering and all my father's house. And the name of the second called he Ephraim (*Fruitful*); for God hath caused me to be fruitful in the land of my affliction.

Now the seven years of plenty that was in the land of Egypt came to an end; and there was famine in all lands; but in all the land of Egypt there was bread. And all the earth came into Egypt to Joseph to buy grain, because the famine was sore in all the world.

Now when Jacob saw that there was grain in Egypt, Jacob said unto his sons: Why do ye look one upon another? And he said: Behold, I have heard that there is grain in Egypt; get you down thither, and buy for us from thence; that we may live and not die. So Joseph's ten brethren went down to buy grain in Egypt. But Benjamin, Joseph's brother, Jacob sent not with his brethren; for he said: Lest peradventure mischief befall him. And the sons of Israel came among others who came to buy grain; for the famine was in the land of Canaan.

Now Joseph was governor over the land; he it was that sold grain to all the people of the land. And Joseph's brethren came and bowed themselves down before him with their faces to the earth. And Joseph saw his brethren and recognized them, but he dissembled with them and spake harshly unto them. And he said unto them: Whence come ye? And they said: From the land of Canaan to buy food. And Joseph knew his brethren, but they did not know him. And Joseph remembered the dreams which he had dreamed of them, and said unto them: Ye are spies; to see the nakedness of the land are ye come. And they said unto him: Nay, my lord; but thy servants have come to buy food. We are all one man's sons; we are true men; thy servants are not spies. And he said unto them: Nay, but to see the nakedness of the land are ye come. And they said: Thy servants are twelve brethren, the sons of one man in the land of Canaan; and behold, the youngest is this day with our father, and one is not. And Joseph said unto them: This is what I spake unto you, saying: Ye are spies. Hereby ye shall be proved. As Pharaoh lives, ye shall not go hence unless your youngest brother come hither. Send one of you that he may bring your brother, and ye shall be bound, that your words may be proved whether there be truth in you; but if not, as Pharaoh lives ye are spies. And he put them in ward for three days. And on the third day Joseph said unto them: This do and live, for I fear God. If ye be true men, let one of your brethren be bound in your prison-house; and go ye, carry again for the famine in your houses; and bring your youngest brother unto me; so shall your words be verified, and ye shall not die. And they did so. And they said one to another: Truly we are guilty concerning our brother when we saw the anguish of his soul as he besought us and we would not hear. Therefore is this distress come upon us. And Reuben answered them, saying: Spake I not unto you saying, Sin not against the boy; and ye would not hear? Therefore behold, his blood is required. And they knew not that Joseph understood them, for he had spoken to them through an interpreter. And he turned away from them and wept. And he turned back to them and spake unto them; and he took Simeon from among them and bound him before their eyes. Then Joseph commanded to fill their sacks with grain, and to restore every man's money into his sack, and to give them provision for the way; and thus was it done unto them. And they laded their asses with the grain, and departed thence. And as one of them opened his sack to give his ass provender in the inn, he espied his money; for behold, it was in his sack's mouth. And he said unto his brethren: My money is restored, and lo, it is even in my sack. And their heart failed them, and they said anxiously one to another, What is this that God hath done unto us?

And they came unto Jacob their father unto the land of Canaan, and told him all that had befallen them, saying: The man, the lord of the land, spake roughly to us, and took us for spies of the country. And we said unto him: We are true men, we are no spies; we are twelve brethren, sons of one father; one is not, and the youngest is this day with our father in the land of Canaan. And the man, the lord of the country, said unto us: Hereby shall I know that ye are true men. Leave one of your brethren with me, and take food for the famine of your households, and go. And bring your youngest brother unto me; then shall I know that ye are no spies but true men. Your brother will I give unto you, and ye shall traffic in the land.

Now it came to pass, as they emptied their sacks, that behold, every man's bundle of money was in his sack; and when they and their father saw their bundles of money, they were afraid. And Jacob their father said unto them: Me have ye bereaved. Joseph is not and Simeon is not, and ye will take Benjamin away; all these things are against me. And Reuben spake unto his father, saying: Slay my two sons, if I bring him not to thee. Put him into my hand, and I will bring him back to thee. And he said: God Almighty give you mercy before the man, that he may send away your other brother and Benjamin. And as for me, if I be bereaved of my children, I am bereaved.

*   *   *   *   *   *   *

Now there stood no man with him when Joseph made himself known unto his brethren. And he wept aloud; and the Egyptians and the house of Pharaoh heard. And Joseph said unto his brethren: I am

Joseph; doth my father yet live? And his brethren could not answer him, for they were troubled at his presence: [and he said] Be not angry with yourselves, for God did send me before you to preserve life. For these two years hath the famine been in the land, and there are five more years in which there will be neither plowing nor harvest. And God sent me before you to save your lives by a great deliverance. so now it was not you that sent me hither, but God. And He hath made me a father to Pharaoh and lord of all his house, and a ruler throughout all the land of Egypt. Haste ye and say [*unto my father:*] Thus saith thy son Joseph, God hath made me lord of all Egypt; and thou shalt be near unto me. And ye shall tell my father of all my glory in Egypt and of all that ye have seen; and ye shall haste and bring my father down hither. Then he kissed all his brethren and wept over them, and after that his brethren talked with him.

And the fame thereof was heard in Pharaoh's house, that Joseph's brethren were come; and it pleased Pharaoh and his servants well. And Pharaoh said unto Joseph: Say unto thy brethren: This do ye; lade your beasts and go, get you unto the land of Canaan, and take your father and your households and come unto me; and I will give you the good of the land of Egypt, and ye shall eat the fat of the land. So Joseph gave them wagons, according to the commandment of Pharaoh, and gave them provision for the way. To each one of them he gave changes of raiment; but to Benjamin he gave three hundred pieces of silver and five changes of raiment. And to his father he sent after this manner: ten asses laden with the good things of Egypt, and ten asses laden with grain and bread and meat for his father by the way. So he sent his brethren away, and they departed; and he said unto them: See that ye fall not out by the way.

And they went up out of Egypt, and came into the land of Canaan unto Jacob their father, and told him, saying: Joseph is yet alive, and he is governor over all the land of Egypt. And Jacob's heart fainted, for he believed them not. But when he saw the wagons which Joseph had sent to carry him, the spirit of Jacob their father revived. And he went to Beersheba, and offered sacrifices unto the God of his father Isaac. And God spake to Israel in visions of the night, and said: Jacob! Jacob! And he said: Here am I. And he said: I am God, the God of thy father. Fear not to go down into Egypt, for I will there make of thee a great nation. I will go down with thee into Egypt, and I will surely bring thee up again; and Joseph shall put his hand upon thine eyes. And Jacob rose up from Beersheba; and the sons of Israel carried Jacob, their father, and their little ones and their wives, in the wagons which Pharaoh had sent to carry him.

And Pharaoh spake unto Joseph, saying: Thy father and thy brethren are come unto thee; the land of Egypt is before thee; in the best of the land make thy father and thy brethren to dwell.

And it came to pass after these things, that one said to Joseph: Behold, thy father is sick. And he took with him his two sons, Manasseh and Benjamin. And one told Jacob: Behold, thy son Joseph cometh unto thee. And Israel strengthened himself, and sat up on the bed. And Israel beheld Joseph's sons, and said: Who are these? And Joseph said unto his father: They are my sons, whom God hath given me here. And he said: Bring them unto me, I pray thee, and I will bless them. (Now the eyes of Israel were dimmed with age, so that he could not see.) And he brought them near unto him; and he kissed them and embraced them. And Israel said unto Joseph: I had not thought to see thy face, and lo, God hath showed me also thy seed. And Joseph brought them out from between his knees, and bowed his face to the earth.

And Joseph took them both, Ephraim in his right hand toward Israel's left hand and Manasseh in his left hand towards Israel's right hand, and brought them near unto him. And Israel stretched out his right hand and laid it upon Ephraim's head who was the younger, and his left hand upon Manasseh's head, guiding his hands wittingly; for Manasseh was the first-born. And he blessed Joseph and said: The God before whom my fathers Abraham and Isaac did walk, the God who hath been my shepherd all my life long unto this day, the Messenger who hath redeemed me from all evil, bless the lads; and let my name be named in them, and the name of my fathers Abraham and Isaac, and let them grow into a multitude in the midst of the earth. Now when Joseph saw that his father was laying his right hand on the head of Ephraim it displeased him; and he held up his father's hand to remove it from Ephraim's head unto Manasseh's head. And Joseph said unto his father: Not so, my father, for this is the first-born; put thy right hand upon his head. And his father refused and said: I know it, my son, I know it; he also shall become a great people, and he also shall be great; howbeit, his younger brother shall be goodlier than he, and his seed shall become a multitude of nations. And he blessed them that day, saying: By thee shall Israel bless, saying: God make thee as Ephraim and as Manasseh. And he set Ephraim before Manasseh. And Israel said unto Joseph: Behold, I die; but God will be with you and bring you back unto the land of your fathers. Moreover, I have given unto thee one portion above thy brethren, which I took out of the hand of the Amorite with my sword and with my bow.

Now, when Joseph's brethren saw that their father was dead, they said: Joseph peradventure will hate us, and he will certainly requite us all the evil which we did unto him. And they did plead with Joseph, saying: Thy father did command before he died, saying: Thus shall ye say unto Joseph: Forgive, I pray thee now, the trespass of thy brethren and their sin; for they did unto thee evil. And now, we pray thee, forgive the trespass of the servants of the God of thy father.

And Joseph wept when they spake unto him. And his brethren also went and fell down before him and they said: Behold, we are thy servants. And Joseph said unto them: Fear ye not! for am I in the place of God? Ye indeed devised evil against me, but God meant it for good, in order that he might do as at this day,—save much people alive. And now, fear ye not; I will nourish you and your little ones. Thus he comforted them and spake kindly unto them.

And Joseph dwelt in Egypt, he and his father's house. And Joseph lived a hundred and ten years. And Joseph saw Ephraim's children of the third generation; the children also of Machir, the son of Manasseh, were brought up upon Joseph's knees. And Joseph said unto his brethren: I am dying; but God will surely visit you and bring you up from this land unto the land which he confirmed by oath to Abraham, to Isaac and to Jacob. Then Joseph took an oath of the Children of Israel, saying: God will surely visit you, and ye will carry up my bones from here.

So Joseph died, being a hundred and ten years old; and they embalmed him, and he was put in a sarcophagus in Egypt.

C.   THE BLESSING OF JACOB [1]
(Gen. xlix, 1-27, 33)

And Jacob called unto his sons and said: Gather yourselves together
that I may tell you what shall befall you in the last days.

Come together and hear, ye sons of Jacob,
And hearken unto Israel, your father!

Reuben, my first-born art thou,
My might and the beginning of my strength.
The excellency of dignity and the excellency of power.
Unstable as water, thou shalt not excel,
For thou didst go up to thy father's bed.
Thus didst thou defile it;   he went up to my couch!

Simeon and Levi are brthren;
Weapons of oppression are their swords.
Enter not into their secret, my mind!
Be not joined with their assembly, my soul!!
In their wrath, they slew a man,   and in their self-wll
They houghed oxen.
Cursed be their wrath, for it was fierce,
And their anger, for it was cruel.
I will divide them in Jacob, and scatter them in Israel.

Judah, thee shall thy brethren praise,
Thy hand is in the neck of thine enemies.
Unto thee shall bow down the sons of thy father.
Thy whelp of a lion is Judah;
From the prey, my son, thou hast risen.
He stooped, he lay in wait like a lion, and like a lioness;
Who shall arouse him?
The sceptre shall not depart from Judah,
Nor a law-giver from between his feet,
Until he shall come to Shiloh
And the obedience of the people is his.
Binding his foal to the vine, the she-ass's colt to the choice vine.
He hath cleansed his garments in wine,
And his vesture in the blood of grapes.

Zebulon on the sea-coast shall dwell, he shall be a haven for ships.
And his border shall stretch to Zidon.
Issachar is a well-grown ass settling down between burdens;
And he saw a resting-place, that it was good,
And the land, that it was pleasant;
And he bowed his shoulder to bear
And became a servant to tribute.

Dan shall judge his people like one of the tribes of Israel;
Dan shall be a serpent on the way, an adder upon the path,
That biteth the horse's heels,
So that the rider falleth backwards.
I have waited for thy salvation, Yahweh!

Gad! a troop shall press upon him; he shall press upon their heel.
Asher! his bread shall be rich;
He shall yield dainties for kings.
Naphtali is a hind let loose; he giveth goodly words.

[1] A late poem in the form of a prophecy, which gives the conditions of the tribes in
E's day, and which is generally attributed to him. Dr. Driver gives it to J.

Joseph is a fruitful bough,
A fruitful bough by a fountain, the branches run over the wall.
The archers have sorely provoked him
And shot at and strongly attacked him,
But his bow preserved its strength,
And active was the power of his hands.
Through the hands of the Mighty One of Jacob,
(Thence the Shepherd, the Rock of Israel),
Through the God of thy father who shall help thee,
And the Almighty who shall bless thee
With blessings of the heaven above,
Blessings of the deep lying beneath,
Blessings of the breast and of the womb.
The blessings of thy father have prevailed
Above the blessings of my fore-fathers,
Unto the utmost bounds of the everlasting hills.
They shall be upon the head of Joseph,
Upon the crown of the head of him
Who was separated from his brethren.

Benjamin shall ravin as a wolf
In the morning he shall devour the prey,
And in the evening he shall apportion the spoil.

All these are the twelve tribes of Israel; and this is it which their father spake unto them and blessed them. Then he gathered up his feet into the bed, and yielded up the ghost; and he was gathered unto his people.

IV

OF MOSES, THE LIBERATOR OF HIS PEOPLE

A. His birth and training. His commission to liberate his people. The crossing of the Red Sea. The battle with the Amalekites. (Exodus, i, 15-23; ii, 1-14; iii, 1, 4b, 6, 9-15, 19-22; iv, 14, 18, 20b-21, 27-28; v, 4; vi, 1; vii, 15, 17b, 20b, 25; ix, 22-23a, 25a, 35a; x, 12-13a, 14a, 15b, 20-23, 27; xi, 1-3; xii, 31-36, 38-39, 42a; xiii, 17-19; xiv, 8-9, 10b, 19a, 26-29; xv, 1, 20-21; xvii, 1-6, 8-10.)

Now the king of Egypt spake to the Hebrew midwives, of whom the name of the one was Shiphrah and the name of the other Puah, and said: When ye shall deliver the Hebrew women and see them on the birth-stool, if it be a son then ye shall kill him; but if it be a daughter, then she shall live. But the midwives feared God and did not as the King of Egypt commanded them, but saved the men-children alive. And the king of Egypt called for the midwives and said unto them: Why have ye done this thing and saved the men-children alive? And the midwives said unto Pharaoh: Because the Hebrew women are not like the Egyptian women, for they are vigorous and are delivered before the midwives come in to them. Therefore God dealt well by the midwives; and because the midwives feared God, he made them houses. And Pharaoh charged all the people, saying: Every son that is born, ye shall cast into the river, and every daughter ye shall save alive.

Now a man of the house of Levi went and took to wife a daughter of Levi. And the woman conceived and bare a son; and when she saw that he was a goodly child, she hid him three months. And when she could no longer hide him, she took for him an ark of papyrus reed and covered it with bitumen and with pitch, and she put the child in it and set it among the reeds by the river's brink; and his sister took her stand at a distance to see what would happen to him. And the daughter of Pharaoh came down to the river to bathe, and her maidens walked along by the riverside, and she saw the ark among the reeds and sent her maid to get it; and she opened it and saw the child, and behold, the babe was weeping. And she had compassion on him and said: This is one of the Hebrews' children. Then said his sister to Pharaoh's daughter: Shall I go and call thee a nurse from the Hebrew women that she may nurse the child for thee? And Pharaoh's daughter said to her: Go. And the maiden went and called the babe's mother. And Pharaoh's daughter said unto her: Take this child away and nurse him for me, and I will give thee thy wages. And the woman took the child and nursed him. And the child grew, and she brought him to the daughter of Pharaoh and he became her son. And she called his name Moses; and she said: Because I drew him out of the water.

And it came to pass in those days when Moses was grown, that he went forth among his brethren, and saw their heavy tasks; and he saw an Egyptian beating a Hebrew, one of his brethren. And he looked this way and that way; and, when he saw there was no one, he killed the Egyptian and buried him in the sand. And he went forth a second day, and behold, two Hebrew men fighting. And he said to the aggressor: Why are you beating your neighbor? And he said: Who has made you a prince and a judge over us? Art thou thinking to kill me, as thou didst the Egyptian? And Moses feared and said: Surely this thing is known.

* * * * * * *

Now Moses kept the flock of Jethro, his father-in-law, the priest of Midian; and he led the flock to the back of the wilderness, and came to the mountain of God, to Horeb. And God called unto him out of the midst of the bush, and said: Moses, Moses! And he said: Here am I. And He said: I am the God of thy father, the God of Abraham, the God of Isaac and the God of Jacob. (And Moses hid his face, for he was afraid to look upon God.) Now, therefore, behold, the cry of the Children of Israel is come unto Me, and I have also seen the oppression wherewith the Egyptians oppress them. Come now, therefore, and I will send thee unto Pharaoh, that thou mayest bring forth My people, the Children of Israel, out of Egypt. And Moses said unto God: Who am I that I should go unto Pharaoh, and that I should bring forth the Children of Israel out of Egypt? And He said: Surely I will be with thee; and this shall be a token unto thee that I have sent thee. When thou hast brought forth the people out of Egypt, thou shalt serve God upon this mountain. And Moses said unto God: Behold, when I come to the Children of Israel and say unto them: The God of your fathers hath sent me unto you; and they shall say unto me: What is His name? what shall I say unto them? And God said unto Moses: I AM THAT I AM. And He said: Thus shalt thou say unto the Children of Israel; I AM hath sent me unto you. And God said further unto Moses: Thus shalt thou say unto the Children of Israel: YAHWEH, the God of your fathers, the God of Abraham, the God of Isaac and the God of Jacob, hath sent me unto you. And I am sure that the king of Egypt will not let you go, save by a strong hand. And I will stretch out My hand and smite Egypt with all My wonders which I will do in the midst thereof; and after that, he will let you go. And I will give this people favor in the sight of the Egyptians. And it shall come to pass that, when ye go, ye shall not go empty, but every woman shall borrow of her neighbor and of her that sojourneth in her house, jewels of silver and jewels of gold and raiment; and ye shall spoil the Egyptians. And thou shalt take this rod in thine hand, wherewith thou shalt do signs.

And Moses went and returned to Jethro, his father-in-law, and said unto him: Let me go, I pray thee, and return to my brethren which are in Egypt, and see whether they be yet alive. And Jethro said unto Moses: Go in peace. And Moses took the rod of God in his hand. And Yahweh [1] said unto Moses: When thou goest back into Egypt, see that thou doest all the wonders before Pharaoh that I have put in thine hand. But I will harden his heart that he shall not let My people go.

And Yahweh said unto Aaron: Go into the wilderness to meet Moses. And he went and met him in the Mount of God and kissed him. And Moses told Aaron all the words of Yahweh wherewith He had sent him, and all the signs which He had commanded him. . . . And the king of Egypt said unto them: Why do ye, Moses and Aaron, distract the people from their work? Get you unto your tasks.

Then Yahweh said unto Moses: Now shalt thou see what I will do unto Pharaoh, for with a strong hand shall he expel them, and with a strong hand shall he drive them out of his land. Get thee unto Pharaoh in the morning; lo, he goeth out unto the water. And thou shalt stand by the river's brink against he come. And thou shalt smite with the rod that is in thine hand upon the waters, and they shall be turned to blood. And he lifted up the rod and smote the waters in the river, in the sight of Pharaoh and in the sight of his seranvts; and all the waters that were in the river were turned into blood. And Pharaoh turned and went into his house.

And Yahweh said unto Moses: Stretch forth thine hand toward heaven, that there may be hail in all the land of Egypt, upon man and upon beast and upon every herb of the field throughout the land of Egypt. And Moses stretched forth his rod toward heaven, and Yahweh sent thunder and hail, and the fire ran along upon the ground. And the hail smote throughout all the land of Egypt all that was in the field, both man and beast; and the heart of Pharaoh was hardened, neither would he let the Children of Israel go.

And Yahweh said unto Moses: Stretch out thine hand over the land of Egypt for the locusts, that they may come up upon the land of Egypt and eat every herb of the land, even all that the hail hath left. And Moses stretched forth his rod over the land of Egypt, and the locusts went up over all the land of Egypt, and rested in all the coasts of Egypt; and they did eat every herb of the land and all the fruit of the trees which the hail had left. But Yahweh hardened Pharaoh's heart, so that he would not let the Children of Israel go.

And Yahweh said unto Moses: Stretch out thine hand toward heaven, that there may be darkness over the land of Egypt, even darkness that may be felt. And Moses stretched forth his hand toward heaven, and there was a thick darkness in all the land of Egypt three days; they saw not one another, neither rose any from his place for three days. But all the Chidren of Israel had light in their dwellings. But Yahweh hardened Pharaoh's heart, and he would not let them go.

And Yahweh said unto Moses: Yet will I bring one plague more upon Pharaoh and upon Egypt, after which he will let you go hence; when he sends you away, he will surely thrust you out hence. Speak now in the ears of the people that they shall borrow every man of his neighbor

[1] Note the change from the word *God* to that of *Yahweh* for the Deity of Israel.

and every woman from her neighbor, jewels of silver and jewels of gold. And Yahweh gave the people favor in the sight of the Egyptians; (also the man Moses was very great in the land of Egypt in the sight of Pharaoh's servants and in the sight of the people.) . . .

And Pharaoh called for Moses and Aaron by night and said: Rise up and get you forth from among my people, both ye and the Children of Israel; and go, serve Yahweh, as ye have said. Also take your flocks and your herds, as ye have said, and be gone; and bless me also. And the Egyptians were urgent upon the people, that they might send them out of the land in haste; for they said: We be all dead men. And the people took their dough before it was leavened, their kneading-troughs being bound up in their clothes upon their shoulders. And the Children of Israel did according to the word of Moses; and they borrowed of the Egyptians jewels of silver and jewels of gold, and raiment. And Yahweh gave the people favor in the sight of the Egyptians, so that they lent unto them; and they spoiled the Egyptians. And a mixed multitude went up also with them, and flocks and herds, even very much cattle. And they baked unleavened cakes of the dough which they brought forth out of Egypt, for it was not leavened because they could not tarry, neither had they prepared for themselves any victual. It is a night to be much observed unto Yahweh for bringing them out from the land of Egypt.

And it came to pass when Pharaoh had let the people go, that God did not lead them by the way of the land of the Philistines, although that was near; for God said: Lest the people repent when they see war, and they return into Egypt. But God led the people about by way of the wilderness of the Red Sea. And the Children of Israel went up well equipped out of the land of Egypt. And Moses took the bones of Joseph with him; for he had strictly sworn the Children of Israel, saying: God will surely visit you, and ye shall carry up my bones hence with you.

Now Yahweh hardened the heart of Pharaoh, king of Egypt, and he pursued after the Children of Israel; for the Children of Israel went out with a high hand. And the Egyptians pursued after them and overtook them encamping by the sea. And the Children of Israel cried out unto Yahweh. And Yahweh said unto Moses: Wherefore criest thou unto Me? Speak unto the Children of Israel that they go forward. And lift thou up thy rod and stretch out thy hand over the sea, and divide it, and the Children of Israel shall go into the midst of the sea on dry ground. And the messenger of God, who went before the camp of Israel, removed from before them and stood behind them. And Moses stretched forth his hand over the sea, and the waters were divided, and the Children of Israel went into the midst of the sea upon dry ground, and the waters were a wall unto them on their right hand and on their left. And the Egyptians went in after them into the midst of the sea. And Yahweh said unto Moses: Stretch out thy hand over the sea, that the waters may come back upon the Egyptians. And Moses stretched forth his hand over the sea; and the waters returned and covered the chariots and the horsemen, even all the host of Pharaoh that went after them into the midst of the sea; there remained not so much as one of them. But the Children of Israel walked upon dry land in the midst of the sea; and the waters were a wall upon their right hand and on their left.

Then sang Moses and the Children of Israel this song unto Yahweh, and spake, saying:

I will sing unto Yahweh, for He is highly exalted,
  The horse and his rider hath He thrown into the sea.

For the horses of Pharaoh went in with his chariots and with his horsemen into the sea, and Yahweh brought back the waters of the sea upon them, but the Children of Israel walked on dry land in the midst of the sea.

And Miriam the prophetess, the sister of Aaron, took a timbrel in her hand; and all the women went out after her, with timbrels and with dances. And Miriam sang unto them:

> Sing ye unto Yahweh, for He is highly exalted;
> The horse and his rider hath He thrown into the sea.

Now the people thirsted there for water. And the people murmured against Moses and said: Wherefore is this, that thou hast brought us out of Egypt to kill us and our cattle with thirst? And Moses cried unto Yahweh, saying: What shall I do unto this people? they be almost ready to stone me. And Yahweh said unto Moses: Go on before the people, and take with thee of the elders of Israel; and thy rod wherewith thou didst smite the river, take in thy hand and go. Behold, I will stand before thee upon the rock in Horeb; and thou shalt smite the rock, and there shall come water out of it that the people may drink. And Moses did so in the sight of the elders of Israel.

Then came Amalek and fought with Israel in Rephidim. And Moses said unto Joshua: Choose us out men, and go out, fight with Amalek. To-morrow I will stand on the top of the hill with the rod of God in my hand. So Joshua did as Moses had said to him, and fought with Amalek; and Moses, Aaron and Hur went up to the top of the hill. And it came to pass, when Moses held up his hand, that Israel prevailed; and when he let down his hand, Amalek prevailed. But Moses's hands were heavy; and they took a stone, and put it under him, and he sat thereon. And Aaron and Hur stayed up his hands, the one on the one side and the other on the other side; and his hands were steady until the going down of the sun. And Joshua discomfited Amalek and his people with the edge of the sword. And Yahweh said unto Moses: Write this for a memorial in a book, and rehearse it in the ears of Joshua; for I will utterly put out the remembrance of Amalek from under heaven. And Moses built an altar, and called the name of it Yahweh-nissi (*Yahweh my banner*); for he said: By the throne of Yah, Yahweh will have war with Amalek from generation to generation.

B. The Feast of the Covenant. The Legislation of Moses. The people ratify the Covenant. Moses returns to the mount. The apostasy of the people, and the sin of Aaron. The anger of Moses. The command to leave Horeb. The form of worship in the wilderness. (Exodus, xviii; xix, 2b-19; xx, 1-21; xxiii, 20-23; xxiv, 3-8, 12-14, 18b; xxxi, 18b; xxxii, 1-8, 15-35; xxxiii, 1-11.)

When Jethro the priest of Midian, the father-in-law of Moses, heard of all that God had done for Moses and for Israel his people, and that Yahweh had brought Israel out of Egypt, then Jethro took Zipporah, Moses's wife, after he had sent her back, and her two sons (of whom the name of the one was Gershom, for he said: I have been a *stranger* in a foreign land; and the name of the other Eliezer (*God my help*)— for the God of my father, said he, was my help and delivered me from the hand of Pharaoh);—and Jethro, Moses's father-in-law, came with his sons and his wife into the wilderness unto Moses where he was encamped at the mount of God. And he said unto Moses: I, thy father-in-law, am come unto thee and thy wife and her two sons with her. And

Moses went out to meet his father-in-law and did obeisance and kissed him. And they asked each other of their welfare, and they came into the tent. And Moses told his father-in-law all that Jahweh had done to Pharaoh and the Egyptians for Israel's sake, all the travail that had come upon them by the way, and how Yahweh had delivered them. And Jethro rejoiced for all the goodness which Yahweh had showed to Israel, whom He had delivered out of the hand of the Egyptians; and Jethro said: Blessed be Yahweh who hath delivered you out of the hand of the Egyptians and out of the hand of Pharaoh. Now know I that YAHWEH is greater than all the gods; for in the matter wherein they dealt proudly, He was above them. And Jethro took a burnt-offering and sacrifices for God; *and Aaron came and all the elders of Israel to eat bread with Moses's father-in-law before God.*

And it came to pass, on the morrow, that Moses sat to judge the people; and the people stood by Moses from morning unto the evening. And when Moses's father-in-law saw all that he did for the people, he said: What is this thing that thou doest for the people? Why sittest thou thyself alone, and all the people are attendant upon thee from morning until evening? And Moses said unto his father-in-law, Because the people come to me to enquire of God. When they have a matter, they come unto me, and I judge between one and another, and I make them know the statutes of God and His laws. And Moses' father-in-law said unto him: The thing that thou doest is not good. Thou wilt surely wear away, both thou and this people that is with thee, for this thing is too heavy for thee; thou art not able to perform it thyself alone. Hearken now unto my voice. I will give thee counsel, and God shall be with thee. Be thou for the people instead of God, that thou mayest bring their causes unto God. And thou shalt teach them ordinances and laws, and shalt show them the way wherein they must walk and the work that they must do. And thou shalt select out of all the people able men, such as fear God, men of truth, hating covetousness, and place over them as rulers of thousands, rulers of hundreds, rulers of fifties and rulers of tens, and let them judge the people at all seasons. And it shall be that every great matter they shall bring to thee, but every small matter they shall judge. So shall the burden be lessened for thee, and they shall bear it with thee. If thou shalt do this thing, and God command thee so, then thou shalt be able to endure, and all these people shall go to their places in peace.

So Moses hearkened to the voice of his father-in-law and did all that he had said. And Moses chose able men out of all Israel and made them heads over the people, rulers of thousands, rulers of hundreds, rulers of fifties and rulers of tens. And they judged the people at all seasons; the hard causes they brought unto Moses, but every small matter they judged themselves. And Moses let his father-in-law depart, and he went his way into his own land. And Israel encamped before the mount.

And Moses went up unto God, and He called unto him out of the mountain, saying: Thus shall ye say to the house of Jacob, and tell the Children of Israel. Ye have seen what I did to the Egyptians, and how I bare you on eagles' wings, and brought you unto Myself. Now therefore, if ye will obey My voice indeed and keep My covenant, then ye shall be a peculiar treasure unto Me above all people; for all the earth is Mine; and ye shall be unto Me a kingdom of priests, and a holy nation.

And Moses came and called for the elders of the people, and laid before them all these words which Yahweh had commanded him. And all the people answered together and said: All that Yahweh hath spoken will we do. And Moses reported the words of the people unto Yahweh.

And Yahweh said unto Moses: Go unto the people and let them sanctify themselves to-day and to-morrow, and let them wash their clothes and be ready against the third day; for the third day Yahweh will come down in the sight of all the people upon mount Sinai. And thou shalt set bounds unto the people round about, saying, Take heed to yourselves in going up to the mount, lest ye touch the border of it; whosoever toucheth the mount shall surely die. No hand shall touch it but he shall surely be stoned or shot; whether beast or man, it shall not live. And Moses went down from the mount and sanctified the people, and they washed their clothes. And he said unto the people: Be ready against the third day; come not near a woman.

And it came to pass on the third day in the morning, that there were thunders and lightnings and a thick cloud upon the mount, and the voice of a trumpet, exceeding loud. And Moses brought forth the people out of the camp to meet God; and they stood at the nether part of the mount. And Mount Sinai was altogether on smoke, because Yahweh descended upon it in fire. And the smoke thereof ascended as the smoke of a furnace, and the whole mount quaked greatly. And when the voice of the trumpet sounded long and waxed louder and louder, Moses spake, and God answered him by a voice. And God spake all these words, saying:

I am YAHWEH thy GOD, which brought thee out of the land of Egypt, out of the house of bondage. Thou shalt have none other gods before Me.

Thou shalt not make unto thee any graven image, or any likeness of anything that is in heaven above, or that is in the earth beneath, or that is in the water under the earth. Thou shalt not bow down thyself to them nor serve them; for I, Yahweh, thy God, am a jealous God, visiting the iniquity of the fathers upon the children unto the third and fourth generation of them that hate Me; and showing mercy unto thousands of them that love Me and keep My commandments.

Thou shalt not take the name of Yahweh, thy God, in vain; for Yahweh will not hold him guiltless that taketh His name in vain.

Remember the sabbath day to keep it holy. Six days shalt thou labor and do all thy work; but the seventh day is the sabbath of Yahweh thy God. In it thou shalt not do any manner of work; thou, nor thy son nor thy daughter, thy manservant nor thy maidservant nor thy cattle, nor the stranger within thy gates. For, in six days Yahweh made heaven and earth, the sea, and all that in them is, and rested the seventh day; wherefore Yahweh blessed the seventh day and hallowed it.

Honor thy father and thy mother, that thy days may be long in the land which Yahweh, thy God, giveth thee.

Thou shalt not kill.

Thou shalt not commit adultery.

Thou shalt not steal.

Thou shalt not bear false witness against thy neighbor.

Thou shalt not covet thy neighbor's house; thou shalt not covet thy neighbor's wife; nor his man-servant, nor his maid-servant, nor his ox nor his ass, nor anything that is thy neighbor's.

And all the people saw the thunderings and the lightnings and the noise of the trumpet and the mountain smoking; and when the people saw it, they trembled and stood afar off. And they said unto Moses: Speak thou with us and we will hear; but let not God speak with us lest we die. And Moses said unto the people: Fear not; for God is come to prove you, and that His fear may be before you, that ye sin not. And the people stood afar off, and Moses drew near to the thick darkness where God was. And Yahweh said unto Moses: Thus shalt thou say unto the Children of Israel: Ye have seen that I have talked with you from heaven. Ye shall not make with Me gods of silver, nor gods of gold shall ye make unto you. An altar of earth thou shalt make unto Me, and shalt sacrifice thereon thy burnt offerings and thy peace offerings, thy sheep and thine oxen; in all places where I record My name, I will come unto thee and I will bless thee. And if you wilt make an altar of stone, thou shalt not build it of hewn stone; for, if thou lift up thy tool upon it, thou hast polluted it. Neither shalt thou go up by steps unto mine altar, that thy nakedness be not discovered thereon.

Behold, I send a messenger before thee, to keep thee by the way and to bring thee into the place which I have prepared. Take heed of him, and hearken unto his voice. Be not rebellious against him, for he will not pardon thy transgression; for My name is in him. But, if thou wilt indeed hearken unto his voice, and do all that I command, then will I be an enemy unto thine enemies, and an adversary unto thy adversaries. For My messenger shall go before thee, and bring thee in unto the Amorite and the Hittite, the Perizzite, the Canaanite, the Hivite and the Jebusite, and I will cut them off.

And Moses came and told the people all the words of Yahweh, and all the ordinances; and all the people answered with one voice, and said: All the words which Yahweh hath spoken we will do. And Moses wrote all the words of Yahweh, and rose up early in the morning, and builded an altar under the mount, and twelve pillars according to the twelve tribes of Israel. And he sent the young men of the Children of Israel who offered burnt-offerings and sacrificed peace-offerings unto Yahweh. And Moses took half of the blood and put it in basins, and half the blood he dashed against the altar. And he took the Book of the Covenant, and read in the hearing of the people; and they said: All that Yahweh hath spoken will we do, and obey. And Moses took the blood and sprinkled it upon the people, and said: Behold, the blood of the Covenant which Yahweh hath made with you, in agreement with all these words.

And Yahweh said unto Moses: Come up to Me into the mount, and be there; and I will give thee the tables of stone, and the Law of the Covenant which I have written, that thou mayest teach them. And Moses rose up, and Joshua his servant; and Moses went up to the mount of God. And unto the elders he said: Tarry ye here for us, until we come back to you; and behold, ye have Aaron and Hur with you; whosoever hath a cause, let him come near unto them. And Moses was in the mount forty days and forty nights.

And He gave unto Moses, when He had made an end of speaking with him upon the mount, the two tables of the testimony, tables of stone, written with the finger of God.

And when the people saw that Moses delayed to come down out of the mount, the people gathered themselves together unto Aaron, and said unto him: Up, make us gods that shall go up before us; for as for this Moses, the man who brought us up out of the land of Egypt, we know not what has become of him. And Aaron said unto them: Break off the golden rings which are in the ears of your wives, of your sons and of your daughters, and bring them to me. And all the people brake off the golden rings which were in their ears and brought them to Aaron. And he received it at their hand and fashioned it with a graving tool and made a molten calf. And they said: These be thy gods, O Israel, which brought thee up out of the land of Egypt. And when Aaron saw this, he built an altar before it; and Aaron cried aloud and said, To-morrow shall be a feast to Yahweh. And they rose up early on the morrow and offered burnt-offerings, and brought peace-offerings. And the people sat down to eat and to drink, and rose up to play.

And Yahweh said unto Moses: Go, get thee down; for thy people, which thou didst bring up out of the land of Egypt, have corrupted themselves. They have turned aside quickly out of the way which I commanded them. They have made them a molten calf and have worshiped it, and have sacrificed unto it and said: These be thy gods, O Israel, which brought thee up out of the land of Egypt.

And Moses turned and went down from the mount, with the two tables of the testimony in his hand, tables of stone written with the finger of God; the tables were written on both their sides, on the one side and on the other were they written. And the tables were the work of God, and the writing was the writing of God graven upon the tables. And when Joshua heard the noise of the people as they shouted, he said unto Moses: There is a sound of battle in the camp. And he said: This is not the shout of victory, nor is it the cry of the conquered; it is the voice of singing that I hear. And it came to pass, as soon as he came nigh to the camp, that he saw the calf and the dancing. And Moses' anger waxed hot, and he cast the tables out of his hands and brake them beneath the mount. And he took the calf which they had made and burnt it with fire, and ground it to powder, and strewed it upon the water, and made the Children of Israel to drink of it.

And Moses said unto Aaron: What did this people do unto thee, that thou hast brought so great a sin upon them? And Aaron said: Let not the anger of my lord wax hot. Thou knowest the people that they are set on evil; for they said unto me: Make us gods which shall go before us, for as for this Moses, the man who brought us up out of the land of Egypt, we know not what has become of him. And I said unto them: Let them break off their gold for me; and they gave it me, and I threw it into the fire, *and there came out this calf*. And when Moses saw that the people had become unruly (for Aaron had let them loose to be mocked of their enemies), then Moses stood at the entrance to the camp, and said: Whoso is for Yahweh, let him come unto me. And all the sons of Levi gathered themselves unto him. And he said unto them: Thus saith Yahweh, the God of Israel: Put ye every man his sword upon his thigh, and go to and fro from gate to gate throughout the camp, and slay every man his brother and every man his neighbor and every man his companion. And the sons of Levi did according to the words of Moses; and there fell of the people that day about three thousand men. Then Moses said: Consecrate your-selves to-day to Yahweh, even every man against his son and against his brother, that He may bestow upon you a blessing this day. And it came to pass on the morrow, that Moses said unto the people: Ye have sinned a great sin; and now I will go up unto Yahweh; peradventure I shall make atonement for your sin. And Moses returned unto Yahweh, and said: Alas, this people have sinned a great sin, and have made them gods of gold. Yet now, if Thou wilt, forgive their sin; and if not, blot me, I pray thee, out of the book which Thou hast written. And Yahweh said unto Moses: Whosoever hath sinned against Me, him will I blot out of My book; therefore now go, lead the people to the place of which I have spoken unto thee. Behold, My messenger shall go before thee. Nevertheless, in the day when I visit, I will visit their sin upon them. And Yahweh plagued the people, because they made the calf which Aaron made.

And Yahweh said unto Moses: Depart and go up hence, thou and the people which thou hast brought up out of the land of Egypt, unto the land which I sware unto Abraham, to Isaac and to Jacob, saying: Unto thy seed will I give it. And I will send a messenger before thee (and I will drive out the Canaanite, the Amorite, and the Hittite and the Perizzite, the Hivite and the Jebusite), unto a land flowing with milk and honey; but I will not go up in the midst of thee (for thou art a stiffnecked people), lest I consume thee in the way. And when the people heard these evil tidings, they mourned, and no man did put on him his ornaments. For Yahweh had said unto Moses: Say unto the Children of Israel: Ye are a stiffnecked people; I will come up into the midst of thee in a moment and consume thee; therefore now put off thy ornaments from thee, that I may know what to do unto thee. And the Children of Israel stripped themselves of their ornaments from mount Horeb onwards.

Now Moses used to take the tent and pitch it without the camp, afar off from the camp, and he called it the Tent of Meeting. And it came to pass that everyone who sought Yahweh went out to the Tent of Meeting which was without the camp. And it came to pass when Moses went out to the Tent, that all the people rose up and took his stand, every man at his tent door, and looked after Moses until he was gone into the Tent. And it came to pass when Moses entered into the Tent, the pillar of cloud descended and stood at the door of the Tent, and Yahweh spake with Moses. And all the people saw the pillar of cloud stand at the door of the Tent, and all the people rose up and worshipped, every man at his tent door. And Yahweh spake with Moses face to face, as a man speaketh unto his friend. And he returned into the camp; but his servant Joshua the son of Nun, a young man, departed not out of the Tent.

C. The Journey northward from Sinai. The Jealousy of Aaron and Miriam. Moses sends men to survey Canaan. They report favorably, but the people refuse to advance. Yahweh sends upon them the plague of the fiery serpents. Moses raises for their cure the Brazen Serpent. Moses and Aaron are debarred from entering Canaan. Moses conquers Sihon king of the Amorites, and Israel dwells in their land. Balak, king of Moab, sends for Balaam to curse them. The Blessing of Balaam. Joshua is charged with the leadership of the people, and Moses dies in Moab. (Numbers, x, 33-36; xi, 1-4, 16-17, 24-30; xii, 1-16; xiv, 1a, 5-7, 10, 37-38; xx, 1b, 3a, 5, 7, 8b, c, 9-11, 13-18, 22a, c, 28b; xxi, 4b-9, 11b-15, 21-24a; xxii, 2-3a, 5a, 6a, c, 8-10, 12-16, 18a, 19-21a, c, 37-38, 40-41; xxiii, 1-26; xxiv, 25; xxv, 1a, 3, 5; Deut. xxxi, 14-15, 23; xxxiv, 5-6.)

Then they set forward from the mount of God three days' journey; and the ark of the covenant of Yahweh went before them three days' journey to seek a resting-place for them. And the cloud of Yahweh was over them by day, when they set forward from the camp. And when the ark set forward, Moses said: Rise up, O Yahweh, and let Thine enemies be scattered, and let them that hate Thee flee before Thee. And when it rested, he said: Return, O Yahweh, unto the ten thousands of Israel.

Now Yahweh heard the people as they were complaining, and it displeased Him, and his anger was kindled; and the fire of Yahweh burnt among them, and consumed those who were in the uttermost parts of the camp. And the people cried unto Moses, and, when Moses prayed unto Yahweh, the fire was quenched. And he called the name of the place Taberah (*a burning*); because the fire of Yahweh had burnt among them.

Then Yahweh said unto Moses: Gather unto Me seventy men of the elders of Israel whom thou knowest to be the elders of the people, and officers over them, and bring them unto the Tent of Meeting, that they may stand there with thee. And I will come down and talk with thee there. And I will take of the spirit which is upon thee, and will put it on them; and they shall bear the burden of the people with thee, that thou bear it not thyself alone. So he gathered seventy men of the elders of the people, and set them round about the tent. And Yahweh came down in a cloud and spake unto him, and took of the spirit that was upon him, and gave it to the seventy elders; and it came to pass when the spirit rested upon them, they prophesied; but no longer. But there remained two men in the camp (the name of the one was Eldad, and the name of the other, Medad), and the spirit rested upon them, and they were of them who were registered, but went not out to the tent. Then a young man ran and told Moses, saying: Eldad and Medad are prophesying in the camp. Then Joshua the son of Nun who was attending Moses,—one of his chosen men,—answered and said: My lord Moses, forbid them. And Moses said unto him: Art thou jealous for my sake? Would that Yahweh would make all the people prophets, that He would put His spirit upon them! And Moses gat him into the camp, he and all the elders of Israel.

Now Miriam and Aaron spake against Moses because of the Cushite woman whom he had married, for he had married a Cushite woman. And they said: Hath Yahweh spoken indeed only by Moses? hath He not also spoken by us? And Yahweh heard. Now the man Moses was very humble, above all the men who were on the earth. And Yahweh said suddenly unto Moses and to Aaron and to Miriam: Come out, ye three, to the Tent of Meeting. And they three came out. And Yahweh came down in a pillar of cloud and stood in the door of the tent, and called Aaron and Miriam; and they both came forth. And He said:

Hear now My words! If there be a prophet among you,
In a vision will I make Myself known, in a dream will I speak to him.
Not so with My servant Moses, who is faithful in all My house;
Mouth to mouth will I speak to him, plainly and not in parables;
The similitude of Yahweh shall he see;
Then wherefore do ye not fear to speak
Against My servant Moses?

And the anger of Yahweh was kindled against them, and He departed. And when the cloud removed from the tent, behold, Miriam was leprous, white as snow. And Aaron looked upon Miriam, and behold, she was leprous.

Then Aaron said unto Moses: Alas, my lord, I beseech thee, lay not upon us as sin this folly we have committed and wherein we are guilty. Let her not, I pray thee, be as one dead, whose flesh is half consumed when he cometh out of his mother's womb. And Moses cried unto Yahweh, saying: Heal her, God, I beseech Thee! And Yahweh said unto Moses: If her father had but spit in her face, should she not be ashamed seven days? Let her be shut out from the camp seven days, and after that, let her be brought in again. And Miriam was shut out from the camp seven days; and the people journeyed not till Miriam was brought in again.

Then Moses sent men to spy out the land of Canaan, and said unto them: Go up into the mountains, and see what the land is, whether it be fat or lean, whether there be wood there or not. And be of good courage, and bring back some of the fruit of the land. Now the time was the time of the first-ripe grapes. And they came to the brook Eshcol. (The place was called the Valley of Eshcol because of the cluster of grapes which the Israelites cut down from there.) And they returned from spying out the land, and they spread an evil report of the land, saying: The land through which we have passed is a land that eateth up the inhabitants thereof, and all the men we saw were of great stature. And there we saw the Nephilim; and we were in our own sight as grasshoppers, and so we were in their sight.

And all the congregation lifted up their voice and cried aloud. And all the Children of Israel murmured against Moses and against Aaron; and the whole congregation said unto them: Would that we had died in Egypt, or would we had died in the wilderness! Then Moses and Aaron fell on their faces before all the assembly of the congregation of the Children of Israel. And Joshua the son of Nun and Caleb the son of Jephunneh, who were of them that spied out the land, rent their clothes; and they spake unto all the congregation of the Children of Israel, saying: The land which we passed through to survey it is an exceedingly good land. But all the congregation bade stone them with stones. Then the glory of Yahweh appeared in the Tent of Meeting unto all the Children of Israel. Then those men that did bring up an evil report of the land died by the plague before Yahweh; but Joshua the son of Nun and Caleb the son of Jephunneh remained alive of those men that were sent to spy out the land.[1]

Now the people were dwelling in Kadesh; and Miriam died there and was buried there. And the people strove with Moses, and spake, saying: Wherefore have ye made us come up out of Egypt to bring us to this evil place? It is no place of seed or of figs, or of vines or of pomegranates, neither is there any water to drink. And Yahweh spake unto Moses, saying: Take the rod, and thou shalt bring forth water for them out of the rock. And Moses took the rod from before Yahweh, as He commanded him. And Moses and Aaron gathered the assembly together before the rock, and Moses said unto them: Hear, now, ye rebels; are we to bring you water out of this rock? And he lifted up his hand and smote the rock with his rod twice; and water came forth abundantly, and the congregation drank, and their cattle. And Yahweh said unto Moses and unto Aaron: Because ye believed not in Me, to sanctify Me in the eyes of the Children of Israel, therefore ye shall not bring this people into the land which I have given them. These are the waters of Meribah, where the Children of Israel strove with Yahweh, and He was sanctified in them.

From Kadesh, Moses sent messengers unto the king of Edom, saying: Thus saith thy brother Israel: Thou knowest all the travail that hath befallen us; how our fathers went down into Egypt, and we dwelt in

---

[1] Chapters xv, xviii, xix, added by P, are entirely concerned with the duties, positions and emoluments of the priests and Levites. The rebellion of Korah also interwoven by P with that of Dathan and Abiram, told by J, in Ch. xvii, will be found in Part II.

Egypt a long time; and the Egyptians dealt ill with us and our fathers. And when we cried unto Yahweh, He heard our voice, and sent a messenger and brought us out of Egypt. Now behold, we are in Kadesh, a city in the uttermost of thy border. Let us pass, I pray thee, through thy land; we will not pass through the fields or through the vineyards, neither will we drink of the water of thy wells; we will not turn to the right hand nor to the left until we have passed thy border. And Edom said unto him: Thou shalt not pass through me, lest I come out against thee with the sword. Thus Edom refused to give Israel passage through his border. And they departed from Kadesh and pitched in Mount Hor, which is in the edge of the land of Edom. And Aaron died there in the top of the mount.

Now the soul of the people was discouraged because of the way; and the people spake against God and against Moses: Wherefore have ye brought us up out of Egypt to die in the wilderness? for there is neither bread nor water, and our soul doth loathe this good-for-nothing food. Then Yahweh sent fiery serpents among the people and they bit the people, so that many of the people of Israel died. And the people came to Moses, and said: We have sinned, because we have spoken against Yahweh and against thee; pray unto Yahweh, that He take away the serpents from us. And Moses prayed for the people. And Yahweh said unto Moses: Make thee a fiery serpent and set it upon a pole. And it shall come to pass that every one that is bitten, when he looketh upon it shall live. And Moses made a serpent of brass, and put it upon a pole; and it came to pass that, if a serpent had bitten any man, when he looked upon the serpent of brass, he lived.

Then they encamped in the wilderness which is before Moab, toward the sun-rising. Thence they journeyed and pitched in the valley of Zered. Thence they removed and encamped on the other side of Arnon, which is in the wilderness that cometh out of the border of the Amorites; for the Arnon is the boundary of Moab, between Moab and the Amorites. Wherefore it is said in the "Book of the Wars of Yehweh"

*   *   *   *   *   Through Vaheb to Suphneh,
And the valleys of Arnon,   and the slope of the valleys
That inclineth to the site of Ar,   and lieth on the border of Moab.

Then Israel sent messengers to Sihon, king of the Amorites, saying: Let me pass through thy land. We will not turn into the fields or the vineyards, we will not drink of the water of the wells, but we will go along the king's highway until we be past thy borders. But Sihon would not suffer Israel to pass through his border; and Sihon gathered all his people together, and went out against Israel into the wilderness. And he came to Jahaz and fought against Israel. And Israel smote him with the edge of the sword, and possessed his land from Arnon unto Jabbok, even to the children of Ammon. Thus Israel dwelt in the land of the Amorites.

Now Balak the son of Zippor saw all that Israel had done to the Amorites, and Moab was sore afraid of the people, because they were so many. And he sent to Balaam, to Pethor which is on the river Euphrates, saying: [Come, curse me this people] for I know that he whom thou blessest is bessed, and he whom thou cursest is cursed. And he said unto them: Lodge here this night, and I will bring you word again as Yahweh shall speak to me. And the princes of Moab abode with Balaam.

And God came unto Balaam, and said: What men are these with thee? And Balaam said unto God: Balak the son of Zippor, king of Moab, hath sent unto me. And God said unto Balaam: Thou shalt not go with them; thou shalt not curse the people, for they are blessed. And Balaam rose up in the morning, and said unto the princes of Balak: Get you into your land; for Yahweh refuseth to give me leave to go with you. And the princes of Moab rose up, and they went unto Balak, and said: Balaam refuseth to come with us. But Balak again sent princes, more and more honorable than they. And they came to Balaam, and said to him: Thus saith Balak the son of Zippor: Let nothing, I pray thee, hinder thee from coming unto me. And Balaam said: Tarry ye also here this night, I pray you, that I may know what Yahweh will say unto me more. And God came unto Balaam at night, and said unto him: Since the men have come to implore thee, rise up and go with them; but only the thing that I shall say unto thee, that shalt thou do.

So Balaam rose up in the morning and went with the princes of Moab. Then Balak said unto Balaam: Did I not urgently send unto thee to call thee? Wherefore camest thou not unto me? Am I not able indeed to promote thee to honor? And Balaam said unto Balak: Lo, I am come unto thee. Have I now any power at all to say anything? The word that God shall put into my mouth, that shall I speak. And Balak offered oxen and sheep, and sent to Balaam and to the princes that were with him.

And it came to pass in the morning, that Balak took Balaam and brought him to the high places of Baal, that thence he might see the utmost part of the people. And Balaam said unto Balak: Build me here seven altars, and prepare me here seven bullocks and seven rams. And Balak did as Balaam had commanded, and offered on each altar a bullock and a ram. And Balaam said unto Balak: Stand by thy burnt-offering and I will go; peradventure Yahweh will come to meet me; and whatever He sheweth me, I will tell thee. And he went to a high place.

And God met Balaam; and he said unto Him: I have prepared seven altars, and I have offered upon each altar a bullock and a ram. And Yahweh put a word in Balaam's mouth, and said: Return to Balak, and thus thou shalt speak. And he returned unto him, and lo! he stood by his offering, he and all the princes of Moab. And he took up his parable, and said:

> From Aram hath Balak, king of Moab brought me,
> From the mountains of the East,
> Saying: Come, curse me Jacob, and come, execrate Israel!
> How shall I curse whom God hath not cursed?
> And how shall I denounce whom God hath not denounced?
> For, from the top of the rocks can I see him,
> And from the heights I behold him.
> Lo, a people dwelling apart,
> Not counting itself among the nations!!
> Whol shall weigh the dust of Jacob, or number a fourth of Israel?
> Let me die the death of the righteous,
> And let my last end be like his!

Then said Balak to Balaam: What hast thou done unto me? I took thee to curse mine enemies; and behold, thou hast blssed them exceedingly. And he answered and said: Must I not speak what Yahweh putteth into my mouth? And Balak said unto him: Come, I pray thee, with me into another place, whence thou mayest see them; thou shalt

see but the utmost part of them, and shall not see them all, and denounce me them from thence. And he took him into the field of Zophim,
to the top of Pisgah, and built seven altars, and offered a bullock and a
ram upon every altar. And he said unto Balak: Stand here by thy
burnt-offering, while I meet Yahweh yonder. And Yahweh met Balaam,
and put a word into his mouth, and said: Go again to Balak, and say
thus. And when he came to him, behold, he stood by his burnt-offering,
and the princes of Moab with him. And Balak said unto him: What
hath Yahweh spoken?

And he took up his parable, and said:

> Rise up, Balak, and hear! Hearken unto me, thou son of Zippor!
> God is not a man, that He should lie,
> Nor the son of man, that He should repent.
> Hath He not said, and shall He not do it?
> Or spoken, and will He not confirm it?
> Lo, I have received commandment to bless,
> He hath blessed, and I cannot reverse it.
> He hath not beheld iniquity in Jacob,
> Nor hath He seen wrong-doing in Israel.
> Yahweh, his God, is with him, and rejoicing for kings is in Him.
>
> God is bringing him forth from Egypt,
> Strength as of a wild-ox is his.
> No sorcery will avail against Jacob, nor divination against Israel.
> In due time shall it be said of Jacob and of Israel:
> What hath God wrought!
> Behold, the people riseth up as a lion,
> As a lioness he raiseth himself up.
> He lieth not down till he eateth the prey,
> And drinketh the blood of the slain.

And Balak said unto Balaam: Neither curse them at all, nor bless
them at all. And Balaam answered and said unto Balak: Did I not
speak unto thee, saying: All that Yahweh speaketh, that I must do?
Then Balaam rose up and went, and returned to his place; and Balak also
went his way.

And Israel abode in Shittim; and Israel became devoted to the Baal
of Peor. And Moses said unto the judges of Israel: Slay ye every one
his men that have served the Baal of Peor.

[Then Yahweh said unto Moses: Behold, the days draw near when
thou must die. Call Joshua, and present yourselves in the Tent of
Meeting, that I may give him a charge. And Moses and Joshua went,
and presented themselves in the Tent of Meeting. And Yahweh appeared in the tent in a pillar of cloud; and the pillar of cloud stood over
the door of the tent. And He gave Joshua the son of Nun a charge,
saying: Be strong and of a good courage; for thou shalt bring the
Children of Israel into the land which I sware unto them; and I will
be with thee.

So Moses, the servant of Yahweh, died there in the land of Moab. And
He buried him in the valley of the land of Moab, over against Baal-
Peor; but no man knoweth his sepulchre unto this day. D₂]

V

OF JOSHUA, LEADER OF THE TRIBES INTO CANAAN

THE CROSSING OF THE JORDAN.   THE CIRCUMCISION OF ALL THE HOST.   THE
TAKING OF JERICHO AND AI.   JOSHUA'S ADDRESS TO ALL
ISRAEL AND HIS DEATH.

(Joshua, ii, 13a, b, 4a, 5a, c, 7, 9a, 12a, 13-14a, 20, 15c, 16, 22-24;
iii, 1b, 2, 12, 6, 14, 17; iv, 4-5, 7b, 8a, 20; v, 2-3, 9; vi, 1-2a, 4-5b, 6, 9,
12b-13, 15-16, 20b, 22-23; viii, 8-13, 14b, 15a, 16b, 17a, 18, 24-26,
28; ix, 3, 6-9a, 11-15a, 16a, 22a, 24-27a; x, 1b-5a, 9b-11, 15; xiv,
1-30, 32-33.)

Joshua, the son of Nun, sent out from Shittim secretly two men as
spies, saying: Go, view the land and Jericho. And they went, and came
into the house of a harlot, and lodged there. And the king of Jericho
sent to Rahab, saying: Bring forth the two men that came to thy
house. Now the woman had taken the two men and hidden them when
it was dark, at the time of the shutting the gate. And she said thus:
Pursue after them quickly, and ye will overtake them. And the men
pursued after them on the road to Jordan unto the fords. And as soon
as they that pursued had gone out, they shut the gates. But Rahab
said unto the men: Swear that ye will save alive my father and my
mother and my brethren and my sisters and all that they have, and
deliver our lives from death. And the men said unto her: Our lives for
yours, if ye do not betray our business here. But, if thou disclose this
our business, then we shall be quit of this oath which thou hast made
us swear. Then she let them down by a rope through the window; for
her house was upon the town wall, and she dwelt upon the wall. And
she said unto them: Get you to the mountains, lest the pursuers meet
you, and hide yourselves there three days until the pursuers be returned; and afterward ye may go your way. And they went and came
unto the mountain and abode there three days, until the pursuers were
returned; and the pursuers sought them on every road, but found them
not. So the two men turned back and descended from the mountain,
and passed over and came to Joshua the son of Nun, and told him
all that had befallen them. And they said unto Joshua: Truly Yahweh
hath delivered all the land into our hands. Then they removed from
Shittim.

Now at the end of three days, the officers went through the camp,
and commanded the people, saying: When ye see the ark of Yahweh,
your God, and the priests bearing it, then ye shall remove from your
place and go after it. Also, take you twelve men from the tribes of
Israel, out of every tribe a man. And Joshua spake unto the priests,
saying: Take up the ark, and pass over before the people. And it
came to pass when the people removed from their tents to pass over
the Jordan, with the priests bearing the ark before the people, that
the priests that bare the ark of Yahweh stood firm on dry ground in
the midst of the Jordan, and all the Israelites passed over on dry ground,
until all the cattle had completed the crossing of the Jordan.

Then Joshua called the twelve men of the Children of Israel whom
he had appointed, out of every tribe a man; and Joshua said unto them:
Pass over before the ark of Yahweh your God into the midst of the
Jordan, and let every man of you take up a stone upon his shoulder,
according to the number of the twelve tribes of Israel; and these stones

shall be for a memorial unto the Children of Israel for ever. And the Children of Israel did so, according as Joshua commanded. And these twelve stones which they took out of Jordan did Joshua set up in Gilgal.

At that time Yahweh said unto Joshua: Make thee knives of flint, and circumcise the Children of Israel. Then Joshua made him knives of flint, and circumcised the Children of Israel at Gibeah Araloth (*Hill of the Foreskins*); and Yahweh said unto Joshua: To-day have I rolled away the reproach of Egypt from off you. Wherefore the name of that place is called Gilgal (*rolling*) to this day.

Now Jericho was fast closed and barred, because of the Children of Israel; none went out and none came in. And Yahweh said unto Joshua: Seven priests shall bear before the ark seven trumpets of ram's horns, and ye shall compass the city seven times while the priests blow the trumpets; and it shall be that when they make a long blast with the ram's horn, when ye hear the sound of the trumpet, all the people shall shout a great shout, and the wall of the city will fall down. Then Joshua the son of Nun called the priests, and said unto them: Take up the ark, and let seven priests bear seven trumpets of ram's horns before the ark of Yahweh; and the seven priests bearing the seven trumpets of ram's horns before Yahweh shall pass on while they blow the trumpets with the ark of Yahweh following them, and the armed men going before the priests who blow the trumpets, and the rearguard following the ark of Yahweh, while they continually blow the trumpets. Then the priests took up the ark of Yahweh, and the seven priests bearing the seven trumpets of ram's horns before the ark of Yahweh continued to advance; and they blew the trumpets, and the armed men went before them, and the rearguard followed the ark of Yahweh, blowing the trumpets continually. And on the seventh time that the priests blew the trumpets, it came to pass, as the people heard the sound of the trumpet, then the people shouted with a great shout, and the wall fell down.

Then Joshua said to the two men who had spied out the land: Go into the house of the harlot, and bring out thence the woman and all that she hath, as ye sware unto her. And the young men, the spies, went in and brought out Rahab and her father and her mother and her brethren and all that she had; and they brought out all her kindred. But the city and all that was in it they burnt with fire.

Then all the people drew near, and pitched on the north side of Ai; and there was a valley between them and Ai. And he [Joshua] took about five thousand men and set them in ambush between Bethel and Ai, on the east side of the city. And they stationed the people, all the host that was to the north of the city, and those lying in wait to the west of the city; but Joshua went that night into the middle of the valley. Then the men of the city rose up early and went out against Israel to battle; but Joshua and all Israel made as if they were beaten by them. So they pursued after Joshua, and were drawn away from the city. And there was not a man left in Ai or Bethel who went not out after Israel. Then Yahweh said unto Joshua: Stretch forth the spear in thy hand towards Ai, for I will give it into thy power. And Joshua stretched forth the spear that was in his hand toward the city. And as soon as he had stretched out his hand, they [the men in ambush] ran and entered the city and took it. And when Joshua and all Israel saw that the ambush had taken the city, they turned back and slew the men of Ai. And when Israel had made an end of slaying all the inhabitants of Ai, and they all, even to the last man, had fallen by the edge of the sword, then all the Israelites returned to Ai, and smote it with the edge of the sword. And all that fell that day, both of men and women, were twelve thousand, even all the men of Ai. For Joshua drew not back his hand wherewith he stretched out the spear, until all the inhabitants of Ai were utterly destroyed. Then Joshua burnt Ai and made it a heap forever, a desolation unto this day.

Now when the inhabitants of Gibeon heard what Joshua had done to Jericho and to Ai, they went to Joshua unto the camp at Gilgal, and said to Joshua: We are thy servants. And Joshua said unto them: Who are ye? and whence come ye? And they said unto him: From a very far country are thy servants come; and our elders and all the inhabitants of our country said unto us: Take provisions in your hand for the journey, and go to meet them, and say unto them, We are your servants. So Joshua made peace with them. But it came to pass at the end of three days, that they heard that they were their neighbors. Then Joshua summoned them and spake unto them, saying: Why have ye deceived us? And they answered Joshua and said: Behold, we are in thy hand; do unto us what seemeth good and right unto thee to do unto us. And so did he unto them, and delivered them out of the hand of the Children of Israel that they slew them not. But Joshua made them hewers of wood and drawers of water.

Now when the people of Jerusalem heard how the inhabitants of Gibeon had made peace with Israel, they feared greatly; because Gibeon was a great city like one of the royal cities, and because it was greater than Ai and all her men were warriors. So the king of Jerusalem sent to the kings of the Amorites, saying: Come up unto me and help me, that we may smite Gibeon; for it hath made peace with Joshua and with the Children of Israel. Then the five kings of the Amorites went up and made war against it. And the men of Gibeon sent to Joshua, saying: Come up to us quickly and help us; for all the kings of the Amorites who dwell in the hill-country are gathered together against us. So he went up from Gilgal that night. And Yahweh discomfited them before Israel, and slew them with a great slaughter at Gibeon; and they chased them by the way of Beth-horon. And as they fled from the face of Israel, while they were on the descent of Beth-horon, Yahweh cast down great stones from heaven upon them unto Azekah, and they died. They were more who died from the hailstones, than they whom the Children of Israel slew with the sword. And Joshua and all Israel with him returned unto Gilgal.

Then Joshua gathered all the tribes of Israel to Shechem, and called for all the elders of Israel and for their chiefs and for their judges and for their officers; and they presented themselves before God. And Joshua said to all the people: Thus saith Yahweh, the God of Israel. Your fathers dwelt of old beyond the River, and they served their gods. But I took your father Abraham from beyond the River, and led him through all the land of Canaan, and multiplied his seed, and gave him Isaac. And I gave Isaac, Jacob and Esau; and I gave unto Esau mount Seir; but Jacob and his children went down into Egypt. Then I sent Moses and Aaron; and when I had plagued Egypt according to what I did among them, afterward I brought you out. And ye came to the sea, and the Egyptians pursued after your fathers with chariots and with horsemen unto the Red Sea. And when they cried unto Yahweh, he put darkness between you and the Egyptians, and brought the sea upon them and covered them; and your eyes saw what I did in Egypt. And ye dwelt a long time in the wilderness. Then I brought you into the land of the

Amorites who lived beyond the Jordan, and they fought with you; but I gave them into your hand that ye might possess the land, and I destroyed them before you. Then Balak, the son of Zippor, king of Moab, arose and fought against Israel; and he sent and called Balaam the son of Beor to curse you; but I would not hearken to Balam, and he blessed you instead. So I delivered you out of his power. Then ye came across the Jordan, even unto Jericho; and the men of Jericho fought against you, and I delivered them into your hand. And I sent before you the hornet, even the two kings of the Amorites, which drave them out before you.

Now, therefore, fear Yahweh and serve Him in sincerity and truth; and put away the gods which your fathers served beyond the River [Euphrates] and in Egypt, and serve Yahweh. If, however, it seem evil to you to serve Yahweh, choose for yourselves whom ye will serve—whether the gods which your fathers served beyond the River, or the gods of the Amorites in whose land ye dwell; but as for me and my house, we will serve Yahweh.

And the people answered and said: God forbid that we should forsake Yahweh to serve other gods. For Yahweh, our God, He it is that brought us and our fathers up out of the land of Egypt, from the house of bondage, and which did great signs in our sight, and preserved us in all the way wherein we went, and among all the people through which we passed. And Yahweh drove out before us all the people, even the Amorites which dwelt in the land. Therefore will we also serve Yahweh, for He is our God.

And Joshua said unto the people: Ye cannot serve Yahweh, for He is a holy God; He is a jealous God; He will not forgive your transgressions nor your sins. If ye forsake Yahweh and serve strange gods, then He will turn and do you hurt and consume you, after that He hath done you good. But the people said unto Joshua: Nay, but we will serve Yahweh.

Then Joshua said unto the people: Ye are witnesses against yourselves that ye have chosen for yourselves Yahweh, to serve Him. (And they said: We are witnesses.) Now therefore, put away the strange gods which are among you, and incline your heart unto Yahweh, the God of Israel. And the people said unto Joshua: Yahweh our God will we serve, and His voice will we obey. Thus Joshua made a covenant with the people that day, and set them a statute and an ordinance in Shechem.

Then Joshua wrote these words in the book of the law of God, and he took a great stone and set it up there under the oak that was by the sanctuary of Yahweh. And Joshua said unto all the people: Behold, this stone shall be a witness unto us, for it hath heard all the words of Yahweh which He hath spoken unto us; therefore it shall be a witness unto you, lest ye deny your God. Then Joshua sent away the people, each to his own possession.

And after these things, Joshua the son of Nun died, being an hundred and ten years old. And they buried him in the land of his inheritance, in Timmath-serah which is in Mount Ephraim, on the north side of the hill of Gaash. And the bones of Joseph, which the Children of Israel had brought up out of Egypt, buried they in Shechem in the parcel of ground which Jacob bought of the sons of Hazor, the father of Shechem, for a hundred pieces of silver; and they became the possession of the sons of Joseph. And Eleazar the son of Aaron died, and they buried him in the hill of Phinehas, his son, which was given him in Mount Ephraim.

VI

OF DEBORAH, BARAK AND JAEL

Deborah summons Barak from Naphtali to head an uprising of the central tribes against Jabin, King of Canaan. Sisera heads the Canaanite host against them. He is defeated at the River Kishon, and flees on foot and alone, and takes refuge in the tent of Heber the Kenite. Jael, the wife of Heber, slays Sisera, and delivers him to Barak. A preface to the tale giving the political situation is prefixed by D₂, a writer of the 7th Cent. (Judges, iv, 1-3, [*the preface*] iv, 4-23; by E. Verse 24, a comment by D₂.)

(*Preface by D₂.* The Israelites offended Yahweh when Ehud was dead, and He sold them into the hand of Jabin, the King of Canaan who reigned in Hazor, the captain of whose host was Sisera, who dwelt in Harosheth of the Gentiles. And the Israelites cried unto Yahweh for help; for Jabin had nine hundred iron chariots, and for twenty years he mightily oppressed the Children of Israel. Now a prophetess, Deborah, wife of Lapidoth, was judging Israel at that time.)

She sent and summoned Barak, the son of Abinoam, from Kedesh in Naphtali, and said unto him: Hath not Yahweh, the God of Israel, commanded, saying: Go and draw toward mount Tabor, and take with thee ten thousand men of the children of Naphtali and the children of Zebulon? And I will draw unto thee to the brook Kishon Sisera with his chariots and his multitudes, and I will deliver him into thy hand. And Barak said unto her: If thou wilt go with me, I will go; but if thou wilt not go with me, then I will not go. And she said: I will surely go with thee; notwithstanding, the journey shall not be for thine honor, for Yahweh shall sell Sisera into the hands of a woman. And Deborah arose and went with Barak to Kedesh.

Then Barak called Zebulon and Naphtali to Kedesh; and there went up with him ten thousand men, and Deborah went with him.

Now Heber the Kenite had severed himself from the Kenites and pitched his tent as far away as the tree of Zaannaim which is near Kedesh.

And they told Sisera that Barak the son of Abinoam was gone up to Mount Tabor. And Sisera gathered together all his chariots, even nine hundred chariots of iron, and all the people that were with him, from Harosheth of the Gentiles unto the brook Kishon. And Deborah said unto Barak: Up, for this is the day in which Yahweh hath delivered Sisera into thy hand. Is not Yahweh going before thee? So Barak went down from Mount Tabor and ten thousand men after him. And Yahweh discomfited Sisera[1] and all his chariots and all his host with the edge of the sword before Barak; and Sisera alighted from his chariot, and fled away on foot.

But Barak pursued after the chariots and after the host unto Harosheth of the Gentiles; and all the host of Sisera fell upon the edge

[1] In the great Ode of Deborah given in J's History, this discomfiture is attributed to a great hail-storm and rain that filled the brook Kishon to overflowing.

of the sword; there was not a man left. Howbeit, Sisera fled away on foot to the tent of Jael, wife of Heber the Kenite.

And Jael went out to meet Sisera and said unto him: Turn in, my lord, turn in to me; fear not. And when he had turned in to her in the tent, she covered him with a rug. And he said unto her: Give me, I pray thee, a little water to drink, for I am thirsty. And she opened a bottle of milk and gave him drink, and covered him. Again he said unto her: Stand in the door of the tent; and it shall be when any man doth come and inquire of thee, and say: Is there any man here? that thou shalt say, No. Then Jael, Heber's wife, took a nail of the tent and a mallet in her hand, and went softly unto him, and smote the nail into his temples and fastened it into the ground; for he was fast asleep and weary. So he died.

And behold, as Barak pursued Sisera, Jael came out to meet him, and said unto him: Come in, and I will show thee the man whom thou seekest. And when he came in lo, Sisera lay dead, and the nail was in his temples.

(*Comment by D₂.* Thus God on that day enabled the Israelites to subdue Jabin, the King of Canaan. And the power of the Israelites prevailed more and more until they had destroyed Jabin, King of Canaan.)

VII

OF GIDEON[1]

(Judg. vi, 1-5b, 33, 36-40; vii, 2-8, 16a, 17b-20, 24-25b; viii, 1-3, 22-23, 30-31.)

Preface by D₂.—The Israelites again did evil in the sight of Yahweh, and Yahweh delivered them into the hands of Midian seven years. And because of the Midianites, the Israelites made themselves hiding-places in the mountains and caves and fastnesses. For, when Israel had sown, the Midianites and Amalekites and the eastern Bedouin would come up and encamp against them, and destroy the increase of the earth till thou comest to Gaza, and they left no sustenance for Israel, neither sheep nor ox nor ass. For they came up with their cattle and their tents, and they came as grasshoppers for multitude, and their camels were without number.

Now all Midian had gathered together and crossed the Jordan, and encamped in the plain of Jezreel. Then Gideon said unto God: If Thou wilt save Israel by my hand, as Thou hast spoken, behold, I will put a fleece of wool on the threshing-floor; if there be dew on the fleece only and it be dry on all the ground, then shall I know that Thou wilt save Israel by my hand as Thou hast spoken. And it was so; for he rose up early on the morrow and wrung out dew out of the fleece, a bowlful of water. And Gideon said unto God: Let not Thine anger be kindled against me; let me make trial, I pray Thee, with the fleece but this once more; let it be dry only upon the fleece, and upon the ground let there be dew. And God did so that night; for it was dry upon the fleece only, and there was dew on all the ground. . . . Then Yahweh

------

[1] Called also Jerubbaal, who freed Israel from the annual raids of the Midianites (Bedouin). Possibly E here combines the exploits of two different men.

said to Gideon: The people who are with thee are too many for Me to give the Midianites into their hand; lest Israel vaunt itself against Me, saying: Mine own power hath saved me. Now, therefore, proclaim in the hearing of the people: Whosoever is afraid and timid, let him return and depart early from Mount Gilead. And there returned twenty and two thousand; but there remained ten thousand. And Yahweh said unto Gideon: There are yet too many; bring them down to the water, and I will try them for thee there; and it shall be that of whom I shall say unto thee; This shall go with thee, the same shall go with thee. And of whomsoever I say unto thee: This shall not go with thee, the same shall not go. So he brought the people down to the water; and Yahweh said unto Gideon: Every man that lappeth of the water with his tongue as a dog lappeth, him shalt thou set by himself; likewise every one that boweth down upon his knees to drink. And the number of them that lapped, putting their hand to their mouth, was three hundred men; but all the rest bowed down upon their knees to drink water. And Yahweh said unto Gideon: By the three hundred men that lapped will I save you, and will deliver Midian into thy hand; let all the rest of the people go home. So they took victuals of the people in their hands, and their horns; and he sent all the men of Israel to their tents; and retained only the three hundred men.

Then he divided his three hundred men into three companies, and furnished them all with horns. And he said: When I come to the outmost edge of the camp, it shall be that as I do, so shall ye do. When I blow the horn, I and all that are with me, then do ye also blow the horns on every side of the camp. Now Gideon and the hundred men with him reached the edge of the camp in the beginning of the middle watch, and they blew their horns; then the three companies blew their horns; and Yahweh set every man's sword against his fellow, throughout all the host. And the men of all Manasseh were called out, and pursued Midian. Gideon also sent messengers through all the hill-country of Ephraim, saying: Come down to meet Midian and hold the streams against them as far as Beth-barah; so all the men of Ephraim were called out, and held the waters as far as Beth-barah. And they took the two princes of Midian, Oreb and Zeeb, and slew Oreb at the Rock of Oreb, and Zeeb they slew at the wine-press of Zeeb. Then the Ephraimites said to Gideon: Why hast thou served us thus, that thou didst not call us when thou wentest to fight with Midian? And they did chide with him sharply. But he answered them: What have I now done? Is not the gleaning of Ephraim better than the vintage of Abi-ezer? God hath given into your hand the princes of Midian, Oreb and Zeeb. What was I able to do in comparison with you? When he had said that, their anger was appeased.

Then the men of Israel said unto Gideon: Rule thou over us, both thou and thy son, and thy son's son; for thou hast saved us out of the hand of Midian. And Gideon said unto them: I will not rule over you, neither shall my son rule over you; Yahweh shall rule over you. So Jerubbaal son of Joash went and dwelt in his own house.[1]

---

[1] ["Now Gideon had seventy sons, all begotten by him, for he had many wives. And his concubine also, who lived in Shechem, bore him a son whom he named Abimelech." *Added by P.* The additions of pre-exilic editors are given with due notice in the text.]

VIII

OF ABIMELECH KING IN SHECHEM, AND JOTHAM HIS BROTHER
(Judg. ix, 1-21, 22c, 23, 25, 42-56a.)

Abimelech ben Jerubbaal went to Shechem unto his mother's brethren and spake with them and with all the family of his mother's father, saying: Speak, I pray you, in the ears of all the men of Shechem, saying: Which is better for you, that all the sons of Jerubbaal, who are threescore and ten persons, rule over you, or that one rule over you? Remember also that I am your bone and your flesh. And his mother's brethren spake of him in the ears of all the men of Shechem all these words and their hearts inclined to follow Abimelech; for they said: He is our brother. And they gave him threescore and ten pieces of silver out of the house of Baal-berith, wherewith Abimelech hired worthless fellows who followed him. And he went unto his father's house at Ophrah, and slew his brethren, the sons of Jerubbaal, being threescore and ten persons, on one stone; but Jotham, the youngest son of Jerubbaal, was left; for he hid himself. And all the men of Shechem assembled themselves together, and all Beth-Millo, and went and made Abimelech king by the terebinth of the pillar that was in Shechem.

And when they told it to Jotham, he went and stood on the top of Mount Gerizim and lifted up his voice and cried unto them:

Hearken unto me, ye men of Shechem, that God may hearken to you! The trees went forth on a time to anoint a king over them. And they said to the olive tree: Reign thou over us! But the olive tree said unto them: Shall I leave my fatness seeing that through me gods and men are honored, and come to hold sway over the trees? And the trees' said to the fig-tree: Come thou, and reign over us! But the fig-tree said unto them: Shall I leave my sweetness and my good fruitage, and go to reign over the trees? And the trees said unto the vine: Come thou, and reign over us! And the vine said unto them: Shall I leave my wine, which gladdens gods and men, and go to hold sway over the trees? Then said all the trees unto the bramble: Come thou, and reign over us! And the bramble said unto the trees: If in truth ye anoint me king over you, then come and take refuge under my shadow; and if not, let fire come out of the bramble and devour the cedars of Lebanon.

Now therefore, if ye have dealt truly and uprightly in that ye have made Abimelech king, and if ye have dealt well with Jerubbaal and his house, and have done unto him according to his deserts—for my father fought for you and adventured his life, and delivered you out of the hand of Midian; and ye are risen up against my father's house this day, and have slain his sons, threescore and ten men on one stone; and have made Abimelech, the son of his maid-servant, king over the men of Shechem because he is your kinsman—if ye then have dealt truly and uprightly with Jerubbaal and his house this day, then rejoice ye in Abimelech, and let him also rejoice in you. But if not, let fire come out from Abimelech and devour the men of Shechem and Beth-Millo; and let fire come out from the men of Shechem and from Beth-Millo and consume Abimelech. And Jotham ran away and fled and went to Beer and dwelt there, for fear of Abimelech, his brother.

After Abimelech had ruled three years, God sent a spirit of discord between Abimelech and the men of Shechem, and the men of Shechem dealt treacherously with Abimelech. And the men of Shechem set liers-in-wait on the hilltops, and they robbed all that came along that way; and it was told Abimelech.

And on the following day, the people went out into the field, and it was told Abimelech. And he took the people and divided them into three companies and lay in wait in the field; and he looked and behold, the men were coming forth out of the city; and he rose against them and smote them. And Abimelech and the companies that were with him rushed forward and stood in the entrance of the gate of the city, and the two other companies rushed upon all that were in the field and smote them. And Abimelech fought against the city all that day, and took the city and slew all the people that were therein; and he razed the city and sowed it with salt.

And when the men of the tower of Shechem heard thereof, they went into the crypt of the temple of El-berith; and it was told Abimelech that all the men of the tower of Shechem were gathered there. And Abimelech gat him up to Mount Zalmon, he and all the people that were with him; and Abimelech took an axe in his hand and cut down a bough from the trees and took it up and laid it on his shoulder; and he said to the men who were with him: Make haste, and do what ye have seen me do. And all the people likewise cut down every man his bough, and followed Abimelech and put them to the crypt, and set fire to the crypt upon the men in it; so that all the men of the tower of Shechem died also, about a thousand men and women.

Then went Abimelech to Thebez, and encamped against Thebez and took it. But there was a strong tower within the city, and thither fled all the men and women of the city and shut themselves in, and gat them up to the roof of the tower. And Abimelech came unto the tower and went close under the door of the tower to burn it with fire. And a certain woman cast an upper millstone upon Abimelech's head, and broke his skull. Then he called hastily to his armor-bearer who attended him, and said unto him: Draw thy sword and kill me; that men may not say of me: A woman slew him. And his young man thrust him through, and he died. And when the men of Israel saw that Abimelech was dead, they departed every man to his place.

(Thus God requited the wickedness of Abimelech which he committed against his father in slaying his seventy brethren; and all the wickedness of the men of Shechem did God requite upon their heads; and thus the curse of Jotham ben Jerubbaal came upon them all.)[1]

IX

OF JEPHTHAH THE GILEADITE WHO DELIVERED GILEAD FROM THE AMMONITES

Judg. x, 6a, c, 7; xi, 1a, 3-11, 30-40; xii, 1-6.)

(*Preface by D₂*.—And the Israelites again offended Yahweh and served the Baalim and the Ashtoreth, and forsook Yahweh and did not serve Him. And Yahweh was incensed against Israel, and sold them into the power of the Philistines and into the power of the Ammonites.)[2]

Now Jephthah the Gileadite was a great warrior, and he was the son of a harlot. And Jephthah fled from his brethren, and dwelt in

[1] Comment of a pre-exilic editor; possibly also the interpolator of the prefaces to these tales of the "Judges".

[2] The mention of the Philistines seems to indicate that E, too, recounted some exploits of Samson's; but those that have been embodied in "Judges" are by J, and belong to his "History".

the land of Tob, and there gathered about him worthless fellows who went out with him. And it came to pass after a while that the Ammonites made war upon Israel. And the elders came to fetch Jephthah out of the land of Tob; and they said unto him: Come and be our chief, that we may fight against the Ammonites. And Jephthah said unto the elders of Gilead: Did not ye hate me, and drive me out of my father's house? Why are ye come unto me now, when ye are in distress? And the elders of Gilead said unto Jephthah: Therefore are we now returned to thee, that thou mayest go with us and fight with the Ammonites; and thou shalt be our chief over all the inhabitants of Gilead. And Jephthah said unto the elders of Gilead: If ye bring me back home to fight against the Ammonites, and Yahweh deliver them over to me, then I will be your chief. And the elders of Gilead said unto Jephthah: Yahweh shall be witness between us; surely, according to thy word, so will we do. Then Jephthah went with the elders of Gilead, and the people made him chief and commander over them; and Jephthah spake all his words before Yahweh at Mizpah.

And Jephthah vowed a vow unto Yahweh, and said: If Thou wilt indeed deliver the Ammonites into my hand, then it shall be that whatsoever cometh forth of the doors of my house to meet me, when I return in peace from the Ammonites, it shall be Yahweh's, and I will offer it up as a burnt-offering. Then Jephthah passed over to the Ammonites to fight against them; and Yahweh delivered them into his hand. And he smote them from Aroer until thou come to Minneth, and even to Abel-cheramim, with a very great slaughter. So the Ammonites were subdued before the Children of Israel.

And Jephthah came to Mizpah, to his house; and behold, his daughter came out to meet him with timbrels and with dances; and she was his only child; besides her he had neither son nor daughter. And it came to pass, when he saw her, that he rent his clothes and cried: Alas, my daughter! thou hast brought me very low, thou art become my ruin; for I have vowed a vow unto Yahweh, and I cannot go back from it! And she said unto him: My father, thou hast vowed a vow unto Yahweh; do unto me according to that which thou hast vowed; forasmuch as Yahweh hath wrought vengeance for thee on thy foes, even on the children of Ammon. And she said unto her father: Let this thing be done for me; let me alone two months that I may depart and go to the mountains and bewail my virginity, I and my companions. And he said: Go. And he sent her away for two months; and she went, she and her companions, and bewailed her virginity upon the mountains. And at the end of two months she returned to her father; and he did with her according to the vow which he had vowed; and she had not known man. Thus it became a custom in Israel that the daughters of Israel went yearly to lament the daughter of Jephthah the Gileadite four days in a year.

Now the men of Ephraim were gathered together and passed over to Zaphon. And they said to Jephthah: wherefore didst thou pass over to fight with the Ammonites and didst not summon us to go with thee? We will burn thy house over thee with fire. And Jephthah said unto them: I and my people were at great strife with the children of Ammon; and when I called you, ye saved me not out of their hand. And when I saw that ye were not going to help me, I took my life in my hand and passed over against the Ammonites, and Yahweh delivered them into my hand. Wherefore, then, have ye come up unto me this day to fight against me? Then Jephthah gathered together all the men of Gilead, and fought with Ephraim; and the men of Gilead smote Ephraim, because they said: Ye are fugitives of Ephraim, ye Gileadites, in the midst of Ephraim, and in the midst of Manasseh.

And the Gileadites took the fords of the Jordan against the Ephraimites; and it was so, that when any of the fugitives of Ephraim said: Let me go over, the men of Gilead said unto them: Art thou an Ephraimite? If he said: Nay, then said they unto him: Say now *Shibboleth;* and he said: *Sibboleth,* for he could not pronounce it aright. Then they laid hold on him, and slew him at the fords of the Jordan. And there fell of Ephraim that time forty and two thousand.

X

OF ELI THE PRIEST AND THE CHILD SAMUEL

(1 Sam'l, i, 1-28; ii, 11-36; iii, 1-21; iv, 1b, 2a, c, 3b, 4a, c, 6a, 7a, 8, 9b, c, 11-22.)

Now there was a certain man of Ramathaim-sophim, of the hill-country of Ephraim, whose name was Elkanah the son of Jeroham, the son of Elihu, the son of Tohu, the son of Zuph, an Ephrathite. And he had two wives; the name of the one was Hannah, and the name of the other Peninnah. And Peninnah had children, but Hannah had no children. And this man went up out of his city from year to year to worship and to offer sacrifices unto Yahweh Sabaoath in Shiloh. (Now the two sons of Eli, Hophni and Phineas, were priests there unto Yahweh.) And when a day came that Elkanah sacrificed, he gave portions to Peninnah his wife and to all her sons and daughters; but to Hannah he gave a double portion, for he loved Hannah. But Yahweh had shut up her womb; and her rival vexed her sore so as to make her fret, because Yahweh had shut up her womb. And as he did so year by year when she went up to the house of Yahweh, so she vexed her; therefore she wept and would not eat. And her husband Elkanah said unto her: Hannah, why weepest thou? and why eatest thou not? Am I not better unto thee than ten sons?

Now Eli the priest sat upon a seat by the door-post of the temple of Yahweh. And Hannah rose up after they had eaten in Shiloh and after they had drunk, and she was in bitterness of soul. And she prayed unto Yahweh and wept sore; and she vowed a vow, and said: O Yahweh Sabaoth, if Thou wilt look upon the afflictions of Thine handmaid, and remember me and not forget Thine handmaid, but wilt give me a manchild, then I will give him unto Yahweh all the days of his life, and there shall no razor come upon his head.

Now it came to pass, as she prayed long before Yahweh, that Eli watched her mouth. Now Hannah spake in her heart; only her lips moved, but her voice could not be heard; therefore Eli thought she had been drunken. And Eli said unto her: How long wilt thou be drunken? Put away thy wine from thee. And Hannah answered and said: Nay, my lord, I am a woman of sorrowful spirit. I have drunk neither wine nor strong drink, but I was pouring out my soul before Yahweh. Count not thine handmaid for a wicked woman, for out of the abundance of my complaint and my vexation have I spoken hitherto.

Then Eli answered and said: Go in peace; and may the God of Israel grant thy petition that thou hast asked of Him. And she said: Let thine handmaid find grace in thy sight. So the woman went her way and did eat, and her countenance was no more sad. And they rose up in the morning early and worshipped before Yahweh, and returned and came to their house in Ramah. And Elkanah knew Hannah his wife, and Yahweh remembered her. And it came to pass when the time was come about, that Hannah conceived and bare a son; and she called his name Samuel: Because I have asked him of Yahweh.

And the man Elkanah and all his house went up to offer the yearly sacrifice to Yahweh and his vow; but Hannah went not up, for she said unto her husband: Not until the child be weaned; then I will bring him, that he may appear before Yahweh, and abide there for ever. And Elkanah her husband said unto her: Do what seemeth unto thee good; tarry until thou have weaned him; only may Yahwah establish His word. So the woman tarried and gave her son suck until she weaned him. And when she had weaned him, she took him up with her, with three bullocks and one ephah of meal and a bottle of wine, and brought him unto the house of Yahweh in Shiloh; and the child was young. And when the bullock was slain, they brought the child unto Eli. And she said: O my lord, as thy soul liveth, my lord, I am the woman that stood by thee here, praying unto Yahweh. For this child I prayed, and Yahweh hath granted my petition which I asked of Him; therefore I also have lent him to Yahweh; as long as he liveth he is lent to Yahweh. And he worshipped Yahweh there. And Elkanah went to Ramah to his house. And the child did minister unto Yahweh before Eli the priest.[1] Now the sons of Eli were base men; they knew not Yahweh. And the custom of the priests with the people was that, when any man offered sacrifice, the priest's servant came, while the flesh was seething, with a flesh-hook of three teeth in his hand and struck it into the pan or kettle or cauldron or pot; all that the flesh-hook brought up the priest took. So they did unto all the Israelites that came thither in Shiloh. Yea, before they burnt the fat, the priest's servant came and said to the man that sacrificed: Give flesh to roast for the priest; for I will not have sodden flesh of thee, but raw. And if the man said unto him: Let them not fail to burn the fat presently, and then take as thy soul desireth; then he would say: Nay, but thou shalt give it me now; and if not, I will take it by force. And the sin of the young men was very great before Yahweh; for the men dealt contemptuously with the offering of Yahweh.

But Samuel ministered before Yahweh, being a child girded with a linen ephod. Moreover his mother made him a little robe and brought it to him from year to year, when she came up with her husband to offer the yearly sacrifice. And Eli would bless Elkanah and his wife, and say: May Yahweh give thee seed of this woman for the loan which was lent to Yahweh. And they would go to their own house. So Yahweh remembered Hannah, and she conceived and bare three sons and two daughters. And the child Samuel grew before Yahweh.

Now Eli was very old; and he heard all that his sons did unto all Israel, and how they lay with the women that did service at the door of the Tent of Meeting. And he said unto them: Why do ye such things? for I hear evil reports concerning you from all this people. Nay, my sons; for it is no good report which I hear the people of Yahweh do spread abroad. If one man sin against another, the judge shall judge him; but if a man sin against Yahweh, who shall entreat for him? But

---

[1] The "Prayer of Hannah" (ch. ii, 1-10) is a late triumphal ode, recording the success of a king. See verses 4 and 10b.

they hearkened not unto the voice of their father, because Yahweh would slay them. And the child Samuel grew on, and increased in favor both with Yahweh and with men.

And there came a man of God unto Eli, and said unto him: Thus saith Yahweh, Did I reveal Myself unto the house of thy father when they were in bondage in Egypt to Pharaoh's house? And did I choose him out of all the tribes of Israel to be My priest, to go up unto Mine altar, to burn incense, to wear an ephod before Me? And did I give unto the house of thy father all the offerings of the Children of Israel made by fire? Wherefore kick ye at My sacrifice and at Mine offering, which I have commanded in My habitation, and honored thy sons above Me, to make yourselves fat with the chiefest of all the offerings of Israel My people? Therefore said Yahweh, the God of Israel: I said indeed that thy house and the house of thy father should walk before Me for ever; but now saith Yahweh: Be it far from Me; for them that honor Me I will honor, and they that despise Me shall be lightly esteemed. Behold, the days come that I will cut off thine arm, and the arm of thy father's house, that there shall not be an old man in thine house. And thou shalt behold a rival in My habitation in all the good that shall be done to Israel; and there shall not be an old man in thy house for ever. Yet will I not cut off every man of thine from Mine altar, to make thine eyes to fail and thy heart to languish; but all the increase of thine house shall die young men. And this shall be the sign unto thee,—that which shall come upon thy two sons, on Hophni and Phinehas; in one day they shall die, both of them. And I will raise Me up a faithful priest, that shall do according to that which is in My heart and in My mind; and I will build him a sure house, and he shall walk before Mine anointed for ever. And it shall come to pass, that every one that is left in thine house shall come and bow down to him for a piece of silver and a loaf of bread, and shall say: Put me, I pray thee, into one of the priests' offices, that I may seat a morsel of bread.

And the child Samuel ministered to Yahweh before Eli. And the word of Yahweh was precious in those days; there was no frequent vision. And it came to pass at that time, when Eli was lain down in his place,—now his eyes had begun to wax dim that he could not see,—and ere the lamp of Yahweh was gone out, and Samuel had lain down in the temple of Yahweh, where the ark of God was, that Yahweh called, Samuel! and he said: Here am I. And he ran to Eli, and said: Here am I, for thou calledst me. And he said: I called not; lie down again. And he went and lay down. And Yahweh called yet again: Samuel! And Samuel arose and went to Eli, and said: Here am I; for thou didst call me. And he answered: I called not, my son; lie down again. Now Samuel did not yet know Yahweh, neither was the word of Yahweh yet revealed unto him. And Yahweh called Samuel the third time. And he arose and went to Eli, and said: Here am I; for thou *didst* call me. And Eli perceived that Yahweh was calling the child. Therefore Eli said unto Samuel: Go, lie down; and it shall be, if thou be called, that thou shalt say: Speak, Yahweh! for Thy servant heareth. So Samuel went and lay down in his place. And Yahweh came, and stood, and called as at other times: Samuel! Samuel! Then Samuel said: Speak, for Thy servant heareth. And Yahweh said to Samuel: Behold, I will do a thing in Israel, at which both the ears of every one that heareth it shall tingle. In that day, I will perform against Eli all that I have spoken concerning his house, from the beginning even to the end. For I have told him that I will judge his house for ever for his iniquity, in that he knew that his sons did bring a curse upon themselves, and he rebuked them not. And therefore I have sworn unto the house of Eli, that the iniquity of Eli's house shall not be expiated with sacrifice nor offering forever.

And Samuel lay till the morning, and opened the doors of the house of Yahweh. And Samuel feared to tell Eli the vision. Then Eli called Samuel, and said: Samuel, my son! And he said: Here am I. And he said: What is the thing that He hath spoken unto thee? I pray thee, hide it not from me. God do so to thee and more also, if thou hide any thing from me of all the things that He spake unto thee. And Samuel told him all the words, and hid nothing from him. And he said: It is Yahweh; let Him do what seemeth Him good.

And Samuel grew, and Yahweh was with him, and did let none of his words fall to the ground. And all Israel from Dan unto Beersheba knew that Samuel was established to be a prophet of Yahweh. And Yahweh appeared again in Shiloh; for Yahweh revealed Himself to Samuel in Shiloh by the word of Yahweh.

Now Israel went out against the Philistines to battle, and pitched beside Ebenezer, and the Philistines pitched in Aphek; and when the battle was joined Israel was smitten before the Philistines. Then the elders of Israel said: Wherefore hath Yahweh smitten us to-day before the Philistines? Let us bring the ark of our God out of Shiloh, that He may come among us and save us from the hand of our enemies.

Now the two sons of Eli, Hophni and Phineas, were there with the ark of God. And when the ark of God came into the camp, all Israel shouted with a great shout. And when the Philistines heard the noise of the shout, they said: What is this noise of great shouting in the camp of the Hebrews? And the Philistines were afraid; for they said: God is come into their camp. Woe unto us! Who shall deliver us out of the hand of these mighty gods? These are the gods that smote the Egyptians with all manner of plagues and pestilence. Quit yourselves like men, O ye Philistines, that ye be not slaves unto the Hebrews, as they have been slaves to you. And Israel was smitten, and fled every man to his tent. And there fell of Israel thirty thousand footmen. And the ark of God was taken; and the two sons of Eli, Hophni and Phineas, were slain.

And a Benjamite ran out of the army and came to Shiloh the same day with his clothes rent and with earth on his head. And as he came, lo, Eli was sitting on his seat by the gate, watching; for his heart trembled for the ark of God. And when the man came into the city and told it, all the city cried out. And when Eli heard the noise of the crying, he said: What is this noise of tumult? And the man made haste and told Eli. And the man said unto Eli: I am he that came out of the army, and I fled to-day out of the army. And he said: How went the matter, my son? And he that brought the tidings answered and said: Israel is fled before the Philistines, and there hath been also a great slaughter among the people, and thy two sons also, Hophni and Phinehas, are dead, and the ark of God is taken. And it came to pass, when he made mention of the ark of God, that Eli fell from off his seat backward by the side of the gate, and his neck brake and he died; for he was an old man and heavy.

And his daughter-in-law, Phinehas's wife, was with child, about to be delivered; and when she heard the tidings that the ark of God was taken, and that her father-in-law and her husband were dead, she bowed herself and brought forth; for her pains came suddenly upon her.

And about the time of her death the women who stood by her said unto her: Fear not, for thou hast brought forth a son. But she answered not, neither did she regard it. But she named the child Ichabod [*dishonored*]. And she said: The glory hath departed from Israel, for the ark of God is taken. And the Philistines took the ark of God, and brought it from Ebenezer to Ashdod.

XI

OF SAMUEL THE SEER

Samuel urges the people to put away foreign gods. They obey, and gather for a fast at Mizpah. The Philistines attack them, but are pursued and smitten. Samuel is judge of a small circuit. The people demand a king; Samuel details the evils of monarchy, but finally yields and anoints Saul, a Benjamite, king. Saul's son, Jonathan, routs a garrison of the Philistines. Saul rashly assumes the office of priest and is rejected by Yahweh. Samuel is sent by Yahweh to anoint David of Bethlehem as Saul's successor. Samuel dies. (1 Sam'l, vii, 2b; viii, 22; x, 17-27; xiii, 3-6, 7b-15; xv, 24-31; xvi, 1-13; xxv, 1a.)

And all the house of Israel yearned after Yahweh. And Samuel spake unto all the house of Israel, saying: If ye do return unto Yahweh with all your heart, then put away the foreign gods and the Ashtoreth from among you, and direct your hearts unto Yahweh and serve Him only, and He will deliver you out of the hand of the Philistines. Then the Children of Israel did put away the Baalim and the Ashtoreth and served Yahweh only.

And Samuel said: Gather all Israel to Mizpah, and I will pray for you unto Yahweh. And they gathered together to Mizpah, and drew water and poured it out before Yahweh, and fasted on that day, and said there: We have sinned against Yahweh. And Samuel judged the Children of Israel in Mizpah.

And when the Philistines heard that the Children of Israel were gathered together at Mizpah, the lords of the Philistines went up against Israel. And when the Children of Israel heard it, they were afraid of the Philistines. And they said unto Samuel: Cease not to cry unto Yahweh our God for us, that He may save us out of the hand of the Philistines. And Samuel took a sucking lamb and offered it for a whole burnt-offering unto Yahweh; and Samuel cried unto Yahweh for Israel, and Yahweh answered him. And as Samuel was offering up the burnt-offering, the Philistines drew near to battle against Israel; but Yahweh thundered with a great thunder on that day against the Philistines and discomfited them; and they were smitten down before Israel. And the men of Israel went out of Mizpah and pursued the Philistines; and they smote them until they came under Beth-car.

Then Samuel took a stone and set it between Miszpah and Shen, and called the name of it Ebenezer (*Stone of help*), saying: Hitherto hath Yahweh helped us.[1]

So the Philistines were subdued, and they came no more within the

[1] The hand of the Deuteronomist Redactor, (D₂), is very evident in this part of Samuel's history; but the touch of the marvellous in the battle with the Philistines, and the intimate details are akin to those of the traditions preferred by E. The account of the rise of the monarchy is largely added to by DR (Ch. viii, 8-20).

border of Israel; and the hand of Yahweh was against the Philistines all the days of Samuel. And there was peace between Israel and the Amorites. And Samuel judged Israel all the days of his life. And he went from year to year in circuit to Bethel and Gilgal and Mizpah and judged Israel in all those places. And his return was to Ramah, for there was his house; and there he judged Israel; and he built there an altar unto Yahweh.

Now it came to pass when Samuel was old, that he made his sons judges over Israel. Now the name of his first-born was Joel, and the name of the second, Abijah; they were judges in Beer-sheba. And his sons walked not in his ways, but turned aside after lucre and took bribes, and perverted justice.

Then all the elders of Israel gathered themselves together and came to Samuel at Ramah. And they said unto him: Behold, thou art old, and thy sons walk not in thy ways; now make us a king to judge us like all the nations. But the thing displeased Samuel when they said: Give us a king to judge us. And Samuel prayed unto Yahweh. And Yahweh said unto Samuel: Hearken unto the voice of the people in all that they say unto thee; for they have not rejected thee, but they have rejected Me, that I should not be king over them. Now therefore hearken unto their voices; howbeit thou shalt earnestly forwarn them, and shalt declare unto them the manner of the king that shall reign over them. And Samuel told all the words of Yahweh unto the people that asked of him a king, and he said:

This will be the manner of the king that shall reign over you: he will take your sons and appoint them for himself over his chariots and to be his horsemen; and they shall run before his chariots. And he will appoint them to be captains of thousands and captains of fifties, and to plough his ground and to reap his harvest, and to make his instruments of war and the instruments of his chariots. And he will take your daughters to be perfumers, and to be cooks and to be bakers. And he will take your fields and your vineyards and your olive-yards, even the best of them and give them unto his servants. And he will take the tenth of your produce and of your vineyards, and give to his officers and to his servants. And he will take your men-servants and your maid-servants and your goodliest young men and your asses, and put them to his work. He will take the tenth of your flocks; and ye shall be his servants. And in that day ye shall cry out because of your king whom ye shall have chosen you; and Yahweh will not answer you in that day.

But the people refused to hearken unto the voice of Samuel; and they said: Nay, but there shall be a king over us, that we also may be like all the nations; and that our king may judge us, and go out before us and fight our battles. And Samuel heard all the words of the people, and he spake them in the ears of Yahweh. And Yahweh said to Samuel: Hearken unto their voice, and make them a king. And Samuel said unto the men of Israel: Go ye every man into his own city.

Then Samuel called the people together unto Yahweh to Mizpah. And he said to the Children of Israel: Thus saith Yahweh: I brought up Israel out of Egypt, and delivered you out of the hand of the Egyptians, and out of the hand of all the kingdoms that have oppressed you. But ye have this day rejected your God, who Himself saveth you out of all your calamities and your distresses. And ye have said unto Him: Nay, but set a king over us. Now therefore, present yourselves before Yahweh by your tribes and by your thousands. So Samuel brought all the tribes of Israel near; and the tribe of Benjamin was taken. And he brought the tribe of Benjamin near by their families, and the family of Matri was taken; and Saul the son of Kish was taken; but when they sought him, he could not be found. And they inquired of Yahweh further, if the man should yet come hither. And Yahweh answered: Behold, he hath hidden himself among the stuff. And they ran and fetched him thence; and when he stood among the people, he was higher than any of the people from his shoulders upward. And Samuel said to all the people: See ye him whom Yahweh hath chosen; and all the people shouted, and cried: Long live the king!

Then Samuel told the people the manner of the kingdom, and wrote it in a book, and laid it up before Yahweh. And Samuel sent all the people away, every man to his own home.

Then Saul went to his house in Gibeah; and there went with him the men of valor whose hearts God had touched. But certain base fellows said: How shall this man save us? and they despised him, and brought him no present. But Saul held his peace. Then Jonathan, Saul's son, smote the garrison of the Philistines which was in Geba; and the Philistines heard of it. And Saul blew the horn throughout all the land, saying: Let the Israelites hear. And all Israel heard it said that Saul had smitten the garrison of the Philistines, and that Israel also had made itself odious to the Philistines. And the people gathered themselves together unto Saul in Gilgal. And the Philistines assembled themselves together to fight with Israel thirty thousand chariots and six thousand horsemen, and people as the sand which is on the seashore in multitude; and they came up and pitched in Michmash, eastward of Bethaven. When the men of Israel saw that they were in a strait,—for the people were distressed—then the people did hide themselves in caves and in thickets, and among rocks and holds and in pits. But as for Saul, he was yet in Gilgal.

And he tarried seven days, according to the set time that Samuel had appointed: but Samuel came not to Gilgal; and the people were scattering from him. And Saul said: Bring hither to me the burnt-offerings and the peace-offerings. And he offered the burnt-offering. And it came to pass that, as soon as he had made an end of offering the burnt-offering, that Samuel came; and Saul went out to meet him, that he might salute him. And Samuel said: What hast thou done? And Saul said: I saw that the people were scattering from me, and that thou camest not within the days appointed, and that the Philistines were assembling themselves together against Michmash; therefore said I, now will the Philistines come down upon us in Gilgal, and I have not entreated the favor of Yahweh. I forced myself therefore, and offered the burnt-offering.

And Samuel said unto Saul: Thou hast done foolishly; thou hast not kept the commandment of Yahweh thy God, which He commanded thee. For now would Yahweh have established thy kingdom for ever. But now thy kingdom shall not continue; Yahweh hath sought Him a man after His own heart, and hath appointed him to be a prince over His people, because thou hast not kept that which Yahweh commanded thee.

And Saul said unto Samuel: I have sinned; for I have transgressed the commands of Yahweh, and thy words, because I feared the people and hearkened to their voice. Now therefore, I pray thee, pardon my sin and return with me, that I may worship Yahweh. And Samuel said unto him: I will not return with thee, for thou hast rejected the word of Yahweh, and Yahweh hath rejected thee from being king over Israel.

And as Samuel turned about to go away, he [Saul] laid hold of the skirt of his robe and it rent. And Samuel said unto him: Yahweh hath rent the kingdom of Israel from thee this day, and hath given it to a neighbor of thine who is better than thou. And also, the Glory of Israel will not lie nor repent; for He is not a man, that He should repent. Then he said: I have sinned; yet honor me now, I pray thee, before the elders of the people and before Israel; and return with me, that I may worship Yahweh thy God. So Samuel turned back with Saul; and Saul worshipped Yahweh.

Then Samuel went to Ramah, and Saul went up to his house, to Gibeah of Saul. And Samuel never beheld Saul again until the day of his death. For Samuel mourned for Saul; and Yahweh repented that He had made him king over Israel.

And Yahweh said unto Samuel: How long wilt thou mourn for Saul, seeing I have rejected him from being king over Israel? Fill thy horn with oil and go; I will send thee to Jesse the Bethlehemite; for I have provided Me a king among his sons. And Samuel said: How can I go? If Saul hear it, he will kill me. And Yahweh said: Take a heifer with thee and say: I am come to sacrifice unto Yahweh. And call Jesse to the sacrifice, and I will tell thee what thou shalt do; and thou shalt anoint unto Me him whom I name unto thee.

And Samuel did that which Yahweh spake, and came to Bethlehem. And the elders of the city came to meet him trembling, and said: Comest thou peaceably? and he said: Peaceably. I am come to sacrifice unto Yahweh; sanctify yourselves and come with me to the sacrifice. And he sanctified Jesse and his sons and called them to the sacrifice.

And it came to pass when they were come, that he beheld Eliab, and said: Surely the anointed of Yahweh is before Him. But Yahweh said unto Samuel: Look not on his countenance or on the height of his stature, because I have rejected him; for it is not as man seeth, for man looketh on the outward appearance; but Yahweh looketh on the heart. Then Jesse called Aminadab, and made him pass before Samuel; and he said: Neither hath Yahweh chosen this. Then Jesse made Shemmiah pass by; and he said: Neither hath Yahweh chosen this. And Jesse made seven of his sons pass before Samuel.

And Samuel said unto him: Are here all thy children? And he said: There remaineth yet the youngest; and behold, he keepeth the sheep. And Samuel said unto Jesse: Send and fetch him; for we will not sit down till he come hither. And he sent and brought him in. Now he was ruddy, and withal of beautiful eyes and goodly to look upon. And Yahweh said: Arise, anoint him, for this is he. Then Samuel took the horn of oil and anointed him in the midst of his brethren. And the spirit of Yahweh came mightily upon David from that day forward. So Samuel rose up and returned to Ramah.

And Samuel died; and all Israel gathered themselves together and lamented him. And they buried him in his house at Ramah.

XII

OF SAUL, KING OF BENJAMIN

Saul's success in war throughout the Jordan valley. The Philistines renew their attacks. Their champion, Goliath, challenges the Israelites to furnish a champion to settle their disputes by single combat. David son of Jesse comes to the camp to visit his brothers. He offers himself as the champion of Israel. Slays Goliath. Abner, Saul's general, brings him to Saul. The praise of David's prowess above his own rouses Saul's jealousy. (1 Sam'l, xiv, 47-52; xvii, 1-56; xviii, 6-9.)

Saul took the kingship over Israel,[1] and fought against all his enemies on every side; against Moab and against the children of Ammon, against Edom and against the kings of Zobah, and against the Philistines; and whithersoever he turned, he put them to the worse. And he did valiantly, and smote the Amalekites, and delivered Israel out of the hands of him that spoiled them.

Now the names of the sons of Saul were Jonathan, Ishui, and Malchishua; and the names of his daughters were these: the name of the first-born, Merab; and the name of the younger, Michal. And the name of Saul's wife was Ahinoam, the daughter of Ahimaaz. And the name of the captain of his army was Abner, the son of Ner, Saul's uncle. And Kish was the father of Saul, and Ner, the father of Abner, was the son of Abiel.

And there was sore war against the Philistines all the days of Saul; and when Saul saw any powerful man, or a valiant man, he took him unto him.

Now the Philistines gathered their armies together to battle, and they were assembled at Socoh, which belongeth to Judah, and pitched between Socoh and Abekah, in Ephes-dammim. And Saul and the men of Israel were gathered together, and pitched near the valley of Elah, and set the battle in array against the Philistines. And the Philistines stood on a mountain on the one side, and Israel stood on a mountain on the other side; and a valley was between them.

And there went out a champion out of the camp of the Philistines named Goliath of Gath, whose height was six cubits and a span. And he had a helmet of brass upon his head, and he was armed with a coat of mail; and the weight of the coat was five thousand shekels of brass. And he had greaves of brass upon his legs, and a target of brass between his shoulders. And the staff was like a weaver's beam; and his spear's head weighed six hundred shekels of iron; and one bearing a shield went before him. And he stood and cried unto the armies of Israel, and said unto them: Why are ye come out to set your battle in array? Am not I a Philistine, and ye, servants of Saul? Choose you a man for you, and let him come down to me. If he be able to fight with me and to kill me, then will we be your servants; but if I prevail against him and kill him, then shall ye be our servants, and serve us. And the Philistine said: I defy the armies of Israel this day; give me a man, that we may fight together. When Saul and all Israel heard those words of the Philistine, they were dismayed and greatly afraid.

Now David was the son of that Ephrathite of Bethlehem-Judah,

[1] Saul the Benjamite was king only of the Benjamites, though the other tribes, men of Judah and of Ephraim, nearest to him and to the Philistines, looked to him as their champion, and fought with him. The kingdom of Israel, promised by Samuel, he forfeited by disobedience; either by assuming the priestly office, as given by E, or by not annihilating the Amalekites, as given by J.

whose name was Jesse and who had eight sons; and the man went among men for an old man in the days of Saul. And the three eldest sons of Jesse went and followed Saul to the battle; and the names of the three sons that went to the battle were: Eliab, the firstborn, and next him Ahinadab, and the third, Shammah. And David was the youngest; and the three eldest followed Saul.

And the Philistine drew near morning and evening and presented himself forty days.

And Jesse said unto David his son: Take now for thy brethren an ephah of this parched corn and these ten loaves, and run to the camp to thy brethren, and carry these ten cheeses unto the captain of their thousand, and look how thy brethren fare, and take their pledge. Now Saul, and they and all the men of Israel, were in the valley of Elah, fighting with the Philistines.

And David rose up early in the morning and left the sheep with a keeper, and took, and went, as Jesse had commanded him; and he came to the trench as the army was going forth to the fight and shouting for the battle. For Israel and the Philistines had put the battle in array, army against army. And David left his baggage in the hand of the keeper of the baggage, and ran into the army, and came and saluted his brethren. And as he talked with them, behold, there came up the champion, the Philistine of Gath, Goliath by name, out of the armies of the Philistines, and spake according to the same words; and David heard them. And all the men of Israel, when they saw the man, fled from him and were sore afraid.

And the men of Israel said: Have ye seen this man that is come up? surely to defy Israel is he come up; and it shall be that the man who killeth him, the king will enrich with great riches, and will give him his daughter and make his father's house free in Israel. And David spake to the men that stood by him, saying: What shall be done to the man that killeth this Philistine, and taketh away the reproach from Israel? For, who is this uncircumcised Philistine, that he should defy the armies of the living God? And the people answered him after this manner, saying: So shall it be done to the man that killeth him.

But Eliab his eldest brother heard when he spake unto the men, and his anger was kindled against David, and he said: Why camest thou down hither, and with whom hast thou left those few sheep in the wilderness? I know thy pride and the naughtiness of thy heart; for thou art come down that thou mightest see the battle.

And David said: What have I done now? Is there not a cause? And he turned from him to another, and spake after the same manner; and the people answered him again after the former manner.

And when the words were heard which David spake, they rehearsed them before Saul; and he was taken to him. And David said to Saul: Let no man's heart fail within him; thy servant will go and fight with this Philistine. And Saul said to David: Thou are not able to go against this Philistine to fight with him, for thou art but a youth, and he a man of war from his youth. And David said unto Saul: Thy servant kept his father's sheep, and there came a lion and a bear, and took a lamb out of the flock; and I went out after him and smote him, and delivered it out of his mouth; and when he arose against me, I caught him by the beard and slew him. Thy servant slew both the lion and the bear; and this uncircumcised Philistine shall be as one of them, seeing he hath defied the armies of the living God. David said moreover, Yahweh, who delivered me out of the paw of the bear, He will deliver me out of the hand of this Philistine.

And Saul said unto David: Go, and may Yahweh be with thee.

And Saul armed David with his armor, and he put a helmet of brass upon his head; also he armed him with a coat of mail. And David girded his sword upon his armor, and he essayed to go; for he had not proved it. And David said unto Saul: I cannot go with these, for I have not proved them. And David put them off him. And he took his staff in his hand, and chose him five smooth stones from the brook and put them in a shepherd's bag which he had, even in a scrip; and his sling was in his hand; and he drew near to the Philistine.

And the Philistine drew nearer and nearer unto David, and the man that bare the shield before him. And when the Philistine looked about and saw David, he disdained him; for he was but a youth and ruddy, and of a fair countenance. And the Philistine said: Am I a dog, that thou comest to me with staves? And the Philistine cursed David by his gods. And the Philistine said to David: Come to me, and I will give thy flesh unto the fowls of the air, and to the beasts of the field. Then said David to the Philistine: Thou comest to me with a sword and with a spear, and with a shield; but I come to thee in the name of Yahweh Sabaoth, the God of the armies of Israel, whom thou hast defied. This day will Yahweh deliver thee into my hand; and I will smite thee, and take thine head from thee; and I will give the carcasses of the host of the Philistines this day unto the fowls of the air, and to the wild beasts of the earth; that all the earth may know that there is a God in Israel. And all this assembly shall know that Yahweh saveth not with sword and spear; for the battle is Yahweh's, and He will give you into our hands.

And it came to pass, when the Philistine arose, and came and drew nigh to meet David, that David hasted and ran toward the army to meet the Philistine. And David put his hand in his bag and took thence a stone and slung it, and smote the Philistine in the forehead, so that the stone sank into his forehead; and he fell upon his face to the earth. So David prevailed over the Philistine with a sling and with a stone, and smote the Philistine and slew him; but there was no sword in the hand of David. Therefore David ran and stood upon the Philistine, and took his sword, and drew it out of the sheath thereof, and slew him, and cut off his head therewith.

Now when the Philistines saw that their champion was dead, they fled. And the men of Israel and of Judah arose and shouted, and pursued the Philistines until thou come to the valley and to the gates of Ekron. And the wounded of the Philistines fell down by the way to Shaaraim, even unto Gath and to Ekron. And the Children of Israel returned from chasing after the Philistines, and they destroyed their tents. And David took the head of the Philistine, and brought it to ———. But he put his armor in his tent.

And when Saul saw David go forth against the Philistine, he said unto Abner, the captain of the host: Abner, whose son is this youth? And Abner said: As thy soul liveth, O king, I cannot tell. And the king said: Inquire thou, whose son the stripling is. And as David returned from the slaughter of the Philistine, Abner took him and brought him before Saul with the head of the Philistine in his hand. And Saul said unto him: Whose son art thou, young man? And David answered: I am the son of thy servant, Jesse the Bethlehemite.

Now it came to pass as they came when David was returning from the slaughter of the Philistine, that the women came out of all the cities of Israel to meet king Saul with tabrets, with joy, and with instruments of music. And the women answered one another as they played, and said:

> Saul hath slain his thousands
> And David his ten thousands.

And Saul was very wroth, and the saying displeased him; and he said: They have ascribed unto David ten thousands, and to me they have ascribed but thousands; and what can he have more but the kingdom? And Saul eyed David from that day and forward.

<hr>

XIII

OF JONATHAN AND DAVID

Jonathan's love for David. Saul's hatred of David. Jonathan pleads for him. He plans for David's escape. Saul's anger against Jonathan. David, aided by Jonathan, escapes into a stronghold in the mountains. Their parting. (1 Sam'l, xviii, 1-4; xix, 1-7; xx, 1-34; xxiii, 14-19.)

And it came to pass when he [David] had made an end of speaking unto Saul, that the soul of Jonathan was knit with the soul of David, and Jonathan loved him as he loved his own soul. And Saul took him that day, and would let him go no more home to his father's house. Then Jonathan and David made a covenant, because he loved him as his own soul. And Jonathan stripped himself of the robe that was upon him and gave it to David, and his garments, even to his sword and his bow, and to his girdle.

And Saul spake to Jonathan his son and to all his servants, that they should slay David. And Jonathan told David, saying: Saul my father seeketh to slay thee; now therefore, I pray thee, take heed to thyself in the morning, and abide in a secret place and hide thyself; and I will go out and stand beside my father in the field, and I will speak with my father of thee; and if I see aught, I will tell thee.

And Jonathan spake good of David unto Saul his father, and said unto him: Let not the king sin against his servant, against David; for he hath not sinned against thee, and his work has been very good towards thee; for he put his life in his hand and smote the Philistine, and Yahweh wrought a very great victory for Israel. Thou sawest it and didst rejoice. Wherefore then wilt thou sin against innocent blood, to slay David without a cause? And Saul hearkened unto the voice of Jonathan, and Saul sware: As Yahweh liveth, he shall not be put to death. And Jonathan brought David to Saul, and he was in his presence as aforetime.

And there was war again; and David went out and fought with the Philistines, and slew them with a great slaughter, and they fled before him. And an evil spirit from Yahweh was upon Saul as he sat in his house with his spear in his hand; and David was playing with his hand upon the harp. And Saul sought to smite David even to the wall with the spear; but he slipped away out of Saul's presence, and he smote the spear into the wall; and David fled, and escaped that night.

And David fled from Naioth in Ramah, and came and said unto Jonathan: What have I done? what is mine iniquity? and what is my sin before thy father, that he seeketh my life? And he said unto him: Far from it; thou shalt not die; behold, my father doeth nothing either

great or small, but that he will shew it unto me; and why should my
father hide this thing from me? it is not so. But David sware and
said: Thy father certainly knoweth that I have found favor in thine
eyes: and he saith, Let not Jonathan know this, lest he be grieved;
but truly, as Yahweh liveth, and as thy soul liveth, there is but a step
between me and death.

Then said Jonathan unto David: Whatsoever thy soul desireth, I
will even do it for thee. And David said unto Jonathan: Behold, to-
morrow is the new moon, and I should not fail to sit with the king at
meat; but let me go, that I may hide myself in the field unto the third
day at even. If thy father at all miss me, then say: David asked
leave of me that he might run to Bethlehem, his city; for there is a
yearly sacrifice for all his family. If he say thus: It is well; thy servant
shall have peace; but if he be very wroth, be sure that evil is determined
by him. Therefore thou shalt deal kindly with thy servant; for thou
hast brought thy servant into a covenant of Yahweh with thee. Notwithstanding, if there be in me iniquity, slay me thyself; for why
shouldest thou bring me to thy father?

And Jonathan said: Far be it from thee; for if I knew certainly
that evil were determined by my father to come upon thee, then would
not I tell thee? Then said David to Jonathan: Who shall tell me?
what if thy father answer thee roughly? And Jonathan said unto David:
Come and let us go out into the field. And they went out both of them
into the field. And Jonathan said unto David: By Yahweh, God of
Israel, when I have sounded my father, any time to-morrow or the
third day, and behold, if there be good toward David, and I then send not
word unto thee, and shew it thee; Yahweh do so and more also to
Jonathan; but if it please my father to do thee evil, then I will shew
it thee and send thee away, that thou mayest go in peace, and Yahweh
be with thee, as he hath been with my father. And thou shalt shew
me the kindness of Yahweh not only while yet I live, that I die not,
but thou shalt not cut off thy kindness from my house for ever; no,
not when Yahweh hath cut off the enemies of David every one from
the face of the earth. And Jonathan caused David to swear again
for the love he had to him; for he loved him as he loved his own soul.

And Jonathan said unto him: To-morrow is the new moon, and thou
wilt be missed because thy seat will be empty. And in the third day
thou shalt go quickly, and come down to the place where thou didst hide
thyself in the day of work, and shalt remain by the stone Ezel. And I
will shoot three arrows to the side, as though I shot at a mark. And
behold, I will send the lad: Go, find the arrows. If I say to the lad:
Behold, the arrows are on this side of thee; take them and come, for
there is peace, and no hurt for thee. But if I say thus unto the boy:
Behold, the arrows are beyond thee;—go thy way, for Yahweh hath
sent thee away. And, as touching the matter which I and thou have
spoken of, behold, Yahweh be between thee and me for ever.

So David hid himself in the field. And when the new moon was
come, the king sat him down to eat meat. And the king sat as at other
times on a seat by the wall; and Jonathan stood up, and Abner sat by
Saul's side; but David's place was empty. Nevertheless Saul spake not
any thing that day; for he thought: Something hath befallen him, he
is not clean; surely he is not clean. And it came to pass, on the morrow
after the new moon, the second of the month, that David's place was
empty; and Saul said unto his son: Wherefore cometh not the son of
Jesse to meat, neither yesterday nor to-day? And Jonathan answered

Saul: David earnestly asked leave of me to go to Bethlehem; and he said: Let me go, I pray thee, for our family hath a sacrifice in the city; and my brother, he hath summoned me; and now, if I have found favor in thine eyes, let me get away, I pray thee, and see my brethren. Therefore he is not come to the king's table.

Then Saul's anger was kindled against Jonathan, and he said unto him: Thou son of perverse rebellion, do not I know that thou hast chosen the son of Jesse to thine own confusion, and unto the shame of thy mother's nakedness? For so long as the son of Jesse liveth upon the earth, thou shalt not be established, nor thy kingdom. Wherefore now, send and fetch him unto me, for he shall surely die. And Jonathan answered Saul his father: Wherefore should he be put to death? what hath he done? And Saul cast his spear at him to smite him; whereby Jonathan knew that it was determined of his father to slay David. So Jonathan rose from the table in fierce anger, and did eat no meat the second day of the month, for he was grieved for David, and because his father had put him to shame.

And it came to pass in the morning, that Jonathan went out into the field at the time appointed with David, and a little lad with him. And he said to the lad: Run, find now the arrows which I shoot. And as the lad ran, he shot an arrow beyond him. And when the lad was come to the place of the arrow which Jonathan had shot, Jonathan cried after the lad, and said: Is not the arrow beyond thee? And Jonathan cried after the lad: Make speed, haste, stay not. And Jonathan's lad gathered up the arrows and came to his master. But the lad knew not anything; only Jonathan and David knew the matter. And Jonathan gave his weapons unto his lad and said to him: Go, carry them to the city, And as soon as the lad was gone, David came out of a place toward the south, and fell on his face to the ground, and bowed down three times; and they kissed one another, and wept one with the other until David exceeded. And Jonathan said to David: Go in peace, forasmuch as we have sworn both of us in the name of Yahweh, saying: Yahweh shall be between me and thee, and between my seed and thy seed for ever. And he arose and departed; and Jonathan went into the city. And David abode in strongholds, and remained in a mountain in the wilderness of Ziph. And Saul sought him every day, but God delivered him not into his hand. And Jonathan arose and went to David in the wood, and strengthened his hand in God. And he said: Fear not, for the hand of my father shall not find thee; and thou shalt be king over Israel, and I shall be next unto thee; and that my father knoweth. And David abode in the wood, and Jonathan went to his own house.[1]

[1] There is no evidence that they ever met again; but David wrote the beautiful elegy upon the death of Saul and Jonathan on Mount Gilboa, and fulfilled his promise by caring for Jonathan's afflicted son, Mephibosheth, till the day of his death.

XIV

OF DAVID THE OUTLAW

Saul pursues David who narrowly escapes. David spares Saul's life and
they swear a truce. David's adventures in Carmel. Marries Abigail,
and Ahinoam of Jezreel. Saul gives Michal, David's wife, to another
man. David seeks refuge among the Philistines, but deceives them,
fighting against their allies and sending the spoil to his friends in
Judah. He shows himself both just and generous to his own people.
(1 Sam'l, xxiii, 1-29; xxiv, 1-19; xxv, 2-44; xxviii, 1-12; xxviii, 1;
xxix, 1-11; xxx, 1-31.)

Now the Ziphites came up to Saul at Gibeah, saying: Doth not
David hide himself with us in the strongholds of the wood in the hill
of Hachilah, which is on the south of Jeshimon? Now therefore, O
King, come down according to all the desire of thy soul; come down,
and our part shall be to deliver him up into the king's hand. And Saul
said: Blessed be ye of Yahweh, for ye have had compassion on me.
Go, I pray you, make yet more sure, and know and see the place where
his haunt is, and who hath seen him there; for it is told me that he
dealeth very subtly. See therefore, and take knowledge of all the
lurking-places where he hideth himself, and come ye back to me with
the certainty, and I will go with you; and if he be in the land, I will
search him out among all the thousands of Judah. And they arose and
went to Ziph ahead of Saul. But David and his men were in the
wilderness of Maon, in the Arabah to the south of Jeshimon.

And Saul and his men went to seek him. And they told David;
wherefore he came down to the rock, and abode in the wilderness of
Maon. And Saul went on this side of the mountain, and David and his
men on that side of the mountain; and David made haste to get away,
for fear of Saul; for Saul and his men compassed David and his men
round about, to take them. But there came a messenger to Saul, saying:
Haste thee and come; for the Philistines have made a raid upon the
land. So Saul turned back from pursuing David, and went against the
Philistines; therefore they called that place Sela-hammalekoth (The Rock
of Divisions). And David went up from thence, and dwelt in the
stronghold of Engedi (*the Kid's Fountain*).

Now when Saul returned from following up the Philistines, it was
told him: Behold, David is in the wilderness of Engedi. Then Saul took
three thousand chosen men out of all Israel, and went to seek David
and his men on the rock of the wild goats. And he came to the sheep-
cotes by the way, where was a cave, and Saul went in to cover his feet.
Now David and his men were sitting in the innermost parts of the cave.
And David's men said to him: Behold the day in which Yahweh hath
said unto thee: Lo, I deliver thine enemy into thine hand, and thou
shalt do unto him as shall seem good unto thee. Then David arose, and
cut off the skirt of Saul's robe secretly. And it came to pass afterward,
that David's heart smote him because he had cut off Saul's skirt. And
he said to his men: Yahweh forbid, that I should do this thing to
Yahweh's anointed,—to put forth my hand against him, seeing that he
is Yahweh's anointed. So David checked his men with these words,
and suffered them not to rise against Saul. And Saul rose up out of the
cave, and went his way.

David also arose afterward, and went out of the cave and cried after
Saul, saying: My lord the King! And when Saul looked behind him,

David bowed with his face to the earth, and prostrated himself. And David said to Saul: Wherefore hearkenest thou to men's words, saying: Behold, David seeketh thy hurt? Behold, this day thine eyes have seen how that Yahweh had delivered thee to-day into my hand in the cave; and some bade me kill thee; but mine eye spared thee, and I said: I will not put forth my hand against my lord, for he is Yahweh's anointed. Moreover, my father, see, yea, see the skirt of thy robe in my hand; for in that I cut off the skirt of thy robe and killed thee not; know thou and see that there is neither evil nor transgression in my hand, and I have not sinned against thee, though thou liest in wait for my life to take it. May Yahweh judge between me and thee, but my hand shall not be upon thee. As saith the proverb of the ancients: Out of the wicked cometh forth wickedness; but my hand shall not be upon thee. After whom is the King of Israel come out? after what dost thou pursue? after a dead dog? after a flea? Yahweh judge between me and thee, and see and plead my cause, and deliver me out of thy hand!

And it came to pass, when David had ceased speaking these words unto Saul, that Saul said: Is this thy voice, my son David? And Saul lifted up his voice, and wept. And he said to David: Thou art more righteous than I, for thou hast rendered me good, whereas I have rendered unto thee evil. And thou hast declared this day how thou hast dealt well with me; forasmuch as when Yahweh had delivered me up into thine hand, thou didst not kill me. Swear now therefore unto me by Yahweh, that thou wilt not cut off my seed after me. And David sware unto Saul. And Saul went home; but David and his men gat them up into the stronghold.

Now there was a man in Maon, whose possessions were in Carmel; and the man was very great; and he had three thousand sheep and a thousand goats; and he was shearing sheep in Carmel. And the name of the man was Nabal, and the name of his wife, Abigail. And the woman was of good understanding, and of a beautiful form; but the man was churlish, and evil in his doings; and he was of the house of Caleb. And David heard in the wilderness that Nabal was shearing his sheep. And David sent ten young men, and David said unto the young men: Get you up to Carmel and go to Nabal, and greet him in my name; and thus shall ye say: All hail! and peace be both unto thee and peace be unto thy house, and peace be unto all that thou hast. And now I have heard that thou hast shearers; thy shepherds have now been with us, and we did them no hurt, neither was there aught missing unto them, all the while they were in Carmel. Ask thy young men, and they will tell thee. Wherefore let my young men find favor in thine eyes, for we come on a good day; give, I pray thee, whatsoever cometh to thy hand unto thy servants, and unto thy son David.

And when David's young men came, they spake to Nabal according to all these words in the name of David, and ceased. And Nabal answered David's servants, and said: Who is David? and who is the son of Jesse? There are many servants nowadays that break away every man from his master; shall I then take my bread and my water and my flesh, that I have killed for my shearers, and give it to men of whom I know not whence they are? So David's young men turned on their way and went back, and came and told him according to all these words. And David said unto his men: Gird ye on every man his sword. And they girded on every man his sword; and there went up after David about four hundred men; and two hundred abode by the luggage.

But one of the young men told Abigail, Nabal's wife, saying: Behold,

David sent messengers out of the wilderness to salute our master, and he flew upon them. But the men were very good unto us, and we were not hurt nor missed we anything while we were with them when we were in the fields; they were a wall unto us both by night and by day all the while we were with them keeping the sheep. Now therefore, know and consider what thou wilt do; for evil is determined against our master and against all his house; for he is such a churl that one cannot speak to him.

Then Abigail made haste and took two hundred loaves and two bottles of wine, and five sheep ready dressed and five measures of parched corn, and a hundred clusters of raisins and two hundred cakes of figs, and laid them on asses. And she said unto her young men: Go on before me; behold, I come after you. But she told not her husband Nabal. And it was so, as she rode on her ass and came down by the covert of the hill, that behold, David and his men came down towards her; and she met them. (For David had said: Surely in vain have I kept all that this fellow hath in the wilderness, so that nothing was missed of all that pertained to him; and he hath returned me evil for good. God do so and more also unto the enemies of David, if I leave of all that pertain unto him by the morning light so much as one male.) And when Abigail saw David, she made haste and alighted from her ass, and fell down before David on her face, and bowed to the ground. And she fell at his feet and said: Upon me, my lord, be the iniquity; and let thy handmaid, I pray thee, speak in thine ears, and hear thou the words of thine handmaid. Let not my lord, I pray thee, regard this rude fellow, even Nabal; for as his name is, so is he; Nabal (*fool*) is his name, and folly is with him. But I, thine handmaid, saw not the young men of my lord, when thou didst send them. Now therefore, my lord, as God liveth, and as thy soul liveth, seeing Yahweh hath withholden thee from blood-guiltiness, and from finding redress for thyself with thine own hand,—now therefore, let thine enemies and them that seek evil to my lord, be as Nabal. And now, this present which thy servant hath brought unto my lord, let it be given unto the young men that follow my lord. Forgive, I pray thee, the trespass of thy handmaid; for Yahweh will certainly make my lord a sure house, because my lord fighteth the battles of Yahweh, and evil hath not been found in thee all thy days. And though man is risen up to pursue thee, and to seek thy life, yet the soul of my lord shall be bound in the bundle of life with Yahweh thy God; and the souls of thine enemies them shall He sling out as from the hollow of a sling. And it shall come to pass, when Yahweh shall have done to my lord according to all the good that He hath spoken concerning thee, and shall have appointed thee prince over Israel; that this shall be no stumbling-block unto thee nor offence of heart unto my lord,—either that thou hast shed blood without cause, or that my lord found redress for himself. And, when Yahweh shall have dealt well by my lord, then remember thy handmaiden.

And David said to Abigail: Blessed be Yahweh the God of Israel who sent thee this day to meet me; and blessed be thy discretion, and blessed be thou that hast kept me this day from blood-guiltiness, and from finding redress for myself with mine own hand. For in very deed, as Yahweh the God of Israel liveth, who hath withholden me from hurting thee; except thou hadst made haste and come to meet me, surely there had not been left to Nabal by the morning light so much as one male.

So David received of her hand that which she had brought him;

and he said unto her: Go up in peace to thy house; see, I have hearkened to thy voice, and have accepted thy person.

And Abigail came to Nabal; and behold, he was holding a feast in his house, like the feast of a king; and Nabal's heart was merry within him, for he was very drunken; wherefore she told him nothing, less or more, until the morning light. And it came to pass in the morning, when the wine had gone out of Nabal, that his wife told him these things; and his heart died within him, and he became as a stone. And it came to pass, about ten days after, that Yahweh smote Nabal, so that he died.

And when David heard that Nabal was dead, he said: Blessed be Yahweh, that hath pleaded the cause of my reproach from the hand of Nabal, and hath kept back his servant from evil-doing; and the evil-doing of Nabal hath Yahweh returned upon his own head. And David sent and spake concerning Abigail to take her to wife. And when the servants of David were come to Abigail to Carmel, they spake unto her saying: David hath sent us to thee, to take thee to him to wife. And she arose and bowed down with her face to the earth, and said: Behold, thy handmaid is a servant to wash the feet of the servants of my lord. And Abigail hastened and arose and rode upon an ass, with five damsels of hers that followed her; and she went after the messengers of David, and became his wife.

David took also Ahinoam of Jezreel, and they became both of them his wives. Now Saul had given Michal his daughter, David's wife, to Palti the son of Laish, who was of Gallim.

Then David said in his heart: I shall now be swept away one day by the hand of Saul; there is nothing better for me than that I should escape into the land of the Philistines; then Saul will despair of seeking me any more in all the borders of Israel; so shall I escape out of his hand. And David arose and passed over, he and the six hundred men that were with him, unto Achish the son of Maoch, king of Gath. And David dwelt with Achish at Gath, he and his men, every man with his household, David also with his two wives, Ahinoam, the Jezreelitess, and Abigail, the Carmelitess, Nabal's wife. And it was told Saul that David was fled to Gath; and he sought for him again no more.

And David said unto Achish: If now I have found favor in thy sight, let them give me a place in one of the cities of the country, that I may dwell there; for why should thy servant dwell in the royal city with thee? Then Achish gave him Ziklag that day; wherefore Ziklag belongeth unto the kings of Judah unto this day.

And the number of the days that David dwelt in the country of the Philistines was a full year and four months. And David and his men went up and made a raid upon the Geshurites and the Gizrites and the Amalekites; for these were the inhabitants of the land of old, as thou goest to Shur, even unto the land of Egypt. And David smote the land, and left neither man nor woman alive, and took away the sheep and the oxen and the asses and the camels and the apparel. And he returned and came to Achish. And Achish said: Where have ye made a raid to-day? And David said: Against the south of Judah and against the South of the Jerahmeelites, and against the south of the Kenites. Now David left neither man nor woman alive, to bring them to Gath, saying: Lest they should tell on us, saying: Thus did David, and such hath been his manner all the while that he hath dwelt in the country of the Philistines. And Achish believed David, saying: He hath made his people Israel utterly to abhor him; therefore he shall be my servant for ever.

And it came to pass in those days, that the Philistines gathered their hosts together to fight with Israel. And Achish said unto David: Know thou assuredly that thou shalt go out with me in the host, thou and thy men.

Now the Philistines gathered together all their armies to Aphek; and the Israelites pitched by the fountain which is in Jezreel. And the lords of the Philistines passed on by hundreds, and by thousands; and David and his men passed on in the rearward with Achish. Then said the princes of the Philistines: What do these Hebrews here? And Achish said unto the princes of the Philistines: Is not this David, the servant of Saul the king of Israel, who hath been with me these days or these years, and I have found no fault in him since he fell away unto me unto this day? And the princes of the Philistines were wroth with him; and the princes of the Philistines said unto him: Make this fellow return, that he may go again to his place which thou hast appointed him, and let him not go down with us to battle, lest in the battle he be an adversary to us; for wherewith should he reconcile himself to his master? Should it not be with the heads of these men? Is not this David, of whom they sang:

Saul slew his thousands, and David his ten thousands?

Then Achish called David, and said unto him: Surely, as Yahweh liveth, thou hast been upright, and thy going out and thy coming in with me in the host is good in my sight; for I have not found evil in thee, from the day of thy coming unto me unto this day. Nevertheless, the lords favor thee not. Wherefore, now, return and go in peace, that thou displease not the lords of the Philistines. And David said unto Achish: But what have I done? and what hast thou found in thy servant so long as I have been with thee unto this day, that I may not go and fight against the enemies of my lord the king? And Achish answered and said to David: I know that thou art good in my sight as an angel of God; notwithstanding, the princes of the Philistines have said: He shall not go up with us to the battle. Wherefore, rise thou up early in the morning with thy master's servants that are come with thee; and as soon as ye be up, early in the morning, and have light, depart. So David and his men rose up early in the morning to depart to return into the land of the Philistines; and the Philistines went up to Jezreel.

Now it came to pass, when David and his men were come to Ziklag on the third day, that the Amalekites had invaded the south and Ziklag, and burned it with fire, and had taken the women captives that were therein; they slew not any, either great or small, but carried them away, and went on their way. So David and his men came to the city, and behold! it was burned with fire; and their wives and their daughters were taken captive. Then David and the people that were with him lifted up their voice and wept, until they had no more power to weep. And David's two wives were taken captive, Ahinoam, the Jezreelitess, and Abigail, the wife of Nabal the Carmelite. And David was greatly distressed; for the people spake of stoning him, because the soul of all the people was grieved, every man for his sons and for his daughters; but David strengthened himself in Yahweh his God.

And David said unto Abiathar the priest, Ahimelech's son: I pray thee, bring me hither the ephod. And Abiathar brought thither the ephod to David. And David inquired of Yahweh: Shall I pursue after this troop? Shall I overtake them? And He answered him: Pursue, for thou shalt surely overtake them, and shalt recover them without fail. So David went, he and the six hundred men that were with him, and came to the brook Besor, where those who were left behind stayed. But David pursued, he and four hundred men; for two hundred abode behind, who were so faint, that they could not go over the brook Besor.

And they found an Egyptian in the field and brought him to David, and gave him bread, and he did eat; and they made him drink water; and they gave him a piece of a cake of figs, and two clusters of raisins; and when he had eaten, his spirit came again to him; for he had eaten no bread nor drunk any water three days and three nights. And David *said unto him: To whom belongest thou? and whence are thou? And he said: I am a young Egyptian, servant to an Amalekite; and my master left me, because three days agone I fell sick. We made an invasion upon the south of the Cherethites and upon that which belongeth to Judah and upon the south of Caleb; and we burned Ziklag with fire. And David said unto him: Canst thou bring me down to this company? And he said: Swear unto me by God, that thou wilt neither kill me nor deliver me into the hands of my master, and I will bring thee down to this company.

And when he had brought him down, behold, they were all spread abroad upon the earth, eating and drinking and dancing, because of all the great spoil that they had taken out of the land of the Philistines, and out of the land of Judah. And David smote them from the twilight even to the evening of the next day; and there escaped not a man of them save four hundred young men who rode upon camels and fled. And David recovered all that the Amalekites had carried away; and David rescued his two wives. And there was nothing lacking to them, neither small nor great, neither sons nor daughters, neither spoil nor any thing that they had taken to them. David recovered all. And David took all the flocks and the herds, which they drave before the other cattle, and said: This is David's spoil.

And David came to the two hundred men who were so faint that they could not follow David, whom also they had caused to abide by the brook Besor; and they came forth to meet David, and to meet the people who were with him; and when David came near to the people, he saluted them. Then answered all the wicked and base men of those that had gone with David, and said: Because they went not with us, we will not give them aught of the spoil that we have recovered, save to every man his wife and children, that he may lead them away and depart. Then said David: Ye shall not do so, my brethren, with that which Yahweh hath given unto us, who hath preserved us and delivered the troop that came against us into our hand. For who will hearken unto you in this matter? For as is the share of him who goeth down to the battle, so shall his share be that tarrieth by the baggage; they shall share alike. And it was so from that day forward; and he made it a statute and an ordinance for Israel unto this day.

And when David came to Ziklag he sent of the spoil unto the elders of Judah, to his friends, saying: Behold a present for you of the spoil of the enemies of the Lord; to them which were in Bethel, and to them which were in south Ramoth, and to them which were in Jattir, and to them which were in Aroer, and to them which were in Siphmoth, and to them which were in Eshtemoa, and to them which were in Rachal, and to them which were in the cities of the Jerahmeelites, and to them which were in the cities of the Kenites, and to them which were in Hormah, and to them which were in Chorashan, and to them which were in Athach, and to them which were in Hebron, and to all the places where David himself and his men were wont to haunt.

XV

OF JEROBOAM, FIRST KING OF ISRAEL

The northern tribes revolt against Rehoboam, and recall Jeroboam from Egypt to rule them. He builds altars where his people may worship instead of going to Jerusalem. A man of God prophesies against the king and the altar, but is himself slain for disobedience to God's command. After Nadab, son of Jeroboam, a succession of usurpers rule in Israel, of whom Baasha is the greatest. (1 Kings, xii, 2b, 3a, 20, 25-33; xiii, 1-32; xiv, 1-18, 20; xv, 25-30; xvi, 7, 2-4.)

Jeroboam the son of Nebat was dwelling in Egypt, whither he had fled from the presence of Solomon, and they sent and called him. And when all Israel knew that Jeroboam had returned, they sent and called him unto the congregation, and made him king over Israel. Then Jeroboam fortified Shechem in the hill-country of Ephraim, and dwelt there. And he went out thence and fortified Penuel.

Now Jeroboam said in his heart: The kingdom will surely return to the house of David; if the people go up to offer sacrifices in the house of Yahweh in Jerusalem, then will the heart of the people turn back to their lord, even to Rehoboam, king of Judah. Whereupon Jeroboam took counsel, and made two calves of gold. And he said to the people: Ye have gone up long enough to Jerusalem. Behold thy gods, O Israel, which brought thee out of the land of Egypt! And he put the one in Bethel, and the other he put in Dan. And he made houses for high places, and made priests from among the people that were not of the sons of Levi.

And Jeroboam ordained a feast in the eighth month, like unto the feast that is in Judah, and he went up unto the altar which is in Beth-el to sacrifice unto the calves that he had made; and he placed in Beth-el the priests of the high places that he had made. And he went up unto the altar which he had made in Beth-el on the fifteenth day in the eighth month, even in the month that he had chosen of his own heart; and he ordained a feast for the Children of Israel, and went up to the altar to offer.

And behold, there came a man of God out of Judah by the word of Yahweh unto Beth-el; and Jeroboam was standing by the altar to offer. And he cried against the altar by the command of Yahweh, and said: O altar! altar; thus saith Yahweh: Behold, a son shall be born to the house of David, Josiah by name; and upon thee shall he sacrifice the priests of the high places that offer upon thee, and men's bones shall they burn upon thee. And he gave a sign the same day, saying: This is the sign which Yahweh hath spoken: Behold, the altar shall be rent, and the ashes that are upon it shall be poured out.

And it came to pass, when the king heard the saying of the man of God which he cried against the altar in Beth-el, that Jeroboam put forth his hand from the altar saying: Lay hold on him! And his hand, which he put forth against him, dried up, so that he could not draw it back to him. The altar also was rent and the ashes poured out from the altar, according to the sign which the man of God had given by the word of Yahweh. And the king answered and said unto the man of God: Entreat now the favor of Yahweh, thy God, and pray for me that my hand may be restored me. And the man of God entreated Yahweh, and the king's hand was restored him, and became as it was before. And the king said unto the man of God: Come home with me and refresh thyself, and I will give thee a reward. And the man of God said unto the king: If thou wilt give me half thy house, I will not go in with thee, neither will I eat bread nor drink water in this place. For so was it charged me by the word of Yahweh, saying: Thou shalt eat no bread, nor drink water, neither return by the way that thou camest. So he went another way, and returned not by the way that he came to Beth-el.

Now there dwelt an old prophet in Beth-el; and one of his sons came and told him all the works that the man of God had done that day in Beth-el; and the words which he had spoken unto the king they told them unto their father. And their father said unto them: What way went he? For his sons had seen what way the man of God went that came from Judah. And he said unto his sons: Saddle me the ass. So they saddled him the ass, and he rode thereon. And he went after the man of God, and found him under a terebinth; and he said unto him: Art thou the man of God that camest from Judah? And he said: I am. Then he said unto him: Come home with me and eat bread. And he said: I may not return with thee, nor go in with thee; neither will I eat bread nor drink water with thee in this place. For it was said to me by the word of Yahweh: Thou shalt eat no bread nor drink water there, nor turn back to go by the way that thou camest. And he said unto him: I also am a prophet as thou art; and an angel spake unto me by the word of Yahweh, saying: Bring him back with thee into thy house, that he may eat bread and drink water. (He lied unto him.) So he went back with him, and did eat bread in his house and drank water.

And it came to pass as they sat at the table, that the word of Yahweh came unto the prophet that brought him back; and he said unto the man of God that came from Judah: Thus saith Yahweh: Forasmuch as thou hast rebelled against the word of Yahweh, and hast not kept the commandment which Yahweh, thy God, commanded thee, but camest back, and hast eaten bread and drunk water in the place of which He said to thee: Eat no bread, and drink no water; thy carcass shall not come unto the sepulchre of thy fathers. And it came to pass, after he had eaten bread, and after he had drunk, that he saddled for him the ass, to wit, for the prophet whom he had brought back. Now, when he had started, a lion met him by the way and slew him; and his carcass was cast in the way, and the ass stood by it; the lion also stood by the carcass. And behold, men passed by, and saw the carcass cast in the way, and the lion standing by the carcass; and they came and told it in the city where the old prophet dwelt.

And when the prophet that brought him back from the way heard of it, he said: It is the man of God who rebelled against the word of Yahweh; therefore Yahweh hath delivered him to the lion which hath torn him and slain him, according to the word of Yahweh, which He spake unto him. And he spake to his sons, saying: Saddle me the ass. And they saddled it. And he went and found his carcass cast in the way, and the ass and the lion standing by the carcass; the lion had not eaten the cascass nor torn the ass. And the prophet took up the carcass of the man of God and laid it upon the ass, and brought it back; and he came to the city of the old prophet to lament and to bury him. And he laid his carcass in his own grave, and they made lamentation for him: Alas, my brother! And it came to pass after he had buried him, that he spake to his sons, saying: When I am dead, then bury me in the sepulchre wherein the man of God is buried; lay my bones by his bones. For the saying which he cried by the word of Yahweh against the altar of Beth-el, and against all the houses of the high places which are in the cities of Samaria, shall surely come to pass.

After this thing Jeroboam returned not from his evil way, but made again from among all the people priests of the high places; whosoever would, he consecrated him that he might be one of the priests of the high places. And this thing became sin unto the house of Jeroboam, even to cut it off and to destroy it from the face of the earth.

At that time, Abijah, the son of Jeroboam, fell sick. And Jeroboam said to his wife: Arise, I pray thee, and disguise thyself, that thou be not known to be wife of Jeroboam, and get thee to Shiloh; behold, there is Ahijah the prophet who spake concerning me that I should be king over the people. And take with thee ten loaves and biscuits and a cruse of honey and go to him; he will tell thee what shall become of the child. And Jeroboam's wife did so and arose and went to Shiloh; and she came to the house of Ahijah. Now Ahijah could not see, for his eyes were set by reason of his age. Now Yahweh had said unto Ahijah: Behold, the wife of Jeroboam cometh to inquire of thee concerning her son; for he is sick. Thus and thus shalt thou say unto her; for it will be, when she cometh in, that she will feign herself to be another woman.

And it was so, when Ahijah heard the sound of her feet as she came in at the door, that he said: Come in, thou wife of Jeroboam; why feignest thou thyself to be another? for I am sent to thee with heavy tidings. Go, tell Jeroboam: Thus saith Yahweh, the God of Israel: Forasmuch as I exalted thee from among the people and made thee prince over My people Israel, and rent the kingdom. away from the house of David and gave it thee; and yet thou hast not been as My servant David, who kept My commandments, and who followed Me with all his heart to do that only which was right in Mine eyes; but hast done evil above all that was before thee, and hast gone and made thee other gods and molten images to provoke Me, and hast cast Me behind thy back;—therefore behold, I will bring evil upon the house of Jeroboam, and will cut off from Jeroboam every man-child, both him that is shut up and him that is left at large in Israel, and will utterly sweep away the house of Jeroboam, as a man sweepeth away dung till it be all gone. Him that dieth of Jeroboam in the city shall the dogs eat; and him that dieth in the field shall the fowls of the air eat; for Yahweh hath spoken it. Arise thou therefore, get thee to thy house; and when thy feet enter into the city, the child shall die. And all Israel shall make lamentation for him and bury him; for he only of Jeroboam shall come to the grave; because in him is found some good thing toward Yahweh, the God of Israel, in the house of Jeroboam. Moreover, Yahweh will raise Him up a king over Israel who shall cut off the house of Jeroboam that day. But what is it even then? for Yahweh will smite Israel, as a reed is shaken in the water; and He will root up Israel out of this good land He gave to their fathers, and will scatter them beyond the River; because they have made their Asherim, provoking Yahweh. And He will give Israel up because of the sins of Jeroboam, which he hath sinned, and wherewith he hath made Israel to sin.

And Jeroboam's wife arose and departed, and came to Tirzah; and as she came to the threshold of the house, the child died. And all Israel buried him and made lamentation for him; according to the word of Yahweh, which He spake by the hand of His servant Ahijah the prophet.

And the days which Jeroboam reigned were two and twenty years; and he slept with his fathers; and Nadab his son reigned in his stead.

And Nadab, the son of Jeroboam, began to reign over Israel in the second year of Asa, king of Judah, and he reigned over Israel two years. And he did that which was evil in the sight of Yahweh, and walked in the way of his father and in his sin wherewith he had made Israel to sin. Then Baasha the son of Ahijah of the house of Issachar, conspired against him; and Baasha smote him at Gibbethon which belonged to the Philistines; for Nadab and all Israel were laying siege to Gibbethon. And in the third year of Asa, king of Judah, did Baasha slay him, and reigned in his stead. And it came to pass that, as soon as he was king, Baasha smote all the house of Jeroboam; he left not to Jeroboam any that breathed that he did not destroy him, according to the saying of Yahweh which He spake by the mouth of Ahijah the Shilonite, for the sins of Jeroboam which he sinned, and wherewith he made Israel to sin, and because of the provocation with which he provoked Yahweh, the God of Israel.

But the word of Yahweh came against Baasha and against his house by the hand of the prophet Jehu, the son of Hanani, both because of all the evil he was doing in the sight of Yahweh to provoke Him by the work of his hand, in being like the house of Jeroboam, and because he had destroyed it, and He said: Forasmuch as I exalted thee out of the dust, and made thee ruler over My people Israel; and thou hast walked in the way of Jeroboam, and hast made Israel to sin, to provoke Me with their sins; behold, I will utterly sweep away Baasha and his house; and I will make thy house like the house of Jeroboam the son of Nebat. Him that dieth of Baasha in the city shall the dogs eat; and him that dieth in the field, shall the fowls of the air eat.

And Baasha slept with his fathers, and was buried in Tirzah; and Elah his son reigned in his stead. He reigned two years; and his servant Zimri, captain of half his chariots, conspired against him. Now he was in Tirzah, drinking himself drunk in the house of Arza, who was steward of his house in Tirzah; and Zimri went in and smote him and killed him, and reigned in his stead. And as soon as he sat on the throne, he smote all the house of Baasha; he left hm not a single man-child, neither of his kinsfolk nor of his friends. Thus did Zimri destroy all the house of Baasha, according to the word of Yahweh, which He spake against Baasha by Jehu the prophet.

XVI

OF ELIJAH THE TISHBITE

How he rebuked Ahab, and proclaimed a drought. How he saved a
Phœnician woman, and restored her child to life. How he exter-
minated the priests of Baal, introduced by Jezebel. How Jezebel
decreed his death, and he fled to Horeb. Yahweh's revelation to
him that He dwells in the heart of man. The doom he pronounced
upon Jezebel for her breach of the law. The marvels attributed to
him. His ascension. (1 Kings, xvii-xix; xxi; 2 Kings, i, 2-17;
ii, 1-18.)

A. Elijah the Tishbite, of the inhabitants of Gilead, said unto Ahab:
As Yahweh, the God of Israel, liveth, before whom I stand, there shall
not be dew nor rain these years but according to my word. And the
word of Yahweh came unto him, saying: Get thee hence and turn thee
eastward, and hide thee by the brook Cherith that is before Jordan.
And thou shalt drink of the brook, and I have commanded the ravens
to feed thee there. So he went and did according to Yahweh's word;
for he went and dwelt by the brook Cherith which is before Jordan.
And the ravens brought him bread and flesh in the morning, and bread
and flesh in the evening, and he drank of the brook.

And it came to pass after a while, that the brook dried up because
there had been no rain in the land. And the word of Yahweh came to
him, saying: Arise, get thee to Zarephath which belongeth to Zidon,
and dwell there; behold, I have commanded a widow woman to sustain
thee there. And he arose and went to Zarephath. And when he came
to the gate of the city, behold, the widow woman was there, gathering
sticks; and he called to her, and said: Fetch me, I pray thee, a little
water in a vessel, that I may drink. And as she was going to fetch it,
he called to her, and said: Bring me, I pray thee, a morsel of bread in
thy hand. And she said: As Yahweh, thy God, liveth, I have not a
cake, but an handful of meal in a barrel and a little oil in a cruse; and
behold, I am gathering two sticks, that I may go in and dress it for me
and my son, that we may eat it and die. And Elijah said unto her: Fear
not; go and do as thou hast said; but make me thereof a little cake first
and bring it to me, and afterwards make for thee and thy son. For
thus saith Yahweh the God of Israel: The barrel of meal shall not
waste, neither shall the cruse of oil fail, until the day that Yahweh
sendeth rain upon the earth. And she went and did according to
the saying of Elijah, and she and he and her house did eat many
days.

And it came to pass after these things, that the son of the woman,
the mistress of the house, fell sick; and his sickness was so sore that
there was no breath left in him. And she said to Elijah: What have
I to do with thee, O thou man of God? Art thou come unto me to call
my sin to remembrance, and to slay my son? And he said unto her:
Give me thy son. And he took him out of her bosom and carried him
up unto a loft where he abode, and laid him upon his own bed. And
he cried unto Yahweh, and said: O Yahweh, my God, hast Thou also
brought evil upon the widow with whom I sojourn by slaying her son?
And he stretched himself upon the child three times, and cried unto
Yahweh, and said: O Yahweh, my God, I pray Thee, let this child's
soul come into him again.

And Yahweh heard the voice of Elijah; and the soul of the child came into him again, and he revived. And Elijah took the child and brought him down out of the chamber into the house, and delivered him unto his mother; and Elijah said: See, thy son liveth. And the woman said unto Elijah: Now by this I know that thou art a man of God, and that the word of Yahweh in thy mouth is truth.

And it came to pass after many days, that the word of Yahweh came to Elijah in the third year, saying: Go, show thyself unto Ahab; and I will send rain upon the earth. And Elijah went to show himself unto Ahab.

Now, there was a sore famine in Samaria. And Ahab called Obadiah, which was governor of his house. (Now Obadiah feared Yahweh greatly; for it was so, when Jezebel cut off the prophets of Yahweh, that Obadiah took an hundred prophets and hid them by fifty in a cave, and fed them with bread and water). And Ahab said unto Obadiah: Go into the land unto all fountains of water and unto all brooks; peradventure we may find grass to save the horses and mules alive, that we lose not all the beasts. So they divided all the land between them to pass throughout it. Ahab went one way by himself, and Obadiah went another way by himself.

And as Obadiah was in the way, behold, Elijah met him; and he knew him, and fell on his face, and said: Art thou my lord Elijah? And he answered him: I am. Go, tell thy lord: Behold, Elijah is here. And he said: How have I sinned, that thou wouldst deliver thy servant into the hand of Ahab, to slay me? As Yahweh, thy God, liveth, there is no nation or kingdom whither my lord hath not sent to seek thee; and when they said: He is not here, he took an oath of the kingdom and nation, that they found thee not. And now thou sayest: Go, tell thy lord: Behold, Elijah is here. And it shall come to pass as soon as I am gone from thee, that the Spirit of Yahweh shall carry thee whither I know not; and when I come and tell Ahab, and he cannot find thee, he shall slay me; but I thy servant fear Yahweh from my youth. Was it not told my lord what I did when Jezebel slew the prophets of Yahweh, how I hid an hundred men of Yahweh's prophets in a cave, and fed them with bread and water? And now thou sayest: Go, tell thy lord: Behold, Elijah is here; and he will slay me!

And Elijah said: As Yahweh Sabaoth liveth, before whom I stand, I will surely show myself unto him to-day.

So Obadiah went to meet Ahab, and told him, and Ahab went to meet Elijah. And it came to pass when Ahab saw Elijah, that Ahab said unto him: Is it thou, thou troubler of Israel? And he answered: I have not troubled Israel, but thou and thy father's house, in that ye have forsaken the commandments of Yahweh, and thou hast followed the Baalim. Now therefore, send and gather to me all Israel unto mount Carmel and the prophets of Baal, four hundred and fifty, and the prophets of the groves, four hundred, which eat at Jezebel's table. So Ahab sent unto all the Children of Israel, and gathered the prophets together unto mount Carmel.

And Elijah came near unto all the people, and said: How long halt ye between two opinions? If Yahweh be God, follow Him; but if Baal, follow him. And the people answered him not a word. Then said Elijah unto the people: I, even I only, remain a prophet of Yahweh; but Baal's prophets are four hundred and fifty men. Let them therefore give us two bullocks; and let them choose one bullock for themselves, and cut it in pieces, and lay it on wood, and put no fire under; and I will dress the other bullock, and lay it on wood, and put no fire under. And call ye on the name of your gods, and I will call on the name of Yahweh; and the God that answereth by fire, let Him be God. And all the people answered and said: It is well spoken.

And Elijah said unto the prophets of Baal: Choose you one bullock for yourselves, and dress it first; for ye are many; and call on the name of your gods, but put no fire under. And they took the bullock which was given them, and they dressed it, and called on the name of Baal from morning even until noon, saying: O Baal, hear us! But there was no voice, nor any that answered. And they danced about the altar which was made. And it came to pass at noon, that Elijah mocked them, and said: Cry aloud, for he is a god; either he is talking, or he is pursuing, or he is on a journey, or peradventure he sleepeth and must be awaked. And they cried aloud, and cut themselves after their manner with knives and lancets, till the blood gushed out upon them. And it came to pass when midday was past, that they prophesied until the time of the offering of the evening sacrifice; but there was neither voice, nor any to answer, nor any that regarded.

Then said Elijah unto all the people: Come near unto me. And all the people came near unto him. And he repaired the altar of Yahweh, which was broken down. And Elijah took twelve stones, according to the number of tribes of the sons of Jacob (unto whom the word of Yahweh came, saying: Israel shall be thy name); and with the stones he built an altar in the name of Yahweh; and he made a trench about the altar, as great as would contain two measures of seed. And he put the wood in order, and cut the bullock in pieces, and laid it on the wood. And he said: Fill four jars with water, and pour it on the burnt-sacrifice, and on the wood. And he said: Do it a second time. And they did it a second time. And he said: Do it a third time. And they did it a third time. And the water ran round about the altar, and he filled the trench also with water.

And it came to pass, at the time of the offering of the evening sacrifice, that Elijah the prophet came near, and said: Yahweh, God of Abraham, of Isaac and of Israel, let it be known this day that Thou art God in Israel, and that I am Thy servant, and that I have done all these things at Thy command. Hear me, O Yahweh, hear me; that this people may know that Thou art the God Yahweh, and that Thou hast turned their heart back again.

Then the fire of Yahweh fell and consumed the burnt-sacrifice, and the wood, and the stones and the dust, and licked up the water that was in the trench. And when all the people saw it, they fell on their faces; and they said: Yahweh, He is God! Yahweh, He is God!

And Elijah said unto them: Take the prophets of Baal; let not one of them escape. And they took them; and Elijah brought them down to the brook Kishon, and slew them there.

And Elijah said unto Ahab: Get thee up, eat and drink; for there is a sound of abundance of rain. So Ahab went up to eat and to drink. But Elijah went up to the top of Carmel; and he cast himself down upon the earth and put his face between his knees, and said unto his servant: Go up, look toward the sea. And he went up and looked, and said: There is nothing. And he said: Go again seven times. And it came to pass the seventh time, that he said: Behold, there riseth a little cloud out of the sea, like a man's hand. And he said: Go up, say unto Ahab: Prepare, and get thee down, that the rain stop thee not. And it came to pass in the meanwhile, that the heaven became black with clouds and wind, and there was a great rain. And Ahab rode, and went to Jezreel. And the hand of Yahweh was on Elijah; and he girded up his loins, and ran before Ahab to the entrance of Jezreel.

And Ahab told Jezebel all that Elijah had done; and withal, how he had slain all the prophets with the sword. Then Jezebel sent a messenger unto Elijah, saying: So may the gods do to me and more also, if I make not thy life as the life of one of them by to-morrow, about this time. And when he understood, he arose and went for his life, and came to Beer-sheba which belongeth to Judah, and left his servant there. But he himself went a day's journey into the wilderness, and came and sat down under a broom-tree. And he entreated that he might die, and said: It is enough; now, O Yahweh; take away my life; for I am no better than my fathers. And he lay down and slept under a broom-tree. And, behold, a messenger touched him and said unto him: Arise and eat. And he looked, and behold, there was at his head a cake baked on the hot stones, and a cruse of water. And he did eat and drink, and laid him down again. And the messenger of Yahweh came again a second time and touched him, and said: Arise and eat; for the journey is too great for thee. And he arose and did eat; and he went in the strength of that meal unto Horeb, the mount of God.

And he came thither into a cave and lodged there; and behold. the word of Yahweh came unto him, and He said unto him: What doest thou here, Elijah? And he said: I have been very jealous for Yahweh, the God of hosts; for the Children of Israel have forsaken Thy covenant, thrown down Thine altars, and slain Thy prophets with the sword; and I, even I only am left; and they seek my life to take it away. And He said: Go forth, and stand upon the mount before Yahweh. And behold, Yahweh passed by. And a great and strong wind rent the mountains, and broke in pieces the rocks before Yahweh; but Yahweh was not in the wind. And after the wind, an earthquake; but Yahweh was not in the earthquake. And after the earthquake, fire; but Yahweh was not in the fire. And after the fire, a still, small voice. And it was so, when Elijah heard it, that he wrapped his face in his mantle, and went out and stood in the entrance of the cave. And behold, there came a voice unto him, and said: What doest thou here, Elijah? And he said: I have been very jealous for Yahweh, the God of hosts, for the Children of Israel have forsaken Thy covenant, thrown down Thine altars, and slain Thy prophets with the sword; and I, even I only, am left; and they seek my life to take it away.

And Yahweh said unto him: Go, return on thy way to the wilderness of Damascus. And when thou comest, thou shalt anoint Hazael to be king of Aram; and Jehu the son of Nimshi shalt thou anoint to be king over Israel; and Elisha the son of Shaphat of Abel-meholah shalt thou anoint to be prophet in thy room. And it shall be that him that escapeth from the sword of Hazael shall Jehu slay; and him that escapeth from the sword of Jehu shall Elisha slay. Yet will I leave seven thousand in Israel which have not bowed unto Baal, and every mouth which hath not kissed him.

So he departed thence, and found Elisha the son of Shaphat, who was ploughing with twelve yoke of oxen before him and he with the twelfth. And Elijah passed over unto him, and cast his mantle upon him. And he left the oxen and ran after Elijah, and said: Let me, I pray thee, kiss my father and my mother, and then I will follow thee. And he said unto him: Go back; for what have I done to thee? And he returned from following him, and took the yoke of oxen and slew them, and boiled their flesh with the instruments of the oxen, and gave unto the people, and they did eat. Then he arose, and went after Elijah, and ministered unto him.

Now Naboth the Jezreelite had a vineyard which was in Jezreel, hard by the palace of king Ahab, king of Samaria. And Ahab spake unto Naboth, saying: Give me thy vineyard, that I may have it for a garden of herbs because it is near my house; and I will give thee for it a better vineyard than it; or, if it seem good unto thee, I will give thee the worth of it in money. And Naboth said to Ahab: Yahweh forbid that I should give the inheritance of my fathers unto thee.

And Ahab came into his house heavy and displeased because of the word which Naboth the Jezreelite had spoken unto him; for he had said: I will not give thee the inheritance of my fathers. And he laid him down upon his bed, and turned away his face, and would eat no bread.

But Jezebel his wife came to him, and said unto him: Why is thy spirit so sad, that thou eatest no bread? And he said unto her: Because I spake unto Naboth the Jezreelite, and said unto him: Give me thy vineyard for money; or else, if it please thee, I will give thee another vineyard for it; and he answered: I will not give thee my vineyard. And Jezebel his wife said unto him: Dost thou now govern the kingdom of Israel? Arise and eat bread, and let thine heart be merry; I will give thee the vineyard of Naboth the Jezreelite. So she wrote letters in Ahab's name, and sealed them with his seal, and sent the letters to the elders and to the nobles that were in his city and dwelt with Naboth. And she wrote in the letters, saying: Proclaim a fast, and set Naboth at the head of the people; and set two men, sons of Belial, before him to bear witness against him, saying: Thou didst blaspheme God and the king. Then carry him out and stone him, that he die.

And the men of his city, even the elders and the nobles that dwelt in his city, did as Jezebel had sent unto them, as it was written in the letters which she had sent unto them. They proclaimed a fast, and set Naboth on high among the people. And there came in two men, sons of Belial, and sat before him; and the men of Belial witnessed against him, against Naboth, in the presence of the people, saying: Naboth did blaspheme God and the king. Then they carried him forth out of the city, and stoned him with stones, that he died.

Then they sent word to Jezebel, saying: Naboth is stoned and is dead. And it came to pass when Jezebel heard that Naboth was stoned and was dead, that Jezebel said to Ahab: Arise, take possession of the vineyard of Naboth the Jezreelite, which he refused to give thee for money; for Naboth is not alive, but dead. And it came to pass when Ahab heard that Naboth was dead, that Ahab rose up to go down to the vineyard of Naboth the Jezreelite, to take possession of it. And the word of Yahweh came to Elijah the Tishbite, saying: Arise, go down to meet Ahab, king of Israel, who is in Samaria; behold, he is in the vineyard of Naboth, whither he is gone down to possess it. And thou shalt speak to him, saying: Thus saith Yahweh: Hast thou killed, and also taken possession? And thou shalt speak unto him, saying: Thus saith Yahweh: In the place where dogs licked the blood of Naboth shall dogs lick thy blood, even thine.

And Ahab said to Elijah: Hast thou found me, O mine enemy? And he answered: I have found thee, because thou hast sold thyself to work evil in the sight of Yahweh. Behold, I will bring evil upon thee, and will take away thy posterity, and will cut off from Ahab every man-child, both him that is shut up and him that is left at large in

Israel. And I will make thy house like the house of Jeroboam the son of Nebat, and like the house of Baasha the son of Ahijah, for the provocation wherewith thou hast provoked Me, and hast made Israel to sin. And of Jezebel also spake Yahweh, saying: The dogs shall eat Jezebel by the walls of Jezreel.

And it came to pass when Ahab heard these words, that he rent his clothes, and put sackcloth upon his flesh, and fasted, and lay in sackcloth, and went softly. And the word of Yahweh came to Elijah the Tishbite, saying: Seest thou how Ahab humbleth himself before Me? Because he humbleth himself before Me, I will not bring the evil in his days; but in his son's days will I bring the evil upon his house.[1]

B. And Ahaziah the son of Ahab fell down through the lattice in his upper chamber in Samaria, and was sick. And he sent messengers and said unto them: Go, inquire of Baal-zebub the god of Ekron, whether I shall recover of this sickness. But a messenger of Yahweh said unto Elijah the Tishbite: Arise, go to meet the messengers of the king of Samaria, and say unto them: Is it because there is no God in Israel that ye go to inquire of Baal-zebub the god of Ekron? Now therefore, saith Yahweh: Thou shalt not come down from the bed whither thou are gone up, but shalt surely die. And Elijah departed.

And the messengers returned unto him, and he said unto them: Why is it that ye are returned? And they said unto him: There came up a man to meet us, and he said unto us: Go, return to the king that sent you, and say to him: Thus saith Yahweh: Is it because there is no God in Israel, that thou sendest to inquire of Baal-zebub the god of Ekron? therefore thou shalt not come down from the bed whither thou hast gone up, but shalt surely die. And he said unto them: What manner of man was he that came up to meet you, and told you these words? And they answered him: He was a hairy man, and girt with a girdle of leather about his loins. And he said: It is Elijah the Tishbite.

Then the king sent unto him a captain of fifty with his fifty. And he went up to him; and behold, he sat on the top of a hill. And he spake unto him: O man of God, the king hath said: Come down. And Elijah answered and said: If I be a man of God, let fire come down from heaven and consume thee and thy fifty. And there came down fire from heaven and consumed him and his fifty. And again he sent unto him another captain of fifty with his fifty. And he said unto him: O man of God, thus hath the king said: Come down quickly. And Elijah answered and said unto him: If I be a man of God, let fire come down from heaven, and consume thee and thy fifty. And the fire of God came down from heaven and consumed him and his fifty. And again he sent the captain of a third fifty with his fifty. And the third captain of fifty went up, and fell on his knees before

---

[1] It is now generally admitted that the account of Elijah's missions, even those narrated in 1 Kings, is composite. Critics differ as to the parts to be assigned to the several authors; but all are agreed that chapters xviii and xix of 1 Kings are by a master hand, elsewhere unknown. The story of the widow and her son is probably by E, who was not unequal to the rude tenderness of the latter part of ch. xvii, or to its dramatic opening; but the superb scene on mount Carmel, and the unerring psychology of the influence of the storm upon the great prophet were beyond him. The other story (of 2 Kings, i, 1-17) shows the eagerness of the populace to exaggerate any marvels ascribed to the great wonder-worker. The same is true of the miracles of Elisha. They were all spread abroad and magnified before they were collected by E, and before the advent of the literary prophets of the eighth century. The superstitions are from the people; the setting, the style, and the appeal to the emotions are by E, and not unworthy of the author of parts of Genesis and of Judges.

Elijah, and besought him, and said unto him: O man of God, I pray thee, let my life, and the lives of these fifty thy servants, be precious in thy sight. Behold, there came down fire from heaven, and consumed the two former captains of fifty with their fifties; but now, let my life be precious in thy sight. And the messenger of Yahweh said unto Elijah: Go down with him; be not afraid of him. And he arose, and went down with him unto the king.

And he said unto him: Thus saith Yahweh: Forasmuch as thou hast sent messengers to inquire of Baal-zebub the god of Ekron, is it because there is no God in Israel to inquire of his word? therefore thou shalt not come down from the bed whither thou art gone up, but shalt surely die.

So he died, according to the word of Yahweh which Elijah had spoken.

C. And it came to pass, when Yahweh would take up Elijah by a whirlwind into heaven, that Elijah and Elisha were walking from Gilgal. And Elijah said unto Elisha: Tarry here, I pray thee, for Yahweh hath sent me as far as Beth-el. And Elisha said: As Yahweh liveth, and as thy soul liveth, I will not leave thee. So they went down to Beth-el. And the sons of the prophets that were at Beth-el came forth to Elisha, and said unto him: Knowest thou that Yahweh will take away thy master from thy head to-day? And he said: Yea, I know it; hold ye your peace. And Elijah said unto him: Elisha, tarry here, I pray thee, for Yahweh hath sent me to Jericho. And he said: As Yahweh liveth, and as thy soul liveth, I will not leave thee. And the sons of the prophets that were at Jericho came near to Elisha and said unto him: Knowest thou that Yahweh will take away thy master from thy head to-day? And he answered: Yea, I know it; hold ye your peace. And Elijah said unto him: Tarry here, I pray thee; for Yahweh hath sent me to the Jordan. And he said: As Yahweh liveth, and as thy soul liveth, I will not leave thee. And they two went on.

And fifty men of the sons of the prophets went and stood over against them afar off; and they two stood by the Jordan. And Elijah took his mantle and wrapped it together, and smote the waters, and they were divided hither and thither, so that they two went over on dry ground. And it came to pass when they were gone over, that Elijah said unto Elisha: Ask what I shall do for thee, before I am taken from thee. And Elisha said: I pray thee, let a double portion of thy spirit be upon me. And he said: Thou hast asked a hard thing; nevertheless, if thou see me when I am taken from thee, it shall be so unto thee; but if not, it shall not be so. And it came to pass, as they still went on, that behold, there appeared a chariot of fire and horses of fire, which parted them both asunder; and Elijah went up by a whirlwind into heaven.

And Elisha saw it, and he cried: My father, my father, the chariots of Israel and the horsemen thereof! And he saw him no more. And he took hold of his own clothes, and rent them into two pieces. He took up also the mantle of Elijah that fell from him, and went back and stood by the bank of the Jordan. And he took the mantle of Elijah that fell from him, and smote the waters and said: Where is Yahweh, the God of Elijah? And when he also had smitten the waters, they were divided hither and thither, and Elisha went over.

And when the sons of the prophets that were at Jericho some way off saw him, they said: The spirit of Elijah doth rest on Elisha. And they came to meet him, and bowed down to the ground before him. And they said unto him: Behold now, there are with thy servants fifty strong men; let them go, we pray thee, and seek thy master; lest peradventure the spirit of Yahweh hath taken him, and cast him upon some mountain or into some valley. And he said: Ye shall not send. But when they urged him till he was ashamed, he said: Send. They sent therefore fifty men; and they sought three days, but found him not. And they came back to him while he tarried at Jericho. And he said: Did I not say unto you: Go not!

XVII

OF ELISHA, THE MIRACLE-WORKER AND KING-MAKER

A.   The miracles he performed.[1]   (2 Ki. i, 19-22; iv, 1-37, 38-41, 42-44; viii, 1-6; v, 1-19, 20-27; vi, 1-7, 8-23.)

Now the men of the city [Jericho] said unto Elisha: Behold, we pray thee, the situation of this city is pleasant, as my lord seeth; but the water is bad, and the land miscarrieth. And he said: Bring me a new cruse, and put salt therein. And they brought it to him. And he went forth unto the spring of the waters, and cast salt therein, and said: Thus saith Yahweh: I have healed these waters; there shall not be from thence any more death or miscarrying. So the waters were healed unto this day, according to the word of Elisha which he spake.

And he went up from thence unto Beth-el; and as he was going up by the way, there came forth out of the city little children and mocked him, and said unto him: Go up, thou baldhead! go up thou baldhead! And he looked behind and saw them, and he cursed them in the name of Yahweh. And there came two she-bears out of the wood and tore forty and two of them. And he went thence to mount Carmel, and from thence returned to Samaria.

Now there cried a certain woman of the wives of the sons of the prophets unto Elisha, saying: Thy servant my husband is dead; and thou knowest that thy servant did fear Yahweh; and the creditor is come to take unto him my two children to be bondmen. And Elisha said unto her: What shall I do for thee? Tell me; what hast thou in the house? And she said: Thy handmaid hath not anything in the house, save a pot of oil. Then he said: Go, borrow thee vessels abroad of all thy neighbors, even empty vessels; borrow not a few. And thou shalt go in and shut the door upon thee and thy sons, and pour out into all those vessels; and thou shalt set aside all that are full. So

[1] Close study of the details concerning Elisha in 2 Kings, ii-xiii, reveal in him three prominent traits. He was a kind and efficient helper in distress, whether of men of his own class among the "Schools of the Prophets", of a foreigner, or of the needy and sorrowful among the poor; an able adviser of kings and an ardent patriot, not above using shady or desperate means to further the good of his people; and a worker of miracles. But on first reading, only the last makes any impression. This is due to the editors' efforts to give in words a chronological parallel of the reigns in the two native kingdoms and among the surrounding nations. They may have thought that this was what J (whose methods they closely followed) intended for the Twin Kingdoms; but he was only concerned with the four usurpers in Israel during Asa's long reign in Judah, with each of whom Asa had to do. Their attempt was the more confusing, because of the similarity or exact doubling of the names of the kings in the twin kingdoms. The separation of the prophet's different activities, as here given, is as nearly as possible in accord with their original presentment, as worked out by eminent scholars.

she went from him, and shut the door upon her and upon her sons; they brought the vessels to her, and she poured out. And it came to pass when the vessels were full, that she said unto her son: Bring me yet a vessel. And he said unto her: There is not a vessel more. And the oil stayed. Then she came, and told the man of God. And he said: Go, sell the oil, and pay thy debt, and live thou and thy sons of the rest.

And it fell upon a day, that Elisha passed to Shunem, where was a great woman; and she constrained him to eat bread. And so it was, that as often as he passed by, he turned in thither to eat bread. And she said to her husband: Behold now, I perceive that this is a holy man of God that passeth by us continually. Let us make, I pray thee, a little chamber on the roof, and let us set for him there a bed and a table and a stool and a candlestick; and when it shall be that he cometh to us, he shall turn in thither. And it fell on a day that he came thither; and he turned into the upper chamber, and lay there. And he said to Gehazi, his servant: Call this Shunammite. And when he had called her, she stood before him. And he said unto him: Say now unto her: Behold, thou hast been careful for us with all this care; what is to be done for thee? Wouldest thou be spoken for to the king, or to the captain of the host? And she answered: I dwell among mine own people. And he said: What then is to be done for her? And Gehazi answered: Verily, she hath no son, and her husband is old. And he said: Call her. And when he had called her, she stood in the door. And he said: At this season, when the time cometh round, thou shalt embrace a son. And she said: Nay, my lord, thou man of God, do not lie to thy handmaid. But the woman conceived, and bare a son at that season, when the time came round, as Elisha had said unto her.

Now when the child was grown, it fell on a day that he went out to his father to the reapers. And he said unto his father: My head, my head! And he said to his servant: Carry him to his mother. And when he had taken him and brought him to his mother, he sat on her knees till noon, and then died. And she went up and laid him on the bed of the man of God, and shut the door upon him, and went out. And she called unto her husband, and said: Send me, I pray thee, one of the servants and one of the asses, that I may run unto the man of God, and come back. And he said: Wherefore wilt thou go to him to-day? it is neither new moon nor sabbath. And she said: Well! Then she saddled an ass, and said to her servant: Drive, and go forward; slacken not the riding, except I bid thee. So she went, and came unto the man of God to mount Carmel.

And it came to pass, when the man of God saw her afar off, that he said to Gehazi, his servant: Behold, yonder is that Shunammite. Run now, I pray thee, to meet her, and say unto her: Is it well with thee? is it well with thy husband? is it well with the child? And she answered: It is well. And when she came to the man of God to the hill, she caught hold of his feet. And Gehazi came near to thrust her away; but the man of God said: Let her alone; for her soul is bitter within her, and Yahweh hath hid it from me, and hath not told me. Then she said: Did I desire a son of my lord? did I not say: Do not deceive me? Then he said to Gehazi: Gird up thy loins, and take my staff in thy hand, and go thy way; if thou meet any man, salute him not; and if any salute thee, answer him not; and lay my staff upon the face of the child. And the mother of the child said: As Yahweh liveth, and as thy soul liveth, I will not leave thee. And he arose and followed her. And Gehazi passed on before them, and laid the staff upon the face of the child; but there was neither voice nor hearing. Wherefore, he returned to meet him, and told him, saying: The child is not awaked.

And when Elisha was come into the house, behold, the child was dead, and laid upon his bed. He went in therefore, and shut the door upon them twain, and prayed unto Yahweh. And he went up and lay upon the child, and put his mouth upon his mouth, and his eyes upon his eyes, and his hands upon his hands; and he stretched himself upon him; and the flesh of the child waxed warm. Then he turned, and walked in the house to and fro, and went up, and stretched himself upon him; and the child sneezed seven times, and the child opened his eyes. And he called Gehazi, and said: Call the Shunammite. So he called her. And when she was come in unto him, he said: Take up thy son. Then she went in, and fell at his feet, and bowed down to the ground; and she took up her son, and went out.

And Elisha came again to Gilgal; and there was a dearth in the land; and the sons of the prophets were sitting before him; and he said to his servant: Set on the great pot, and seethe pottage for the sons of the prophets. And one went out into the field to gather herbs, and found a wild vine, and gathered thereof of wild gourds his lapful, and came and shredded them into the pot of pottage; for they knew them not. So they poured out for the men to eat. And it came to pass as they were eating the pottage, that they cried out, and said: O man of God, there is death in the pot. And they could not eat thereof. But he said: Then bring meal. And he cast it into the pot; and he said: Pour out for the people, that they may eat. And there was no harm in the pot.

And there came a man from Baal-shalishah, and brought the man of God bread of the first-fruits; twenty loaves of barley, and fresh ears of corn in his sack. And he said: Give unto the people, that they may eat. And his servant said: How should I set this before a hundred men? But he said: Give the people, that they may eat; for thus saith Yahweh: They shall eat, and shall leave thereof. So he set it before them; and they did eat, and left thereof, according to the word of Yahweh.

Now Elisha had spoken unto the woman whose son he had restored to life, saying: Arise and go, thou and thy household, and sojourn wheresoever thou canst sojourn; for Yahweh hath called for a famine, and it shall come upon the land seven years. And the woman arose and did according to the word of the man of God; and she went with her household and sojourned in the land of the Philistines seven years. And it came to pass at the end of seven years, that the woman returned out of the land of the Philistines; and she went forth to cry unto the king for her house and for her land. Now the king was talking with Gehazi, the servant of the man of God, saying: Tell me, I pray thee, all the great things that Elisha hath done. And it came to pass, as he was telling the king how he had restored to life him that was dead, that behold, the woman whose son he had restored to life, cried to the king for her house and for her land. And Gehazi said: My lord, O king, this is the woman, and this is her son whom Elisha restored to life. And when the king asked the woman, she told him. So the king appointed unto her a certain officer, saying: Restore all that was hers, and all the fruits of the field since the day that she left the land, even until now.

Now Naaman, captain of the host of the king of Aram, was a great man with his master, and held in esteem because by him Yahweh had given victory unto Aram; he was also a mighty man of valor; but he was a leper. And the Aramæans had gone out in bands, and had brought away captive out of the land of Israel a little maid; and she waited on Naaman's wife. And she said to her mistress: Would that my lord were with the prophet that is in Samaria! Then would he recover him of his leprosy. And one went in and told his lord, saying: Thus and thus said the maid that is of the land of Israel. And the king of the Aramæans said: Go now, and I will send a letter to the king of Israel. And he departed, and took with him ten talents of silver, and six thousand pieces of gold, and ten changes of raiment. And he brought the letter to the king of Israel, saying: Now when this letter is come unto thee, behold, I have sent Naaman my servant to thee, that thou mayest recover him of his leprosy. And it came to pass, when the king of Israel had read the letter, that he rent his clothes, and said: Am I God, to kill and to make alive, that this man doth send unto me to recover a man of his leprosy? But consider, I pray you, and see how he seeketh an occasion against me?

And it was so, when Elisha the man of God heard that the king of Israel had rent his clothes, that he sent unto the king, saying: Wherefore hast thou rent thy clothes? let him come now to me, and he shall know that there is a prophet in Israel. So Naaman came with his horses and with his chariots, and stood at the door of the house of Elisha. And Elisha sent a messenger to him, saying: Go and wash in the Jordan seven times, and thy flesh shall come back to thee, and thou shalt be clean. And Naaman was wroth, and went away, and said: Behold, I thought: He will surely come out to me, and stand and call on the name of Yahweh, his God, and wave his hand over the place, and recover the leper. Are not Abana and Pharpar, the rivers of Damascus, better than all the waters of Israel? may I not wash in them and be clean? So he turned and went away in a rage.

And his servants came near, and spake unto him, and said: My father, if the prophet had bid thee do some great thing, wouldest thou not have done it? how much rather then, when he saith to thee: Wash, and be clean! Then went he down, and dipped himself seven times in the Jordan, according to the saying of the man of God, and his flesh came back like unto that of a little child, and he was clean.

And he returned to the man of God, he and all his company, and came and stood before him; and he said: Behold now, I know that there is no God in all the earth, but in Israel. Now therefore, I pray thee, take a present of thy servant. But he said: As Yahweh liveth, before whom I stand, I will receive none. And he urged him to take it; but he refused. And Naaman said: If not, yet I pray thee, let there be given to thy servant two mules' burden of earth; for thy servant will henceforth offer neither burnt-offering nor sacrifice unto other gods, but unto Yahweh. In this thing Yahweh pardon thy servant; when my master goeth into the house of Rimmon to worship there, and he leaneth on my hand, and I prostrate myself in the house of Rimmon, may Yahweh pardon thy servant in this thing. And he said unto him: Go in peace. So he departed from him a little way.

But Gehazi, the servant of Elisha, the man of God, said: Behold, my master hath spared this Naaman the Aramæan, in not receiving at his hand that which he brought. As Yahweh liveth, I will surely run after him, and take somewhat of him. And Gehazi followed after

Naaman. And when Naaman saw one running after him, he alighted from his chariot to meet him, and said: Is all well? And he said: All is well. My master hath sent me, saying: Behold, even now there are come to me from the hill-country of Ephraim two young men of the sons of the prophets; give them, I pray thee, a talent of silver, and two changes of raiment. And Naaman said: Be content; take two talents. And he urged him, and bound two talents of silver, with two changes of raiment, and laid them on two of his servants; and they bare them before him. And when he came to the hill, he took them from their hand, and bestowed them in the house; and he let the men go, and they departed.

But he went in, and stood before his master. And Elisha said unto him: Whence comest thou, Gehazi? And he said: Thy servant went no whither. And he said unto him: Went not my heart with thee, when the man turned back from his chariot to meet thee? Is it time to receive money and to receive garments, and olive-yards and vine-yards, and sheep and oxen, and man-servants and maid-servants? The leprosy of Naaman therefore shall cleave unto thee and unto thy seed, for ever. And he went out of his presence, a leper as white as snow.

And the sons of the prophets said unto Elisha: Behold now, the place where we dwell is too strait for us. Let us go, we pray thee, unto the Jordan, and take thence every man a beam, and let us make us a place there, where we may dwell. And he answered: Go. And one said: Be content, I pray thee, and go with thy servants. And he answered: I will go. So he went with them. And when they came to the Jordan, they cut down wood. But as one was felling a beam, the axe-head fell into the water; and he cried out, and said: Alas, my master! for it was borrowed. And the man of God said: Where fell it? And he showed him the place. And he cut down a stick, and cast it in thither, and made the iron to swim. And he said: Take it to thee. So he put out his hand, and took it.

Now the king of Aram warred against Israel; and he took counsel with his servants, saying: In such and such a place shall be my camp. And the man of God sent unto the king of Israel, saying: Beware that thou pass not such a place, for thither the Aramæans are coming down. And the king of Israel sent to the place which the man of God had told him and warned him of; and he guarded himself there, not once nor twice. And the heart of the king of Aram was sore troubled for this thing; and he called his servants, and said unto them: Will ye not tell me which of us is for the king of Israel? And one of his servants said: Nay, my lord O King, but Elisha, the prophet that is in Israel, telleth the king of Israel the words that thou speakest in thy bed-chamber. And he said: Go and see where he is, that I may send and fetch him. And it was told him: Behold, he is in Dothan.

Therefore sent he thither horses and chariots and a great host; and they came by night, and compassed the city about. And when the servant of the man of God was risen early and gone forth, behold, a host with horses and chariots was round about the city. And his servant said unto him: Alas, my master! how shall we do? And he answered: Fear not, for they that are with us are more than they that are with them. And Elisha prayed, and said: O Yahweh, I pray Thee, open his eyes, that he may see. And Yahweh opened the eyes of the young man, and he saw; and behold, the mountain was full of horses and chariots of fire round about Elisha. And when they came down upon him, Elisha prayed unto Yahweh, and said: Smite this people, I pray Thee, with blindness. And He smote them with blindness, according to the word of Elisha. And Elisha said unto them: This is not the way, neither is this the city, follow me, and I will bring you to the man whom ye seek. And he led them to Samaria.

And it came to pass when they were come into Samaria, that Elisha said: O Yahweh, open the eyes of these men, that they may see. And Yahweh opened their eyes, and they saw that they were in the midst of Samaria. And the king of Israel said unto Elisha, when he saw them: My father, shall I smite them? shall I smite them? And he answered: Thou shalt not smite them. Hast thou taken captive with thy sword and with thy bow these whom thou wouldest smite? Serve bread and water before them, that they may eat and drink, and go to their master. And the bands of Aram came no more into the land of Israel.

B.—Elisha as the Counsellor and Maker of Kings.   (2 Ki. 1; iii, 4-27; vi, 24-33; vii, 1-20; viii, 7-15; ix, 1-37; x, 1-33, 35; xiii, 3-9, 14-25.)

JUDAH	ISRAEL.	ARAM
B.C 930. REHOBOAM son of Solomon.	c. 930. JEROBOAM founds the king-dom. Heads the First Dynasty.	950. Rezon reigns in Damascus.
916-914. Abiah.		
913-873. ASA.	912-911. Nadab.	
	911-888. BAASHA (Usurper) founds the Second Dynasty.	c. 906. BEN HADAD I. (Ally of Asa.)
	888-887. Elah. (Murdered by Zimri)	
	887. Zimri. (Reigns 7 days)	
	887-883. Civil War.	
	883-877. OMRI. Founds Third Dynas-ty. Builds Samaria.	Lays siege to Samaria.
873-849. JEHOSHAPHAT	876-854. AHAB m. (or=) JEZEBEL d. of the King of Zidon. Their d. Athaliah m. Joram.	
	854-853. Ahaziah. Joram, k. of Judah	HAZAEL
849-843. JORAM m. d. of Ahab Atha-liah	853-842. Joram.	"pressed hard on Israel."
843-842. Amaziah		
842-836. ATHALIAH, qu.	842-815. JEHU. (Anointed by Elisha) Founds Fourth Dynasty.	
836-797. JOASH	814-798. Jehoahaz.	
797-779. Amaziah	798-783. Joash.	
779-740. UZZIAH. (Azariah)	783-743. JEROBOAM II [1]	BEN-HADAD II.

Now Moab rebelled against Israel after the death of Ahab. Mesha, the king of Moab, was a sheep-master; and he rendered unto the king of Israel the wool of a hundred thousand lambs and a hundred thousand rams. But it came to pass when Ahab was dead, that the king of Moab rebelled against the king of Israel; and king Jehoram went out of Samaria at that time, and mustered all Israel. And he sent unto Jehoshaphat, king of Judah, saying: The king of Moab hath rebelled against me; will you go with me against Moab to battle? And he said: I will go; I am as thou art, my people as thy people, my horses as thy horses. Which way shall we go up? And he answered: The way of the wilderness of Edom. So the king of Israel went, and the king of Judah and the king of Edom. And they made a circuit of seven

[1] E wrote during the reign of Jeroboam II. when it seemed probable that he would reunite the tribes and regain the territory lost since the time of Solomon. The Chronicler, writing in the fourth century B.C. makes no mention of him at all, but attributes his conquests to his father, Joash.

days' journey. And there was no water for the host, nor for the beasts that followed them.

And the king of Israel said: Alas! for Yahweh hath called these three kings together, to deliver them into the hand of the king of Moab. But Jehoshaphat said: Is there not a prophet here of Yahweh, that we may inquire of Yahweh by him? And one of the servants of the king of Israel said: Elisha the son of Shaphat is here, who poured water on the hands of the prophet Elijah. And Jehoshaphat said: The word of Yahweh is with him. So the king of Israel and Jehoshaphat and the king of Edom went down to him.

And Elisha said unto the king of Israel: What have I to do with thee? Get thee to the prophets of thy father, and to the prophets of thy mother. And the King of Israel answered him: Nay, for Yahweh hath called these three kings together to deliver them into the hand of Moab. And Elisha said: As Yahweh liveth, before whom I stand, surely, were it not that I regard the presence of Jehoshaphat, the king of Judah, I would not look toward thee, nor see thee. But now, bring me a minstrel. And it came to pass, when the minstrel played, that the hand of Yahweh came upon him. And he said: Thus saith Yahweh: Make this valley full of trenches. For thus saith Yahweh: Ye shall not see wind, neither shall ye see rain; yet that valley shall be filled with water, and ye shall drink, both ye and your cattle. And this is but a light thing in the hand of Yahweh; He will also deliver the Moabites into your hand. And ye shall smite every fortified city and every choice city, and shall fell every good tree, and stop all fountains of water, and mar every good piece of land with stones.

And it came to pass in the morning, about the time of making the offering, there came water by the way of Edom, and the country was filled with water.

Now when the Moabites heard that the kings were come up to fight against them, they gathered themselves together, all that were able to put on armor and upward, and stood on the border. And they rose up early in the morning, and the sun shone upon the water; and the Moabites saw the water, some way off, as red as blood; and they said: This is blood; the kings have surely fought together, and they have smitten every man his fellow. Now then, Moab, to the spoil! But when they came to the camp of Israel, the Israelites rose up and smote the Moabites, so that they fled before them. And they smote the land, even Moab, mightily. And they beat down the cities; and on every good piece of land they cast every man his stone, and filled it. And they stopped all the fountains of water, and felled all the good trees until there was left only Kir-Haresheth with the stones of the wall thereof; so the slingers encompassed it and smote it.

And when the king of Moab saw that the battle was too sore for him, he took with him seven hundred men that drew sword to break through unto the king of Edom; but they could not. Then he took his eldest son, that should have reigned in his stead, and offered him for a burnt-offering upon the wall.[1]

---

[1] The "Moabite stone", found at Dibhan in 1868, gives king Mesha's version of this battle. The first tumultuous onslaught, recorded by the Israelites, seems to have been a great success for them, which they naturally magnify. But the tide turned after Mesha sacrificed his son, which sacrifice, he, as naturally, did not record. The result was that the Moabites, believing that their god would now give them success, and also having had time to put their forces in array, brought the "great wrath" on Israel, which Mehsa details in full, and which compelled the retirement of Israel. There is no reason to doubt the sacrifice of Mesha's first-born, which was a recognized rite in Moab, and also in Canaan, until Abraham's revolt from it, as shown in E's account of the Sacrifice of Isaac.

And there came great wrath upon Israel. And they departed from him, and returned to their own land.

Now it came to pass after this, that the king of Aram gathered all his host and went up and besieged Samaria. And there was a great famine in Samaria; and behold, they besieged it until an ass's head was sold for fourscore pieces of silver, and the fourth part of a kab of dove's dung for five pieces of silver. And as the king was passing upon the wall, there cried a woman unto him, saying: Help, my lord, O king! And the king said unto her: If Yahweh do not help thee, whence shall I help thee? out of the threshing-floor, or out of the wine-press? And the king said unto her: What aileth thee? And she answered: This woman said unto me: Give thy son, that we may eat him to-day; and we will eat my son to-morrow. So we boiled my son, and did eat him. And I said unto her on the next day: Give thy son, that we may eat him; and she hath hid her son. And it came to pass when the king had heard the words of the woman, that he rent his clothes—now he was passing by upon the wall—and the people looked, and lo, he had sackcloth within upon his flesh. Then he said: God do so to me and more also, if the head of Elisha the son of Shaphat shall stand upon him this day.

But Elisha sat in his house, and the elders sat with him. And the king sent a man from before him; but ere the messenger came to him, he said to the elders: See ye how this son of a murderer hath sent to take away my head? Look, when the messenger cometh, shut the door, and hold the door fast against him; is not the sound of his master's feet behind him? And while he yet talked, behold, the messenger came down unto him. And he said: [The king saith], Behold, this evil is of Yahweh; why should I wait any longer?

And Elisha said: Hear ye the word of Yahweh: To-morrow about this time shall a measure of fine flour be sold for a shekel, and two measures of barley for a shekel in the gate of Samaria. Then the captain on whose hand the king leaned answered the man of God, and said: Behold, if Yahweh should make windows in heaven, might this thing be? And he answered: Behold, thou shalt see it with thine eyes, but shalt not eat thereof.

Now there were four leprous men that sat at the entrance of the gates, and they said one to another: Why sit we here until we die? If we say, we will enter into the city, then the famine is in the city, and we shall die there; and if we sit here, we die also. Now therefore come, and let us fall unto the host of the Aramæans; if they save us alive, we shall live; and if they kill us, we shall but die. And they rose up in the twilight to go unto the camp of the Aramæans; and when they were come to the outermost part of the camp, behold, there was no man there. For Yahweh had made the host of the Aramæans to hear a noise of chariots, and a noise of horses, even the noise of a great host; and they said one to another: Lo, the king of Israel hath hired against us the kings of the Hittites and the kings of the Egyptians, to come unto us. Wherefore they arose and fled in the twilight, and left their tents and their horses and their asses, even the camp as it was, and fled for their life. And when those lepers came to the outermost part of the camp, they went into one tent, and did eat and drink, and carried thence silver and gold and raiment, and went and hid it; and they came back, and entered into another tent and carried thence also, and went and hid it.

Then they said one to another: We do not well; this day is a day of good tidings, and we hold our peace. If we tarry till the morning light, punishment will overtake us. Now therefore, let us go and tell the king's household. So they came and called unto the porters of the city; and they told them, saying: We came to the camp of the Aramæans, and behold, there was no man there, neither voice of man, but the horses tied and the asses tied, and the tents as they were. And the porters called, and they told it to the king's household within. And the king arose in the night, and said unto his servants: I will now tell you what the Aramæans have done to us. They know that we are hungry; therefore are they gone out of the camp to hide themselves in the field, saying: When they come out of the city, we shall take them alive, and get into the city. And one of his servants answered and said: Let some take, I pray thee, one of the horses that remain, which are left in the city—behold, they are as all the multitude of Israel that are consumed—and let us send and see. They took therefore two chariots with horses; and the king sent after the host of the Aramæans, saying: Go and see. And they went after them unto the Jordan; and lo, all the way was full of garments and vessels which the Aramæans had cast away in their haste. And the messengers returned and told the king.

And the people went out and plundered the camp of the Aramæans. So a measure of fine flour was sold for a shekel, and two measures of barley for a shekel, according to the word of Yahweh. And the king appointed the captain on whose hand he leaned to have the charge of the gate; and the people trod upon him in the gate, and he died, as the man of God had said who spake when the king came down to him. And it came to pass as the man of God had spoken to the king, saying: Two measures of barley for a shekel, and a measure of fine flour for a shekel shall be to-morrow about this time in the gate of Samaria; and that captain answered the man of God, and said: Now behold, if Yahweh should make windows in heaven, might such a thing be? and he said: Behold, thou shalt see it with thine eyes, but shalt not eat thereof; even so it came to pass unto him; for the people trod upon him in the gate and he died.

Now Elisha came to Damascus; and Ben-Hadad the king of Aram was sick, and it was told him, saying: The man of God is come hither. And the king said to Hazael: Take a present in thy hand, and go meet the man of God, and inquire of Yahweh by him, saying: Shall I recover of this sickness? So Hazael went to meet him, and he took a present with him, even of every good thing of Damascus, forty camels' burden, and came and stood before him, and said: Thy son Ben-Hadad, king of Aram, hath sent me unto thee, saying: Shall I recover of this sickness? And Elisha said unto him: Go, say unto him: Thou shalt surely recover; howbeit, Yahweh hath shown me that he shall surely die. And he settled his countenance steadfastly upon him, until he was ashamed. And the man of God wept. And Hazael said: Why weepeth, my lord? And he answered: Because I know the evil that thou wilt do unto the Children of Israel; their strongholds wilt thou set on fire, their young men wilt thou slay with the sword, and wilt dash in pieces their little ones, and rip up their women with child. And Hazael said: But what! Is thy servant a dog, that he should do this great thing? And Elisha answered: Yahweh hath shown me that thou shalt be king over Aram.

Then he departed from Elisha, and came to his master, who said unto him: What said Elisha unto thee? And he answered: He told me that thou wouldest surely recover. And it came to pass on the morrow, that he took the coverlet and dipped it in water, and spread it on his face, so that he died. And Hazael reigned in his stead.

And Elisha the prophet called one of the sons of the prophets, and said unto him: Gird up thy loins, and take this vial of oil in thy hand, and go to Ramoth-Gilead. And when thou comest thither, look out there Jehu the son of Jehoshaphat the son of Nimshi, and go in and make him rise up from among his brethren, and carry him to an inner chamber. Then take the vial of oil, and pour it on his head, and say: Thus saith Yahweh: I have anointed thee king over Israel. Then open the door and flee, and tarry not. So the young man, even the young man the prophet, went to Ramoth-Gilead. And when he came, behold, the captains of the host were sitting; and he said: I have an errand unto thee, O captain. And Jehu said: Unto which of us all? And he said: Unto thee, O captain. And he arose and went into the house. And he poured the oil on his head, and said unto him: Thus saith Yahweh, the God of Israel: I have anointed thee king over the people of Yahweh, even over Israel. And thou shalt smite the house of Ahab thy master, that I may avenge the blood of My servants the prophets, and the blood of the servants of Yahweh at the hand of Jezebel. For the whole house of Ahab shall perish; and I will cut off from Ahab every man-child, and him that is shut up and him that is left at large in Israel. And I will make the house of Ahab like the house of Jeroboam the son of Nebat, and like the house of Baasha the son of Ahijah. And the dogs shall eat Jezebel in the portion of Jezreel, and there shall be none to bury her. And he opened the door and fled.

Then Jehu came forth to the servants of his lord; and one said unto him: Is all well? And he said unto them: Ye know the man and what his talk was. And they said: It is false; tell us now. And he said: Thus and thus spake he unto me, saying: Thus saith Yahweh: I have anointed thee king over Israel. Then they hastened and took every man his garment, and put it under him on the top of the stairs, and blew the horn, saying: Jehu is king!

So Jehu the son of Jehoshaphat the son of Nimshi conspired against Joram.

Now Joram had been guarding Ramoth-Gilead, he and all Israel, because of Hazael king of Aram; but king Joram was returned to be healed in Jezreel of the wound which the Aramæans had given him, when he fought with Hazael, king of Aram. And Jehu said: If this be your mind, then let none escape and go forth out of the city, to go to tell it in Jezreel. So Jehu rode in a chariot and went to Jezreel, for Joram lay there. And Ahaziah, king of Judah, was come down to see Joram.

Now the watchman stood on the tower in Jezreel, and he spied the company of Jehu as he came, and said: I see a company. And Joram said: Take a horseman and send to meet them, and let him say: Is it peace? So there went one on horseback to meet him, and said: Thus saith the king: Is it peace? And Jehu said: What hast thou to do with peace? turn thee behind me. And the watchman told, saying: The messenger came to them, but he cometh not back. Then he sent out a second on horseback, who came to them and said: Thus saith the king: Is it peace? And Jehu answered: What hast thou to do with peace? turn thee behind me. And the watchman told, saying: He came even unto them, and cometh not back; and the driving is like the driving of Jehu the son of Nimshi, for he driveth furiously.

And Joram said: Make ready. And they made ready his chariot. And Joram, king of Israel, and Ahaziah, king of Judah, went out to meet Jehu, each in his chariots; and they went out to meet Jehu and found him in the portion of Naboth the Jezreelite. And it came to pass, when Joram saw Jehu, that he said: Is it peace, Jehu? And he answered: What peace, so long as the harlotries of thy mother Jezebel and her witchcrafts are so many? And Joram turned his hands and fled, and said to Ahaziah: Treachery, O Ahaziah! And Jehu drew his bow with his full strength, and smote Joram between his arms; and the arrow went out at his heart, and he sank down in his chariot. Then said he to Bidkar his captain: Take up and cast him into the portion of the field of Naboth the Jezreelite; for remember how that, when I and thou rode after Ahab his father, Yahweh pronounced this oracle upon him: Surely I have seen yesterday the blood of Naboth and the blood of his sons, saith Yahweh; and I will requite them in this plot, saith Yahweh. Now therefore, take and cast him into this plot of ground, according to the word of Yahweh.

But when Ahaziah, the king of Judah, saw this, he fled by the way of the garden house. And Jehu followed after him, and said: Smite him also in the chariot. And they did so at the ascent of Gur which is by Ibleam. And he fled to Megiddo, and died there. And his servants carried him in a chariot to Jerusalem, and buried him in the sepulchre with his fathers in the city of David.

Now when Jehu was come to Jezreel, Jezebel heard of it, and she painted her eyes, and attired her head, and looked out at a window. And as Jehu entered in at the gate, she said: Had Zimri peace, who slew his master? And he lifted up his face to the window, and said: Who is on my side, who? And there looked out on him two or three servants. And he said: Throw her down. So they threw her down, and some of her blood was sprinkled on the wall, and on the horses; and she was trodden underfoot. And when he was come in, he did eat and drink; then he said: Look now after this cursed woman and bury her, for she is a king's daughter. And they went to bury her; but they found no more of her than the skull and the feet and the palms of her hands. Wherefore they came back and told him. And he said. This is the word of Yahweh, which He spake by His servant Elijah the Tishbite, saying: In the portion of Jezreel shall the dogs eat the flesh of Jezebel; and the carcass of Jezebel shall be as dung upon the face of the field in the portion of Jezreel, so that none shall say: This is Jezebel.

Now Ahab had seventy kinsfolk in Samaria. And Jehu wrote letters and sent to Samaria unto the rulers of Jezreel, even the elders and them that brought up the sons of Ahab, saying: And now, as soon as this letter cometh to you, seeing your master's sons are with you, and there are with you chariots and horses, fortified cities also, and armor; look ye out the best and meetest of your master's sons, and set him on his father's throne, and fight for your master's house. But they were exceedingly afraid, and said: Behold, the two kings stood not before him; how then shall we stand? And he that was over the household, and he that was over the city, the elders also and they that brought up the children, sent to Jehu, saying: We are thy servants, and will do all that thou shalt bid us; we will not make any man king; do that which is good in thine eyes.

Then he wrote a second time to them, saying: If ye be on my side, and if ye will hearken unto my voice, take ye the heads of the men your master's sons, and come to me by to-morrow this time. Now the king's sons, being seventy persons, were with the great men of the city who brought them up. And it came to pass, when the letter came to them, that they took the king's sons and slew them, even seventy persons, and put their heads in baskets, and sent them to him in Jezreel. And there came a messenger and told him, saying: They have brought the heads of the king's sons. And he said: Lay ye them in two heaps at the entrance of the gate until the morning. And it came to pass in the morning, that he went out and stood, and said to all the people: Ye are righteous. Behold, I conspired against my master, and slew him; but who smote all these? Know now that there shall fall to the earth nothing of the word of Yahweh, which Yahweh spake concerning the house of Ahab; for Yahweh hath done that which He spake by His servant Elijah.

So Jehu smote all that remained of the house of Ahab in Jezreel, and all his great men and his familiar friends, and his priests, until there was left him none remaining.

And he arose and departed, and went to Samaria. And as he was at the shearing-house of the shepherds in the way, Jehu met the brethren of Ahaziah, king of Judah, and said: Who are ye? And they answered: We are the brethren of Ahaziah; and we go down to salute the children of the king and of the queen. And he said: Take them alive. And they took them alive, and slew them at the pit of the shearing-house, even two and forty men; neither left he any of them.

And when he was departed thence, he lighted on Jehonadab the son of Rechab; and he saluted him, and said to him: Is thy heart right, as my heart is with thy heart? And Jehonadab answered: It is. If it be, said he, give me thy hand. And he gave him his hand; and he took him up to him into the chariot. And he said: Come with me, and see my zeal for Yahweh. So he made him ride in his chariot. And when he came to Samaria, he smote all that remained unto Ahab in Samaria, till he had destroyed him, according unto the word of Yahweh which He spake to Elijah.

And Jehu gathered all the people together, and said unto them: Ahab served Baal a little, but Jehu will serve him much. Now therefore, call unto me all the prophets of Baal, all his worshippers and all his priests; let none be wanting; for I have a great sacrifice to make to Baal; whosoever shall be wanting, he shall not live. But Jehu did it in subtlety, to the intent that he might destroy the worshipers of Baal.

And Jehu said: Proclaim a solemn assembly for Baal. And they proclaimed it. And Jehu sent through all Israel, and all the worshipers of Baal came, so that there was not a man left that came not. And they came into the house of Baal; and the house of Baal was filled from one end to the other. And he said to him that was over the vestry: Bring forth vestments for all the worshippers of Baal. And he brought them forth vestments. And Jehu went, and Jehonadab the son of Rechab, into the house of Baal; and he said unto the worshippers of Baal: Search, and look that there be here with you none of the servants of Yahweh; but the worshipers of Baal only. And they went in to offer sacrifice and burnt-offerings. Now Jehu had appointed him fourscore men without, and said: If any of the men whom I bring into your hands escape, his life shall be for the life of him.

And it came to pass, as soon as he had made an end of offering the burnt-offering, that Jehu said to the guard and to the captains: Go in and slay them; let none come forth. And they smote them with the edge of the sword; and the guard and the captains cast them out, and went to the city of the house of Baal. And they brought forth the pillars that were in the house of Baal, and burned them. And they broke down the pillar of Baal, and broke down the house of Baal and made it a draught-house unto this day.

Thus Jehu destroyed Baal out of Israel. Howbeit, from the sins of Jeroboam the son of Nebat, wherewith he made Israel to sin,—from them Jehu departed not, the golden calves that were in Beth-el and that were in Dan. But Yahweh said unto Jehu: Because thou hast done well in executing that which is right in Mine eyes, and hast done unto the house of Ahab according to all that was in My heart, thy sons of the fourth generation shall sit on the throne of Israel.

In those days Yahweh began to cut Israel short; and Hazael smote them in all the borders of Israel; from the Jordan eastward, and all the land of Gilead, the Gadites, and the Reubenites, and the Manassites, from Aroer which is by the valley of Arnon,—even Gilead and Bashan. And Jehu slept with his fathers, and they buried him in Samaria; and Jehoahaz his son reigned in his stead.

And the anger of Yahweh was kindled against Israel, and He delivered them into the hand of Hazael, king of Aram, and into the hand of Ben-Hadad his son continually. And Jehoahaz besought Yahweh, and Yahweh hearkened unto him; for He saw the oppression of Israel, how that the king of Aram oppressed them. And Yahweh gave Israel a deliverer, so that they went out from under the hand of the Aramæans; and the Israelites dwelt in their tents, as aforetime. Neither was there left to Jehoahaz of the people but fifty horsemen and ten chariots, and ten thousand footmen; for the king of Aram destroyed them, and made them as the dust in threshing. And Jehoahaz slept with his fathers; and they buried him in Samaria, and Joash his son reigned in his stead.

Now Elisha was fallen sick of his sickness whereof he was to die; and Joash, the king of Israel, came down to him, and wept over him, and said: My father, my father! the chariots of Israel and the horsemen thereof![1] And Elisha said unto him: Take bow and arrows; and he took unto him bow and arrows. And he said unto the king of Israel: Put thy hand upon the bow; and he put his hand upon it. And Elisha laid his hands upon the king's hands. And he said: Open the window outward; and he opened it. Then Elisha said: Shoot; and he shot. And he said: Yahweh's arrow of victory, even the arrow of victory against Aram; for thou shalt smite the Aramæans in Aphek, till thou have consumed them. And he said: Take the arrows; and he took them. And he said unto the king of Israel: Smite upon the ground; and he smote thrice and stayed. And the man of God was wroth with him, and cried: Thou shouldest have smitten five or six times; then hadst thou smitten Aram till thou hadst consumed it; whereas now, thou will smite Aram but thrice.

And Elisha died, and they buried him. Now the bands of the Moabites used to invade the land at the coming in of the year. And it came to pass, as they were burying a man, that behold, they spied a band; and they cast the man into the sepulchre of Elisha; and as soon as the man touched the bones of Elisha, he revived, and stood upon his feet.

[1] Apparently, a popular expression of grief for the loss of a man of distinguished power. It may have been the figure on which was based the tradition of the ascension of Elijah.

Now Hazael, king of Aram, had oppressed Israel all the days of Jehoahaz. But Yahweh was gracious unto them, and had compassion upon them, and had respect unto them, because of his covenant with Abraham, Isaac and Jacob, and would not destroy them; neither hath He cast them from His presence until now. So Hazael, king of Aram, died; and Ben-Hadad, his son, reigned in his stead. And Jehoash,[1] the son of Jehoahaz, took again out of the hand of Ben-Hadad, the son of Hazael, the cities which he had taken out of the hand of Jehoahaz, his father, by war. Three times did Joash smite him, and recover the cities of Israel.

XVIII

HOW JEHOASH CAME TO THE THRONE IN JUDAH

Athaliah, daughter of Ahab and queen-mother in Judah, tries to destroy all the rest of David's line; but Jehoash, her youngest grandson is saved. Judah endures her rule six years; then the high-priest proclaims Jehoash king, and Athaliah is slain. He rules well; but to save his people from war pays tribute to Hazael, king of Aram. His successor Amaziah, declares war against Jehoash, his contemporary in Israel, but is overpowered and Jerusalem is taken. His people revolt, and put his son Azariah (Uzziah) on the throne. At the same time, Jeroboam II, the last great king of Israel, is ruling. (2 Ki. 11, 1-20; xii, 1-19, 21-22; xiv, 2, 5-14, 16-17, 19-21, 23, 25-27.)

Now when Athaliah, the mother of Ahaziah, saw that her son was dead, she arose and destroyed all the seed royal. But Jehosheba, the daughter of king Joram, sister of Ahaziah, took Joash the son of Ahaziah, and stole him away from among the king's sons who were slain, even him and his nurse, and hid him in her bedchamber from Athaliah, so that he was not slain. And he was with her, hid in the House of Yahweh for six years. And Athaliah reigned over the land.

Now in the seventh year, Jehoiada sent and fetched the captains over hundreds of the Carites and of the Guards, and brought them into the house of Yahweh; and he made a covenant with them, and took an oath of them in the House of Yahweh, and he showed them the king's son. And he commanded them, saying: This is the thing that ye shall do; a third part of you, that come in on the sabbath and that keep the watch of the king's house, (now another third part was at the gate Sur, and another third part at the gate behind the guard), they shall keep the watch of the house and be a barrier. And the other two parts of you, even of all that go forth on the sabbath, shall keep the watch of the House of Yahweh about the king. And ye shall compass the king round about, every man with his weapon in his hand; and he that cometh within the ranks, let him be slain; and be ye with the king, when he goeth out and when he cometh in.

And the captains over hundreds did according to all that Jehoiada the priest commanded; and they took every man his men, those that were to come in on the sabbath with those that were to go out on the sabbath, and came to Jehoiada the priest. And the priest delivered to the captains over hundreds king David's spears and shields that were in the house of Yahweh. And the guard stood, every man with his

---

[1] The names Joash and Joram are frequently given also as Jehoash and Jehoram.

weapon in his hand, from the right side of the house to the left side of the house, along by the altar and the house.

Then he brought out the king's son and put upon him the crown, and gave him the testimony; and they made him king, and anointed him; and they clapped their hands, and said: Long live the king!

Now when Athaliah heard the noise of the guard and the people, she came to the people into the House of Yahweh. And she looked, and behold! the king stood by a pillar, as the manner was, and the captains and the trumpeters by the king; and all the people of the land were rejoicing, and they blew with trumpets. And Athaliah rent her clothes, and cried: Treason, treason! And Jehoiada the priest commanded the captains of hundreds, the officers of the host, and said unto them: Have her forth between the ranks; and him that followeth her, kill with the sword. For the priest had said: Let her not be slain in the House of Yahweh. And they laid hands on her; and she went by the way by which the horses came into the king's house; and there she was slain.

And Jehoiada made a covenant between Yahweh and the king and the people, that they should be Yahweh's people; between the king also and the people. And all the people of the land went to the house of Baal, and brake it down; his altars and his images brake they in pieces thoroughly, and slew Mattan the priest of Baal before the altars. And the priest appointed officers over the House of Yahweh. And he took the captains over hundreds, and the Carites, and the guard, and all the people of the land; and they brought down the king from the House of Yahweh, and came by the way of the gate of the guard to the king's house. And he sat on the throne of the kings. And all the people of the land rejoiced, and the city was quiet; and they slew Athaliah by the sword by the king's house.

Jehoash was seven years old when he began to reign. And Jehoash did that which was right in the eyes of Yahweh all his days that Jehoiada the priest instructed him. And Jehoash said to the priests: All the money of the dedicated things which is brought to the House of Yahweh in current money; the money for which each man is rated, and all the money that cometh into any man's heart to bring into the House of Yahweh, let the priests take it to them, every man from him who bestoweth it upon him; and they shall repair the breaches of the house, wheresoever any breach shall be found. But it was so, that in the three and twentieth year of king Jehoash the priests had not repaired the breaches of the house. Then king Jehoash called for Jehoiada the priest and for the other priests, and said unto them: Why repair ye not the breaches of the house? Now therefore, receive ye no more money of your acquaintance, but deliver it for the breaches of the house. And the priests consented to receive no more money of the people, neither repair the breaches of the house.

Then Jehoiada the priest took a chest and bored a hole in the lid of it, and set it beside the altar, on the right side as one cometh into the House of Yahweh; and the priests that kept the door put therein all the money brought into the house of Yahweh. And it was so, that, when they saw there was much money in the chest, the king's scribe and the high priest came up, and they counted and put up in bags the money that was found in the house of Yahweh. And they gave the money that was weighed out into the hands of them that had the oversight of the house of Yahweh; and they paid it out to the carpenters and builders and wrought upon the House of Yahweh, and to masons and hewers of stone, and for buying timber and hewn stone to repair the breaches of the House of Yahweh, and for all that was laid out for the house to repair it. Howbeit, there were not made for the House of Yahweh bowls of silver, snuffers, basins, trumpets, any vessels of gold or vessels of silver, out of the money that was brought into the House of Yahweh; but they gave that to the workmen, and repaired therewith the House of Yahweh. Moreover, they reckoned not with the men into whose hand they delivered the money to give to them that did the work, for they dealt faithfully. The trespass-money and sin-money was not brought into the house of Yahweh; it was the priests'.

Then Hazael, king of Aram, went up and fought against Gath, and took it; and Hazael set his face to go up to Jerusalem. And Jehoash, king of Judah, took all the hallowed things that Jehoshaphat and Jehoram and Ahaziah his fathers, kings of Judah, had dedicated, and his own hallowed things, and all the gold that was found in the treasures of the House of Yahweh, and in the king's house, and sent it to Hazael, king of Aram; and he went away from Jerusalem.

Then his servants arose and made a conspiracy and slew Joash in the house of Millo, that goeth down to Silla. For Jozachar the son of Shimeath, and Jehozabad, the son of Shomer, his servants, smote him; and he died. And they buried him with his fathers in the city of David; and Amaziah his son reigned in his stead. He was twenty and five years old when he began to reign, and he reigned twenty and nine years in Jerusalem. And it came to pass, as soon as the kingdom was confirmed in his hand, that he slew his servants who had slain the king his father; but the children of the murderers he slew not (according to the law of Moses wherein Yahweh commanded, saying: The fathers shall not be put to death for the children, nor the children be put to death for the fathers; but every man shall be put to death for his own sins.) [1] He slew of Edom in the valley of Salt ten thousand, and took Sela by war, and called the name of it Joktheel.

Then Amaziah sent messengers to Jehoash, king of Israel, saying: Come, let us look one another in the face. And Jehoash, king of Israel, sent to Amaziah, king of Judah, saying: The thistle that was in Lebanon sent to the cedar that was in Lebanon, saying: Give thy daughter to my son to wife; and there passed by a wild beast that was in Lebanon, and trod down the thistle. Thou hast indeed smitten Edom and thine heart hath lifted thee up. Glory therein, and stay at home. For why shouldest thou meddle to thy hurt, that thou shouldest fall, thou and Judah with thee?

But Amaziah would not hear. Therefore Jehoash, king of Israel, went up; and he and Amaziah looked one another in the face at Beth-Shemesh, which belongeth to Judah. And Judah was put to the worse before Israel; and they fled every man to their tents.

And Jehoash, king of Israel, took Amaziah, king of Judah, at Beth-Shemesh, and came to Jerusalem, and brake down the wall of Jerusalem from the gate of Ephraim unto the corner gate, four hundred cubits.[2] And he took all the gold and silver, and all the vessels that were found in the House of Yahweh and the treasures that were in the king's house, and hostages also, and returned to Samaria. And Joash slept with his fathers, and was buried in Samaria with the kings of Israel; and Jeroboam, his son, reigned in his stead.

---

[1] The words in parenthesis are probably a late addition. The custom of the day forbade the alleging of such a reason, however humane the individual might have been.
[2] This conquest may account somewhat for the Chronicler's disregard of Jeroboam II. while giving high honor to his father.

And Amaziah, the son of Joash, king of Judah, lived after the death of Jehoash, son of Jehoahaz, king of Israel, fifteen years. Then they made a conspiracy against him in Jerusalem, and he fled to Lachish. But they sent after him to Lachish, and slew him there. And they brought him upon horses, and he was buried in Jerusalem, with his fathers in the city of David. And all the people of Judah took Azariah, who was sixteen years old, and made him king in the room of his father Amaziah.

In the fifteenth year of Amaziah the son of Joash, king of Judah, Jeroboam son of Joash, king of Israel, began to reign. He restored the border of Israel from the entrance of Hamath unto the sea of the Arabah; according to the word of Yahweh, the God of Israel, which He spake by the hand of His servant Jonah, the son of Amittai, the prophet who was of Gath-Hepher. For Yahweh saw the affliction of Israel, that it was very bitter; for there was not any left, shut up nor at large, to be a helper for Israel. But Yahweh had not said that He would blot out the name of Israel from under Heaven; and He saved them by the hand of Jeroboam, the son of Joash.[1]

[1] With this statement of the territory already recovered for Israel by Jeroboam II. and his exultant acclaim of the young king as the future saviour of the whole nation, the Ephraimite author E closes his roll of the Heroes of Israel.

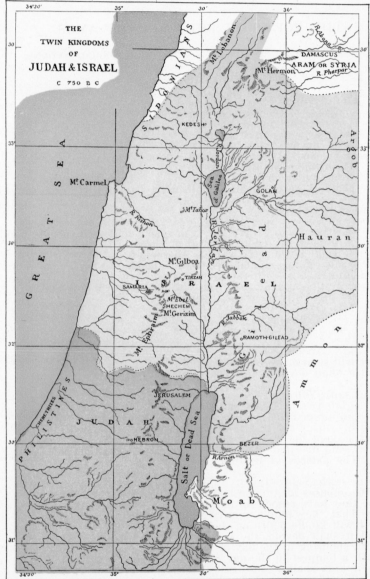

THE
TWIN KINGDOMS
OF
JUDAH & ISRAEL
C 750 B C

GREAT SEA

SIDONIANS

Mt Lebanon

Mt Hermon

DAMASCUS
ARAM OR SYRIA
R. Pharpar

R. Abana

Argob

KEDESH

Sea of Galilee

GOLAN

Hauran

Mt Carmel

R. Kishon

Mt Tabor

R. Jordan

Mt Gilboa

TIRZAH

SAMARIA

I S R A E L

Mt Ephraim

Mt Ebel
SHECHEM
Mt Gerizim

Jabbok

RAMOTH-GILEAD

Ammon

CHERETHITES

JERUSALEM

P H I L I S T I N E S

J U D A H

HEBRON

BEZER

R. Arnon

Salt or Dead Sea

M o a b

THE POEMS OF THE PROPHET AMOS

I. The Judgment to Come Upon the Surrounding Nations, but Chiefly Upon Guilty Israel

(Am. i, 3-15; ii, 1-3, 6-16)[1]

Thus saith Yahweh:
For three offenses of Damascus and for four,   I will not revoke it,
Because they have harrowed Gilead   with harrows of iron.
  So I will send fire into the House of Hazael
  That shall devour the palaces of Ben-Hadad;
Will break the bar of Damascus and cut off
    The dweller in Bikath-Aven,
  And him that holdeth the sceptre   from Beth-eden;
And the people of Aram shall go into exile   unto Kir, saith Yahweh.

Thus saith Yahweh:
For three offenses of Gaza and for four,   I will not revoke it,
Because they bore into exile a whole people   to deliver them to Edom.
  So I will send fire upon the wall of Gaza
  And it shall devour the palaces thereof;
I will cut off the inhabitants from Ashdod
And him that holdeth the sceptre from Ashkelon;
I will turn my hand against Ekron,   and the remnant
    Of the Philistines shall perish, saith Yahweh.

Thus saith Yahweh:
For three offenses of Tyre and for four,   I will not revoke it,
Because they delivered up a whole   captivity unto Edom,
    And remembered not the brotherly covenant.
  So I will send a fire on the wall of Tyre,
  And it shall devour the palaces thereof.

Thus saith Yahweh:
For three offenses of Edom and for four,   I will not revoke it,
Because he pursued his brother with the sword, and cast off pity,
    And his anger did tear perpetually
    And he kept his wrath for ever.
So I will send fire upon Teman;   it shall devour
    The palaces of Bozrah.

Thus saith Yahweh:
For three offenses of Ammon and for four,   I will not revoke it,
Because they have ripped up in Gilead   the pregnant women
    That they might enlarge their borders.
  So I will kindle a fire on the wall of Rabbah
  And it shall devour the palaces thereof,
    With shouting in the day of battle,
    With a tempest in the day of the whirlwind;
And their king shall go into exile,   he and the princes
    Together, saith Yahweh.

[1] Superscription by P (ch. i, 1). "The words of Amos who was among the herdsmen of Tekoa which he saw concerning Israel in the days of Uzziah, king of Judah, and in the days of Jeroboam, son of Joash, king of Israel, two years before the earthquake." Verse 2a is borrowed by P from Joel iv, 16a; and 2b is paraphrased from Joel 10 & 12, where they will be found. They are therefore here omitted.

Thus saith Yahweh:
For three offenses of Moab and for four,   I will not revoke it,
Because he burned the bones of the king of Edom, desecrating the dead.
So I will send fire upon Moab; it shall devour the palaces of Kirioth.
I will cut off the ruler from their midst   and will slay
    All his nobles with him, saith Yahweh.

Thus saith Yahweh:
For three offenses of Israel and for four,   I will not revoke it,
Because they sell the righteous for silver, the needy for a pair of shoes;
That pant after the dust of the earth   on the head of the poor,
    And turn aside the way of the humble.
A man and his father go in to the same maid, to profane My holy name;
They lie down beside every altar upon clothes taken in pledge,
And in the house of their god they drink   the wine of the fined.

Yet destroyed I the Amorite before them,
Whose height was like that of cedars; he was strong as the oaks.
Yet I destroyed his fruit from above and his roots from beneath.
    I brought you out of the land of Egypt
    And led you forty years in the wilderness,
    To possess the land of the Amorites.
I raised up of your sons for prophets, of your youth for Nazarites.
    Is it not even thus, O Children of Israel? saith Yahweh.

But ye gave the Nazarites wine to drink,
    Ye commanded the prophets: Prophesy not!
    Behold, I will make your place to groan
    As a cart groans that is full of sheaves.
Flight shall not avail the swift, the strong shall not use his strength,
The swift of foot shall not escape, nor shall he that rideth a horse.
Nor shall the warrior deliver himself, nor shall he that handleth the bow.
The courageous among the mighty shall flee away naked in that day,
        saith Yahweh.

II. THE COMING JUDGMENT WILL BE SURE AND THOROUGH

(Amos iii, 1-15)

Hear this word that Yahweh hath spoken against you, O Children of Israel, against the whole family which I brought out of the land of Egypt, saying:

You only have I known   of all the families of the earth,
Therefore will I visit upon you   all your iniquities.

Will two walk together   except they be agreed?
Will a lion roar in the forest   when he hath no prey?
Will a lion-cub cry from his den   if he have taken nothing?
Will a bird fall into a snare   if there is no bait set for it?
Shall the trumpet blare in the city   and people not be afraid?
Shall evil befall a city   and Yahweh hath not done it?
Surely Yahweh will do nothing   that He doth not reveal
    His purpose unto His servants, the Prophets!

The lion hath roared;   who will not fear?
The God Yahweh has spoken;   who can but prophesy?
Proclaim on the palaces of Ashdod,   and over the palaces of Egypt;
Gather ye on the mount of Samaria and see the manifold tumults
    And the oppressions in their midst;
For they know not how to do right who store up violence and robbery
    In their palaces, saith Yahweh.

Therefore thus saith the God Yahweh:
    Lo, an enemy surrounds the land;
And he shall strip thee of thy strength;
    Thy palaces shall be plundered.
As the shepherd rescueth out of the mouth of the lion
    Two legs or a piece of an ear,
So shall the dwellers in Samaria escape
    With the corner of a couch or the leg of a bed.

Hear ye and testify against the house of Jacob!
    Saith the God Yahweh, the militant God:
In the day that I shall visit upon Israel his transgressions,
I will visit the altars of Bethel; the horns of the altar
    Shall fall to earth;
Together with the winter-house. will I smite the summer-house;
The houses of ivory shall perish, the great houses be swept away,
        saith Yahweh.

III. AGAINST THE WOMEN OF SAMARIA

(Amos iv, 1-3)

Hear this word, ye kine of Bashan,
    Who dwell in the mount of Samaria;
Ye that oppress the poor, that crush the needy;
That say to your husbands: Bring, that we may feast!
    The God Yahweh hath sworn by His holiness:
    Lo, surely, the days shall come upon you
That ye shall be drawn with hooks, the last of you with fish-hooks,
And ye shall go out at the breaches, every woman straight before her,
    And ye shall be cast into Harmon, saith Yahweh.

IV. ISRAEL'S RELIANCE UPON RITES AND CEREMONIES WHILE BLIND TO THE PURPOSE OF GOD'S JUDGMENT

(Amos iv, 4-15)

Come to Bethel and transgress!
    To Gilgal, and multiply transgression!
Bring your sacrifices in the morning, your tithes after three days!
Offer a sacrifice of thanksgiving of that which is leavened;
Proclaim your free-will offerings! so love ye to do, ye Israelites,
        said the God Yahweh.

But I have given you cleanness of teeth in all your cities,
    And lack of bread in all your palaces;
    Yet have ye not returned unto Me, saith Yahweh.

I have also withheld from you the rain,
    When there were yet three months to harvest
So that two or three cities wandered to one to drink water,
    And were not satisfied.
    Yet have ye not returned unto Me, saith Yahweh.

I smote you with blasting and mildew,
    Laying waste your gardens and vineyards,
And your fig-trees and your olive-trees did the palmer-worm devour;
    Yet have ye not returned unto Me, saith Yahweh,

I have sent among you the pestilence after the manner of Egypt;
  Your youths have I slain with the sword
  And I have carried away your horses;
I have made the stench of your camps come up even unto your nostrils
  Yet have ye not returned unto Me, saith Yahweh.

I have overthrown some of you, as God overthrew Sodom and Gomorrah,
  And ye were as a brand plucked out of the burning;
  Yet have ye not returned unto Me, saith Yahweh.

  Therefore thus will I do unto thee, O Israel!
For this will I do unto thee; Prepare to meet thy God, O Israel!

V. A Lament for the Imminent Destruction of Israel and a
Pleading to Her to Repent

(Amos v, 1-6, 10-17)

  O House of Israel,
Hear the word which I take up,— a lamentation over you.
The Virgin of Israel is fallen, she shall rise no more;
She is cast down upon her land, there is none to take her up.
  For thus saith the God Yahweh:
The city that went forth a thousand shall have a hundred left;
And that which went forth a hundred shall have but ten left.

  For thus saith Yahweh:
  Seek ye Me and live, but seek not Bethel nor enter Gilgal,
    And pass not to Beersheba;
For Gilgal shall go into exile and Bethel shall come to naught.
Seek Yahweh and live, lest He cast fire on the House of Joseph;
  Lest it devour, and there be none to quench it in Bethel.

Ye who turn justice to gall and cast righteousness to the ground,
  That hate him that reproveth in the gate, and abhor him
    That speaketh uprightly!
Lo, because ye trample on the poor and exact of him loads of grain;
Ye have built houses of stone, but ye shall not dwell in them;
Pleasant vineyards ye plant, but wine of them shall ye not drink.
  For I know how manifold are your transgressions
    And how great are your sins,
  Ye that afflict the just, and take a bribe,
  And thrust aside the needy in the gate.
  Wherefore the prudent in such a time will keep silence
    For surely the time is evil.

  Seek good and not evil, that ye may live;
That Yahweh, the militant God, may be with you, as ye have said.
  Hate evil and love the good, and establish justice in the gate;
    It may be that Yahweh Sabaoth will be gracious
      To the remnant of Joseph.
    Therefore thus saith Yahweh Sabaoth:
In all the streets shall be wailing, on the highways the cry, Alas!
  They shall call the husbandman to mourn,
    And to wailing those skilled in lamentation;
In all vineyards shall there be mourning; for through thy midst
    Shall I pass, saith Yahweh.

VI.   THE DAY OF YAHWEH SHALL BE A DAY OF RETRIBUTION

(Amos v, 18-27; vi, 1-14)

Woe unto you that desire the Day of Yahweh!
    Why would ye have the Day of Yahweh?
Darkness it shall be, and not light.
As if a man did flee from a lion, and a bear met him;
Or went into a house, and leaned his hand on the wall,
    And a serpent bit him.
Shall not the day of Yahweh   be darkness and not light?
    Even very dark,   and no brightness in it?

I hate, I despise your feasts,   I take no delight
    In your solemn assemblies;
Yea, though ye offer burnt-offerings and your meal-offerings
    I will not accept them.
Neither will I regard the peace-offerings of your fat beasts.
    Take thou away from Me   the noise of thy songs,
And let Me not hear the melody   of thy psalteries;
    But let Justice well up as spring-waters,
    And Righteousness as a mighty stream.

Did ye offer Me sacrifices in the wilderness
    For forty years, O House of Israel?
But now ye shall take up the tents of your king and the image
    Of your god which ye have made for yourselves,
And I will cause you to go into captivity beyond Damascus,
                    Saith Yahweh.

Woe to those that are at ease in Zion,
    That are secure in the mount of Samaria!
The notable men of the first of the nations,
    To whom the House of Israel resort,
Ye that put off the evil day, yet create a rule of violence!

They lie upon beds of ivory and stretch themselves on their couches
And eat the lambs of the flock   and calves from the inner stall;
That thrum on the psaltery   and devise for themselves
    Instruments of music;
That drink wine by bowlfuls   and with the finest of oils
    Anoint themselves.
But now shall they go captive with the first that go into captivity;
    The revelry of the sprawlers shall come to an end.

The God Yahweh hath sworn by Himself, saith Yahweh Sabaoth:
    I abhor the pride of Jacob and hate his palaces;
    I will deliver up the city with all that is therein;
    For behold, Yahweh commandeth;
    He will smite the great house into splinters,
        And the little ones into chips.

Do horses run upon crags? Do men plough there with oxen,
    That ye have turned justice into gall
    And the fruit of righteousness into wormwood?
Ye that rejoice in a thing of naught, that say: By our own strength
    Have we not taken horns?

Verily, I am raising against you a nation,
    And they shall oppress you, O Israel,
From the entering in of Hamath even to the brook of the Arabah,
    Saith Yahweh, the Militant God.

VII. Two Apologues Upon Recently Averted Misfortunes

(Amos vii, 1-3; 4-6)

Thus Yahweh showed unto me,   and behold, He was forming locusts
When growth of late grass begins,   after the King's sowings;
   Already locusts had made an end of all the growths of the land.
And I said: O Yahweh, forgive,   I beseech Thee;
   How shall Jacob stand?   for he is small.
Yahweh repented concerning it.   It shall not be, said Yahweh.

Thus Yahweh showed unto me and behold, he was calling
   For judgment by fire;
And it devoured the great deep,   and would have eaten the land.
And I said: O Yahweh, cease, I pray Thee! How shall Jacob stand?
   For he is small.
He relented also concerning this.   This too shall not be,
                       said Yahweh.

VIII. A Third Apologue. The Doom of Israel is Sealed

(Amos vii, 7-9)

Then He showed me, and behold, Yahweh stood by a wall, a plumb-
line in His hand. And Yahweh said unto me: Amos! what seest thou?
And I said: A plumb-line. Then said Yahweh:
      Lo, a plumb-line will I set
In the midst of My people Israel.   No more will I parden them.
   The high places of Isaac shall be desolate
   And the sanctuaries of Israel shall be laid waste;
     And I will rise up with a sword against
     The House of Jeroboam.

IX. Amaziah, Priest of Bethel, Is Roused to Action Against this Judaean Prophet

(Amos vii, 10-17)

Then Amaziah the priest of Bethel sent to Jeroboam, king of Israel,
saying: Amos hath conspired against thee in the midst of the house
of Israel; the land is not able to bear his words. For thus Amos saith:
Jeroboam shall die by the sword, and Israel shall surely be led away
captive out of the land.

Then Amaziah said unto Amos: O thou Seer, go, flee away into the
land of Judah, and there eat bread and prophesy there; but prophesy no
more at Bethel; for it is the king's sanctuary, and the king's residence.

Then Amos answered and said unto Amaziah: I was no prophet,
neither was I a prophet's son; but I was a herdsman and a dresser of
sycamore trees. But Yahweh called me from following the flock; and
Yahweh said unto me: Go, prophesy unto My people, Israel. Now,
therefore, hear the word of Yahweh. Thou sayest: Prophesy not
against Israel, and preach not against the House of Isaac. Therefore
thus saith Yahweh:

Thy wife shall be a harlot in the city,   thy sons and daughters
            Shall fall by the sword.
Thy land shall be divided by line,   and thou shalt die
            In an unclean land;
And Israel shall surely be led away   captive from his land.

X. A Vision and a Prophecy, the Time Is at Hand.
(Amos viii, 1-5, 7-10, 14)

Thus the God Yahweh showed me, and lo, a basket of summer fruit.
And He said: Amos, what seest thou? And I said: A basket of summer
fruit. Then said Yahweh:

            The time is come upon My people Israel.
I will not pardon them any more.   In that day the songs
  Of the palace shall be wailings, saith Yahweh Sabaoth.
The dead bodies shall be many;   in all places shall be silence,

Hear this, O ye that trample the needy,
      And destroy the poor of the land;
That say: When will the new moon be gone,
      That we may sell grain?
And the sabbath, that we may set forth grain,
      Making the ephah small, the shekel great,
And falsifying the balances of deceit?

Yahweh hath sworn by the pride of Jacob:
Never shall I forget any of their works. Shall not the land
Tremble for this, and every one that dwelleth therein?
Shall not the whole of it rise as the Nile, be troubled and sink,
      Like the river of Egypt?

It shall come to pass that day   that I will make the sun
  To go down at noon;   and I will darken the earth
      In the clear day,   saith Yahweh.
  I will turn your feasts into mournings, and your songs
            Into lamentations;
I will put sackcloth on all loins,   and baldness on every head,
  And I will make the mourning   as mourning for an only son;
      And the end thereof as a bitter day.

They that swear by the sin of Samaria,
  And say: As thy god, O Dan, liveth!!
And: As the way of Beersheba liveth! shall fall to rise no more.

XI. The Vision of the End
(Amos ix, 1-4, 7-8)

I saw Yahweh, standing beside the altar, and He said:
            Smite the capitals,   that the posts may shake,
      And break them in pieces   on the heads of them all;
And I will slay the residue   of them with the sword.
There shall not one of them escape,   nor shall one flee to safety.
Though they dig through to Sheol,   then shall My hand take them.
And if they climb up to heaven,   thence will I bring them down;
Though they hide themselves   in the top of Carmel,
I will search them out from thence   and take them.

And though they hide from My sight   at the bottom of the sea,
There will I command the serpent,   and he shall bite them.
And though they go into captivity   before their enemies,
There will I command the sword   and it shall slay them,
And I will set Mine eyes upon them   for evil and not for good.
Are ye not as the Cushites to Me,   O Israel, saith Yahweh?
Did I not bring up Israel   out of the land of Egypt,
And the Philistines from Caphtor,   and Aram from Kir?
Behold, the eyes of the God Yahweh   are upon the sinful kingdom,
     And I will destroy it from the face of the earth.

POEMS AND APOTHEGMS OF THE PROPHET HOSEA

THE PROLOGUE [1]
(Ch. i, 2b; ii, 6b, 7a, 4b, 6a; iii, 1-4, 5a, c.)

Now Yahweh said unto Hosea: Go, take thee a wife of whoredoms who will bear you children of whoredoms; for the land is continually committing whoredoms, turning away from Yahweh. So he went and took Gomer, the daughter of Diblaim; and she conceived and bare him a son. And Yahweh said unto him: Call his name *Jezreel;* for yet a little while and I will avenge the blood of Jezreel upon the House of Jehu, and will cause the house of Israel to cease. And it shall come to pass in that day, that I will break the bow of Israel in the valley of Jezreel.

And she conceived again, and bare a daughter. And He said unto him: Call her name Lo-Ruhamah; for I will have *mercy no longer* upon the house of Israel to pardon them in any wise. Now, when she had weaned Lo-ruhamah, she again conceived and bare a son. And He said: Call his name Lo-ammi; for ye are *not My people*, and I will not be your God.

[Then Hosea said] They are children of harlotry; she that conceived them hath done shamefully; she is not my wife, nor will I be her husband, and on her children I will have no pity.

Then Yahweh said unto me; Still, go, love a woman who loveth a paramour, and is an adulteress, even as Yahweh loveth the sons of Israel, though they turn unto other gods, and love cakes of raisins. (So I bought her unto me for fifteen pieces of silver and a homer of barley, and a half-homer of barley. And I said unto her: Thou shalt sit solitary for me many days; thou shalt not play the harlot, and thou shalt not be any man's wife, nor will I have to do with thee.) Even so, the Israelites shall sit solitary many days without king and without prince and without sacrifice and without pillar and without ephod or teraphim. Afterward shall they come trembling to Yahweh and to His goodness in the end of days.

I. YAHWEH PLEADS WITH HIS PEOPLE
(Ch. ii, 4a, c, 5, 7b-9a, 21-25)

Plead with thy mother, plead!
That she put her harlotries out of her sight,
Her adulteries from between her breasts;
Lest I strip her naked and set her   as on the day of her birth,
And make her like a wilderness,   like a land without water,
And discipline her with thirst.
For she saith: I will go   after my lovers who gave me
My bread and my water, my wool   and my flax, my oil and wine.

[1] Hosea gives some personal experiences in which he sees a similarity to the relations between Yahweh and Israel, His Chosen People. In chapters i and ii, Hosea speaks of himself in the third person. In chap. iii, he uses the first person.

263

Behold, I will hedge up her way with thorns,
And build up a wall about her, that she shall not find her way,
She shall pursue her paramours but shall not overtake them.
She shall seek them but she shall not find them.
For she did not know that it was I that gave her
The corn and the wine and oil and multiplied her silver,
And her gold that they used for Baal.

Therefore I will take back my corn and my wine in its season;
I will take back my wool and flax given to cover her nakedness,
Now will I uncover her shame in the sight of her lovers,
And none shall deliver her out of My hand.
I will cause her mirth to cease, her feasts and her new moons,
Her sabbaths and her appointed seasons.
I will lay waste her vines, her fig trees whereof she said:
These are my hire, that my lovers have given me;
And I will make them a forest, where beasts of the field shall eat.

I will visit upon her the days of the Baalim
Wherein she offered unto them,
And decked herself with her ear-rings and jewels,
And went after her lovers, and forgat Me, saith Yahweh.

Therefore I will allure her, and bring her into the desert;
I will speak kindly to her, and will give her vineyards
And the valley of Achor for a door of hope.
And she shall respond there as in the days of her youth,
As in the day when she came up out of the land of Egypt.

And it shall be in that day that she shall call to her lord
And shall call no more on the Baalim;
And I will take the names of the Baalim out of her mouth,
And they shall be mentioned no more by their names,
And I will betroth her to Me forever,
Yea, I will plight her to Me in righteousness
In justice and loving-kindness, in mercy, yea, in fidelity,
And she shall know Yahweh, saith Yahweh.

And it shall come to pass that day, that I will speak, saith Yahweh,
I will speak to the heavens, and they shall speak to earth;
The earth shall speak to the corn, to the wine and to the oil,
And they shall speak to Jezreel, I will sow her to Me in the land.
And I will have mercy on her that had not obtained mercy;
And I will say to Lo-Ammi, Thou art My people;
And they shall say to Me, Thou art my God.

II. THE CHARGE AGAINST THE PEOPLE OF ISRAEL THAT THEY HAVE NOT KNOWN YAHWEH

(Ch. iv, 1-14, 16-19)

Hear the word of Yahweh, O Israel! for Yahweh hath a charge
Against the inhabitants of the land;
For therein is neither truth, mercy nor knowledge of God.
But perjury, lying and murder stealing and adultery.
They break all bounds, and blood answereth for blood.
Therefore the land mourneth, all its inhabitants languish
With the beasts of the field and the fowls of heaven,
Yea, the fish of the sea also are swept away.

Yet, let no man bring charges,   let none reprove another,
For My people are neither worse   nor better than the priests.
So thou shalt stumble by day,   the priest will fall by night,
     And I will destroy thy mother.

My people are destroyed   for lack of knowledge;
Because thou hast rejected knowledge, I will also reject thee,
     That thou shalt be no priest to Me.
Since thou forgettest the law of thy youth,
     I will also forget thy children.

The more they increased, the more they sinned against Me.
I will change their glory to shame; they feed on My people's sin;
It is like priest, like people; they have set their heart on evil.
     But I will punish them both for their ways,
     And I will reward them their doings.
They shall eat and not be satisfied   shall commit whoredom and find no
                                               [delight,
     Because they have ceased to heed Yahweh.

Whoredom and wine and new wine   becloud the understanding.
My people ask counsel of a stock,   and their staff speaketh wisdom.
    For the spirit of harlotry   hath caused them to err,
And they have gone a-whoring   not following their God.
They sacrifice on mountaintops   and burn incense on the hills,
Under oaks and poplars and holms   because their shade is good.
Therefore your daughters are harlots, and your brides adulterous.

I will not punish your daughters   when they play the harlot
    Nor your wives when they commit adultery;
    For they have consorted with lewd women,
They have sacrificed with the sacred prostitutes,
     Thus were they misled.
For Israel hath been stubborn   like a stubborn heifer.
Will Yahweh now feed them   as a lamb in a broad pasture?

Ephraim is joined to his idols,   let him alone!
When their carouse is over   they betake them to harlotry.
    Their rulers shamefully hold out the hand: Give ye!
The wind shall bind them up in her wings, and they
    Shall be shamed because of their sacrifices.

III. AGAINST PRIESTS AND RULERS

(Ch. v, 1-14)

Hear this, O ye Priests!   and attend, O House of Israel!
And give ear, O house of the king,   for to you pertaineth judgment.
A snare have ye been at Mizpah,   and a net spread out on Tabor.
    The apostates have plunged deep in slaughter,
    And I am rejected of them all.

I know Ephraim well indeed,   and Israel is not hid from Me,
    For thou, O Ephraim,   hast played the harlot;
     Israel is defiled.
Their deeds do not suffer them   to return unto their God.
The spirit of harlotry is in them, and they know not Yahweh.
    For the pride of Israel will testify before Him,
    And Ephraim and Israel shall stumble in their guilt.

With flocks will they seek Yahweh, but they shall not find Him,
For they have been faithless to Yahweh, and begotten strange children.
Now shall the new moon devour them and their portions.

Blow ye the trumpet in Gibeah,   sound the horn in Ramah!
Raise an alarm in Bethel,   making Benjamin tremble!
Ephraim shall be a desolation   in the day of visitation;
Among the tribes of Israel do I unfold what shall surely be.

The princes of Jacob have become like those who remove landmarks.
I will pour out My wrath   upon them like water.
Oppressed is Ephraim, crushed in his right, because he steadfastly
        pursued evil.
        Therefore am I to Ephraim like a moth
        Like rottenness to the House of Jacob.

When Ephraim saw his sickness,   and Israel his wound,
        Ephraim went to Assyria,   Israel to one who could not heal
        Nor cure him of his wound.
But I will be like a lion to Ephraim, like a young lion to Israel.
I, even I will rend and go My way,   I will carry away
        And there shall be none to deliver.

IV.   YAHWEH LAMENTS THE FICKLENESS OF ISRAEL

(Ch. v, 15; vi, 1-10; vii, 1-7)

I will go and return to My place until they confess their guilt,
        And seek My presence.
        In their affliction they will seek Me, saying:
        Come, let us return to Yahweh!
He hath smitten, He will heal us; after two days He will raise us.
        And we shall live in His presence.
        Yea, let us know, let us eagerly seek to know Yahweh.
His coming is as sure as morning; He will come to us as the rain,
        As the spring rain   that gently waters the earth.

        O Ephraim, what shall I do unto thee?
        O Israel, what shall I do unto thee?
        For your goodness is like a morning cloud,
        And as the early dew it passeth away.
I have hewed them by the prophets,   I have slain them
        By the words of My mouth,
That their judgments might be as the light when it goeth forth.
        For I desired mercy and not sacrifice,
        The knowledge of God more than burnt-offerings.
        But they, like men, have broken the covenant,
        They have been faithless to Me.
Gilead is a city of evil-doers,   it is polluted with blood;
And as bandits lie in wait for a man, so doth a band of priests
        Murder on the way to Schechem;
        They commit deliberate crimes.

        In Bethel have I seen a horrible thing;
There doth Ephraim commit whoredom, there is Israel defiled.
When I would have healed Israel, then is the guilt of Ephraim revealed.
And the thief entereth in, while bandits make a raid without.
Let them not say in their heart that I store up all their guilt,
For their continuous deeds which are ever in My sight betray them.

They delight the king with their wickedness,
  And the princes with their lies.
  They are all of them adulterers.
They make our king ill, the princes are fevered with wine.
  They join hands with dissolute fellows.
For like an oven, their heart burns all night with treachery.
Through the night it slumbers; at morn, it blazes into a flame.
  All of them glow like an oven, and they consume their judges;
  All their kⁱngs have succumbed; none of them call unto Me.

V. A Second Arraignment of the Nation

(Ch. vii, 8-16; viii, 1-3)

Ephraim! He letteth himself be mixed with foreign nations!
Ephraim is a cake unturned. Strangers devour his strength
    And he knoweth it not.
Gray hairs are here and there upon him, but he knoweth it not.
   Israel's arrogance is in his face,
 And they return not unto Yahweh, their God.
   And in all this they seek him not.

   Ephraim is become like a silly dove;
  To Egypt they call, after Assyria they go.
  Even as they go, I will spread My net upon them.
Like birds of the heavens, I will bring them down,
  I will chastise them because of their wickedness.

Woe to them that they have strayed! Destruction,
   Because they are untrue to Me!
Although it was I who redeemed them, they spake lies about Me,
  And they have not cried unto Me with their heart,
   Though they wail upon their beds.
  They assemble themselves for corn and wine,
   But they rebel against Me.

Though I have trained their arms and strengthened them,
  They devise evil against Me, they turn ever to Baal.
  They are become like a deceitful bow;
  Their princes fall by the sword,
  Because of the falseness of their tongues.
  In the land of Egypt they will lick the dust,
  For as an eagle, I will swoop down upon My house.
To Me continually they cry; My God, we of Israel know Thee!
Israel hath rejected that which is good;
   Let the enemy pursue him.

VI. Yahweh Repudiates Israel's Kings and Idols

(Ch. viii, 4-13)

They have set up kings, but not by Me;
They have made princes without My knowledge;
Of their silver and their gold, they have made them idols,
   That they may be cut off.
  Thy Calf, O Samaria, hath cut thee off!
  Mine anger is kindled against them!
How long will it be that they escape punishment?
For this too is from Israel; the craftsman made it; thus it is
   no God.

Yea, the Calf of Samaria shall be broken to slivers.
For they have sown the wind   and shall reap the whirlwind.
They are a shoot that hath no stalk, and yieldeth no fruit;
    If it shall yield, strangers must devour it.

Israel is swallowed up.
Already are they among the nations as a vessel of no value.
For they are gone up to Assyria like a wild ass all alone.
    Ephraim hath hired lovers.
Yea, though they hire among the nations, I will gather them up.
They begin to be diminished for the burden of kings and princes.
    Though Ephraim hath built up many altars,
        All of them are altars for sin.
    Though I wrote for him all My great Laws,
        They were accounted as a stranger's.

As for their sacrifices made by fire unto Me,
    Let them sacrifice flesh and eat it,
For Yahweh accepteth them not; but He will remember their guilt
And punish their sins.   They shall return into Egypt.

VII.   Israel Shall Again Be Taken Captive
(Ch. ix, 1-16)

Rejoice not, O Israel, unto exultation   like the nations,
For thou hast strayed from thy God;   thou hast loved
        A harlot's hire upon every corn-floor.
The threshing-floor and the wine-press shall not feed them,
        And the new wine shall fail her.
They shall not dwell in Yahweh's land,   but Ephraim shall return
    Into Egypt.   They shall eat unclean food in Assyria.

They shall pour no wine-offerings to Yahweh, neither shall they
            Be pleasing to Him.
    Their bread shall be as bread of mourners;
    They that eat thereof shall be polluted;
    For their bread shall be for their hunger,
    It shall not come into the house of Yahweh.
What will ye do on the festival-day, the Day of Feast to Yahweh?

For lo, they are gone away from destruction,
Yet Egypt shall gather them up;   Memphis shall bury them;
Their precious treasures of silver,   nettles shall cover them;
        Thorns shall be in their tents.
The days of visitation are come,   days of recompense are at hand.
        Israel shall know it.
The prophet is a fool?   The man inspired is raving mad?
For the multitude of thine iniquities, the enmity is great.

Ephraim was a watchman with my God!
As for the prophet, a fowler's snare is in all his ways.
        And enmity in the house of his God.
They have deeply corrupted themselves as in the days of Gibeah.
    He will remember their guilt,   He will punish their sin.

I found Israel like grapes in the wilderness;
    I saw your fathers as the first-ripe fruit of the fig-tree
        In her first season.
    But as soon as they came to Baal-Peer,
        They gave themselves up unto shame,
And became as detestable as that which they loved.

As for Ephraim—like a bird   his glory shall fly away.
There shall be no birth, none with child, and no conception.
Though they bring up their children, I will bereave them;
                No son shall be left.
        Yea, woe be unto them   when I turn away from them!

Ephraim, as I have seen Tyre,   is planted in a pleasant place.
Yet Ephraim must himself lead out   his children to slaughter.
Give them, O Yahweh—   what wilt Thou give?
Give them a miscarrying womb,   and dry breasts!

Their wickedness came to a head in Gilgal; there I hated them.
    For their evil-doing, I will drive them out of Mine house.
    I will love them no more.   All their rulers are rebellious.
Ephraim is smitten; their root is dried up; they shall bear Me
                No more fruit.
    Yea, though they bring forth,   I will destroy
        The beloved fruit of their womb.

VIII. A LAMENTATION FOR THE COMING RUIN

(Ch. x, 1-6)

Israel was a luxuriant vine   which put forth fruit freely.
But, as the fruit increased,   he increased his altars.
The more goodly was his land,   the more goodly were his pillars.
    Their heart is divided,   now shall they bear their guilt.
Yahweh shall raze their altars,   He shall spoil their idols.
            Surely they will now say:
    We have no king because we feared not Yahweh,
            But what could a king do for us?
But the dwellers in Samaria shall fear for the Calf of Beth-Aven;
            For the people thereof shall mourn
        And the priests shall tremble for him;
For the glory wherein they rejoiced hath departed from him.
It also shall be borne to Assyria   for a present to the great king.
    Ephraim shall be disgraced,   Israel shall be ashamed
                Of its idol.
        As for Samaria, her king is cut off
        As foam from the face of the waters.
The high places of Aven, the sin of Israel, shall be destroyed.
Thorns and thistles shall come up   upon their altars,
And they shall cry to the mountains: Cover us!
        And to the hills: Fall upon us!

IX. THE JUDGMENT THAT ISRAEL HAS EARNED

(Ch. x, 9-15)

    O Israel, thou hast sinned   from the days of Gibeah!
There they stood; no battle would overtake them in Gibeah!
    In My wrath I will come and chastise them,
    The nations shall be gathered against them,
        To chastise them for their double crime.

Ephraim is a heifer well-broken   that loveth to thresh;
I Myself laid a yoke on her fair neck; Ephraim was to ride;
    Israel was to plough,   Jacob to break up the clods.
But ye have ploughed wickedness,   ye have reaped iniquity.
        Ye have eaten the fruit of lies.

Because thou didst trust in thine own way,
In the multitude of thy warriors,
Therefore shall a tumult arise   among thy hosts;
Thy fortresses shall be spoiled   as Shalman [ezer?] spoiled
Beth-Arba in the day of battle.
The mother was dashed in pieces   with her children.
Thus will I do unto you   because of your great sins.
Early in the morning   shall the king of Israel
Be utterly cut off.

X. THE LOVING KINDNESS OF YAHWEH

(Ch. xi, 1-9.)

When Israel was a child   then I loved him
And out of Egypt   I called My sons;
But the more I called them,   the more they went away.
They sacrificed unto the Baalim   and made offerings to idols.
Yet it was I who taught Ephraim to walk,
Taking them by their arms;
But they knew not that I healed them.

I drew them with cords of a man, with bands of love;
I was to them as one who removeth the yoke from the jaws of an ox.
And I set their food before them.
He shall not return to the land of Egypt;
The Assyrian shall be his king,
Because they refused to return unto Me;
And the sword shall fall upon his cities, and shall destroy
His fortresses.

How can I give up, Ephraim!   How can I surrender thee, Israel!
How can I make thee as Admah!   How can I set thee as Zeboim!
My heart is turned within Me,   My compassion glows for thee.
I will not carry out the fierceness of Mine anger,
I will not return to destroy Ephraim.
For I am God and not man;   the Holy One in the midst of Thee.
And I will not come in wrath.

XI. YAHWEH REVIEWS THE HISTORY AND FIXED INGRATITUDE
OF ISRAEL

(Ch. xii, 1-4a, 8-11, 14-15, 12)

Ephraim compasses Me about with lies,
And the House of Israel with deceit,
And towards the Holy One,   who is faithful?
Ephraim feedeth upon wind   and hunteth the east wind.
All day long he heapeth up   falsehood and desolation.
He maketh a league with Ashur   and carrieth oil to Egypt.
Yahweh hath a charge against Jacob and will punish Israel
According to his deeds.
In the womb he supplanted his brother;
In his hand are false balances,   he loveth to oppress.
For Ephraim saith: I have become rich;
Surely I have gained me wealth.
All his gains will not secure him immunity for his sin.

But I am Yahweh, thy God   since the land of Egypt.
   I will again make thee dwell in tents
      As ye did in the days of old.
Yet I spake to you by prophets.   and I multiplied visions,
And through the mouths of prophets I spake in parables.
And by a prophet I, Yahweh,   brought Israel out of Egypt,
   And by a prophet   was he preserved.

Ephraim hath given bitter provocation, therefore shall his blood
      Be cast upon him;
  And Yahweh will return upon him his reproach.

THE APOTHEGMS OF HOSEA
(Ch. xiii)

I. When Isreal spake trembling, he exalted himself in Israel,
    But when he offended through Baalim, he died.

II. They sin more and more, having made themselves molten images
    of silver;
    Idols of their own devising; all of the craftmen's work;
    Of them they say: They that sacrifice men, kiss calves.

III. They shall be as the morning cloud, and as the early dew that
    passeth away;
    As the chaff that is driven by the whirlwind from the threshing-
    floor, and as the smoke out of the chimney.

IV. I am Yahweh, thy God, from the land of Egypt; thou shalt know
    no God but Me; for besides Me there is no saviour.

V. I did know thee in the wilderness, in the land of great drought;
    According to their pasture, so were they filled.
    They were filled and their heart was exalted; therefore have they
    forgotten Me.

VI. I will be unto them as a lion; as a leopard will I watch them by
    the way.
    •I will meet them as a bear bereaved of her whelps, and will rend
    the caul of their hearts. There will I devour them like a
    lioness; as a wild beast will I tear them.

VII. O Israel, thou hast destroyed thyself; but in Me is thy help.
    I am thy King. Where in all thy cities is a king that can save
    thee? and the judges to whom thou saidst: Give us a king
    and princes?
    I gave thee a king in Mine anger, and take him away in wrath.

VIII. The iniquity of Ephraim is wrapped up; his sin is laid up in
    store.
    The throes of a travailing woman are come upon him. He is
    unwise; for this is no time to linger in the place of the break-
    ing forth of children.

IX. Shall I ransom them from the power of the grave? Shall I
    redeem them from danger?
    O Death! I will be thy plague. O Grave! I will be thy destruction.
    Repentance shall be hid from Mine eyes.

X. Though he be fruitful among the reed-grass, an east wind shall
    come. The wind of Yahweh shall come up from the wilder-
    ness, and his spring shall become dry, and his fountain shall
    be dried up.

XI. He shall despoil thee of thy treasure, all thy precious things.

THE POEMS OF THE PROPHET ISAIAH

A. EARLY POEMS WRITTEN DURING THE REIGNS OF
JOTHAM AND AHAZ, KINGS OF JUDAH

(Ch. ii, 5-10, 20-21, 11-17, 22; iii, 1, 4-5,
8-9, 12-15; iii, 16-17, 24, iv, 1; v, 1-7.)

I. ON THE IMPENDING DAY OF YAHWEH

O House of Israel! Come, let us walk in the light of Yahweh!
For Thou, Yahweh, hast renounced   Thy people, the House of Jacob.
  For they are full   of diviners from the East,
 And of soothsayers,   like the Philistines.
Israel's land is full of silver and gold,
  His treasures are endless.
His land is full of horses,   there is no end of his chariots.
His land is full of idols,   he worships the work of his hands.
To them the mean man boweth down,   the great man humbleth himself:
 Therefore Thou canst not forgive them.

Go into clefts of the rock,   and hide thyself in the dust,
From the terror of Yahweh   and for the glory of His majesty,
 When He ariseth to shake terribly the earth.

 * * * * * * *

 * * * * *   to the moles and to the bats
Shall men cast away that day   the idols of silver and of gold
Which they made to bow down to,   that they may go in that day
Into the clefts of the rocks   and into the holes in the dust,
From before the terror of Yahweh   and for the glory of His majesty,
 When He ariseth to shake terribly the earth.

II. ON THE SAME SUBJECT [1]

 * * * * * * *
The haughtiness of Mankind shall be bowed down
And the loftiness of men brought low,
And in that day shall Yahweh alone be exalted.

For a day of doom hath Yahweh Sabaoth
For all that is proud and lofty,   for all that is lifted up and high.
For all the lofty cedars of Lebanon   and for all the oaks of Basham;
For all the mountains the lofty,   and for all the uplifted hills.
 For every high tower   and for every fortified wall.
For all the ships of Tarshish   and for all the stately vessels.
The haughtiness of Mankind shall be bowed down
And the loftiness of men brought low,
And in that day shall Yahweh alone be exalted.

O cease trusting in man in whose nostrils is but a breath,
For how little is he to be trusted. . . . .

[1] These fragments of separate poems on the Judgment to Come are distinguishable by
their refrains.

III. A Fragment on the Fall of Judah.

*   *   *   *   *

For behold, Yahweh Sabaoth removes   from Jerusalem and from Judah
Every stay and support; every stay   of bread and stay of water.

*   *   *   *   *

I will make youths their princes,   insulting boys shall rule them.
The people shall tyrannize one over another, neighbor over neighbor.
They shall be insolent, the boy to the aged, the base to the noble.
    For Jerusalem cometh to ruin   and Judah is falling,
Because their tongue and their deeds   are against Yahweh
        To defy His glorious eyes.
    Their observance of persons   testifieth against them,
    And the sin of Sodom   they publish without disguise.
Woe unto them! for they have wrought their own misfortunes.

My People! a boy is their ruler,   and women rule over them.
My People; thy guides lead thee astray, they have confused thy ways.
Yahweh cometh forward to plead,   He stands to judge His people.
He enters into judgment with nobles,   with the elders of His people.
It is ye who eat up the land; the spoil of the poor is in your houses.
What mean ye by crushing My people,   grinding the face of the needy?
      Saith Yahweh, the Militant God.

IV. A Charge Against the Women of Judah

Because the daughters of Zion   are haughty
And walk with neck thrown back   and leering eyes,
Tripping along as they go,   making a chime with their anklets,
Yahweh will encrust with scabs   the crowns of their heads;
     Yahweh will expose   their shames.
Instead of perfumes shall he decay   and instead of a girdle, a rope;
Instead of curled hair, baldness,   of a mantle, girding of sackcloth.
And in that day, seven women   will seize on one man, saying:
Our own bread will we eat,   we will wear our own garments,
Only let us be called by thy name!   Take away our reproach!

V. The Parable of the Vineyard

A song will I sing of my friend,   a love-song touching his vineyard.
A vineyard belongs to my friend   on a hill that is very fruitful.
He digged it and cleared it of stones and planted in it choice vines.
He built a tower in the midst   and hewed therein a wine-vat.
He looked to find choice grapes;   and it bare only the wild!

    Ye in Jerusalem dwelling,   ye that are freemen of Judah,
     Judge ye now, I pray,   between me and my vineyard.
What could have been done more   than I had done for my vineyard?
When I looked to find fine grapes,   why bare it only the wild?

And now I will have you know   what I will do to my vineyard.
Its hedge will I take away   that it be eaten up.
I will break through its walls   that it be trodden down;
I will make it a waste   neither pruned nor weeded;
It shall bear only briers and thorns; I will command the clouds
     That they rain no rain upon it.

For the vineyard of Yahweh Sabaoth   is the House of Israel;
And the men of Judah are   His cherished plantation.
   And He looked for peace,   and behold, bloodshed!
   For righteousness,   but behold, an outcry!

VI. THE VISION OR CALL OF ISAIAH
(Ch. vi, 1-13)

In the year that King Uzziah died [740 B.C.] I saw Yahweh sitting on a high and uplifted throne, and the train of His robe filled the temple. Above Him stood the seraphim; each one had six wings; with twain he covered his face, with twain he covered his loins, and with twain he did fly. And again and again, one cried to another, and said:

Holy, holy, holy is Yahweh Sabaoth!
The whole earth is full of His glory.

And the foundations of the thresholds shook at the sound of their voices, and the temple was filled with smoke. And I said: Woe is me! I am undone! I am a man of unclean lips. Mine eyes have seen the King, Yahweh Sabaoth.

Then flew one of the seraphim unto me with a glowing coal in his hand that he had taken from off the altar, and with it he touched my lips, and said:

Lo, this hath touched thy lips;
Thine iniquity is taken away, and thy sin forgiven.

And I heard the voice of Yahweh, saying:

Whom shall I send?   who will go for Me?

Then said I: Here am I; send me. And He said:
Go and say to this people:
Hear Me, but understand not!   See on, but perceive not!
Make fat this people's heart, make dull their ears and dim their eyes
Lest they see with their eyes,   and hear with their ears,
And understand with their hearts   and return, and be healed.
And I said: O Yahweh, how long? And He said:
Until cities be waste   without inhabitant,
And houses without men,   and the land be left
A desolation,
And Yahweh have removed the men afar,
And in the heart of the land the deserted regions be wide.
And if a tenth part be left therein, this also will be consumed
Like the terebinth and the oak,
Whereof the stock, after felling, remaineth.

VII. THE SIXFOLD DENUNCIATION OF THE SINS OF ISRAEL
(Is. v, 8-24. Written c. 735 B.C.)

Woe unto those who join house to house and add field to field
Till there be no more room,   and ye are settled
Alone in the midst of the land.
Therefore thus hath Yahweh Sabaoth revealed himself in mine ears.
Surely your many houses shall become a desolation,
Your great and fair palaces without an inhabitant.
Two acres of vineyard shall yield one bath,
And the seed of an homer but an ephah.

Woe to those who rise at dawn   to revel in strong drink!
Who tarry late into the night   inflamed with wine!
At their banquets are flute and harp, tabret, flute and wine;
But they regard not Yahweh's ways, nor ponder His handiwork.
Therefore My people shall go   into exile unawares,
      Their honored men shall be weak for hunger,
      Their multitudes parched for thirst.
Therefore Sheol gapes ravenously and opens widely her mouth,
    And their glory, their busy throngs and joyous ones,
      Plunge headlong in.
      Lambs shall graze where they dwelt,
    Wanderers shall feed in their desert wastes.

Woe unto them that draw guilt to them with cords of iniquity
      And sin as with a cart-rope;
Who say: Let Him hasten His work, let it speed
      That we may see it!
    Let the purpose of Israel's Holy One be revealed
      That we may know it!

Woe unto them that call evil good and good evil,
    Who put darkness for light and light for darkness;
    Who put bitter for sweet and sweet for bitter!
Woe unto those who are wise—in their own eyes,
    And keen-witted in their own conceit!
Woe unto them who are mighty—in drinking wine,
      And well-skilled—in mixing drinks!
Who justify the wicked for a bribe,
And strip the righteous of his integrity!

As the tongue of fire devoureth hay and stubble shrivels in flame,
    So shall their root become rottenness,
    And their blossom go up like dust;
    Because they have rejected the Law of Yahweh Sabaoth,
    And spurned the word of Israel's Holy One.

VIII. The Imminent Punishment of Israel [1]

(Ch. ix, 8-21; x, 1-4b; v, 26-29, 25c.)

Written 734 B.C.

A word hath Yahweh sent unto Jacob, and it shall light upon Israel.
And all the people shall know it; Ephraim and the men of Samaria,
    Who have stiffened their necks in pride,
      And in stoutness of heart, saying:
    Bricks have fallen down,   but we will build with stone!
Sycamores have been felled,   cedars will fill their places!
    Hence Yahweh hath stirred up their foe,
And spurred on their enemies against them;   ffl
Aram on the east, the Philistines on the west, and they devour
      Israel greedily.
    Because of all this, His anger is not turned away,
      But His hand is stretched out still.

    Yet the people turn not to Him that smote them,
      And Yahweh do they not regard;
    So from Israel Yahweh will cut off head and tail,
      Palm-branch and rush in one day.[2]

---

[1] From this point, Isaiah's poems are amazingly dislocated; but his frequent use of refrain, and the individuality of his style have gone far in enabling scholars to restore them in large measure.

[2] Vv. 15-16 are an inserted marginal gloss which destroys the force of the preceding figure; they are therefore omitted.

Therefore Yahweh spareth not their youths,
    Nor pitieth their orphans and widows;
Because every one is impious and an evil-doer,
    And every mouth speaketh folly.
For all this, His anger is not turned away,
But His hand is stretched out still.

For wickedness burneth as a fire,
    It consumeth briars and thorns;
Yea, it kindleth the thickets of the forest;
    They whirl upward in columns of smoke.
By the fury of Yahweh the land is burned up,
    The people become food for the flame.
One snatcheth on the right, yet is famished,
    On the left-hand, and still is hungry.
Everyone eateth his neighbor's flesh,
    None hath pity on his fellow.
Manasseh devoureth Ephraim, Ephraim Manasseh,
    And both together against Judah.
For all this, His anger is not turned away
But His hand is stretched out still.

Woe to them that set up unjust decrees,
    To the scribes who write iniquity!
Who turn aside justice from the helpless,
And despoil the poor of My people of their rights,
That widows may be their prey,
    And that orphans may be their plunder.
What then will ye do in the day of punishment,
    Of crashing storm that comes from afar?
To whom will ye flee for aid,
    And where will ye leave your wealth?
For all this, His anger is not turned away,
    But His hand is stretched out still.

So He will raise a signal to a distant nation,[1]
And hiss to them to come from the end of the earth;
And lo, speedily, swiftly they come.
None there is weary, and among them none stumbles;
The zone of their loins is not loosened;
Of their sandals there tears not a thong.
Their arrows are sharpened, all their bows are bent,
The hoofs of their horses are counted as flint,
    And as a whirlwind their wheels.
Their roaring is like that of the lion,
    Yea, like young lions they roar, and growl,
        and seize the prey,
And carry it off safe and none rescues it.
For all this, His anger is not turned away,
    But His hand is outstretched still.[2]

[1] This fine strophe, the appropriate conclusion of the poem, we find misplaced in chapter v.

[2] This superb translation of Isaiah's great ode is borrowed from the works of the late Canon Cheyne, to whose profouud exegesis and literary acumen every Bible student is deeply indebted.

B. Events and Poems of the Year 734 b.c., During
the Campaign of Tiglath Pileser III, In Syria

I. Isaiah's Counsel to Ahaz (Ch. vii. 2-16.)

And it was told the House of David that Aram was confederate with Ephraim. And the heart of Ahaz was moved and the heart of his people, as the trees of the forest are moved by the wind. Then said Yahweh unto Isaiah: Go forth now to meet Ahaz, thou and thy son Shear-jashub, at the end of the conduit of the upper pool on the highway by the fuller's field, and say to him: Be wary, and keep thyself calm; fear not, neither let thy heart be faint because of these two fagends of smoking firebrands, for the fierce anger of Rezin and Syria and of Ben-Remaliah. Because Aram hath proposed evil against thee with Ephraim and Ben-Remaliah, saying: Let us go up against Judah and distress it and win it for ourselves, and appoint Ben-Tabel to be king therein, thus saith Yahweh:

> It shall not stand, neither shall it come to pass.
> For the head of Syria is Damascus,
> And the head of Damascus is Rezin;
> And the head of Ephraim is Samaria,
> And the head of Samaria is Ben-Remaliah.
> If ye will not have faith, ye shall not be established.

And Isaiah spake further unto Ahaz, saying: Ask thee a sign of Yahweh, thy God; ask it either in the deep below or in the height above. But Ahaz said: I will not ask, neither will I test Yahweh. Then Isaiah said: Hear now, O House of David; Is it a small thing for you to weary man, and will ye weary God also? Therefore, Yahweh himself will give you a sign. Behold, a young woman shall conceive and bear a son, and will call his name Immanuel; because, before the boy shall know how to refuse the evil and choose the good, the land, of whose two kings thou art sore afraid, shall be unpeopled.

II. Prophecies of the Ruin of Damascus and Samaria

(Ch. vii, 18-20; viii, 1-4; viii, 5-7; viii, 20b-22)

> Yahweh will hiss unto the flies and to the bees, and they
> Will come and settle between the steep heights
> And in the clefts of the rocks,
> And in all thorn-hedges and in all pastures.
> Yahweh will shave, with the razor that is hired
> Beyond the River,
> The head and the hidden hair, and the beard also
> Will He take away.

Yahweh said unto me: Take thee a large tablet, and write upon it in plain characters, "SWIFT SPOIL, SPEEDY PREY"; and take for Me as faithful witnesses Uriah the priest and Zechariah Ben-Jeberechiah. And I went in unto the prophetess and she conceived and bare a son. Then said Yahweh unto me: Call his name, Maher-shalal-hash-baz;[1] for before the boy shall know how to cry "my father" and "my mother", the riches of Damascus and the spoil of Samaria shall be carried away before the king of Assyria.

[1] The Hebrew words written on the tablet and translated "swift spoil, speedy prey."

Yahweh said further unto me: Forasmuch as this people have rejected the waters of Shiloh that flow softly, and despond because of Rezin and Ben-Remaliah; now, therefore, behold:

Yahweh bringeth on them the waters of the mighty River and great;
It shall rise above all its channels, and overflow all its banks
And sweep onward unto Judah,   flow over and pass beyond,
Reaching even unto the neck   .   .   .   .   .
Yahweh's outspread wings shall cover the full breadth of the land.

Know, ye peoples, and give ear,   all ye far lands of the earth!
Gird yourselves,   yet ye shall be terror-stricken;
Gird yourselves,   yet ye shall be terror-stricken.
Devise a plan,   it shall come to naught;
Declare a word,   but it shall not stand.
For thus Yahweh hath said unto me   calming me with His hand,
Warning me not to follow   the custom of the people:
Call not all a conspiracy that this people call conspiracy;
That which they fear, fear not ye, nor count it
worthy of dread.
Yahweh Sabaoth,   Him count ye holy;
Let Him be your fear,   and let Him be your dread.

He shall be a stone to strike against,
A rock of stumbling, a trap and a snare
To both Houses of Israel, to the dwellers in Jerusalem.
Many shall stumble thereover and fall,
And be broken, and be snared and be taken.

On the Despair of the People

.   .   .   .   he,   for whom there is no daybreak;
And he will pass through it,   hard-pressed and famishing.
And when he is famished,   he will be enraged:
And he will curse his king   and his God, and look upward
.   .   .   .   .   and then to earth will he look,
And behold, distress and gloom,   a dark veil of anguish,
And thick darkness   .   .   .   .   .   .

III.   The Downfall of Damascus and Israel
(Ch. xvii, 1-11)

Lo, the day is at hand when Damascus shall cease to be a city;
Forsaken shall be the cities thereof; they shall become a ruin;
They shall be for flocks lying down,   with none to afright them,
Ephraim shall lose her fastnesses,   Damascus her sovereignty,
And the remnant of Aram shall be   like the glory of Israel,
Saith Yahweh Sabaoth.

In that day shall the glory of Jacob grow dim
And the fatness of his flock become lean.
It shall be as when a harvester gathers standing wheat
And reapeth the ears with his arm.
Yet it shall be as when he gathers ears in the vale of Rephaim,
And gleanings thereof shall be left like beatings of olives,
Two or three on the uppermost bough, four or five
On the boughs of fruit-trees, saith Yahweh Sabaoth.

In that day shall thy cities be deserted
    Like the deserted places of the Hivites and the Amorites
Because thou hast forgotten the God of thy safety,
    And hast not remembered the rock that is thy bulwark.
Therefore, though thou plantedst little gardens
        With shoots for Adonis,
And didst set them with slips from a stranger's garden;
    Though, as soon as thou didst plant them,
        Thou didst fence them in,
And didst early bring thy shoots to blossom;
The harvest shall vanish in a day of sickness,
        And desperate pain.

C.   Poems of the Year 722 b.c. When the Kingdom of Israel
    Was Destroyed, and the Ten Tribes Carried Away

I. The Signal—Remarkable Preservation of Judah
(Ch. xvii, 12-14 [1])

Woe! the tumult of many nations!
Like the tumult of the seas is their uproar;
    And the tumult of rushing nations,
Like the roaring of mighty waters is their roar.
But when He rebukes them, they flee afar off,
And are driven like the chaff of mountain threshing-floors
        Before the wind,
    And like whirling dust before the tempest.

At eventide, behold terror! Before morning, they are gone!
Be this the lot of our spoilers, the lot of our plunderers!

II. A Lament on the Fall of Samaria
(Ch. xxviii, 1-4)

Woe! the proud coronets of the drunkards of Ephraim!
And the fading flower of her glorious beauty
    Which crowned the rich valley of those
        Who by wine are down-smitten!

Behold, Yahweh hath at hand a mighty weapon.
    Like a storm of hail,   a destroying tempest,
Like a storm of rushing   overflowing waters,
He casts down to earth   with violence.
    They shall be trampled underfoot,
    The proud coronets of the drunkards of Ephraim
And the fading flower of her beauteous adornment
    Which crowned the rich valley,—
They shall be like an early fig before the fruit-season
Which, as soon as a man has in his hand, he swalloweth.

III. A Fragment on the Same Subject
(Ch. i, 29-31)

Because of the terebinths in which ye had pleasure,
        Ye shall be shamed,
And will blush for the gardens which ye have chosen!
For ye shall be like a terebinth whose eaves
        Are withered,

[1] There is an interval of eleven years between Ch. xvii, 11, and the addition, vv. 12-14; during which time Tiglath Pileser III began, and Shalmanezer IV, and Sargon completed the conquest of all Syria (Aram) and Israel. But Judah was mercifully spared.

And like a garden that hath no water.
The strong man will be as tow, his work as a spark,
They shall both burn together, and none will quench them.

ON THE FATE OF THE PHILISTINES (c. 720 B.C.)
(Ch. xiv, 29-32)

Rejoice not in all thy borders, Philistia,[1]
That the rod that smote thee is broken!
For out of the serpent's root will issue a basilisk,
And a flying dragon will be its fruit.

The poor will feed on My meadows,
And the needy will lie down securely;
But thy seed will I kill with famine,
And thy remnant will I slay.

Howl, O gate! Cry, O city!
Faint in all thy borders, Philistia!
For out of the north cometh the smoke of the foe,
And no straggler is found in his levies.

And what will the king of My people answer
If messengers of a nation should ask of him?
That Yahweh hath founded Zion,
And in her shall the afflicted of His People find refuge.

D. THE LAST DECADE OF ISAIAH'S CAREER
AS POET AND COUNSELLOR TO THE KING

(711-701 B.C.)

I. OF ASSYRIA, THE INSTRUMENT OF YAHWEH'S JUDGMENTS
(Ch. x, 5-9, 13-14; xiv, 24-26; xii, 27-32)

Woe! Asshur, the rod of Mine anger,
    And the staff of Mine indignation!
Against an impious nation am I wont to send him
And against the objects of My wrath to give him a charge
    To take the spoil   and to seize the booty
And to trample them down   like mire in the streets.

Howbeit, he meaneth not so   nor doth his mind so plan;
To destroy in his intent,   to cut off nations not a few,
    Are not my captains   all kings? he saith
    Hath not Calno fared   like Carchemish?
Is not Hamath as Arpad,   Or Samaria like Damascus?
    By the strength of my hand have I done it,
    By my wisdom,   for I am prudent.
I have changed the bounds of the peoples
And I have robbed their treasuries,
And I have brought low,   those that were seated high.
    My hand hath found the riches of the peoples
        As in a nest,
    As one gathereth eggs that are forsaken
    Have I carried off all the earth.
None fluttered a wing or opened a beak or chirped.

    Therefore Yahweh Sabaoth hath sworn:
Surely, as I have planned,   so shall it be;
And as I have purposed   so it shall stand.

That I will break Asshur in My land,
And upon My mountains I will tread him underfoot.
This is the purpose that is purposed upon the whole earth
This is the hand outstretched,   over all nations.
Yahweh Sabaoth hath purposed,   who shall thwart Him?
His is the outstretched hand,   who can turn it back?

His burden will be removed from thy shoulder,
And his yoke shall no more press thy neck.

A FRAGMENT UPON THE SAME SUBJECT

Behold!   .   .   .   .   the foe hath come to Aiath!
He hath passed through Migron   he layeth up his baggage
                    At Michmash.
He goes over the pass;   in Geba he halts for the night.
Ramah is terror-stricken,   Saul's Gibeah is fleeing!
Cry with a shrill voice,   O daughter of Gallim!
Hearken, O Laish! answer her, Anathoth! Madmenah is in flight.
The dwellers in Gebim flee to cover;
This very day he will halt in Nob; he shaketh his fist at Zion,
                    At the hill of Jerusalem!

II.   CONCERNING THE CAPTIVITY OF EGYPT AND ETHIOPIA

(Ch. xx, 1-6)

In the year that the Tartan came to Ashdod, sent by Sargon, king of Assyria, and assaulted Ashdod and took it, Yahweh said unto Isaiah the son of Amoz: Go, and loose the sackcloth from thy loins, and put off thy shoe from off thy foot; and he did so, walking naked and barefoot. And Yahweh said: Like as My servant Isaiah hath gone naked and barefoot three years as a sign and a warning to Egypt and Ethiopia, so will the king of Assyria lead away the captives of Egypt and the exiles of Ethiopia, young and old, naked and barefoot, and their bodies exposed. And those who looked to Ethiopia and boasted of Egypt will be dismayed and disappointed. And the inhabitants of this coast will say in that day: Truly, if such is the plight of those to whom we looked, and to whom we fled for help to be delivered from the king of Assyria, how can we ourselves hope to escape?

III.   WARNING TO JERUSALEM, SEEING THAT SHE HAS LEARNED NOTHING FROM THE FALL OF ISRAEL

(Ch. xxviii, 7-22)

*   *   *   *   *   *   *

But these also reel with wine, and stagger with strong drink!
The priest and the prophet are confused because of wine.
They reel, telling their visions; they totter, giving judgment.
        Their tables are full   of filthy vomit;
                No place is clean.

"To whom," say they, would he teach knowledge, and to whom explain a revelation? To weanlings just parted from the breast? For he is ever gibbering in a strange tongue; çav la çav, çav la çav, qav la qav, qav la qav; here a word, there a word. Will he verily speak to this people with stammering lips and in an alien tongue,[1]—he, who used to say to them: This is the true rest, give ye rest to the weary; this is the true refreshment?" But they would not hear. So to them the word of Yahweh shall indeed come çav la çav, çav la çav; qav la qav, qav la qav, here a word, there a word; so that, as they go, they may stumble and fall backward, and be shattered, be ensnared, and be taken.[1]

Wherefore, hear the word of Yahweh,   ye scoffers!
 Rulers of the people which is in Jerusalem,
Because ye have said: We have made a covenant with death,
 And with Sheol we are in agreement;
The overwhelming scourge, when it passes, will not reach us,
For we have made lies our refuge; by deceit are we hidden,—
 Therefore thus saith Yahweh:
Behold, I lay in Zion a stone,   a tried and precious stone,
A foundation corner-stone.   He who believes
 Will be firmly planted.
 I will make justice the measuring-line
 And righteousness the plumb-weight.
Hail shall sweep away your hiding-place,
 Waters shall overwhelm the hiding-place,
And your covenant with death shall be annulled;
 Your agreement with Sheol shall not stand.
 When the whelming scourge passeth through,
 By it shall ye be beaten down.
As often as it passeth through, it shall bear you away.
Morning by morning shall it pass through, by day and night.
Then shall it be sheer terror to understand the message.

 For Yahweh will rise up as in Mount Perazim,
 (He will be wroth as in the valley of Gibeon)
 To do His work (strange is His work),
 To carry through His task (strange is His task)!

Now therefore, be ye not scoffers lest your bands be made strong.
For a decree of utter destruction have I heard from
          Yahweh Sabaoth.

IV. THE FATE OF JERUSALEM, OF ARIEL, THE ALTAR OF GOD
OR HIS HEARTH-FIRE

(Written c. 703)

(Ch. xxix, 1-6, 9-10, 13-14)

Alas, Ariel! Ariel! city against which David encamped!
Add ye year to year!   Let feasts run their full course!
Then will I distress Ariel,   there shall be moaning
 And bemoaning;
And she shall be to Me   a true Hearth-of-God.
Like David will I encamp against thee,
And will lay siege against thee.
I will close thee in with mounds,
 And will set up forts against thee.
Then, being humbled, thou wilt speak from the ground.
And thy speech will come   submissively out of the dust.

 * * * * * * *

[1] No one has yet found these syllables in any ancient or newly-discovered language. To the early translators they represented words of wisdom; they are but the gibberish by which the scoffers mock at Isaiah's warnings, unintelligible to them.

Then suddenly, full suddenly,   shall Ariel be punished.
Yahweh Sabaoth will send   thunder and earthquake,
The noise of a whirlwind   and tempest, with flame
          Of devouring fire.

*   *   *   *   *   *   *

Stupefy yourselves, and be stupid! Blind yourselves and be blind!
Be ye drunken but not with wine; stagger, but not with strong drink!
For Yahweh hath poured out upon you a spirit of deep sleep,
And hath closed your ears, and covered your hands.

Thus saith Yahweh: Forasmuch as this people draw near Me with
their mouth, and honor Me with their lips, but their heart they keep
from Me, and their fear of Me is but a precept of men, learned by rote;
therefore, behold,

I will again do a marvelous work   among this people,
•   Even an astonishing work   and a wonder; so that
The wisdom of their wise men   shall perish,
The discernment of their sages   shall disappear.

V. Fragments Against the Egyptian Alliance
(Ch. xxix, 15; xxx, 1-5, 6-7a)

Woe unto those who from Yahweh   deeply hide their purpose
So that their work is done   in the dark; and they say:
    Who seeth us? and who knoweth of us?   .   .   .
Woe to the unruly sons, saith Yahweh; carrying out
A purpose that is not Mine   and concluding a treaty
    Contrary to My spirit, adding sin to sin!

Who set forth on the way to Egypt without asking
          My counsel,
To flee to the strength of Pharaoh, and take shelter
          In the shadow of Egypt.
Such shelter will turn to your shame, and the refuge
          To your confusion,
For though the princes of Zoan are his vassals,
And his messengers have come to Hanes,
They will all be ashamed of a people that cannot profit them
          Which bring neither help nor profit,
          But disappointment and disgrace.

Through a land of disgrace and anguish, of roaring lions,
    Whence come the viper,   and the flying serpent,
    They bring their wealth   on the backs of young asses,
    And their treasures   upon the humps of camels,
To a people that can profit no one, whose help
          Is but vapor and emptiness.

VI. On the Coming Ruin of the State, and Its Cause
(Ch. xxx, 8-17)

Now, go in, write it down on a tablet,
          Inscribe it on a scroll,
That it may serve in days to come as a testimony for ever.
For it is a rebellious people, lying children,
Children that refuse to hear the teaching of Yahweh.

That say to the seers: See not! to the prophets:
    Do not prophesy to us right things!
Speak unto us smooth things,   prophesy delusions.
    Turn out of the way,   go aside from the path!
    Trouble us no more   with Israel's Holy One!

Thus saith therefore Israel's Holy One: Because ye despise this word, and trust in oppression and perversity and rely thereon, therefore this iniquity shall be unto you as a breach swelling out in a high wall, ready to fall, whose breaking cometh suddenly, in a moment. Yea, it breaketh as one dasheth a potter's vessel to pieces, shattering it ruthlessly, so that there shall not be found a sherd among its pieces with which to take up fire from a hearth, or to draw water out of a cistern. For thus saith Yahweh your God, Israel's Holy One:

In returning and quietness shall be your safety,
    In quietness and faith shall be your strength.

But ye have refused, saying:

Nay, for we will fly upon horses.   Therefore shall ye flee!
We will ride upon swift ones.   They that pursue you shall
    be swift.
Ye shall flee at a war-cry of five, till your remnant shall be
As a pole on the top of a mountain, as a signal set on a hill.

VII. ANOTHER FRAGMENT ON THE EGYPTIAN ALLIANCE

(Ch. xxxi, 1-3)

Woe unto those that go down   to Egypt for help!
Who rely on horses and trust in chariots, because they are many;
And in horsemen because they are exceedingly strong;
But they look not to the Holy One of Israel, nor seek Yahweh!

Yet He too is wise, and bringeth evil to pass,
    Nor hath He recalled His words.
He will arise against the house of evil-doers,
    And against those who help the workers of wickedness.

But the Egyptians are men, not God;
    Their horses are flesh, not spirit.
Yahweh will stretch out His hand, he that helpeth will stumble
    And he that is helped shall fall.
    All shall come to an end together.

VIII. ANOTHER FRAGMENT ON THE SAME

(xxxi, 4)

Thus hath Yahweh said unto me:
Like as the old or the young lion growls over his prey
When the band of shepherds is summoned against him,
But at their shouting is not dismayed,
    and by their noise is not daunted,
So will Yahweh Sabaoth come down to fight
Against Mount Zion, and against the hill thereof.

IX. AGAINST THE PREFECT OF THE PALACE
(Ch. xxii, 15-18)

Thus saith Yahweh Sabaoth: Go to the Prefect and say, What right hast thou here and what kin hast thou here, that thou hast hewn out a sepulchre for thyself here? Thou that hast hewn out a sepulchre for thyself in the rock, behold, Yahweh will hurl thee up and down; yea, He will wind thee round and round; He will violently roll and toss thee like a ball into a wide-stretching land. Thither shalt thou go to die, and thither will go thy splendid chariots, thou disgrace of the house of thy master!

X. TWO FRAGMENTS ON WHICH LATER WRITERS BUILT UP THE ORACLE ON MOAB (Ch. xv-xvi) AND THAT ON KEDAR (Ch. xxi, 11-15)

In three years, exactly measured, shall Moab's glory become contemptible, despite all that great tumult; and the remnant shall be very small and without strength.

In a year more, exactly measured, all the glory of Kedar shall be past; and the number of the archers, the mighty men of the Children of Kedar, shall be diminished. Yahweh, the God of Israel, hath spoken it.

(Ch. xvi, 14; xxi, 16-17)

XI. THE DESTRUCTION OF THE ASSYRIAN ARMY
(Ch. xviii, 1-6)

Ah, land of the shrill buzzing of insects' wings,
Which sendest ambassadors by the sea in skiffs of papyrus
Over the waters!
Depart, ye fleet messengers, to a nation tall and of glossy skin,
To a people dreaded far and wide, a nation sturdy and heroic,
Whose land rivers divide!
All ye inhabitants of the world and dwellers on the earth,
When an ensign is lifted up on the mountains, see ye!
When the horn is blown, hear ye!
For thus hath Yahweh said unto me:
I will hold Me still and look on from My dwelling-place.
Like clear heat in sunshine, as the dewy mist during harvest.
Before the harvest, when the bloom is over,
And the bud becometh a ripening grape,
He will lop off the branches with pruning-hooks,
And cut off and cast away the young shoots.
Both will be left for ravenous birds, and for beasts of prey,
Thereon the wild birds will summer, and the beasts of the land
shall winter.

XII. THE POET'S LAST APPEAL TO HIS PEOPLE TO REPENT
701 B.C. (Ch. i, 2-26)

Hear, O heavens, and give ear, O earth! for Yahweh hath spoken.
Sons have I reared and set on high
But they have rebelled against Me.
The ox knoweth its owner, and the ass his master's crib,
But Israel doth not know, My people do not consider.

Ah, sinful people! seed of evil-doers!
Guilt-laden nation, degenerate children!
They have forsaken Yahweh, spurned Israel's Holy One!
They have turned away backward.

On what part can ye still be smitten,
Seeing ye revolt more and more?
The whole head is sick, and the whole heart faint;
From the sole of the foot to the head, there is no sound part.
Nothing but wounds and bruises and putrefying sores,
That have not been pressed nor bound up nor softened with oil.
Your land is a desolation, your cities are burned with fire;
Your arable land, strangers devour it before your face,
Zion is left like a booth in a vineyard,
As a lodge in a garden of cucumbers, as a besieged city.
Except Yahweh Sabaoth had left us a very small remnant,
We should have been as Sodom, like unto Gomorrah.

Hear the word of Yahweh, ye rulers of Sodom!
Give ear to the law of our God, ye people of Gomorrah!
To what purpose is the multitude of your sacrifices unto Me?
Saith Yahweh.
I am sated with burnt-offerings of rams, with the fat of beasts;
In the blood of bullocks and lambs and goats, I have no delight.
When ye come before My holy court, who hath required this of you?

No more may ye trample My courts nor bring Me vain oblations;
They are an abomination unto Me; neither can I endure
Your new moons and sabbaths, your fasts, your calling of
assemblies and solemn meetings;
They are an encumbrance to Me, I am tired of hearing them.

If ye spread forth your hands, I will hide Mine eyes from you;
Yea, when ye make many prayers, I will not hear;
Your hands are full of blood.
Wash you, make you clean! Let Me see the evil of your doings no more.
Seek justice, relieve the oppressed; right the orphan;
Plead for the widow.

Come now, and let us reason together; saith Yahweh.
Though your sins be as scarlet, they may become white as snow;
Though they be red as crimson, they may become as wool.
If ye be willing and obedient, ye shall eat the good of the land.
But if ye refuse and rebel, by the sword ye shall be eaten.
The mouth of Yahweh hath spoken.

O, how hath she become a harlot, the faithful city!
Zion, which was full of justice, where righteousness abode!
Thy silver is changed to dross, thy wine is a mixed juice;
Thy rulers are unruly, they are companions of thieves.
Every one loveth bribes and runneth after rewards;
The cause of the widow is disregarded,
They right not the fatherless one.

Therefore this is the oracle of Yahweh,
The hero of Israel.
Aha, I will ease Me of Mine adversaries,
And take vengeance on Mine enemies!
I will turn Mine hand against thee,
In the furnace I will smelt out thy dross.
I will take away all thine alloy.
I will restore thy judges to be as at first,
And thy counsellors as at the beginning.

Thereafter, thou shalt be called
THE CITY OF RIGHTEOUSNESS. THE FAITHFUL CITY.

XIII. ISAIAH'S LAST POEM (701 B.C.)

A LAMENT OVER THE USELESSNESS OF HIS PREACHING, AND HIS PREVISION OF THE END.

(Ch. xxii, 1-14)

What aileth thee now, that all thy people
    Are gone up to the house-tops?
Thou that art full of uproar, a tumultuous city, a joyous town?
Thy slain are not slain with the sword, nor fallen in battle;
All thy chieftains fled together without the shooting of a bow.
    They were made prisoners;   all thine who were seized
Were made prisoners together,   though they had fled far away.

Therefore I say: Look away from me! Let me weep bitterly!
    Strive not to comfort me for the destruction of my people!
For a day of tumult, of trampling and of confusion cometh
    From Yahweh Sabaoth.
In the Valley of Vision they break down the wall, and their cry
    Reacheth the mountains.

They come from far; a great nation from the ends of the earth
Elam took up the quiver; they came with troops of men,
    Yea, even horsemen!
And Kir uncovered the shield; thy fairest vales were full of chariots.
And the horsemen set them in array against the gates,
And the enemy drew aside the screen of Judah.

Then ye looked to the armor   in the House of the Forest,
And ye saw that the breaches   in David's city were many;
But ye looked not to Him   who had prepared all this,
And Him ye did not regard   who fashioned it long ago.
Then did Yahweh Sabaoth call you   to weeping and lamentation,
    To baldness and to girding   with sackcloth;
But behold! joy and gladness,   slaughtering of sheep
And killing of oxen; eating and drinking; for ye thought:
    To-morrow we may die!

But thus Yahweh Sabaoth hath revealed Himself in mine ears;
NEVER CAN THIS YOUR INIQUITY BE CANCELLED TILL YE DIE![1]

[1] Chapters xxxvi-xxxix, formerly included in Part I of the Book of Isaiah, ascribed to Isaiah I, are also, almost *verbatim*, in 2 Kings, xviii 13-xx, 18. Both may have been derived from the same records, but evidently neither was written by Isaiah. There are even, in both, two different descriptions of the same event.

THE POEMS OF THE PROPHET MICAH

I. The Coming of Yahweh in Judgment
(Ch. i, 2-ii, 11)

Hear, all ye people!
Hearken, O Earth,   and all that is therein,
And let the God Yahweh   be witness against you,
Yahweh, from His holy temple.

For behold! Yahweh cometh forth out of His place,
And will come down and tread upon the high places of earth.
And the mountains shall be smitten under Him,
And the valleys shall be cleft,
As wax before the fire, and as waters poured down
A steep place.
For the transgression of Jacob is all this,
For the sins of the House of Israel.

What is the transgression of Jacob? Is it not Samaria?
And what the high places of Judah? Is it not Jerusalem?
Therefore I will make Samaria a heap in the field,
A place for planting vineyards,
I will pour down the stones thereof into the valley,
And the foundations thereof I will uncover.
All her graven images   shall be beaten to pieces,
And all her hires   shall be burned with fire;
For of the hire of a harlot hath she gathered them,
And unto the hire of a harlot shall they return.

For this I will wail and howl, I will go stripped and naked;
I will make a wail like jackals and a mourning like owls.
For her wound is incurable,   it is come even to Judah.
It runneth to the plate of My people.
Even to Jerusalem.

Declare ye it not in Gath,   weep ye not at all!
In the house of Aphrah,   roll ye in the dust!
Pass on, thou woman of Saphir in nakedness and shame!
He shall take from you   the standing-place therof.
For the dweller in Haroth   waiteth anxiously for good;
But from Yahweh evil cometh unto the gates of Jerusalem.

Bind the chariot to swift steeds, O dweller in Lachish!
She was the beginner of sin   to the daughter of Zion.
For the offenses of Israel   are found in thee,
Therefore shalt thou give a parting-gift to Moresh-Gath.
The houses of Achzib shall be deceitful things
To the kings of Israel.

Yet will I bring thee an heir, O inhabitant of Mareshah;
The glory of Israel shall come even unto Adullam.
Make thee bald and poll thee   for thy delicate children;
      Make thee bald as the eagle,
        For they go from thee into exile.

Woe to them that devise iniquity and work evil upon their beds!
When the morning is light they act, since it is in their power.
They covet fields and seize them, and houses and take them.
      Thus they oppress a man and his house,
        Yea, a man and his heritage.
      Therefore thus saith Yahweh:
Behold, against this family   do I devise an evil,
      From which ye shall not save your necks.
Neither shall ye walk haughtily, for it shall be an evil time.

      In that day shall they take up a parable against you,
        And lament with a doleful lamentation, and say:
We are utterly ruined; He changeth the portion of my people.
      How He hath removed it from me!
      Instead of restoring our fields, he divideth them.
Therefore thou shalt have none to cast a lot
      In the congregation of Yahweh.

      Prophesy not! say they to the prophets.
They will not be prophesied to that they need not be shamed.
      O thou that is called the House of Jacob!
      Is the Spirit of Yahweh bound?
      Are these His ways?
Do not My words do good to him that walketh aright?
      But of late, My people is risen up as an enemy;
      With the mantle, ye strip away the garment
From men that are passing quietly, as those averse to contention.
      The women of My people have ye cast out
      From their pleasant houses;
From their young children ye take away My glory forever.

Arise now and get you gone, for this is no place to rest!
      Because of its foulness,
It shall destroy you with a great destruction.

II. AGAINST THE CRIMES OF THOSE IN HIGH PLACES
(Ch. iii, 1-12)

Hear now, ye heads of Jacob
And ye judges of the House of Israel!
      Ought ye not to know justice,
Ye haters of good, and lovers of evil?
Who strip off My people's skin, and their flesh from their bones;
      Who devour My people's flesh,
Break their bones and chop them in pieces,
Like that which is in the pot, like meat in the cooking-pot.

Then will they cry to Yahweh, but He will not answer;
      Yea, then will He hide His face from them
      According to the evil of their doings.

Thus saith Yahweh to the prophets that make my people to err,
That cry: Peace! when they have anything between their teeth;
      And whoso putteth not into their mouths,
      Against him they prepare war.

Therefore it shall be night unto you that ye shall have no vision,
And it shall be dark unto you that ye may not divine.
And the sun shall go down upon the prophets
And the day shall be dark over them;
And the seers shall be put to shame, and the diviners baffled.
They shall cover their lips, for Yahweh shall return no answer.

But I, verily, am full of power, of justice and might,
By the Spirit of Yahweh,
To declare unto Jacob his transgression,
And to Israel his sin.

Hear this, I pray you, ye Heads of the House of Jacob,
And ye Rulers of the House of Israel!
That abhor justice and pervert all equity;
That build up Zion with blood, and Jerusalem with iniquity.
And her prophets divine for money; yet they lean upon Yahweh.
And say: Is not Yahweh in the midst of us?
No evil shall come upon us!

Therefore, for your sake, shall Zion be ploughed as a field,
And Jerusalem! She shall become heaps of ruins,
And the mount of Yahweh's House as the high forest-places.

III. AN EXHORTATION TO REPENTANCE AND COURAGE
(Ch. iv, 9-14)

Now, why dost thou cry out aloud?
Is there no king in thee?   Is thy counsellor perished,
That pangs have taken thee   as of a woman in travail?
Be in pain and labor to bring forth,
O daughter of Zion,   as doth a woman in travail.
For now thou shalt go forth from the city,
And shalt dwell in the field.
There shalt thou be rescued, there shall Yahweh redeem thee
From the hand of thine enemies.

And now many nations are assembled against thee,
They say: Let her be defiled, and let our eye gaze on Zion!
But they know not the thoughts of Yahweh,
Neither understand they His counsel;
For He hath gathered them as sheaves to the threshing-floor.

Arise and thresh, O daughter of Zion!
For I will make thy horns iron, I will make thy hoofs brass,
And thou shalt beat in pieces many peoples.
And thou shalt devote their gain unto Yahweh.
And consecrate their substance unto the Lord of the earth.

Now, gather thyself in troops, O daughter of troops!
They have laid siege against us.
They smite the Judge of Israel
With a rod upon the cheek.

IV. Two Fragments Attributable to Micah [1]

(Ch. vi, 1-4b; vv. 6, 8)

Hear ye now what Yahweh saith!
Arise, contend thou before the mountains,
   And let the hills hear thy voice.
Hear, O ye mountains, Yahweh's controversy,
And ye enduring rocks, the foundations of the earth.
For Yahweh hath a controversy with His people,
   And He will plead with Israel.

O My people, what have I done unto thee,
   And wherein have I wearied thee?
     Testify against Me.
For I brought thee up out of the land of Egypt,
And redeemed thee out of the house of bondage.

    *   *   *   *

Wherewith shall I come before Yahweh,
   And bow myself before God on high?

    *   *   *   *

It hath been told thee, O man, what is good,
And what Yahweh doth require of thee;
Only to do justly,   and love mercy,
And to walk humbly with thy God.

[1] The rest of the "Book of Micah," viz., chapters five and seven, are indisputably post-exilic, although some fragments of Micah's sayings may be preserved in them; to this period alsc belong the few lines omitted from chapters two and three, and most of chapter four. All these passages will be found in Part II.

SUPPLEMENT TO J'S HISTORY OF THE PEOPLE
OF ISRAEL

BY JE, COMPILER OF THE WORKS OF J AND E

SECTION I.—The death of Jeroboam II, king of Israel, and the accesion of Azariah (Uzziah) to the throne of Judah. The swift succession of usurpers in Israel. The reign of Pekah (Pekaiah?) and the first invasion by Assyria. The reigns of Jotham and Ahaz in Judah. Hoshea reigns in Israel. The second invasion of Assyria; the siege of Samaria, and the fall of the Northern Kingdom (2 Ki. xv-xvii.) *Materials:* Chiefly the "Chronicles" of the kings of Judah and of Israel, constantly referred to by JE; but evidently also, accounts of eye-witnesses, himself and others; probably too the Temple Records.

Now the rest of the acts of Jeroboam, and all that he did, and his might, how he warred, and how he recovered Damascus and Hamath for Judah in Israel, are they not written in the book of the chronicles of the kings of Israel? And Jeroboam slept with his fathers, even with the kings of Israel; and Zechariah his son reigned in his stead.[1]

In the twenty and seventh year of Jeroboam, king of Israel, began Azariah son of Amaziah, king of Judah, to reign. Sixteen years old was he when he began to reign; and he reigned two and fifty years in Jerusalem; and his mother's name was Jecoliah of Jerusalem. And he did right in the sight of Yahweh, according to all that his father Amaziah had done. But Yahweh smote the king so that he was a leper to the day of his death; and he dwelt in a house apart. And Jotham, the king's son was over the household, judging the people of the land. Now the rest of the acts of Azariah, and all that he did, are they not written in the book of the Chronicles of the Kings of Judah? And Azariah slept with his fathers; and they buried him with his fathers in the city of David; and Jotham his son reigned in his stead.

In the thirty and eighth year of Azariah king of Judah did Zechariah the son of Jeroboam reign over Israel in Samaria six months. And Shallum the son of Jabesh conspired against him, and smote him before the people, and slew him, and reigned in his stead. Now the rest of the acts of Zechariah; behold, they are written in the book of the Chronicles of the Kings of Israel. This was the word of Yahweh which He spake unto Jehu, saying: Thy sons to the fourth generation shall sit upon the throne of Israel. And so it came to pass.

---

[1] As E wrote only of the earlier acts of Jeroboam, it is presumable that he died before him, and it was left to JE to record his death. The apparent abruptness of the above opening is therefore due to the fact that JE was merely continuing the formulæ he had used before in trying to combine and synchronize the works of J and E. See table of Kings in Story of Elisha, p. 245.

Shallum the son of Jabesh began to reign in the nine and twentieth year of Uzziah (Azariah) king of Judah; and he reigned the space of a month in Samaria. And Menahem, the son of Gadi, went up from Tirzah and came to Samaria, and smote Shallum the son of Jabesh in Samaria, and reigned in his stead. Now the rest of the acts of Shallum and the conspiracy that he made, behold, they are written in the book of the Chronicles of the Kings of Israel.

Then Menahem smote Tiphsah and all that were therein, because they opened not to him, therefore he smote it; and all the women with child he ripped up. In the nine and twentieth year of Azariah, king of Judah, began Menahem the son of Gadi to reign over Israel; and he reigned ten years in Samaria. There came against the land Pul [Tiglath Pileser III] the king of Assyria; and Menahem gave Pul a thousand talents of silver, that his hand might be with him to confirm the kingdom in his hand. And Menahem exacted the money of Israel, even of all the mighty men of wealth, of each man twenty shekels of silver to give to the king of Assyria. So the king of Assyria turned back, and stayed not there in the land. Now the rest of the acts of Menahem, and all that he did, are they not written in the book of the chronicles of the kings of Israel? And Menahem slept with his fathers; and Pekaiah his son reigned in his stead.[1] In the fiftieth year of Azariah, king of Judah, Pekaiah the son of Menahem began to reign over Israel in Samaria; and he reigned two years. And Pekah the son of Remaliah, his captain, conspired against him, and smote him in Samaria, in the castle of the king's house, by Argob and by Arieh; and with him were fifty men of the Gileadites; and he slew him, and reigned in his stead. Now the rest of the acts of Pekaiah, and all that he did, behold, they are written in the book of the Chronicles of the Kings of Israel.

In the two and fiftieth year of Azariah, king of Judah, Pekah the son of Remaliah began to reign over Israel in Samaria, and reigned twenty years. In the days of Pekah, king of Israel, came Tiglath Pileser, king of Assyria, and took Ijon and Abel-beth-Maacah, and Janoah and Kedesh and Hazor, and Gilead, all the land of Napthtali; and he carried them captive to Assyria.

And Hoshea the son of Elah made a conspiracy against Pekah the son of Remaliah and smote him, and slew him, and reigned in his stead, in the twentieth year of Jotham the son of Uzziah. Now the rest of the acts of Pekah, and all that he did, behold, they are written in the book of the Chronicles of the Kings of Israel.

In the second year of Pekah the son of Remaliah, began Jotham the son of Uzziah king of Judah to reign. Five and twenty years old was he when he began to reign; and he reigned sixteen years in Jerusalem; and his mother's name was Jerusha, the daughter of Zadok. And he did that which was right in the sight of Yahweh; he did according to all that his father Uzziah had done. He built the upper gates of the House of Yahweh. Now the rest of the acts of Jotham, and all that he did, are they not written in the book of the Chronicles of the Kings of Judah?

In those days Yahweh began to send against the house of Judah Rezin the king of Aram, and Pekah the son of Remaliah. And Jotham slept with his fathers, and was buried with his fathers in the city of David his father; and Ahaz his son reigned in his stead.

In the seventeenth year of Pekah the son of Remaliah, Ahaz the son of Jotham, king of Judah, began to reign. Twenty years old was Ahaz

---

[1] It is generally doubted whether there was ever a king Pekaiah, or whether the name was not due to a scribal error, followed up by the ordinary formula. As yet there is no proof on either side. We have not those chronicles.

when he began to reign, and he reigned sixteen years in Jerusalem; and he did not that which was right in the sight of Yahweh his God, like David his father, but he walked in the ways of the kings of Israel; yea, and he made his son to pass through fire, according to the abominations of the heathen whom Yahweh cast out from before the Children of Israel. Then Rezin, king of Aram, and Pekah son of Remaliah, king of Israel, came up to Jerusalem to war; and they besieged Ahaz, but could not overcome him. At that time, Rezin king of Aram, recovered Elath for Aram, and drove the Israelites from Elath; and the Edomites came to Elath, and dwell there unto this day.

So Ahaz sent messengers to Tiglah Pileser, king of Assyria, saying: I am thy servant and thy son. Come up and save me out of the hand of the king of Aram, and out of the hand of the king of Israel, who rise up against me. And Ahaz took the silver and gold that was found in the house of Yahweh and in the treasure of the king's house, and sent it for a present to the king of Assyria. And the king of Assyria hearkened unto him; and the king of Assyria went up against Damascus, and took it, and carried the people of it captive to Kir, and slew Rezin.

And king Ahaz went to Damascus to meet Tiglath-Pileser, king of Damascus, and saw the altar that was at Damascus; and king Ahaz sent to Urijah the priest the fashion of the altar and the pattern of it, according to all the workmanship thereof. And Urijah the priest built an altar; according to all that king Ahaz had sent from Damascus, so did Urijah the priest make it against the coming of king Ahaz from Damascus. And when the king was come from Damascus, the king saw the altar; and the king drew near unto the altar, and offered thereon. And he offered his burnt-offering and his meal-offering, and poured his drink-offering, and dashed the blood of the peace-offerings against the altar. And the brazen altar which was before Yahweh, he brought from the forefront of the house, from between his altar and the House of Yahweh, and put it on the south side of his altar. And King Ahaz commanded Urijah the priest, saying: Upon the great altar offer the morning burnt-offering and the evening meal-offering, and the king's burnt-offering and his meal-offering with the burnt-offering of all the people of the land, and their meal-offerings and their drink-offerings; and dash against it all the blood of the burnt-offering, and all the blood of the sacrifice. But the brazen altar shall be for me to look to. Thus did Urijah the priest, according to all that king Ahaz commanded.

And king Ahaz cut off the borders of the bases, and removed the laver from off them; and took down the sea from off the brazen oxen that were under it, and put it on a pavement of stone. And the covered place for the sabbath that they had built in the house and the king's entry without, turned he unto the House of Yahweh because the king of Assyria. Now the rest of the acts of Ahaz which he did, are they not written in the book of the Chronicles of the Kings of Judah? And Ahaz slept with his fathers, and was buried with his fathers in the city of David. And Hezekiah his son reigned in his stead.

In the twelfth year of Ahaz the king of Judah began Hoshea the son of Elah to reign in Samaria over Israel, and he reigned nine years. Against him came up Shalmaneser, king of Assyria, and Hoshea became his servant, and made him presents. But the king of Assyria found conspiracy in Hoshea; for he had sent messengers to So, king of Egypt, and offered no present to the king of Assyria as he had before done year by year. Therefore the king of Assyria shut him up and bound him in prison. Then the king of Assyria came up throughout all the land, and went up to Samaria and besieged it three years. In the ninth year of king Hoshea, the king of Assyria took Samaria, and carried Israel away unto Assyria, and placed them in Halah and in Habor on the river of Gozan, and in the cities of the Medes.

And the king of Assyria brought men from Babylon and from Cutha, and from Avva and from Hamath and from Sepharvaim, and placed them in the cities of Samaria instead of the Children of Israel; and they possessed Samaria, and dwelt in the cities thereof. And so it was at the beginning of their dwelling there, that they feared not Yahweh; therefore Yahweh sent lions among them which killed some of them. Wherefore they spake to the king of Assyria, saying: The nations which thou hast removed and placed in the cities of Samaria, know not the manner of the God of the land; therefore He hath sent lions among them; and behold, they slay them, because they know not the manner of the God of the land.

Then the king of Assyria commanded, saying: Carry thither one of the priests whom ye brought from thence, and let them go and dwell there, and let him teach them the manner of the God of the land. So, one of the priests whom they had carried away from Samaria came and dwelt in Beth-el, and taught them how they should reverence Yahweh. Howbeit, every nation made gods of their own, and put them in the houses of the high places which the Samaritans had made, each nation in the city wherein they dwelt. And the men of Babylon made Succoth-benoth, and the men of Cuth made Nergal, and the men of Hamath made Niblas and Tartak; and the Sepharvites burnt their children in the fire to Adrammelech and Anammelech, the gods of the Sepharvaim. So they feared Yahweh, and served their own gods, after the manner of the nations from among whom they had been carried away. Unto this day, they do after their former manners.

SECTION II.—The Reign of Hezekiah in Judah. His care for the worship of Yahweh alone. His successful campaign against the Philistines. A second and fuller account of the fall of the Kingdom of Israel. The Invasion of Judah by Sennacherib. Details of his campaign, and its end. The appearance of Isaiah the prophet as counsellor of the king. Hezekiah's illness. The embassy from Babylon upon his recovery; the king's imprudence in displaying his treasures, and Isaiah's foresight of the result. Death of Hezekiah and accession of Manasseh. (2 Kings, xviii-xx.)

Materials: From the "Chronicles of the Kings of Judah" combined with two remarkable accounts, from different hands, of the Assyrian invasion.

Now it came to pass in the third year of Hoshea son of Elah, king of Israel, that Hezekiah the son of Ahaz, king of Judah, began to reign. Twenty and five years[1] old was he when he began to reign; and he reigned twenty and nine years in Jerusalem; and his mother's name was Abi, the daughter of Zechariah. And he did right in the sight of Yahweh, according to all that David his father had done. He brake in pieces the brazen serpent that Moses had made, for unto those days the Children of Israel did burn incense to it; and he called it Nehushtan (a thing of brass). He trusted in Yahweh, the God of Israel; for he clave

[1] A mistake of the editor. Hezekiah was at his accession certainly under twenty; some say but fifteen years of age.

to Yahweh; he departed not from following Him, but kept His commandments which Yahweh had commanded Moses. And Yahweh was with him; whithersoever he went forth he prospered. He smote the Philistines to Gaza and the borders thereof, from the tower of the watchmen to the fortified city.

And it came to pass in the fourth year of king Hezekiah, which was the seventh year of Hoshea son of Elah, king of Israel, that Shalmaneser, king of Assyria, came up against Samaria and besieged it. And at the end of three years they took it; even in the sixth year of Hezekiah, which was the ninth year of Hoshea, king of Israel, Samaria was taken. And the king of Assyria carried Israel away unto Assyria and put them in Halah, and in Habor, on the river of Gozan, and in the cities of the Medes; because they hearkened not to the voice of Yahweh their God, but transgressed His covenant, even all that Moses the servant of Yahweh commanded, and would not hear it nor do it.

And it came to pass that Sennacherib, king of Assyria, came up against all the fortified cities of Judah and took them. And Hezekiah, king of Judah, sent to the king of Assyria to Lachish, saying: I have offended; return from me; that which thou puttest on me, I will bear. And the king of Assyria appointed unto Hezekiah, king of Judah, three hundred talents of silver and thirty talents of gold. And Hezekiah gave him all the silver which was found in the House of Yahweh and in the treasures of the king's house. At that time did Hezekiah cut off the gold from the doors of the temple of Yahweh, and from the doorposts which he had overland, and gave it to the king of Assyria.

[1] And the king of Assyria sent the Rab-shakeh from Lachish to king Hezekiah with a great force unto Jerusalem. And he took up his position by the conduit of the upper pool, which is in the highway of the fuller's field. And there went out to him Eliakim the son of Hilkiah who was over the household, and Shebna the scribe, and Joab the son of Asaph, the recorder.

And the Rab-shakeh said unto them: Say, I pray you, unto Hezekiah: Thus saith the king of Assyria: What is this confidence that thou dost cherish? Thinkest thou that a mere word of the lips is counsel and strength for war? Now in whom dost thou trust, that thou rebellest against me? Surely thou dost trust in the staff of that splintered reed, even upon Egypt, whereon, if a man lean, it wil run into his hand and pierce it. So is Pharaoh, king of Egypt, unto all that trust in him. Now, therefore, I pray thee, make a wager with my master the king of Assyria: I will give thee two thousand horses, if thou be able on thy part to set riders upon them. How then canst thou repel the onset of one captain, even of the least of my master's servants? And yet thou puttest thy trust on Egypt for chariots and for horsemen. Have I now come up against this land without Yahweh to destroy it? Yahweh Himself said unto me: Go up against that land, and destroy it.

Then said Eliakim and Shebna and Joab unto the Rab-shakeh: Speak, we pray, to thy servants in Aramaic, for we understand it; and speak not with us in Hebrew in the ears of the people that are on the wall. But the Rab-shakeh said unto them: Is it to thy master and to thee that my master hath sent me to speak these words? Is it not to the men that sit on the wall that he hath sent me, and to those who will be compelled to eat and drink filthy food with you? Then the Rab-shakeh stood forth, and cried with a loud voice and said in Hebrew: Hear ye the word of the great king, the king of Assyria. Thus saith the

[1] The first account of Sennacherib's frustrated attempt to take Jerusalem.

king: Let not Hezekiah beguile you; for he is not able to rescue you out of his hand; and let not Hezekiah make you trust in Yahweh, saying: Yahweh will surely rescue us, and this city will not be given into the hand of the king of Assyria. Hearken not to Hezekiah; for thus saith the king of Assyria: Make your peace with me, and come out to me; and ye shall eat, every one, of his own vine and of his fig-tree, and every one shall drink the water of his own cistern, until I come and take you away to a land like your own land, a land of wheat and new wine, a land of olive-yards and vineyards, of bread and of honey, that ye may live and not die.

But the people held their peace, and answered him not a word; for the king's commandment was: Answer him not. Then came Eliakim the son of Hilkiah, the governor of the palace, and Shebna the scribe, and Joab the son of Asaph, the recorder, to Hezekiah with their clothes rent; and told him the words of the Rab-shakeh.

And when king Hezekiah heard it, he rent his clothes and covered himself with sackcloth, and went into the house of Yahweh. And he sent Eliakim, the governor of the palace, and Shebna the scribe, and the elders of the priests unto Isaiah the prophet, the son of Amoz. And they said unto him: Thus saith Hezekiah: This is a day of trouble and of rebuke and of contumely, for children are come to the birth, and there is no strength to bring forth. It may be that Yahweh thy God will hear all the words of the Rab-shakeh, whom the king of Assyria his master hath sent to taunt the living God, and will punish the words which Yahweh, thy God, hath heard. Wherefore, make prayer for the remnant which is left.

So the servants of King Hezekiah came to Isaiah; and Isaiah said unto them: Thus shall ye say to your master: Thus saith Yahweh: Be not afraid of the words that thou hast heard, wherewith the servants of the king of Assyria have blasphemed Me. Surely I will strike him with a groundless fright, that when he shall hear a rumor of ill, he shall return to his own land; and I will cause him to fall by the sword in his own land.

Then the Rab-shakeh returned, and found the king of Assyria still at Lachish. And he heard say of Tirhakah, king of Ethiopia: Behold, he is come out to fight against thee; and when he heard that, he departed. So Sennacherib, king of Assyria, returned and dwelt at Nineveh. And as he was worshipping in the house of Nisroch his god, Adrammelech and Sarezer, his sons, slew him with the sword. But they escaped into the land of Ararat. And Esarhaddon, his son, reigned in his stead.

(SECOND ACCOUNT OF THE WITHDRAWAL OF SENNACHERIB)

And Sennacherib was warring at Libnah; and he sent messengers to Hezekiah saying: . . . . Let not thy God in whom thou trustest deceive thee, saying: Jerusalem shall not be given into the hand of the king of Assyria. Behold, thou thyself hast heard what the kings of Assyria have done to all lands, destroying them utterly; and shalt thou be delivered? Did the gods of the nations which my fathers destroyed deliver them,—Gozan, and Haran, and Reseph, and the Edenites in Telassar? Where is the king of Hamath, and the king of Arpad, and the king of Sepharvaim, of Hena and Ivva? Which among all the gods of these countries have rescued their land out of my hand, that Yahweh should rescue Jerusalem out of my hand?

And Hezekiah took the letter out of the hand of the messengers, and read it, and went up to the House of Yahweh. And Hezekiah spread it before Yahweh and prayed, saying: O Yahweh, the God of Israel, that sittest upon the cherubim! Thou art the God, even Thou alone, of all the kingdoms of the earth; Thou hast made heaven and earth. Incline Thine ear, O Yahweh, and hear; open Thine eyes, O Yahweh, and see; and hear the message of Sennacherib, wherewith he would insult the Living God. Of a truth, O Yahweh, the kings of Assyria have laid waste the nations and their lands, and have cast their gods into the fire; for they were no gods, but the work of men's hands, wood and stone. Therefore they could destroy them. Now, therefore, O Yahweh, our God, save Thou me, I beseech Thee, out of his hand, that all the kingdoms of the earth may know that Thou, Yahweh, Thou alone art God.

Then Isaiah the son of Amoz sent to Hezekiah, saying: Thus saith Yahweh, the God of Israel: Whereas thou hast prayed to Me concerning Sennacherib, king of Assyria, thus saith Yahweh concerning the king of Assyria:

He shall not come into this city,   nor shoot an arrow into it,
Nor come before it with a shield,   nor cast up a mound against it.
        For I will guard this city   that I may save it
              For Mine own Name's sake,
        And for the sake of David, My servant.

And it came to pass that night, that the messenger of Yahweh went forth, and smote in the camp of the Assyrians a hundred and fourscore and five thousand; and when men arose early in the morning, behold, all those men were stark dead.)

In those days was Hezekiah sick unto death. And Isaiah the prophet, the son of Amoz, came to him and said unto him: Thus saith Yahweh: Set thine house in order; for thou shalt die, and not live. Then he turned his face to the wall, and prayed unto Yahweh, saying: Remember now, O Yahweh, I beseech Thee, how I have walked before Thee in truth and with a whole heart, and have done that which is good in Thy sight. And Hezekiah wept sore. And it came to pass, before Isaiah was gone out of the gate, that the word of Yahweh came to him, saying: Return, and say to Hezekiah, the prince of My people: Thus saith Yahweh, the God of David thy father: I have heard thy prayer, I have seen thy tears, I will heal thee; on the third day thou shalt go up into the house of Yahweh. And I will add unto thy days fifteen years; and I will deliver thee and this city out of the hand of the king of Assyria; and I will defend this city for Mine own sake, and for My servant David's sake. And Isaiah said: Take a cake of figs. And they took it and laid it on the boil, and he recovered.

And Hezekiah said unto Isaiah: What shall be the sign that Yahweh will heal me, and that I shall go up unto the house of Yahweh the third day. And Isaiah said: This shall be the sign unto thee from Yahweh, that Yahweh will do the thing that He hath spoken; shall the shadow go forward ten degrees, or go back ten degrees? And Hezekiah answered: It is a light thing for the shadow to decline ten degrees; nay, but let the shadow return backward ten degrees. And Isaiah the prophet cried unto Yahweh; and He brought the shadow ten degrees backward, by which it had gone down on the dial of Ahaz.

At that time the king of Babylon, Merodach-Baladan son of Baladan, sent a letter and a present unto Hezekiah; for he had heard that Hezekiah had been sick. And Hezekiah had pleasure in this, and showed them his treasure-house, the silver and the gold, and the spices and the precious oil, and the house of his armor, and all that was found in his stores; there was nothing in his house nor in his dominion that Hezekiah showed them not. Then came Isaiah the prophet unto king Hezekiah, and said unto him: What said these men, and from whence came they unto thee? And Hezekiah said: They are come from a far country, even from Babylon. And he said: What have they seen in thine house? And Hezekiah answered: All that is in my house have they seen; there is nothing among my treasures that I have not shown them.

Then Isaiah said unto Hezekiah: Hear the word of Yahweh: Behold, the days come, that all that is in thine house, and that which thy fathers have laid up in store unto this day, shall be carried to Babylon; nothing shall be left, saith Yahweh. And of thy sons that shall issue from thee they shall take away; and they shall be officers in the palace of the king of Babylon. Then said Hezekiah unto Isaiah: Good is the word of Yahweh which thou hast spoken. He said, moreover: Is it not so, if peace and truth shall be in my days?

Now the rest of the acts of Hezekiah, and all his might, and how he made the pool and the conduit and brought water into the city, are they not written in the book of the chronicles of the kings of Judah? And Hezekiah slept with his fathers, and Manasseh his son reigned in his stead.[1]

[1] The last three chapters (ch. xviii-xx, A .V.), with the exception of two verses in ch. xviii and some slight changes in phraseology in the other two, are also found in the Book of Isaiah, (A. V. ch. xxxvi-xxxix), where they form a transition from the works formerly all attributed to the prophet of the eighth century to the treasury of poems by unknown writers of the exilic and post exilic ages, (ch. xl-lxvi). It is barely possible that they were collected and inserted in his compilation by JE, for there are indications that he lived until the age of Manasseh; but the vivid realism of the dialogue in ch. xviii, and the noble prayer of Hezekiah in ch. xx, could not have been from his pen. They are now held by many scholars to be by different Deuteronomists; but they are retained here since the question is still not decided. On the other hand, the "Poem of Derision" on Sennacherib (ch. xix, 21-31), is certainly post-exilic, and is therefore omitted.

FROM THE REIGN OF MANASSEH TO THE EXILE (698-584 B.C.)

COMPILED BY P.[1]

(2 Kings, xxi-xxv)

Materials: Chronicles of the kings of Judah, Temple Records, Biography of Jeremiah, and the narratives of eye-witnesses of the events handed down from father to son.

Manasseh was twelve years old when he began to reign, and he reigned five and fifty years in Jerusalem, and his mother's name was Hephzibah. And he did that which was evil in the sight of Yahweh, after the abominations of the nations whom Yahweh had driven out before the Children of Israel. For he built again the high places which his father Hezekiah had destroyed, and he reared up altars for Baal, and made an Asherah, as did Ahab king of Israel, and worshipped all the host of heaven, and served them. And he built altars in the House of Yahweh, whereof Yahweh had said: In Jerusalem have I put My name. And he built altars for all the host of heaven in the two courts of the House of Yahweh. And he made his son to pass through fire, and practised soothsaying, and used enchantments, and appointed them that divined by a ghost or a familiar spirit; he wrought much evil in the sight of Yahweh, to provoke Him. And he set the graven image of the Asherah he had made, in the house of which Yahweh had said to David and to Solomon his son: In this house, and in Jerusalem, which I have chosen out of all the tribes of Israel, will I put My name for ever; neither will I cause the feet of Israel to wander any more out of the land which I gave to their fathers; if only they will observe to do according to all that I have commanded them, and according to all the law that My servant Moses commanded them. But they hearkened not; and Manasseh seduced them to do that which is evil more than did the nations whom Yahweh destroyed before the Children of Israel.

And Yahweh spake by His servants the prophets, saying: Because Manasseh, king of Judah, hath done these abominations, and hath done wickedly above all that the Amorites did that were before him, and hath made Judah also to sin with his idols; therefore thus saith Yahweh, the God of Israel. Behold, I bring much evil upon Jerusalem and Judah, that whosoever shall hear of it, both his ears shall tingle. And I will stretch over Jerusalem the line of Samaria, and the plummet of the house of Ahab; and I will wipe Jerusalem as a man wipeth a dish, wiping it and turning it upside down. And I will cast off the remnant of Mine inheritance, and deliver them into the hand of their enemies; because they have done that which is evil in My sight, and have provoked

[1] P may stand for one writer or many. Possibly they may have been a self-perpetuating committee, appointed by the Sanhedrim at the beginning of the Persian period to arrange the Canon. It is certain that many additions were made even after the LXX translation had been completed.

Me since the day their fathers came forth out of Egypt, even unto this day.

Moreover Manasseh shed very much innocent blood, till he had filled Jerusalem from one end to the other, besides his sin wherewith he made Judah to sin in doing that which was evil in the sight of Yahweh. Now the rest of the acts of Manasseh, and all that he did, and his sin that he sinned, are they not written in the book of the Chronicles of the Kings of Judah? And Manasseh slept with his fathers, and was buried in the garden of his own house, in the garden of Uzzah; and Amon his son reigned in his stead.

Amon was twenty and two years old when he began to reign; and he reigned two years in Jerusalem; and his mother's name was Meshulle-meth, the daughter of Haruz of Jotbah. And he did that which was evil in the sight of Yahweh, as did Manasseh his father. And he walked in all the way that his father had walked in, and served the idols that his father had served, and worshipped them. And he forsook Yahweh, the God of his fathers, and walked not in the way of Yahweh.

And the servants of Amon conspired against him, and put the king to death in his own house. But the people of the land slew all them that had conspired against king Amon; and the people of the land made Josiah his son king in his stead. Now the rest of the acts of Amon which he did, are they not written in the Chronicles of the Kings of Judah? And he was buried in the sepulchre in the garden of Uzzah and Josiah his son reigned in his stead.

Josiah was eight years old when he began to reign; and he reigned thirty and one years in Jerusalem; and his mother's name was Jedidah, the daughter of Adaiah of Bozkath. And he did that which was right in the eyes of Yahweh, and walked in all the way of David his father, and turned not aside to the right hand or to the left.

And it came to pass in the eighteenth year of king Josiah, that the king sent Shaphan the son of Azaliah, the son of Meshullam the scribe, to the House of Yahweh, saying: Go up to Hilkiah the high-priest, that he may sum the money which is brought into the house of Yahweh, which the keepers of the door have gathered of the people; and let them deliver it into the hand of the workmen that have the oversight of the House of Yahweh; and let them give it to the workmen that are in the House of Yahweh to repair the breaches of the house; unto the carpenters, and to the builders, and to the masons; and for buying timber and hewn stone to repair the house. Howbeit there was no reckoning made with them of the money that was delivered into their hand; for they dealt faithfully.

And Hilkiah the high-priest said unto Shaphan the scribe: I have found the Book of the Law in the house of Yahweh. And Hilkiah delivered the book to Shaphan, and he read it. And Shaphan the scribe came unto the king, and reported unto the king, and said: Thy servants have poured out the money that was found in the house, and have delivered it into the hand of the workmen that have oversight of the house of Yahweh. And Shaphan the scribe told the king, saying: Hilkiah the priest hath delivered me a book. And Shaphan read it before the king. And it came to pass when the king had heard the words of the Book of the Law, that he rent his clothes. And the king commanded Hilkiah the priest, and Ahikam the son of Shaphan, and Achbor the son of Micaiah, and Shaphan the scribe, and Asaiah, the king's servant, saying: Go ye, inquire of Yahweh for me, and for the people, and for all Judah, concerning the words of this book that is found; for great is the wrath of Yahweh that is kindled against us, because our fathers have nct hearkened unto the words of this book, to do according to all that which is written concerning us.

So Hilkiah the priest, and Ahikam and Achbor and Shaphan and Asaiah, went unto Huldah the prophetess, the wife of Shallum the son of Tikvah, the son of Harbas, keeper of the wardrobe,—now she dwelt in Jerusalem in the second quarter—and they spake with her. And she said unto them: Thus saith Yahweh, the God of Israel: Tell ye the man that sent you unto me: Thus saith Yahweh: Behold, I will bring evil upon this place, and upon the inhabitants thereof, even all the words of the book which the king of Judah hath read; because they have forsaken Me, and have offered unto other gods, that they might provoke Me with all the work of their hands; therefore My wrath shall be kindled against this place, and it shall not be quenched. But unto the king of Judah, who sent you to inquire of Yahweh, thus shall ye say to him: Thus saith Yahweh, the God of Israel: As touching the words which thou hast heard; because thy heart was tender, and thou didst humble thyself before Yahweh, when thou heardest what I spake against this place, and against the inhabitants thereof, that they should become an astonishment and a curse, and hast rent thy clothes and wept before Me, I also have heard thee, saith Yahweh. Therefore behold, I will gather thee to thy fathers, and thou shalt be gathered to thy grave in peace, neither shall thine eyes see all the evil which I will bring upon this place. And they brought back word unto the king.

And the king sent, and they gathered unto him all the elders of Judah and of Jerusalem. And the king went up to the House of Yahweh, and all the men of Judah and all the inhabitants of Jerusalem with him, and the priests and the prophets and all the people, both small and great; and he read in their ears all the words of the book of the covenant, which was found in the house of Yahweh. And the king stood on the platform, and made a covenant before Yahweh, to walk after Yahweh and to keep His commandments, and His testimonies, and His statutes, with all his heart, and all his soul, to confirm the words of this covenant that were written in this book; and all the people stood to the covenant.

And the king commanded Hilkiah the high-priest, and the priests of the second order, and the keepers of the door, to bring forth out of the temple of Yahweh all the vessels that were made for Baal and for the Asherah, and for all the host of heaven; and he burned them without Jerusalem in the fields of Kidron, and carried the ashes of them unto Beth-el. And he put down the idolatrous priests whom the kings of Judah had ordained to burn incense in the high places in the cities of Judah, and in the places round about Jerusalem; them also that offered unto Baal, to the sun, and to the moon, and to the planets, and to all the host of heaven. And he brought out the Asherah from the House of Yahweh without Jerusalem unto the brook Kidron, and stamped it small to powder, and cast the powder thereof upon the graves of the common people. And he broke down the houses of the sodomites that were in the House of Yahweh, where the women wove coverings for the Asherah. And he brought all the priests out of the cities of Judah, and defiled the high places where the priests had burned incense, from Geba to Beer-sheba; and he broke down the high places of the gates at the entrance of the gate of Joshua the governor of the city, which were on a man's left hand as he entered the gate of the city. (Nevertheless the priests of the high places came not up to the altar of Yahweh in Jerusalem, but they did eat unleavened bread among their brethren.)

And he defiled Topheth which is in the valley of the sons of Hinnom, that no man might make his son or his daughter pass through the fire to Molech. And he took away the horses that the kings of Judah had given to the sun, at the entrance of the House of Yahweh, by the chamber of Nethan-melech, the officer which was in the precincts; and he burned the chariots of the sun with fire. And the altars that were on the roof of the upper chamber of Ahaz, which the kings of Judah had made, and the altars which Manasseh had made in the two courts of the House of Yahweh, did the king break down and beat them down from thence, and cast the dust of them into the brook Kidron. And the high places that were before Jerusalem, which were on the right hand of the mount of corruption, which Solomon had built for Ashtoreth the abomination of the Zidonians, and for Chemosh the abomination of the Moabites, and for Milcom the abomination of the Ammonites, did the king defile. And he brake in pieces the pillars, and cut down the Asherim, and filled their places with the bones of men.

Moreover, the altar that was at Beth-el, and the high place which Jeroboam the son of Nebat, who made Israel to sin, had made; even that altar and the high place he brake down, and he burned the high place and stamped it small to powder, and burned the Asherah. And as Josiah turned himself, he spied the sepulchres that were there in the mount; and he sent and took the bones out of the sepulchres, and burned them upon the altar and defiled it, according to the word of Yahweh, which the man of God proclaimed who prophesied these things. Then he said: What monument is that which I see? And the men of the city told him: It is the sepulchre of the man of God, who came from Judah and prophesied these things that thou hast done against the altar of Beth-el. And he said: Let him be; let no man move his bones. So they let his bones alone, with the bones of the prophet that came out of Samaria. And all the houses also of the high places that were in the cities of Samaria, which the kings of Israel had made to provoke Yahweh, Josiah took away, and did to them all that he had done in Beth-el. And he slew all the priests of the high places that were there upon the altars, and burned men's bones upon them. So he returned to Jerusalem.

And the king commanded all the people, saying: Keep the Passover unto Yahweh your God, as it is written in this book of the covenant. And there was not kept such a passover from the days of the judges that judged Israel, nor in all the days of the kings of Israel, nor of the kings of Judah; but in the eighteenth year of king Josiah was this passover kept to Yahweh in Jerusalem. Moreover them that divined by a ghost or by a familiar spirit, and the teraphim, and the idols, and all the detestable things that were spied in the land of Judah and in Jerusalem, did Josiah put away, that he might perform the words of the law which were written in the book that Hilkiah the priest found in the House of Yahweh. And like him was there no king before him, that turned to Yahweh with all his heart, and with all his soul, and with all his might, according to the law of Moses; neither after him was there any like him.

Now the rest of the acts of Josiah, and all that he did, are they not written in the book of the Chronicles of the Kings of Judah? In his days, Pharaoh-Necho, king of Egypt, went up against the king of Assyria to the river Euphrates, and king Josiah went against him; and he slew him at Megiddo. . . . And his servants carried him in a chariot dead from Megiddo, and brought him to Jerusalem, and buried him in his own sepulchre. And the people of the land took Jehoahaz the son of Josiah, and anointed him and made him king in his father's stead.

Jehoahaz was twenty and three years old when he began to reign, and he reigned three months in Jerusalem, and his mother's name was Hamutal, the daughter of Jeremiah of Libnah. And he did that which was evil in the sight of Yahweh, according to all that his fathers had done. And Pharaoh-Necho put him in bonds at Riblah that he might not reign in Jerusalem; and put the land to a fine of a hundred talents of silver, and a talent of gold. And Pharaoh-Necho made Eliakim the son of Josiah king in the room of Josiah his father, and changed his name to Jehoiakim; but he took Jehoahaz away; and he came to Egypt and died there. And Jehoiakim gave the gold and the silver to Pharaoh; but he taxed the land to give the money according to the commandment of Pharaoh; he exacted the silver and the gold of the people of the land, of every one according to his taxation, to give it to Pharaoh-Necho.

Jehoiakim was twenty and five years old when he began to reign, and he reigned eleven years in Jerusalem; and his mother's name was Zebudah, the daughter of Pedaiah of Rumah. And he did that which was evil in the sight of Yahweh, according to all that his fathers had done. In his days Nebuchadrezzar king of Babylon came up, and Jehoiakim became his servant three years. Then he turned and rebelled against him. And Yahweh sent aganist him bands of the Chaldæans, and bands of the Aramæans, and bands of the Moabites, and bands of the children of Ammon, and sent them against Judah to destroy it, according to the word of Yahweh which He spake by the hand of His servants the prophets. Surely at the commandment of Yahweh came this upon Judah to remove them out of His sight, for the sins of Manasseh according to all that he did; and also for all the innocent blood that he shed; for he filled Jerusalem with innocent blood, and Yahweh would not pardon.

Now the rest of the acts of Jehoiakim, and all that he did, are they not written in the book of the Chronicles of the Kings of Judah? So Jehoiakim slept with his fathers; and Jehoiachin his son reigned in his stead. And the king of Egypt came not again out of his land; for the king of Babylon had taken, from the brook of Egypt unto the river Euphrates, all that pertained to the king of Egypt.

Jehoiachin was eighteen years old when he began to reign, and he reigned in Jerusalem three months; and his mother's name was Nehushta the daughter of Elnathan of Jerusalem. And he did that which was evil in the sight of Yahweh, according to all that his father had done. At that time, the servants of Nebuchadrezzar, king of Babylon, came up to Jerusalem, and the city was besieged. And Nebuchadrezzar, king of Babylon, came unto the city while his servants were besieging it. And Jehoiachin the king of Judah went out to the king of Babylon, he, and his mother, and her servants, and his princes, and his officers; and the king of Babylon took him in the eighth year of his reign. And he carried out thence all the treasures of the House of Yahweh, and the treasures of the king's house, and cut in pieces all the vessels of gold which Solomon, king of Israel, had made for the temple of Yahweh, as Yahweh had said. And he carried away all Jersualem,—all the princes and all the mighty men of valor, even ten thousand captives, and all the craftsmen and the smiths; none remained save the poorest sort of the people of the land. And he carried away to Babylon Jehoiachin, and the king's mother, and the king's wives and his officers and the chief men of the land carried he into captivity from Jerusalem to Babylon. And all the men of might, even seven thousand, all of them strong and apt for war, even them the king of Babylon brought captive to Babylon.

And the king of Babylon made Mattaniah, his father's brother, king in his stead, and changed his name to Zedekiah.

Zedekiah [1] was twenty and one years old when he began to reign, and he reigned eleven years in Jerusalem; and his mother's name was Hamutal the daughter of Jeremiah of Libnah. And he did that which was evil in the sight of Yahweh, according to all that Jehoiakim had done. For through the anger of Jahweh did it come to pass in Jerusalem and Judah, until He had cast them out from His presence.

And Zedekiah rebelled against the king of Babylon. And it came to pass in the ninth year of his reign, in the tenth month, in the tenth day of the month, that Nebuchadrezzar, king of Babylon, came, he and all his army, against Jerusalem, and encamped against it; and they built forts against it round about. So the city was besieged until the eleventh year of king Zedekiah. On the ninth day of the fourth month the famine was sore in the city, so that there was no bread for the people of the land. Then a breach was made into the city, and all the men of war fled by night by the way of the gate between the two walls which was by the king's garden (now the Chaldæans were close to the city round about), and the king went by the way of the Arabah. But the army of the Chaldæans pursued after the king, and overtook him in the plains of Jericho; and all his army was scattered from him. Then they took the king, and carried him up to the king of Babylon to Riblah; and they gave judgment upon him. And they slew the sons of Zedekiah before his eyes, and put out the eyes of Zedekiah, and bound him in fetters, and carried him to Babylon.

Now in the fifth month, on the seventh day of the month, which was the nineteenth year of Nebuchadrezzar, king of Babylon, came Nebuzaradan, the captain of the guard, a servant of the king of Babylon, unto Jerusalem. And he burnt the House of Yahweh, and the king's house; and all the houses of Jerusalem, even every great man's house, burnt he with fire. And all the army of the Chaldæans that were with the captain of the guard-temple, brake down the walls of Jerusalem round about. And the residue of the people that were left in the city, and those that fell away, that fell to the king of Babylon, and the residue of the multitude, did Nebuzaradan, the captain of the guard, carry away captive. But the captain left of the poorest of the land to be vine-dressers and husbandmen.

And the pillars of brass that were in the House of Yahweh, and the bases and the brazen sea that were in the House of Yahweh, did the Chaldæans break in pieces and carry the brass of them to Babylon. And the pots and the shovels and the snuffers and the pans, and all the vsesels of brass wherewith they ministered, took they away. And the fire-pans and the basins, that which was of gold, in gold, and that which was of silver, in silver, the captain of the guard took away. The two pillars, the one sea, and the bases which Solomon made for the House of Yahweh, the brass of these vessels was beyond weight. The height of the one pillar was eighteen cubits, and a capital of brass was upon it, and the height of the capital was three cubits, with network and pomegranates upon the capital round about, all of brass; and like unto these had the second pillar with network.

And the captain of the guard took Seraiah, the chief priest, and Zephaniah the second priest, and the three keepers of the door; and out

[1] The concluding chapter of the Book of Jeremiah, A. V. is taken almost verbatim either from this account in 2 Kings (ch. xxiv, 18-xxv, 30) or from the records used by the historian. For fuller details of the siege and the events following the sack of the city, see Jer. ch. xxxix-xliv, A. V. or Booklet VI of this edition.

of the city he took an officer that was set over the men of war; and
five men of them that saw the king's face, who were found in the city;
and the scribe of the captain of the host, who numbered the people of
the land; and threescore men of the people of the land, that were found
in the city. And Nebuzaradan, the captain of the guard, took them, and
brought them to the king of Babylon to Riblah. And the king of Babylon slew them and put them to death at Riblah in the land of Hamath.

So Judah was carried away captive out of his land. And as for the
people that were left in the land of Judah whom Nebuchadrezzar, king
of Babylon, had left, over them he made Gedaliah the son of Ohikam, the
son of Shaphan, governor.

Now when all the captains of the forces, they and their men, heard
that the king of Babylon had made Gedaliah governor, they came to Gedaliah to Mizpah, even Ishmael the son of Nethaniah, and Johanan the
son of Kareah, and Seraiah the son of Tanhumeth, and Jaazaniah the
son of the Maacathite, they and their men. And Gedaliah sware to them,
and to their men, and said unto them: Fear not because of the servants
of the Chaldæans. Dwell in the land, and serve the king of Babylon,
and it shall be well with you.

But it came to pass in the seventh month, that Ishmael the son of
Nethaniah the son of Elishama of the seed royal, came, and ten men
with him, and smote Gedaliah, that he died, and the Jews and the Chaldæans that were with him at Mizpah. And all the people, great and
small, and the captains of the forces, arose and came to Egypt; for they
were afraid of the Chaldæans.

Now it came to pass in the seven and thirtieth year of the captivity
of Jehoiachin, king of Judah, in the twelfth month, on the seven and
twentieth day of the month, that Evil-merodach, king of Babylon, in the
year that he began to reign, did lift up the head of Jehoiachin, king of
Judah, out of prison. And he spake kindly unto him, and set his throne
above the thrones of the kings that were with him in Babylon. And he
changed his prison garments, and did eat bread before him continually
all the days of his life. And for his allowance, there was a continual
allowance given him of the king, every day a portion, all the days of
his life.

THE
GOLDEN AGE OF HEBREW LITERATURE

SECOND PERIOD

FROM ZEPHANIAH'S WARNING OF A WORLD-WIDE DOOM

TO THE PROPHECY OF ISRAEL'S WORLD-WIDE MISSION

THE POEM OF ZEPHANIAH, "THE DAY OF YAHWEH"

THE BOOK OF THE LAW (DEUTERONOMY) BY D.

THE BOOK OF JEREMIAH

THE PRAISE OF WISDOM

THE POEMS OF NAHUM ON THE FALL OF NINEVEH

THE POEM OF HABAKKUK

THE TWO "POEMS OF THE SERVANT"

THE POEM OF THE PROPHET ZEPHANIAH

THE DAY OF YAHWEH

PART I. ITS IMMINENT ADVENT
(Ch. 1, 7, 2-6, 8-18)[1]

Hold thy peace at the presence of Yahweh,
    For the Day of Yehweh is at hand,
For Yahweh hath prepared a sacrifice, He hath bidden His guests.

I will utterly consume everything from off the land, saith Yahweh.
I will take away the fowls of heaven and the fishes of the sea.
The stumbling-blocks with the wicked, and mankind from the earth.

    I will stretch out My hand upon Judah
    And upon all the dwellers in Jerusalem.
From this place I will cut off the remnant of Baal,
    The very name of its priests,
And them who worship on the house-tops the host of heaven,
And the worshipers of Yahweh who also swear by Malcham;
Them also who are apostate to Yahweh, who have not sought Him,
    Nor inquired of Yahweh.

And it shall come to pass in the day of Yahweh's sacrifice,
That I will punish the princes and the king's children,
    And all those that clothe themselves in foreign apparel.
    I will also punish those who leap over the threshold,
    Who fill their masters' houses with violence and deceit.

Hark! a cry from the Fishgate and a wailing from the New Quarter
    And a great crashing from the hills,
    And a wailing from the dwellers in Maktesh.
    For all the merchants are cut down,
    All they that have silver and gold are cut off.
    And I will search Jerusalem with lamps,
    And punish those settled upon their lees;
That say in their hearts: Yahweh will do us no good;
    Neither will He do evil.
Therefore their wealth shall become a prey, and their house,
    A desolation.

For the Day of Yahweh is near; near, and hasteneth greatly;
The outcry of the Day of Yahweh wherein the strong man
    Shall cry bitterly.
That day is a day of wrath, a day of trouble and distress;
    A day of destruction and desolation,
    A day of darkness and gloom;
    A day of clouds and thick darkness,
    A day of the trumpet and the alarum

---

[1] (Superscription by P. Ch. i, 1.) "The word of Yahweh which came to Zephaniah the son of Cushi, the son of Gedaliah, the son of Amariah, the son of Hezekiah, in the days of Josiah the son of Amon, king of Israel."

Against the fortified cities and against the high battlements.
>   And I will bring distress upon men
>   That they shall walk as the blind;
And their blood shall be poured out as dust,
>   And their flesh shall be as dung.
Neither their silver nor their gold shall serve to deliver them
>   In the day of the wrath of Yahweh;
But the whole land shall be devoured by the fire of His jealousy
>   For He shall make a speedy riddance of all those
>   That dwell in the land.

PART II. THE RUIN SHALL BE WORLD-WIDE
(Ch. ii, 1-6, 7b, 6-10, 12-15)

>   Gather yourselves together!
>   Yea, gather together, O shameless nations!
Before the decree is passed that ye shall be as drifting chaff,
>   Before the fierce wrath of Yahweh shall come upon you!
Seek ye Yahweh, all ye meek upon earth, ye who obey His Laws!
Seek righteousness, seek meekness; it may be ye shall be hid
>   In the day of the wrath of Yahweh.

>   For Gaza shall be forsaken, Askelon, a desolation;
They shall drive out Ashdod at noon, Ekron shall be uprooted.
Woe to the dwellers by the sea, the nation of the Cherethites!
The word of Yahweh is against you, O Canaan, land of Philistines!
I will so destroy thee that there shall be no inhabitant.
And the sea-coast shall be pastures, meadows for shepherds,
>   And folds for flocks.
>   In the palace of Askelon shall they lie down in the evening,
>   By the sea shall they feed.

I have heard the taunt of Moab, the reviling of the children of Ammon.
>   Wherewith they have taunted My people,
>   Magnifying themselves against them.
>   Therefore as I live saith Yahweh, the God of Israel,
Surely Moab shall be as Sodom, and the children of Ammon
>   Like Gomorrah;
Even salt-pits, the breeding-place of nettles, a desolation forever.
>   The residue of My people shall spoil them,
>   And the remnant of it shall possess them.

>   Ye Ethiopians also, ye shall be slain by My sword;
>   And He will stretch out His hand against the north,
>   And destroy Assyria,
And will make Nineveh a desolation, and dry as the desert.
Beasts of every kind shall lie down in the midst of her;
The pelican and the bittern shall lodge in her lintels.
Their cries shall be heard in her ruined windows;
>   Desolation shall be on her thresholds,
>   And the cedar-work thereof shall lie bare.

>   This is the joyous city that dwelt without care!
That said in her heart: There is none like unto me!
How is she become a desolation, a den for jackals!
>   Every passer-by shall hiss at her,
>   And wag his head.

PART III.   A GLEAM OF HOPE FOR JUDAH

(Ch. iii, 1-7)

Woe to her that is filthy and polluted!   Woe to the oppressing city!
She heeded not the warning voice, she accepted no reproof;
She trusted not in Yahweh; she drew not near to her God.
Her rulers in her midst are roaring lions; her judges, ravening wolves.

They leave not a bone for the morrow.
Her prophets are dissolute and faithless men,
Her priests profane what is holy.
And do violence to the Law.

Yet Yahweh, the Just One, is in her midst,
He will not do unrighteousness.
Morning by morning He maketh clear His law,
He faileth not to do right.
He saith: I have cut off the nations; destroyed their walls.
I have laid waste their streets and none pass over them.
Desolate are their cities, without a man, not an inhabitant.

Surely thou, (Jerusalem) wilt fear Me! Thou wilt accept rebuke!
So that her dwelling shall not be destroyed,
After all I have visited upon her!
But despite all this, she hath made all her doings corrupt!

PART IV.   A PSALM OF REJOICING [1]

(Ch. iii, 14-20)

Sing, O daughter of Zion!   Shout, O Israel!
Be glad and rejoice with all thy heart, O Daughter of Jerusalem!
Yahweh hath taken away thy judgments, He hath cast out thy foe.
The king of Israel, even Yahweh, is in the midst of thee.
Thou shalt not fear evil any more.

O Zion, let not thy hands be slack; thy God, Yahweh, is in thy midst,
A Mighty One, who will save.
He will rejoice over thee with joy, He will love thee in silence,
He will joy over thee with singing.

I will gather them that are far from the solemn assembly,
Who are of thee,—who grieved for the burden of reproach upon it.
Behold, at that time, I will undo all that afflicted thee.
And I will succour her that halteth, and rescue her that was outcast.
And I will cause them to receive praise and a name,
Whose shame hath been in all the earth.

[1] Probably written by Zephaniah after the Great Reformation of Josiah, 621 B.C.
Vv, 8-13 are evidently post-exilic and therefore omitted.

THE BOOK OF THE LAW

(DEUTERONOMY)

SUPERSCRIPTION

(Ch. i, 1, 4-5)

These are the words that Moses spake unto all Israel beyond Jordan in the wilderness, in the plain over against the Red Sea between Paran and Tophel and Laban and Hazeroth and Dizahab, after he had slain Sihon, the king of the Amorites which dwelt in Heshbon, and Og, the king of Bashan which dwelt at Ashtaroth in Edrei.[1]   Beyond Jordan, in the land of Moab, began Moses to declare this law, saying:

THE EXORDIUM

(Ch. i, 6-46; ii, 1-9, 13-19, 24-37; iii, 1; iv, 28, 32-40)

Yahweh, our God, spake unto us in Horeb, saying: Ye have dwelt long enough in this mount. Turn you and take your journey, and go to the mount of the Amorites and all places thereunto in the plain, in the hills and in the vale and in the south and by the seaside, to the land of the Canaanites, and unto Lebanon unto the great river, the river Euphrates. Behold, I have set the land before you. Go in and possess the land which Yahweh sware unto your forefathers, Abraham, Isaac and Jacob, to give unto them and to their seed after them. And I spake unto you at that time, saying: I am not able to bear you myself alone. Yahweh, your God, hath multiplied you, and behold, ye are this day as the stars of heaven for multitude. (May Yahweh, the God of your fathers, make you a thousand times as many more, and bless you, as He hath promised you!) How can I myself alone bear your cumbrance and your burden and your strife? Take you wise and intelligent men and known among your tribes, and I will make them heads over you. And ye answered and said: The thing which thou hast spoken is good. So I took the chief men of your tribes, wise men and full of knowledge, and made them heads over you; captains over hundreds and captains over fifties, and captains over tens, and officers among your tribes. And I charged your judges at that time, saying: Hear the causes between your brethren, and judge righteously between a man and his brother, and the stranger that is with you. Ye shall not respect persons in judgment; ye shall hear the small as well as the great. Ye shall have no fear of men, for the judgment is God's. And the cause that is too hard for you, bring it to me and I will hear it. And I commanded you at that time all the things which you should do.

And when we departed from Horeb, we went through all that great and terrible wilderness which ye saw, by the way of the hill-country of the Amorites, as Yahweh our God commanded us. And we came to

---

[1] Vv. 2-3 added by the Redactor are omitted.

Kadesh-barnea. And I said unto you: We are come unto the hill-country of the Amorites, which Yahweh, our God, is giving unto us. Behold, Yahweh thy God hath set the land before thee; go up and take possession, as Yahweh, the God of thy fathers, hath spoken; fear not, neither be dismayed. And ye came near unto me, every one of you, and said: Let us send men before us that they may search the land for us and bring us back word by what way we must go up, and unto what cities we shall come. And the saying pleased me well. And I took twelve men of you, one for each tribe; and they turned and went up into the mountain, and came unto the valley of Eshcol and searched it out. And they took of the fruit of the land in their hands, and brought it down to us; and brought us word and said: It is a good land which Yahweh, our God, hath given us. Yet ye would not go up, but rebelled against the commandment of Yahweh, your God; and ye murmured in your tents, and said: Because Yahweh hated us, hath He brought us forth out of the land of Egypt to deliver us into the hands of the Amorites to destroy us. Whither are we going up? Our brethren have discouraged our heart, saying: The people are greater and taller than we; the cities are large, and fortified up to heaven; moreover we have seen the sons of the Anakim there.

Then I said unto you: Fear not, neither be afraid of them. Yahweh, your God, which goeth before you, He shall fight for you, according to all that He did for you in Egypt before your eyes; and in the wilderness, where thou hast seen how that Yahweh thy God bare thee, as a man beareth his son, in all the way that ye went until ye came to this place. Yet in this thing ye do not believe Yahweh your God, who went in the way before you to search out a place for you to pitch your tents, in fire by night to show you what way ye should go, and in a cloud by day.

And Yahweh heard the voice of your words and was wroth, and sware, saying: Surely there shall not one of these men of this evil generation see that good land which I sware to give unto your fathers, save Caleb the son of Jephunneh. He shall see it; and to him will I give the land that he hath trodden upon and to his children, because he hath wholly followed Yahweh. Also, Yahweh was angry with me for your sakes, saying: Thou also shalt not go thither; Joshua, the son of Nun, which standeth before thee, he shall go in thither; encourage thou him, for he shall cause Israel to inherit it. Moreover, your little ones, which ye said should be a prey, and your children which this day have no knowledge of good and evil,—they shall go in thither and unto them will I give it, and they shall possess it. But as for you, turn you and take your journey into the wilderness by the way to the Red Sea.

Then ye answered and said unto me: We have sinned against Yahweh. We will go up and fight, according unto all that Yahweh our God hath commanded us. And when ye had girded on every man his weapons of war, ye were ready to go up the hill. But Yahweh said unto me: Say unto them, Go not up, neither fight, for I am not among you; lest ye be smitten by your enemies. So I spake unto you, but ye would not hear, but rebelled against the commandment of Yahweh, and went up presumptuously into the hill. And the Amorites which dwelt in that mountain came out against you and chased you, as bees do, and beat you down in Seir, even unto Hormah. And ye returned and wept before Yahweh; but Yahweh would not hearken unto your voice, nor give ear unto you. So ye abode in Kadesh many days, according unto the days that ye abode there.

Then we turned and took our journey into the wilderness by the way to the Red Sea, as Yahweh said unto me; and we compassed Mount Seir many days. Then Yahweh spake unto me, saying: Ye have compassed this mountain long enough; turn you northward. And command thou the people, saying: Ye are to pass through the border of your brethren, the Children of Esau, which dwell in Seir; and they will be afraid of you. Take good heed unto yourselves therefore; meddle not with them; for I will not give you of their land, no, not so much as a foot-breadth; for I have given Mount Seir unto Esau for a possession. Ye shall buy meat of them for money, that ye may eat; and ye shall also buy water of them for money, that ye may drink. For Yahweh thy God, hath blessed thee in all the works of thy hand. He knoweth how thou hast come through this great wilderness; these forty years Yahweh, thy God, hath been with thee; thou hast lacked nothing.[1]

Now when we had passed beyond our brethren the Children of Esau, who dwelt in Mount Seir, by the way of the plain from Elath even to Ezion-geber, we turned and passed by the wilderness of Moab. And Yahweh said unto me: Be not at enmity with Moab, neither contend with him in battle; for I will not give thee of his land for a possession, because I have given Ar unto the Children of Lot for a possession. Rise up and get you over the brook Zered. So we went over the brook Zered. And the space from the days when we left Kadesh-Barnea until we crossed over the brook Zered was thirty and eight years; until all the generation of the men of war were wasted out from the host, as Yahweh had sworn unto them. Then Yahweh spake unto me, saying: Thou art this day to pass over the border of Moab, even Ar. And when thou comest nigh over against the Children of Ammon, harass them not, nor contend with them; for I will not give thee the land of the Children of Ammon for a possession, because I have given it unto the Children of Lot for a possession. Rise up, take your journey over the valley of Arnon; behold, I have given into thy hand Sihon the Amorite, King of Heshbon, and his land; begin to possess it and contend with him in battle.

This day will I begin to put the dread of thee and the fear of thee upon the peoples that are under the whole heaven who shall report of thee; and they shall tremble and be in anguish because of thee.

Then I sent messengers out of the wilderness of Kedemoth unto Sihon king of Heshbon with words of peace, saying: Let me pass through thy land. I will go by the highway; I will neither turn to the right hand nor to the left. Thou shalt sell me meat for money, that I may eat; and give me water for money, that I may drink; only let me pass through on my feet; as the Children of Esau that dwell in Seir, and the Moabites that dwell in Ar did unto me; until I shall pass over the Jordan into the land which Yahweh, our God, is giving us. But Sihon, king of Heshbon, would not let us pass by him; for Yahweh had hardened his spirit and made his heart obstinate, that He might deliver him into thy hand, as appeareth this day.

And Yahweh said unto me: Behold, I have begun to deliver up

---

[1] Vv. 10-12 and 20-23 of Chap. ii are evidently interpolations, interrupting the address; but they present local traditions too interesting to be omitted, and are therefore given here. Vv. 10-12. "The Emim dwelt therein in times past, a people great and many and tall like the Anakim; which also were accounted giants (*Rephaim*) but the Moabites called them *Anakim*. The Horim also dwelt in Seir beforetime; but the Children of Esau succeeded them when they had destroyed them, and dwelt in their stead; *as Israel did unto the land of their possession which Yahweh gave unto them.*" Vv. 20-23. "That also was accounted a land of giants; giants dwelt therein of old time, and the Ammonites call them *Zamzummim.* . . . But Yahweh destroyed them before them (the Ammonites) and they succeeded them and dwelt in their stead. As He did to the Children of Esau which dwelt in Seir after He had destroyed the Horim before them. . . . And the Avim, which dwelt in Hazerim unto Azzah, the Caphtorim which came forth out of Caphtor (*Crete*) destroyed, and dwelt in their stead."

Sihon and his land unto thee; begin to possess his land. Then Sihon came out against us, he and all his people, unto battle at Jahaz. And Yahweh, our God, delivered him up before us, and we smote him and his sons and all his people. And we took all his cities at that time, and utterly destroyed every city, the men and the women and the little ones; we left none remaining; only the cattle we took unto ourselves for a prey, with the spoil of the cities we had taken. From Aroer, which is on the edge of the valley of Arnon, and from the city that is in the valley, even unto Gilead,—there was not a city too high for us; Yahweh, our God, delivered them all up before us. Only to the land of the Children of Ammon thou camest not near; all the sides of the river Jabbok, and the cities of the hill-country, and wheresoever Yahweh forbade us.

Then we turned and went up the way to Bashan; and Og the king of Bashan came out against us, he and all his people, unto battle at Edrei. And Yahweh said unto me: Fear him not; for I have delivered him and all his people and his land into thine hand; and thou shalt do unto him as thou didst unto Sihon king of the Amorites who dwelt at Heshbon. So Yahweh, our God, delivered into our hand Og also, the king of Bashan, and all his people; and we smote him until none was left to him remaining. And we took all his cities at that time; there was not a city which we took not from them; three-score cities, all the region of Argob, the kingdom of Og in Bashan (all these cities were fortified cities with high walls, gates and bars), besides unwalled towns a great many. And we utterly destroyed them as we did unto Sihon king of Heshbon, utterly destroying the men, women and children of every city. But all the cattle and the spoil of the cities we took for ourselves. And we took at that time out of the hand of the two kings of the Amorites the land that was on this side Jordan, from the river of Arnon unto Mount Hermon,[1] all the cities of the plain, and all Gilead, and all Bashan unto Salchah and Edrei, cities of the kingdom of Og in Bashan. For only Og remained of the remnant of the giants (*Rephaim*); behold his bedstead was a bedstead of iron; is it not in Rabbah of the cities of Ammon? Nine cubits the length thereof, and four cubits the breadth of it, after the cubit of a man. And this land which we took possession of at that time, from Aroer which is by the river Arnon, and half Mount Gilead and the cities thereof, gave I unto the Reubenites and the Gadites. And the rest of Gilead and all Bashan, the kingdom of Og, gave I unto the half-tribe of Manasseh; all the region of Argob with all Bashan which was called the land of giants.[2] . . . . .

And I commanded you at that time, saying: Yahweh, your God, hath given you this land to possess it. Ye shall pass over armed before your brethren the Children of Israel, all that are fit for war. But your wives and your little ones and your cattle,—for I know that ye have much cattle,—shall abide in your cities which I have given you until Yahweh have given rest unto your brethren as well as unto you; and until they also possess the land which Yahweh your God shall give them beyond Jordan. Then shall ye return, every man unto his possession which I have given you.

And I commanded Joshua at that time, saying: Thine eyes have seen all that Yahweh, your God, hath done unto these two kings; so shall Yahweh do unto all the kingdoms whither thou goest. Ye shall not fear them: for Yahweh, your God, He shall fight for you. And I besought

---

[1] V. 10, a gloss, inappropriate to the address, is here omitted.
[2] Vv. 15-17. Statistics, after the manner of P and therefore omitted.

Yahweh at that time, saying: O God Yahweh! thou hast begun to show Thy servant Thy greatness and Thy mighty hand. For what God is there in heaven or earth that can do according to Thy works and according to Thy might? I pray Thee, let me go over and see the good land that is beyond Jordan, that goodly hill-country and Lebanon! But Yahweh was wroth with me on your account and would not hear me. And Yahweh said unto me: Let it suffice thee; speak no more unto Me of the matter. Get thee up into the top of Pisgah, and lift up thine eyes westward and northward and southward and eastward, and behold it with thine eyes; for thou shalt not go over this Jordan. But charge Joshua, and encourage and strengthen him; for he shall go over before this people, and he shall cause them to inherit the land which thou shalt see. So we abode in the valley over against Beth-Peor.

Now, therefore, hearken, O Israel, unto the statutes and unto the judgments which I teach you to do them; that ye may live, and go in and possess the land which Yahweh, the God of your fathers, giveth you. Ye shall not add unto the word which I command you, neither shall ye diminish aught from it, that ye may keep the commandments of Yahweh, your God, which I command you. Your eyes have seen what Yahweh did because of Baal-Peor; for all the men that followed Baal-Peor did Yahweh thy God destroy from among you. But ye that did cleave unto Yahweh your God are alive every one of you this day. Behold, I have taught you statutes and judgments, even as Yahweh my God commanded me that ye should do in the land whither ye go to possess it. Keep therefore, and do them; for this is your wisdom and your understanding in the sight of the nations which shall hear of these statutes and judgments, and say: Verily, this great nation is a wise and understanding people! For what nation is there that hath God so nigh unto them as is Yahweh our God, in all that we call upon Him for? And what nation hath statutes and judgments so righteous as all this law which I set before you this day? Only take heed unto thyself, and keep thy soul diligently lest thou forget the things which thine eyes have seen, and lest they depart from thy heart all the days of thy life. And do thou teach them to thy sons and thy sons' sons; of the day thou didst stand before Yahweh, thy God, in Horeb, when Yahweh said unto me: Gather Me the people together; and I will make them hear My words, that they may learn to fear Me all the days that they shall live upon the earth, and that they may teach their children. And ye came and stood under the mountain; and the mountain burned with fire unto the heart of heaven with darkness, clouds and thick darkness. And Yahweh spake unto you out of the midst of the fire. Ye heard the sound of the words, but saw no similitude; only ye heard a voice. And He declared unto you His covenant which He commanded you to perform, even the Ten Words; and He wrote them upon two tables of stone.

And Yahweh commanded me at that time to teach you statutes and judgments that ye might do them in the land whither ye are going over to possess it. Take ye therefore good heed unto yourselves (for ye saw no manner of similitude on the day that Yahweh spake unto you in Horeb out of the midst of the fire), lest ye corrupt yourselves and make you a graven image, the likeness of male or female, the likeness of any beast that is on the earth, the likeness of any winged fowl that flieth in the air, the likeness of any thing that creepeth on the ground, the likeness of any fish that is in the waters beneath the earth; and lest thou lift up thine eyes unto heaven, and when thou seest the sun and the

moon and the stars, even all the host of heaven, shouldest be induced
to worship them and serve them, which Yahweh, thy God, hath allotted
to all nations under the whole heaven.

But you hath Yahweh taken and brought forth out of the iron
furnace, even out of Egypt, to be unto Him a people of inheritance, as
ye are this day. Furthermore, Yahweh was angry with me on your
account, and sware that I should not go over Jordan—that I should not
go in unto that good land which Yahweh, thy God, is giving thee for an
inheritance; but I must die in this land. I must not go over Jordan;
but ye shall go over and possess that good land. Take heed unto yourselves, let ye forget the covenant which Yahweh, your God, made with
you, and make you a graven image or the likeness of any thing which
Yahweh, thy God, hath forbidden thee. For Yahweh, thy God, is a
consuming fire,—a jealous God.

When thou shalt beget children and children's children and shalt have
remained long in the land; if ye shall corrupt yourselves and make a
graven image of any thing, and shalt do evil in the sight of Yahweh
thy God to provoke Him to anger; I call heaven and earth to witness
against you this day, that ye shall soon perish from off the land whereunto ye are going over Jordan to possess it. Ye shall not prolong your
days upon it, but shall utterly be destroyed. And Yahweh will scatter
you among the nations, and ye shall be few in number among the
heathen whither Yahweh shall lead you. And there ye shall serve gods,
the work of men's hands, wood and stone, which neither see nor hear
nor eat nor smell.

For ask now of the days that are past, which were before thee, since
the day that God created man upon the earth, and from one end of
heaven unto the other, whether there hath been anything like this
great thing, or hath been heard like it? Did ever people hear the voice
of God speaking out of the midst of the fire, as thou hast heard, and
live? Or hath God essayed to take Him a nation from the midst of
another nation by trials, by signs and by wonders and by war, and by a
mighty hand, and by a stretched out arm, and by great terrors, according
unto all that Yahweh, your God, did for you in Egypt before your eyes?
Unto thee it was showed, that thou mightest know that Yahweh, He is
God; there is none else beside Him. Out of heaven He made thee to hear
His voice, that He might instruct thee; and upon earth He showed thee
His great fire, and thou didst hear His voice out of the midst of the
fire. And because He loved thy fathers, therefore He chose their seed
after them, and brought thee out in His sight by His mighty power out
of Egypt, to drive out nations before thee greater and mightier than
thou, to bring thee in and to give thee their land for an inheritance,
as it is this day.

Know therefore this day, and consider in thine heart, that Yahweh
is God in heaven above and upon the earth beneath; there is no other.
Therefore shalt thou keep His statutes and His commandments which
I command thee this day; that it may go well with thee and with thy
children after thee; and that thou mayest prolong thy days upon the
earth which Yahweh thy God giveth thee for ever.[1]

[1] Chapter iv, 41-v, 1, are late interpolations foreign to the context.

THE STATEMENT OF THE LAWS
AND THE CHOICE OF MOSES AS THEIR EXPOSITOR
(Ch. v, 4-30)

Hear, O Israel, the statutes and the ordinances which I speak in your ears this day, that ye may learn them, and observe to do them. Yahweh, our God, made a covenant with us in Horeb. Yahweh made not this covenant with our fathers, but with us, even US, who are all of us here alive this day. Yahweh spake with you face to face in the mount out of the midst of the fire,—(I stood between Yahweh and you at that time, to declare unto you the word of Yahweh; for ye were afraid of the fire, and went not up into the mount),—saying:

I am Yahweh, thy God, who brought thee out of the land of Egypt, from the house of bondage. Thou shalt have no other gods before Me.

Thou shalt not make thee any graven image, or any likeness of anything that is in heaven above, or that is in the earth beneath, or that is in the water under the earth. Thou shalt not bow down unto them nor serve them; for I, Yahweh thy God am a jealous God, visiting the iniquity of the fathers upon the children, and upon the third and fourth generation of them that hate Me, and showing mercy unto the thousandth generation of them that love Me, and keep My commandments.

Thou shalt not take the name of Yahweh, thy God, in vain; for Yahweh will not hold him guiltless, that taketh His name in vain.

Observe the sabbath day to keep it holy, as Yahweh, thy God, commanded thee. Six days shalt thou labor, and do all thy work; but the seventh day is the sabbath of Yahweh, thy God. In it thou shalt do no work, thou, nor thy son, nor thy daughter, nor thy man-servant, nor thy maid-servant, nor thine ox nor thine ass nor any of thy cattle, nor any stranger that is within thy gates; that thy man-servant and thy maid-servant may rest as well as thou. For thou shalt remember that thou wast a servant in the land of Egypt; and Yahweh thy God brought thee out thence by a mighty hand and a stretched-out arm; therefore Yahweh thy God hath commanded thee to keep the sabbath day.

Honor thy father and thy mother, as Yahweh thy God commanded thee; that thy days may be prolonged, and that it may go well with thee upon the land which Yahweh thy God giveth thee.

Thou shalt not murder.

Neither shalt thou commit adultery.

Neither shalt thou steal.

Neither shalt thou bear false witness against thy neighbor.

Neither shalt thou covet thy neighbor's house, his field, or his man-servant, or his maid-servant, his ox or his ass, or anything that is thy neighbor's.

These words Yahweh spake unto all your assembly in the mount out of the midst of the fire, of the cloud, and of the thick darkness, with a great voice, and He added no more. And He wrote them upon two tablets of stone and gave them unto me. And it came to pass, when ye heard the voice out of the midst of the darkness while the mountain did burn with fire, that ye came near unto me, even all the heads of your tribes and your elders; and ye said: Behold, Yahweh our God hath shown us His glory and His greatness, and we have heard His voice out of the midst of the fire. We have seen this day that God doth talk with man and he liveth. Now, therefore, why should we die? for this great fire will consume us; if we hear the voice of Yahweh our God any more, then we shall die. For who is there of all flesh, that hath heard the voice of the living God speaking out of the midst of the fire, as we have, and lived? Go thou near and hear all that Yahweh may say; and thou shalt speak unto us all that Yahweh our God may speak unto thee; and we will hear it and do it.

And Yahweh heard the sound of your words when ye spoke unto me; and Yahweh said unto me: I have heard the voice of the words of this people which they have spoken unto thee; they have well said all that they have spoken. Oh, that they had such a heart as this alway, to fear Me and to keep My commandments, that it might be well with them and with their children for ever. Go, say to them: return ye to your tents. But as for thee, stand thee here by Me, and I will speak unto thee all the commandment, and the statutes and the ordinances which thou shalt teach them, that they may do them in the land which I am giving them to possess it. Ye shall observe therefore to do as Yahweh your God hath commanded you; ye shall not turn aside to the right hand or to the left. Ye shall walk in all the way which Yahweh your God hath commanded you, that ye may live; and that it may be well with you, and that ye may prolong your days in the land which ye shall possess.

EXPOSITION OF THE FULL MEANING OF THE LAWS OF THE FIRST TABLET

(Ch. vi, 4; xiii, 18)

Hear, O Israel! Yahweh, our God, is One God. Thou shalt love Yahweh thy God with all thy heart, and with all thy soul, and with all thy might. And these words, which I command thee this day, shall be upon thy heart; and thou shalt teach them diligently unto thy children. And shalt talk of them when thou sittest in thine house, and when thou walkest by the way, and when thou liest down, and when thou risest up. And thou shalt bind them for a sign upon thine hand, and they shall be for frontlets between thine eyes. And thou shalt write them upon the door-posts of thy house, and upon thy gates.

And it shall be, when Yahweh thy God shall bring thee into the land which He sware unto thy fathers, to Abraham, to Isaac and to Jacob, to give thee,—great and goodly cities which thou didst not build, and houses full of good things which thou didst not fill, and cisterns hewn out which thou didst not hew, vineyards and olive-trees which thou didst not plant and thou shalt eat of the fruit and be satisfied; then beware lest thou forget Yahweh, who brought thee out of the land of Egypt, out of the house of bondage. Thou shalt fear Yahweh thy God; Him shalt thou serve, and by His name shalt thou swear. Ye shall not go after other gods, gods of the peoples that are round about you; for a jealous God, even Yahweh thy God, is in the midst of thee; lest the anger of Yahweh my God be kindled against thee, and He destroy thee from the face of the earth.

Ye shall not tempt Yahweh thy God as ye tempted Him in Massah. Ye shall diligently keep the commandments of Yahweh your God, and His testimonies and His statutes which He hath commanded thee. And thou shalt do that which is right and good in the sight of Yahweh; that it may be well with thee, and that thou mayest go in and possess the good land which Yahweh sware unto thy fathers, to thrust out all thine enemies from before thee, as Yahweh thy God hath spoken.

When thy son asketh thee in time to come, saying: What mean the testimonies and the statutes and the ordinances which Yahweh hath commanded you? then thou shalt say unto thy son: We were Pharaoh's bondmen in the land of Egypt; and Yahweh brought us out of Egypt with a mighty hand. And Yahweh showned signs and wonders, great and sore, upon Egypt, upon Pharaoh, and upon all his house before our eyes. And He brought us out from thence that He might bring us into and give us the land which He sware unto our fathers. And Yahweh commanded us to do all these statutes, to fear Yahweh our God for our good always, that He might preserve us alive as it is this day. And it shall be our righteousness, if we observe to do all these commandments before Yahweh our God, as He hath commanded us.

When Yahweh thy God shall bring thee into the land whither thou goest to possess it, and hath cast out many nations before thee,—the Hittites and the Girgashites and the Amorites and the Canaanites and the Perizzites and the Hivites and the Jebusites, seven nations greater and mightier than thou; and when Yahweh thy God shall deliver them up before thee, and thou shalt smite them; then thou shalt utterly destroy them; thou shalt make no covenant with them, nor show mercy unto them; neither shalt thou make marriages with them. Thy daughter shalt thou not give unto his son, nor his daughter shalt thou take unto thy son; for they will turn away thy children from following Me, that they may serve other gods; so will the anger of Yahweh be kindled against you, and He will destroy thee suddenly. But thus shall ye deal with them: ye shall break down their altars, and dash in pieces their pillars and hew down their Asherim, and burn their graven images with fire. For thou art a holy people unto Yahweh thy God; Yahweh thy God hath chosen thee to be His own treasure, above all peoples on the face of the earth. Yahweh did not set His love upon you, nor choose you, because ye were more in number than any people,—for ye were the fewest of all peoples; but because Yahweh loved you, and because He would keep the oath which He sware unto your fathers, hath Yahweh brought you out of the house of bondage, from the hand of Pharaoh, king of Egypt.

Know therefore that Yahweh, thy God, He is God; the faithful God, who keepeth covenant and mercy with them that love Him and keep His commandments to a thousand generations; and repayeth them that hate Him to their face, to destroy them; He will not be slack to him that hateth Him; He will repay him to his face. Thou shalt therefore keep the commandment and the statutes and the ordinances which I command thee this day to do them.

Wherefore it shall come to pass, if ye hearken to these ordinances, and keep and do them, Yahweh thy God will keep with thee the covenant and the mercy which He sware unto thy fathers, and He will love thee, and bless thee and multiply thee; He will also bless the fruit of thy body, and the fruit of thy land, thy corn and thy wine and thine oil, the increase of thy kine and the young of thy flock, in the land which He sware unto thy fathers to give thee. Thou shalt be blessed above all peoples; there shall not be male or female barren among you, or among your cattle. And Yahweh will take away from thee all sickness; and He will put upon thee none of the evil diseases of Egypt which thou knowest; but will lay them upon all them that hate thee. And thou shalt consume all the peoples that Yahweh thy God shall deliver unto thee; thine eye shall not pity them; neither shalt thou serve their gods, for that will be a snare unto thee.

If thou shalt say in thine heart: These nations are more than I;

how can I dispossess them? thou shalt not be afraid of them; thou shalt well remember what Yahweh thy God did unto Pharaoh and unto all Egypt; the great temptations which thine eyes saw, and the signs and the wonders, and the mighty hand and the outstretched arm, whereby Yahweh thy God brought thee out; so shall Yahweh thy God do unto all the peoples of whom thou art afraid. Moreover Yahweh thy God will send the hornet among them, until they that are left and they that hide themselves shall perish from before thee. Thou shalt not be afraid of them, for Yahweh thy God is in the midst of thee, a God mighty and terrible. And Yahweh thy God will cast out those nations before thee by little and little; thou mayest not consume them quickly, lest the beasts of the field increase upon thee. But Yahweh thy God shall deliver them up before thee, and shall discomfit them with a great discomfiture, until they be destroyed. And He shall deliver their kings into thy hand, and thou shalt make their name to perish from under heaven; there shall no man be able to stand before thee until thou have destroyed them. The graven images of their gods shall ye burn with fire; thou shalt not covet the silver or the gold that is on them, nor take it unto thee lest thou be snared therein; for it is an abomination to Yahweh thy God. And thou shalt not bring an abomination into thy house; lest thou be a cursed thing like it; thou shalt utterly detest it, and thou shalt utterly abhor it; for it is a cursed thing.

All the commandments which I command thee this day shall ye observe to do, that ye may live and multiply and go in and possess the land which Yahweh sware unto your fathers. And thou shalt remember all the way which Yahweh thy God hath led thee these forty years in the wilderness, that He might afflict thee to prove thee, to know what was in thine heart, whether thou wouldest keep His commandments or no. And He afflicted thee and suffered thee to hunger, and fed thee with manna which thou knewest not, neither did thy fathers know; that He might make thee know that man doth not live by bread only, but by every word that proceedeth out of the mouth of Yahweh doth man live. Thy raiment waxed not old upon thee, neither did thy foot swell, these forty years. And thou shalt consider in thine heart, that, as a man chasteneth his son, so Yahweh thy God chasteneth thee. And thou shalt keep the commandments of Yahweh thy God, to walk in His ways and to fear Him. For Yahweh thy God bringeth thee into a good land, a land of brooks, of fountains and pools of water, springing forth in valleys and hills; a land of wheat and barley, and vines and pomegranates and fig-trees, a land of olive-trees and honey; a land where thou shalt eat bread without scarceness; thou shalt not lack anything in it; a land whose stones are iron, and out of whose hills thou mayest dig brass. And thou shalt eat and be satisfied, and bless Yahweh thy God for the good land which He hath given thee. Beware lest thou forget Yahweh thy God in not keeping His commandments and His ordinances and His statutes, which I command thee this day; lest when thou hast eaten and art full, and hast built goodly houses and dwelt therein; and when thy herds and thy flocks multiply, and thy silver and thy gold is multiplied, and all that thou hast is multiplied; then thy heart be lifted up, and thou forget Yahweh thy God who brought thee out of the land of Egypt, out of the house of bondage; who led thee through the great and terrible wilderness, wherein were serpents, fiery serpents and scorpions, and thirsty ground where was no water; who brought thee forth water out of the rock of flint; who fed thee in the wilderness with manna, which thy fathers knew not; that He might afflict thee, and that He might prove thee to do thee good in the end; and thou say in thine heart: *My* power and the might of *my* hand hath gotten me this wealth. But thou shalt remember Yahweh thy God; for it is He that giveth thee power to get wealth, that He may establish His covenant which He sware unto thy fathers, as it is thy day.

And it shall be, if thou shalt forget Yahweh thy God, and walk after other gods and serve them and worship them, I forewarn you this day, that ye shall surely perish, because ye would not hearken unto the voice of Yahweh your God.

Hear, O Israel! Thou art to pass over the Jordan this day, to go in and dispossess nations greater and mightier than thyself, whose cities are great and fortified up to heaven; a people great and tall, the sons of the Anakim of whom thou knowest, and of whom thou hast heard say: "Who can stand before the sons of Anak?" Know therefore this day that Yahweh thy God is He that goeth before thee as a devouring fire. He will destroy them, and He will bring them down before thee; so shalt thou drive them out, and make them to perish quickly, as Yahweh hath spoken unto thee. Speak not thou in thine heart, after that Yahweh thy God hath thrust them out before thee, saying: Because of my righteousness hath Yahweh brought me in to possess this land; whereas, for the wickedness of those nations doth Yahweh drive them out from before thee. Not for thy righteousness, nor for the uprightness of thy heart, dost thou go in to possess the land; but for the wickedness of these nations doth Yahweh thy God drive them out from before thee, and that He may establish the word which He sware unto thy fathers, to Abraham, to Isaac and to Jacob. Know therefore, that it is not for thy righteousness that Yahweh thy God giveth thee this good land to possess it; for thou art a stiff-necked people.

Remember, forget thou not, how thou didst provoke Yahweh thy God to wrath in the wilderness; from the day thou didst go forth from the land of Egpyt until ye came unto this place, ye have been rebellious against Yahweh. Also in Horeb ye made Yahweh wroth, and Yahweh was angry with you to have destroyed you. When I was gone up into the mount to receive the tables of stone, even the tables of the covenant which Yahweh made with you, then I abode in the mount forty days and forty nights; I did neither eat bread nor drink water. And Yahweh delivered unto me the two tables of stone written with the finger of God; and on them was written according to all the words which Yahweh spake with you in the mount out of the midst of the fire, in the day of the assembly. And it came to pass, at the end of forty days and forty nights, that Yahweh gave me the two tables of stone, even the tables of the covenant. And Yahweh said unto me: Arise, get thee down quickly from hence, for thy people that thou hast brought forth out of Egypt have acted wickedly; they have turned aside out of the way that I commanded them; they have made them a molten image. Furthermore Yahweh spake unto me, saying: I have seen this people, and behold, it is a stiff-necked people. Let Me alone that I may destroy them, and blot out their name from under heaven. And I will make of thee a nation mightier and greater than they.

So I turned and came down from the mount, and the mount burned with fire; and the two tables of the covenant were in my two hands. And I looked, and behold, ye had sinned against Yahweh your God; ye had made you a molten calf; ye had turned aside quickly out of the way which Yahweh had commanded you. And I took hold of the two tables and cast them out of my two hands, and I brake them before your eyes. And I fell down as at the first before Yahweh; I did neither eat bread nor drink water, because of all your sin which ye sinned, in doing that which was evil in the sight of Yahweh, to provoke Him. For I was in dread of the anger and hot displeasure wherewith Yahweh was wroth against you to destroy you. But Yahweh hearkened unto me that time also. Moreover, Yahweh was very angry with Aaron to have destroyed him; and I prayed for Aaron also the same time. And I took your sin, the calf that ye had made, and burnt it with fire and beat it in pieces, grinding it very small until it was as fine as dust; and I cast the dust thereof into the brook that descended out of the mount. And at Taberah, and at Massah, and at Kibroth-hattaavah ye made Yahweh wroth. And when Yahweh sent you from Kadesh-barnea, saying: Go up, and possess the land which I have given you! then ye rebelled against the commandment of Yahweh your God, and ye believed Him not nor hearkened to His voice. Ye have been rebellious against Yahweh from the day that I knew you. So I fell down before Yahweh forty days and forty nights; because Yahweh had said He would destroy you. And I prayed unto Yahweh, and said: O God Yahweh! destroy not Thy people and Thy inheritance that Thou hast redeemed through Thy greatness, that Thou hast brought forth out of Egypt with a mighty hand. Remember Thy servants, Abraham, Isaac and Jacob; look not upon the stubbornness of this people, nor upon their wickedness nor their sin; lest the land whence Thou broughtest us say: Because Yahweh was not able to bring them into the land which He promised them, and because He hated them, He hath brought them out to slay them in the wilderness. Yet they are Thy people and Thine inheritance, that Thou didst bring out by Thy great power and by Thine out-stretched arm.

At that time Yahweh said unto me: Hew thee two tables of stone like unto the first, and come up unto Me into the mount, and make thee an ark of wood. And I will write on the tables the words that were on the first tables which thou didst break; and thou shalt put them into the ark. So I made an ark of acacia-wood, and hewed two tables of stone like unto the first, and went up into the mount, having the two tables in my hand. And He wrote on the tables, according to the first writing, the ten words which Yahweh spake unto you in the mount out of the midst of the fire in the day of the assembly; and Yahweh gave them unto me. And I turned and came down from the mount, and put the tables in the ark which I had made; and there they are, as Yahweh commanded. I had stayed in the mount as at the first time forty days and forty nights; and Yahweh hearkened unto me that time also; Yahweh would not destroy thee. And Yahweh said unto me: Arise, go before the people, causing them to set forward, that they may go in and possess the land which I sware unto their fathers to give them.

And now, Israel, what doth Yahweh thy God require of thee but to fear Yahweh thy God, to walk in all His ways, and to love Him, and to serve Yahweh thy God with all thy heart and with all thy soul; to keep the commandments of Yahweh and His statutes which I command thee this day for thy good? Behold, unto Yahweh thy God belongeth the heaven and the heaven of heavens, the earth with all that therein is. Only Yahweh had a delight in thy fathers to love them, and He chose their seed after them, even you, above all peoples, as it is this day. Circumcise, therefore, the foreskin of your heart, and be no more stiff-necked. For Yahweh, your God, He is God of gods, and Lord of lords, the great God, the Mighty and the Awful, who regardeth not persons nor taketh reward. He doth execute justice for the fatherless and the widow, and loveth the stranger in giving him food and raiment. Love ye, therefore, the stranger; for ye were strangers in the land of Egypt. Thou shalt fear Yahweh thy God; Him thou shalt serve, and to Him shalt thou cleave, and by His name thou shalt swear. He is thy glory and He is thy God that hath done for thee great and tremendous things, which thine eyes have seen. Thy fathers went down into Egypt with threescore and ten persons; and now Yahweh thy God hath made thee as the stars of heaven for multitude.

Therefore, thou shalt love Yahweh thy God and keep His charge, and His statutes and His ordinances and His commandments alway. And know ye this day—and I speak not to your children that have not known and have not seen the chastisement of Yahweh your God, His greatness, His mighty hand and His stretched out arm, and His signs and His wonders which He did in the midst of Egypt unto Pharaoh, the king of Egypt, and unto all his land; and what He did unto the army of Egypt, unto their horses and to their chariots; how He made the water of the Red Sea to overflow them as they pursued after you, and how Yahweh hath destroyed them unto this day. And what He did unto you in the wilderness until ye came unto this place; and what He did unto Dathan and Abiram, the sons of Eliab, the son of Reuben; how the earth opened her mouth and swallowed them up, and their households and their tents, and all the substance in their possession before all Israel; but your eyes have seen all the acts of Yahweh which He did. Therefore shall ye keep all the commandment which I command thee this day, that ye may be strong, and go in and possess the land whither ye go over to possess it; and that ye may prolong your days upon the land which Yahweh sware to give unto your fathers and to their seed, a land flowing with milk and honey.

For the land whither thou goest in to possess it is not as the land of Egypt, from whence ye came out, where thou didst sow thy seed, and didst water it with thy foot like a garden of herbs; but the land whither ye go over to possess it is a land of hills and valleys, and drinketh water as the rain of heaven cometh down; a land which Yahweh thy God careth for. The eyes of Yahweh thy God are always upon it, from the beginning of the year even unto the end of the year.

And it shall come to pass, if ye shall hearken diligently unto my commandments which I command you this day, to love Yahweh your God and to serve Him with all your heart and with all your soul, that He will give the rain of your land in its season, the former rain and the latter rain, that thou mayest gather in thy corn and thy wine and thine oil. And He will give grass in thy fields for thy cattle, that thou mayest eat and be full. Take heed to yourselves lest your heart be deceived, and ye turn aside and serve other gods, and worship them; and the wrath of Yahweh be kindled against you, and He shut up the heaven so that there shall be no rain, and the ground shall not yield her fruit, and ye perish quickly from off the good land which Yahweh giveth you. Therefore shall ye lay up my words in your heart and in your soul; and ye shall bind them for a sign upon your hand, and they shall be for frontlets between your eyes. And ye shall teach them your children, talking of them when thou sittest in thine house and when thou walkest by the way, and when thou liest down and when thou risest up. And thou shalt write them upon the door-posts of thy house, and upon thy gates; that your days may be multiplied, and the days of your children, upon the land which Yahweh sware unto your fathers to give them, as the days of heaven upon the earth.

For ye shall diligently keep all these commandments which I command you to do them; to love Yahweh your God, to walk in all His ways and to cleave unto Him. Then will Yahweh drive out all these nations from before you, and ye shall dispossess nations greater and mightier than yourselves. Every place whereon the sole of your foot shall tread shall be yours; from the wilderness and Lebanon, from the River, the river Euphrates, even unto the hinder sea shall your land be. There shall no man be able to stand before you. Yahweh your God shall lay the fear of you and the dread of you upon all the land that ye shall tread upon, as He hath spoken unto you.

Behold, I set before you this day a blessing and a curse: the blessing, if ye shall hearken unto the commandments of Yahweh your God which I command you this day; and the curse, if ye shall not hearken unto the commandments of Yahweh your God, but turn aside out of the way which I command you this day to go after other gods which ye have not known. And it shall come to pass, when Yahweh thy God shall bring thee into the land whither thou goest to possess it, that thou shalt set the blessing upon mount Gerizim, and the curse upon mount Ebal. Are they not on the other side Jordan, by the way where the sun goeth down, in the land of the Canaanites that dwell in the Arabah, over against Gilgal, beside the terebinth of Moreh? For ye are to pass over Jordan to go in to possess the land which Yahweh your God giveth you; and ye shall possess it and dwell therein. And ye shall observe to do all the statutes and ordinances which I set before you this day.

These are the statutes and the ordinances which ye shall observe to do in the land which Yahweh, the God of your fathers, hath given you to possess it all the days that ye live upon the earth. Ye shall surely destroy all the places wherein the nations ye are to dispossess served their gods, upon the high mountains and upon the hills and under every leafy tree. And ye shall break down their altars, and break their pillars and burn their Asherim with fire; and ye shall hew down the graven images of their gods, and ye shall destroy their names out of that place. Ye shall not do so unto Yahweh your God. But unto the place that Yahweh your God shall choose out of all your tribes to put His name there, even His habitation shall ye seek, and thither shalt thou come. And thither shall ye bring your burnt-offerings and your sacrifices, and your tithes and the offering of your hand, and your vows and your free-will offerings, and the firstlings of your herds and of your flocks; and there shall ye eat before Yahweh your God, and ye shall rejoice in all that ye put your hand unto, ye and all your households wherein Yahweh thy God hath blessed thee. Ye shall not do after all that we do here this day, every man whatsoever is right in his own eyes; for ye are not as yet come to the rest and to the inheritance which Yahweh thy God giveth thee. But when ye go over the Jordan, and dwell in the land which Yahweh your God causeth you to inherit, and when He giveth you rest from all your enemies round about, so that ye dwell in safety; then there shall be a place which Yahweh your God shall choose to cause His name to dwell there; thither shall ye bring all that I command you,—your burnt-offerings and your sacrifices, your tithes and the offering of your hand, and all your choice vows which ye vow unto Yahweh. And ye shall rejoice before Yahweh your God, ye and your sons and your daughters, and your man-servants and your maid-servants, and the stranger that is within your gates.[1] Take heed to thyself that thou offer not thy burnt-offerings in every place that thou seest; but in the place which Yahweh shall choose in one of your tribes, there thou shalt offer thy burnt-offerings, and there shalt thou do all that I command thee. Notwithstanding thou mayest kill and eat flesh within all thy gates after all the desire of thy soul, according to the blessing of Yahweh thy God which He hath given thee; the unclean and the clean may eat thereof, as of the gazelle and as of the hart. Only ye shall not eat the blood; thou shalt pour it cut upon the earth as water.

Thou must not eat within thy gates the tithe of thy corn, or of thy wine or of thine oil, or of the firstlings of thy herd or of thy flock; nor shalt thou pay there any of thy vows which thou vowest, nor thy free-will offerings, nor the heave-offering of thy hand; but thou must eat them before Yahweh thy God in the place that He shall choose, thou and thy son and thy daughter, thy man-servant and thy maid-servant and the stranger that is within thy gates; and thou shalt rejoice before Yahweh thy God, in all that thou puttest thine hand unto.

When Yahweh thy God shall enlarge thy border, as He hath promised thee, and thou shalt say: I will eat flesh, because thy soul desireth to eat flesh; thou mayest eat flesh after all the desire of thy soul, if the place which Yahweh thy God shall choose to put His name there be too far from thee; then thou shalt kill of thy herd and of thy flock which Yahweh hath given thee, as I have commanded thee, and thou shalt eat within thy gates after all the desire of thy soul. Howbeit as the gazelle and as the hart is eaten, so shalt thou eat thereof; the unclean and the clean may eat thereof alike. Only be steadfast in not eating the blood; for the blood is the life; and thou shalt not eat the life with the flesh. Thou shalt not eat it; thou shalt pour it out upon the earth as water. Thou shalt not eat it, that it may be well with thee and with thy children after thee, when thou shalt do that which is right in the eyes of Yahweh. Only thy holy things which thou hast and thy vows, thou shalt take and go unto the place which Yahweh shall choose; and thou shalt offer thy burnt-offerings, the flesh and the blood, upon the altar of Yahweh thy God; and the blood of thy sacrifices shall be poured out upon the altar of Yahweh thy God, and thou shalt eat the flesh. Observe and hear all these words which I command thee, that it may go well with thee and with thy children after thee, when thou doest that which is right and good in the eyes of Yahweh thy God.

When Yahweh thy God shall cut off the nations from before thee whither thou goest to dispossess them, and thou succeedest them and dwellest in their land; take heed unto thyself, that thou be not ensnared to follow them, after that they are destroyed from before thee; and that thou inquire not after their gods, saying: How did these nations serve their gods? so will I do likewise. Thou shalt not do so unto thy God Yahweh; for every abomination to Yahweh which He hateth have they done unto their gods; for even their sons and their daughters do they burn in the fire to their gods.

All this word that I command you, that shall ye observe to do; thou shalt not add thereto nor diminish from it.

If there rise in the midst of thee a prophet or a dreamer of dreams, and he give thee a sign or a wonder, and the sign or the wonder come

---

[1] V. 12c is a late addition by a too careful scribe to accord with the conditions of his own day; v. 19 is also omitted for the same reason.

to pass whereof he spake unto thee, saying: Let us go after other gods, which thou hast not known and let us serve them; thou shalt not hearken unto the words of that prophet or that dreamer of dreams. For Yahweh your God is putting you to proof, to know whether ye indeed love Yahweh your God with all your heart and with all your soul. After Yahweh your God shall ye walk, and Him shall ye fear, and His commandments shall ye keep; and obey His voice, and ye shall serve Him and cleave unto Him. And that prophet or that dreamer of dreams, shall be put to death; for he hath spoken to turn you away from Yahweh your God, which brought you out of the land of Egypt and redeemed you out of the house of bondage, to thrust thee out of the way which Yahweh thy God commanded thee to walk in. So shalt thou put evil away from the midst of thee.

If thy brother, the son of thy mother, or thy son or thy daughter, or the wife of thy bosom, or thy friend which is as thine own soul entice thee secretly, saying: Let us go and serve other gods,—which thou hast not known, thou, nor thy fathers; of the gods of the peoples that are round about you, nigh unto thee or far off from thee, from the one end of the earth even unto the other end of the earth; thou shalt not consent unto him nor hearken unto him, neither shall thine eye pity him, neither shalt thou spare, neither shalt thou conceal him; but thou shalt surely kill him. Thy hand shall be first upon him to put him to death, and afterwards the hand of all the people. And thou shalt stone him with stones that he die; because he hath sought to draw thee away from Yahweh thy God, who brought thee out of the land of Egypt, out of the house of bondage. And all Israel shall hear and fear, and shall no more do any such wickedness as this is among you.

If thou shalt hear it said of any one of thy cities which Yahweh thy God giveth thee to dwell therein: Certain base fellows have gone out from among you, and have drawn away the inhabitants of their city, saying: Let us go and serve other gods which ye have not known; then thou shalt inquire and make search and ask diligently; and behold, if it be truth and it be certain that such abomination is wrought among you, thou shalt surely smite the inhabitants of that city with the edge of the sword, destroying it utterly and all that is therein, even the cattle thereof, with the edge of the sword. And thou shalt gather all the spoil of it into the midst of the great square, and shalt burn with fire the city and all the spoil thereof, every whit, before Yahweh thy God. And it shall be a heap for ever; it shall not be rebuilt. And there shall cleave naught of the cursed thing to thy hand; that Yahweh may turn from the fierceness of His anger, and show thee mercy, and have compassion upon thee and mutiply thee, as He hath sworn to thy fathers to do, when thou shalt hearken to the voice of Yahweh thy God to keep all His commandments which I command thee this day, to do right in the eyes of Yahweh thy God.

EXPOSITION OF THE LAWS OF THE SECOND TABLET

(Ch. xiv, 1—xxvi, 19)

Ye are the children of Yahweh your God. Ye shall not cut yourselves, nor make any baldness between your eyes for the dead. For thou art a holy people unto Yahweh thy God, and Yahweh hath chosen thee to be a peculiar people unto Himself above all the nations that are upon the face of the earth. Thou shalt not eat any abominable thing. These are the beasts that ye shall eat: the ox, the sheep and the goat,

the hart and the gazelle, the roebuck, the wild-goat, the pygarg, the ante-
lope and the mountain-sheep; and every beast that parteth the hoof
and cleaveth the cleft into two claws, and cheweth the cud among the
beasts, that ye may eat. Nevertheless these ye shall not eat of; them
that only chew the cud, or them that only have the hoof cloven: the
camel and the hare and the coney, because they chew the cud but part
not the hoof; they are unclean unto you; and the swine, because he
parteth the hoof but cheweth not the cud, he is unclean unto you; of
their flesh ye shall not eat, and their carcasses ye shall not touch.

These ye may eat of all that are in the waters: whatsoever hath fins
and scales, ye may eat; and whatsoever hath not fins and scales ye shall
not eat; it is unclean for you.

Of all clean birds ye may eat. But these are they of which ye shall
not eat: the great vulture and the bearded vulture and the ospray;
and the glede and the falcon and the kite after its kinds; and every raven
after its kinds; and the ostrich and the night-hawk, and the sea-mew,
and the hawk after its kinds; the little owl and the great owl and the
horned owl; the pelican and the carrion-vulture and the cormorant;
and the stork, and the heron after its kinds, the hoopoe and the bat.
And all winged swarming things are unclean unto you; they shall not
be eaten. Of all clean winged things ye may eat.

Ye shall not eat of anything that dieth of itself; thou mayest give
it unto the stranger that is within thy gates, that he may eat it; or
thou mayest sell it unto a foreigner; but thou art a holy people unto
Yahweh thy God. Thou shalt not seethe the kid in its mother's milk.

Thou shalt surely tithe all the increase of thy seed, that which is
brought forth in the field from year to year. And thou shalt eat
before Yahweh thy God, in the place which He shall choose to cause
His name to dwell there, the tithe of thy corn, of thy wine and of thine
oil, and the firstlings of thy herd and of thy flock; that thou mayest
learn to fear Yahweh thy God always. But, if the way be too long for
thee, so that thou art not able to carry it because the place is too far
from thee which Yahweh thy God shall choose to set His name there,
when Yahweh thy God shall bless thee; then thou shalt turn it into
money and bind up the money in thy hand, and shalt go up unto the
place which Yahweh thy God shall choose. And thou shalt bestow the
money for whatsoever thy soul desireth, for oxen or for sheep, or for
strong drink, or for whatsoever thy soul asketh of thee; and thou
shalt eat these before Yahweh thy God, and thou shalt rejoice, thou and
thy household.[1]

At the end of every three years, even in the same year, thou shalt
bring forth all the tithe of thine increase, and shalt lay it up within
thy gates. And the [2]stranger and the fatherless and the widow that
are within thy gates shall come, and shall eat and be satisfied; that
Yahweh thy God may bless thee in all the work of thy hand which
Thou doest.

At the end of every seven years thou shalt make a release. And this
is the manner of the release; every creditor shall release that he hath
lent unto his neighbor; he shall not exact it of his neighbor and his
brother, because Yahweh's release hath been proclaimed. Of a foreigner
thou mayest exact it; but whatsoever is thine with thy brother, thy
hand shall release. Howbeit there shall be no needy among you,—for
Yahweh will surely bless thee in the land which Yahweh thy God giveth

---

[1] V. 27 is interpolated; it belongs to the later legislation, and is here omitted.
[2] The enjoining of charity for the Levite is contrary to the Mosaic legislation; v. 29a
is therefore omitted.

thee for an inheritance to possess it,—if only thou diligently hearken to the voice of Yahweh thy God, to observe to do all this commandment that I command thee this day. For Yahweh thy God will bless thee as He promised thee; and thou shalt lend unto many nations, but thou shalt not borrow; and thou shalt rule over many nations, but they shall not rule over thee.

If there be among you a needy man, one of thy brethren, within any of thy gates in the land which Yahweh thy God giveth thee, thou shalt not harden thy heart nor shut thine hand from thy needy brother; but thou shalt surely open thine hand unto him, and shalt surely lend him sufficient for his need in that which he lacketh. Beware that there be not a base thought in thy heart, saying: The seventh year, the year of release is at hand; and thine eye be evil against thy needy brother, and thou give him nought, and he cry unto Yahweh against thee, and it be sin in thee. Thou shalt surely give to him, and thy heart shall not be grieved when thou givest unto him; because that for this thing Yahweh will bless thee in all thy work, and in all that thou puttest thine hand unto. For the poor shall never cease out of the land; therefore I command thee, saying: Thou shalt surely open thy hand unto thy poor and needy brother in thy land.

If thy brother, a Hebrew man or a Hebrew woman, be sold unto thee, he shall serve thee six years; and in the seventh year thou shalt let him go free from thee. And when thou lettest him go free from thee, thou shalt not let him go empty; thou shalt furnish him liberally out of thy flock, and out of thy threshing-floor, and out of thy wine-press; of that wherewith Yahweh thy God hath blessed thee, thou shalt give unto him. And thou shalt remember that thou wast a bondman in the land of Egypt, and that Yahweh thy God redeemed thee; therefore I command thee this thing to-day. And it shall be, if he say unto thee: I will not go out from thee, because he loveth thee and thy house, because he fareth well with thee; then thou shalt take an awl and thrust it through his ear and into the door, and he shall be thy bondman for ever. And also unto thy bondwoman thou shalt do likewise. It shall not seem hard unto thee when thou lettest him go free from thee; for to the double of the hire of an hireling hath he served thee six years; and Yahweh thy God will bless thee in all that thou doest.

All the firstling males that are born of thy herd and of thy flock thou shalt sanctify unto Yahweh thy God; thou shalt do no work with the firstling of thine ox, nor shear the firstling of thy flock. Thou shalt eat it before Yahweh thy God year by year, in the place which Yahweh shall choose, thou and thy household. And if there be any blemish therein, lameness or blindness, any ill blemish whatsoever, thou shalt not sacrifice it unto Yahweh thy God. Thou shalt eat it within thy gates; the unclean and the clean may eat it alike, as the gazelle, and as the hart. Only thou shalt not eat the blood thereof; thou shalt pour it out upon the ground as water.

Observe the month Abib, and keep the passover unto Yahweh thy God; for in the month of Abib Yahweh thy God brought thee forth out of Egypt by night. And thou shalt sacrifice the passover-offering unto Yahweh thy God, of the flock and the herd, in the place which Yahweh shall choose to cause His name to dwell there. Thou shalt eat no leavened bread with it; seven days shalt thou eat unleavened bread therewith, even the bread of affliction; for in haste didst thou come forth out of the land of Egypt; that thou mayest remember the day when thou camest forth out of the land of Egypt all the days of thy life. And there shall no leaven be seen with thee in all thy borders seven days; neither shall any of the flesh which thou dost sacrifice the first day at even remain with thee until the morning. Thou mayest not sacrifice the offering of the passover within any of thy gates, which Yahweh thy God hath given thee; but at the place which Yahweh thy God shall choose to cause His name to dwell in, there shalt thou sacrifice the passover-offering at even, at the going down of the sun, at the season that thou camest forth out of Egypt. And thou shalt roast and eat it in the place which Yahweh thy God shall choose; and thou shalt turn in the morning and go unto thy tents. Six days thou shalt eat unleavened bread; and on the seventh day shall be a solemn assembly to Yahweh thy God; thou shalt do no work therein.

Seven weeks shalt thou number unto thee; from the time the sickle is first put to the standing corn shalt thou begin to number seven weeks. And thou shalt keep the feast of weeks unto Yahweh thy God after the measure of the freewill-offering of thy hand, which thou shalt give according as Yahweh thy God blesseth thee. And thou shalt rejoice before Yahweh thy God, thou and thy son and thy daughter and thy man-servant and thy maid-servant and the Levite that is within thy gates, and the stranger and the fatherless and the widow that are in the midst of thee, in the place which Yahweh thy God shall choose to cause His name to dwell there. And thou shalt remember that thou wast a bondman in Egypt; and thou shalt observe and do these statutes.

Thou shalt keep the feast of tabernacles seven days, after that thou hast gathered in from thy threshing-floor and from thy wine-press. And thou shalt rejoice in thy feast, thou and thy son and thy daughter, and thy man-servant and thy maid-servant, and the Levite and the stranger, and the fatherless and the widow that are within thy gates: Seven days shalt thou keep a feast unto Yahweh thy God in the place which Yahweh shall choose; for Yahweh thy God shall bless thee in all thine increase and in all the work of thine hands, and thou shalt be altogether joyful.

Three times in a year shall all thy males appear before Yahweh thy God in the place which He shall choose: On the feast of unleavened bread, and on the feast of weeks, and on the feast of tabernacles; and they shall not appear empty; every man shall give as he is able, according to the blessing of Yahweh thy God which He hath given thee.

Judges and officers shalt thou make thee in all thy gates, which Yahweh thy God giveth thee, tribe by tribe; and they shall judge the people with righteous judgment. Thou shalt not wrest judgment; thou shalt not have regard to persons; neither shalt thou take a gift, for a gift doth blind the eyes of the wise and pervert the words of the righteous. Justice, justice shalt thou follow, that thou mayest live and inherit the land, which Yahweh thy God giveth thee.

Thou shalt not plant thee an Asherah of any kind of tree beside the altar of Yahweh thy God, which thou shalt make thee. Neither shalt thou set thee up a pillar which Yahweh thy God hateth.

Thou shalt not sacrifice unto Yahweh thy God an ox or a sheep wherein is a blemish or any evil thing; for that is an abomination unto Yahweh thy God.

If there be found in the midst of thee, within any of the gates which Yahweh thy God giveth thee, man or woman, that doeth that which is evil in the sight of Yahweh thy God in transgressing His covenant, and who hath gone and served other gods and worshipped them, or the sun or the moon or any of the host of heaven which I have commanded not, and it be told thee, and thou hear it; then shalt thou inquire diligently, and behold, if it be true, and the thing certain that such abomination is wrought in Israel, then thou shalt bring forth that man or that woman who hath done this evil thing unto thy gates, even the man or the woman; and thou shalt stone them with stones, that they die. At the mouth of two witnesses or three witnesses, shall he that is to die be put to death; at the mouth of one witness shall he not be put to death. The hand of the witnesses shall be first upon him to put him to death, and afterward the hand of all the people. So shalt thou put away the evil from the midst of thee.

If there arise a matter too hard for thee in judgment, between blood and blood and between plea and plea, between stroke and stroke, even matters of controversy within thy gates; then shalt thou arise and get thee up unto the place which Yahweh thy God shall choose. And thou shalt come unto the priests the Levites, and unto the judge that shall be in those days, and thou shalt inquire; and they shall declare unto thee the sentence of judgment. And thou shalt do according to the tenor of the sentence which they shall declare unto thee from that place which Yahweh thy God shall choose; and thou shalt observe to do according to all that they shall teach thee. According to the law which they shall teach thee, and according to the judgment which they shall tell thee, thou shalt do; thou shalt not turn aside from the sentence which they shall declare unto thee, to the right hand or to the left. And the man that doeth presumptuously in not hearkening to the priest that standeth to minister there before Yahweh thy God, or unto the judge, even that man shall die; and thou shalt exterminate the evil from Israel. And all the people shall hear, and fear, and act no more presumptuously.

When thou art come unto the land which Yahweh thy God giveth thee, and shalt possess it and shalt dwell therein, and shalt say: I wilt set a king over me, like all the nations that are round about me; thou shalt in any wise set him king over thee whom Yahweh thy God shall choose; one from among thy brethren shalt thou set as king over thee; thou mayest not put a foreigner over thee, who is not thy brother. Only he shall not multiply horses to himself, nor cause the people to return to Egypt, to the end that he should multiply horses; forasmuch as Yahweh hath said unto you: Henceforth ye shall return no more that way. Neither shall he multiply wives unto himself, that his heart turn not away; neither shall he multiply to himself silver and gold. And it shall be, when he sitteth upon the throne of his kingdom, that he shall write him a copy of this law in a book, out of that which is before the priests the Levites. And it shall be with him, and he shall read therein all the days of his life; that he may learn to fear Yahweh his God, to keep all the words of this law and these statutes, to do them; that his heart be not lifted up above his brethren, and that he turn not aside from the commandment to the right hand or to the left; to the end that he may prolong his days in his kingdom, he and his children, in the midst of Israel.

The priests, the Levites, eevn all the tribe of Levi, shall have no portion nor inheritance with Israel; they shall eat the offerings of Yahweh made by fire which are His inheritance. And they shall have no inheritance among their brethren; Yahweh is their inheritance, as He hath spoken unto them.

And this shall be the priests' due from the people, from them that offer sacrifice, whether it be ox or sheep; that they shall give unto the priest the shoulder and the two cheeks and the maw. The first-fruits of thy corn and of thy wine and of thine oil, and the first of the fleece of thy sheep, shalt thou give him. For Yahweh thy God hath chosen him out of all thy tribes, to stand to minister in the name of Yahweh, him and his sons for ever.

And if a Levite come from any of thy gates out of all Israel, where he sojourneth, and come with all the desire of his soul unto the place which Yahweh thy God shall choose; then he shall minister in the name of Yahweh his God, as all his brethren the Levites do, who stand there before Yahweh. They shall have like portions to eat, besides that which is his due according to the fathers' houses.

When thou art come into the land which Yahweh thy God giveth thee, thou shalt not learn to do after the abominations of those nations. There shall not be found among you any one that maketh his son or his daughter to pass through fire, or that useth divination, a soothsayer, an enchanter, or a sorcerer, or a charmer or a consulter with familiar spirits, or a wizard or a necromancer. For all that do these things are an abomination to Yahweh; and because of these abominations doth Yahweh thy God drive them out from before thee. Thou shalt be perfect with Yahweh thy God. For these nations which thou shalt dispossess hearkened unto soothsayers and unto diviners; but as for thee, Yahweh thy God hath not suffered thee so to do.

A Prophet will Yahweh thy God raise up unto thee from the midst of thee, one of thy brethren like unto me; unto him shall ye hearken, according to all that thou didst desire of Yahweh thy God in Horeb, in the day of the assembly, saying: Let me not hear again the voice of Yahweh my God, neither let me see this great fire any more, that I die not. And Yahweh said unto me, They have well spoken. I will raise up a Prophet from among their brethren like unto thee; and I will put My words in his mouth; and he shall speak unto them all that I command him. And it shall come to pass, that whosoever will not hearken to My words which he shall speak in My name, I will require it of him. But the prophet who shall presume to speak a word in My name which I have not commanded him to speak, or who shall speak in the name of other gods, that same prophet shall die. And if thou say in thine heart: How shall we know the word which Yahweh hath not spoken? When a prophet speaketh in the name of Yahweh, if the thing follow not nor come to pass, that is the thing which Yahweh hath not spoken; the prophet hath spoken it presumptuously; thou shalt not be afraid of him.

When Yahweh thy God hath cut off the nations whose land Yahweh thy God giveth thee, and thou succeedest them and dwellest in their cities, and in their houses; thou shalt separate three cities for thee in the midst of the land which Yahweh thy God giveth thee to possess it. Thou shalt prepare thee a way, and divide the borders of thy land, which Yahweh thy God giveth thee to inherit, into three parts, that every slayer may flee thither.

And this is the case of the man-slayer which shall flee thither, that he may live: Whoso killeth his neighbor ignorantly, whom he hated not in time past; as when a man goeth into the wood with his neighbor to hew wood, and his hand fetcheth a stroke with the axe to cut down the tree, and the head slippeth from the helve, and lighteth upon his neighbor that he die; he shall flee to one of those cities and live; lest the avenger of blood pursue the slayer while his heart is hot, and overtake him because the way is long, and slay him; whereas he was not worthy of death, inasmuch as he hated him not in time past. Wherefore I command thee, saying: Thou shalt separate three cities for thee.

And if Yahweh thy God enlarge thy border, as He hath sworn to thy fathers, and give thee all the land which He promised to give unto thy fathers; if thou shalt keep all these commandments to do them, which I command thee this day; to love Yahweh thy God, and to walk ever in His ways; then thou shalt add three cities more for thee, besides these three; that innocent blood shall not be shed in thy land, which Yahweh thy God giveth thee for an inheritance, and so blood be upon thee.

But if any man hate his neighbor, and lie in wait for him and rise up against him, and smite him mortally that he die, and fleeth unto one of these cities; then the elders of his city shall send and fetch him thence, and deliver him into the hand of the avenger of blood, that he may die. Thine eye shall not pity him, but thou shalt put away the blood of the innocent from Israel, that it may be well with thee.

Thou shalt not remove thy neighbor's landmark, which they of old time have set in thine inheritance, which thou shalt inherit in the land that Yahweh thy God giveth thee to possess it.

One witness shall not rise up against a man for any iniquity or for any sin, in any sin that he sinneth; at the mouth of two witnesses or the mouth of three witnesses shall the matter be established. If a false witness rise up against any man to testify against him wrongly; then both the men between whom is the controversy shall stand before Yahweh, before the priests and the judges which shall be in those days; and the judges shall make diligent inquisition; and behold, if the witness be a false witness, and hath testified falsely against his brother; then shall ye do unto him as he had thought to do unto his brother; so shall ye put away the evil from among you. And those that remain shall hear, and fear, and shall henceforth commit no more any such evil among you. And thine eye shall not pity; life for life, eye for eye, tooth for tooth, hand for hand, foot for foot.

When thou goest out to battle against thine enemies, and seest horses and chariots and a people more than thou, be not afraid of them; for Yahweh thy God is with thee, which brought thee up out of the land of Egypt. And it shall be, when ye are come nigh unto the battle, that the priest shall approach and speak unto the people, and shall say unto them: Hear, O Israel! ye approach this day unto battle against your enemies; let not your hearts faint; fear not, and do not tremble, neither be ye terrified because of them; for Yahweh your God goeth with you to fight for you against your enemies to save you. And the officers shall speak unto the people, saying: What man here hath built a new house, and hath not dedicated it? let him go and return to his house, lest he die in battle, and another man dedicate it. And what man hath planted a vineyard, and hath not yet eaten of it? let him go and return unto his house, lest he die in battle, and another man use the fruit thereof. And what man hath betrothed a wife, and hath not taken her? let him go and return to his house, lest he die in battle, and another man take her. And the officers shall speak further unto the people, and say: What man is fearful and faint-hearted? let him go and return unto his house, lest his brethren's heart faint as well as his heart. And it shall be, when the officers have made an end of speaking unto the people, that they shall make captains of the armies to lead the people.

When thou comest nigh unto a city to fight against it, then proclaim peace unto it. And it shall be, if it make thee answer of peace and open unto thee, then it shall be that all the people found therein shall be tributaries unto thee, and they shall serve thee. But if it will make no peace with thee and will make war against thee, then thou shalt besiege it; and when Yahweh thy God hath delivered it into thy hands, thou shalt smite every male thereof with the edge of the sword; but the women and the little ones and the cattle, and all that is in the city, all the spoil thereof, shalt thou take unto thyself; and thou shalt consume the spoil of thine enemies, which Yahweh thy God hath given thee. Thus shalt thou do unto all the cities which are very far off from thee, which are not of the cities of these nations. But of the cities of these people which Yahweh thy God doth give thee for an inheritance, thou shalt save alive nothing that doth breathe; thou shalt utterly destroy them: the Hittites, and the Amorites, the Canaanites and the Perizzites, the Hivites and the Jebusites,[1] as Yahweh thy God hath commanded thee; that they teach you not to do after all their abominations, which they have offered unto their gods; and so ye sin against Yahweh your God.

When thou shalt besiege a city a long time, in making war against it to take it, thou shalt not destroy the trees thereof by wielding an axe against them; for thou mayest eat of them, but thou shalt not cut them down; for is the tree of the field man, that thou shouldest besiege it? Only the trees of which thou knowest that they are not trees for food, them thou mayest destroy and cut down, that thou mayest build bulwarks against the city that maketh war against thee, until it be subdued.

If one be found slain in the land which Yahweh thy God giveth thee to possess it, lying in the field, and it be not known who hath slain him; then thy elders and thy judges shall come forth, and they shall measure unto the cities round about him that is slain; and it shall be that the city nearest unto the slain man, even the elders of that city shall take an heifer which hath not been wrought with, nor hath drawn in the yoke; and the elders of that city shall bring down the heifer to a rough valley which is neither ploughed nor sown, and strike off the heifer's neck there in the valley; and the priests the sons of Levi shall come near—for them hath Yahweh thy God chosen to minister unto Him, and to bless in the name of Yahweh, and according to their decision shall be every controversy and every stroke. And all the elders of the city nearest to the slain man shall wash their hands over the heifer that is beheaded in the valley. And they shall speak and say: Our hands have not shed this blood, neither have our eyes seen it. Be merciful, O Yahweh, unto Thy people Israel whom Thou hast redeemed, and lay not innocent blood to the charge of Thy people Israel. And the blood shall be forgiven them. So shalt thou put away innocent blood from among you, when thou doest right in the sight of Yahweh.

When thou goest forth to war against thine enemies, and Yahweh thy God hath delivered them into thine hands, and thou hast taken them captive, and seest among the captives a beautiful woman and hast a

---

[1] All these peoples had conquered Canaanite territory, and intermarried with the original settlers and had thereby become contaminated.

desire for her, that thou wouldest have her to wife; then thou shalt bring her home to thy house, and she shall shave her head and pare her nails; and she shall put off from her the raiment of her captivity and shall remain in thine house and bewail her father and her mother a full month; and after that thou shalt go in unto her and be her husband, and she shall be thy wife. And it shall be, if thou have no delight in her, then thou shalt let her go whither she will; but thou shalt not sell her at all for money; thou shalt not make merchandise of her, because thou hast humbled her.

If a man have two wives, one beloved and another hated, and they have both borne him children, and the first-born son be hers that was hated; then it shall be, when he maketh his sons to inherit that which he hath, that he may not make the son of the beloved first-born before the son of the hated who is indeed the first-born; but he shall acknowledge the son of the hated first-born by giving him a double portion of all that he hath; for he is the beginning of his strength; the right of the first-born is his.

If a man have a stubborn and rebellious son which will not obey the voice of his father or the voice of his mother, and who, when they have chastened him, will not hearken unto them; then shall his father and his mother lay hold on him and bring him unto the elders of his city and unto the gate of his place; and they shall say unto the elders of the city: This our son is stubborn and rebellious; he will not obey our voice; he is a glutton and a drunkard. And all the men of his city shall stone him with stones, that he die. So shalt thou put away evil from among you; and all Israel shall hear, and fear.

And if a man have committed a sin worthy of death, and he be put to death, and thou hang him on a tree; his body shall not remain all night upon the tree, but thou shalt in any wise bury him that day, for he that is hanged is accursed of God, that the land be not defiled, which Yahweh thy God giveth thee for an inheritance.

Thou shalt not see thy brother's ox or his sheep go astray, and hide thyself from them; thou shalt in any case bring them again to thy brother. And if thy brother be not nigh unto thee, or if thou know him not, then thou shall bring it unto thine own house, and it shall be with thee until thy brother seek after it; then thou shalt restore it unto him again. In like manner shalt thou do with his ass; and so shalt thou do with his raiment; and with every thing of thy brother's which he hath lost and thou hast found, shalt thou do likewise. Thou mayest not hide thyself.

Thou shalt not see thy brother's ass or his ox fall down by the way and hide thyself from them; thou shalt surely help him to lift them up again.

The woman shall not wear that which pertaineth to a man, neither shall a man put on a woman's garment; for all that do so are abomination unto Yahweh thy God.

If a bird's nest chance to be before thee in the way, in any tree or on the ground, with young ones or eggs and the dam sitting upon the young or upon the eggs, thou shalt not take the dam with the young; thou shalt in any wise let the dam go, and take the young to thee; that it may be well with thee, and that thou mayest prolong thy days.

When thou buildest a new house, then thou shalt make a battlement for thy roof that thou bring not blood upon thine house, if any man fall from thence.

Thou shalt not sow thy vineyard with divers seeds, lest the fullness of the seed which thou hast sown and the fruit of thy vineyard alike deteriorate.

Thou shalt not plough with an ox and an ass together. Thou shalt not wear a garment of mixed goods, as of woollen and cotton together. Thou shalt make thee twisted cords upon the four corners of thy vesture, wherewith thou coverest thyself.[1]

*   *   *   *   *   *   *

When thou comest into thy neighbor's vineyard, thou mayest eat thy fill of grapes at thine own pleasure; but thou shalt not put any in thy vessel. When thou comest into thy neighbor's standing corn, thou mayest pluck the ears with thy hand; but thou shalt put no sickle into thy neighbor's standing corn.

No man shall take the mill nor the upper mill-stone to pledge; for he taketh a man's life to pledge.

When thou dost lend thy neighbor any manner of loan, thou shalt not go into his house to fetch the pledge; thou shalt stand without, and the man to whom thou dost lend shall bring forth the pledge without unto thee. And if he be a poor man, thou shalt not sleep retaining his pledge; thou shalt surely restore the pledge to him when the sun goeth down, that he may sleep in his garment and bless thee; and it shall be righteousness unto thee before Yahweh thy God.

Thou shalt not oppress a hired servant that is poor and needy, whether he be of thy brethren or of the strangers that are in the land within thy gates. In the same day thou shalt give him his hire, neither shall the sun go down upon it; for he is poor and setteth his heart upon it; lest he cry against thee unto Yahweh, and it be sin in thee.

When thou reapest the harvest in thy field, and hast forgot a sheaf, thou shalt not go back to fetch it; it shall be for the stranger, for the fatherless and for the widow. When thou beatest thine olive-tree, thou shalt not go over the boughs again; it shall be for the stranger, for the fatherless and for the widow. When thou gatherest the grapes of thy vineyard, thou shalt not glean it after thee; it shall be for the stranger, for the fatherless and for the widow. And thou shalt remember that thou wast a bondman in the land of Egypt; therefore I command thee to do this thing.

If there be a controversy between men and they come unto judgment, then the judges shall justify the righteous and condemn the wicked. And it shall be, if the wicked man be worthy to be beaten, that the judge shall cause him to lie down and be beaten before his face according to his fault by a certain number. Forty stripes he may give him, but not more; lest, if he exceed and beat him above these with many stripes, then thy brother should be dishonored before thine eyes.

Thou shalt not muzzle the ox when he treadeth out the corn.

Thou shalt not have in thy bag diverse weights, a great and a small. Thou shalt not have in thy house diverse measures, a great and a small. Thou shalt have a perfect and just weight, a perfect and just measure shalt thou have; that thy days may be long in the land which Yahweh thy God hath given thee. For all that do such things, and all that do unrighteously, are an abomination unto Yahweh thy God.

Remember what Amalek did unto thee by the way, when thou wast

---

[1] Ch. xxii, 13-xxv, 12, contain chiefly expansions of the laws for the regulation of the domestic life of the Israelites given in the "Law of Holiness." A few excerpts given below show the Deuteronomic insistence upon justice, mercy, and benevolence in the smallest details in the life of the community, and the scrupulous care for the feelings of the recipient of kindnesses.

come out of Egypt; how he met thee by the way and smote the hind-most of thee, even all that were feeble behind thee, when thou wast faint and weary; and he feared not God. Therefore it shall be, when Yahweh thy God hath given thee rest from all thine enemies round about, in the land which Yahweh thy God giveth thee for an inheritance to possess it, that thou shalt blot out the remembrance of Amalek from under heaven; thou shalt not forget it.

And it shall be, when thou art come in unto the land which Yahweh thy God giveth thee for an inheritance, and dost possess it and dwell therein, that thou shalt take of the first of all the fruit of the earth which thou shalt bring forth of the land that Yahweh thy God giveth thee, and shalt put it in a basket and shalt go unto the place which Yahweh thy God shall choose to place His name there. And thou shalt go unto the priest that shall be in those days, and shalt say unto him:

I profess this day unto Yahweh thy God, that I am come unto the land which Yahweh sware unto our fathers to give us.

And the priest shall take the basket out of thine hands, and set it down before the altar of Yahweh thy God.

And thou shalt speak and say before Yahweh thy God: A Syrian ready to perish was my father; and he went down into Egypt and so-journed there with a few, and became there a nation, great, mighty and populous; and the Egyptians evil-entreated us, and laid upon us hard bondage; and when we cried unto Yahweh, the God of our fathers, He heard our voice and looked upon our affliction and our labor and our oppression; and Yahweh brought us forth out of Egypt with a mighty hand, with an outstretched arm, and with great terribleness and with signs and with wonders; and He hath brought us unto this place, and hath given us this land that floweth with milk and honey. And now, behold, I have brought thee first-fruits of the land which Thou, O Yahweh, hast given me.

And thou shalt set it before Yahweh thy God, and worship before Yahweh thy God; and thou shalt rejoice in every good thing which Yahweh thy God hath given unto thee and thine house, thou and the Levite, and the stranger that is with you.

When thou hast made an end of tithing all the tithes of thine in-crease the third year, the year of tithing; and hast given unto the Levite, the stranger, the fatherless and the widow, that they may eat within thy gates and be filled; then thou shalt say before Yahweh thy God:

I have put away the hallowed things out of my house, and have also given them to the Levite and unto the fatherless and the widow, and unto the stranger, according to all the commandments which Thou hast commanded me; I have not transgressed Thy commandments, neither have I forgotten Thee; I have not eaten thereof in my mourn-ing, neither have I taken away thereof for unclean use, nor given thereof for the dead. I have hearkened unto the voice of Yahweh my God, and have done according to all that Thou hast commanded me. Look down from heaven, Thy holy habitation, and bless Thy people Israel and the land which Thou hast given us, as Thou swarest unto our fathers, a land that floweth with milk and honey.

This day Yahweh thy God hath commanded thee to do these statutes and ordinances; thou shalt therefore observe and do them with all thine heart and with all thy soul. Thou hast this day avouched Yahweh to be thy God, and to walk in His ways and keep His statutes, His com-mandments and His ordinances, and to hearken to His voice; and Yahweh hath this day avouched thee to be His peculiar people, as He hath promised thee, if thou keep all His commandments, and to make thee high above all nations which He hath made in praise, and in name, and in honor; that thou mayest be an holy people unto **Yahweh thy God,** as He hath spoken.

SUMMATION OF THE RESULTS OF OBEDIENCE AND OF DISOBEDIENCE TO THESE COMMANDMENTS
(Ch. xxviii, 1-68)

[1] And it shall come to pass, if thou wilt hearken diligently unto the voice of Yahweh thy God, to observe and to do all His commandments which I have commanded thee this day, that Yahweh thy God will set thee high above all nations of the earth; and all these blessings shall come on thee and overtake thee, if thou wilt hearken unto the voice of Yahweh thy God.

Blessed shalt thou be in the city, and blessed shalt thou be in the field.

Blessed shall be the fruit of thy body, and the fruit of thy ground, and the fruit of thy cattle, the increase of thy kine and the young of thy flock.

Blessed shall be thy basket and thy store.

Blessed shalt thou be when thou comest in, and blessed shalt thou be when thou goest out.

Yahweh shall cause thine enemies that rise up against thee to be smitten before thee; they shall come out against thee one way, and flee before thee seven ways.

Yahweh shall command the blessing upon thee in thy storehouses, and in all that thou settest thine hand unto; and He shall bless thee in the land which Yahweh thy God giveth thee.

Yahweh shall establish thee an holy people unto Himself, as He hath sworn unto thee if thou shalt keep the commandments of Yahweh thy God, and walk in His ways. And all people of the earth shall see that thou art called by the name of Yahweh, and they shall be afraid of thee.

And Yahweh shall make thee plenteous in goods, in the fruit of thy body, and in the fruit of thy cattle, and in the fruit of thy ground, in the land which Yahweh sware unto thy fathers to give thee. Yahweh shall open unto thee His good treasure: the heaven to give the rain unto thy land in its season, and to bless all the work of thine hand.

And thou shalt lend unto many nations, and thou shalt not borrow. And Yahweh shall make thee the head, and not the tail; and thou shalt be above only; thou shalt not be beneath; if that thou hearken unto the commandments of Yahweh thy God, which I command thee this day, to observe and to do them. And thou shalt not go aside from any of the words which I command thee this day, to the right hand or the left, to go after other gods to serve them.

But it shall come to pass, if thou wilt not hearken unto the voice of Yahweh thy God, to observe to do all His commandments and His statutes which I command thee this day, that all these curses shall come upon thee and overtake thee.

Cursed shalt thou be in the city and cursed shalt thou be in the field.

[1] Ch. xxvii is recognized by all critics to be either an addition or out of place. In either case, it interrupts the sequence of the argument, and is therefore omitted.

Cursed shall be thy basket and thy store.

Cursed shall be the fruit of thy body, and the fruit of thy land, the increase of thy kine and of the young of thy flock.

Cursed shalt thou be when thou comest in and cursed when thou goest out.

Yahweh shall send upon thee cursing, vexation, and rebuke in all that thou settest thy hand unto, until thou be destroyed, and until thou perish quickly; because of the wickedness of thy doings, whereby thou hast forsaken Me.

Yahweh shall make the pestilence cleave unto thee, until He have consumed thee from off the land which thou goest over to possess.

Yahweh shall smite thee with a consumption, and with a fever, and with an inflammation and with an extreme burning, and with the sword, and with blasting, and with mildew; and they shall pursue thee, until thou perish. And the heaven that is over thy head shall be brass, and the earth that is under thee, iron. Yahweh shall make the rain of thy land powder and dust; from heaven shall it come down upon thee, until thou be destroyed.

Yahweh shall cause thee to be smitten before thine enemies; thou shalt go one way against them, and flee seven ways before them; and thou shalt be removed into all the kingdoms of the earth. And thy carcass shall be meat unto all the fowls of the air, and unto the beasts of the earth, and no man shall fray them away.

Yahweh will smite thee with the boil of Egypt, and with the emerods, and with the scab, and with the itch, whereof thou canst not be healed.

Yahweh shall smite thee with madness and blindness and with astonishment of heart; and thou shalt grope at noonday, as the blind gropeth in darkness, and thou shalt not prosper in thy ways. And thou shalt be perpetually oppressed and robbed, and no man shall save thee.

Thou shalt betroth a wife, and another man shall lie with her; thou shalt build an house, and thou shalt not dwell therein; thou shalt plant a vineyard, and shall not gather the grapes thereof. Thine ox shall be slain before thine eyes, and thou shalt not eat thereof; thine ass shall be violently taken away before thy face, and shall not be restored to thee; thy sheep shall be given unto thine enemies and thou shalt have none to rescue them. Thy sons and thy daughters shall be given unto another people, and thine eyes shall look and fail with longing for them all the day long; and there shall be no might in thine hand. The fruit of thy land and of all thy labors shall a nation that thou knowest not eat up; and thou shalt be only oppressed and crushed alway; so that thou shalt be mad for the sight of thine eyes that thou shalt see.

Yahweh shall smite thee in the knees, and in the legs, with a sore boil that cannot be healed, from the sole of thy foot unto the crown of thy head.

Yahweh shall bring thee, and thy king which thou shalt set over thee unto a nation that neither thou nor thy fathers have known; and there shalt thou serve other gods, wood and stone. And thou shalt become an astonishment, a proverb and a byword among all nations whither Yahweh shall lead thee.

Thou shalt carry much seed out into the field, and shalt gather little in, for the locust shall consume it. Thou shalt plant and dress vineyards, but thou shalt neither drink the wine, nor gather the grapes, for the worms shall eat them. Thou shalt have olive-trees throughout all thy borders, but thou shalt not anoint thee with the oil, for thine olives shall drop off. All thy trees and fruit of thy land shall the locust consume.

Thou shalt beget sons and daughters, but thou shalt not enjoy them; for they shall go into captivity. The stranger that is in the midst of thee shall mount above thee higher and higher, and thou shalt come down lower and lower. He shall lend to thee, and thou shalt not lend to him; he shall be the head, and thou shalt be the tail.

And all these curses shall come upon thee, and shall pursue thee and overtake thee, till thou be destroyed; because thou hearkenedst not unto the voice of Yahweh thy God, to keep His commandments and His statutes which He commanded thee; and they shall be upon thee for a sign and for a wonder, and upon thy seed for ever. Because thou servedst not Yahweh thy God with joyfulness and with gladness of heart by reason of the abundance of all things; therefore shalt thou serve thine enemy whom Yahweh shall send against thee, in hunger and in thirst and in nakedness and in want of all things; and He shall put a yoke of iron upon thy neck until He have destroyed thee.

Yahweh shall bring a nation against thee from far, from the end of the earth, as the vulture sweepeth; a nation whose tongue thou shalt not understand; a nation of fierce countenance, which shall not regard the person of the old, nor show favor to the young; and he shall eat the fruit of the herds and the fruit of thy ground, until thou be destroyed; who shall not leave thee corn, wine, or oil, the increase of thy kine, nor the young of thy flocks until he have destroyed thee. And he shall besiege thee in all thy gates, until thy high and fortified walls wherein thou didst trust come down throughout all thy land; and he shall besiege thee in all thy gates throughout all the land which Yahweh thy God hath given thee. And thou shalt eat the fruit of thine own body, the flesh of thy sons and of thy daughters, which Yahweh hath given thee, in the siege and in the straitness with which thine enemies shall distress thee. The man that is tender among you and very delicate, his eyes shall be evil toward his brother, and toward the wife of his bosom, and toward the remnant of his children remaining; so that he will not give any of them of the flesh of his children to eat; because he hath nothing left him for the siege and the straitness wherewith thine enemies shall distress thee in all thy gates. The tender and delicate woman among you, which would not adventure to set the sole of her foot upon the ground for delicateness and tenderness, her eye shall be evil toward the husband of her bosom, and toward her son and toward her daughter and toward the babes that she shall bear; for she shall eat them, for want of all things, secretly in the siege and distress wherewith thine enemy shall distress thee in thy gates.

If thou wilt not observe to do all the words of this law that are written in this book, that thou mayest fear this glorious and fearful name, YAHWEH THY GOD; then Yahweh will make thy plagues wonderful, and the plagues of thy seed, great plagues and of long continuance, and sore sicknesses of long continuance. Moreover He will bring upon thee all the diseases of Egypt, which thou wast afraid of; and they shall cleave unto thee. Also every sickness and every plague which are not written in the book of this law, them will Yahweh bring upon thee, until thou art destroyed.

And ye shall be left few in number, whereas ye were as the stars of heaven for multitude; because thou wouldest not obey the voice of Yahweh thy God. And it shall come to pass, that as Yahweh rejoiced over you to do you good, and to multiply you; so Yahweh will rejoice over you to destroy you, and to bring you to naught; and ye shall be plucked from off the land whither thou goest to possess it.

And Yahweh shall scatter thee among all people, from the one end of the earth even unto the other; and there thou shalt serve other gods, which neither thou nor thy fathers have known, wood and stone. And among these nations shalt thou find no ease, neither shall the sole of thy feet have rest; but Yahweh shall give thee a trembling heart, and failing eyes, and sorrow of mind; and thy life shall hang in doubt before thee; and thou shalt fear day and night, and shall have none assurance of thy life. In the morning thou shalt say: Would God it were evening! and at even thou shalt say: Would God it were morning! for the fear of thine heart wherewith thou shalt fear, and for the sight of thine eyes which thou shalt see.

And Yahweh shall bring thee into Egypt again with ships, by the way whereof I said unto thee: Ye shall see it no more again. And there ye shall be sold unto your enemies for bondmen and bondwomen, and no man shall buy you.

THE PERORATION
(Ch. xxix, 9-14, 29; xxx, 11-20.)

Ye stand this day, all of you, before Yahweh your God; your captains of tribes, your elders and your officers with all the men of Israel, your little ones, your wives, and the stranger that is in thy camp, from the hewer of thy wood unto the drawer of thy water, that thou shouldest enter into covenant with Yahweh thy God, and into His oath which Yahweh thy God maketh with thee this day; that He may establish thee to-day for a people unto Himself, and that He may be thy God, as He hath said unto thee, and as He hath sworn unto thy fathers, unto Abraham, to Isaac and to Jacob. Neither with you only do I make this covenant and this oath, with him that standeth here with us this day before Yahweh our God; but also with him that is not here this day; lest there should be any man among you, or woman, or family, or tribe, whose heart turneth away this day from Yahweh our God, to go and serve the gods of these nations; lest there should be among you a root that beareth gall and wormwood; and it come to pass, when he heareth the words of this curse, that he bless himself in his heart, saying: I shall have peace, though I walk in the imaginations of mine heart to add drunkenness to thirst,—Yahweh will not spare him; but the anger of Yahweh and His jealousy shall smoke against that man, and all the curses that are written in this book shall lie upon him, and Yahweh shall blot out his name from under heaven.

The secret things belong unto Yahweh our God; but those revealed belong unto us and to our children forever, that we may do all the words of this law.

For this commandment which I command thee this day, it is not hidden from thee, neither is it far off. It is not in heaven, that thou shouldest say: Who shall go up for us to heaven and bring it us, that we may hear it and do it? Neither is it beyond the sea, that thou shouldest say: Who shall go over the sea for us and bring it us, that we may hear it and do it? But the word is very nigh unto thee, in thy mouth and in thy heart, that thou mayest do it.

See, I have set before thee this day life and good, and death and evil, in that I command thee this day to love Yahweh thy God, to walk in His ways and to keep His commandments and His statutes and His ordinances, that thou mayest live and multiply; and Yahweh thy God shall bless thee in the land whither thou goest to possess it. But if thine heart turn away so that thou wilt not hear, but shalt be drawn away and worship other gods, and serve them; I denounce unto you this day that ye shall surely perish, and that ye shall not prolong your days upon the land whither thou goest over Jordan to possess it.

I call heaven and earth to witness this day against you, that I have set before you life and death, blessing and cursing; therefore choose life, that both thou and thy seed may live; that thou mayest love Yahweh thy God, that thou mayest obey His voice, and that thou mayest cleave unto Him. For He is thy life and the length of thy days. That thou mayest dwell in the land which Yahweh sware unto thy fathers, unto Abraham, to Isaac and to Jacob, to give them.

APPENDIX BY A LATER WRITER, OR POSSIBLY BY D. HIMSELF AS EDITOR OF THE ORATION

(Ch. xxxi, 9-13.)

[And Moses wrote this law and delivered it unto the priests the sons of Levi which bare the ark of the covenant of Yahweh, and unto all the elders of Israel. And Moses commanded them, saying: At the end of every seven years, in the solemnity of the year of release, in the feast of tabernacles, when all Israel is come to appear before Yahweh thy God in the place which He shall choose, thou shalt read this law before all Israel in their hearing. Gather the people together, men and women and children, and the stranger that is within thy gates, that they may hear and that they may learn, and fear Yahweh your God, and observe to do all the words of this law; and that their children, which have not known, may hear and learn to fear Yahweh your God, as long as ye live in the land whither ye go over to possess it.]

SECOND APPENDIX, MUCH LATER

(Ch. xxxi, 1-8.)

[And Moses went and spake these words unto all Israel, and said unto them: I am an hundred and twenty years old this day. I can no more go out and come in; also Yahweh hath said unto me: Thou shalt not go over this Jordan. Yahweh thy God, He will go over before thee; He will destroy these nations from before thee, and thou shalt dispossess them. And Joshua shall go over before thee, as Yahweh hath said. And Yahweh shall do unto them as He did to Sihon and to Og, kings of the Amorites, and unto the land of them whom He destroyed. And Yahweh shall give them up before your face, that ye may do unto them according unto all the commandments which I have commanded you. Be strong and of a good courage; fear not, nor be affrighted by them, for Yahweh thy God is He that goeth with thee; He will be with thee, He will not fail thee nor forsake thee; fear not, neither be dismayed.

And Moses called unto Joshua, and said unto him in the sight of all Israel: Be strong and of a good courage; for thou shalt go with this people into the land which Yahweh hath promised unto their fathers to give them; and thou shalt cause them to inherit it. And Yahweh, He it is that goeth before thee. He will be with thee. He will not fail thee, nor forsake thee. Fear not, neither be dismayed.]

THE BOOK OF JEREMIAH

FIRST BOOKLET

A. THE CALL OF JEREMIAH (c. 627 B.C.)
(Jer. i, 4-14)[1]

The word of Yahweh came unto me, saying:

Before I found thee in the belly, I knew thee;
Before thou camest forth from the womb, I sanctified thee;
   I ordained thee a prophet unto the nations.

Then said I: Ah, God Yahweh, behold, I cannot speak, for I am a child. But Yahweh said: Say not unto Me, I am a child; for thou shalt go to all to whom I shall send thee; and whatsoever I command thee, thou shalt speak. Be not afraid of their faces, for I am with thee to deliver thee. Then Yahweh put forth His hand and touched my mouth. And Yahweh said unto me:

  Behold, I have put My words in thy mouth.
See, I have this day set thee over the nations and kingdoms
To root out and to pull down, to destroy and to throw down,
   To build and to plant.

Moreover, the word of Yahweh came to me, saying: What seest thou? And I said: I see a twig of an almond-tree. Then said Yahweh unto me: Thou hast well seen; for I will hasten My word to perform it.

And the word of Yahweh came to me a second time, saying: What seest thou? And I said: I see a seething pot, and the face of it is from the north. Then Yahweh said unto me:

Evil breaketh forth from the north on all who dwell upon earth;
For lo, I call upon all peoples of the kingdoms of the north.
   They shall come, and each shall set up his throne
     Before the gates of Jerusalem,
Against all her walls round about, and all the cities of Judah.
I will utter My judgments against them for all their offenses,
In that they have forsaken Me and burned incense to alien gods,
     And have bowed themselves down to worship
       The works of their own hands.
     Now gird up thy loins and arise
     And say to them all that I bid thee.
       Be not dismayed before them,
    Lest I confound thee before them,
For lo, I make thee this day a fortress, an iron pillar
   And brazen walls against all the land, the kings of Judah

---

[1] Native editor's preface (Ch. i, 1-3.) "The words of Jeremiah the son of Hilkiah, of the priests that were in Anathoth in the land of Benjamin; to whom the word of Yahweh came in the days of Josiah, the son of Amon, king of Judah, in the thirteenth year of his reign. It came also in the days of Jehoiakim, king of Judah, unto the eleventh year of Zedekiah the son of Josiah, king of Judah, until the carrying away captive of Jerusalem in the fifth month."

And the princes thereof, and against the priests thereof
And her common people.
And they shall fight against thee, but shall not overcome thee,
For I am with thee to deliver thee, saith Yahweh.

B. JEREMIAH'S FIRST DISCOURSE (c. 625 B.C.)

(Ch. ii, 2-13, 20-37; iii, 1-5)

Thus saith Yahweh:
I remember the piety of thy youth,   the love of thine espousals,
Thy following Me in the wilderness,   the uncultivated land.
Israel was dedicated to Yahweh,   the first-fruits of His care.
All that molest him shall be held guilty;
Evil shall come upon them, saith Yahweh.

Hear the word of Yahweh, O House of Jacob,
All the families of the House of Israel!
What iniquities have your fathers found in Me
That they removed themselves far from Me?
And have not said: Where is Yahweh that brought us up
Out of the land of Egypt,
Our Leader through the wilderness, the land of deserts and pits,
The land of drought and of terror, a land traversed by none,
And no man dwelt therein?

I brought you into a fertile land to eat its fruit and goodness,
But when ye entered, ye defiled My land
And made Mine heritage an abomination.
The priests said not: Where is Yahweh?
They that handle the law knew Me not; the rulers
Transgressed against Me;
The prophets prophesied by Baal, and bowed to gods that help not.

Therefore, I will yet plead with you, with your sons' sons will I plead.
For, pass over the Isles of Chittim, and see!
Send now to Kedar, and closely consider
Whether ever a thing like this hath been.
Hath any nation changed its gods, though no gods they were?
But My people have changed its glory for what profiteth not!
Be astonished at this, ye heavens! Yea, shudder and be amazed!

For My people have committed two evils;
Me have they forsaken, the fountain of living waters,
And hewed them out wells, broken wells, which hold no water.

In the old days I broke thy yoke, I pulled off thy fetters.
And thou saidst: I will not transgress;
Yet upon every high hill and under every leafy tree
Thou hast bowed down, playing the harlot.

Yet I planted thee a noble vine, altogether of noble seed;
How art thou changed!—to a degenerate plant to Me unknown;
For though thou wash thee with potash, and use much soap,
Still thine iniquity is recorded before Me, saith Yahweh.

How canst thou say: I am not defiled,
After Baalim have I not gone!
See thy path in the valley; know what thou hast done.
Thou art a swift young camel, traversing her ways,
A wild ass of the wilderness in the flush of her craving;

She snuffeth up the scent of her desire;
    Who shall restrain her?
Let not those that seek her weary themselves;
    In her month they shall find her.
Save thy foot from being unshod, thy throat from thirst.
But thou saidest: There is no hope, for I have loved aliens
    And after them will I go.

As a thief is ashamed when he is caught, so is the House of Israel.
They, their kings, their nobles, their priests and prophets;
    Who say to a tree: Thou art my father!
    To a stone: Thou hast brought me forth.
For their back they have turned to Me, and not their faces.
    Yet, in the time of trouble, they will say:
    Arise, and save me!
Now, where are thy gods, that thou madest for thyself?
Let them arise in the time of thy trouble
    If they can save thee;
For, as the number of thy cities are thy gods, O Judah!

    Why do ye strive against Me?
    Ye have all transgressed against Me.
In vain do I smite your children, they accept no correction.
Your own sword hath slain your prophets, like a ravening lion.
    And ye were not afraid!
    Hear, now, the words of Yahweh!
Have I been a desert to Israel? a land of utter darkness?
    Then why say My people: We will rule ourselves;
    We will come no more to Thee?

Will a maiden forget her adornments,   or a bride her girdle?
Yet My people have forgotten Me,   days without number.
    How hath it profited, thy way of seeking love?
Whereby thou hast taught thyself   the ways of wickedness.
    Yea, on thy hands is found   the blood of the guiltless;
    Not only on law-breakers is it found,
    But upon all these people.

Yet sayest thou: Surely His anger is turned away from me;
    I am innocent.
    Behold I condemn thee, because thou hast said:
    I have not sinned.

How greatly dost thou cheapen thyself,—to change thy way!
    Through Egypt shalt thou be shamed, as thou wast by Ashur.
    From this one, too, shalt thou go forth,
    Thy hands upon thy head.
    For Yahweh hath rejected those thou dost trust in,
    Nor shalt thou thrive by them.

If a man put away his wife,   and she have belonged to another,
Shall he turn to her again?   Is she not greatly polluted?
    Yet thou hast played the harlot with many lovers,
    And wouldst thou return unto Me?
    Lift thine eyes to the high places, and see!
    Where hast thou not embraced them?
On the roads hast thou embraced them
    As an Arab in the wilderness.
Thou hast polluted the land with thy harlotry and thy crimes.
    Thine is the forehead of an abandoned woman,
    Thou hast refused to be ashamed.

Dost thou not, even now, call Me, Father? saying:
"The guide of my youth art Thou!"
Behold, thus thou speakest,
And doest wicked deeds when thou canst.

C.   A Prophecy of a Scythian Invasion (c 625 b.c.)

(Ch. iv, 3-31; v, 1-31; vi, 1-30)

Thus saith Yahweh to the men of Judah and Jerusalem:

Break up your fallow ground,   and sow not among thorns.
Circumcise yourselves to Yahweh;   put away uncleanness
From among you.
Lest My wrath go forth like a fire and burn,
And there be no quenching it,
Because of the wickedness of your deeds.

Declare in Judah, announce in Jerusalem, and say:
Blow the trumpet in the land!   Cry aloud, help each other,
Get together; say: Let us go to the fortified cities;
Raise the standard towards Zion, flee in haste, stay not!
For calamity cometh from the north and a great destruction.

A lion hath risen from his lair, a destroyer of nations
Hath broken camp, gone forth from his place to make
Thy land desolate.
To lay thy cities waste,   without an inhabitant.
For this, gird you with sackcloth,   lament and wail,
For the fierce anger of Yahweh is not turned from us.

In that day, the heart of the king shall fail,
And the heart of the princes,
And the priests shall be appalled, the prophets struck with awe.
Then shall they say: Alas, O God Yahweh,
Thou hast greatly deceived this people and Jerusalem, saying:
Ye shall have peace.
Whereas the sword pierceth to our soul.

At that time it shall be said to this people and to Jerusalem:

A dry wind from the hills in the wilderness
Cometh towards My people,
Not to winnow and not to cleanse,   a strong, powerful wind.
Lo, it mounteth like clouds!   Like a whirlwind its chariots,
Swifter than eagles its horses!   Woe to us! We are destroyed!
For rumor gives warning from Dan   of distress to Mount Ephraim:
Make it known to the nations,   make Jerusalem heed!
Heralds from a far country   proclaim danger for Judah.
As keepers of a field do they   compass her about
Because she hath been rebellious   against Me, saith Yahweh.

Thy customs and thy deeds   have brought it upon thee,
This thy calamity; bitter it is;   it pierceth unto thy heart.
O Jerusalem, cleanse thy heart   from evil, that Thou be saved!
How long shall evil devices   be harbored within thee?

(My anguish! my anguish! I writhe;   the walls of my heart are racked,[1]

[1]Having heretofore spoken as the mouthpiece of Yahweh, the young prophet is here overcome by the purport of his message, and pours forth his own anguish over the coming woe.

My heart groans aloud within me   I cannot keep silence.
For I hear the sound of a horn,   I hear the alarum of war.
Ruin on ruin is declared,   all the land is laid waste.
Suddenly are my tents despoiled,   in a twinkling my curtains!
How long shall I see the standard   or hear the voice of horns?)

My people have no discernment,   they have not known Me;
Foolish children they are,   devoid of understanding,
Keen are they to do evil;   to do right is beyond them.

(I beheld the earth, and lo!   It was formless and void.
    And the heavens had no light.
I beheld the mountains,   and lo! they quaked,
    And the hills moved to and fro.
I beheld, and lo! there was no man, the birds of the air had flown.
I beheld, and lo! the fruitful land was waste, and its cities
    were broken down
Before the face of Yahweh, and the fierceness of His anger.)

    For thus Yahweh hath said: The whole land shall be desolate.
For this shall the earth mourn and the heavens be obscured,
Because I have spoken it, I have purposed it, I will not repent,
    Neither will I turn back from it.
    Before the noise of the horsemen and bowmen,
    The whole city shall flee.
They shall creep into thickets and caves and climb upon cliffs;
Every city shall be abandoned   and not a man shall dwell therein.

    When thou art ruined, what wilt thou do?
    Though thou clothe thyself with crimson,
    Though thou deck thee with jewels of gold
    And paint thine eyelids with kohl,
In vain dost thou make thyself fair, thy lovers will scorn thee.
    They will seek thy life.

The noise of a woman in travail have I heard,
The anguish of one bringing forth her first-born child.
The voice of the daughter of Zion; she gasps, she spreadeth her hands.
Woe is me! for my soul fainteth because of the murderers!

Run through the streets of Jerusalem,   and see now and know!
Seek in her spacious squares   if ye can find a man,
If there be one who doeth right or earnestly seeks for truth.
Yet they say: By the life of Yahweh! Surely they swear falsely,
    O Yahweh; do not Thine eyes look for truth?
    Thou hast smitten them but they have not grieved;
    They have made their faces harder than rock
They refuse to accept correction, and to return unto Me.

Then said I: Surely these are poor men   and they are stupid;
They know not the way of Yahweh,   nor the law of their God.
To the nobles I will betake Me,   I will speak with them;
For they know the way of Yahweh,   the law of their God.
Verily, these also have broken the yoke and burst the bonds.

Wherefore a lion out of the forest shall slay them,
An evening wolf shall spoil them; a leopard shall prowl
About their cities, and all who go forth shall he rend.
For many are their offenses, their backslidings are many.
How can I pardon thee for this? Thy children have forsaken Me
    And sworn by them that are no gods.

When I had fed them to the full,   they became adulterous,
And into the houses of harlots   they trooped together.
Like lusty stallions, each one neighed after his neighbor's wife.
For these things shall I not punish? saith Yahweh.
     Shall I not be avenged   on such a nation?
Go up against her walls and destroy; take away her branches,
     They are not Yahweh's.
For they have dealt very treacherously with Me, saith Yahweh.
They have belied Yahweh, and said: It is not He,
Nor shall evil come upon us, nor shall we see sword nor famine.
And the prophets shall be as wind; they have no message.

Therefore thus saith Yahweh Saboath: Thus shall be done to them;
Because they speak thus, behold!   in thy mouth will I make
     My word fire. And this people, wood;
         And it shall devour them.
I will bring upon you a distant nation, O House of Israel.
     An ancient nation,   a mighty nation,
Whose tongue thou knowest not,   nor understandest what they say.
(Their quiver is like an open sepulchre; they are all men of might.)
It shall eat up thy harvest and thy bread, thy flocks and herds,
     It shall eat up thy sons and daughters, thy vines and fig-trees;
     It shall batter thy fortified cities in which thou didst trust.

     And it shall come to pass when they shall say: Wherefore doth
Yahweh, our God, these things unto us? then thou shalt answer them:

     Like as ye have forsaken Me and served alien gods in your land,
     So shall ye serve strangers in a land that is not yours.

Hear now this, ye foolish people,   and without understanding,
Which have eyes and see not,   which have ears and hear not!
Fear ye not Me? saith Yahweh,   will ye not tremble before Me?

     But this people hath a stubborn and fractious mind;
         They have revolted and gone;
     Neither say they in their hearts: Let us fear Yahweh,
That giveth rain, the early rain, the latter rain in its season.
     Who reserveth for us the weeks appointed for the harvest.
     Your iniquities have changed all this,
     Your sins have withheld good things from you.

     For among My people are found wicked men
     Lying in wait as one crouching to lay snares;
         That set a trap,   they lay hold upon men.
As a cage is full of birds, so their houses are full of deceit.
     They plan, yea, they carry through wicked things,
         They defend not the cause of the orphan,
         They succeed, though they vindicate not
         The rights of the poor;
Therefore have they become great, and they prosper and wax fat.

     For these things shall I not punish? saith Yahweh,
Or shall not My soul be avenged on such a nation as this?
     A fearful and a wonderful thing is done in the land.
The prophets prophesy falsely, and the priests rule by their word.
     And My people love to have it so!
     What then will ye do in the end thereof?

     Be bold, ye sons of Benjamin! From the midst of Jerusalem
Blow a blast on the trumpet, raise a signal on Beth-haceren!
For calamity appears from the North, and a great destruction.

Shall I liken the daughter of Zion to a delightful pasture?
  Unto her come shepherds with their flocks;
  They pitch their tents round about her;
Each feedeth his flocks where he chooseth.

Suddenly war is determined against her: "Arise, let us go up at noon!"
  (Woe to us, for the day is declining,
  The shadows of evening are lengthening!
"Arise, let us go up by night, and let us destroy her palaces!
  Hew down trees, and cast up a mound against Jerusalem!"

For thus saith Yahweh: This city is to be punished.
  Oppression is in the midst of her.
As waters gush from a fountain, so doth her wickedness overflow.
  Violence and wrong-doing are heard in her;
  Suffering and slaughter are ever before Me.
Take warning, O Jerusalem, lest I depart from thee!
Lest I make thee desolate, an uninhabited land.

Thus saith Yahweh: Ye shall thoroughly glean, as a vine,
  The remnant of Israel.
Like the grape-gatherer, thrust in again thy hand among
  The thick-woven branches.
To whom shall I speak and give warning, that they may hear?
Behold, their ear is dulled,   the people cannot attend.
  Lo, to them the word of Yahweh is a reproach,
  They take no delight in it.
Therefore I am full of the wrath of Yahweh.
  I am tired of holding it in.

I will pour it out on the children in the street,
  In assemblies of noble youths.
Both husband and wife shall be taken, the aged with men in their prime.
Their houses shall be turned over to others, fields and wives together.
  For I will stretch out My hand
  On the dwellers in the land, saith Yahweh.

From the least of them even to the greatest, everyone
  Is greedy of gain.
From the prophet to the priest,   everyone dealeth falsely.
They treat the wound of My people as if it were slight;
  Saying: Peace! Peace! when there is no peace.
Were they ashamed when they committed the abominable act?
  Nay, they were not at all ashamed, nor could they blush.
  Therefore they shall fall among the slain;
When I punish them, they shall be completely overthrown.

      Thus saith Yahweh:
Stand in the highways and look, and ask for the old ways:
"Where is the good way?" and walk therein, and ye shall find
      Rest for your souls.
  But they said: "We will not walk therein."
Yet I had appointed for thee watchmen, to say:
  Listen for the sound of the trumpet!
  But they said: "We will not listen."

    Wherefore hear, ye nations,
And understand, ye shepherds of their flocks!
Behold, I am bringing evil upon this people,
  The fruit of their evil devices.
Because they have not listened to My words,
  And My Law they have rejected.

To what end do they bring unto Me incense from Sheba,
    And sweet cane from a distant land?
Your burnt-offerings are not acceptable unto Me,
    Nor your sacrifices sweet.

Therefore thus saith Yahweh: Behold, I will lay
    Stumbling-blocks before this people;
Fathers and sons together shall stumble upon them,
    Neighbors and friends shall perish together.

      Thus saith Yahweh:
  Behold, a people cometh   from the land of the north,
A great nation is stirring   from the confines of the earth.
They lay hold on bow and spear,   they are cruel, they have no mercy.
Their voices roar like the sea;   they ride upon horses
    Against thee, O daughter of Zion,
    Like men marshalled for battle.

We have heard the rumor thereof,   our hands are enfeebled;
Anguish seizeth upon us and pains,   as of a woman in travail.
    Go not out in the fields,   nor walk upon the highway,
For there is the sword of the foe,   terror is all about us.

    O daughter of My people!
  Gird thee with sackcloth,   roll thyself in the dust.
Make a mourning as for an only son,   a bitter lamentation;
For suddenly is the destroyer   coming upon us.

Thee have I set among My people   as a refiner of gold,
    That thou mayest know   and purify their way.
    Brass and iron are they all,   all grossly corrupt.
    They are the most rebellious of rebels,
    Going about with slanders.
The bellows is fiercely blown,   the lead is molten by fire;
In vain the smelter refineth,   the slag is not purged away.
    Refuse silver shall they be called,
    For Yahweh hath rejected them.

D.   THE COMMAND GIVEN TO JEREMIAH AFTER THE FINDING OF
THE BOOK OF THE LAW (621 B.C.)

(Ch. xi, 1-9)

The word that came to Jeremiah from Yahweh, saying: Hearken to
the words of this covenant, and speak unto the men of Judah and to
the inhabitants of Jerusalem, and say unto them: Thus saith Yahweh,
the God of Israel: Cursed be the man that obeyeth not the words of this
covenant which I did set before your fathers in the day that I brought
them forth out of the land of Egypt from the iron furnace, saying:
Hearken to My voice and do according to all that I command you, and ye
shall be My people and I will be your God, that I may perform the oath
which I sware to your fathers to give them a land flowing with milk
and honey, as it is this day.   Then answered I and said: So be it,
O Yahweh.

Then Yahweh said unto me: Proclaim all these words in the cities
of Judah and in the streets of Jerusalem, saying: Hear ye the words of
this covenant and do them; for I earnestly adjured your fathers in the
day that I brought them forth from the land of Egypt even unto this

day, rising early and admonishing them, saying: Obey My voice; but they obeyed not, but walked every one in the stubbornness of his evil heart. So I brought upon them all the judgments of this covenant, if they performed not what I commanded them to do.

E. THE GREAT TEMPLE-DISCOURSE

(Ch. vii, i—ix, 22; x, 17)

The word that came to Jeremiah from Yahweh, saying: Stand in the gates of the house of Yahweh, and there proclaim this word: Hear the word of Yahweh the God of Israel, all ye of Judah who are entering in at these gates! Amend your ways and your deeds, and I will cause you to dwell in this place. Trust ye not in vain repetitions, saying: The Temple of Yahweh, the Temple of Yahweh are these! For if ye thoroughly amend your ways and your doings; if ye faithfully execute judgment between a man and his neighbor; if ye oppress not the stranger, the fatherless and the widow, and shed not innocent blood in this place, neither walk after other gods to your hurt; then will I cause you to dwell in this place, in the land which I gave your fathers, for-ever and ever.

Behold, ye trust in lying words that profit nothing. Will ye steal, murder, and commit adultery and swear falsely, and offer incense to Baal and go after other gods whom ye know not, and then come and stand before Me in this house which is called by My name, and say: We are free to do all these abominations? Is this house which is called by My name become a den of robbers in your eyes? Behold, I have surely seen it, saith Yahweh.

Go now to My place in Shiloh, where I caused My name to dwell at the first, and see what I did to it on account of the wickedness of My people Israel. And now, because ye have done all these deeds, saith Yahweh, and I spake unto you, rising up early and speaking, and ye heeded not; and I called you but ye answered not; I will do unto the house which is called by My name, wherein ye trust, and to the place which I gave to you and to your fathers, as I did unto Shiloh; and I will cast you out of My sight as I have cast out all your brethren, even the whole seed of Ephraim.

> Therefore, pray not thou for this people,
> Neither lift up in their cause cry nor prayer.
> Neither make intercession with Me, for I will not hear thee.

Seest thou not what they are doing in the cities of Judah,
       And in the streets of Jerusalem?
The children gather wood, and the fathers kindle the fire,
And the women knead the dough into cakes for the queen of heaven
       And pour out drink-offerings to other gods,
          That they may provoke Me to anger.

Do they provoke Me to anger? saith Yahweh.
Do they not rather provoke themselves to their own shame?
          Therefore thus saith Yahweh:
Behold, Mine anger and My fury shall be poured out on this place
Over man and over beast, upon the trees of the field
          And the fruit of the ground.
And it shall burn, it shall not be quenched.

Thus saith Yahweh Sabaoth, the God of Israel: Add your burnt-offerings to your sacrifices, and eat flesh. For I spake not unto your fathers nor commanded them, in the day that I brought them out of the land of Egypt, concerning burnt-offerings or sacrifices, but this thing I did command them: Hearken to My voice, and I will be your God and ye shall be My people; and walk ye in all the ways that I have commanded you, that it may be well with you. But they hearkened not nor inclined their ear, but walked in the stubbornness of their wicked heart, backward and not forward. Since the day that your fathers came forth out of the land of Egypt even unto this day, I have sent unto you all My servants the prophets, rising early and sending; yet they hearkened not unto Me nor gave heed, but became more stubborn than their fathers. Therefore thou shalt speak this word unto them:

This is the nation that hath not hearkened
    To the voice of Yahweh, their God,
Nor accepted correction; truth hath perished and is cut off
    From their mouth.
Cut off thy hair, O Judah, cast it away; raise a lamentation
    On the high places;
For Yahweh hath rejected and forsaken the generation of His wrath.

For the children of Judah have done evil in Mine eyes, saith Yahweh. They have set up their abominations in the house which is called by My name to pollute it; they have built the high places of Topheth in the Valley of Ben-Hinnom, to burn their sons and daughters in the fire, which I commanded not nor thought of. Wherefore behold, the days come, saith Yahweh, that it shall no more be called Topheth, nor the Valley of Ben-Hinnom, but the Valley of Slaughter. For in Topheth they shall bury till there be no more room. And the carcasses of this people shall be meat for the fowls of the heaven and for the beasts of the earth, and none shall frighten them away.

Then will I cause to cease from the cities of Judah
    And from the streets of Jerusalem,
The sound of joy and the sound of gladness,
The voice of the bridegroom and the voice of the bride,
    And the land shall become a desolation.

At that time, saith Yahweh, they shall bring out the bones of the kings of Judah and the bones of his nobles, and the bones of the priests and of the prophets and the bones of the inhabitants of Jerusalem, out of their graves; and they shall spread them before the sun and the moon, and all the host of heaven whom they have loved and whom they have served, whom they have sought and whom they have worshipped; they shall not be gathered nor buried; they shall be for dung on the face of the earth. And death shall be chosen rather than life by all the residue of them that remain of this people which remain in all the places whither I have driven them, saith Yahweh.
    Thus saith Yahweh:

Shall men fall and not rise?   Does one turn away and not return?
Why then is this people given   to persistent backsliding?
They hold fast to deceit;   they refuse to return.
I have hearkened and heard, but no man repenteth of his guilt.
    Every one dasheth on in his course,
    As a horse rushing headlong into battle.
Even the stork in the heavens   knoweth her seasons;
The turtle, the swallow, the crane observe the time of their coming
    But My people will not foresee the judgment of Yahweh.

How can ye say: We are wise, and the law of Yahweh is with us?
Then surely, the mischievous pens of scribes have made it a lie
And have rejected the word of Yahweh. And what is their wisdom?
        I will scrape up their fruits, saith Yahweh [1]
        But there are no grapes on the vine,
          Nor figs on the fig-tree, and the foliage is withered.

Let us enter the fortified cities,   and be destroyed there.
For Yahweh, our God, hath destroyed us; let us drink poppy-juice
          Because we have sinned against Him.
      We expected peace, but no good came!
      A time of healing, but behold, terrors!
The snorting of his horses   was heard from Dan;
At the sound of the neighing of his strong ones
        The whole land trembled.
Lo, they have come and have devoured the land,
      The city and they that dwell in her.

    For behold, I send against you serpents,
    Vipers, against which there is no charm,
        And they shall bite you, saith Yahweh.

    (My cheerfulness is crushed beyond recovery,
        My heart is faint within me.
    Lo, the cry of the daughter of my people
        From a far-distant land!)
Is not Yahweh in Zion?   Is there no king in her?
Why have they moved Me to anger with their graven images?
        With strange vanities?

(The harvest is past, the summer ended, and we are not saved!
Because of the destruction of my people, I am destroyed;
        I mourn, desolation hath fastened upon me.
    Is there no balm in Gilead?   Is no physician there?
Why then is there no healing   for the daughter of my people?
O that my head were waters   and mine eyes a fount of tears!
      That I might weep day and night for the slain
        Of the daughter of my people!

    O, that I had in the desert   a traveller's lodge
    That I might leave my people   and go far from them!
    For they are all adulterers,   an assembly of deceivers.
    And they bend their tongues   like their bow, to lies.
And they are not valiant for truth in the land.)
      They proceed from evil to evil, and know not Me, saith Yahweh.

      Let everyone keep watch on his neighbor,
        Nor confide in his brother;
      For every brother will supplant his brother,
And every neighbor will go about, slandering.
And each will deceive his neighbor, and will not speak the truth.

They have taught their tongue to speak lies, they exhaust
        Themselves in perversity.
      Thy dwelling is in the midst of deceit;
      Through deceit they refuse to know Me, saith Yahweh.

      Therefore thus saith Yahweh:
Behold, I will smelt them and purify them, for what else
        Can I do for My people?

[1] The three verses omitted are repeated from ch. vi, 12-15.

Their tongue is a sharp arrow.   deceit is the word of their mouth.
One greets his neighbor with "Peace!" but inwardly plots against him.
    Shall I not punish them for these things? saith Yahweh;
    Upon such a nation as this,   shall I not avenge Myself?
Upon the mountains I will lift up   a weeping and a wailing,
A lamentation over the pastures   now laid waste;
    Because they are burned up   and no man passeth.
    Both the birds of the heavens   and the beasts are fled, gone.
And I will make Jerusalem ruins,   a den of jackals;
The cities of Judah I will give   to destruction,
    With not an inhabitant.

    Who is the man so wise that he may understand this?
To whom hath the mouth of Yahweh   spoken, that he may declare
Why the land is ruined, burned up,   like a desert untravelled?
Because they have forsaken My law   which I set before them,
And have not obeyed My voice   nor walked accordingly;
But have walked after the Baalim   as their fathers taught them.
They have walked according to the obstinacy of their own heart.

    Therefore thus saith Yahweh, the God of Israel:
    Behold, I will feed this people with wormwood,
    I will give them juice of poppies to drink;
        I will scatter them also among peoples
    Whom neither they nor their fathers have known;
And I will send after them the sword, until I have consumed them.

Send for the mourning women that they may come!
    Send for the wise women! Let them make haste
        And raise up for us a wailing;
That our eyes may pour down tears, our eyelids flow with water.
    For a sound of wailing is heard from Zion;
        How are we ruined!
We are put to exceeding shame,   for our dwellings cast us out!

    Hear, O women, and let your ears receive My words!
    Teach your daughters wailing, each to her neighbor a dirge.
Death hath come up into our windows, hath entered our palaces,
    To cut off our children from the streets,
    The youths from the broad, open courts.
The dead bodies of men fall as dung upon the open field,
As the handful after the harvester, and no one gathers them.

        Gather up thy wares from out the land,
        Thou that restest in a place besieged
            For thus saith Yahweh:
I am hurling out at once   the inhabitants of this land,
And I will harass them   that they may be saved.

F. The Poet's Lamentation for the Imminent Destruction
of his People

(Ch. x, 18-24)

    Woe is me for my hurt!   my wound is grievous!
    But I said: This is my grief, and I must bear it.
My tent is ruined, and all my cordage is torn away.
My children are gone forth from me,   and lo, they are not!
None any more to spread my tent, and to put up my curtains!

For the shepherds are become as brutes
  And have not inquired of Yahweh.
Therefore they have not taught wisely,
  And all their flocks are scattered.

Hark! News! Lo, it cometh,   a mighty din from the northland!
To make the cities of Judah a waste,   a haunt of wild beasts!
I know, O Yahweh, it is not for man   to choose his way;
To no one living is it given   to direct his steps.
Correct us, O Yahweh, but leniently   and not in wrath,
    Lest Thou leave us few!

G. AFTER THE REACTION FROM JOSIAH'S GREAT REFORM
(Ch. xi, 9-14)

Yahweh said unto me: A conspiracy is discovered among the men of Judah and among the inhabitants of Jerusalem. They are turned back to the iniquities of their fathers which refused to hear my words and went after other gods to serve them; the house of Israel and the house of Judah have broken the covenant which I made with their fathers. Therefore thus saith Yahweh: Behold, I will bring evil upon them which they shall be unable to escape; and, though they shall cry unto me, I will not hearken unto them. Let the cities of Judah and the inhabitants of Jerusalem go and cry unto the gods to whom they offer incense; but these will not save them in the time of trouble. For, as the number of thy cities are thy gods, O Judah; and to the number of the streets of Jerusalem have ye set up altars to the shameful thing, —altars to burn incense unto Baal. Therefore, pray not thou for this people, nor lift up a cry nor a supplication for them; for I will not hearken when they shall cry unto me in their trouble.

H. ON A CONSPIRACY OF HIS FELLOW-TOWNSMEN AGAINST HIM
(Ch. xi, 15-18)

.   .   .   . and Yahweh gave me knowledge of it.
And I knew of it;   .   . Yea, Thou didst show me their doings.
    But I was like a lamb, an ox led to the slaughter;
I knew not that they had devised such machinations against me;
"Let us hew down the tree in its freshness,
Let us cut him off from the land of the living,
    That his name be no more remembered."
But Thou, O Yahweh, that judgest righteously,
    Proving the reins and the heart,
Make me to see Thy vengeance upon them, for unto Thee
    Have I revealed my cause.

Therefore, thus saith Yahweh concerning the men of Anathoth that seek my life, saying: "Prophesy not in the name of Yahweh, that thou diest not at our hands."

Behold, I will punish them. The youths shall die by the sword,
    Their sons and their daughters shall die by famine
    And no remnant of them shall be saved.
For I will bring evil upon the men of Anathoth
    In the year of their visitation.

I. Two Symbolic Illustrations of the Corruption of the Nation, and the Prophecy of Punishment for Prophets and People

(Ch. xiii, 2-11; 12-14, 18-22)

Then Yahweh said unto me: Go, buy thee a linen waist-cloth, and put it about thy loins, but put it not in water. So I bought a waist-cloth, according to the word of Yahweh, and put it on my loins. And the word of Yahweh came to me a second time, saying: Take the waist-cloth which thou didst buy, which is upon thy loins, and arise, go to Perath, and hide it there in a cleft in the rock. So I went and hid it near Perath, as Yahweh commanded me.

And it came to pass, after many days, that Yahweh said to me: Arise, go to Perath, and take thence the waist-cloth which I commanded thee to hide there. Then I went to Perath and digged, and took the waist-cloth from the place where I had hid it; and behold, the waist-cloth was ruined; it was not fit for anything.

Then the word of Yahweh came unto me, saying: Thus saith Yahweh, even so will I destroy the pride of Judah and the arrogance of Jerusalem. This wicked people, which refuse to heed My words, which go after other gods to serve them and to worship them, shall be like this waist-cloth which is fit for nothing. For, as the waist-cloth clingeth to the loins of a man, so have I called the whole house of Israel and of Judah to cleave to me, saith Yahweh, to be My people for My renown and for My praise and My glory; but they would not hear.

And thou shalt also say unto them this: Thus saith Yahweh, the God of Israel: Every bottle is to be filled with wine. And they will say unto thee: Do we not know very well that every bottle is to be filled with wine? Then thou shalt say to them this: Thus saith Yahweh, Behold, I will fill all the inhabitants of this land, even the kings that sit upon David's throne and the priests and the prophets and all the inhabitants of Jerusalem, with drunkenness. And I will dash them one against another, the fathers and the sons together, saith Yahweh. I will not pity nor have mercy, nor spare from destroying them.

Say to the king and the queen; Humble yourselves! sink down!
For your princedoms shall fall, even the crown of your glory.
The cities of the south shall be closed, with none to open them.
All Judah shall go into exile, her wealth all stripped away.

Lift up your eyes and see these who come from the north!
Where is the herd once given thee, thy glorious flock?
  What canst thou say when He punisheth thee?
  For thou hast trained these to be captains,
    Yea, to be lords over thee.
Shall not sorrows take thee, like those of a woman in travail?
  And if thou say in thine heart:
  Whence come these things unto me?
For the greatness of thy sins are thy skirts uncovered,
    Thy heels laid bare.

J. Written During a Famine

(Ch. xiv, 1, 10-16)

The word of Yahweh that came to Jeremiah concerning the dearth.[1] Thus saith Yahweh unto this people: They have so loved to wander and have not refrained their feet, that Yahweh doth not accept them; He will now remember their iniquity, and visit their sins. Then said Yahweh unto me: Pray not for this people, that it may be well with them. When they fast, I will not hear their cry; and when they offer burnt-offering and an oblation, I will not accept them; but I will consume them by the sword and by the famine, and by the pestilence.

Then said I: Ah, Yahweh, our God, behold, the prophets say unto them, Ye shall not see the sword, neither shall ye have famine; but I will give you assured peace in this place. Then said Yahweh unto me: The prophets prophesy lies in My name; I sent them not, neither have I commanded them, neither spake I unto them. They prophesy unto you a false vision and divination, a thing of naught and the deceit of their own heart.

Therefore thus saith Yahweh: Concerning the prophets that prophesy in My name and I sent them not, yet they say: Sword and famine shall not be in this land,—by sword and famine shall those prophets be consumed. And the people to whom they prophesy shall be cast out into the streets of Jerusalem because of the famine and the sword, and there shall be none to bury them,—them, their wives, their sons and their daughters; for I will pour out their wickedness upon them.

(The Same Continued, Ch. xv, 1-4)

Then said Yahweh unto me: Though Moses and Samuel stood before Me, yet would not My soul be inclined toward them. Send this people from before My face; let them go forth. And if they shall say unto thee: Whither shall we go? then say thou unto them:

Thus saith Yahweh: Such as are for death, to death;
 Those for the sword, to the sword;
 Such as are for famine, to famine;
 Such as are for exile, to exile.
 And I will appoint for them, four dooms:
The sword to slay, the dogs to tear; the fowls of heaven
 And the beasts of the earth
  To devour and to destroy.
And I will cause them to be removed
Into all the kingdoms of the earth.

K. On the Condition of Zion After the Fall of the City

(Ch. xv, 5-9)

Who will have pity upon thee, or who shall bemoan thee,
Or who shall turn aside to ask, O Jerusalem, of thy welfare?
Thou hast rejected Me, saith Yahweh; thou hast gone backward.
And I have stretched out My hand and have destroyed thee.
 I am weary of repenting.

[1] Vv. 2-9, omitted here, are an exquisite lament by a late poet upon a dearth in his own day. Some editor has inserted it here as appropriate to these conditions, although its feeling is quite opposed to Jeremiah's. It will be found in the Appendix to Booklet I.

I will fan them with a fan in the gates of the land.
I bereave them of children, I destroy My people,
        Since they reform not their ways.
Their widows are increased in My sight above the sand of the sea.
Against the mother of youths I have brought a spoiler at noon
To fall upon her suddenly, and terrors upon the city.
        She that hath borne seven shall languish,
            Her spirit droopeth.
Her sun hath gone down while it is yet day; she is ashamed
            And confounded.
        And the residue of them will I deliver to the sword
        Before their enemies, saith Yahweh.

L. The Poet's Complaint for His Nation and the Answers
            of Yahweh

(Ch. xv, 10-18; xvi, 5-12, 21)

        Woe is me, my mother,   that thou hast borne me,
A man of strife and a man of contention to the whole earth.
I have neither lent on usury, nor have men lent me on usury,
        Yet every one of them doth curse me.

        Yahweh saith:
    Verily, it shall be well with thee; I will even cause
            The enemy to help thee
    In the time of evil,   and in the time of affliction.
Can iron be broken? Lo!   armor of brass is thy strength.

O Yahweh, Thou knowest!   Remember me and think of me,
    And avenge me of my persecutors.
Let me not pass away,   for Thou art long-suffering!

Thy commands were discovered,   and I made them my joy;
    Thy words were a joy to me   and a gladness for my heart,
        Because I am called by Thy name,
            O Yahweh, Thou God of Hosts!
I sat not nor rejoiced in   the assembly of the merry-makers;
Because of Thy hand I sat apart, for Thou hast filled me
            With indignation.
    Why is my pain perpetual,   my wound incurable,
        Refusing to be healed?
Wilt Thou be to me as a transient brook, as waters that fail?

Thus saith Yahweh: Enter not into the house of mourning
    Neither go to lament nor bemoan them.
    My peace have I taken from this people,
        My loving-kindness and My mercies.
Both great and small shall die, they shall not be buried,
Nor shall men lament nor cut themselves, nor for them
        Make themselves bald.
    Neither shall men break bread for the mourners,
        To comfort them for the dead,
    Nor shall they bring them the cup of consolation.
        To drink for their father or mother.
Thou shalt not go with them into the house of feasting
        To sit with them to eat and to drink.

    For thus saith Yahweh Sabaoth, the God of Israel:
        Behold, I will cause to cease in this place,
            In your eyes and in your day,
        The voice of mirth and the voice of gladness,
    The voice of the bridegroom and the voice of the bride.

And it shall come to pass, when thou shalt show this people all these words and they shall say unto thee: Wherefore hath Yahweh pronounced all this great evil against us? or, What is our iniquity or our sin that we have committed against Yahweh, our God? then thou shalt say unto them:

Because your fathers forsook Me   and walked after other gods,
And served them and worshiped them,   and did not keep My laws.
      And ye have done worse than your fathers;
            For behold, ye walk each one
      In the obstinacy of his evil heart,
            So that ye hearken not to Me;
Therefore I cast you out of this land into a land that ye know not,
      And neither did your fathers.
      There shall ye serve other gods, day and night.
Behold, this once I will cause them to know My hand and My might,
      They shall know that My name is Yahweh.

M. The Parable of the Potter.

(Ch. xviii, 1-17)

The word which came to Jeremiah from Yahweh, saying: Arise, and go down to the potter's house, and there will I cause thee to hear My words. Then I went down to the potter's house, and there he was making a vessel on the wheel. And the vessel he was making of clay was marred in the hand of the potter; and he made it again into another vessel, as seemed good in the eyes of the potter.

Then came to me the word of Yahweh, saying: O House of Israel, can I not do with thee as doth this potter? Behold, as the clay in the hand of the potter, so art thou in My hand, O House of Israel. At the moment that I shall speak concerning a nation and concerning a kingdom, to uproot and to pull down and to destroy it; if that nation against whom I have spoken shall turn from its evil-doing, I will repent of the evil that I thought to do unto them. Also, in the moment that I am speaking concerning a nation and concerning a kingdom, to build and to plant it; if it do evil in my sight that it obey not My voice, then I will repent of the good wherewith I said I would benefit them.

Now, therefore, go, speak to the men of Judah and to the inhabitants of Jerusalem, saying: Thus saith Yahweh, Behold, I am framing evil against you and devising a plan against you; return now everyone from his evil way, and make your ways and your doings good. But they answer: We have no hope; for according to our own devices we will walk, and after the evil imaginations of our hearts we will do. Therefore thus saith Yahweh:

Ask ye now among the nations: Who hath heard such things?
An exceedingly horrible thing   hath the virgin of Israel done.
Doth the snow of Lebanon fail   from under the rock in the field?
Or shall the cooling showers   for heaven be dried up?
But My people have forgotten Me; they have burned incense in vain;
They have stumbled in their course from the ancient paths
To walk in untrodden ways;   to make their land desolate,
            A lasting scorn.
Everyone passing by her shall be amazed, and shall shake his head.
I will scatter them as with an east wind before the enemy.
      I will show them My back and not My face
      In the day of their calamity.

N. The Plot Against Jeremiah

(Ch. xviii, 18)

Then they said: Come ye, let us devise a plot against Jeremiah; for instruction shall not perish from the priest, nor counsel from the wise, nor the word from the prophet. Come and let us smite him-with-the-tongue, and let us not give heed to any of his words.

O. Jeremiah's Prayer

(Ch. xviii, 19-23)

Give heed unto me, O Yahweh, and listen to the voice of mine adversaries. Shall good be repaid with evil? for they have digged a pit for my soul? Remember that I stood before Thee to speak good for them, and to turn away Thy wrath from them. Therefore, deliver up their children to the famine, and pour out their blood by the edge of the sword; let their wives be bereaved of their children, and become widows; let their men be put to death, and their young men be slain by the sword in battle. Let a cry be heard from their houses, when Thou shalt bring a troop suddenly upon them; for they have digged a pit to catch me, and laid snares for my feet. And Thou, O Yahweh, knowest all their counsel against me to slay me; forgive not their iniquity, neither blot out their sins from Thy sight; but let them be overthrown before Thee. Deal with them in the time of Thine anger.

P. The Parable of the Broken Bottle

(Ch. xiv, 1-15)

Thus said Yahweh: Go and get an earthenware bottle of the potter, and certain elders of the people and of the priests, and go forth to the Valley of Ben-Hinnom which is near the entrance of the east gate, and proclaim there the words that I shall tell thee, and say: Hear ye the word of Yahweh, O kings of Judah, and inhabitants of Jerusalem!

Thus saith Yahweh Sabaoth, the God of Israel: Behold, I will bring evil upon this place, so that the ears of every one that heareth of it shall tingle. Because they have forsaken Me and made this place alien to Me and have burned incense therein to other gods whom neither they nor their fathers have known, nor the kings of Judah; and have filled this place with the blood of innocents, and have built also the high places of Baal to burn their sons with fire as burnt-offerings unto Baal, which I commanded not, nor spake it, neither came it into My mind; therefore, behold, the days come, saith Yahweh, that this place shall no more be called Topheth nor the Valley of Ben-Hinnom, but the Valley of Slaughter. And I will make void the counsel of Judah and Jerusalem in this place; and I will cause them to fall by the sword before their enemies, and by the hands of them that seek their lives; and their carcasses will I give to be meat for the fowls of the heavens and for the beasts of the earth. And I will make this city desolate and an hissing; every one that passeth thereby shall be astonished and hiss because of the plagues thereof. And I will cause them to eat the flesh of their sons and the flesh of their daughters, and they shall eat every one the flesh of his friend in the siege and straitness, wherewith their enemies, and they that seek their lives, shall straiten them.

Then shalt thou break the bottle in the sight of the men that go with thee, and shalt say unto them: Thus saith Yahweh Sabaoth: Even so will I break this people and this city as one breaketh a potter's vessel that cannot be made whole again. And they shall bury in Topheth till there be no place to bury. Thus will I do to this place, saith Yahweh, and to the inhabitants thereof, and even make this city as Topheth; and the houses of Jerusalem and the houses of the kings of Judah shall be defiled as the place of Topheth, because of all the houses upon whose roofs they have burned incense unto all the host of heaven, and have poured out drink-offerings to other gods.

Then came Jeremiah from Topheth, whither Yahweh had sent him to prophesy; and he stood in the court of the house of Yahweh, and said to all the people: Thus saith Yahweh Sabaoth, the God of Israel: Behold, I will bring upon this city and upon all her villages all the evil that I have pronounced against it, because they have stiffened their necks, that they might not hear My words.

R. JEREMIAH IS PUT IN THE STOCKS

(Ch. xx, 1-6)

Now Pashhur, son of Immer the priest, who was governor in the house of Yahweh, heard that Jeremiah prophesied these things. Then Pashhur smote Jeremiah the prophet, and put him in the stocks that were in the high gate of Benjamin, near the house of Yahweh. And it came to pass on the morrow, that Pashhur brought forth Jeremiah out of the stocks. Then said Jeremiah unto him, Yahweh hath not called thy name Pashhur (*Redeemed*) but Magor-missabib (*Terror-on-every-side*). For thus saith Yahweh: Behold, I will make thee a terror to thyself and to all thy friends; and they shall fall by the sword of their enemies, and thine eyes shall behold it. And I will give all Judah into the hand of the king of Babylon, and he shall carry them captive into Babylon, and shall slay them with the sword. Moreover, I will deliver all the strength of this city and all the gains thereof, and all the precious things thereof, and all the treasures of the kings of Judah into the hands of their enemies which shall spoil them and take them and carry them to Babylon. And thou, Pashhur, and all that dwell in thine house shall go into captivity; and thou shalt come to Babylon, and there thou shalt die and shalt be buried, thou and all thy friends to whom thou hast prophesied lies.[1]

S. IN SPITE OF HIS PERSECUTIONS, JEREMIAH WILL STILL CONTINUE HIS WARNINGS

(Ch. xx, 7-12)

O Yahweh, Thou didst entice me,	and I was enticed.
Thou art stronger than I,	and hast prevailed.
I am in derision daily,	every one mocketh me;
For as often as I speak, I predict	violence and destruction.
The word of Yahweh hath become	my daily taunt and reproach.
Then I said: I will not mention Him nor speak in His name.	

[1] Verses 1-6 are probably taken from the Biography of the prophet to explain the triumphant strophes with which Booklet I closes.

But then there burned in my heart   as it were a fire in my bones;
I grew weary of keeping silence,   I could no longer forbear.
For I heard the defaming of many,   Terror on every side.
"Prophesy!" cried my familiar friends, lying in wait for my halting;
(Perchance he may be enticed   and we shall entrap him,
            And wreak our vengeance upon him.)

But Yahweh is on my side   as a mighty warrior;
Verily, my persecutors shall stumble,   they shall not prevail;
They shall be greatly ashamed,   for they shall not prosper,
Their everlasting confusion   shall never be forgotten.

            Sing unto Yahweh!   Praise ye Yahweh!
            Sing unto Yahweh! Praise ye Yahweh!
        For he hath delivered the soul of the needy
        From the hands of evil-doers.

APPENDIX TO BOOKLET I

GIVING NON-JEREMIANIC PASSAGES FOUND IN IT

A LATE INTERPOLATION IN JEREMIAH'S FIRST DISCOURSE (B)[1]
(Ch. ii, 14-19)

Is Israel a servant or home-born slave?   Why is he now a prey?
Over him young lions are roaring.   They gave forth their cry;
They have laid his land waste;   his cities are burned up,
            Without an inhabitant.
        The children of Noph and Tahpanhes also
        Have broken the crown of his head.

        Hast thou not brought this on thyself?
    Thou didst forsake Yahweh, thy God, who led thee on thy way.
        Now why art thou on the road to Egypt?
        Is it to drink of the waters of Sihor?
        Or why art thou on the road to Assyria?
            To drink of the great river?

        Thy offenses shall be a punishment to thee,
            Thy backslidings shall judge thee.
    Know now and see, that thy forsaking of Yahweʌ
            Was evil and bitter to thee,
    And that no fear of Me is in thee, saith Yahweh, thy God.

A VERY LATE
PREFACE TO THE PROPHECY OF THE SCYTHIAN INVASION (C)
(Ch. iii, 6-iv, 2; ix, 1-2)

Yahweh said unto me in the days of Josiah the king: Hast thou seen what backsliding Israel hath done? She hath gone up on every high mountain and under every green tree, and there hath played the harlot. And I said, after she had done all these things: Turn thou unto Me. But she returned not, and her faithless sister Judah saw it. And I saw that when, for all the causes whereby backsliding Israel had committed adultery, I had put her away and given her a bill of

---

[1] The capital letters in parentheses refer the reader to the divisions in the preceding Booklet, from which these are excerpted.

divorce, yet her faithless sister Judah feared not, but went and played the harlot also. And it came to pass, through the lightness of her whoredom, that she defiled the land and committed adultery with stocks and stones. And yet, for all this, her faithless sister Judah hath not turned unto Me with all her heart, but feignedly, saith Yahweh.

And Yahweh said unto me: Apostate Israel hath justified herself more than treacherous Judah. Go and proclaim these words towards the north; and thou shalt say:

> Return, O apostate Israel! No longer will I look
> In anger upon you, for I am merciful.
> I will not keep Mine anger for ever;
> Only acknowledge thy guilt, for against thy God thou hast sinned,
> And hast opened thy ways to aliens under every green tree.
> But unto My voice thou hast not listened, saith Yahweh.

> Return, O apostate children, saith Yahweh, for I am married to you.
> I will choose you, one of a city and two of a family,
> And I will bring you to Zion.
> And I will give you shepherds after My own heart,
> Who shall feed you with knowledge and wisdom.
> And when ye shall be multiplied and increased in the land.
> No more shall ye say "The Ark of the Covenant of Yahweh,"
> Nor shall it come to mind: none shall remember it,
> Nor visit it, nor shall it be made again.

> In that day they shall call Jerusalem the Throne of Yahweh;
> And to her shall be gathered all nations
> To the name of Yahweh, to Jerusalem;
> And no more shall they walk in the obstinacy of their evil heart.
> The House of Judah shall walk with the House of Israel;
> Together shall they come from the northland to the land
> That I gave to their fathers for a possession.

> Then I said: How like sons I will treat thee,
> And give thee a pleasant land!
> A glorious inheritance among the nations!
> And I said: Thou shalt call Me "My Father",
> Thou shalt not turn aside from Me.
> But as a woman is faithless to her lover, so verily have ye
> Been faithless unto Me, O House of Israel.

> A voice is heard in the high places,
> Weeping and prayers of the Children of Israel,
> For they have perverted their way,
> They have forgotten Yahweh, their God.

> Return, ye apostate sons, and I will heal your apostasy!
> Behold, we come unto Thee, for Thou art Yahweh, our God.
> Truly, in vain from the hills, from the crowds on the mountains,
> Is salvation for Israel; only from Yahweh, our God.
> For, from our youth, Baal hath devoured
> The fruit of our fathers' toil,—
> Their flocks and their herds, their sons and their daughters.
> We lie down in our shame, and shame is our covering.
> For against Yahweh, our God, we have sinned,
> We, and our fathers.
> From our youth even unto this day we have not obeyed
> The voice of Yahweh, our God.

If thou wilt return, O Israel, return unto Me,
If thou wilt put thine abominations away,
Thou shalt not be thrust away.
And thou shalt swear "By the life of Yahweh" in truth,
In justice and righteousness;
And in Him shall the nations be blessed,
And in Him shall they glory.

A LATE APPENDIX TO THE TEMPLE DISCOURSE (E)
(Ch. ix, 22-24, x, 1-16)

Thus saith Yahweh:
Let not the wise man glory in his wisdom, nor the mighty man
Glory in his might.
Let not the rich man glory in riches; but let him
That glorieth, glory in this,
That he understandeth and knoweth Me: that I am Yahweh,
Who doth act with Mercy, Justice, and Righteousness
In the earth;
For in these things I delight, saith Yahweh.

Behold, the days come, saith Yahweh, that I will punish all them that
are circumcised in their uncircumcision: Egypt, and Judah, and Edom,
and the children of Ammon, and Moab, and all that have the corners of
their beards polled that dwell in the wilderness.

For all the nations are uncircumcised; but the House of Israel
Are uncircumcised in the heart.

Hear ye the word which Yahweh speaketh unto you, O House of Israel!
Thus saith Yahweh:
Learn not ye the way of the nations   and be not dismayed
At the signs of the heavens, because the nations are dismayed.
For the rites of these peoples are vain.
One heweth a tree of the forest for the work of the artisan;
They adorn it will silver and gold, with hammers and nails;
They fasten it that it be not unsteady.
Like a palm-tree of graven work,   they cannot speak,
They must needs be carried,   for they cannot walk.
Be not afraid of them;   they can do no harm;
But neither have they power   to do any good.

There is none like unto Thee, O Yahweh; great Thou art,
And great is the power of Thy name.
Who would not reverence Thee,   O King of Nations!
For to Thee is reverence due.
Among all the wise men of the nations, in all their kingdoms,
There is none like unto Thee!
They are altogether foolish and brutish.
Their religion is one of frauds,   of gods made of trees;
Plates of beaten silver are brought from Tarshish,
And gold from Uphaz;
Work from the hand of the smelter, and of the graver;
Their clothing of blue and purple, the work of skilled men.

But the true God, the Living God,   is Yahweh, the Eternal King.
At His wrath the earth shall tremble, the Nations are unable
To abide His indignation.
Thus shall ye say unto them:

The gods which have not made   the heavens and the earth,
Shall perish from the earth,   from beneath these heavens.
He hath made the earth by His power, and established the world
           By His wisdom,
   And hath stretched out the heavens by His discretion.

When He giveth forth His voice,   lo, a tumult of waters in heaven!
   He maketh vapors arise   from the ends of the earth.
       He maketh lightnings with rain
     And bringeth forth wind from His treasures.

All mankind is brutish   and is without knowledge.
   Every artist is put to shame by his molten image,
For his castings are falsehood,   there is no breath in them.
   They are all vanity,   the creations of delusion.
In the time of their visitation   they shall perish.

   Not like these is the Portion of Jacob.
       The Framer of All Things is He,
   And Israel is the tribe of His inheritance;
       Yahweh Sabaoth is His name.

A Fragment

(Ch. x, 25)[1]

Pour out Thy fury upon the nations   that know Thee not,
Upon the families that call not   upon Thy name;
   For they have devoured Jacob   and he is destroyed;
They have put an end to him and made his habitation desolate.

Another Fragment

(Ch. xi, 13-15)

     What hath My beloved to do in My house,
       Who hath wrought evil with many?
The holy flesh hath passed from thee, because of thy wickedness.
An olive-tree, fresh and fair of form, once thou wert called.
       With a noise of great tumult,
   Fire is burning and destroying thy branches;

   For Yahweh Sabaoth who planted thee hath pronounced evil against thee, because of the evil of the House of Israel and of the House of Judah, which they have wrought for themselves in provoking Me by offering incense to Baal.

Six Fragments Preserved in Chapter XII [2]

Righteous art Thou, O Yahweh! but let me talk of Thy judgments.
Why doth the way of the wicked prosper, yet cheats and traitors are at
     ease?
Thou hast planted them, they take root, they grow and bear fruit.
Near art Thou to their mouth, but far from their inward parts.
But Thou, O Yahweh, knowest me, Thou hast seen and proved my heart.
       Pull them out, like sheep for the slaughter.
       Prepare them for the day of slaughter.
                        (Ch. xii, 1-3)

[1] A prayer for vengeance upon the people who have already despoiled Judah. Exilic.
[2] Chapter xii is a collection of short poems showing no trace of Jeremianic authorship, picturing in varying imagery the desolation of Zion and the misery of her exiled people. The last one gives a promise of restoration, which suggests that it is of a later date than the rest.

How long shall the land mourn,   and every herb wither
          For the wickedness of them that dwell therein?
               The beasts are consumed, and the birds,
          For they have said: He shall not see
                    The end of us all.

                                                  (Ch. xii, 4)

If thou have run with the footmen, and they have wearied thee,
          How canst thou contend with war-horses?
     If thou didst put thy trust in a land of peace,
          How wilt thou do in the swelling of Jordan?
     For even thy brethren and thy father's house,
          Even they have betrayed thee;
Believe them not then, though they speak fairly to thee.

                                                  (Ch. xii, 5-6)

     I have forsaken My house, I have given up My heritage;
I have given the beloved of My soul into the hands of foes.
     Mine heritage is to Me like a lioness in the forest.
          She hath given forth her voice against Me,
               Therefore have I hated her.
     Mine heritage is to Me like a bird of prey;
          The birds round about are against her.
     Many shepherds have ruined My vineyard,
          They have trodden My lot underfoot;
     They have made My pleasant portion a desolate wilderness.
     They have made it desolate; and, desolate, it mourneth to Me.

The whole land is made desolate, because no man careth for it.
Upon all the bare heights in the desert have spoilers come.
          From one end of the land even to the other,
               No flesh shall have peace.
          They have sown wheat, but shall reap thorns,
     They shall put themselves to pain, but profit not.
          They shall be ashamed of their harvest
               Because of the fierce wrath of Yahweh.

                                                  (Ch. xii, 7-12)

     Thus saith Yahweh: As for all My neighbors that touch the inherit-
ance which I have caused My people Israel to inherit, behold, I will
pluck them up from all their land, and will pluck up the House of
Judah from among them.

And it shall come to pass, after I have plucked them out,
          That I will have compassion upon them,
     And I will return and bring them again
Every one to his heritage, and every one to his land.
     And if they will diligently learn the ways of My people,
To swear by My name, the Living Yahweh, as they taught My sons
               To swear by Baal,
     They shall then be built up in the midst of My people;
But, if they will not obey, I will root out and destroy
               That nation, saith Yahweh.

                                                  (Ch. xii, 14-17)

A WARNING AND A GLOSS INTERPOLATED IN (J)

(Ch. xiii, 15-17; 25-27)

Hear ye and give ear; be not proud, for Yahweh speaketh.
Give glory to Yahweh, your God, before He spreadeth darkness.
Before He cause your feet to stumble on the dark mountains;
And while ye wait for light, He turn it into the shadowof Death,
    And into swart darkness.
But, if ye will sit and hear it, My soul in secret places
Shall weep because of your pride, because the flock of Yahweh
    Is held captive.

Can a Cushite change his skin or a leopard his spots? then may ye
also become good, who have chosen the evil. Therefore will I scatter
them as chaff passeth away before the wind of the desert. This is thy
lot, the portion meted out to thee by Me, saith Yahweh, because thou
hast forgotten Me, and hast trusted to falsehood. Therefore will I pull
thy skirts over thy face, that thy shame may appear. Woe to thee,
Jerusalem! When shall it be?

A POEM ON A LATE DROUGHT APPLIED TO THE EARLIER ONE LAMENTED
BY JEREMIAH (L)

(Ch. xiv, 2-6, 8-9)

Judah mourneth and the gates thereof languish,
  They bow down in gloom even to the ground.
   The cry of Jerusalem riseth.
Her nobles have sent their little ones to the waters
  They came to the wells, but found no water;
   They returned with their vessels empty.
They were ashamed and confounded, and covered their heads.
The parched ground is cracked, for there have been no showers
   In the land.
The ploughmen feel disgraced; they have hidden their faces.
  Even the doe in the field hath dropped her young
   And forsaken it, because there is no herbage.
Upon the bare heights, the wild asses stand waiting,
They snuff up the wind like jackals; their eyes are failing
   Because there is no grass.[1]

 . . . .

O Thou Hope of Israel; The Saviour thereof in time of trouble!
Why shouldest Thou be as a stranger in the land,
  And as a sea-faring man that turneth aside
   To tarry for a night?
  Why shouldest Thou be as a man overcome,
   A warrior that cannot save?
Yet Thou, O Yahweh, art in the midst of us!
  And we are called by Thy name.
   O leave us not!

[1] Verse 7, which introduces a very different note, is omitted. Probably a gloss.

LATE INTERPOLATIONS IN CHAPTERS XIV AND XV
(Ch. xiv, 19-21)

Hast Thou utterly rejected Judah?   Hath Thy soul loathed Zion?
Why hast Thou smitten us, and there is no healing for us?
We looked for peace,   and there is nothing good!
For the time of healing,   and behold, trouble!
        We acknowledge our wickedness, O Yahweh,
        And the iniquity of our fathers;
    For we have sinned against Thee; do not despise us,
            For Thy name's sake.
    Do not disgrace the throne of Thy glory!
    Remember!   Break not Thy covenant with us.
                                                    (Ch. xiv, 19-21)

Are there any among the idols of the nations
        That can cause rain?
    Or can the heavens bestow showers?
    Art Thou not He, O Yahweh, our God?
Therefore will we wait upon Thee, for Thou hast made
        all these things.
                                                    (Ch. xiv, 22)

    Yahweh hath said: Verily, it shall be well with thy remnant; verily,
I will cause the enemy to treat thee well in the time of evil and in the
time of affliction.   Shall iron break the northern iron and the steel?
Thy substance and thy treasures will I give to the spoil without price,
and that for all thy sins, even in all thy borders.   And I will make thee
to pass with thine enemies into a land thou knowest not; for a fire is
kindled in Mine anger which shall burn forever.
                                                    (Ch. xv, 11-14)

Thus saith Yahweh: If thou repent, then will I restore thee,
        And thou shalt stand before Me;
    And if thou separate the precious from the vile,
        Thou shalt be as My mouth.
Let them return unto thee, but return not thou unto them,
And I will make thee unto this people a brazen fenced wall.
        And they shall fight against thee,
        But they shall not prevail against thee.
    For I am with thee to save thee
    And to deliver thee, saith Yahweh.
And I will deliver thee out of the hand of the wicked,
And I will redeem thee out of the hand of the terrible.
                                                    (Ch. xv, 19-21)

FRAGMENTS OF PROSE AND VERSE
INTERWOVEN BY A LATE EDITOR TO MAKE A CONTINUOUS NARRATIVE
(Ch. xvi, 14-xvii)

    Behold, the days come, saith Yahweh, that it shall no more be said:
Yahweh liveth that brought up the children of Israel out of the land of
Egypt; but Yahweh liveth that brought up the children of Israel from
the land of the north, and from all the lands whither He had driven them;
and I will bring them again into their own land which I gave their
fathers.
                                                    (Ch. xvi, 14-15)

Hast thou utterly rejected Yahweh?   Doth thy soul loathe Zion?
Lo, I will send for many fishers,   and they shall fish them;
Then will I send for many hunters,   and they shall hunt them
   Out of the holes of the rocks of every mountain and of every hill.
Mine eyes are upon all their ways;   they are not hid from Me,
Neither is their dwelling-place   hid from Mine eyes.
And first I will repay double   their iniquity and their sin;
Because they have defiled My land,   they have filled My heritage
   With the carcasses of their detestable and abominable things.

                                       (Ch. xvi, 16-18)

O Yahweh, my strength and my fortress, my refuge in the day of
                                           [affliction!
  The nations shall come to Thee from the ends of the earth,
And say: Surely, our fathers have inherited lies,
    And vanities wherein is no profit.
    Shall a man make gods for himself
       Which yet are no gods?

                                       (Ch. xvi, 19-20)

    The sin of Judah is written with a pen of iron,
       With the point of a diamond.
  It is graven upon the tablet of their heart,
     Upon the horns of their altars;
  Upon every green tree, upon the high hills,
     And upon the mountains in the field.
Thy wealth, all thy treasures, will I give as a spoil,
     Thy high places of sin throughout all thy borders.
  And thou shalt loosen thy hand from the possessions
     That I gave thee;
  And I will cause thee to serve thine enemies
    In the land thou knowest not
For ye have kindled a fire in Mine anger
    That shall burn forever.

                                   (Ch. xvii, 1-4)

       Thus saith Yahweh:
    Cursed is the man that trusteth in man,
And maketh flesh his arm, and whose heart departeth from Yahweh!
  For he shall be like heath in the desert, and shall not see
       When good cometh;
  He shall dwell in the parched places in the wilderness,
    A salt land, and not inhabited.

Blessed is the man that trusteth in Yahweh, whose hope is Yahweh;
    For he shall be as a tree planted by the waters,
      That spreadeth out her roots to the river;
    It shall not fear when heat cometh,
      For her leaf shall be green;
  In the year of drought she shall not pine,
    Nor cease from bearing fruit.

                                   (xvii, 5-8)

The heart is deceitful above all things, and desperately wicked.
         Who can know it?
  I, Yahweh, search the heart, probing the inward parts,
    That I may pay every man according to his ways,
      According to the fruit of his doings.

As the partridge sitteth on eggs that she hath not laid,
  So is he that getteth riches, but not with justice.
  In the midst of his days they shall leave him,
    And at his end, he shall be a fool.

(xvii, 9-11)

A glorious exalted throne is the place
    Of our sanctuary.
O Hope of Israel, Yahweh! all that forsake Thee
    Shall be ashamed.

They that depart from Me
    Shall be written in the earth,
Because they have forsaken Yahweh,
    The fountain of living waters.

(xvii, 12-13)

Heal me, O Yahweh, and I shall be healed; save me, and I shall be saved; for Thou art my praise. Behold, they say unto me: Where is the promise of Yahweh? Let it come now. As for me, I have not fled from a shepherd's tent to follow Thee; neither have I desired the woeful day. Thou knowest. What hath come forth from my lips hath been righteous before Thee. Let them be confounded that persecute me, but let not me be confounded. Let them be dismayed, but let not us be dismayed; bring upon them the day of evil, and destroy them with a double destruction.

(xvii, 14-18)

Yahweh Sabaoth, that triest the righteous,
  And seest the reins and the heart,
    Let me see Thy vengeance upon them,
    For unto Thee have I opened my cause.

(Ch. xx, 12)

Sing unto Yahweh!   Praise ye Yahweh!
For He hath delivered the soul of the poor
    From the hand of evil-doers!

(xx, 13)

Cursed be the day wherein I was born
Let not the day be blessed that my mother brought me forth!
Cursed be the man who brought tidings to my father,
Saying: A man-child is born to thee,—making him very glad.
    And let that man be as the cities
    Which Yahweh overthrew and hath not repented,
    And let him hear a cry in the morn
      And an alarum at noon-tide;
Because He slew me not from the womb,
Or that my mother might have been my grave.

Wherefore came I forth out of the womb to see labor and sorrow?
  And that my days should be consumed with shame.

(xx, 13-18)

N. B. A study of this collection of incongruous passages, and especially of chapters xvi and xvii, wherein laments and rejoicings, prayer, praise and proverbs are jumbled together, with their several causes far to seek, is convincing for the necessity of drastic revision.

THE SECOND BOOKLET

THE WORDS OF JEREMIAH DURING THE REIGN OF JEHOIAKIM

(Ch. xxvi, 1-24; xxii, 1-9, 10-12; xxxvi, 1-32; xlv, 1-5; xlvi, 3-12; xxii,
13-23; xxiii, 1-2, 9-18, 21-29; xxii, 24-30; xxiv, 1-16.)

In the beginning of the reign of Jehoikim the son of Josiah, king
of Judah, came this word from Yahweh, saying: Thus saith Yahweh:
Stand in the court of the house of Yahweh and speak unto all the
cities of Judah which come to worship in the house of Yahweh all the
words that I command thee to speak to them; diminish not a word.
It may be they will hearken and turn every man from his evil way,
that I may repent Me of the evil which I purpose to do unto them,
because of the evil of their doings.   And thou shalt say unto them,
Thus saith Yahweh: If ye will not hearken to Me to walk in My law
which I have set before you, to hearken to the words of My servants
the prophets whom I send unto you, even sending them betimes and
often but ye have not hearkened; then will I make this house like
Shiloh, and this city will I make a curse to all the nations of the earth.
Now the priests and the prophets and all the people heard Jeremiah
speaking these words in the house of Yahweh.   And it came to pass
when Jeremiah had made an end of speaking all that Yahweh had
commanded him to speak unto all the people, that the priests and
the prophets and all the people laid hold on him, saying: Thou
shalt surely die; why hast thou prophesied in the name of Yahweh,
saying: This house shall be like Shiloh, and this city shall be desolate,
without an inhabitant?   And all the people were gathered together
against Jeremiah in the House of Yahweh.

When the princes of Judah heard these things, they came up from
the king's house to the House of Yahweh; and they sat in the entrance
of the new gate of the House of Yahweh.   Then spake the priests
and the prophets unto the princes and to all the people, saying: This
man is worthy of death, for he hath prophesied against this city, as
ye have heard with your own ears.   Then spake Jeremiah unto all the
princes and to all the people, saying: Yahweh sent me to prophesy
against this house and against this city all the words that ye have
heard.   Therefore now, amend your ways and your doings and hearken
unto Yahweh, your God, and Yahweh will repent Him of the evil that
He hath pronounced against you.   But as for me, I am in your hand;
do with me as is good and right in your eyes.   Only, know ye for
certain that, if ye put me to death, ye will bring innocent blood upon
yourselves and upon this city and upon the inhabitants thereof; for
of a truth, Yahweh hath sent me unto you to speak all these words in
your ears.   Then said the princes and all the people unto the priests
and to the prophets: This man is not worthy of death, for he has
spoken to us in the name of Yahweh our God.

Then rose up certain of the elders of the land and spake to all the
assembly of the people, saying: Micah the Morasthite prophesied in
the days of Hezekiah, king of Judah, saying:

Zion shall be ploughed as a field, Jerusalem shall become heaps;
The hill of the Temple shall be as the high places of a forest.

Did Hezekiah, king of Judah, and all Judah put him to death?   Did
he not fear Yahweh and entreat the favor of Yahweh?   And Yahweh
repented Him of the evil which He had pronounced against them.
Thus might we procure great evil upon our own souls.   Now there
was another man that prophesied in the name of Yahweh,—Uriah the

son of Shemaiah of Kiriath-jearim; and he prophesied against this
city and against this land according to all the words of Jeremiah; and
when the king and all the princes heard his words, the king sought to
put him to death. But when Uriah heard it, he was afraid and fled,
and went into Egypt. But Jehoiakim the king sent men into Egypt,
Elnathan the son of Achbor and certain men with him; and they
fetched forth Uriah out of Egypt and brought him to Jehoiakim the
king, who slew him with the edge of the sword, and cast his dead
body into the graves of the common people. But the hand of Ahikam
the son of Shaphan was with Jeremiah, so that they did not give him
into the hand of the people to put him to death.

The word that came to Jeremiah concerning all the people of Judah
in the fourth year of Jehoiakim the son of Josiah, king of Judah,
(which was the first year of Nebuchadrezzar, king of Babylon) which
Jeremiah the prophet spake unto all the people of Judah and to all
the inhabitants of Jerusalem, saying: From the thirteenth year of
Josiah son of Amon, king of Judah, even unto this day, these three
and twenty years, the word of Yahweh hath come unto me and I have
spoken unto you, speaking betimes and often; but ye have not hearkened. And Yahweh hath sent unto you all his servants the prophets,
sending them betimes and often, (but ye have not hearkened neither
inclined your ears to hear), saying: Return ye now, every one from
his evil way, from the evil of his doings, and dwell in the land that
Yahweh hath given unto you and to your fathers for ever and ever;
go not after other gods to serve them and to worship them; and
provoke Me not with the work of your own hands; then will I do you
no hurt. Yet ye have not hearkened unto Me, saith Yahweh, but have
provoked Me with the work of your own hands to your hurt. Therefore thus saith Yahweh Sabaoth: Because ye have not obeyed My
words, behold, I will send and take all the families of the earth,
saith Yahweh, and I will send unto Nebuchadrezzar the king of Babylon,
My instrument, and will bring them against this land, and against all
the inhabitants thereof, and against all these nations round about;
and I will utterly destroy them, and make them an astonishment and
a hissing and perpetual desolations. Moreover, I will cause to cease
from among them the voice of mirth and the voice of gladness, the
voice of the bridegroom and the voice of the bride, the sound of the
millstones and the light of the lamp. And the whole land shall be a
desolation and a waste.

For thus saith unto me Yahweh, the God of Israel: Take the cup
of the wine of this fury from My hand, and cause all the nations to
whom I send thee to drink it; and they shall drink, and reel to and
fro, and be like unto madmen, because of the sword that I am sending
among you. Then I took the cup from the hand of Yahweh, and I
caused all the nations to whom Yahweh had sent me to drink; Jerusalem and the cities of Judah, the kings thereof and the princes thereof;
Pharoah, king of Egypt, his servants and princes, and all his people,
and all the foreign peoples; and all the kings of the land of Uz, and
all the kings of the land of the Philistines, of Askelon and Gaza, Ekron
and all the remnant of Ashdod, Edom and Moab and the Ammonites and
all the kings of Tyre, and all the kings of Sidon; and the kings of the
isle which is beyond the sea, Deden and Tema and Buz,—all of those
that have the corners of their hair shorn, and all the kings of the mingled peoples that live in the desert.

Thus said Yahweh: Go down to the house of the king of Judah and speak there this word, and say: Hear the word of Yahweh, O king of Judah, that sitteth upon the throne of David, thou, and thy servants, and thy people that enter in by these gates. Thus saith Yahweh: Execute ye justice and righteousness, and deliver the oppressed out of the hand of the oppressor; and do no wrong; do no violence to the stranger, the fatherless nor the widow, neither shed innocent blood in this place. For, if ye do this wrong indeed, then shall there enter in by the gates of this house kings to sit upon the throne of David, riding in chariots and on horses, he and his servants and his people. But if ye will not hear these words, I swear by Myself, saith Yahweh, that this house shall become a desolation. For thus saith Yahweh concerning the house of the king of Judah:

Thou art Gilead unto Me, the head of Lebanon;
Yet surely I will make thee a desert, like uninhabited cities.
I will bring destroyers against thee, every one with his weapons;
Thy choice cedars shall be cut down, and cast into the fire.

And many nations shall pass by this city, and they shall say, every man to his neighbor: Wherefore hath Yahweh done thus unto this great city? Then they shall answer: Because they forsook the covenant of Yahweh, their God, and worshiped other gods, and served them.

A Lament for the Discrowned King [1]

Weep not for the dead,   neither bemoan him;
But weep sore for him that goeth away,
For he shall return no more,
Nor see his native land.

For thus saith Yahweh touching Shallum the son of Josiah, king of Judah, who reigned instead of Josiah his father, and who went forth out of this place:

He shall return hither no more, but shall die in the place
Whither they have led him captive,
And shall see this land no more.

How the Scroll of Jeremiah's Sermons Came to be Burned

(Ch. xxxvi) [2]

It came to pass in the fourth year of Jehoiakim the son of Josiah, king of Judah, that this word came unto Jeremiah from Yahweh, saying: Take thee a roll of a book, and write therein all the words that I have spoken to thee against Israel and against Judah and against all the nations, from the day that I spake unto thee in the days of Josiah even unto this day. It may be that the house of Judah will listen

[1] Shallum, who is also called Jehoahaz, and who succeeded Josiah after the battle of Megiddo in 608 B.C. whereby Judah became subject to Egypt, reigned but three months, was then deposed by Necho and taken to Egypt. His brother Eliakim was put on the throne, and his name changed to Jehoiakim. The touching little elegy in v. 10, enforces through this recent event the warnings of the preceding section.

[2] This chapter, probably an excerpt from a Biography of the prophet, does not belong to the Second Booklet; but from its superscription it must come before the great deliverance from the rule of Egypt; after which the current of events runs steadily on to the Babylonian Captivity. It is therefore inserted here by the editor.

to all the evil which I purpose to do unto them, and return every man from his evil way; and that I may forgive their iniquity and their sin.

Then Jeremiah called Baruch the son of Neriah; and Baruch wrote from the mouth of Jeremiah all the words of Yahweh which He had spoken unto him upon a roll of a book. And Jeremiah commanded Baruch, saying: I am prevented; I cannot go into the House of Yahweh; therefore go thou and read from the roll which thou hast written from my mouth the words of Yahweh in the ears of the people in the House of Yahweh upon a fast-day; and also thou shalt read them in the ears of all the people of Judah that come out of their cities. It may be that they will present their supplication before Yahweh, and will return every man from his evil way; for great is the anger and the fury that Yahweh hath pronounced against this people. And Baruch the son of Neriah did according to all that Jeremiah commanded him, reading from the book the words of Yahweh in Yahweh's House.

Now it came to pass in the fifth year of Jehoiakim the son of Josiah, king of Judah, in the ninth month, that they proclaimed a fast before Yahweh, all the people in Jerusalem and all the people that came from the cities of Judah unto Jerusalem. Then did Baruch read from the book the words of Jeremiah in the House of Yahweh, in the chamber of Gemariah the son of Shaphan the scribe, in the upper court at the entrance of the new gate of the House of Yahweh, in the ears of all the people. And when Micaiah the son of Gemariah the son of Shaphan had heard the words of Yahweh, he went down into the king's house, into the scribe's chamber; and lo, all the princes were sitting there, Elishama the scribe, Delaiah the son of Shemaiah, Elnathan the son of Achbor, Gemariah the son of Shaphan and Zedekiah the son of Hananiah, and all the princes. Then Micaiah declared unto them all the words that he had heard, when Baruch read the book in the ears of all the people. Therefore all the princes sent Jehudi the son of Nethaniah, the son of Shelemiah, the son of Cushi, unto Baruch, saying: Take in thy hand the roll wherein thou hast read in the ears of the people, and come. So Baruch the son of Neriah took the roll in his hand and came unto them. And they said unto him: Sit down now and read it in our ears. So Baruch read it in their ears. Now it came to pass, when they had heard all the words, they turned in fear one toward another, and said unto Baruch: We will surely tell the king of these words. And they asked Baruch, saying: Tell us now; how didst thou write all these words at his mouth? Then Baruch answered them: He pronounced all these words unto me with his mouth, and I wrote them with ink in the book. Then said the princes to Baruch: Go, hide thee, thou and Jeremiah; and let no man know where ye are. And they went in unto the king in the court; (but they had deposited the roll in the chamber of Elishama the scribe) and they told all the words in the ear of the king. So the king sent Jehudi to fetch the roll; and he took it out of the chamber of Elishama the scribe. And Jehudi read it in the ears of the king and of all the princes that stood beside the king. Now the king was sitting in the winter-house in the ninth month; and the brazier was burning before him. And it came to pass, when Jehudi had read three or four columns, that he [the king] cut it with a paper-knife, and cast it into the fire that was in the brazier, until all the roll was consumed. Yet they were not afraid, nor rent their garments, neither the king nor any of his servants that heard all these words. Moreover Elnathan and Delaiah had entreated the king not to burn the roll; but he would not listen to them. And the king commanded Jerahmeel the king's son and Seraiah the son of Azriel and Shelemaiah the son of Abdeel, to take Baruch the scribe and Jeremiah the prophet; but Yahweh hid them.

Then the word of Yahweh came to Jeremiah, after that the king had burned the roll and the words which Baruch wrote at the mouth of Jeremiah, saying: Take thee again another roll, and write in it all the former words that were in the first roll, which Jehoiakim, the king of Judah, hath burned. And concerning Jehoiakim, king of Judah, thou shalt say: Thus saith Yahweh: Thou hast burned the roll, saying: Why hast thou written therein saying: The king of Babylon shall certainly come and destroy this land, and shall cause to cease from it man and beast? Therefore thus saith Yahweh concerning Jehoiakim, king of Judah: He shall have none to sit upon the throne of David; and his dead body shall be cast out in the day to the heat, and in the night to the frost. And I will visit upon him and his seed and his servants their iniquity; and I will bring upon them and upon the inhabitants of Jerusalem and upon the men of Judah all the evil that I have pronounced against them, and they hearkened not.

Then Jeremiah took another roll and gave it to Baruch the scribe, the son of Neriah; who wrote therein from the mouth of Jeremiah all the words of the book which Jehoiakim the king of Judah had burned in the fire; and there were added besides unto them many like words.

The word that Jeremiah the prophet spake unto Baruch, the son of Neriah, when he wrote the words in a book at the mouth of Jeremiah, in the fourth year of Jehoiakim the son of Josiah, king of Judah, saying: Thus saith Yahweh, the God of Israel, concerning thee, O Baruch. Thou didst say:

Woe is me now, for Yahweh hath added sorrow to my pain!
I am weary with my groaning, and I find no rest.

Thus shalt thou say unto him, saith Yahweh:
Behold, that which I have built will I break down,
And that which I have planted will I pluck up.
And this is the whole land.
And seekest thou great things for thyself?
Seek thou not!

For behold, I will bring evil upon all flesh, saith Yahweh; but thy life will I give thee for booty in all places whithersoever thou goest.

A SONG OF TRIUMPH FOR THE DEFEAT OF PHARAOH NECHO
AT THE BATTLE OF CARCHEMISH, B.C. 605

Make ready buckler and shield and draw near to battle!
Harness the horses and mount, ye horsemen,
And stand forth with your helmets!
Furbish the spears, put on the coats of mail.
Why do I see them dismayed and turned backward?

Their mighty ones are beaten down; they flee apace
And look not back.
Terror is on every side, saith Yahweh.
The swift cannot flee away, nor the mighty warrior escape.
In the north by the River Euphrates
Have they stumbled and fallen.

Who is this that riseth up like the Nile,
    Whose waves toss themselves like the River?
Saying: I will rise up, I will cover the earth;
    I will destroy all its inhabitants?
Prance, ye horses, rush madly, ye chariots!
Let the mighty warriors go forth!
Cush and Put, that handle the shield,
And the Ludim that bend the bow!

But that day is Yahweh's Day of Vengeance,
    That He may avenge Him of His adversaries.
The sword shall devour and be satiate,
    And shall drink its fill of their blood.
For Yahweh Sabaoth hath a sacrifice in the Northland
    By the River Euphrates.

Go up to Gilead and take balm, O virgin daughter of Egypt!
    In vain wilt thou use many medicines;
        There is no cure for thee!
The nations have heard of thy shame,
    The earth is full of thy cry;
For hero hath stumbled against hero;
    And both are fallen together.[1]

THE FAST-APPROACHING DOOM OF JEHOIAKIM

Woe to him that buildeth his house by unrighteousness,
    And his chambers by injustice!
    Using his neighbors' service without wages,
        Giving him not his hire!
That saith: I will build me a vast house
    With spacious chambers and many windows;
And it is ceiled with cedar   and painted with vermilion.
Shalt thou reign because thou dost strive to excel in cedar?
    Did not thy father eat and drink
        And execute law with justice?
    He judged the cause of the poor and needy
        And that was well.
    Is not this to know Me? saith Yahweh.

But thine eyes and thine heart are bent on dishonest gain,
On the shedding of innocent blood, on oppression and violence.
Therefore thus saith Yahweh,   concerning Jehoiakim,
    The son of Josiah,   king of Judah:
They shall not lament for him, Alas, my brother! Alas, my sister!
They shall not lament for him, Alas, my lord! or Alas, my glory!
He shall be buried as an ass is buried, drawn and cast forth
        Beyond the city-gates.

Go up to Lebanon and cry aloud! Lift up thy voice in Bashan!
        And cry out from Mount Abarim!
    For all that loved thee are destroyed.
In thy prosperity, I spake unto thee; but thou saidst:
        I will not hear.
    This hath been thy way from thy youth
    That thou hearkenedst not to My voice.
    The wind shall feed upon thy shepherds,
    Thy lovers shall go into captivity.

----

[1] The authorship of this ode is warmly disputed; but many authorities find in it special marks of Jeremiah's style.

Surely then shalt thou be ashamed,
And confounded for all thy wickedness.
O inhabitant of Lebanon, thou that art nestled in the cedars,
How wilt thou groan
When pangs come upon thee, as of a woman in travail!

Concerning the Prophets

Woe to the Shepherds that scatter and destroy
The sheep of My pasture!
Thus saith Yahweh against the men that feed My people, Israel:
Ye have scattered My flock and driven them away;
Ye have taken no care of them.
Behold, I will have a care of you; I will visit on you your deeds.

(My heart within me is broken   all my bones do shake.
I am like a drunken man   whom wine hath overcome,
Because of Yahweh and because of His holy commands.
For the land is full of adulterers,
Their course is evil, their force not right.
For both prophet and priest are ungodly,)
Yea, in My House have I found their wickedness.
Therefore their way shall be unto them
Like slippery paths in the darkness.
They shall be thrust down and fall therein
For I will bring evil upon them in the time of their visitation,
                                        [saith Yahweh.

In the prophets of Samaria have I seen wickedness
They prophesied by Baal, they caused My people to err;
But in the prophets of Jerusalem have I seen a horrible thing.
They commit adultery and walk in lies
And they strengthen the hands of evil-doers.
They are all to Me like Sodom, its inhabitants like Gomorrah.

Therefore thus saith Yahweh Sabaoth concerning the Prophets:
Behold, I will feed them with wormwood
And make them drink water of gall
For from the prophets of Jerusalem is gone forth
Ungodliness in the land.

Hearken not to the prophets that feed you with vain hopes, that
speak the desires of their own hearts and not out of the mouth of
Yahweh; that say continually to them that despise Me: Thus saith
Yahweh, ye shall have peace;—and to him that walketh in his self-
will: No evil shall come upon you. For who hath stood in the council
of Yahweh, that he should perceive and hear His word? Who hath
hearkened to His word and obeyed it?

I have not sent these prophets,   yet they ran;
I have not spoken unto them,   yet they have prophesied.
If they had stood in My council,   they had caused My people
To hear My words:
They had turned them from their evil way,
And from their evil-doing.
Am I a God near at hand, saith Yahweh, and not far-off?
Can a man hide himself in secret places that I shall not see him?
Do not I fill both heaven and earth? saith Yahweh.

I have heard what the prophets say   that prophesy lies in My name,
    Saying: I have dreamed,   I have dreamed!
        How long shall this be?
Is My word in the hearts of prophets that prophesy lies?
    That prophesy the deceit of their heart,
Thinking to cause My people to forget My name,
By the dreams they tell every man to his neighbor,
    As their father forgot My name for Baal.

The prophet that hath a dream, let him tell his dream;
And let him speak My word faithfully that hath My word.
    What hath the straw to do with the wheat? saith Yahweh,
        Is not My word like a fire,
        Like a hammer that shatters the rocks?

The Doom of Jehoiachin (Coniah)

WHO SUCCEEDED JEHOIAKIM, AND REIGNED THREE MONTHS

As I live, saith Yahweh, though Coniah the son of Jehoiakim, king of Judah, were the signet upon My right hand, yet would I pluck him thence. And I will give thee into the hand of them that seek thy life, and into the hand of them of whom thou art afraid, even into the hand of Nebuchadrezzar, king of Babylon, and into the hand of the Chaldæans. And I will cast thee out, and thy mother that bare thee, into another country in which ye were not born, and there shall ye die. But to the land whereunto they long to return, thither shall they not return.

    Is this man Coniah a despised, broken image?
    Is he a vessel wherein is no pleasure?
    Wherefore are they cast out, he and his seed,
And are cast into the land which they know not?
    O land, land, land! hear the word of Yahweh?
Thus saith Yahweh: Write this man childless;
    A man that shall not prosper in his days.
    For no man of his seed shall prosper
Sitting upon the throne of David, and ruling any more
        In Judah.

After Nebuchadrezzer, king of Babylon, had carried away captive Jeconiah the son of Jehoiakim, king of Judah, and the princes of Judah with the craftsmen and smiths from Jerusalem, and had brought them to Babylon, Yahweh showed me two baskets of figs, set before the temple of Yahweh. One basket had very good figs, like the figs that are first ripe; and the other basket had very bad figs, which could not be eaten, they were so bad. Then Yahweh said unto me: What seest thou, Jeremiah? And I said: Figs; the good figs, very good; and the bad, very bad, that cannot be eaten, they are so bad. Thereupon the word of Yahweh came unto me, saying:

Thus saith Yahweh, the God of Israel: Like these good figs, so will I regard for good the captives of Judah whom I have sent out of this place into the land of the Chaldæans. And I will keep Mine eyes upon them, and I will bring them back to this land; and I will build them up and not pull them down, and I will plant them and not pluck them up; and I will give them a heart to know Me, that I am Yahweh; and they shall be My people, when they shall return unto Me with their whole heart, and I will be their God. But as for the bad figs that cannot be eaten, they are so bad—surely thus saith Yahweh: So will I make Zedekiah, the king of Judah, and his princes, and the residue of Jerusalem that remain in this land, and them that dwell in the land of Egypt,—I will even make them a horror among all the nations of the earth, and they shall be a reproach and a proverb, a taunt and a curse in all places whither I shall drive them. And I will send the sword, the famine and the pestilence among them, till they be consumed from off the face of the land that I gave to their fathers.

THE THIRD BOOKLET

WHICH BEGINS WITH THE ACCESSION OF ZEDEKIAH, (597 B.C.)[1]

(Ch. xxvii, 1-22; xxviii, 1-17; xxix, 1-32)

In the beginning of the reign of Zedekiah, came this word unto me from Yahweh, saying: Make thee bands and bars and put them upon thy neck, and send to the kings of Edom, of Moab, of the Ammonites, of Tyre and of Sidon, by the messengers that have come to Zedekiah, king of Judah, and give them a charge to their masters, saying: Thus saith the militant God Yahweh, the God of Israel: Thus shall ye say to your masters: I have made the earth, the man and the beast that are upon the face of the earth by My great power and by Mine outstretched arm; and I give it unto whom it seemeth right to Me. And now I have given the earth unto Nebuchadrezzar, king of Babylon, My servant, and the beasts of the field to serve him; and the people and the kingdom which will not serve this same Nebuchadrezzar, king of Babylon, and that will not put their neck under the yoke of the king of Babylon, will I punish, saith Yahweh, with the sword and with famine and with pestilence until I have consumed them by his hand.

But as for you, hearken not to your prophets nor to your diviners nor to your dreamers nor to your soothsayers and sorcerers, who say: Ye shall not serve the king of Babylon! For they prophecy a lie to you to remove you far from your land; and that I should drive you out, and ye should perish. But the nation that shall bring its neck under the yoke of the king of Babylon and serve him, that nation will I leave in their own land, saith Yahweh, and they shall till it and dwell therein.

And to Zedekiah, king of Judah, spake I the same words, saying: Bring your neck under the yoke of the king of Babylon, and serve him and his people and live. Why will ye die, thou and thy people, by the sword, by famine and by pestilence, as Yahweh hath spoken concerning the nation that will not serve the king of Babylon? Hearken not unto the words of the prophets that speak unto you, saying: Ye shall not serve the king of Babylon; for they prophesy a lie unto you. For I have not sent them, saith Yahweh; they are prophesying falsely in My name, that they may drive you out and that ye may perish, ye, and the prophets that prophesy unto you.

Also, I spake to the priests and to all the people, saying: Thus saith Yahweh: hearken not to the words of your prophets that say:

---

[1] In A. V. as also in the Heb. the booklet opens "In the beginning of the reign of *Jehoiakim*": but that this is a scribal error is immediately evident, for Zedekiah is the only king of Judah mentioned throughout. He, also, was a son of Josiah. The three chapters of this little booklet have noteworthy peculiarities found nowhere else in the whole book; among others, the fact that Jeremiah speaks directly in the first person.

Behold, the vessels of Yahweh's House shall now shortly be brought back from Babylon; for they prophesy a lie upon you. Hearken not unto them; serve the king of Babylon and live; why should the city become desolate? But if these be prophets, and if the word of Yahweh be with them, let them now make intercession with Yahweh the militant, that the vessels that are left in the House of Yahweh and in the house of the king of Judah and at Jerusalem, go not to Babylon. For thus saith Yahweh Sabaoth concerning the pillars and the sea and the bases and the residue of the vessels that remain in the city, which Nebuchadrezzar, king of Babylon, took not when he carried away captive Jeconiah the son of Jehoiakim, king of Judah, from Jerusalem to Babylon, and all the nobles of Judah and Jerusalem; yea, thus saith Yahweh Sabaoth, the God of Israel, concerning the vessels that remain in the House of Yahweh and in the house of the king of Judah, and at Jerusalem: They shall be carried to Babylon, and there shall they be until the day that I remember them, and bring them up and restore them to this place.

And it came to pass the same year in the beginning of the reign of Zedekiah, in the fourth year, in the fifth month, that Hananiah, son of Azzur, the prophet, who was of Gibeon, spake unto me in the House of Yahweh, in the presence of the priests and of all the people, saying: Thus saith Yahweh Sabaoth, the God of Israel; I have broken the yoke of the king of Babylon. Within two full years I will bring back into this place all the vessels of the House of Yahweh that Nebuchadrezzar, king of Babylon, took away from this place and carried them to Babylon. And I will bring back to this place Jeconiah, the son of Jehoiakim, king of Judah, with all the captives of Judah that went into Babylon, saith Yahweh, for I will break the yoke of the King of Babylon. Then the prophet Jeremiah said unto the prophet Hananiah in the presence of the priests, and in the presence of all the people that stood in the House of Yahweh: Amen! May Yahweh do so; May Yahweh perform thy words which thou hast prophesied, to bring again the vessels of Yahweh's House and all that is carried away captive, from Babylon into this place. Nevertheless, hear thou now this word that I speak in thine ears, and in the ears of all the people: The prophets that have been before me and before thee of old prophesied both against many countries and against great kingdoms, of war and of evil, and of pestilence. The prophet that prophesieth of peace, when the word of that prophet shall come to pass it shall be known that Yahweh hath truly sent him.

Then Hananiah the prophet took the yoke from off the neck of the prophet Jeremiah, and brake it. And Hananiah spake in the presence of all the people, saying: Thus saith Yahweh: Even so will I break the yoke of Nebuchadrezzar, king of Babylon, from the neck of all nations within the space of two full years. And the prophet Jeremiah went his way.

Then the word of Yahweh came unto Jeremiah after that Hananiah the prophet had broken the yoke from off the neck of the prophet Jeremiah, saying: Go, and tell Hananiah, saying: Thus saith Yahweh: Thou hast broken the yokes of wood, but thou shalt make instead of them yokes of iron. For thus saith Yahweh Sabaoth, the God of Israel: I have put a yoke of iron upon the neck of all these nations, that they may serve Nebuchadrezzar, king of Babylon; and they shall serve him.

Then said the prophet Jeremiah unto Hananiah the prophet: Hear now, Hananiah; Yahweh hath not sent thee, but thou makest this people to trust in a lie. Therefore thus saith Yahweh: Behold, I will cast thee from off the face of the earth. This year thou shalt die, because thou hast taught rebellion against Yahweh. So Hananiah the prophet died the same year, in the seventh month.

These are the words of the letter that Jeremiah the prophet sent from Jerusalem unto the elders of the captives, whom Nebuchadrezzar had carried away captive, by the hand of Eleazar the son of Shaphan and Gemariah the son of Hilkiah, whom Zedekiah, king of Judah, sent to the king of Babylon.

Thus saith Yahweh Sabaoth, the God of Israel, unto all whom I have caused to be carried away from Jerusalem unto Babylon: Build ye houses, and dwell in them; and plant gardens, and eat the fruit of them; take ye wives, and beget sons and daughters, and take wives for your sons and give your daughters to husbands, that ye may be increased there and not diminished. And seek the peace of the city whither I have caused you to be carried away captives, and pray unto Yahweh for it; for in the peace thereof shall ye have peace.

For thus saith Yahweh Sabaoth: Let not your prophets and your diviners in the midst of you deceive you, neither heed the dreams which they dream. For they prophesy falsely unto you in My name. I have not sent them.

For thus saith Yahweh: After seventy years be accomplished at Babylon, I will visit you, and perform My good word toward you, in causing you to return to this place. For I know My thoughts toward you, saith Yahweh, thoughts of peace and not of evil, to give you a hoped-for end. Call upon Me and pray unto Me, and I will hearken unto you. And when ye shall seek for Me and search for Me with all your heart, ye shall find Me.

Because ye have said: Yahweh hath raised up prophets for us in Babylon, thus saith Yahweh Sabaoth of Ahab the son of Kolaiah, and of Zedekiah son of Maaseiah: Behold, I will deliver them into the hand of the king of Babylon, and he shall slay them before your eyes. And of them shall be taken up a curse by all the captivity of Judah which are in Babylon, thus: May Yahweh make thee like Zedekiah and like Ahab whom the king of Babylon roasted in the fire; because they have wrought villainy in Israel and have committed adultery with their neighbors' wives, and have spoken in My name that which I have not commanded them; verily, I know, and am the witness, saith Yahweh. Thou shalt also speak to Shemaiah the Nehelemite, saying:

Because this one wrote to Zephaniah the son of Maaseiah the priest, saying: Yahweh hath made thee priest in the stead of Jehoiada the priest, that thou shouldest be overseer in the House of Yahweh over every madman who pretendeth to be a prophet, that thou shouldst put him in the stocks and in the collar; now therefore, why hast thou not reproved Jeremiah of Anathoth, which pretendeth to be a prophet to you? For he sent to us in Babylon, saying: This captivity will be long; build ye houses and dwell in them, and plant gardens, and eat the fruit of them. And Zedekiah the priest read this letter in the ears of Jeremiah the prophet.

Then came the word of Yahweh to Jeremiah, saying: Send to all them of the captivity, saying: Thus saith Yahweh concerning Shemaiah the Nehelemite: Because Shemaiah hath prophesied unto you, but I sent him not, and he hath caused you to trust in a lie; therefore thus saith Yahweh: Behold, I will punish Shemaiah the Nehelemite and his seed; he shall not have one to dwell among you who shall see the good that I will do for My people, saith Yahweh; because he hath spoken perversely against Yahweh.

THE FOURTH BOOKLET

THE COUNSELS AND WARNINGS OF JEREMIAH BEFORE THE DESTRUCTION OF JERUSALEM AND THE KINGDOM OF JUDAH (B.C. 586)

(Ch. xxxvii, 1-3, 5-10; xxi, 3-10; xxxvii, 11-22, 4; xxxviii, 1-13, 28; xxxiv, 1-22; xxxii, 1a, 2a, 6-15; xxxix, 1a, 3, 14-18)

Zedekiah the son of Josiah reigned as king instead of Coniah the son of Jehoiakim, whom Nebuchadrezzar the king of Babylon made king in the land of Judah. But neither he nor his servants nor the people of the land hearkened unto the words of Yahweh, which He spake by the prophet Jeremiah.

And Zedekiah the king sent Jehucal the son of Shelemiah, and Zephaniah the son of Maaseiah the priest to the prophet Jeremiah, saying: Pray now unto Yahweh, our God, for me. Now Jeremiah came in and went out among the people; for they had not yet put him in prison. And Pharaoh's army was come forth out of Egypt; and when the Chaldæans that were besieging Jerusalem heard tidings of them, they broke up from before Jerusalem. Then came the word of Yahweh unto the prophet Jeremiah, saying: Thus saith the God of Israel, Yahweh: Thus shalt thou say unto the king of Judah that sent thee unto Me to inquire of Me: Behold, Pharaoh's army which is come forth to help you shall return to Egypt, to their own land. And the Chaldæans shall return and fight against this city; and they shall take it and burn it with fire. Thus saith Yahweh: Deceive not yourselves, saying: The Chaldæans shall surely depart from us; they shall not depart. For though ye had smitten the whole army of the Chaldæans that fight against you, and there remained but wounded men among them, yet should they rise up every man in his tent, and burn this city with fire.

Then said Jeremiah unto them: Thus shall ye say to Zedekiah: Thus saith Yahweh the God of Israel: Behold, I will turn back the weapons of war that are in your hands wherewith ye fight against the king of Babylon and the Chaldæans, which besiege you without the walls, and I will gather them into the midst of this city. And I Myself will fight against you with an outstretched arm and with a strong hand, even in anger and in fury, and in great wrath. And I will smite the inhabitants of this city, both man and beast; they shall die of a great pestilence. And afterward, saith Yahweh, I will deliver Zedekiah, king of Judah, and his servants and the people and such as are left in this city from the pestilence, from the sword and from the famine, into the hand of Nebuchadrezzar, king of Babylon, and into the hand of their enemies, of those that seek their life; and he shall smite them with the edge of the sword; he shall not spare them, neither have pity, nor have mercy.

And unto this people thou shalt say, Thus saith Yahweh: Behold, I set before you the way of life and the way of death. He that abideth in the city shall die by the sword and by the famine and by the pestilence; but he that goeth out and falleth to the Chaldæans that besiege you, he shall live, and his life shall be unto him for a prey. For I have set My face against this city for evil and not for good, saith Yahweh; it shall be given into the hand of the king of Babylon, and he shall burn it with fire.

Behold, I am against thee, O inhabitant of the valley,
Rock of the plain!
Ye that say: Who can come against us?
Who can enter our strongholds?
I will punish you according to the fruit of your deeds, saith Yahweh.
I will kindle a fire in her forest that shall consume
Alll that is round about her.

And it came to pass that, when the army of the Chaldæans was broken up for fear of Pharoah's army, that Jeremiah went forth out of Jerusalem to go into the land of Benjamin to receive his portion there in the midst of his people. And when he was in the Gate of Benjamin, a captain of the ward, whose name was Irijah, took Jeremiah the prophet, saying: Thou fallest away to the Chaldæans. Then said Jeremiah: It is false; I fall not away to the Chaldæans. But he hearkened not to him; so Irijah took Jeremiah and brought him to the princes. Wherefore the princes were wroth with Jeremiah and smote him, and put him in prison in the house of Jonathan the scribe; for they had made that the prison.

When Jeremiah was come into the dungeon-house and into the cells, and had remained there many days, Zedekiah the king sent and took him out; and the king asked him secretly in his house, and said: Is there any word from Yahweh? And Jeremiah said: There is; for, said He, thou shalt be delivered into the hand of the king of Babylon. Moreover Jeremiah said unto King Zedekiah, What have I done against thee, or against thy servants, or against this people, that ye have put me in prison? Where now are your prophets that prophesied unto you, saying: The king of Babylon shall not come against you, nor against this land? And now, hear, I pray thee, O my lord the king; let my supplication, I pray thee, be presented before thee, that thou cause me not to return to the house of Jonathan the scribe, lest I die there.

Then Zedekiah the king commanded, and they committed Jeremiah to the court of the guard; and they gave him daily a loaf of bread out of the bakers' street, until all the bread in the city was spent. Thus Jeremiah remained in the court of the guard, and went in and out among the people, for they had not put him in durance.

Now Shephatieth the son of Mattan, and Gedaliah the son of Pashhur, and Jucal the son of Shelemiah, and Pashhur the son of Malchiah heard the words that Jeremiah spake unto all the people, saying: Thus saith Yahweh: He that remaineth in this city shall die by the sword, by the famine and by the pestilence; but he that goeth forth to the Chaldæans shall live, and his life shall be unto him for a prey. Thus saith Yahweh: This city shall surely be given into the hand of the king of Babylon, and he shall take it. Then the princes said unto the king: Let this man, we pray thee, be put to death; forasmuch as he weakeneth the hands of the men of war that remain in this city, and the hands of all the people in speaking such words as these. For this man seeketh not the welfare of this people, but the hurt. Then said Zedekiah the king: Behold, he is in your hand; for the king is not he that can do anything against you. Then took they Jeremiah and cast him into the pit of Malchiah, the king's son, that was in the court of the guard; and they let him down with cords. And in the pit there was no water, but mire; and Jeremiah sank in the mire.

Now when Ebed-melech the Ethiopian, an officer who was in the king's house, heard that they had put Jeremiah into the pit, (the king then sitting in the Gate of Benjamin) Ebed-melech went forth out of the king's house and spake to the king, saying: My lord the king, these men have done evil in all that they have done to Jeremiah the prophet, whom they have cast into the pit; and he is like to die in the place where he is on account of the famine; for there is no more bread in the city. Then the king commanded Ebed-melech the Ethiopian, saying: Take from hence thirty men with thee, and take up Jeremiah the prophet out of the pit before he die.   So Ebed-melech took the men with him, and went into the house of the king under the treasury, and took thence worn clouts and rags, and let them down by cords into the pit to Jeremiah.   And Ebed-melech the Ethiopian said unto Jeremiah: Put now these old worn-out clouts and rags under thine armpits under the cords. And Jeremiah did so.   So they drew up Jeremiah by the cords, and took him out of the pit; and Jeremiah remained in the court of the guard, and abode in the court of the guard until the day that Jerusalem was taken.[1]

The word which came to Jeremiah from Yahweh when Nebuchadrezzar, king of Babylon, and all his army and all the kingdoms of the land of his dominion and all the peoples, fought against Jerusalem and against all the cities of Judah.

Thus saith Yahweh: Go to Zedekiah, king of Judah, and tell him: Thus saith Yahweh: Behold, I will give this city into the hand of the king of Babylon, and he shall burn it with fire; and thou shalt not escape out of his hand.   And thine eyes shall behold the eyes of the king of Babylon, and he shall speak with thee mouth to mouth, and thou shalt go to Babylon.   Yet hear the word of Yahweh, O Zedekiah, king of Judah; thus saith Yahweh concerning thee: Thou shalt not die by the sword, thou shalt die in peace; and like the burnings of thy fathers, the kings that were before thee, so shall they make a burning for thee; and they shall lament thee,—Ah, lord! for I have spoken the word, saith Yahweh.

Thus Jeremiah the prophet spake all these words unto Zedekiah, king of Judah, while the king of Babylon's army was besieging Jerusalem and all the cities of Judah that were left, Lachish and Azekah; for these alone remained of the fortified cities of Judah.

The word that came to Jeremiah from Yahweh, after the king Zedekiah had made a covenant with all the people that were at Jerusalem to proclaim unto them a liberation: that every man should let his manservant and his maid-servant go free, if they were Hebrews; that none should make bondmen of them, being Judæans, his brethren; and all the princes and all the people hearkened, and entered into the covenant and let them go free.   But afterwards they turned and caused the servants and the handmaids, whom they had let go free, to return, and brought them into subjection again.   Therefore the word of Yahweh came to Jeremiah, saying:

Thus saith Yahweh the God of Israel: I made a covenant with your fathers in the day that I brought them forth out of the land of Egypt, out of the house of bondage, saying: At the end of seven years ye shall let go every man that is Hebrew that hath been sold unto thee and hath served thee six years; thou shalt let him go free; but your fathers hearkened not unto Me, nor inclined their ear.   But ye had

[1] Verses 14-27 are a later and inaccurate version of the secret interview between Jeremiah and the king, already given in Ch. xxxvii. It gives the impression of two such interviews, where a closer study shows that there was but one.   It is an excellent illustration of the difficulty of reconciling the accounts in the several booklets which has not yet been entirely overcome.

now turned and had done that which is right in Mine eyes, in proclaiming liberty every man to his neighbor; and ye had made a covenant before Me in the house which is called by My name. Now ye have turned and profaned My name, and caused, every man of you, his servant and his handmaid whom ye had let go free at his pleasure, to return and be in subjection again. Therefore thus saith Yahweh: Ye have not hearkened unto Me to proclaim freedom every man to his brother, and every man to his neighbor;—now I proclaim for you freedom, saith Yahweh, to become the prey of the sword and of famine and of the pestilence; and I will make you a horror to all the kingdoms of the earth. And I will give the men that have transgressed My covenant, that have not performed the words of the covenant they made before Me,— when they cut the calf in twain, and passed between the parts thereof,— the princes of Judah and the rulers of Jerusalem, the officers and the priests and all the people; I will even give them into the hand of their enemies, and into the hand of them that seek their life, and their dead bodies shall be for food unto the fowls of heaven, and to the beasts of the earth. And Zedekiah, king of Judah, and his princes will I give into the hand of their enemies, even into the hand of the king of Babylon's army, which has gone away from you. Behold, I will command, saith Yahweh, and cause them to return to this city, and they shall fight against it and take it, and burn it with fire; and I will make the cities of Judah a desolation, without inhabitant.

A word came to Jeremiah from Yahweh, while the king of Babylon was besieging Jerusalem. And Jeremiah said, The word of Yahweh came unto me, saying: Behold, Hanamel, the son of Shallum thine uncle, shall come unto thee, saying: Buy my field that is in Anathoth, for the right of redemption to buy it is thine. So Hanamel, mine uncle's son, came to me in the court of the guard according to the word of Yahweh, and said unto me: Buy my field, I pray thee, that is in Anathoth in the land of Benjamin; for the right of inheritance is thine, and the redemption is thine. Buy it for thyself. Then I knew that it was the word of Yahweh. And I bought the field that was in Anathoth of mine uncle's son, and weighed him the money, even seventeen shekels of silver. And I signed the deed and sealed it and called witnesses, and weighed him the money in the balances. Then I took the deed of the purchase, both that which was sealed containing the terms and conditions, and that which was open; and I delivered the deed of the purchase unto Baruch the son of Neriah, the son of Maaseiah, in the presence of Hanamel mine uncle's son, and in the presence of the witnesses that subscribed the deed of the purchase, before all the Judæans that sat in the court of the guard. And I charged Baruch before them, saying: Thus saith Yahweh, the God of Israel: Take these deeds, this deed of purchase which is sealed, and this deed which is open; and put them in an earthen vessel, that they may remain many days. For thus saith Yahweh Sabaoth, the God of Israel: Houses and fields and vineyards shall yet again be bought in this land.

And it came to pass, when Jerusalem was taken, that all the princes of the king of Babylon came in and sat in the middle gate,—Nergalsharezer, Nebushazban, and all the rest of the princes of the king of Babylon. And they sent and took Jeremiah out of the court of the guard, and committed him unto Gedaliah the son of Ahikam son of Shaphan, that he should carry him home. So he dwelt among the people.

Now the word of Yahweh had come unto Jeremiah, while he was shut up in the court of the guard, saying: Go and speak to Ebed-melech the Ethiopian, saying: Thus saith Yahweh Sabaoth, the God of Israel: Behold, I will bring to pass My words for evil upon this city, and not for good; and they shall be accomplished before thee in that day. But I will deliver thee in that day, saith Yahweh, and thou shalt not be given into the hands of the men of whom thou art afraid. For I will surely deliver thee, and thou shalt not fall by the sword; but thy life shall be for a prey unto thee, because thou hast put thy trust in Yahweh.

THE FIFTH BOOKLET

EVENTS IN JUDAH AFTER ITS CONQUEST, AND THE PART TAKEN BY JEREMIAH IN THE DISSENSIONS OF THE PEOPLE (584 B.C.)

(Ch. xxxix, 1b, 2, 4-12; xl, 1-16; xli, 1-18; xlii, 1-22; xliii, 1-13)

In the ninth year of Zedekiah, king of Judah, in the tenth month, came Nebuchadrezzar, king of Babylon, and all his army against Jerusalem and beseiged it; in the eleventh year of Zedekiah, in the fourth month, the ninth day of the month, a breach was made in the city wall. And when Zedekiah, the king of Judah, and all the men of war saw it, they fled and went forth out of the city by night by the way of the king's garden, by the gate betwixt the two walls; and he went out toward the Arabah. But the army of the Chaldæans pursued after them and overtook Zedekiah in the plains of Jericho; and when they had taken him, they brought him up to Nebuchadrezzar, king of Babylon, to Riblah in the land of Hamath, and he passed judgment upon him. Then the king of Babylon slew the sons of Zedekiah in Riblah before his eyes; also he slew all the nobles of Judah. Moreover he put out the eyes of Zedekiah, and bound him in fetters to carry him to Babylon. And the Chaldæans burned the king's house and the houses of the people with fire, and broke down the walls of Jerusalem.

Then Nebuzaradan, the captain of the guard, carried away captive to Babylon the remnant of the people that remained in the city, the deserters also that fell away to him; but Nebuzaradan left the poor of the people, who had nothing, in the land of Judah, and gave them vineyards and fields in that day.

Now Nebuchadrezzar, king of Babylon, gave charge concerning Jeremiah to Nebuzaradan, the captain of the guard, saying: Take him, and look well to him, and do him no harm; but do unto him even as he shall say unto thee.

The word which came to Jeremiah from Yahweh, after that Nebuzaradan the captain of the guard had let him go from Ramah, whither he had taken him bound in chains among all the captives of Jerusalem and Judah that were being carried away captive unto Babylon. And the captain of the guard took Jeremiah, and said unto him: Yahweh thy God pronounced this evil upon this place and Yahweh hath brought it and done according as He spake; because ye have sinned against Yahweh, and have not hearkened to His voice; therefore is this thing come upon you. And now, behold, this day I loose thee from the chains which are upon thy hand. If it seem good to thee to come with me to Babylon, come; and I will look well unto thee. But if it seem ill unto thee to come with me to Babylon, forbear; behold, all the land is before thee; whither it seemeth good and right unto thee to go, go thither. (Yet he would not go). Go back then to Gedaliah the son of

Ahikam, the son of Shaphan, whom the king of Babylon hath made governor over all the cities of Judah, and dwell with him among the people; or go whithersoever it seemeth right unto thee to go. Then the captain of the guard gave him an allowance and a present, and let him go. Then went Jeremiah unto Gedaliah the son of Ahikam to Mizpah, and dwelt with him among the people that were left in the land.

Now when all the captains of the forces that were in the fields, even they and their men, heard that the king of Babylon had made Gedaliah, son of Ahikam, governor in the land, and had committed unto his care men and women and children and of the poorest of the land of them that were not carried away captive to Babylon, they came to Gedaliah, even Ishmael the son of Nethaniah, and Johanan and Jonathan, sons of Kareah, and Seraiah the son of Tanhumeth, and the sons of Ephai the Netophathite, and Jezaniah the son of the Maacathite, they and their men. And Gedaliah the son of Ahikam the son of Shaphan spake earnestly unto them and to their men, and said: Fear not to serve the Chaldæans; dwell in the land and serve the king of Babylon, and it shall be well with you. As for me, I will dwell in Mizpah, to meet the Chaldæans that may come unto us; but ye, gather ye wine and summer fruits and oil, and put them in your vessels, and dwell in the cities you have taken.

Likewise, when all the Judæans that were in Moab and in Edom and in all the countryside, heard that the king of Babylon had left a remnant of Judah, and that he had set over them Gedaliah son of Ahikam, then all the Judæans returned out of all the places whither they had been driven, and came to the land of Judah to Gedaliah, to Mizpah, and gathered wine and summer fruits in great abundance.

Moreover, Johanan the son of Kareah and all the captains of the forces that were in the fields, came to Gedaliah at Mizpah, and said unto him: Dost thou know that Baalis, the king of the Ammonites, hath sent Ishmael the son of Nethaniah to take thy life? But Gedaliah son of Ahikam believed them not. Then Johanan son of Kareah spake to Gedaliah in Mizpah secretly, saying: Let me go, I pray thee, and I will slay Ishmael the son of Nethaniah, and no man shall know it; wherefore should he take thy life, that all the Judæans that are gathered unto thee should be scattered, and the remnant of Judah perish? But Gedaliah the son of Ahikam said unto Johanan the son of Kareah: Thou shalt not do this thing; thou speakest falsely.

Now it came to pass in the seventh month, that Ishmael the son of Nethaniah, the son of Elishama of the seed royal, and one of the chief officers of the king, and ten men with him, came unto Gedaliah the son of Ahikam to Mizpah; and there they did eat bread together in Mizpah. Then arose Ishmael the son of Nethaniah and the ten men that were with him, and smote Gedaliah the son of Ahikam with the sword and slew him whom the king of Babylon had made governor over the land. Ishmael also slew all the Judæans who were with Gedaliah at Mizpah, and the Chaldæans that were found there, even the men of war.

Now it came to pass the second day after he had slain Gedaliah, and no man knew it, that there came certain men from Shechem, from Shiloh and from Samaria, even fourscore men, having their beards shaven and their clothes rent and having cut themeslves, with meal-offerings and frankincense in their hand, to bring to the House of Yahweh. And Ishmael the son of Nethaniah went forth from Mizpah to meet them, weeping all along as he went. And when he met them, he said unto them: Come to Gedaliah the son of Ahikam. And it was so, that when they came into the middle of the city, Ishmael the son of

Nethaniah slew them and cast them into the midst of the pit, he and the men who were with him. But ten were found among them who said: Slay us not; for we have stores hidden in the field of wheat, of barley, of oil and of honey. So he forbare, and slew them not among their brethren. Now the pit wherein Ishmael cast all the dead bodies of the men whom he had slain by the side of Gedaliah, was that which Asa the king had made for fear of Baasha, king of Israel; the same Ishmael the son of Nethaniah filled with them that were slain. Then Ishmael carried away captive all the residue of the people that were in Mizpah, even the king's daughters, and all the people that remained in Mizpah whom Nebuzaradan had committed to Gedaliah the son of Ahikam; Ishmael the son of Nethaniah carried them away captive, and departed to go over to the children of Ammon.

But when Johanan the son of Kareah, and all the captains of the forces that were with him heard of all the evil that Ishmael had done, they took all the men and went to fight with Ishmael, and they found him by the great waters that are in Gibeon. Now, when all the people that were with Ishmael saw Johanan the son of Kareah, and all the captains of the forces that were with him, they were glad. So all the people that Ishmael had carried away captive from Mizpah cast about, and returned, and went unto Johanan the son of Kareah. But Ishmael escaped from Johanan with eight men, and went to the children of Ammon.

Then took Johanan the son of Kareah, and all the captains of the forces that were with him, all the remnant of the people from Mizpah whom he had recovered from Ishmael, son of Nethaniah, after he had slain Gedaliah, son of Ahikam,—even the men of war, the women and the children, and the officers whom he had brought back from Gibeon; and they departed and dwelt in Geruth Chimham which is near Bethlehem, to be on the road to Egypt. For he was afraid of the Chaldæans, because Ishmael had slain Gedaliah, the son of Ahikam, whom the king of Babylon had made governor over the land.

Then all the captains of the forces, and Johanan the son of Kareah, and Jezaniah, the son of Hoshaiah, and all the people from the least even unto the greatest, came near and said unto Jeremiah the prophet: Let our supplication be accepted before thee, we pray thee; do thou pray for us unto Yahweh thy God for all this remnant; (for we are left but a few out of many, as thine eyes do see us) that Yahweh thy God may tell us the way wherein we should walk, and the thing that we should do. Then Jeremiah the prophet said unto them: I have heard you. Behold, I will pray unto Yahweh your God according to your words. And it shall come to pass that whatsoever thing Yahweh shall answer you, I will declare it unto you; I will keep nothing back from you. Then they said to Jeremiah: Yahweh be a true and faithful witness against us if we do not faithfully according to all the word wherewith Yahweh thy God shall send thee to us. Whether it be good or whether it be evil, we will hearken to the voice of Yahweh our God, to whom we send thee; that it may be well with us when we hearken to the voice of Yahweh our God.

And it came to pass after ten days, that the word of Yahweh came unto Jeremiah. Then called he Johanan the son of Kareah and all the captains of the forces that were with him, and all the people from the least unto the greatest, and said unto them: Thus saith Yahweh, the God of Israel, unto whom ye sent me to present your supplication before Him: If ye will still abide in this land, then will I build you and not pull you down, and I will plant you and not pluck you up; for I repent Me of the evil I have done unto you. Be not afraid of the king of Babylon, of whom ye are afraid; be not afraid of him, saith Yahweh; for I am with you to save you and to deliver you out of his hand. And I will grant you compassion, that he may have compassion upon you, and cause you to return to your own land. But if ye say: We will not abide in this land, so that ye hearken not to the voice of Yahweh your God, saying: No; but we will go into the land of Egypt, where we shall see no war, nor hear the sound of the horn nor have hunger for bread; there will we abide; then, hear ye the word of Yahweh, O remnant of Judah. Thus saith Yahweh Sabaoth, the God of Israel: If ye wholly set your faces to enter Egypt and go to sojourn there, then it shall come to pass that the sword which ye fear shall overtake you there in the land of Egypt; and the famine, whereof ye are afraid, shall follow hard after you there in Egypt, and there ye shall die. So shall it be with all the men that set their faces to go into Egypt to sojourn there; they shall die by the sword, by the famine and by the pestilence; and none of them shall remain, or escape from the evil that I will bring upon them. For thus saith Yahweh Sabaoth, the God of Israel: As Mine anger and My fury hath been poured forth upon the inhabitants of Jerusalem, so shall My fury be poured forth upon you, when ye shall enter Egypt; and ye shall be an execration and an astonishment and a curse and a reproach, and ye shall see this place no more. Yahweh hath spoken concerning you, O remnant of Judah. Go ye not into Egypt. Know certainly that I have forewarned you this day.

For ye have dealt deceitfully against your own souls; for ye sent me unto Yahweh your God, saying: Pray for us unto Yahweh our God, and according unto all that Yahweh our God shall say, so declare unto us, and we will do it. And I have this day declared it unto you; but ye have not hearkened to the voice of Yahweh your God in anything for which He hath sent me unto you. Now therefore, know certainly that ye shall die by the sword, by the famine and by the pestilence in the place whither ye desire to go, to sojourn there.

And it came to pass that, when Jeremiah had made an end of speaking unto all the people all the words of Yahweh their God, wherewith Yahweh their God had sent him to them, even all these words, Azariah, the son of Hoshaiah, and Johanan, the son of Kareah, and all the proud men spake, saying unto Jeremiah: Thou speakest falsely; Yahweh our God hath not sent thee to say: Ye shall not go to Egypt to sojourn there; but Baruch, the son of Neriah, setteth thee on against us, to deliver us into the hands of the Chaldæans, that they may put us to death or carry us away captive to Babylon. So Johanan the son of Kareah and all the captains of the forces took all the remnant of Judah that were returned from all the nations whither they had been driven to sojourn, the men and the women and the children and the king's daughters, and every person that Nebuzaradan the captain of the guard had left with Gedaliah the son of Ahikam the son of Shaphan, and Jeremiah the prophet and Baruch the son of Neriah; and they came into the land of Egypt; for they hearkened not to the voice of Yahweh. And they came to Tahpanhes.

Prophecies of the Restoration of Israel, Mostly Exilic, But Pre-
serving Passages Attributable to Jeremiah

(Ch. xxx, 1-9, 12-21; xxxi, 2-9, 15-20, 27-34, 38-40; xxxii, 24-33;
xxxiii, 1, 4-13)

The word that came to Jeremiah from Yahweh, saying: Thus
speaketh Yahweh, the God of Israel: Write all these words which I
have spoken unto thee in a book. For lo, the days come when I will
turn the captivity of My people Israel and Judah, and I will cause thee
to return to the land that I gave to their fathers, and they shall possess it.

These are the words which Yahweh spake concerning Israel and
Judah. For thus saith Yahweh:

We have heard a cry of terror,   of fear and not of peace.
Ask ye now and see whether a man doth travail with child?
Wherefore do I see every man with his hands on his loins
          As a woman in travail,   and all faces turned pale?

Alas; for that day is great, so that none is like it;
A time of trouble unto Jacob,   but out of it he shall be saved.
    And it shall be in that day,   saith Yahweh Sabaoth,
I will break his yoke from thy neck, and will burst thy bonds.
          Strangers shall no more enslave them,
      But they shall serve Yahweh, their God.
      Shall serve David their king, whom I
          Will raise up to them.

Thus saith Yahweh: Thy hurt is incurable;
  Thy wound is grievous; none thinketh it may be bound up,
          Nor hast thou healing medicines.
All thy lovers have forgotten thee, they seek thee not;
  For I have wounded thee with the wound of an enemy,
          With a cruel chastisement,
      For the greatness of thine iniquity,
      Because thy sins were increased.

Why criest thou for thy hurt, that thy pain exceedeth?
For the greatness of thine iniquity have I thus punished thee.
    But all they that devour thee shall be devoured,
And all thy opponents, yea all, shall go into captivity.
      They that spoil thee shall be a spoil,
      All that prey upon thee shall be a prey;
      But I will restore health unto thee,
      And I will heal thee of thy wounds.

Because they have called thee an outcast,—
      She is Zion; none careth for her!
          Thus saith Yahweh:
Behold, I will turn the captivity of Jacob's tents,
    I will have compassion upon her dwelling-places.
The city shall be rebuilt on her own hill,
    The palace shall be inhabited as of old.
Out of them shall proceed thanksgiving, and the voice
          Of them that make merry;
And I will multiply them; they shall not be diminished.
I will greatly increase them; they shall not dwindle away.

Their children also shall be as aforetime,
Their congregation shall be established before Me
And I will punish all that oppress them.
Their princes shall be of themselves,
Their ruler shall come from their midst,
And I will cause him to draw near, he shall approach Me.
Now, who is he that hath pledged his heart to draw
Near unto Me? saith Yahweh.

Thus saith Yahweh: The people that were left of the sword
Have found grace in the wilderness,
Even Israel, when I shall go to cause him to rest.
I have loved thee with an enduring love, therefore
With love have I drawn thee.
Again will I build thee and thou shalt be built,
O virgin of Israel;
Again shalt thou be adorned with tabrets,
And go forth to dances of merry-making;
Again shalt thou plant vineyards upon the mountains of Samaria.
The planters shall plant, and shall have the use thereof.

There shall yet be a day that watchmen
Shall call on Mount Ephraim:
Arise ye and let us go up to Zion, to Yahweh our God!
For thus saith Yahweh: Rejoice for Jacob, shout aloud
At the head of the nations,
Announce ye, praise ye, and say:
O Yahweh, save Thy people, the remnant of Israel!

Behold, I will bring them from the north country,
And gather them from the uttermost parts of the earth;
And with them the blind and the lame,
The woman that bringeth her child
And her that travaileth with child, together.
A great company shall they return; they shall come a-weeping,
With supplications will I make them to walk; I will lead them
By rapid rivers, in a narrow path, but they shall not stumble;
For I am become a Father to Israel
And My first-born is Ephraim.

———

Thus saith Yahweh: A voice is heard in Ramah,
Lamentation and bitter weeping, Rachel weeping for her children;
She refuseth to be comforted for her children,
Because they are not.
Thus saith Yahweh: Refrain thy voice from weeping
And thine eyes from tears,
For thy work shall be rewarded.
They shall come back from the enemy's land,
Yea, there is hope for thy future!
That thy children shall return to their own border.

I surely heard Ephraim making a moan,—
Thou hast chastised me, and I was chastised as a calf untrained
Turn thou me and I shall be turned, for Thou art Yahweh, my God.
Surely, after I was turned, I repented;
After I was taught I smote upon my thigh.
I was ashamed, yea, even confounded,
Because I did bear the reproach of my youth.

Is Ephraim a darling son unto Me? a child that is fondled?
For as oft as I do speak of him, I remember him earnestly still.
Therefore doth my heart yearn for him;
I will surely have pity upon him.

Set thee up way-marks,　　make thee guide-posts!
Set thy heart toward the highway,
Even the way thou didst go.
Return, O virgin of Israel, return to these thy cities!
How long wilt thou turn away coyly,
O thou back-sliding daughter?
Yahweh hath created a new thing on earth,
A woman shall woo a man.

Thus saith Yahweh Sabaoth, the God of Israel:
Yet again shall they use this speech in the land of Judah
And in her cities,
When I shall turn their capitivity.
May Yahweh bless thee, O home of Righteousness
O mountain of Holiness!
And Judah and all the cities thereof
Shall dwell therein together;
The husbandmen and they that guide the flocks,
For I have satisfied the weary soul,
And every pining soul have I comforted.

Upon this, I awaked and beheld,
And my sleep was sweet to me.

Behold, the days come, saith Yahweh, that I will sow the house of
Israel and the house of Judah with the seed of man and the seed of
beast. And it shall come to pass that like as I have watched over
them to pluck up and to break down, and to overthrow and to destroy
and to afflict, so will I watch over them to build and to plant, saith
Yahweh.

In those days they shall say no more:

The fathers have eaten sour graps, and the children's teeth are set
on edge, but every one shall die for his own iniquity; every man that
eateth the sour grapes, his teeth shall be set on edge.

Behold, the days come, saith Yahweh, that I will make a NEW
COVENANT with the house of Israel and with the house of Judah. Not
according to the covenant that I made with their fathers in the day
that I took them by the hand to bring them out of the land of Egypt;
forasmuch as they broke My covenant, although I was an husband
unto them, saith Yahweh; but this is the covenant that I will make with
the house of Israel. AFTER THOSE DAYS, SAITH YAHWEH, I WILL PUT MY
LAW IN THEIR INWARD PARTS AND IN THEIR HEART WILL I WRITE IT. AND I
WILL BE THEIR GOD, AND THEY SHALL BE MY PEOPLE. AND THEY SHALL NO
MORE TEACH EVERY MAN HIS NEIGHBOR, AND EVERY MAN HIS BROTHER,
SAYING: KNOW YAHWEH; FOR THEY SHALL ALL KNOW ME, FROM THE LEAST
OF THEM UNTO THE GREATEST OF THEM, SAITH YAHWEH. FOR I WILL
FORGIVE THEIR INIQUITY, AND THEIR SIN WILL I REMEMBER NO MORE.

Behold, the days come, saith Yahweh, that the city shall be built
to Yahweh from the tower of Hananel unto the gate of the corner,
and the measuring line shall yet go out straight forward unto the hill
Gareb, and shall turn about unto Goah. And the whole valley of the

dead bodies and of the ashes, and all the fields unto the brook Kidron, unto the corner of the horse-gate toward the east, shall be holy unto Yahweh. It shall not be plucked up nor thrown down any more forever.

[Then said Jeremiah:] Behold the mounds! They are come unto the city to take it, and the city is given into the hand of the Chaldæans that are fighting against it, and what Thou hast spoken is come to pass; and behold, Thou seest it. Yet Thou hast said unto me, O God Yahweh; Buy thou the field for money, and call witnesses;[1] whereas the city is given into the hand of the Chaldæans.

Then came the word of Yahweh to Jeremiah, saying: Behold, I am Yahweh, the God of all flesh; is there any thing too hard for Me? Behold, I will give this city into the hand of the Chaldæans, and into the hand of Nebuchadrezzar, king of Babylon, and he shall take it; and the Chaldæans that fight against this city shall come and set this city on fire and burn it with the houses upon whose roofs they have offered unto Baal, and poured out drink-offerings unto other gods, to provoke Me. For the Children of Israel and the Children of Judah have done only that which was evil in My sight from their youth; for the Children of Israel have only provoked Me with the work of their hands.

For this city hath been to Me a provocation of Mine anger and of My fury from the day they built it even unto this day, that I should remove it from before My face; because of all the evil which they have done to provoke Me, they and their kings, their princes, and their priests, and their prophets and the men of Judah and the inhabitants of Jerusalem. And they have turned unto Me the back and not the face; and though I taught them, teaching them betimes and often, yet they have not hearkened to receive instruction.

But they set their abominations in the house which is called by My name to defile it. And they built the high places of Baal which are in the Valley of the Son of Hinnom, to set apart their sons and daughters unto Melech; which I commanded them not, neither came it into My mind that they would do this abomination, to cause Judah to sin.

And now thus saith Yahweh, the God of Israel, concerning this city, whereof ye say: It is given into the hand of the king of Babylon by the sword and by the famine and by the pestilence,—Behold, I will gather them out of all countries whither I have driven them in Mine anger and in My fury and in My great wrath; and I will bring them again into this place, and I will cause them to dwell safely. And they shall be My people, and I will be their God; and I will give them one heart and one way, that they may fear Me for ever, for the good of them and of their children after them. And I will make an everlasting covenant with them, that I will not turn away from them to do them good, but I will put My fear in their hearts, that they shall not depart from Me. Yea, I will rejoice over them to do them good, and I will plant them in this land assuredly with My whole heart and My whole soul.

For thus saith Yahweh: Like as I have brought this great evil upon this people, so will I bring upon them all the good that I have promised them. And fields shall be bought in this land, whereof ye say: It is desolate, without man or beast; it is given into the hands of the Chaldæans. Men shall buy fields for money and subscribe deeds,

---

[1] Referring to the sale of land to his cousin Hanameel, given in its chronological order in Booklet IV (Ch. xxxii, 6-15). The prayer following it is exilic and will be found in Appendix II.

and seal them, and call witnesses in the land of Benjamin and in the places about Jerusalem and in the cities of Judah, and in the cities of the hill-country, and in the cities of the Lowland, and in the cities of the South; for I will cause their captivity to return, saith Yahweh.

Moreover the word of Yahweh came unto Jeremiah the second time, while he was yet shut up in the court of the guard, saying: Thus saith Yahweh, the God of Israel, concerning the houses of this city and concerning the houses of the kings of Judah which are broken down for mounds and for ramparts whereon they come to fight with the Chaldæans; even to fill them with the dead bodies of men whom I have slain in Mine anger and in My fury, and for all for whose wickedness I have hid My face from this city. Behold I will bring it healing and cure, and I will cure them; and I will reveal unto them the abundance of peace and truth. And I will cause the captivity of Judah and the captivity of Israel to return, and will build them as at the first.
I will gather the remnant of My flock out of all the countries against Me; and I will pardon all their iniquities whereby they have sinned against Me, and whereby they have transgressed against Me. And this city shall be to Me for a name of Joy, for a praise and for a glory, before all the nations of the earth, which shall hear the good that I do unto them, and shall fear and tremble for all the good and for all the peace that I shall procure for it.
Thus saith Yahweh: Yet again shall there be heard in this place, whereof ye say: It is waste, without man and without beast, even in the cities of Judah and in the streets of Jerusalem that are desolate without man and without inhabitant, and without beast,—the voice of them that say: Give thanks to Yahweh Sabaoth, for Yahweh is good, for His mercy endureth for ever; even of them that bring offerings of thanksgiving into the House of Yahweh. For I will cause the captivity of the land to return as at the first, saith Yahweh.
Thus saith Yahweh Sabaoth: Yet again shall there be in this place which is waste, without man and without beast, and in all the cities thereof, a habitation of shepherds causing their flocks to lie down. In the cities of the hill-country, in the cities of the Lowland, in the cities of the South and in the land of Benjamin, and in the places about Jerusalem and in the cities of Judah, shall the Flocks again pass under the hands of Him that counteth them, saith Yahweh.

[The Seventh Booklet of the "Book of Jeremiah" (Ch. xliii, 7b-13; xliv, 1-30; xlvi, 13-28; xlvii-li) was all added very late, and will therefore be found in Part II in the order of the events which inspired the various poems on the fate of the nations akin to Israel. Some legends concerning Jeremiah in Egypt also belong there; the oldest and most persistent one, however, is given here in Appendix II to Booklets II-V. Chapter lii is taken with but slight change from the same records or traditions used by P in 2 Kings, xxiv, 15-20; xxv, 1-21, 27-30; it is already given in P's supplement to J's History. —Editor.]

APPENDIX II

Passages Found in Booklets II-V, Written Presumably Between 598 and 584, but not by Jeremiah, and Quite Opposed to His Prophecies.

I will gather the remnant of My flock out of all the countries whither I have driven them, and will bring them back to their folds; and they shall be fruitful and multiply. And I will set up shepherds over them who shall feed them; and they shall fear no more, nor be dismayed; neither shall any be lacking, saith Yahweh.

Behold, the days come, saith Yahweh,
That I will raise to David a righteous shoot;
He shall reign as king and prosper, and shall execute justice
    And righteousness in the land.
In his days shall Judah be saved, and Israel dwell safely.
And this is the name whereby He shall be called,
    YAHWEH. OUR RIGHTEOUSNESS.

Therefore behold, the days come, saith Yahweh, that they shall
no more say: As Yahweh liveth that brought up the Children of Israel
out of the land of Egypt; but, As Yahweh liveth that brought up and
led the seed of the house of Israel out of the north country, and from
all the countries whither I had driven them; and they shall dwell in
their own land.

(Ch. xxiii, 3-8)

Behold, a storm of Yahweh is gone forth in fury,
    Yea, a whirling storm!
It shall whirl on the head of the wicked.
The anger of Yahweh shall not abate
Till He have effected, and have performed
    The purpose of His heart.
In the end of days ye shall consider it.[1]

(xxiii, 19-20)

Behold, I am against the prophets, saith Yahweh, that steal My
words every one from his neighbor. Behold, I am against the prophets,
saith Yahweh, that use their own tongues, yet say: He saith. Behold,
I am against them that prophesy lying dreams, saith Yahweh, and do
tell them, and do cause My people to err by their lies, and by their
wantonness. Yet I sent them not, nor commanded them; neither can
they profit these people at all, saith Yahweh.

And when this people or the prophet or a priest shall ask thee,
saying: What is the burden of Yahweh? thou shalt answer them:
What burden? I will cast you off, saith Yahweh. And as for the
prophet and the priest and the people that shall say: The burden
(or oracle) of Yahweh,—I will even punish that man and his house.

Thus shall ye say, every one to his neighbor, and every one to his
brother: What hath Yahweh answered? or, What hath Yahweh spoken?
And the burden of Yahweh shall ye mention no more; for every man's
own word shall be his burden. Would ye pervert the words of the
living God? of Yahweh Sabaoth, our God? Thus shalt thou say to
the prophet: What hath God answered thee? and, What hath Yahweh
spoken? But if ye say: The burden of Yahweh—thus saith Yahweh;
because ye say this word: The burden of Yahweh; and I have sent
unto you saying: Ye shall not say: The burden of Yahweh; Behold,
I will utterly tear you out, and I will cast you and the city that
I gave you and your fathers, away from My presence; and I will bring
an everlasting reproach upon you, and a perpetual shame which shall
not be forgotten.[2]   (xxiii, 30-40)

[1] This little poem appears again in Ch. xxx, 23-24.
[2] The remarkable attempt of some prosaic commentator to expound Jeremiah's great
condemnation of false prophets, which is as clear and forceful as this exposition is the
reverse.

And it shall come to pass, when seventy years are accomplished, that I will punish the king of Babylon and that nation and the land of the Chaldæans for their iniquity, saith Yahweh, and I will make it perpetual desolation. And I will bring upon that land all My words which I have pronounced against it, even all that is written in this book, which Jeremiah hath prophesied against all the nations. For many nations and great kings shall make bondmen of them also; and I will recompense them for their deeds, and according to the work of their own hands.   (Ch. xxv, 12-14.)

Fear thou not, O Jacob, My servant,
    Nor be dismayed, O Israel!
For lo, I will save thee from afar, and bring
    Thy seed from the land of their exile.
Jacob shall again be quiet and at ease,
    And none shall make him afraid.
For I am with thee, saith Yahweh, to save thee.
For I will make a full end of all nations
    Whither I have scattered thee;
But of thee I will make no full end.
Though I will correct thee in measure,
    I will not utterly destroy thee.[1]

                                        (Ch. xxx, 10-11.)

A PROPHECY OF THE NATION'S TRIUMPHANT RETURN TO JUDAEA

Hear the word of Yahweh, ye Nations; declare it
    In the isles afar off.
He that scattered Israel gathereth him,
    And keepeth him from the hand of him
        That is stronger than he.
And they shall come and sing in the height of Zion,
And shall flow together to the goodness of Yahweh,
    To the corn and the wine and the oil.
    To the young of the flock and the herd.
Their soul shall be as a watered garden; they shall sorrow
        No more at all.
    Then shall the virgin rejoice in the dance,
        The youths and old men together;
    For their mourning will I turn to joy,
I will comfort them and make them rejoice from their sorrow.
And I will satiate the soul of the priests with fatness.
And My people shall be satisfied with My goodness, saith Yahweh.
                                        (Ch. xxxi, 10-14.)

Thus saith Yahweh, who giveth the sun for a light by day,
The laws of the moon and the stars for a light by night,
Who stirreth up the sea, that the waves thereof roar,—
        Yahweh Sabaoth is His name,—
    If these statutes depart from Me, saith Yahweh,
The seed of Israel shall also cease from being a nation for ever
        From before Me.
If heaven above can be measured and earth's foundations
        Searched out from beneath,
    Then I also will cut off Israel's seed
    For all that they have done, saith Yahweh.
                                        (xxxi, 35-37.)

---

[1] Found again in Ch. xlvi, 27-28 in a fitting connection. Here it is out of harmony with the succeeding strophe.

O God, behold, Thou hast made the heaven and the earth by Thy great power, and by Thy stretched-out arm, and there is nothing too hard for Thee, who showest mercy unto thousands, and dost recompense the iniquity of the fathers into the bosom of their children after them,—the great, the mighty GOD, Yahweh Sabaoth is His name, great in counsel and mighty in work; whose eyes are open upon all the ways of the sons of men, to give to every one according to his way and according to the fruit of his doings; who didst signs and wonders in the land of Egypt, even unto this day, both in Israel and among other men; and madest Thee a name as at this day; and didst bring forth Thy people Israel out of the land of Egypt with signs and wonders and with a strong hand and with an outstretched arm and with great terror; and gavest them this land which Thou didst swear unto their fathers to give them, a land flowing with milk and honey; and they came in and possessed it; but they hearkened not to Thy voice, neither walked in Thy laws; they have done nothing at all that Thou didst command them to do; therefore Thou hast caused all this evil to befall them . . .[1]

(Ch. xxxii, 17-23.)

Thus saith Yahweh, the Maker thereof, Yahweh who formed it
To establish it; (Yahweh is His name),
Call unto Me and I will answer thee, and will tell thee
Great things and hidden,
Which thou knowest not.

(Ch. xxxiii, 2-3.)

And the word of Yahweh came to Jeremiah, saying: Considerest thou not what this people have spoken, saying: The two families which Yahweh did choose, He hath cast them off? And they contemn My people, that they should no longer be a nation before them. Therefore thus saith Yahweh: If My covenant be not with day and night; if I have not appointed the laws of heaven and earth; then will I also cast away the seed of David My servant, so that I will not take of his seed to be rulers over the seed of Abraham, of Isaac and Jacob; for I will cause their exiles to return, and I will have compassion upon them.

(xxxiii, 23-26.)

A LEGEND OF A PROPHECY CONCERNING THE FATE OF BABYLON WHICH WAS CAST INTO THE RIVER EUPHRATES

The word which Jeremiah the Prophet commanded Seraiah the son of Neriah, the son of Maaseiah, when he went with Zedekiah the king of Judah to Babylon in the fourth year of his reign. Now Seraiah was quarter-master. And Jeremiah wrote in one book all the evil that should come upon Babylon, even all these words which are written concerning Babylon. And Jeremiah said to Seraiah: When thou comest

---

[1] Compare with Jeremiah's prayer, (Ch. xviii, 19-23). The conclusion of this prolix preamble has been given in its proper connection in Booklet V, a simple, earnest prayer of the perplexed prophet for guidance.

[2] Ch. xxxiii, 14-18; 19-22; are slight re-arrangements of xxiii, 5-7 and xx, 35-37, given above. Ch. xxxviii, 14-20 is a second version of xxxvii, 18-21. It is unnecessary to give these repetitions here.

to Babylon, then see that thou read all these words, and say: O Yahweh! Thou hast spoken concerning this place to cut it off, that none shall dwell therein, neither man nor beast, but that it shall be desolate for ever. And it shall be, when thou hast made an end of reading this book, that thou shall bind a stone to it, and cast it into the midst of the Euphrates. And thou shalt say: Thus shall Babylon sink, and shall not rise again because of the evil that I will bring upon her; and they will be weary.

(Ch. li, 59-64.)

THE PRAISE OF WISDOM

(Proverbs, i, 2-ix, 18. A. V.) [1]

SUPERSCRIPTION

To know Wisdom and Instruction, to discern words of understanding;
To receive the discipline of wisdom in justice and right and equity;
To give prudence to the simple, to the young knowledge and discretion
That the wise may hear and increase in learning;
And the man of understanding may attain to wise counsels.
To understand a proverb and a figure,
The words of the wise and their dark sayings.

(Ch. i, 2-6.)

The Fear of Yahweh is the beginning of knowledge,
But the foolish despise wisdom and instruction.

Hear, my son, the instruction of thy father, and forsake not
the teaching of thy mother,
For they shall be a chaplet of grace to thy head,
and chains about thy neck.

My son, if sinners entice thee, consent thou not.
If they say: Come with us, let us lie in wait for blood;
Let us lurk for the innocent causelessly,
Let us swallow them alive like Sheol,
And whole, as those that go down into the pit;
We shall find all precious substance,
We shall fill our houses with spoil;
Thou shalt cast in thy lot with us,
We will all have one purse,—
My son, walk not thou in the way with them,
Restrain thy feet from their path.

For their feet run to evil, they make haste to shed blood.
But in vain the net is spread in the sight of any bird;
And these lie in wait for their own blood,
That lurk privily for their own lives.
So are the ways of every one that is greedy of gain;
It taketh away the lives of the owners thereof.

(Ch. i, 7-19.)

Wisdom crieth aloud in the street,
She uttereth her voice in the broad places,
She crieth in the market of commerce,
At the entrance of the city-gates she uttereth her voice:
How long, ye thoughtless ones, will ye love thoughtlessness?

[1] Indisputably post-Deuternomic; written as an introduction to the extant collections of proverbs, and to emphasize the necessity for wisdom in overcoming the special temptations of the author's day. The title was first applied by Prof. Ewald, of Göttingen, c. 1840, and has since been generally accepted.

And scorners take delight in scorning, and fools hate wisdom?
Turn you at my reproof! Behold, I will pour out
My spirit upon you,
I will make known my words unto you.

Because I have called, and ye refused,
I have stretched out my hand, and no man regarded,·
But ye set at naught my counsel, and would none of my rebuke,—
I also will laugh in the day of your calamity,
I will mock when your fear cometh;
When your fear cometh as a storm,
And your calamity cometh on as a whirlwind,
When distress and anguish come upon you;
Then shall they call upon me, but I will not answer;
They shall seek me diligently, but they shall not find me.
For that they hated knowledge, and did not choose
the Fear of Yahweh.
They would none of my counsel, they despised my reproof,
Therefore shall they eat of the fruit of their own way,
And be filled with their own devices.
For the waywardness of the thoughtless shall slay them
And the confidence of fools shall destroy them;
But whoso hearkeneth unto me shall dwell securely,
And shall be quiet, without fear of evil.

(Ch. i, 20-33.)

My son, if thou wilt hear my words
And lay up my commandments within thee,
So that thou incline thine ear unto wisdom ,
And apply thy heart to understanding;
Yea, if thou call for understanding,
And lift up thy voice for discernment;
If thou seek her as silver, and search for her
as for hid treasures;
Then shalt thou understand the Fear of Yahweh,
And find the knowledge of God.

For Yahweh giveth wisdom.
Out of His mouth cometh knowledge and discernment.
He layeth up sound wisdom for the upright,
He is a shield to them who walk in integrity,
That He may guard the paths of justice,
And preserve the way of His saints.

Then shalt thou understand righteousness and justice and equity,
Yea, every good path.
For wisdom shall enter into thine heart,
And knowledge be pleasant unto thy soul;
Discretion shall watch over thee, discernment shall guard thee,
To deliver thee from the way of evil,
From the men that speak froward things.
(Who leave the paths of uprightness to walk in ways of darkness;
Who rejoice to do evil, and delight in the frowardness of evil;
Who are crooked in their ways, and perverse in their paths.)
To deliver thee from the strange woman,
From the stranger of flattering words,
That forsaketh the lord of her youth,
And forgetteth the covenant of her God.
(For her house sinketh down to death, her paths unto the shades;
None that go unto her return, nor attain unto the paths of life.)
That thou mayest walk in the way of good men,

And keep the paths of the righteous.
For the upright shall dwell in the land,
And the whole-hearted shall remain in it.
But the wicked shall be cut off from the land,
And the faithless shall be plucked up out of it.
(Ch. ii, 1-22.)

My son, forget not my teaching,
But let thy heart keep my commandments.
For length of days and years of life and peace
Will they add to thee.
Let not kindness and truth forsake thee
Bind them about thy neck, write them on the table of thy heart.
So shalt thou find favor and good repute in the eyes of God and man.

Trust in Yahweh with all thy heart
And lean not upon thine own understanding!
In all thy ways acknowledge Him, and He will direct thy paths.
Be not wise in thine own eyes,
Fear Yahweh and depart from evil;
It shall be health to thy navel, and marrow to thy bones.

Honor Yahweh with thy substance,
And with the first-fruits of all thine increase;
So shall thy barns be filled with plenty,
And thy vats overflow with new wine.

My son, despise not the chastening of Yahweh
Neither spurn his correction.
For whom Yahweh loveth, He chasteneth
Even as a father the son in whom he delighteth.

Happy is the man that findeth Wisdom
And the man that getteth understanding,
For the merchandise of it is better than that of silver,
And the gain thereof than wrought gold.

She is more precious than rubies;
All the things that thou canst desire are not to be compared
unto her.
Length of days is in her right hand;
In her left are riches and honor.
Her ways are ways of pleasantness, and all her paths are peace.
She is a tree of life to them that lay hold on her,
And happy is every one that holdeth her feet.

Yahweh by wisdom founded the earth,
By understanding, He established the heavens;
By His knowledge the depths were broken up,
And the skies drop down the dew.
(Ch. iii, 1-20.)

My son, keep sound wisdom and discretion,
Let them not depart from thine eyes;
So shall they be life to thy soul, and grace to thy neck.
Then shalt thou walk in thy way securely,
And thy feet shall not stumble.
When thou liest down, thou shalt not be afraid;
Yea, thou shalt lie down, and thy sleep shall be sweet.

Be not afraid of sudden terror,
Neither of the destruction of the wicked when it cometh;
For Yahweh shall be thy confidence,
And shall keep thy foot from being caught.

(Ch. iii, 21-26.)

Withold not good from him to whom it is due,
When it is in the power of thy hand to do it.
Say not to thy neighbor: Go, and come again,
When thou hast it by thee, saying:
To-morrow I will give.

Devise not evil against thy neighbor,
Seeing he dwelleth securely by thee.
Strive not with a man without cause,
If he have done thee no harm.
Envy thou not the man of violence, and choose none of his ways;
For the perverse is an abomination to Yahweh,
But his counsel is with the upright.
The curse of Yahweh is in the house of the wicked,
But He blesseth the habitation of the righteous.
Though He scorneth the scorners,
He giveth grace to the humble.
The wise shall inherit honor;
But shame shall be the promotion of fools.

(Ch. iii, 27-35.)

Hear, ye children, the instruction of a father,
And attend to know understanding.
For I give you good doctrine; forsake ye not my teaching.
For I was a son unto my father,
Tender and only beloved in the sight of my mother.
And he taught me and said unto me:
Let thy heart hold fast my words; keep my commandments and live.
Get wisdom, get understanding, forget it not;
Nor decline from the words of my mouth.
Forsake her not, and she will preserve thee;
Love her, and she will keep thee.

Wisdom is the principal thing, therefore get wisdom!
Yea, with all thy getting, get understanding!
Exalt her, and she will exalt thee;
She will bring thee to honor, if thou embrace her.
She will give to thy hand a chaplet of grace,
A crown of glory will she bestow upon thee.

(Ch. iv, 1-9.)

Hear, O my son, and receive my sayings,
And the years of thy life shall be many.
I have taught thee in the way of wisdom,
I have led thee in the paths of righteousness.
When thou goest, thy steps shall not be straightened,
And if thou runnest, thou shalt not stumble.
Take fast hold of instruction, let her not go; keep her,
For she is thy life.

Enter not into the path of the wicked,
And walk not in the way of evil men.
Avoid, pass not by it, turn from it and pass on.
For they sleep not, unless they have done evil.
Their sleep is taken away unless they cause some one to fall.
For they eat the bread of wickedness and drink the wine of violence.
But the path of the righteous is as the light of dawn
That shineth more and more unto the perfect day.
The way of the wicked is as darkness,
They know not at what they stumble.

My son, attend to my words; incline thine ear to my sayings;
Let them not depart from thine eyes,
Keep them in the midst of thy heart;
For they are life to them that find them,
And health to all their flesh.

Above all that thou guardest, keep thy heart,
For out of it are the issues of life.
Put away from thee a froward mouth,
And perverse lips put far from thee.
Let thine eyes look right on,
And let thine eyelids look straight before thee.
Make plain the ways of thy feet,
And let all thy ways be established.
Turn not to the right hand, nor to the left.
Remove thy foot from evil.

(Ch. iv, 10-27.)

My son, attend to my wisdom,
Incline thine ear to my understanding;
That thou mayest preserve discretion,
And that thy lips may keep knowledge.
For the lips of a strange woman drop honey,
And her mouth is smoother than oil.
But her end is bitter as wormwood, sharp as a two-edged sword.
Her feet go down to death, her steps take hold on Sheol;
Lest she should walk the level paths of life,
Her ways are unstable, and she knoweth it not.

Now then, ye children, hearken unto me,
And depart not from the words of my mouth.
Remove thy way far from her
And come not near the door of her house;
Lest thou give thy vigor unto others,
And thy years to the cruel;
Lest strangers be filled with thy strength,
And thy labors be in the house of an alien.
And thou moan when thine end cometh,
And thy flesh and thy body be consumed.
And thou say: How have I hated instruction,
And my heart despised reproof!
Neither have I hearkened to the voice of my teachers,
Nor inclined mine ear to them that instructed me.
I was well nigh in all evil,
In the midst of the congregation and the assembly.

Drink waters out of thine own cistern,
And running waters out of thine own well.
Should thy springs be dispersed abroad,
And rivers of water in the streets?
Let them be for thyself alone, and not for strangers with thee.
Let thy fountain be blessed,
And have joy of the wife of thy youth.
As a lovely hind and a graceful doe,
Let her breasts satisfy thee at all times;
With her love be thou ravished always.
Why then wilt thou, my son, be ravished with a strange woman?
And embrace the bosom of an alien?

For the ways of men are before the eyes of Yahweh,
And He maketh level all His paths.
His own iniquities shall ensnare the wicked,
And he shall be holden with the cords of his sin.
He shall die for lack of instruction,
And in the greatness of his folly go astray.
(Ch. v, 1-23.)

My son, if thou art become surely for a stranger,
If thou hast struck thy hands for a stranger,
Thou art snared with the words of thy mouth,
Art taken by the words of thy mouth.
Do this now, my son, and deliver thyself,
Seeing thou art come into the hands of thy neighbor,
Go, humble thyself, and importune thy neighbor.
Give not sleep to thine eyes, nor slumber to thine eyelids;
Deliver thyself as a gazelle from the hands of the hunter
And as a bird from the hand of the fowler.
(Ch. vi, 1-5.)

Go to the ant, thou sluggard, consider her ways and be wise.
Which having no chief, overseer or ruler,
Provideth her bread in the summer, and gathereth her food in the
harvest.
How long wilt thou sleep, thou sluggard?
When wilt thou arise out of thy sleep?
Yet a little sleep, a little more slumber,
A little folding of the hands to sleep!
So shall thy poverty come as a runner,
And thy want, as an armed man.
(Ch. vi, 6-11)

A base person, a man of iniquity
Is he that walketh with a froward mouth, that winketh with his eyes,
That scrapeth with his feet, that pointeth with his fingers.
Frowardness is in his heart; he deviseth evil continually;
He soweth discord.
Therefore shall his calamity come suddenly;
On a sudden shall he be broken, and that without remedy.

There are six things which Yahweh hateth,
Yea, seven which are an abomination unto Him.
Haughty eyes, a lying tongue, hands that shed innocent blood,
A heart that deviseth evil things,
And feet that are swift in running to mischief.
A false witness that uttereth lies,
And he that soweth discord between brethren.
(Ch. vi, 12-19)

My son, keep the commandment of thy father,
And forsake not the teaching of thy mother.
Bind them continually upon thy heart, tie them about thy neck.
When thou walkest it shall lead thee; when thou liest down,
    It shall watch over thee,
And when thou wakest, it shall talk with thee.

For the commandment is a lamp, and the law is light;
And the reproofs of instruction are the way of life,
    To keep thee from the evil woman,
From the smoothness of the silken tongue.
Lust not after her beauty in thy heart
        Nor let her snare thee with her eyelids.
For because of a harlot, a man is brought to a piece of bread,
And the adulteress hunteth for the precious life.

Can a man take fire in his bosom and his clothes not be burned?
Or can one walk on hot coals, and his feet not be scorched?
    So he that goeth to his neighbor's wife;;
Whoever toucheth her shall not go unpunished.

Men do not despise a thief if he steal
To satisfy his need when he is hungry;
But, if he be found, he must restore seven-fold;
He must give all the substance of his house.

He that committeth adultery is void of understanding.
    He that doeth it would destroy his own soul.
        Wounds and dishonor shall he get,
And his reproach shall not be wiped away.
    For jealousy is the rage of a man,
And he will not spare in the day of vengeance.
        He will not regard any ransom;
Neither will he be content though thou givest many gifts.
                                    (Ch. vi, 20-35)

        My son, keep my words
And lay up my commandments with thee.
    Keep my commandments and live,
And my teaching as the apple of thine eye.
        Bind them upon thy fingers,
    Write them upon the tablet of thy heart.
Say unto Wisdom: Thou art my sister;
    And call understanding thy kins-woman
    That they may keep thee from the strange woman,
From the stranger that flattereth with her words.

At the window of my house, I looked forth through my lattice;
I discerned among the youths, I beheld among the thoughtless
    A young man, void of understanding,
Passing through the street near her corner.
        And he went the way to her house.
    In the twilight, in the evening of the day,
    In the blackness of night and the darkness,
Behold, there met him a woman with the attire of a harlot,
        And wily of heart.

    She is riotous and rebellious;
    Her feet abide not in her house;
Now she is in the streets, now in the broad squares,
    And she lieth in wait at every corner.
    So she caught him and kissed him,

And with impudent face said unto him:
Sacrifices of peace-offerings were due from me;
This day I have paid my vows.
Therefore came I forth to meet thee,
To seek thy face, and I have found thee.
I have decked my couch with coverlets,
With striped cloths of the yarn of Egypt.
I have perfumed my bed with myrrh, aloes and cinnamon.
Come, let us take our fill of love until the morning,
Let us solace ourselves with loves.
For my husband is not at home; he hath gone a long journey;
He hath taken with him the bag of money;
He will come home at the full moon.

With her much fair speech she causeth him to yield;
With the blandishment of her lips she enticeth him away.
He goeth after her straightway, as an ox goeth to the slaughter,
Or as one in fetters to the correction of the fool,
Till an arrow strike through his liver;
As the bird hasteneth to the snare, and knoweth not
That it is at the cost of his life.

Now therefore, O ye children, hearken unto me,
And attend to the words of my mouth.
Let not thy heart decline to her ways;
Go not astray in her paths.
For she hath cast down many wounded,
Yea, a mighty host are all her slain.
Her house is the way to Sheol, going down to the chambers of Death.

(Ch. vii, 1-27)

Doth not Wisdom call, and Understanding put forth her voice?
In the top of high places by the way,
Where the paths meet she standeth.
Beside the gates, at the entry of the city,
At the coming in at the doors, she crieth aloud:
Unto you, O men, I call, and my voice is to the sons of men.
O ye thoughtless, understand prudence!
Ye fools, be of an understanding heart!
Hear, for I will speak excellent things,
And the opening of my lips shall be right things,
For my mouth shall utter truth.

Wickedness is an abomination to my lips.
All the words of my mouth are righteousness,
In them there is nothing crooked or perverse.
They are all plain to him that understandeth,
And right to them that find knowledge.
Receive my instruction and not silver, and knowledge, rather than
choice gold;
For wisdom is better than rubies.
And all desirable things are not comparable unto her.

I, Wisdom, dwell with prudence, and find out knowledge of devices.
The Fear of Yahweh is to hate evil;
Pride and arrogancy and the froward mouth do I hate.
Counsel is mine, and sound judgment; I am understanding;
Power is mine; by me kings reign, and princes decree justice.
I love them that love me,
And they that seek me earnestly shall find me.
Riches and honor are with me, yea, enduring riches and righteousness.

My fruit is better than gold, yea, than fine gold,
    And my revenue than choice silver.
I walk in the way of righteousness,
    In the midst of the paths of justice,
That I may cause those that love me to inherit substance.
    And that I may fill their treasuries.

Yahweh made me in the beginning of His way.
    Before His works of old.
I was set up from everlasting, from the beginning,
    Or ever the earth was.
When there were no depths, I was brought forth;
When there were no fountains, abounding in water.
Before the mountains were settled; before the hills
    Was I brought forth,
While as yet He had not made the earth nor the fields,
Nor the beginning of the dust of the world.

When He established the heavens, I was there.
When He set a circle upon the face of the deep,
    When He made firm the skies above,
When the fountains of the deep showed their might,
    When He gave to the sea His decree,
That the waters should not transgress His command;
When He appointed the foundations of the earth,
    Then I was by Him a nursling,
And I was always His delight, playing always before Him,
    Playing in His habitable earth;
And my delight was with the sons of men.

Now therefore, ye children, hearken unto me,
    For happy are they that keep my ways.
Hear instruction, and be wise and refuse it not.
Happy is the man that hearkeneth to me, watching daily at my gates,
    Waiting at the posts of my desire.
For whoso findeth me, findeth life
    And obtaineth favor of Yahweh.
But he that refuseth me wrongeth his own soul;
    All they that hate me love death.

(Ch. viii, 1-36)

Wisdom hath builded her house,
    She hath hewn out her seven pillars;
She hath prepared her meat, she hath mingled her wine;
    She hath also furnished her table.
    She hath sent forth her maidens;
She calleth aloud on the highest places of the city:
    Whoso is thoughtless, let him turn in hither.

As for him that lacketh understanding, to him she saith:
    Come, eat of my bread,
And drink of the wine that I have mingled!
    Forsake all thoughtlessness, and live,
And walk in the way of understanding.

He that correcteth a scorner, getteth unto himself shame;
And he that reproveth a wicked man, getteth himself a blot.
    Reprove not a scorner, lest he hate thee;
    Reprove a wise man, and he will love thee.
Give to a wise man, and he will be yet wiser;
Teach a righteous man, and he will increase in learning.

The Fear of Yahweh is the beginning of Wisdom,
And knowledge of the Holy One is understanding.
For by me shall thy days be multiplied,
And the years of thy life shall be increased.
If thou art wise, thou art wise for thyself,
And if thou scornest, thou alone shalt bear it.

(Ch. ix, 1-12)

The woman Folly is clamorous;
She is thoughtless, and knoweth nothing,
And she sitteth at the door of her house,
On a seat in the high places of the city
To call to them that pass by, going right on their ways:
"Whoso is thoughtless, let him turn in hither,"
And as for him that lacketh understanding, she saith to him:
"Stolen waters are sweet, and bread eaten in secret
Is pleasant."
But she knoweth not that the dead are there,
That her guests are in the depths of Sheol.

(Ch. ix, 13-18)

THE POEM OF NAHUM THE ELKOSHITE

Upon the Impending Fall of Nineveh

(Nahum, i, 2—iii, 19)

Yahweh is a jealous God, Yahweh avengeth and is full of wrath.
    Yahweh taketh vengeance on His foes,
    He reserveth His wrath for His enemies.
Yahweh waiteth long, but, great in power,
    He will by no means acquit the guilty.
His path is the whirlwind and the storm,
    The clouds are the dust of His feet;
He rebuketh the sea and maketh it dry,
    And drieth up all the rivers.
    Bashan languisheth and Carmel,
And the flower of Lebanon is withered.

Before Him the mountains quake, and the little hills dissolve;
    The earth is upheaved at His presence,
    Yea, the world and all that is therein.
    Who can stand before His indignation?
    Who can abide the fierceness of His anger?
    His fury is poured out like fire,
And the rocks are broken asunder before Him.

    Good is Yahweh! a refuge in time of trouble;
    He knoweth them that put their trust in Him,
    But darkness shall pursue His enemies,
And with an overwhelming flood will He make an utter end
        Of the place thereof.

    What devise ye against Yahweh?
    He will put an utter end to it.
    Trouble shall not arise a second time.
    For though they be tangled up like thorns,
    And drenched with copious drinking,
They shall be consumed like stubble that is fully dry.
    Out of thee came he forth that deviseth evil,
    That counselleth wickedness against Yahweh,
    Though they be at peace and many in number,
Yet shall they be shorn, and he shall pass away.
    Though I have afflicted thee, O Judah,
    I will afflict thee no more, saith Yahweh.
    Now will I break his yoke from off thee,
    And will burst thy bonds asunder.

    Behold on the mountains the feet of him
That bringeth good tidings, that publisheth peace!
Keep thy solemn feasts, O Judah! perform thy vow.
For no more shall the wicked molest thee; he is utterly cut off.
    Yahweh hath given command concerning thee
    That thy name shall be known no more.
Out of the house of thy gods will I destroy
    The graven image, the molten image;
    Yea, I will make thy grave, for thou art vile.

He that dasheth to pieces cometh up before thy face.
Guard thy defenses, watch the roads,
Make thy loins strong, increase thy powers!
For Yahweh restoreth the pride of Jacob,
Yea, the excellency of Israel.
The shield of his mighty ones is red,
His warriors are dyed in scarlet.
The sheen of the chariots is like fire,
The horses are curbed in the day of preparing;
Along the streets the chariots are raging,
They jostle one another in the broad squares
Their appearance is like torches, they speed like lightning.

He numbers his nobles; they succeed in their onset;
They rush to the wall,   they set up their mantelet!
But the gates of the river are opened,
The gate of the palace is in ruins.
The queen is uncovered, she is carried away,
And her maids moan like doves taboring on their breasts.

Nineveh was once like a pool of water;
Now her waters are flowing away.
Stand, stand! they cry, but not one looketh back.
Take ye spoil of silver and spoil of gold
For there is no end to the store,
And the glory of all the infinite wealth of precious things.
She is empty and desolate and waste;
The heart melteth, the knees knock together;
Convulsion is in all loins, and the faces of all grow dark.

Where is the den of the lions and the lair of the young lions,
Where the lion and the lioness walked
And the whelps,
And none made them afraid?
The lion tore in pieces enough for his whelps,
For the lioness he strangled the prey,
And he filled his caves with ravin, and his lairs with spoil.

Woe to the city of bloodshed, full of lies and rapine!
Behold, I am against thee, saith Yahweh Sabaoth.
I will burn thy chariots in the smoke;
The sword shall devour the young lions;
I will cut off thy prey from the earth,
And there shall no more be heard the voice of thy messengers.

Woe to the city of bloodshed, full of lies and rapine!
There is no end to the spoil.
Hark, the whip! and hark, the rattling wheels!
The noise of prancing horses, of bounding wheels!
Of horsemen charging with flaming swords
With the lightning of the spear!
There is a multitude of slain, a great number of carcasses.
There is no end to the corpses; they stumble over the bodies.
Because of the multitude of the harlotries
Of the well-favored harlot;
The mistress of whoredoms,
That selleth nations through her whoredoms, and peoples
Through her witchcrafts.

Behold, I am against thee, saith Yahweh Sabaoth,
And I will uncover thy skirts before thy face.
I will show the nations thy nakedness,
And the kingdoms thy disgrace.
I will cast loathsome filth upon thee;
I will make thee vile, and set thee up for a gazing-stock.
All that look upon thee shall flee before thee, saying:
Nineveh is laid waste; who will bemoan her?
Whence shall I seek comforters for thee?

Art thou better than mighty No-Amon
Which lay among many streams?
Waters were round about her, her bulwark was the sea,
Her wall was the sea.
Her strength was Ethiopia and Egypt,
Put with her countless cities, and Libya her help.
Yet was she carried away, she went into captivity;
Her young children were dashed in pieces
At the top of all her streets.
Her captors cast lots for her honored men,
And all her great men were bound in chains.

Thou also shalt be drunken,
Thou too shalt swoon.
Thou too shalt seek a refuge because of the enemy.
All thy strongholds shall be like fig-trees
With first-ripe figs;
If they be shaken the figs shall drop
Into the mouth of the eater.
Behold, thy populace are but women;
Fire hath consumed thy defenses;
The gates of thy land are set wide open to thine enemies.

Draw thee water for the siege, strengthen thy fortresses!
Go into the clay-pits and tread the clay,
Make sure of the brick-moulds!
There the fire will consume thee,
The sword shall cut thee down.
It shall destroy thee, though thou increase and make thyself many,
As doth the canker-worm, or like a swarm of locusts.
Thou hast multiplied thy merchants above the stars of heaven;
Thy exalted ones are as the locusts,
Thy captains as swarms of grasshoppers
Which camp in the hedges on a cold day;
But when the sun rises they fly away,
And the place where they are is unknown.

Thy shepherds slumber, O king of Assyria, thy nobles rest.
The people are scattered upon the mountains,
And there is none to recall them.
There is no healing for thy hurt, thy wound is fatal.
All that hear report of thee shall clap their hands over thee;
For upon whom hath not thy wickedness fallen continually?

THE POEM OF HABAKKUK

ARRAIGNING THE JUSTICE OF YAHWEH

(Ch. i, 2-4, 12a, 13; ii, 1-4; i, 5-12b, 14-17; ii, 5b-13, 15-17, 19, 18, 20)

How long, O Yahweh, shall I cry, and Thou wilt not hear?
I cry out unto Thee of violence, and Thou wilt not save!
  Why dost Thou make me look upon wickedness
   And behold grievance?
  Why are rapine and violence before us,
   And strifes and contentions?
  Therefore law is perverted and right judgment
   Is never pronounced;
  For the wicked beset the righteous,
   And wrong judgment is wrested from them.

  Art Thou not from everlasting, O Yahweh,
   My God, my Holy One,
  With eyes too pure to behold evil,
  That canst not gaze on iniquity?
  Wherefore, then, dost thou look favorably
   On them that deal treacherously?
  And art silent when the wicked devoureth
   The man more righteous than he?
I will stand upon the watch, I will set me on my tower
   To see what He will say to me,
  And what I shall answer unto His reproof.

  Then did Yahweh answer me and say:
   Write down the vision and make it plain
That a man may read it readily when running swiftly.
   For the vision is for a time appointed;
  It declareth the end; it will not lie.
   Though it tarry, wait thou for it,
  Because it will surely come; it cannot delay.

Behold, the haughty of soul hath no uprightness in him;
  But he that walketh righteously.
  Shall live because of his faith.
Look around you among the nations, observe and ponder
   And marvel!
  For I will work a work in your days
  Which ye will not believe for the telling.
  For behold, I am raising the Chaldæans
  Against that bitter, impetuous nation
  That marcheth throughout the earth to possess
   Dwelling-places not theirs.
Terrible, dreadful are they,—a law unto themselves.

Their horses are swifter than leopards,
More fierce than wolves of the desert.
Their horsemen spread them abroad, yea, they come from far;
They fly like vultures hastening to devour.
All of them come to do violence,
Their faces sup up the east wind.
They gather up captives as the sand,
And they do scoff at kings.
To them princes are a derision, strongholds they deride.
For they heap up earthworks and take it.
Then their spirit swells to overflowing,
They impute their strength to their god.

Thou, O Yahweh, hast ordained them for judgment;
Thou, O Rock, hast established them for correction.
For they make men as fish of the sea,
As worms that have no ruler.
They take them all up with their hook,
They catch them in their net,
They gather them in with their drag-net.
Therefore they rejoice and are glad,
They sacrifice unto their net,
And burn incense unto their drag-net.
For through these their portion is fat, their meat plenteous.
Shall they, therefore, empty their net,
Nor cease to slay whole nations?

Woe to that proud and treacherous one
Who transgresseth by wine, nor stayeth at home,
But maketh his desire as large as Sheol,
And is as unsatisfied as Death!
Who gathereth unto himself all nations,
And heapeth unto himself all peoples.
Shall not all these take up a proverb against him?
And make against him a taunting song, and say:

Woe to him that heapeth up what is not his,
That loadeth himself with many pledges!
Shall not thy creditors suddenly arise?
Shall not they wake to vex thee, shall not they
Make thee their prey?
Because thou hast spoiled many nations, all they,
The remaining peoples, shall make thee their prey.
For thy shedding of blood, for violence done to the land,
To the city and to all that dwell therein.

Woe to him that covereth evil gains for his house,
That he may set his nest on high,
And be secured from the power of evil!
Thou hast devised shame for thy house
By cutting off many people.
Thou hast forfeited thy life.
For the stone shall cry out of the wall,
And the beam of timber shall answer it.

Woe to him that buildeth a town with blood,
And establisheth a city by iniquity!
So that the people labor even in the fire
And the nations weary themselves for naught!
Woe to him that giveth his neighbor to drink
From the cup of his wrath, till he be drunken,
That he may gaze on his nakedness!

Thou shalt be filled with shame instead of glory;
The cup of Yahweh's right hand shall be turned unto thee.
Drink thou also, and be uncovered!
Filthiness shall be upon thy glory.
For the violence done to Lebanon shall be on thee,
And the destruction of beasts which made them afraid,
For the shedding of man's blood,
For the violence done to the land,
To the city and to all that dwell therein.

Woe unto him that saith unto the wood: Awake!
To the dumb stone: Arise!
What profiteth it the graven image
That the maker thereof hath graven it?
Even the molten image, and the teacher of lies?
Doth the maker of his work trust therein
That maketh dumb idols?   Can this teach?

Behold, it is overlaid with gold and with silver
And there is no breath in its midst;
But Yahweh is in his holy temple.
Let all the earth keep silence before Him.[1]

[1] The superb ode that follows in (Ch. iii, A. V.), known as the "Prayer of Habakkuk," belongs to a different age and different circumstances. It will be found in Part II in the Appendix to the Psalms.

TWO POEMS UPON THE MISSION OF ISRAEL

THE SERVANT OF YAHWEH

(Isaiah xlii, 1-4; xlix, 1-6)

[*Yahweh speaks*]

Behold My Servant, whom I uphold, My Chosen One,
    In whom My soul delighteth.
    I have put My spirit upon him.
He will set forth the Law to the Nations.

He will not cry aloud nor roar as a lion,
Nor will he raise his voice to be heard in the street.
    A bruised reed will he not break;
    A dim-burning wick will he not quench;
    Faithfully will he set forth the law.
He will not burn dimly, nor be crushed in spirit
Till he have established the Law in the earth
And for his instruction the far countries wait.

———————

[*The Servant speaks*]

Hearken, ye far countries to me, and listen,
        Ye distant peoples!
    Yahweh hath called me from the womb
    From my mother's lap hath He honored my name.
    He made my mouth like a sharp sword,
    In the shadow of His hand He hid me;
He made me a polished shaft, in His quiver He stored me.
He said to me: Thou art My Servant in whom I will glorify Me.
I was honored in the sight of Yahweh; my God became my strength.

But I,—I said: I have labored in vain;
    For naught and vanity have I spent my strength.
    Yet surely, my cause is before Yahweh,
        And my recompense with my God.

And now saith Yahweh, He who from the womb
    Formed me to be a servant to Him;
To bring back Jacob to life, to assemble Israel together:

IT IS TOO LIGHT A THING THAT THOU SHOUDST RAISE UP
    THE TRIBES OF ISRAEL,
AND RESTORE THE PRESERVED OF ISRAEL;
THEREFORE I SET THEE TO BE A LIGHT TO THE NATIONS,
THAT MY DELIVERANCE MAY BE TO THE ENDS OF THE EARTH.

[1] The unknown author of these two poems sees in the experiences of his nation a Divine preparation for a world-wide spiritual leadership. He may or may not be the great prophet of the "New Covenant" (Jer. xxxi, 31-34) which proclaims the essence of religion for the individual; but the same lofty idealism informs his view of permanent international relations. He is inspired by the same joy of unexpected return to Zion; possibly by recognition of the thinness of the veil that separates his faith from that of his new beneficent masters.

The other two poems usually grouped with these (Is. l, 4-9 and lii, 13-liii, 12) show a very different background, and are now attributed to an author of the time of Artaxerxes III (B.C. 389-338), when the Jews were again subjected to very grievous persecution.

APPENDICES

APPENDICES

APPENDIX A

EARLY BELIEFS CONCERNING THE HEBREW SCRIPTURES

I. THE CANON ACCORDING TO THE JEWS.

    a. According to JOSEPHUS in "Against Apion", Century I., A.D.

"We have not an innumerable multitude of books among us disagreeing from and contradicting one another, but only twenty-two books which contain records of all past times, which are justly believed to be divine. And of these five belong to Moses, which contain his laws and the traditions of mankind until his death. . . . But as to the time from the death of Moses till the reign of Aryaxerxes, king of Persia, the prophets who were after Moses wrote down what was done in their times in thirteen books. The remaining four books contain hymns to God and precepts for the conduct of human life." (Bk. I.8.)

    b. According to THE TALMUD. Cent. V-IX. (Baba Bathra, xiv, b)

MOSES wrote his own Book, the section on Balaam and Job.

JOSHUA wrote his own Book, and eight verses of the law.

SAMUEL wrote his own Book and Judges and Ruth.

JEREMIAH wrote his own Book, the Book of Kings and Lamentations.

HEZEKIAH and his College wrote Isaiah, Proverbs, Song of Songs and Koheleth *(Ecclesiastes)*.

MEN OF THE GREAT SYNAGOGUE wrote Ezekiel, The Twelve *(the Minor Prophets)*, Daniel and Esther.

EZRA wrote his own Book and the Genealogies of Chronicles, as far as himself".

II. THE MATERIAL THEN AT HAND FOR EXAMINATION OF THE TEXTS.

    a. The Samaritan Pentateuch (time of Nehemiah). Cent. V. B.C.

The Septuagint Translation (LXX). Cent. III. and later.

Targums (Aramaic paraphrases of O. T.) beginning Cent. IV.

    b. Oldest Hebrew Text, by R. Aqiba (recovered from texts used by the Masoretes). Cent. II. A.D.

Literal Translation of Aqiba's text, word for word into Greek, by Aqila, Cent. II. (Used by Origen).

Origen's "Tetrapla" and "Hexapla". Cent. III. A.D.

Jerome's Translation of the Hebrew Scriptures into Latin, Cent. V. A.D.

Targum of Onkelos. Cent. V. A.D.

(N.B.—The opinion that Ezra closed the Canon (c. 440 B.C.) rests only on a conjecture offered in the XVIth cent. by Elias Levita, who wrote on "The Origin and Nature of the Masorah" in 1538; edited by Ginsburgh, 1867.)

APPENDIX B

STEPS TOWARD A FULLER UNDERSTANDING OF THE OLD TESTAMENT

I. THE EARLIEST CRITICS.

    Philo of Alexandria. Origen of Alexandria and Palestine. Augustine, Bishop of Hippo. Cent. II.-V.

    Jewish critics in Babylonia. Cent. VIII.-IX.

II. FIRST CRITICAL ANALYSIS ON MODERN LINES.

    Abraham Ibn Ezra maintains "Isaiah" to be the work of two authors. Opinion received in France. Cent. XII.

    David Kimchi continues the work of scientific exegesis. Cent. XIII.

    Spinoza's "Tractatus Theologico-Politicus" (1669), the first defense of liberty of thought and speech in regard to the Scriptures.

    Jean Astruc, a French physician, points out two separate sources for Genesis (1753).

    Robert Lowth, Professor of Poetry in Oxford, lectures on the "Laws of Hebrew Poetry" (1753), applying them to the analysis of "Isaiah".

III. ADVANCE IN SCIENCE, GIVING RISE TO DOUBTS OF ASSERTION IN THE SCRIPTURES.

    Birth of Modern Philosophy, and New Departures in Science. Cent. XVII.

    Birth of Geology and Comparative Anatomy. Cent. XVIII.

    Study of Comparative Grammar and Philology. Cent. XIX.

    Sciences of Archæology and Ethnology founded. Cent. XIX.

APPENDIX C

DISCOVERIES IN THE NEAR EAST DURNG THE LAST CENTURY

1798. NAPOLEON takes to Egypt forty *savants* who make an exhaustive study of the ruins then visible. These he publishes with full text and superb colored plates as a "Description of Egypt", better known as "The Napoleon Books" (1809-1813).

1799. BOUSSARD discovers the "Rosetta Stone"; General Desaix finds another tri-lingual inscription in Upper Egypt. From these, CHAMPOLLION deciphers the clue to the ancient language of Egypt (1821-1826).

1845-1847. LAYARD (Austen Henry) discovers the ruins of Nineveh on the Tigris, and the palaces of Sennacherib and other rulers of Assyria.

1846-1851. RAWLINSON (Henry C.) discovers the tri-lingual inscription of Darius I. on the "Rock of Behistun" in Persia, and deciphers the one in wedge-shaped characters, thus recovering the lost language of Babylonia-Assyria.

1842-1845. LEPSIUS (Karl R.) explores all Upper Egypt, and publishes his *finds* in 1859.

1850-1880. MARRIETTE (Augustus) makes many remarkable discoveries at Abydos; finds the rock-temple of Seti I. (Dyn. XIX.) and its "List of Kings" in Egypt from Mena down.

1881-1910. MASPERO (Gaston) succeeds Marriette as Director of the Cairo Museum. Discovers the great *cache* of Royal Mummies at Deir el Bahri, where they had lain undisturbed since the time of Solomon. His many writings upon everything concerned with discoveries in Egypt are most valuable.

1887. Discovery of the "Tel el Amarna Letters" from the governors of the Syrian provinces to their Overlord, AMENHOTEP III., imploring aid against the *Khabiri* or Arab raiders of their lands. Others contain the negotiations for the marriage of Amenhotep IV. (IKH-N-ATON) with a princess of the Mitanni.

1901. Discovery of the CODE OF LAWS OF KHAMMURABI, king of Babylonia (2200 B.C.).

1907. Discovery of the tomb of QUEEN TIY and the mummy of HER SON, IKH-N-ATON, THE ARTIST, POET AND RELIGIOUS REFORMER OF Dyn. XVIII.

RESULTS OF THESE DISCOVERIES

The making over of Ancient History, and the clearing up of many obscure points in the History of the Israelites and the Development of their Religion.

Major authority upon the History of Egypt, SIR WILLIAM FLINDERS-PETRIE.

Major authority upon that of Babylonia-Assyria, the late MORRIS JASTROW, JR., of the Univ. of Pennsylvania.

APPENDIX D

EASILY ATTAINABLE WORKS OF LEADING AUTHORITIES IN THE DEVELOPMENT OF BIBLICAL CRITICISM

1837–1841. EWALD, G. HEINRICH A., "Prophets of the Old Testament" (trans. 1877).

1845.   "   "   "   "History of Israel" (trans. 1867–1874).

1860. KUENEN, ABRAHAM, "The Religion of Israel" (trans. 1875).

1875.   "   "   "The Prophets and Prophecy of Israel" (trans. 1877).

1869–1872. COLENSO, J. W. (Bp. of Natal), "Treatises on the Pentateuch".

1881–1889. SMITH, W. ROBERTSON, "The Old Testament in the Jewish Church"; "The Prophets of Israel"; "On the Religion of the Semites".

1882. WELLHAUSEN, JULIUS, "Prolegomena to the History of Israel" (trans. 1885).

1880–1886. DILLMAN, C. F. A., Studies of "Exodus", "Leviticus", "Numbers", "Deuteronomy", "Joshua".

1887–1898. STADE, BERNHARD. Many valuable articles contributed to Biblical Encyclopedias and Reviews. Major works not yet translated.

1888. DELITZSCH, FRANZ, "Commentaries", "Daniel".

1891. DRIVER, SAMUEL R., "Introduction to the Literature of the Old Testament."

1898. CHEYNE, THOMAS K., "Jewish Religious Life After the Exile".

1899. BUDDE, KARL, "Religion of Israel to the Exile".

1900. GUNKEL, HERRMAN, "Legends of Genesis" (trans. 1904).

AMONG AMERICAN SCHOLARS

1891–1894. BACON, BENJAMIN W., "The Genesis of Genesis"; "The Triple Tradition of the Exodus".

1899. BRIGGS, CHARLES A., "Introduction to the Study of the Holy Scriptures".

1898. HARPER, WILLIAM R. Articles on "Amos" and "Hosea" in the International Critical Commentary.

1900. MOORE, GEORGE F., "Critical Edition of 'Judges' ".

1903. HARPER, ROBERT. Monograph on the "Battle of Kadesh", between Ramses II. and the Hittites (Kheta). Published in the *Decennial Books* of the Chicago University.

1904–1921. KENT, CHARLES F., Five Vols. of "The Student's Bible" (not yet finished).

1916. BARTON, GEORGE A., "Archæology and the Bible".

Excellent articles upon almost every possible subject connected with the Bible may be found in the Encyc. Brit. More detailed scholarly ones in Hastings' Dict. of the Bible and The Encyclopaedia Biblica, edited by Prof. Cheyne. For the Geology and Physiography of Bible-lands, see "The Face of the Earth," vol. III, by E. Suess; "Researches in Sinai" (1906) by Prof. Flinders-Petrie; "Historical Geography of the Holy Land," by Geo. Adam Smith, D.D. Many younger men, especially in Canada and the United States, are now making notable contributions to the elucidation of important points to which these have shown the way.

18633